WARFARE IN THE WESTERN WORLD

MILITARY OPERATIONS SINCE 1871
VOLUME II

Robert A. Doughty | George C. Herring | Ira D. Gruber
Donald D. Horward | Roy K. Flint | John A. Lynn
Mark Grimsley | Williamson Murray

CENGAGE
Learning

Australia • Brazil • Japan • Korea • Mexico • Singapore • Spain • United Kingdom • United States

CENGAGE
Learning™

WARFARE IN THE WESTERN WORLD
MILITARY OPERATIONS SINCE 1871
VOLUME II

Robert A. Doughty | George C. Herring
Ira D. Gruber | Donald D. Horward
Roy K. Flint | John A. Lynn
Mark Grimsley | Williamson Murray

Executive Editor:
Maureen Staudt
Michael Stranz

Senior Project Development Manager:
Linda de Stefano

Marketing Specialist:
Sara Mercurio

Senior Production/Manufacturing Manager:
Donna M. Brown

PreMedia Supervisor:
Joel Brennecke

Rights & Permissions Specialist:
Todd Osborne

Cover Image: iStockphoto
Cover Designer: Brian Moore

For product information and technology assistance, contact us at
Cengage Learning Customer & Sales Support, 1-800-354-9706
For permission to use material from this text or product, submit all requests online at **cengage.com/permissions**
Further permissions questions can be emailed to
permissionrequest@cengage.com

This book contains select works from existing Cengage Learning resources and was produced by Cengage Custom Solutions for collegiate use. As such, those adopting and/or contributing to this work are responsible for editorial content, accuracy, continuity and completeness.

Compilation Copyright © 2009 Cengage Learning

ISBN-13: 978-0-618-98164-9

ISBN-10: 0-618-98164-0

Cengage Learning
5191 Natorp Boulevard
Mason, Ohio 45040
USA

Cengage Learning is a leading provider of customized learning solutions with office locations around the globe, including Singapore, the United Kingdom, Australia, Mexico, Brazil, and Japan. Locate your local office at: **international.cengage.com/region**

Cengage Learning products are represented in Canada by Nelson Education, Ltd.

For your lifelong learning solutions, visit **www.cengage.com/custom**

Visit our corporate website at **www.cengage.com**

PREFACE

We first talked of writing a history of warfare in the Western world during the spring of 1985. We knew that a number of books dealt broadly with the history of war, usually emphasizing the relationships between war and society. We also knew that there were several multi-volume histories of military operations as well as a multitude of books treating particular wars and campaigns. But we could not find a general history of military operations in the Western world that was both comprehensive and coherent. We decided, therefore, to write such a book. We intended that our book should be sound and readable and that it should appeal to students, to general readers, and to anyone seeking an authoritative reference on warfare.

To give our book the depth and breadth we thought essential to understanding four centuries of warfare, we planned a work of two volumes and six parts. The first volume, which begins with Gustavus Adolphus's synthesis of early seventeenth-century European warfare, analyzes the development of limited warfare in seventeenth and eighteenth-century Europe; the emergence of the citizen soldier and mobile, decisive warfare in the era of the French Revolution and Napoleon; and the adoption of near total warfare in the United States Civil War and the application of Prussian organizational skills to European warfare of the mid-nineteenth century. The second volume, which begins with the small wars of the late nineteenth century, considers successively the systematic harnessing of human and material resources for the total warfare of the First World War, the continuation of total warfare in an even more virulent form during the Second World War, and the resort to varieties of limited warfare since 1945, since the creation of atomic and nuclear weapons.

Because each of the parts of our history is self-sufficient and because several deal with topics that are of special interest to readers, those parts are published separately. Three are available as individual volumes: *The American Civil War: The Emergence of Total Warfare*; *World War II: Total Warfare Around the Globe*; and *Limited Warfare in the Nuclear Age*. A fourth volume, drawn broadly from *Warfare in the Western World*, is titled *American Military History and the Evolution of Warfare in the Western World*. Each of these derivative volumes, like its parent, is profusely illustrated; indeed, *Warfare in the Western World* contains more than 150 photographs and an equal number of maps drawn especially for the work.

In undertaking a book on such an extensive and often fragmented subject as four centuries of warfare in the West, we knew that we would need the help of other scholars. Our work, then, has been a cooperative effort from its inception. Ira Gruber wrote chapters 1–5; John Lynn, chapter 6; Donald Horward, chapters 7–9; Mark Grimsley, chapters 10–14; Williamson Murray, chapters 15 and 21–26; Robert Doughty, chapters 16–20, 27, and

30–31; Roy Flint, chapter 28; and George Herring, chapter 29. Doughty and Gruber contributed the Introduction and Conclusion and helped each other and the other authors to develop unifying themes.

Each of us has, of course, drawn upon the work of scores of other scholars; and each has benefited from the comments of specialists, colleagues, and students who have read portions of this history. We are particularly indebted to Richard Kohn and John Shy, who read carefully an entire draft of the text and drew upon their remarkable understanding of military history and sharp critical judgment to suggest ways for improving the whole. We, and our fellow authors, are grateful to all who have had a part in creating this book. We do not imagine that we will have satisfied our critics; we do hope that they and other readers will continue to share their knowledge of warfare with us.

R. A. D. and I. D. G.

CONTENTS IN BRIEF

CONTENTS

MAP SYMBOLS

The symbols shown below are used on the maps in this volume. Most of the symbols suggest the organization of units in particular campaigns or battles. The reader should understand that the organization of military units has changed over time and has varied from army to army or even within armies. For example, the composition and size of Napoleon's corps varied within his own army and differed from those of his opponents; they also differed dramatically from those of armies later in the nineteenth century. The symbols thus indicate the organization of a unit at a particular time and do not indicate its precise composition or size.

Division	
Corps	
Army	
Army Group	
Cavalry Screen	• • •
Armor	
Airborne	
Fort	
Mine	o—o—o—o
Bridge	
Boundary between Units	——xxxxx——

LIST OF MAPS

INTRODUCTION

Warfare in the Western World is a history of military operations in the West from the seventeenth century to the present; it is not a comprehensive history of warfare or of wars. It concentrates on selected campaigns in major wars and explains how political and military leaders have used armies to wage war effectively—to defeat the enemy's army, occupy his territory, or break the will of his people. It considers war aims and strategy, the overall goals of a war and the use of military forces to achieve those goals. It also considers tactics, the particular measures taken by a commander to defeat enemy forces engaged in battle with his own. But it focuses on operations, the employment of relatively large forces within a specific theater of war. To make its analysis of operations meaningful, it touches on the history of warfare at sea and in the air and on joint actions involving land, sea, and air forces; and it sometimes discusses warfare throughout the world. But this is primarily a history of military operations in Europe and North America, an explanation of how armies have been used and how the waging of war has changed over the past four centuries.

We emphasize warfare in the Western world in part because the West has had its own separate and remarkably successful way of waging war and in part because this book is intended primarily for readers in the United States, whose military institutions and practices are clearly Western in their origins. Europeans have not always been able to generate superior military power, but from the beginning of the seventeenth until the end of the nineteenth century they were more successful in waging war than any other people on earth. Their experience in warfare has had a global influence, and their methods, somewhat modified, have helped the United States preserve its union and become one of the greatest military powers of the twentieth century. So it is that a book intended for readers in the United States concentrates on the remarkable history of warfare in the Western world.

Our story begins in the early seventeenth century when European warfare was becoming decidedly modern. Improvements in firearms had already rendered medieval fortifications obsolete, given musketeers a marked advantage over soldiers equipped with pikes or swords, and driven the most affluent states of western Europe to invest in ever-larger armies and more elaborate fortresses. But not until the beginning of the seventeenth century were commanders able to take full advantage of firearms in their operations, and no one was more successful than King Gustavus Adolphus of Sweden in exploiting and improving upon contemporary practices. He showed not only how handguns and artillery might be combined to generate devastating firepower and make an army formidable offensively and defensively but also how one small state might draw upon its own resources and those of other states to wage war on an unprecedented scale. This book begins, then, with a principal figure in one of the most significant episodes in the history of warfare—the prolonged European adjustment to improvements in firearms that marked the transition from medieval to modern warfare.

In the nearly four centuries since the death of Gustavus Adolphus, warfare in the West has undergone further dramatic changes, and this book attempts to identify and explain them. From the sprawling campaigns of Gustavus Adolphus to the sieges and skirmishes of the age of limited war; from the sustained marches and decisive battles of Napoleon to the even more rapid deployments, larger forces, and costlier battles that came with railroads and rifled weapons in the mid-nineteenth century; and from the land, sea, and air battles that destroyed soldiers and civilians alike in the world wars of the twentieth century to the geographically and militarily more limited operations of the nuclear age; warfare has undergone substantial and unpredictable changes. In the past four centuries operations have increased fundamentally in scale, speed, complexity, and destructiveness. Those increases, however, have at times been interrupted or even reversed, and they have not made warfare progressively more decisive. To what extent have changes in warfare been affected by underlying developments in the population, food supply, industry, and technology of the Western world? To what extent have changes in warfare been the result of deliberate alterations in the ways that leaders have chosen to organize, train, equip, and employ their forces? We hope that this history will suggest answers to these and other fundamental questions about warfare in the Western world.

P A R T

★ ★ ★ ★

Total War and the Great War

16

MAKING WAR MORE LETHAL, 1871–1914

New Technologies,
Institutions, and Ideas

Small Wars and Regional
Wars Before 1914: Mixing
the Old and the New

The wars of the late nineteenth century shattered the hopes of those who believed that the world was entering an era of enduring peace. Instead of peace, the Western world experienced increased tension and heightened nationalism and endured a wave of "new imperialism." As Western states added to their territorial possessions, particularly in Africa and Asia, industrial production increased, and numerous technological advances occurred. At the same time, the powers of central governments expanded, and more resources became available to the military. Important changes also occurred in the methods, organizations, and equipment for waging war. Of the many changes taking place in the military in the late nineteenth century, some of the most important stemmed from the introduction of much more effective and lethal weapons. Advances in artillery, rifles, and machine guns profoundly affected the waging of war on land, while improvements in naval technology and design—particularly the introduction of the HMS *Dreadnought*—made the older battleships of the world's fleets obsolete. Other changes came from improved military organizations. As recognition of the expanding scope of war became apparent, some nations attempted to copy the example of the Prussians in the fielding and employment of mass armies and in the functioning of a general staff. New ideas—such as those of Captain Alfred Thayer Mahan on the importance of sea power—also had an effect. By 1914, the world's armies and navies bore little resemblance to those of 1815.

The decades before World War I did not include a war between two of the major Western powers, but numerous conflicts did occur as regional wars broke out and as the Western powers used their military advantages

to expand their control over the globe. Between 1800 and 1914 they expanded their global empires from about 35 percent of the world's land surface to
about 84 percent. Among the conflicts occurring before World War I, the
Spanish-American War of 1898, the Boer War of 1898, and the Russo-Japanese
War of 1904–1905 tested and demonstrated new methods of waging war
across a broad spectrum of conflict. The victory of the Japanese over the
Russians, however, signaled the eventual end of the Western monopoly over
the new methods. That same war also provided hints about the future scale
and destructiveness of the two world wars of the twentieth century.

New Technologies, Institutions, and Ideas

Throughout the nineteenth century, the effects of the industrial revolution
profoundly influenced the waging of war. Important technological advances
began to affect military weapons and equipment and eventually altered the
way in which wars were fought. In the latter part of the century, steam
power replaced sails on the oceans. At the same time, the Bessemer process
permitted the making of cheap steel, and chemists produced powerful new
explosives. Along with the technological advances came substantial increases in population. In Europe alone, the population went from about 266
million in 1850 to about 401 million in 1900. With industries capable of
producing massive amounts of advanced weapons and ammunition, with
countries having many more citizens available for military service, and with
steam locomotives and ships capable of moving huge quantities of men and
equipment, the wars of the late nineteenth century assumed new dimensions
in scale and lethality.

One of the most incisive observers of these changes was Ivan S.
Bloch, a Polish banker and railway magnate. In 1897–1898 he published an
elaborate, multivolume treatise on modern warfare, *The Future of War in its
Technical, Economic, and Political Relations.* Bloch recognized that the character of war had changed as many nations had passed from agricultural into
industrial societies. Believing that war had become "impossible, except at
the price of suicide," Bloch argued that technological advances had transformed war into an endless cycle of attrition and had made warring nations
vulnerable to social upheaval. He warned of the dangers of unparalleled
slaughter and noted:

> The outward and visible sign of the end of war was the introduc-
> tion of the magazine rifle, . . . smokeless powder, . . . the quick-
> firing gun, . . . and higher explosives. . . . The first thing every man
> will have to do . . . will be to dig a hole in the ground, and throw up
> as strong an earthen rampart as he can to shield him from the hail
> of bullets. . . . When you must dig a trench before you can make
> any advance, your progress is necessarily slow. Battles will last for

days, and at the end it is very doubtful whether any decisive victory
can be gained.

In most countries, the military ignored the warnings of Bloch, who was not
a professional soldier and whose emphasis on the destructiveness of war
aroused strong pacifist sentiments. Most armies and navies experimented
with new technologies and ideas and adopted new weapons and methods,
but almost none recognized the extent of the profound changes occurring
in warfare.

Smokeless Powder

Most of the new weapons introduced in the decades before World War I cap-
italized on the perfection of a noncorrosive smokeless powder that gave its
user significant tactical advantages. In the 1860s a smokeless powder was
introduced, but it was often unstable and dangerous in storage. Then in
1884 a French chemist, Paul M. E. Vieille, invented a safer, more powerful,
and more stable powder. By primarily producing gases and almost no solid
byproducts, the new powder eliminated the cloud of smoke that accompanied the firing of black powder, enabling soldiers to see and fire more effectively. It also allowed soldiers to conceal their firing position from the
enemy. The clouds of smoke from burning black powder, which had been a
conspicuous feature of previous battles, all but disappeared.

The smokeless powder had other important technical advantages.
As a clean-burning propellant, it left the firing mechanism and bore of a
weapon relatively clear of the residue that had plagued weapons using black
powder. In contrast to the extremely rapid burning of black powder, the
new powder burned more evenly and produced a prolonged power impulse
with a relatively low chamber pressure. This yielded greater range and penetrating power. The introduction of smokeless powder proved to be one of
the most important steps in the wave of innovations occurring at the end of
the nineteenth century.

Advances in weapons at the end of the nineteenth century, however,
depended on improvements other than the introduction of smokeless powder. For example, after the development of picric acid as a high explosive
(also known as mélinite or lyddite) in the late 1880s, the military began
using it as a bursting charge in shells. During the next two decades, TNT
(or, trinitrotoluene) replaced picric acid in artillery shells, thereby increasing
the bursting power of shells more than twenty times over the pre-picric acid
versions. Additionally, the development of better and more dependable steel
was particularly significant, for it enabled technicians to improve the design
of weapons. The result was lighter weapons with greater lethality, longer
ranges, better accuracy, and vastly greater rates of fire.

Artillery

Significant changes in the technical characteristics and role of artillery occurred at the end of the nineteenth century. Instead of projectiles following

a fairly flat trajectory, they began following a high, round trajectory; and instead of batteries firing from positions alongside the infantry, they began firing from behind it. The major changes in artillery began in the middle of the nineteenth century. Although the Germans used steel breech-loading cannon in the Franco-Prussian War, the guns lacked a recoil mechanism and thus had to be pushed forward and relaid after each firing. After firing, a gun could roll backwards for several yards depending on its size and the force of the propelling charge. By the end of the nineteenth century most cannon had a recoil mechanism that absorbed much of the shock from firing and that permitted repeated firings without having to relay the piece.

The perfection of a recoil system using a hydrostatic buffer and recuperator system enabled the French to build their first 75-mm field gun in 1893 and adopt it as standard in 1897. This extremely light and highly mobile piece became the first of many "quick-firing" guns. Since the gun recoiled into its cradle, the breech could be easily opened and the gun reloaded and fired in a matter of seconds. Though the standard rate of fire was six rounds per minute, a much higher rate of twenty rounds per minute could be attained in an emergency. The introduction of the French 75-mm gun soon forced most armies to spend vast sums modernizing their artillery.

Although the French remained content with their revolutionary 75-mm gun and neglected the development of heavier, longer-range artillery, the Germans recognized the need for heavy artillery. Before 1870 the Krupp steel-making firm had prodded the German military into capitalizing on the use of steel in making breech-loading artillery; and in the late 1870s the firm gave several spectacular demonstrations on the capabilities of extremely large artillery pieces. For a time the German navy took more advantage of the large Krupp pieces than did the army, but after carefully studying the Russo-Japanese War of 1904–1905 and observing the vulnerability of guns in the open, the German army increased its heavy artillery in its divisions, corps, and field armies. By 1914, the possession of this heavy artillery and its long-range and plunging fire gave the Germans an advantage over most other armies.

Machine Guns

As artillery was shifted from a short-range, direct-fire role to a longer-range, indirect-fire role, the machine gun began providing close-range fire support for the infantry. Just as the French failed to recognize the potential of the *mitrailleuse* in 1870, however, most armies failed to recognize the potential of the machine gun and eventually entered World War I with only a small number in each infantry division. Before 1914, most military leaders had reservations about the reliability and utility of the awkward, heavy weapons. Prior to 1884, machine guns depended on some sort of external power source, such as the hand-cranking motion required to fire the Gatling gun. When the American Hiram S. Maxim produced the first self-powered machine gun in the spring of 1884, the weapon became truly automatic for the first time.

Actuated by the recoil that came from the firing of the shell, the new gun attained a rate of fire of over 600 rounds per minute.

One of the first nations to recognize the potential of the machine gun was Russia. After testing two Gatling guns in 1865, the Russians ordered more than one hundred and then began manufacturing their own. By the time of the Russo-Turkish War of 1877–1878, they had over 400 Gatling guns and used them extensively in that war. By the time of the Russo-Japanese War of 1904–1905, each Russian division had its own machine-gun company. The Japanese were not as enthusiastic about the new weapon, but its use by the Russians convinced them of its value and they too soon supplied each of their divisions with twenty-four machine guns.

By 1914, most armies had supplied their infantry divisions with machine guns and often organized them into separate companies or batteries, rather than integrating them into regiments or battalions. Though not completely portable, the new weapons were much more mobile than the older ones. In 1912, for example, the British adopted the new Vickers Maxim, which was water-cooled but weighed only thirty-eight pounds, significantly lighter than the sixty pounds of the older model. The Vickers was Britain's principal heavy machine gun in both world wars.

At the beginning of World War I, each British, French and German infantry battalion had two heavy machine guns. By the end of 1918, British and German battalions had about fifty light and heavy machine guns, while French battalions had about forty. This dramatic increase clearly illustrates how battlefield experience overcame the reservations most armies had about machine guns.

Gatling guns at their Washington trials, May 6, 1866. Dr. Richard Gatling invented the gun, which consisted of rifled barrels revolving around a central fixed axis. Hiram S. Maxim's automatic machine gun soon made the Gatling gun obsolete.

Rifles

Even though breech-loading, bolt-action rifles were used in the Franco-Prussian War, the introduction of smokeless powder, adoption of magazines, and perfection of metallic cartridges greatly improved the rifle before 1914. The first widely used European breechloader was the Prussian needle gun, which used paper cartridges and a bolt. Its design provided the basis for future improvements. In 1871, a German, Peter Paul Mauser, introduced one of the first successful metallic-cartridge, bolt-action rifles. The next fifteen years saw other important advances. One of the most significant improvements came with the introduction of magazines that increased a rifle's rate of fire. Instead of a soldier having to load each round awkwardly by hand, magazines enabled him to load another round by simply opening the bolt and then pushing it forward. In 1885, an Austrian inventor, Ferdinand Ritter von Mannlicher, introduced the clip-loading magazine system that soon became a common feature on many modern rifles.

After the French in 1886 adopted the Lebel rifle, which used smokeless powder, most states recognized the need to improve their rifles. By the early 1890s, every major army in the world—except the United States—had adopted bolt-action, magazine-fed rifles that used smokeless powder. In 1893, after a decade of tedious testing, the U.S. Army finally adopted its first general-issue magazine rifle, the .30-caliber, 5-shot Krag-Jorgensen. Named for its Scandinavian designers, the bolt-action rifle used smokeless powder and rivaled in range and accuracy most European rifles of its time. Despite the sturdiness of the "Krag," the Spanish-American War revealed it was not as good as the Spanish Mauser, and in 1903 the United States adopted the bolt-action Springfield, which quickly earned a reputation for excellence and reliability.

Improvements in weapons were not the only technological advances that affected the waging of war. As the telegraph and telephone became more common, commanders no longer had to rely solely on messengers or semaphores to communicate. Decades would pass, however, before reliable wireless telegraphy became commonplace. Despite the wave of new weapons that began to appear at the end of the nineteenth century, most armies made only moderate changes in their methods at the beginning of the twentieth century and did not make more extensive changes until after August 1914. Most remained content with incremental rather than radical change.

The Example of the Prussian System

While technological advances exercised great influence over the waging of war, changes in the social and political structures of Western states expanded the scale and scope of modern war throughout the nineteenth century. At the same time, the expanding influence of governments over the lives of their citizens contributed to a greater reliance on mass armies. As governments grappled at the end of the nineteenth century with the complexities of organizing and fielding mass armies, intense debates occurred over the question of creating more modern military systems and a more professional corps of officers.

After Germany's quick victories over the Austrian Empire and France in 1866 and 1871, most states attempted to copy or at least borrow from the Germans. Every major power studied the German system of mobilizing and fielding a mass army as well as their system of higher military education. Military leaders recognized that the German general staff provided new levels of expertise and effectiveness to military administration. Some even credited the Germans with having achieved a revolution in military organization.

In the years following the Franco-Prussian War, the German general staff expanded greatly in influence and size, increasing from 64 in 1857, to 135 in 1871, to 239 in 1888, to 625 in 1914. At the *Kriegsakademie*, technical studies were completely under the control of the general staff. Similarly, its influence over the railway system increased as intricate plans for the mobilization and concentration of armies were completed. Another important step in its growing influence occurred in 1883, when the chief of the general staff received permission to have direct access to the kaiser, even in peacetime. The wine-red stripe on the collar and trousers of the uniform of the general staff officers became a symbol not only for the highest standards of competence and professionalism, but also of an elite and highly influential group.

After the Franco-Prussian War, Great Britain finally initiated long-overdue reforms to overcome weaknesses that had become apparent in the Crimean War. These reforms are normally associated with the name of Edward Cardwell, the secretary of war, and included abolishing the purchase of commissions, shortening the term of service for soldiers, creating a larger reserve, and streamlining the army's command structure. Although the reforms did not establish a carbon copy of the German army in Great Britain and did not create a general staff, they did permit the British army to function more efficiently and effectively in the later years of the nineteenth century.

France borrowed ideas more heavily from the Germans than did the British. Following its defeat in 1871, France carefully studied German methods of education and organization and made several important reforms. Among these were improvements in its military schools and in the preparation of its general staff officers. France was reluctant, nevertheless, to give its general staff officers special responsibilities and authority, and its reorganized military schools became even more technical than those in Germany. Staff officers remained technicians and never had the influence of German general staff officers.

Though French military leaders supported the adoption of conscription and accepted the necessity to create a mass army, they were reluctant to rely as extensively on reserve units as did the Germans. They did create reserve units and developed a more efficient system of mobilization, but reserves were relegated to a secondary role. Similarly, France made some changes in the command structure of its army, but republican leaders refused to appoint a single commander-in-chief who could provide firm leadership. They appointed one officer to be chief of the general staff and designated another to assume command of the army in the event of war.

In the United States, some fears surfaced about the wisdom of following the German model of a general staff and a massive army. The U.S. Congress debated the ideas of Brevet Major-General Emory Upton about organizing an expansible army with a large cadre of professional soldiers, but many congressional leaders remained fearful of "Germanizing" the U.S. Army and giving it influence over other governmental institutions. The few military reforms that occurred in the United States came through the efforts of Elihu Root, who served as secretary of war from 1899 to 1904. Root succeeded in increasing the size of the army and in partially reorganizing and reforming the War Department general staff, but he accomplished these reforms only after encountering numerous difficulties during the Spanish-American War.

While the United States remained uninterested in establishing a large military force, General William Tecumseh Sherman made advanced education for U.S. Army officers possible with the establishment of the School of Application for Infantry and Cavalry at Fort Leavenworth, Kansas, in 1881. During the next two decades, officers such as John F. Morrison, Eben Swift, and Arthur Wagner guided the transformation of the school from a technical school of tactics to a true staff college preparing officers for high-level duties. Sherman also influenced Commodore Stephen B. Luce who persuaded the navy to establish the Naval War College at Newport, Rhode Island, in 1884. Among Luce's most important accomplishments at the Naval War College was his selection of Alfred Thayer Mahan to join the faculty. In 1901, two of Sherman's protégés, Tasker H. Bliss and William H. Carter, played key roles in the establishment of the Army War College. The establishment of advanced military schools by the army and navy demonstrated American recognition of the requirement for officers to study their professions in depth. In the broadest sense, however, American improvements in professional military education and high-level staffs were part of a wave of reforms that swept most military forces of the industrialized world at the turn of the century.

Throughout the Western world, the years between 1871 and 1914 witnessed the emergence of a more professional corps of officers who devoted their lives to mastering the highly technical skills of their profession. Almost none of these professionals, however, anticipated the sort of fighting that would be encountered after the opening battles of World War I. Most believed that improvements in technology favored the offense and made battle more decisive. Expecting heavy casualties in future battles, they demanded larger armies and prepared them to fight in highly mobile and short campaigns. They refused to believe that any country would endure for very long the huge costs of fielding and supporting large forces or would accept the heavy casualties modern weapons could inflict. Despite their increased professionalism, the campaigns they foresaw in the future resembled those of 1870 more than they did those of 1914–1918.

The New "Navalism"

Throughout the 1870s and part of the 1880s, most Western nations placed a stronger emphasis on armies than on navies. Expenditures on navies remained relatively moderate in the years following the American Civil War and the Franco-Prussian War. Nations remained indifferent to overseas empires from the end of the Napoleonic Wars through the mid-1870s, but beginning in the mid-1870s many began placing an increasing emphasis on naval power.

As Western powers expanded their navies, intense rivalries emerged between the British, on the one hand, and the French and Russians, on the other. At the end of the nineteenth century the Germans also applied their considerable industrial capabilities to the creation of a powerful naval force. The emergence of a strong German fleet came from the efforts of Admiral Alfred von Tirpitz, who dominated the German navy from the early 1890s through 1916. The British in particular became concerned about the growth of naval power in other countries, and in 1888 a special committee of British admirals recommended that "no time should be lost in placing the British navy beyond comparison with that of any two powers." The British government endorsed this proposal and by 1890 had considerably increased its naval expenditures. France and Russia reacted promptly by increasing their naval budgets as well. A second British building program began in 1893–1894 and a third in 1904 after Germany decided to build up its navy.

The United States also became deeply involved in the naval rivalry. In the short period from the early 1880s through 1908, the United States went from having a navy inferior to many second-rate powers to having the second-largest fleet in the world. In 1890 the United States decided to build three battleships, the *Indiana, Massachusetts,* and *Oregon.* By 1898, the U.S. Navy had four "first-class" battleships, plus numerous other modern ships. In keeping with the tenor of the times, the navy was designed as a "blue-water" force for controlling the sea.

The naval competition and buildup that emerged at the end of the nineteenth century was a result not only of competition over the size of fleets but also of the technology used in ships. With the greatly increased use of steel and the almost universal adoption of better gunpowder, navies concentrated on improving the size and firing range of guns, the thickness of armor protection, and the speed of their ships. Advances occurred in the development of new armor-piercing shells and the adoption of hydraulic recoil mechanisms for the powerful weapons. Changes also occurred in ship design with the introduction of turrets and barbettes that permitted all-around fire and significantly increased the firing power of the battleship.

In 1906 the launching of the HMS *Dreadnought* by the British admiralty made all other battleships obsolete. Older battleships had carried a mixture of guns of varying ranges and calibers. The *Dreadnought,* however, was an "all big-gun" ship. Although it did have an antitorpedo-boat battery of twenty-four 12-pounders, its main armament was ten 12-inch guns, each of which could fire an 850-pound projectile. With firepower on the new ship being more than double that of other battleships, most navies had no choice but to build "dreadnoughts" if they hoped to maintain their status as naval powers. Ironically, the idea for an all big-gun ship came from an Italian designer, and the United States and Japan were already moving in the direction of larger, faster, more heavily gunned ships when the British launched the *Dreadnought*.

Naval Theorists

As naval officers reflected on the effects of the changes occurring in naval warfare at the end of the nineteenth century, new ideas began to emerge. In France, Admiral H. L. T. Aube became the main spokesman for what was known as the *Jeune École*. According to members of this school of thought, technological advances in mines and torpedoes had rendered the older and much more expensive approaches to naval warfare obsolete and had ended the dominance of the battleship over the sea. Aube and his followers believed that relatively inexpensive torpedo boats, mines, and small warships could launch raids on commercial shipping (*guerre de course*) and could thereby have a significant strategic effect. Most of the proponents of the *Jeune École* came from France, where the allure of a technological alternative seemed to offer a way of establishing France as a naval power without having to build an extraordinarily expensive fleet based on battleships.

Despite the appeal of a less costly alternative, the most important theorist of naval power during this period of profound change was the American Captain Alfred Thayer Mahan, whose work, *The Influence of Sea Power upon History* (1890), became the bible for most navies at the turn of the century. Instead of focusing on the technology and costs of war, Mahan concentrated on history. As one of the few original American theorists on military or naval affairs, he studied history to determine the experience and characteristics of nations that had been great sea powers. While arguing that the greatest nations had been those with sea power, he observed that certain natural factors affected the ability of a state to become a sea power. These factors included geographic position, extent of territory, availability of ports, size and character of population, and attitude of government. According to Mahan, England was especially well-suited to be a great sea power because it was surrounded by water and thus had little need for a large army; it also had numerous ports, an expanding population interested in trade and commerce, and a government favoring industrial, commercial, and naval activities. Mahan concluded that the United States also possessed most of these factors and had the potential to be a great sea power.

Mahan looked beyond the factors influencing the development of sea power and addressed how it should be used. The principal purpose of a navy was to gain "command of the sea" by controlling the areas of sea communication. This could be attained by securing sea communications for one's own cargo vessels while denying their use by an enemy. Rejecting completely the ideas of the *Jeune École*, which stressed raids on commercial shipping, Mahan argued that only the destruction or neutralization of an enemy's fleet with a more powerful fleet could lead to securing the sea for one's own use. Mahan's message was clear: no nation could maintain world-wide influence and commercial greatness without a large battle fleet. He also insisted that concentration was the "predominant principle" of naval warfare and concluded, "Never divide the fleet!"

Although Mahan's ideas initially were not well received in the United States, his works were read widely throughout the world, particularly in Britain, Germany, and Japan. Indeed many naval officers agreed with Mahan's theory. As for the practicality of *guerre de course*, naval officers agreed that such ideas were appropriate only for inferior powers who did not have the resources or will to construct powerful fleets.

One of the most important alternatives to Mahan's ideas came from Sir Julian S. Corbett, a lecturer at the British Royal Naval War College who made significant contributions to the concept of maritime strategy. In 1911 he published *Some Principles of Maritime Strategy*, which became very controversial in naval circles. He defined maritime strategy as the "principles which govern a war in which the sea is a substantial factor." He added, "The paramount concern . . . of maritime strategy is to determine the mutual relations of your army and navy in a plan of war." Corbett argued that it was "almost impossible" for a war to be "decided by naval action alone." He explained:

> Since men live upon the land and not upon the sea, great issues between nations at war have always been decided—except in the rarest of cases—either by what your army can do against your enemy's territory and national life, or else by fear of what the fleet makes it possible for your army to do.

Corbett differed from Mahan in that he believed command of the sea was only a means to an end. In the decades before 1914, when Western states used naval and land forces to project power around the globe, the role of naval power more closely resembled the ideas of Corbett than those of Mahan or the *Jeune École*. Most naval officers, however, preferred Mahan's arguments, for his emphasis on sea power and the clash of battle fleets, rather than maritime strategy, suggested that the fleet was the most crucial element of national power.

Small Wars and Regional Wars Before 1914: Mixing the Old and the New

At the end of the nineteenth century, Western states greatly enlarged their territorial possessions around the world in what has been called the "new imperialism." With Social Darwinism encouraging the notion of competition between races, the French often spoke of their "civilizing mission," and

Rudyard Kipling passionately exhorted the British to "take up the White Man's Burden." The hope of converting people to Christianity encouraged numerous missionaries to seek converts. Economic considerations also had an effect. Though the new possessions often proved unprofitable and expensive, the Western powers sought natural resources and new markets in their far-flung empires. With tariff barriers rising in the late nineteenth century, they feared being locked out of vast areas of the globe. Many of those who participated in the new imperialism believed foreign possessions enhanced the prestige of their country, adding to its status as a world power. After the completion of the Suez Canal in 1869, the British aggressively safeguarded this important link to their imperial possessions in South Asia; and for similar reasons the United States established firm control over the Panama Canal in 1903.

The expansion of steam power contributed to the expansion of the Western powers' territories. As screw propellers replaced paddle wheels, more efficient steam engines reduced fuel consumption and increased ships' range. With transportation costs declining, the shipment of goods and low-priced raw materials between continents became common, and large passenger liners frequently plied the oceans. As intercontinental trade prospered, the capability to transport troops and supplies improved, and the projection of power across vast portions of the globe became more efficient. Without this naval capability, the Western states could not have expanded their influence and territories so easily.

As the Western powers expanded their empires around the globe, they became involved occasionally in what were called "small wars" to conquer or to police their colonial possessions. In some cases, a show of naval strength—gunboat diplomacy—enabled them to influence or gain control over a city or a region. When a show of force did not work, the threat of a bombardment (such as American Commodore Matthew C. Perry's threatening Tokyo in March 1854) or the actual bombardment of a city (such as the British shelling of Alexandria, Egypt, in July 1882) sometimes compelled a ruler to yield to Western demands. In many cases, however, the Western powers used land forces to achieve their objectives. In *Queen Victoria's Little Wars*, for example, Byron Farwell listed some 230 "wars, military expeditions, and campaigns" conducted by the British from 1837 through 1901.

By the end of the nineteenth century, the French and British had developed highly effective methods for conducting operations in distant regions. The French often conducted offensive operations with what they called "mobile columns"; these were heavily armed, highly mobile forces, consisting primarily of professional soldiers and members of the French Foreign Legion. The mobile columns would conduct forced marches deep into enemy territory, seize key terrain or important enemy leaders, and seek to end the fighting in a swift, sure strike. In 1899, Major Charles E. Callwell of the British army wrote a book entitled *Small Wars: Their Principles and Practice*. He focused on the operations of well-equipped and well-trained forces against poorly equipped and trained opponents and suggested that such conditions led intervening forces to rely primarily on offensive operations. While advocating methods similar to those used by the French, Callwell warned of the difficulty of striking a decisive blow against a foe who operated by different rules and who probably had greater mobility. He also warned of the difficulties of obtaining adequate information about the enemy. Nonetheless, he argued that intervening forces would face their greatest challenges in dealing with questions of transport and supply. According to Callwell, the nature of such campaigns was completely different from that of "modern regular warfare."

Not all wars at the end of the nineteenth century resulted from attempts by Western states to expand their colonial empires; some stemmed from traditional power politics, economic rivalries, and long-term animosities. Examples of these wars are the War of the Pacific in 1879–1884 between Chile, Peru, and Bolivia, the Russo-Turkish War of 1877–1878, the Sino-Japanese War of 1894–1895, the Greek and Turkish War of 1896, the Tripolitan War of 1912 between Italy and Turkey, and the First and Second Balkan Wars of 1912 and 1913. Though most of the "small wars" were short and did not involve new methods or weapons, military leaders studied them carefully. Unfortunately for the soldiers of 1914, most armies would learn little about future warfare from the numerous conflicts at the end of the nineteenth century.

The Spanish-American War

Of the several wars fought around the turn of the century, the Spanish-American War represented a transition between the old and the new. This was due in part to Spain's declining power and the rising world power of the United States. The Americans expected to achieve a quick and relatively painless victory, but while the navy performed superbly, the army, which was unprepared for war, experienced significant difficulties during the early days of the conflict. The fighting against Spain lasted only four months with the most important land fighting lasting only one month. But the United States also became involved in putting down the Philippine insurrection, a bitter guerrilla war that lasted more than three years. What was supposed to be a "splendid little war" turned out to be something far different.

The war began because of American concern over Spanish presence and activities in Cuba. After the outbreak of a rebellion in Cuba in 1895 and another in the Philippines in 1896, American sentiment strongly supported the Cubans against the Spanish, who were accused of employing barbarous methods to suppress the rebellion. President William McKinley hoped to achieve a diplomatic solution to the Cuban problem, but two events occurred that aroused a storm of public indignation in the United States. One of these was the publication of a private letter from the Spanish minister in Washington expressing strong criticisms of President McKinley. Another was the sinking of the battleship *Maine* in Havana harbor with the loss of 260 lives. Though the explosion that sank the ship may have come from ammunition in its hold, an outpouring of demands for war literally overwhelmed the American government, leading it to make a formal declaration of war on April 25, 1898.

The U.S. Navy was well prepared for the war because it had five battleships, four of which were new and rated as first class. The Spanish could not match American sea power since they had only one battleship and it was rated as second class. The American advantage in sea power greatly affected the outcome of the war, because, as suggested by Corbett, it enabled the United States to land and support armies in Cuba, Puerto Rico, and the Philippines. It also blocked Spain from reinforcing and resupplying its threatened possessions.

Compared to the preparedness of the navy, the army was not ready to fight a modern war. With a regular army of about 28,000 and a National Guard of about 100,000, the United States was neither organized nor trained to fight a war outside the mainland. The army had an inefficient staff in Washington, no system of effective mobilization, no up-to-date knowledge of the Spanish forces, no accurate maps of Cuba or the Philippines, and very few modern weapons. With no unit larger than a regiment, the regular army was accustomed to operating in small units and employing tactics that worked well against the Indians but not against a foreign power. The National Guard was especially unprepared, for its units had little practical experience other than close-order drill. Subsequent difficulties and misfortunes stemmed primarily from this unpreparedness and from the complexities of implementing policies rapidly with too few trained soldiers and inadequate supplies.

Except for a naval plan that called for blockading Cuba, isolating Spanish forces on the island, and attacking a Spanish squadron in Philippine waters, no war plans existed. With no clear strategic objective in mind, the army prepared to send a corps under General William R. Shafter against Havana. Shafter was supposed to capture a port city near Havana and, after the arrival of additional forces, attack the capital city.

The outpouring of volunteers and demands for use of the National Guard quickly swamped the War Department, and by July the United States had mustered more than 270,000 troops and rushed them to camps in the southern states. Since the supply services had maintained stockpiles for a force of only 40,000, the assembled forces could not be issued essential items such as uniforms, shoes, socks, and underwear. For weapons, the regular forces were armed with the newly adopted Krag-Jorgensen rifle, but the National Guard and the volunteers carried the obsolete .45-70 Springfield, a single-shot breechloader that used black powder.

The Spanish navy was reluctant to engage the U.S. Navy, but in April a small Spanish fleet under Admiral Pascual Cervera y Topete sailed slowly from Spain toward the Caribbean. When information about the sortie became known in Washington on April 29, a panic spread along the American east coast, and for a time the navy and army were overwhelmed with calls for coastal defense. The response of the navy was to divide the North Atlantic Squadron into two main parts, even though the action violated Mahan's precept about never dividing a fleet. Under the command of acting Rear Admiral William T. Sampson, the first part prepared for offensive action against Cuba and Puerto Rico. The second, known as the "Flying

Squadron," was under the command of Commodore Winfield Scott Schley and prepared itself to protect the Atlantic seaboard.

While the U.S. Navy searched the Atlantic for Cervera's ships, Commodore George Dewey audaciously steamed into Manila harbor in the Philippines on the night of April 30; the following morning in a battle lasting only a few hours, he destroyed the entire Spanish fleet in the harbor. Dewey had an overwhelming advantage: the seven Spanish vessels outnumbered his six, but his were more modern, had armored decks, and carried longer-range guns. More importantly, intense training before the fight had made American guns much more effective than they otherwise may have been. His crushing victory made him a national hero overnight.

Meanwhile, in the Caribbean, Cervera could not get sufficient coal at other ports, so he put into the harbor of Santiago de Cuba, the only unblocked Cuban port. By chance the Americans discovered him, and soon the squadrons of Sampson and Schley assumed blockading positions off the harbor. By blockading Cervera, the navy had secured the fundamental objective of the naval campaign in the Caribbean—command of the sea. The United States could now operate at will against Cuba and Puerto Rico. The Spanish fleet, however, could not be destroyed without the elimination of the Spanish shore batteries around the harbor. Admiral Sampson soon called for army troops to eliminate these batteries.

General Shafter's corps received the mission of landing in Cuba, and he chose to land at Daiquiri, about twenty miles from Santiago's harbor, rather than storm the 250-foot bluffs at the harbor's entrance. Though unopposed, the landing did not go smoothly. The lack of coordination, the unwillingness of the civilian transport captains to bring their vessels close to shore, and the lack of sufficient lighters to carry troops and equipment from ship to shore caused the landing to drag on for four days.

As soon as a sizable contingent of troops was on shore, Shafter ordered his advance guard to occupy Siboney (about eight miles closer to Santiago), which was better suited than Daiquiri for landings. After assembling sufficient forces and supplies, he planned on pushing westward from Siboney toward the high ground known as San Juan Heights, overlooking Santiago. But his advance guard disregarded his orders and advanced quickly toward the city; the Americans brashly attacked the Spanish rear guard about three miles northwest of Siboney and suffered severe casualties.

News of the clash forced Shafter to move forward and take personal command of his forces. After analyzing the situation and terrain, he decided to launch a two-staged attack, first clearing his right flank by assaulting the fortified village of El Caney, two miles to the north, and then advancing west toward the San Juan Heights, which consisted of San Juan Hill and Kettle Hill. He asked local insurgents to block a road running north out of Santiago and thereby prevent the arrival of Spanish reinforcements. Anticipating the easy capture of El Caney and the San Juan Heights, Shafter expected to enter Santiago quickly.

Unfortunately for the Americans, the Spanish were strongly entrenched and fortified at El Caney. Using their excellent Mauser rifles with great effectiveness, the 521 Spaniards held off the 5,400 Americans for more than eight hours. American artillery, which consisted of four light guns, provided some support, but only in the final hours of fighting, when the guns concentrated their fire against a stone fort, did they open the way for a final charge against the Spanish position.

Meanwhile, two divisions moved slowly along the road to Santiago. They raised an inflatable, hot-air balloon to improve observation, but the Spanish used it as an aiming point for their artillery and inflicted heavy casualties on the Americans who were struggling to move forward. Similarly, the Americans opened fire on the San Juan Heights with four light guns, but smoke from the guns' black powder revealed their location to the enemy and brought in highly effective counterbattery fire. With plunging fire coming from the heights to their front, the situation became even more confused when the leading regiment—the 71st New York Volunteers—panicked and refused to advance.

The Americans finally began their attack even though they did not have artillery support and had to move through barbed-wire entanglements. The attack on San Juan Hill succeeded only because of the fortunate placing of fire on the Spanish position by six Gatling guns under the control of Second Lieutenant John H. Parker. Kettle Hill, which was just north of San Juan Hill, fell under the assault of the African-American troops of the Ninth Cavalry with the First Cavalry and Rough Riders following closely behind.

Instead of continuing on to Santiago, the Americans immediately halted and prepared for a counterattack. Shafter reinforced the San Juan Heights and abandoned all thoughts of moving quickly toward Santiago. The Americans were disorganized and shaken. They had taken 1,385 casualties at El Caney and the San Juan Heights, but the strongest defenses still

African-American troops in the Spanish-American War. Members of the Ninth Cavalry distinguished themselves in the fighting and led the assault on Kettle Hill.

lay to their front. Colonel Theodore Roosevelt, who had participated in the charge, wrote to a friend, "We are within measurable distance of a terrible military disaster."

Concluding that he could not penetrate the Spanish second line of defense, Shafter cabled the War Department and asked permission to withdraw toward Siboney until the arrival of reinforcements and additional supplies. After the secretary of war ordered him to hold his position, he turned to the navy and asked Admiral Sampson to force his way into the harbor. This seemed a ridiculous request to Sampson, who argued that his ships could not enter the harbor until the army destroyed the shore batteries at its mouth.

While the admiral and general debated what was to be done, the entire situation changed abruptly on July 3 when Admiral Cervera received orders from Spanish authorities in Havana to flee the harbor at Santiago. Though such a move would be suicidal, Cervera obeyed, and American naval forces soon destroyed his entire fleet in a running fight that lasted less than four hours. Knowing the destruction of the Spanish fleet had completely isolated the defenders of Santiago, Shafter demanded their surrender. After a long-range naval bombardment on July 10 and 11, the commander in Santiago agreed to surrender his garrison and all troops in eastern Cuba. On July 17, 1898, American troops entered Santiago. Less than a month later, forces under General Nelson Miles easily secured Puerto Rico.

As for the Philippines, an American army corps under the command of General Wesley Merritt had departed for Manila on May 25, before the landing in Cuba at Daiquiri. With about 8,500 troops, Merritt's corps took

Capron's battery firing on the morning of July 1. The battery provided support in the assault on the Spanish fortified position at El Caney. Note the clouds of smoke caused by the burning of black powder.

up positions behind a Filipino insurgent army under Emilio Aguinaldo, who had proclaimed himself the leader of the independence movement and whose forces surrounded the Spanish in Manila. After a sharp fight on August 13, in which the Americans lost 17 killed and 105 wounded, the Spanish surrendered. Tragically, the battle occurred two days after Spain and the United States agreed to an armistice.

After the United States formally proclaimed possession of the Philippines in January 1899, Aguinaldo and other insurgent leaders were outraged, for they did not intend meekly to accept the exchange of one foreign ruler for another. Their insurrection proved to be much more difficult and prolonged than the war against Spain. After several years of fighting, the collapse of the Filipino resistance accelerated rapidly in 1901 when American soldiers captured Aguinaldo in a daring raid. Though the insurrection continued, resistance eventually collapsed. On July 4, 1902, President Roosevelt announced that the war had ended.

Public outrage at the difficulties encountered in the Philippine Insurrection and in the Spanish-American War led to several reforms, most notably the creation of a War Department general staff by Elihu Root. Clearly, modern war required trained staffs and technicians who could plan and execute complex operations. Root also improved the army's school system, making it more comprehensive and adding the War College. Recognizing the difficulties encountered in organizing forces for the war, Congress passed the Dick Act of January 1903, which ensured better coordination between the active army forces and the National Guard. Tactically, the war demonstrated the advantages of smokeless powder, but it also demonstrated the difficulty of overcoming a well-organized defense. Neither the Americans nor the Europeans, however, learned very much from the fighting in Cuba.

The Boer War

Of the numerous wars fought around the turn of the century, the Boer War in South Africa had a significant influence on military thinking because of the demonstrated effect of firepower. The Boers were hardy people whose ancestors were Dutch colonists. When Great Britain annexed the Cape of Good Hope after the Napoleonic Wars (subsequently naming it Cape Colony), many Boers made the "Great Trek" north to avoid the British mandate of 1834 to emancipate their slaves. They soon established the two republics of Transvaal and the Orange Free State, and between 1852 and 1854 Britain recognized their independence.

The discovery of vast quantities of diamonds in the Transvaal renewed Britain's interest in the region. In 1877, it annexed the Transvaal as the first step in an attempt to expand its control over South Africa. In December 1880, however, the Boers proclaimed their independence and inflicted several defeats on the British. Prime Minister William E. Gladstone was unwilling to continue the war and in April concluded a treaty that gave the Transvaal its independence.

The discovery of huge gold deposits in the southern Transvaal soon precipitated another crisis. Waves of British people and capital poured into southern Africa, and the mistreatment of some of the immigrants by the Boers caused great concern in London. When negotiations collapsed, Great Britain sent reinforcements to Cape Colony. As British troops arrived in Cape Town, the two Boer republics decided to attack instead of waiting for an invasion. They hoped to capture several key ports and enormous quantities of artillery and supplies before the British had sufficient forces in place to defeat them. They also hoped that a rapid strike against key points would shake the entire British Empire.

With a strength greater than 40,000, the Boers initially swept easily through British Rhodesia, Natal, and Cape Colony in October 1899 and besieged British garrisons at several key cities. In addition to being extremely fine marksmen, the Boers had a small number of modern artillery pieces, including 75-mm, 120-mm, and 155-mm guns and howitzers. Even though the British slowly increased their strength from about 15,000 to more than 60,000, they suffered several sharp and costly defeats in their attempts to relieve the besieged garrisons.

The British commander, General Sir Redvers Buller, recognized the Boers' strengths and began altering his tactics among which were modifications in old-fashioned methods of using artillery. Given the range and accuracy of modern rifles, the artillery pieces could no longer deploy on line in the open and fire over open sights at a visible target. Against exposed artillery, a rifleman could conceal himself and deliver deadly, accurate fire. Artillerymen quickly learned the advantages of firing from a concealed position or behind folds in the ground. To deliver their fire accurately from these concealed positions, they had to develop new and improved methods of indirect fire. They also learned how to fire rounds behind ridges and hills where an enemy had previously been safe from artillery projectiles. Another important advance was the coordinating of artillery and infantry actions more closely. British infantry learned to crawl along the ground with a slowly advancing curtain of shell fire to their front. These and other improvements, such as better use of cover and advancing by rushes, soon enabled the British to move more effectively against the Boers.

While the British improved their tactical methods, Field Marshal Frederick S. Roberts, who had gained fame in the second Afghanistan War, replaced General Buller as commander of British troops in December 1899. General Horatio H. Kitchener became his second-in-command. During 1900, Roberts' forces increased to some 200,000, and they attacked deeply into Boer territory, relieving several besieged garrisons. After the defeat of the main Boer forces, Roberts departed for England, leaving Kitchener in charge. As he left, he was certain the war was practically over.

Unwilling to concede defeat, however, the Boers changed their strategy. The arrival of large numbers of British troops and the loss of several important battles convinced the Boers that they could not attack their enemies directly and that instead they had to employ guerrilla tactics. With the supply lines of the British spread over thousands of square miles, the Boers struck again and again at vulnerable points and inflicted significant losses.

Boer soldiers proved to be excellent marksmen. Their long-range, smokeless, magazine rifles proved highly effective against British soldiers who were wearing gleaming insignia, stars, buttons, and buckles.

British Campaign Against the Boers, 1899–1900

Kitchener believed he had little choice but to conduct large operations in search of his elusive enemy. He and his men began defining success in terms of the number of enemy killed and captured. He also decided to sweep the countryside clear of anything that could give sustenance to the guerrillas. As part of this effort, he concentrated women and children in protected "laagers" alongside railway lines and even resorted to reducing their rations to force their husbands and fathers to surrender. Because of poor diet and inadequate sanitation practices, thousands of Boers died in these concentration camps. By the time the fighting ended, the cost in lives was about 22,000 British soldiers, 7,000 Boer soldiers, 18,000 to 28,000 Boers in the camps, and more than 12,000 black Africans.

In addition to learning more about the coordination of artillery and infantry, the British left the Boer War with a greater respect for rifle fire. They recognized the importance of accurate, rapid fire from modern rifles and concentrated on improving the marksmanship of their infantry. Well-trained British soldiers prided themselves on being able to fire as many as fifteen rounds a minute. By 1914, Great Britain placed a stronger premium on rifle fire than any other European nation.

Even though the experience of the Boer War taught most British officers the importance of firepower and impressed on them the difficulty of crossing an area covered by small arms and machine-gun fire, they tended to downplay the effect of firepower on tactics and concluded that a war on the European continent would be different from the Boer War. Most believed the effect of modern weapons could be overcome by stronger discipline and better training rather than improvements in infantry tactics and in coordination between the artillery and infantry. Although the British military did institute some changes, they brushed aside their most important experiences in the Boer War.

The Russo-Japanese War

In the Far East, the Russo-Japanese War of 1904–1905 demonstrated both the complexities of employing large mass armies and the effect of the new, highly lethal weapons. The root of that conflict came from the intentions of both Russia and Japan to expand into the territory of the declining Chinese Empire. Japan was particularly interested in Korea's serving as a base for further expansion into China and a way to prevent a rival nation from transforming the jutting Korean peninsula into "a dagger pointed at Japan's heart." Russia wanted to expand its influence into neighboring Manchuria, Korea, and perhaps Mongolia as part of its centuries-old expansion toward the Pacific. Convinced that a partition of China by the Great Powers would soon occur, both Russia and Japan hastened to establish themselves in Korea and Manchuria.

After Japan soundly defeated China in the Sino-Japanese War of 1894–1895, it won control over part of the Liaotung Peninsula in the southern extremity of Manchuria, lying just west of Korea and projecting into the Yellow Sea. The diplomatic intervention of Russia, France, and Germany, however, forced Japan to relinquish its control over the Liaotung Peninsula and Port Arthur on the southern tip of the peninsula. Russia soon gained permission from China to build the eastern section of the Trans-Siberian Railway through Manchuria and in 1897 acquired a lease over the Liaotung Peninsula and Port Arthur. In addition, Russia extended a spur of the Trans-Siberian Railway south to Port Arthur. Amidst growing resentment over being "robbed" of their victory over the Chinese, the Japanese became even more angry when Russian designs on Korea became apparent; many Japanese officials regarded war as inevitable.

Russia had several advantages—primarily its huge army and relatively large fleet. However, it could reinforce its troops in east Asia only by moving them along the lengthy, single-track trans-Siberian Railway; and its fleet was split between the Baltic, the Black Sea, and the Far East. Though Japan had a smaller army and navy, it had the advantage of being close to the Liaotung Peninsula. If the Japanese could concentrate their forces and defeat the Russians before the arrival of reinforcements, they had a solid chance of victory.

Around midnight on February 8, 1904, the Japanese launched a surprise attack against the Russians at Port Arthur. Using destroyers in a night torpedo attack, Vice Admiral Togo Heihachiro struck the force of Russian battleships and cruisers. Though he hit two battleships and one cruiser, he failed to destroy the fleet, and for the next six months, the Russian fleet remained trapped in Port Arthur.

The Russo-Japanese War, 1904–1905

Shortly after the attack on Port Arthur, elements of the Japanese First Army began landing in Korea at Chemulpo (near Seoul) and moving north toward the Yalu River. Despite the bitter cold of the Korean winter, the Japanese reached the Yalu River at the beginning of April. After defeating the Russian forces along the river, the First Army began moving northwest toward Liaoyang. In early May, the Japanese Second Army landed about seventy-five miles north of Port Arthur under the protection of Togo's fleet and moved down the Liaotung Peninsula toward Port Arthur. The Japanese hoped to reduce Port Arthur quickly and then to concentrate against the remaining Russian forces.

After Japanese forces closed in on the area around Port Arthur, the Russian fleet in the port made a dash for safety. Though the Russians escaped the Japanese fleet, Togo soon forced most of the ships back into Port Arthur. Initially believing they could capture Port Arthur as easily as they had in 1894, the Japanese drove what were described as "waves of living flesh and blood" against the modern weapons and trenches of the Russians. After suffering fearful losses, they turned to using parallel trenches and mining to soften the Russian defenses, but the Russian will to resist did not collapse until the Japanese began using 11-inch howitzers firing 485-pound shells. In January 1905, after a siege of 240 days, the Russians surrendered at Port Arthur, but not before scuttling the last of their ships. During the fighting

To capture Russian defensive positions the Japanese relied on massive infantry charges. Japanese infantry are shown here forming lines prior to a charge.

around the port, the Japanese suffered about 60,000 casualties and the Russians about 30,000.

Before the fall of Port Arthur, the Russian commander, General Aleksei N. Kuropatkin, hoped to gain time for reinforcements and supplies to arrive. He decided to withdraw without fighting so the Japanese could be drawn inland and be weakened by their extended supply lines. Late in August, the Russians concentrated about 150,000 soldiers in entrenchments near Liaoyang (about 200 miles northeast of Port Arthur), and the Japanese concentrated about 120,000. After a confusing battle in which each side sustained about 20,000 casualties, the Russians withdrew toward Mukden. Following a disastrous Russian counteroffensive at Sha Ho in which they suffered 41,000 casualties, Kuropatkin continued withdrawing his forces toward Mukden. The stage was now set for the final battle.

By the end of February, the opposing forces faced each other along a line at Mukden that extended about seventy-five miles but that had heavy concentrations of troops along forty miles. The Russians had 275,000 infantry, 16,000 cavalry, and 1,219 artillery pieces; the Japanese had 200,000 infantry, 7,350 cavalry, and 992 artillery pieces. The only area in which the Japanese had an advantage was in machine guns, for they now had more than the Russians.

Kuropatkin attempted to attack first, but a Japanese attack on February 26 preempted him. The Japanese commander, Field Marshal Oyama Iwao, decided to attack all along the front with three field armies and then, in a feint, to move one of his five armies against the Russians' eastern flank. As Russian reserves moved toward the east, Oyama intended to send another army around the Russians' western wing, enveloping their flank and cutting their line of retreat. The Japanese endured heavy casualties in their frontal attack against the Russians, but they managed to envelop the western flank of the Russians. They failed, however, to cut off the enemy's line of retreat. At the end of the three-week battle, the Russians had suffered about 65,000 casualties and 20,000 prisoners, while the Japanese lost about 41,000. Despite their victory, the Japanese did not pursue the defeated Russians. Oyama had used up much of his army and was aware that only a small portion of the Russian forces had arrived in east Asia.

The final blow against the Russians came with the defeat of their Baltic Fleet near Tsushima Strait between Japan and Korea. Departing from the Baltic in October 1904, the Russian fleet set out for Vladivostok, 18,000 miles away. The Russians were ostensibly more powerful at Tsushima than the Japanese, yet Admiral Togo's superior leadership and actions proved decisive. Following the crushing victory of the Japanese on May 27, 1905, only a cruiser and two destroyers from the fifty-three ships that had departed

Admiral Togo Heihachiro was the Japanese
naval hero of the Russo-Japanese War. His
defeat of the Russian fleet near Tsushima
Strait enabled the Japanese to maintain a sea
link to their forces in Manchuria.

from the Baltic managed to reach Vladivostok. Much in accordance with
Mahan's ideas, Togo's decisive victory prevented the Russians from severing
Japan's sea link to its armies in Manchuria and provided the Japanese a sig-
nificant advantage.

The defeats at Port Arthur, Mukden, and Tsushima angered the
Russians, but their resentment focused more on their own government than
on the Japanese. Rebellion soon forced the Russians to seek peace and on
September 5, 1905, at Portsmouth, New Hampshire, the two nations signed
a treaty ending the conflict. Under the terms of the treaty, Japan gained control over Port Arthur and the Liaotung Peninsula and acquired a preferred
position in Manchuria and a protectorate over Korea. It also received the
southern half of the island of Sakhalin. The first war between major powers
since 1871 had ended with an Asian power defeating a Western power. As a
result of an intense period of industrialization and modernization, the Japanese had successfully learned about Western military organization, equipment, and methods and had defeated the largest power in Europe. They had
mastered the technologies and techniques that previously had given only the
Western powers the capacity to dominate other areas of the world, and they
had interrupted three centuries of Western success.

☆   ☆   ☆   ☆

The years before 1914 profoundly changed warfare. The introduction of
new weapons, the adoption of new techniques of organizing and controlling

armies, and the outbreak of numerous small wars required members of the military to reconsider many of their methods and the structure of their forces. In 1866 and 1870, the Prussians had demonstrated new ways of organizing, supplying, and moving a mass army, but advances in weapons had caused only small changes in tactics and organizations. By 1914 improvements in rifles, machine guns, and artillery had greatly increased the lethality of weapons. Moreover, increased industrial production and the enhanced power of central governments over bigger populations made even larger military forces possible; improved staffs and communications also made their organization and employment more efficient and effective. Total war of unparalleled lethality had become possible.

Beyond the importance of the rise of a new power in east Asia and the subsequent outbreak of revolution in Russia in 1905, the Russo-Japanese War provided valuable insights into how the waging of war had changed at the beginning of the twentieth century. Increases in firepower from artillery and machine guns had compelled the opposing forces to disperse and make wide use of entrenchments and barbed-wire entanglements. Communications had improved with the introduction of the telegraph and field telephone, which linked forward positions to headquarters. As most armies analyzed the Russo-Japanese War, they concluded that despite the advantages provided to the defense by the new weapons, the offensive remained supreme. The deadly effect of Boer marksmanship had shaken faith in the offensive, but Japanese success restored confidence in the offensive. The superior morale and determination of the Japanese to advance often enabled them to seize positions defended by Russians who usually waited passively behind their entrenchments. Tragically for many of the soldiers who would die in futile charges in 1914, European military leaders concluded erroneously that superior morale could prevail against modern firepower.

Similarly, the Russo-Japanese War provided ammunition for those arguing that future wars had to be short. Many believed, as did Ivan S. Bloch, that no nation could endure such losses for a long period. After all, the Japanese had experienced significant financial difficulties and the Russians had had a revolution at home. Many military leaders believed that the effects of increased industrialization, the introduction of the mass army, the perfection of new, more lethal weapons, and the vastly increased costs of waging war could lead only to shorter, not longer wars. Rarely have military leaders been so wrong.

SUGGESTED READINGS

Abrahamson, James L. *America Arms for a New Century* (New York: The Free Press, 1981).

Armstrong, David A. *Bullets and Bureaucrats: The Machine Gun and the United States Army, 1861–1916* (Westport, Conn.: Greenwood Press, 1982).

Bidwell, Shelford, and Dominick Graham, *Fire-Power: British Army Weapons and Theories of War 1904-1945* (London: George Allen & Unwin, 1982).

Callwell, C. E. *Small Wars: Their Principles and Practice* (London: Her Majesty's Stationery Office, 1899).

Corbett, Sir Julian Stafford. *Some Principles of Maritime Strategy* (London: Longmans, 1911).

Cosmas, Graham A. *An Army for Empire: The United States Army in the Spanish-American War* (Columbia, Mo.: University of Missouri Press, 1971).

Crowl, Philip A. "Alfred Thayer Mahan: The Naval Historian," in Peter Paret, ed., *Makers of Modern Strategy* (Princeton, N.J.: Princeton University Press, 1986), pp. 444–477.

Ellis, John. *The Social History of the Machine Gun* (Baltimore: Johns Hopkins University Press, 1975).

Farwell, Byron. *Queen Victoria's Little Wars* (New York: W.W. Norton, 1972).

Gates, John Morgan. *Schoolbooks and Krags: The United States Army in the Philippines, 1898–1902* (Westport, Conn.: Greenwood Press, 1973).

Goerlitz, Walter. *History of the German General Staff, 1657–1945*, trans. Brian Battershaw (New York: Frederick A. Praeger, 1953).

Gudmundsson, Bruce I. *On Artillery* (Westport, Conn.: Greenwood Press, 1993).

Headrick, Daniel R. *The Tools of Empire: Technology and European Imperialism in the Nineteenth Century* (New York: Oxford University Press, 1981).

Hogg, Ian V. *The Guns, 1914–18* (New York: Ballantine Books, Inc., 1971).

Huntington, Samuel P. *The Soldier and the State: The Theory and Politics of Civil-Military Relations* (Cambridge, Mass.: Harvard University Press, 1957).

Hutchison, G. S. *Machine Guns: Their History and Tactical Employment* (London: Macmillan & Co., 1938).

Mahan, Alfred T. *The Influence of Sea Power upon History, 1660–1783* (Boston: Little, Brown, & Company, 1894).

McNeill, William H. *The Pursuit of Power: Technology, Armed Force, and Society Since A.D. 1000* (Chicago: The University of Chicago Press, 1982).

Pakenham, Thomas. *The Boer War* (New York: Random House, 1979).

Potter, Elmer B., and Chester W. Nimitz, eds. *Sea Power: A Naval History* (Englewood Cliffs, N.J.: Prentice-Hall, Inc., 1960).

Ralston, David B. *The Army of the Republic: The Place of the Military in the Political Evolution of France, 1871–1914* (Cambridge: M.I.T. Press, 1967).

Trask, David F. *The War With Spain in 1898* (New York: Macmillan, 1981).

Westwood, J. N. *Russia Against Japan, 1904-1905: A New Look at the Russo–Japanese War* (Albany: State University of New York Press, 1986).

17

THE GREAT WAR:
AN INDECISIVE BEGINNING

Planning for a Short,
Decisive War

Failures of Conception and
Execution: The Western
Front, August-September 1914

Stabilizing the Eastern
Front, August–December
1914

Before the war of 1914–1918 became known as the World War, and later as World War I, it was known to those who experienced it as the Great War. It occurred in an era when increases in population, growth of industry, expansion of roads and railroads, and increases in the powers of central governments permitted the mobilizing and equipping of huge armies. Nearly 50 million men served in military units during the war, and millions more men and women supported them by working in factories, transportation systems, hospitals, and numerous other war-related positions. The major campaigns of the Great War pitted the Central Powers (Germany and Austria-Hungary) against the Allies (Great Britain, France, Russia, Italy, and eventually the United States), but more than thirty states ultimately became belligerents, including several from Asia, South America, and Africa. In every sense the Great War was the first world war.

When the war began, most participants expected it to be short; they believed no country would be able to endure for very long the huge costs of fielding and supporting large forces or accept the heavy casualties modern weapons could inflict. The first battles, however, proved indecisive, and as the war progressed both sides found themselves struggling to meet the voracious demands of their armed forces. As the Great War evolved into a total war, many of the belligerents had to commit a significant portion of their population and resources to the war effort, surpassing the commitments of the Napoleonic Wars and the American Civil War. Never before had so many countries and large armies engaged in battles of such magnitude and with such lethal and numerous weapons. Compulsory military service became the norm, and centralized economic planning and industrial mobilization became an essential aspect of most governments' war efforts. Throughout the war, both sides devised new strategies and tactics and shifted the focus of their efforts among the various fronts; they also made significant progress in the development of new weapons such as the airplane, submarine, and tank. Rarely have so many important innovations in warfare occurred in such a brief period.

The Great War witnessed vastly larger armies, unparalleled industrial output, and numerous innovations in technology and methods. Momentous changes stemming from the war initiated an era of remarkable political, economic, and social change throughout Europe and the world. But the costs were high: until the even larger losses of World War II, the unequaled material destruction and loss of lives of World War I surpassed those of any other war in human history. Casualties numbered about 8.5 million killed and 20 million wounded.

As chief of the German general staff, Count Alfred von Schlieffen did not win great victories like Moltke the Elder or execute grand plans as Moltke the Younger did, but he did devise Germany's war plan of 1914.

Planning for a Short, Decisive War

World War I was the first war in which the opponents went to war prepared with detailed and precise plans that had been written in the years preceding the outbreak of hostilities. Most of the plans used in 1914 were based upon the assumption that a future war would be short and that decisive results could be achieved only through the offensive. Of these war plans, none was more ambitious than Germany's.

Count Alfred von Schlieffen, who served as the chief of the German general staff from 1891 until 1906, was primarily responsible for originating the war plan used by Germany in 1914. For some time the general staff had recognized the difficulties inherent in waging a two-front war against France and Russia. Germany's initial strategy sought to cripple both opponents by a sequence of attacks first against Russia and then against France. With the conclusion of the Franco-Russian Alliance in 1894, however, the threat of a two-front war against Germany intensified, and the search for a response to this danger led to a daring strategy—Germany would use its central position and the excellent striking power of its armies to gain a decisive victory over France and then to turn against Russia.

Schlieffen initially planned for German forces to move through eastern Belgium and around the French fortress system on its northeastern frontier (along the Meuse River between Verdun and Toul). By 1905, however, he planned to have the "hammer," or right wing, of the German army march through western Belgium, the Netherlands, and northern France before circling to the west of Paris and driving the opposing armies against the "anvil" of the German forces in Lorraine. By sending the right wing of his army through Belgium and the Netherlands in a gigantic wheeling movement, he sought a huge *Kesselschlacht* (battle of encirclement) and a quick, decisive victory in the west. He intended to destroy France before Russia could mount an effective offensive against the weak forces on Germany's eastern frontier.

To concentrate sufficient power on the right flank of his attack against France and to make the wheeling movement possible, Schlieffen planned on placing five armies on his right wing and two on his left. The mission of the right wing was to pivot on a point north of Metz and to deliver the decisive blow, while the mission of the left wing was to mislead the French and draw them toward the east. Schlieffen expected the French to attack into the difficult terrain of Alsace and Lorraine and thus wanted the German left wing to oppose this advance without becoming decisively engaged and by withdrawing if necessary. When the heavily weighted right wing reached the Franco-Belgian border, the left wing would hold its ground, enabling the extreme tip of the right wing to speed around Paris and fall upon the flanks and rear of the French army.

After General Helmuth von Moltke (the Younger) became chief of the general staff in 1906, he maintained the basic thrust of the Schlieffen Plan but made several important modifications to it. As evidence began to mount of the Russians' having recovered surprisingly quickly from their defeat in 1905, Moltke moved four-and-one-half corps from the west to the east to protect East Prussia. He also had reservations about the wisdom of violating the Netherlands' neutrality and soon modified the sweep of the right wing so the Germans would not enter the Netherlands. After changing the path of the right wing, he also modified the mission of the left wing. Not wanting to lose the valuable coal and iron mines of the Saar and Rhineland, Moltke ordered his left wing to delay the advance of the French initially but then to counterattack and drive them back. In essence, he weakened the right wing and strengthened the left wing without abandoning the idea of sweeping around Paris. As a result of these changes, the plan departed sharply from its original spirit, which was exemplified in Schlieffen's supposed dying words, "Keep the right wing strong."

Despite these modifications, the plan retained its fundamental inadequacies and contradictions, one of which was the German army's never having sufficient forces for a two-front war against a numerically superior coalition. Moltke's hasty shifting of forces from one front to the other might not have been necessary if he had had additional forces. The lack of sufficient forces could have been partially offset through better coordination with

Austria-Hungary, but both states jealously pursued their own strategies. After Germany decided to follow its highly risky strategy, much depended on the enormous logistical effort of moving hundreds of thousands of men and horses, as well as their equipment, from Aachen to around Paris in slightly more than five weeks. The intricate plan ignored the possibility of every lucky break not being in the Germans' favor.

The plan also deprived German political leaders of any flexibility; in fact, the German Chancellor and War Ministry remained ignorant of the new plan until 1912. Since the general staff had prepared only for attacking France first and then Russia, no changes could be made on the afternoon of August 1, 1914, when Kaiser William II asked for the army to be deployed in the east instead of the west. Because of the technical difficulties associated with changing the location and movement of armies, the Germans had no alternative other than a two-front war, and they had to launch their attack—military leaders believed—before the Russians or the French could snatch the initiative from their hands.

Germany thus accepted the waging of "war by timetable," and it chose to ignore many of the factors that might disrupt the timetable. That Germany came so close to victory in 1914 comes more from France's having played into its hands than from the brilliance of the plan itself.

War Plans: France

In the decades after 1871, the French army became increasingly influenced by the idea of the offensive, and on the eve of the Great War adopted an extreme doctrine, known as the *offensive à outrance*, according to which commanders would break the enemy's will to fight by an aggressive infantry assault. After gaining superiority of fire from their rifles, machine guns, and 75-mm cannon, the attacking French infantry would charge the enemy soldiers and finish them with their bayonets. The key to success, in the French view, lay in the will of the attacking commander and in the courage and determination of his troops to complete the attack regardless of losses.

French strategy in 1914 also emphasized the offensive, but unlike the Schlieffen Plan, their Plan XVII provided few details on operations and no clear strategic objective other than to fight a decisive battle with the Germans. General Joseph Joffre, commander of the French forces, retained the flexibility to shift his attacks, for his goal was to bring about a decisive battle. Nonetheless, his principal option was a two-pronged offensive with forces advancing into Lorraine on each side of the Verdun-Toul line. Forces in the southern attack would move from the vicinity of Toul toward the east, and those in the northern attack would move from the north of Verdun toward the east. One field army served as a strategic reserve and had the mission of moving on order and entering the anticipated decisive battle. If the Germans attempted to envelop their left flank, the French intended to attack north into Belgium, but they had to depend on assistance from the Belgians and the British. Despite the absence of any clear strategic objectives, the French firmly believed that their offensive would be successful.

By charging into Lorraine, however, the French played directly into the Germans' hands. As has often been said, the situation was somewhat analogous to a revolving door. While the French pushed hard on one side, the Germans would push on the other and seek to strike them in the rear.

War Plans: Other Powers

In contrast to France and Germany, Great Britain was foremost a naval power with the world's finest navy and a small yet capable army. Though reluctant to become embroiled in a war on the Continent, Britain became increasingly committed to France during the years before 1914, particularly through naval agreements.

As the size and capability of the German fleet increased, Britain began orienting its strategy and war plans toward concentrating its naval forces in the North Sea and withdrawing them from the Mediterranean. On the eve of the war, France agreed to concentrate its naval forces in the Mediterranean, while Britain concentrated its forces in the north near the main ports of the German fleet. The British also accepted the moral obligation of defending France's coast along the English Channel, since France had concentrated its naval forces in the Mediterranean.

Beginning in 1906, secret Franco-British military staff talks obliged the British to send the small British Expeditionary Force (BEF) to the Continent and for it to operate on the left of the French army. Though no formal commitments existed, these arrangements bound Britain to France in the event of an attack from Germany. Like France, Britain had no clear strategic objective other than the defeat of Germany.

In the east, the Russians intended to follow a strategy that, in consonance with the actions of France, would force a two-front war upon Germany and Austria-Hungary. Unlike France and Germany, which had only single strategies, Russia prepared two major plans, one offensive and the other defensive. In Plan G, which assumed Germany would attack Russia with the bulk of its forces, Russia prepared to defend against attacks coming from East Prussia and Austria-Hungary while it completed its mobilization and prepared to counterattack. In Plan A, which assumed Germany would attack first toward France, Russia prepared to advance into Austria-Hungary and East Prussia, followed by an advance into Silesia (eastern Germany). The Russian military hierarchy viewed this plan as the more likely alternative. When faced with the choice of concentrating in the southwest against the Austro-Hungarians or in the northwest against the Germans, the Russians prepared—in accordance with Plan A—to launch serious offensives on both fronts, thereby dispersing their first efforts. Adding to their difficulties, they also accepted France's demand to place some 800,000 soldiers in the field by the fifteenth day of mobilization and to begin offensive operations against Germany as soon as possible.

Prior to the outbreak of war, Austria-Hungary confronted especially difficult strategic problems, because it faced potentially hostile powers in three different directions: Italy in the southwest, Serbia in the south, and

Russia in the east. Austrian military leaders divided the army into three major groups and made plans for a large war (designed as Case I for Italy and Case R for Russia) and a small war against Serbia and Montenegro (Case B). The main force could be deployed against either Italy or Russia; the second could be deployed against Serbia; and the third could reinforce either of the other two forces. The situation of the Austrians was made even more complicated by the existence of a dozen nationalities in the army and the absence of a common language, except for a limited vocabulary of German words used in giving commands. Despite these complexities, Field Marshal Franz Conrad von Hötzendorf, chief of the general staff, failed to complete detailed plans for coordinated actions with the Germans. Not until May 1914 did the Germans tell him they would turn their main strength from France toward Russia six weeks after beginning operations.

The strategies and war plans of the major powers thus strongly emphasized the offensive. Confident of their armies and their leaders, most Europeans greeted the beginning of hostilities in 1914 with relief and in some cases with celebration. The long period of tension and crisis had ended, and many now believed that long-festering problems would soon be resolved. Consequently, thousands of soldiers marched or rode off to battle amid cheering crowds who expected their sons and neighbors to return soon as heroes. The soldiers, however, soon found themselves trapped in a long and brutal war with no apparent route to victory. Despite years of preparation and planning, the armies of Europe were unprepared for the situations they faced and surprised at the nature of the fighting they encountered.

Failures of Conception and Execution: The Western Front, August–September 1914

The rush to war began on June 28, 1914, with the assassination in Sarajevo of Archduke Francis Ferdinand, heir apparent to the Habsburg throne of Austria-Hungary, by a young Bosnian revolutionary. Convinced that the assassination had occurred with the knowledge and perhaps assistance of Serbian officials, Austria-Hungary decided to punish the Serbs. After Kaiser William II provided unconditional assurance of German support, Austria-Hungary issued an ultimatum to Serbia on July 23 that insisted upon Austrian participation in the investigation and punishment of the assassins.

In the following week, the chain of alliances and the web of military plans expanded a single terrorist act into a vast war. When Serbia received support from Russia, which refused to allow Austria-Hungary to destroy Serbia, the possibility of a limited Austro-Serbian conflict was replaced by a much more dangerous Austro-Russian one. After Serbia rejected part of the ultimatum as being an infringement on its sovereignty, Austria-Hungary declared war on July 28. Attempting to curtail expansion of the conflict, Russia first began a partial mobilization against the Austrians, but then on July 30 ordered a complete mobilization.

Since military leaders believed that the first nation to mobilize would have the advantage, Germany demanded an end to the Russian mobilization on its border. It also sent an ultimatum to France asking what actions it would take in the event of a Russo-German conflict. Receiving no response from Russia, Germany began its own general mobilization on August 1, followed the same day by a declaration of war against Russia. When France replied that it would follow the dictates of its own interests, Germany declared war on it on August 3.

As the first step in its move toward France, Germany demanded that Belgium acquiesce in its crossing Belgian territory, but the small country refused to permit the violation of its neutrality. Following the violation of Belgian neutrality, Great Britain declared war on Germany on August 4. Finally, on August 6, Austria-Hungary declared war on Russia.

The Great War had begun, and Europe was divided into two opposing camps. Germany and its allies became known as the Central Powers; and Great Britain, France, Russia, and other participating powers were known as the Allies.

The Opening Battles in the West

During the first month of the war, things went pretty much as military leaders had imagined they would before August 1914. The bulk of the German army moved through Belgium in an attempt to envelop the French flank; most of the French army attacked German positions in Alsace and Lorraine. The Russians moved against East Prussia and Austria-Hungary; the Austrians attacked Serbia and Russia. On all fronts, gigantic offensives threw millions of men into strategic maneuvers. Yet not until after the first month did the real character of the war become apparent and the errors in conception become evident.

The campaign in the west began with the attack into Belgium, and despite some difficulties in the initial fighting, adhered relatively closely to the tightly constructed schedule. The Germans did not expect significant opposition from the Belgians, but the decision by Moltke to avoid violating the neutrality of the Netherlands carried with it the decision to crowd the German First and Second armies, which constituted the heavy end of the right wing, through a bottleneck that included the fortification system around Liège. While the fighting elements of the two field armies could have bypassed the Liège fortress system, the all-important logistical elements behind them could not. The system of six main forts and six smaller forts arranged in a circle around the citadel in the city blocked the important railway and road network that passed directly through it.

The Germans had long recognized the importance of the obstacle formed by Liège and organized a special task force of six infantry brigades and three cavalry divisions to reduce the area. They planned on clearing the Belgians from the fortress system in the two weeks required to mobilize the entire army. Shortly after the Germans issued on August 4 a final note to the Belgian government that amounted to a declaration of war, elements of the special task force crossed the Belgian frontier and moved toward Liège. When German cavalry threatened to encircle the Belgians in Liège, the Belgians pulled their infantry out of the intervals between the forts on August 6, leaving the forts as the only opposition to the Germans. The Germans had foreseen the necessity to employ heavy siege artillery against the forts, and on August 12, the Krupp 420-mm howitzer, soon to become known as the "Big Bertha," and the 305-mm Skoda guns, which had been borrowed from the Austrians, began shelling the forts. Since the forts had been designed to withstand only 210-mm fire, the siege artillery easily destroyed them, the last two forts falling on the morning of August 16.

The Germans completed the mobilization and concentration of their army on August 14 and began moving forces forward before the capture of the last fort. The German First Army, commanded by General Alexander von Kluck, advanced on the extreme right of the entire German force, and the Second Army, commanded by General Karl von Bülow, moved forward on its left. Because of the great distance between Moltke (the German chief of staff was in Koblenz but soon moved to Luxembourg) and his subordinate army commanders, Moltke attempted to ensure coordination between his two right-wing armies by placing Kluck under the operational control of Bülow. By August 20, Louvain and Brussels had fallen to the First Army, and the remnants of the Belgian army were withdrawing toward Antwerp.

The French Offensive

Despite reports of heavy fighting around Liège, the French remained focused on executing Plan XVII. General Joffre dismissed the attack on Liège as a feint and expected the Belgians and the soon-to-arrive British to halt what he believed to be a relatively small German force moving through central Belgium. As a precaution, a French cavalry corps moved north into Belgium on August 6 but failed to penetrate the German cavalry screen.

Oblivious to the giant sweep of the Schlieffen wheel, Joffre pressed forward with his plan for a two-pronged attack—one south and the other north of the Verdun-Toul Line. The First and Second armies prepared to launch the southern attack, while the Third and Fifth armies made ready to launch the northern attack. Joffre ordered the southern attack to begin on the thirteenth day of mobilization, August 14. Conscious of the importance of convincing the French public that their army was confident and prepared, he also launched a small offensive on August 7 by elements of the First Army. Meanwhile, he ordered the Fourth Army, which could have functioned as a strategic reserve, to enter the line between the Third and Fifth armies and to advance with the northern attack. If the unexpected occurred, he had little or no means of response.

On the morning of August 14, Joffre's First and Second armies began the southern attack and advanced into Lorraine. Just as planned, the German Sixth and Seventh armies fell back skillfully, making the advancing French columns pay dearly. Attack after attack, the French infantry gallantly moved forward, charging in the open with their bayonets fixed, often without artillery support, but German artillery and machine guns killed and wounded thousands of them. The two French armies crossed the frontier on August 15, but their forward progress was halted by August 19.

As the attack of the French First and Second armies ground to a halt, the German Sixth and Seventh armies under Crown Prince Rupprecht of Bavaria launched a surprise counterattack at noon on August 20. While the First French Army withdrew in relatively good order, the Second Army had two corps that were almost routed, and by August 22, the two French armies had withdrawn to their starting positions.

The second French offensive was supposed to move in a northeasterly direction from Verdun into the Belgian Ardennes and then turn east. To protect his center, Joffre formed the "Army of the Lorraine" out of reserve divisions on August 19 and placed it between the forces launching the northern and southern attacks. As the southern attack came to a halt on August

As the French marched into battle they wore blue coats, red trousers, and soft caps. The reality of combat soon compelled them to don steel helmets and more subdued uniforms.

20, he issued orders for the French Third and Fourth armies to attack in a northeasterly direction toward Longwy, Virton, and Neufchâteau. Although Joffre was beginning to realize that significant numbers of Germans were sweeping north of the Meuse through Belgium, he steadfastly refused to change his plan, for he believed the Germans were pursuing retreating Belgians. He thought the Third and Fourth armies had the advantage of surprise and numbers and could strike the flank of enemy forces moving west through Belgium.

As the French Third Army moved forward through difficult terrain, it did not expect to encounter large German forces. Meanwhile, the German Fourth and Fifth armies advanced into eastern Belgium and occupied new positions as they waited for the German First, Second, and Third armies to sweep through the central part of Belgium. And as they waited, they organized strong defenses. On August 22, the French Third Army blindly bumped into the German Fifth Army in eastern Belgium. Hoping to hit an advancing German army in the flank, Third Army instead stumbled into a killing zone and suffered thousands of casualties. The French Fourth Army was no luckier than the Third. Just as in the Lorraine offensive, the French infantry failed to coordinate its actions with those of the artillery and often did not bother to suppress enemy fire before advancing. Following several disastrous actions, Joffre reluctantly permitted the two armies to withdraw.

A final French offensive came from Fifth Army. General Charles L. M. Lanrezac, who commanded Fifth Army on the French left, convinced Joffre to send his army north toward the Sambre River. On August 21 Bülow's Second Army collided with elements of the French Fifth Army on the Sambre and secured a foothold south of the river. While the French launched a series of unsupported, uncoordinated assaults against Bülow's forces, the German Third Army crossed the Meuse River on Lanrezac's right flank on August 23 and forced him to retreat.

The defeat of the French Fifth Army on the Sambre was the final step in the collapse of Plan XVII. Instead of concentrating superior force against a weak or decisive point, Joffre had diffused his offensive power in three separate and almost unrelated attacks. Everything now depended on the small British force on the French left flank and on Joffre's ability to shift his demoralized forces from his right to his left.

The Battle of Mons

As part of the military staff conversations between the French and British before the war, the British had agreed to dispatch an expeditionary force to France four days after Great Britain declared war on Germany. With the first troops embarking on August 9 and the bulk moving on August 12–17, the British landed a cavalry division and four infantry divisions under Field Marshal Sir John D. P. French at Boulogne, Le Havre, and Rouen. Using trains, the entire force then concentrated near Le Cateau on the left flank of the French Fifth Army. Despite the small size of the BEF, it was a well-trained, capable force. On August 19, the Kaiser issued an order to General

Kluck to "exterminate the treacherous English and walk over General French's contemptible little army." Because of this order, the small British force tagged themselves the "Old Contemptibles," a name they carried with great pride.

As late as August 20, Moltke believed no important landings of British troops in France had taken place. On August 21, however, the British began marching toward Mons, directly in the path of the German "hammer." After reaching the small Belgian mining town, they occupied a position to the left of the French Fifth Army. The first German encounter with the BEF occurred when Kluck's First Army changed direction and moved south to support the Second Army's attack on Lanrezac's Fifth Army. A small skirmish between German and British cavalry patrols occurred on August 22, but the next day Kluck launched a full-scale attack against the BEF's II Corps which had solidly dug in along the Mons-Condé Canal. Despite heavy casualties from massing their infantry and charging the rapidly firing British, the Germans managed to push back the British in several places along the canal by mid-afternoon.

Around midnight Sir John French learned that Lanrezac's Fifth Army on his right had pulled back and opened his flank. Having little choice, he ordered his two corps to withdraw south. Unfortunately for the British, the Germans followed the retreating soldiers closely and inflicted a major defeat on II Corps at Le Cateau on August 26 when its commander, General Sir Horace Smith-Dorrien, chose to fight rather than continue withdrawing. Shaken and demoralized, the BEF joined the French Fourth and Fifth armies in retreat.

The German Advance

As the German field armies moved forward, the forced diversion of troops (strategic consumption) gradually weakened them. The First Army had to leave a corps to cover the Belgian army in Antwerp. Second Army left a corps to besiege the fortress of Maubeuge, just south of Mons. Third Army left a division to besiege a small fortress near Givet. After receiving bad news from the east about the Russians attacking into East Prussia, Moltke dispatched two corps to the eastern front from the Second and Third armies.

Though his right wing was becoming overextended, Moltke refused to weaken his left wing. Instead of moving forces from his left to his right, as Schlieffen had envisaged, he directed the Sixth and Seventh armies on his left wing on August 27 to continue their attack against the French, directly into their strong defenses between Toul and Épinal. The French fortifications proved to be strong enough to withstand the enemy's attacks, providing Joffre the opportunity to begin shifting forces from his right flank to his left.

The Germans also began having problems with their transportation system. While they had had the advantage of using their own national railway system to transport and concentrate troops and equipment for the attack into Belgium and France, only a small portion of the Belgian and French railway networks remained intact or could be repaired as the Germans advanced. Nonetheless, the railways carried forward the requisite supplies, for even during the time of greatest demand the Germans managed to have about six trains a day arrive with supplies for each army. Because of the fast rate of advance of the armies, the distances separating units from their railheads gradually increased, as did the difficulties of moving supplies forward from these railheads. Much of the ammunition was moved from railheads to units by motor-transport companies, but by September 1, many of the trucks had broken down, primarily because of shortages in spare parts and tires. Despite occasional ammunition shortages, the Germans managed to provide sufficient supplies to units; no German unit lost a battle in the fall of 1914 because of supply shortages.

The long distances covered in the march of the German right wing across Belgium and France severely tested the soldiers' endurance. Many suffered from the sheer exhaustion of having to march twenty to twenty-five miles a day for many days, with those in the First Army on the right wing marching some 300 miles to the Marne River. During the advance, each German corps consumed about 130 tons of food and fodder each day, and their rapid advance and distance from railheads soon forced them to subsist off the countryside. Though the soldiers had to contend with an occasional hungry day, they did manage to live reasonably well on the food they foraged. The horses were not so fortunate. The Germans brought forward or foraged some fodder for their horses, but exhaustion and starvation soon took their toll. On the eve of the battle of the Marne, German heavy artillery—which was horse-drawn like the rest of the artillery—could no longer keep up with the still-advancing columns.

As logistical difficulties mounted, confusion increased. Even though Moltke moved his headquarters from Koblenz to Luxembourg, he still found himself swamped with messages that were invariably out of date. Communications between him and his subordinate commanders remained problematic because he insisted on using the wireless telegraph, even in cases where messengers would have moved faster. Unfortunately, radio links proved to be inadequate, and overloaded relay stations soon became incapable of handling messages without intolerable delays. To add to these difficulties, messages sometimes had to be transmitted three or four times before they were received correctly. Hot summer storms and interferences emanating from the Eiffel Tower in Paris frequently disrupted transmissions. At lower levels, commanders relied primarily on messengers and an extensive system of liaison officers. As the Germans moved farther into France, communications problems became progressively more difficult.

The Allies, too, became exhausted and hungry, but unlike the Germans, they did not have the exhilaration of victories to sustain their morale. They did have, however, the advantage of Joffre's maintaining close contact with his subordinates and staying abreast of the rapidly changing situation. On several occasions, he moved forward and met with some of his subordinate commanders. Also, the passing of information between headquarters occurred more quickly and dependably. Another key advantage pertained to the Allies falling back on their lines of communication. With French roads and railways radiating out from Paris and with the French railway system continuing to function, Joffre managed successfully to shift troops and equipment from northeastern to northern France.

The French Response

As the German forces pressed forward, Joffre carefully recast French strategy and tactics. German strategy had finally become apparent to him; he abandoned hopes of holding along the frontiers and attempted to establish a second defensive line deeper in France. On August 25, he ordered First and Second armies on his right to hold in place, while Third, Fourth, Fifth, and British armies on his left withdrew to the south, pivoting on Verdun, to a defensive line extending westward from Verdun, to Laon, and almost to Amiens. Joffre also began strengthening his left flank and forming two new armies. Composed primarily of troops transported from Lorraine, the new Sixth Army assembled near Paris under General Michel Maunoury and had the mission of preventing the Germans from enveloping the French flank. The new Ninth Army assembled under General Ferdinand Foch behind the retreating Third and Fourth armies but soon entered the line when a gap opened between the Fourth and Fifth armies.

Joffre also took steps to improve the performance of French units. He informed his army commanders that the infantry should attack only after artillery preparation, and he forbade large attacks. Recognizing the need for

General Joseph Joffre commanded French forces in 1914. Though his initial attacks proved costly and wasteful, he succeeded in shifting his forces from northeastern France and in halting the Germans in the battle of the Marne.

new leadership, Joffre began ruthlessly weeding out officers who had not performed to his expectations, among whom were the commanders of the French Fifth and Third armies. Within a short period he relieved dozens of brigade and divisions commanders, sometimes unjustly, but he wanted hard-nosed, self-confident fighters as commanders.

Still the Allies did not halt the Germans. After learning of the British defeat at Le Cateau on August 26, Joffre ordered Lanrezac's Fifth Army on August 27 to attack westward and strike the flank of the Germans who were pressing the British. Despite Lanrezac's pessimism, he managed to move most of his army to face west, but Bülow's Second Army unexpectedly hit his right flank on August 29 near Guise. Though the Germans initially pushed back the French, a spirited counterattack by a corps under General Louis Franchet d'Esperey momentarily halted Bülow's army. With the rapidly advancing German First Army threatening to envelop Lanrezac's flank, however, Joffre gave him permission to withdraw.

When General Maunoury's Sixth Army began unloading from trains east of Amiens, it encountered the leading elements of the German First Army. Kluck's forces drove Sixth Army southwest toward Paris. With his left flank being pressed hard by the Germans, Joffre had no choice but to abandon the attempt to establish a new line between Verdun and Amiens, and on September 1, he ordered his forces to continue their withdrawal.

As the Allied situation became increasingly difficult, coordination between the French and British worsened. After the shattering loss at Le Cateau and after several instances of the French withdrawing and exposing the British flanks, Sir John French lost confidence in the French army and its leaders. Refusing Joffre's appeals, he hurried his army to the south with the intention of going past Paris. When the possibility of a huge gap in the Allied lines appeared, Lord Horatio H. Kitchener, the British secretary of state for war, hastened to France and convinced Sir John to stop withdrawing and to take part in halting the German advance. These actions left Joffre uncertain about the role the BEF would play in the next phase of the campaign.

The Miracle of the Marne

After Franchet d'Esperey's surprising counterattack, the German Second Army remained in place for about a day and a half, thus enabling the French and British on the left to retreat without interference and allowing the German First Army to move ahead of Second Army. On August 27, Moltke released Kluck's First Army from Bülow's operational control and told him to resume his march in a southwesterly direction and to pass around the western edge of Paris. He also ordered Kluck to be prepared to go to the aid of Bülow's Second Army. On August 30, Kluck received a message from Bülow announcing the defeat of the French at Guise in a "decisive manner" and later received another message from Bülow requesting him to move his army southeast to exploit the victory. Aerial reconnaissance also revealed that the still-forming French Sixth Army was pulling back toward Paris and did not pose a threat to the flank of Kluck's First Army.

Kluck felt torn between Moltke's order on August 27 to move his army to the west of Paris and Bülow's request on August 30 to move his army in a southeasterly direction to the east of Paris. Because of ineffective communications with Moltke and lack of time, Kluck knew he had to make a decision on his own. Certain that a great victory was about to be won, Kluck decided to turn his army toward the south and go around Paris on the east rather than the west. This was a decision that was to have a profound effect on the outcome of the campaign.

By September 2, Kluck's First Army was northeast of Paris, more than a full day's march ahead of the Second Army on its left. To Kluck's amazement, he received a message from Moltke that evening ordering the First Army to follow the Second Army in echelon. When Kluck learned that one of his corps had seized the bridges over the Marne River at Château Thierry about forty miles east of Paris, he did not know whether he should pull back the corps or reinforce its success. Choosing to act boldly but also choosing to violate Moltke's order, he ordered his army forward and left one reserve corps to defend against an attack from Paris. He dispatched a message to Moltke, explaining his decision, and in the last paragraph complained about not receiving "regular information" about the other German armies.

As the Germans approached Paris, the French government departed from Paris for Bordeaux on September 2, leaving General Joseph Gallieni in charge of its defenses. As the strength of the Sixth Army in Paris increased, and as the German First Army's turn to the east of Paris exposed the right flank of the entire German line, Joffre recognized the possibility of an attack against the German flank. He remained uncertain, however, about the willingness of the British to participate in a counterattack. Since the BEF was located just east of Paris and to the left of the French Ninth and Fifth armies, a counterattack probably would have failed without British assistance. Joffre also had reservations about the fighting abilities of the Ninth, Fifth, and Sixth armies under Foch, Franchet d'Esperey, and Maunoury, respectively.

On September 4 the vulnerability of the Germans became apparent to Gallieni in Paris after several aircraft reported that large German forces had crossed the Marne northeast of Paris and had left only one corps behind to protect the entire German flank. Later that evening, Gallieni had a heated telephone conversation with Joffre and urged an immediate attack on the German flank. After visiting the British and convincing Sir John French to participate, Joffre finally decided to launch a counterattack on the morning of September 6.

With reports of French troops being moved from east to west, Moltke recognized by September 4 that the right flank of the entire German line was exposed to an attack from the French Sixth Army in Paris. To avoid a disaster, he halted the advance of the First and Second armies on his right wing and ordered them to face Paris and protect the Germans' right flank. Kluck's First Army was ordered to pull back from its exposed position and stay north of the Marne. Still hoping for a victory, Moltke also ordered the Third, Fourth, and Fifth armies to continue attacking in the center, while the left-wing armies continued attacking in the south.

At 0700 hours,* September 5, eleven hours after Moltke's message had been dispatched, Kluck received the order to pull back. The order included no information about the enemy and made no sense to him; he still believed French forces in Paris were only beginning to assemble and posed no threat to his flank. Convinced that Moltke was poorly informed, he let his army continue moving south of the Marne until the end of the day, but he did take the precaution of ordering one corps to halt where it stood. This left two German corps in the vicinity of Paris and two south of the Marne.

On that same day, September 5, the French Sixth Army began moving east so it could launch the counterattack against the German flank on the following morning. The German reserve corps, which had been left behind by Kluck on September 2, became aware of French units advancing from

---

*The use of a twenty-four-hour clock by the military became common during World War I.

Paris and launched an attack to develop the situation. This bold action prevented the Germans from being completely surprised and provided Kluck time to shift his forces from south of the Marne to face the French attack. As Kluck pushed back the French attack, he stopped Joffre's attempt to roll up the German flank, but the movement of two corps to the north opened a large gap between the German First and Second armies.

Abandoning his effort to destroy the German right, Joffre pushed the BEF and the left of d'Esperey's Fifth Army into the gap that was occupied by only a thin line of German cavalry. The Allies advanced slowly, but the British crossed the Marne near Château Thierry on the morning of September 9, thereby threatening to envelop Kluck and Bülow's flanks. An officer from Moltke's staff had visited Bülow's headquarters and authorized the withdrawal of the Second Army if the enemy actually crossed the Marne. As Bülow's army began pulling back, the First Army had no choice but to pull back as well. The Germans hoped to withdraw only a short distance, but by September 12 the First and Second armies had reached the Aisne River. The concurrent withdrawal of the other armies on their left resulted in a long defensive line running roughly from Noyon east to Verdun, and then extending southeast toward Colmar. The opening campaign of the war on the Western Front had ended.

The Race to the Sea

While Joffre had not saved France from a long and bloody war and had made some terrible mistakes in the opening phases of the campaign, he had won a victory that some have classified as one of the most important battles in military history. If Joffre can receive credit for a victory, Moltke must receive some of the blame for the defeat. In contrast to the more energetic and personal role played by Joffre in rallying his forces and successfully modifying his strategy, Moltke had exerted little influence over several key actions and decisions on his right wing. On September 14 the Kaiser relieved him and secretly replaced him with General Erich von Falkenhayn, the Prussian minister of war.

Though the change did not become official until November 3, the new commander of the Germany army immediately began to amass a strong force on his right wing and attempted to roll up the Allied left. As the Allies also moved to outflank the Germans, a series of bloody struggles occurred with every battle moving farther north. The so-called "Race to the Sea," a "leapfrogging" action as each side tried to outflank the other, had begun.

During these struggles, the British moved farther to the north so they could shorten and secure their lines of communication. Also, the small Belgian army, which had been reinforced by three British marine brigades, remained under siege at Antwerp until the first week of October, when they successfully escaped from the Germans and made their way to the northernmost point of the Allied lines. There they occupied a defensive position on the extreme left of the Allies and remained for the duration of the war. By the second week in October, the two opposing positions stretched from the Swiss border to the English Channel.

As winter approached, the new character of the war on the Western Front became obvious. Barbed wire, entrenchments, and mud became pervasive along the 350-mile front from the English Channel to Switzerland. A war of movement in the brisk autumn air had yielded to a war of trenches in the cold winter wind.

Stabilizing the Eastern Front, August–December 1914

Geographic considerations greatly affected the war on the Eastern Front, which extended more than 1,000 miles from the Baltic Sea, around East Prussia, along the protruding Polish salient, and along the Austro-Hungarian border to the northern tip of neutral Romania. The Eastern Front was much longer than the Western Front and extended even farther after Romania entered the war in August 1916 on the side of the Allies. All the major powers in eastern Europe (Russia, Austria-Hungary, and Germany) confronted the question of military operations in the vast area along this front and worried about the problem presented by the Polish salient. The question of the Eastern Front was magnified for Austria-Hungary by the additional question of the Balkan front that extended from the western tip of Romania, between Austria-Hungary and Serbia, to the Adriatic sea. After Italy entered the war in May 1915 on the side of the Allies, Austria-Hungary's strategic situation became even more difficult.

Though military operations on the Eastern Front often relied heavily on the same types of entrenchments and strong defenses as those on the Western Front, the war of grand maneuvers never disappeared from the Eastern Front. Battles in this region frequently assumed a mobile character that did not exist on the Western Front except for the opening and closing battles of the war. Part of the explanation for this stems from the much greater length of the Eastern Front and the existence of vast plains, but the lack of extensive roads and railways also affected the flow of battles. While large formations could be moved easily in the west to fill a gap, the more primitive lines of communication in the east substantially delayed the movement of operational reserves and hampered efforts by a defender to halt a successful enemy offensive.

The large size of the Russian army also contributed significantly to making the Eastern Front different from the Western Front. During the war the Russians mobilized some 12,000,000 men, as compared to 11,000,000 in Germany and 8,410,000 in France. Immediately after mobilization the army numbered about 6,300,000 men, but almost 5,000,000 had received little or no training. The Russian infantry relied on simple, mass tactics, and

Eastern Europe, 1914

even though they had about as much artillery as the Germans, the Russians had placed much of their most modern heavy artillery in fortresses. Achieving cooperation between the infantry and the artillery was a constant problem for the Russians throughout the war. Despite the large size of their army, the Russians did not have a strongly centralized command system. They referred to their supreme headquarters as *Stavka*, a name given to it by Grand Duke Nicholas Nicholaievich when he arrived there on August 14 and took command; the Grand Duke derived the name from an ancient

Russian chieftain's camp. Real power, however, was held by the generals who commanded the two separate fronts, or army groups (the Northwestern Front faced Germany and the Southwestern Front faced Austria-Hungary). The Grand Duke was reluctant to interfere with their decisions or actions.

Prewar disagreements in Russia between officers who wanted to concentrate either against Germany or against Austria-Hungary were accentuated by the maneuvering of several cliques and by the effects of personality clashes; rivalries among the infantry, artillery, and cavalry worsened the problem. It was common for commanders to dislike their chiefs of staff or not to talk to their neighboring commanders. Amidst an environment of intrigue and status-seeking, military efficiency often was sacrificed for personal gain. In the end, faulty planning and poor command decisions had more to do with the initial Russian disasters than unpreparedness or weakness in equipment and supplies.

The Battle of Tannenberg

The most decisive actions initially occurred in East Prussia and were greatly affected by the chain of Masurian Lakes near its eastern frontier. The lakes channeled advancing armies into two avenues of approach—the first through the gap to the north of the lakes and the second through the Polish salient to the south of the lakes. The Russians eventually decided to send two armies into East Prussia; the First Army under General Paul V. Rennenkampf moved north of the Masurian Lakes, while the Second Army under General Alexander V. Samsonov moved south of the lakes. The two armies were placed under the control of the Northwestern Front commanded by General Yakov G. Zhilinski. The Russians had agreed with France before the war to put 800,000 men in the field fifteen days after mobilization, but after the war began, the French pressured them into sending the two armies of the Northwestern Front into the field on August 15, a week earlier than prewar estimates of readiness.

The goal of German strategy in the east was to avoid defeat and to maintain as stable a front as possible. To delay the Russian advance, the Germans placed the Eighth Army in East Prussia under General Max von Prittwitz. Although Prittwitz's forces were better led, disciplined, and equipped, they had the difficult mission of holding back the Russians' overwhelming numbers until reinforcements were shifted from the Western Front. Prittwitz's initial plan was to spread his forces across the frontier of East Prussia and—depending on the circumstances—to concentrate against the Russians coming either north or south of the Masurian Lakes. When monitoring of the enemy's radio traffic revealed the slow movement of the Russian First Army north of the lakes, Prittwitz decided to concentrate most of the Eighth Army against the Russian Second Army, which was moving south of the lakes. Unfortunately, an overly aggressive corps commander boldly pushed his forces forward and engaged Russian forces north of the lakes, thereby upsetting Prittwitz's plan.

On August 20, Prittwitz attacked the Russian First Army north of the Masurian Lakes with nine divisions. By that evening it was clear that the Russians were winning at Gumbinnen, but more disturbing to Prittwitz were reports of two Russian armies (one of which did not exist) entering East Prussia to his rear, south of the Masurian Lakes. In a telephone communication with the German high command, Prittwitz said he would have to retreat across the Vistula River, more than 125 miles to the west of Gumbinnen. Such a withdrawal would have abandoned East Prussia to the Russians.

After the conversation with the German high command, several of Prittwitz's principal staff officers convinced him to use the superior lateral communications of the German forces to concentrate the bulk of his forces against the slowly advancing Russian Second Army to the south. They suggested leaving only a small force behind in the north to slow the advance of the Russian First Army and to move as many forces as possible by rail to the south. Reassured by his staff, Prittwitz agreed to the moves and thereby set into motion the sequence of events that would lead to the battle of Tannenberg and an important German victory.

Disturbed by Prittwitz's initial proposal to abandon much of East Prussia and by his apparent move to divide his forces in the face of a superior enemy, however, Moltke decided to replace him. On the afternoon of August 22, 1914, the 66-year-old retired General Paul von Hindenburg received a telegram from German headquarters offering him the possibility of returning to active duty. After telegraphing his acceptance, he received a second telegram informing him that Major General Erich Ludendorff—fresh from a remarkable performance at Liège—would visit him that night. Subsequent telegrams informed him that he was to command the German Eighth Army on the Eastern Front and that Ludendorff was to be his chief of staff.

As the two men traveled east to take command of Prittwitz's army, their styles and skills began to meld into an extraordinarily well-matched team. On the one hand, Hindenburg, as the commander, was a solid leader who was loyal, dependable, capable of maintaining morale and confidence, but not extremely intelligent; on the other, Ludendorff, as his chief of staff, had one of the finest minds of the war. A skilled technician, he was tough, aggressive, and attuned to detail. The team functioned smoothly with remarkably few clashes until the end of the war.

Though Prittwitz did not learn of his relief until the last moment, Hindenburg and Ludendorff arrived on August 23 to take over the Eighth Army. Hindenburg concurred with the movement orders and the plan for attacking the Russian Second Army, which had already been initiated by Prittwitz. After the slow advance of the Russian First Army in the north became apparent, Ludendorff rushed four corps toward the south so they could attack Samsonov's Second Army. During these moves Moltke decided to reinforce the Eastern Front by withdrawing two German corps from France. Though the two corps did not participate in the battle of Tannenberg, their departure weakened the German effort in France and thereby lessened the chances of German strategy succeeding.

Despite some confusion among troop units and some ignoring of orders by subordinate commanders, the German attack began on August 26. After repulsing an attack by a Russian corps, two German corps drove south toward the right flank of the Russian Second Army. On Samsonov's left flank, a German corps attacked on the 26th with only limited success but moved forward more energetically on August 27. Failing to recognize the operational goal of the Germans and remaining ignorant of what was happening on his flanks, Samsonov launched an attack toward the northwest on August 28 with his center. This attack thrust the neck of his forces into a

A German machine-gun crew in East Prussia. Though the Eastern Front had many more mobile operations than the Western Front, the Germans, Austrians, and Russians often used strongly fortified positions with entrenchments and barbed wire.

noose. After the attack ground to a halt, the Germans struck the Russian left flank, causing it to disintegrate. As German forces on both Russian flanks moved forward, they surrounded Samsonov's force, allowing only a few units to escape.

After some valiant efforts to escape, the Russian troops began surrendering on August 29. The Germans eventually captured about 92,000 prisoners; the Russians apparently lost about 50,000 killed and wounded; and the Germans lost 10,000–15,000. Samsonov shot himself. The Germans had annihilated the Russian Second Army, but they had gained an operational, not a strategic victory. They had destroyed two Russian corps and almost destroyed two others, but the Russians had mobilized at least thirty-seven corps, as well as several other independent brigades and reserve units.

The Russian defeat was due more to a compromised communications system, confused commanders, and inadequate intelligence about the enemy than to the brilliant performance of Hindenburg and Ludendorff. In reality, Russian soldiers had performed better than their officers, who had been unable to take advantage of their superior numbers or of their soldiers' willingness to fight. Similarly, higher commanders had done very little to coordinate the actions of the two Russian armies battling the Germans in East Prussia. Although opposed by small forces, the Russian First Army moved forward slowly and provided no support to the ill-fated Second Army.

As Hindenburg turned the Eighth Army toward the north he hoped for another Tannenberg, but when the Russian First Army commander recognized the danger facing his forces, he pulled them back across the Russian border on September 13. One week later the Germans encountered stronger opposition, and on September 25 the Russians drove the Eighth Army back to the frontier of East Prussia.

Operations in Galicia and Poland

While the Russians were being driven out of East Prussia, the main Russian forces became heavily engaged with the Austrian forces farther to the south on the Galician front. The Russian Southwest Front was under the command of General Nikolai Ivanov; the Austrian forces were under the command of the elderly Archduke Friederich in theory but actually were under the command of Field Marshal Franz Conrad von Hötzendorf, the chief of the general staff. After the first encounters on August 23, 1914, the Austrian First Army achieved some success at Krasnik in the southern part of the Polish salient, and on its right the Fourth Army pushed the Russians back at Komarov. But poor communications and mobility prevented them from taking advantage of their success. To their right, the Austrian Third Army was routed south of Lemberg by two stronger Russian armies.

To halt the Russian advance in the area of the Third Army, Conrad von Hötzendorf turned the Fourth Army to the south toward Lemberg, hoping to strike the advancing Russians in their flank. The movement of the Fourth Army, however, opened the way for a Russian advance between the First and Fourth armies. When Conrad learned to his horror that large Russian forces were moving through his center, he ordered the withdrawal of his forces. After leaving behind a strong force to defend the fortress of Przemysl, the Austrians pulled back about one hundred miles to the Carpathian Mountains. The Austrians would have suffered even worse defeat had the Russians not been so sluggish in their advance. Nevertheless, the Austrians lost nearly 250,000 killed and wounded, plus an additional 100,000 taken as prisoners. Conrad had little choice but to ask for and await German

Operations in Galicia and Poland, 1914

assistance. Thus by September 11 the Russians had gained an important victory against the Austrians and had inflicted more casualties on the Austrians than they had lost at Tannenberg. The Austrian collapse ended any chances of exploiting the German victory at Tannenberg.

In late September, the Russian *Stavka* began preparations for launching an offensive through the Polish salient into Germany (Silesia) after the Austrian army pulled back toward the Carpathian mountains. Hindenburg recognized the danger of such an attack and moved the newly formed German Ninth Army to the northern flank of the battered Austrian First Army. In subsequent fighting, the Germans and Austrians pushed the Russians back sixty miles, reaching the Vistula-San line and relieving Przemysl. But the Russians counterattacked, pushing back the Germans and the

Austrians by the end of October to their original positions. As the Russians rolled through Poland almost to the German border, Hindenburg and Ludendorff moved the Ninth Army to Thorn on the northern edge of the Polish salient and attacked deep into their rear toward the city of Lodz; the Russians held, almost encircling one German corps. Though fearful of suffering their own Tannenberg, the Germans nonetheless managed to halt the Russian drive toward the west.

The Russian offensive made more gains against the Austrians than against the Germans, and in November the Austrians faced the prospect of

Thousands of soldiers died trying to cross no-man's-land, which was often criss-crossed with miles of barbed wire. When measured against the reality of artillery, machine guns, and barbed wire, prewar notions of bayonet charges and élan seem ridiculous.

the Russians' penetrating into Hungary. With some German assistance, they managed to push the Russians back in early December but were too exhausted to exploit their success.

The Austrians had performed no better against the Serbs. When the Austrians entered Serbia on August 12, the two sides were about equal in numbers, but the Serbs were better trained and led, had combat experience from the Balkan Wars, and had modern artillery. The Austrians achieved some success, but by the end of August the Serbs had driven them back. Another Austrian attack occurred in early September, but it too failed. A third Austrian offensive drove the Serbs back, but a desperate counterattack pushed the Austrians out of Serbia by December 15. Not until late 1915 did the Central Powers return in force and overrun Serbia.

☆   ☆   ☆   ☆

In the broadest sense the Central Powers had failed despite their holding the Russians in the east. German strategy had depended on swift victory in the west, but Joffre had indeed achieved a miracle at the Marne when he shifted sufficient forces to face and then turn back the strong right wing of the German forces. In the east, the Germans had achieved remarkable success at Tannenberg, but with the Austrians' being mauled by the Serbians and the Russians, the situation remained grim for the Central Powers.

All the energy spent on the preparation of plans before 1914 had proved futile; no one had achieved quick victory, and all now faced a long, arduous war. With a stalemate settling on the Western Front and with the Eastern Front momentarily stabilized, both sides struggled desperately to meet the needs of their military forces. All armies were consuming previously unimaginable amounts of ammunition and supplies, forcing the warring states to organize nearly all their citizens and their economies to meet these formidable needs; and military leaders on both sides began searching for new strategies and methods for winning the war.

SUGGESTED READINGS

Barnett, Corelli. *The Sword-Bearers: Supreme Command in the First World War* (New York: William Morrow & Company, 1964).

Bucholz, Arden. *Moltke, Schlieffen, and Prussian War Planning* (Oxford: Berg, 1991).

Howard, Michael. "Men against Fire: The Doctrine of the Offensive in 1914," in Peter Paret, ed., *Makers of Modern Strategy* (Princeton, N.J.: Princeton University Press, 1986), pp. 510–526.

Isselin, Henri. *The Battle of the Marne*, trans. Charles Connell (Garden City, N.Y.: Doubleday & Company, Inc., 1966).

Kennedy, Paul, ed., *The War Plans of the Great Powers, 1880–1914* (London: Allen & Unwin, 1979)

Marshall-Cornwall, James. *Foch as Military Commander* (New York: Crane, Russak & Company, 1972).

Morrow, John H., Jr. *The Great War in the Air: Military Aviation from 1909 to 1921* (Washington: Smithsonian Institution Press, 1993).

Ritter, Gerhard. *The Schlieffen Plan: Critique of a Myth*, trans. Andrew and Eva Wilson (New York: Frederick A. Praeger, 1958).

Rothenberg, Gunther E. "Moltke, Schlieffen, and the Doctrine of Strategic Envelopment," in Peter Paret, ed., *Makers of Modern Strategy* (Princeton, N.J.: Princeton University Press, 1986), pp. 296–325.

_____. *The Army of Francis Joseph* (West Lafayette, Ind.: Purdue University Press, 1976).

Showalter, Dennis. *Tannenberg: Clash of Empires* (Hamden, Conn.: Archon Books, 1991).

Stone, Norman. *The Eastern Front, 1914–1917* (New York: Charles Scribner's Sons, 1975).

Terraine, John. *Mons: The Retreat to Victory* (New York: Macmillan, 1960).

18

ATTEMPTING TO END THE STALEMATE, 1914–1916

1914–1915: Adjusting to the Unexpected and Searching for Alternatives

1916: The Battles of Attrition

Tactical and Technological Innovations

The failure of the belligerents in 1914 to end the war transformed it into a long total war and ultimately into a world war. As the war became deadlocked at the tactical and operational levels, and as the battling armies consumed vast supplies, the belligerents mobilized nearly all their people and economic resources. Despite the terrible casualty lists and huge costs, none of the belligerents chose to quit fighting; instead, other powers, such as Italy and the Ottoman Empire, entered the war. Because of the enormous demands of the war, resources and access to them became crucial, and sea power for obtaining these resources or conversely for preventing an opponent from acquiring them assumed greater importance. The war soon became a vast conflict on air, land, and sea in major portions of the globe.

In the search for ways to win the war, the participants reconsidered their strategies. For the Central Powers, an intense debate began in late 1914 about how Germany should focus its efforts. As Austria-Hungary's situation became more desperate, Falkenhayn reluctantly shifted forces from the Western to the Eastern Front. By remaining on the defensive in the west and moving forces to the east, he hoped to neutralize Russian military power and then to return to the west and deal with the Allies. For the Allies in the west, the alternatives seemed more numerous. While some political and military leaders perceived weakness in Austria-Hungary and the Ottoman Empire and called for the opening of new fronts on the flanks of Europe, others argued for concentrating efforts against German defensive positions on the Western Front and breaking through them. And almost all recognized the importance of blocking the flow of resources to the Central Powers. With the launching in 1915 of major offensives on the Western Front and several peripheral operations, the Allies tried simultaneously to break through German defensive positions on the Western Front and to open new fronts on the flanks of Europe.

The many battles of the war's first two years left the Western Front deadlocked and almost static, while armies on the Eastern Front moved great distances. On the Western Front both sides focused their energy and resources on making a breakthrough and restoring mobility but failed. After the Central Powers broke through Russian defenses at Gorlice-Tarnow and drove forward two hundred miles on the Eastern Front, the Germans turned west and in a grinding battle of attrition at Verdun tried to force France from the war. As the combatants searched for alternatives, they began developing new technologies and methods capable of breaking the stalemate. Though the common view of World War I is one of stagnation, this search for new tactics and technologies resulted in the introduction and development of new methods, weapons, and equipment on a remarkable scale.

1914–1915: Adjusting to the Unexpected and Searching for Alternatives

As fall turned into winter in 1914, the dreams of a highly mobile, short war were replaced by the realities of a destructive, consuming war of position and attrition. The changing situation forced both sides to address fundamentally different problems than the ones they had anticipated. When General von Moltke, who was Chief of the German General Staff, received a letter early in the war outlining the need for better economic planning and controls, he responded, "Don't bother me with economics. I am busy conducting the war." Moltke's views were common among political and military leaders, but it did not take long for them to realize that the waging of modern war demanded the mobilization and marshaling of economic resources.

Germany in particular was in no position to wage a long drawn-out war, for it had to import many raw materials and goods. As soon as the war began, the British navy established a blockade of Germany's coastline and severely curtailed its access to overseas suppliers. Though other navies contributed, the subsequent war at sea was essentially a conflict between the navies of Great Britain and Germany. Although the Germans were not yet willing to give up the possibility of receiving supplies from overseas, they immediately recognized the importance of obtaining resources from the heart of Europe; Walther Rathenau, one of Germany's leading industrialists, led the effort to set up a mixture of government and privately owned companies for obtaining raw materials. He began with no clear plans, but by the spring of 1915 he was able to report to the minister of war that the supply of essential raw materials was sufficient. Germany's industry could supply the army with thousands of items in sufficient numbers and quality. Not until August 1916, when simultaneous battles were being fought on the Somme, on the Meuse, in Galicia, and in Italy did serious shortages again occur. Nonetheless the Allied blockade had an effect; though no substitutes for food could be found, the German government established meatless days and initiated a rigid system of price controls and rationing. When wheat supply grew short, the Germans learned to make "war bread" out of potatoes and turnips. And to take the place of supplies unavailable to the German war economy, scientists created *ersatz* (substitute) materials. The perfection of the nitrogen-fixation process, for example, permitted the manufacture of explosives even though nitrates could no longer be imported. Similarly, cellulose was developed as a substitute for cotton.

In the beginning of the war, France also faced particularly acute problems, for it had conscripted most of its factory and farm workers because of its expectations of a short war. Ammunition shortages appeared almost immediately, and barely two months into the war France began releasing soldiers so they could return to factories and farms and begin producing desperately needed food and matériel. To make matters worse, when the front stabilized, some of France's most important sources of coal and iron lay behind enemy lines; however, it eventually managed to increase the manufacture of war matériel and to lead the Allies in the production of all types of weapons except rifles and machine guns. Nonetheless, France depended on Great Britain and the United States for raw materials and fuel and became increasingly reliant on them for food.

Throughout Europe centrally planned and directed economies emerged as each government set up a system of boards and commissions to coordinate its war effort. The British, for example, formed a ministry of munitions in June 1915 with David Lloyd George as its first head. A large increase in output soon resulted. With many men in the armed services, women—particularly in Britain and France—played an increasingly important role in manufacturing crucially needed war matériel. The industrialization of war had arrived, and each country committed almost all its resources to the war effort. Meeting the demands of the military while simultaneously maintaining popular support for the war in the face of failure and horrendous casualties, however, created many problems for governments and often caused stormy confrontations between political and military leaders.

Searching for Tactical and Strategic Alternatives

As political and military leaders feverishly labored to increase the size of their armies and navies, replace casualties, and obtain sufficient weapons, munitions, equipment, and supplies, both sides continued their attacks on the Western Front. After they failed to outflank each other in the "Race to the Sea," they concentrated on breaking through their opponent's defenses. Before the trench lines reached the English Channel, the Germans attacked

The industrialization of war transformed the home front as well as the battlefield. Many women found jobs in factories that produced vast amounts of weapons, equipment, and ammunition.

around Verdun in September 1914 but did little more than create a salient east of the city of St. Mihiel. Other German attacks near Soissons and in Lorraine in January 1915 also failed to yield substantial results.

The first major opportunity to prevent a deadlock came to the Germans when the escape of the Belgians from Antwerp released the German forces that had besieged them. After combining these forces with other newly formed divisions, the Germans made a strong attack against the extreme western end of the front near the English Channel. When in the middle of October the Belgians opened the sluices and allowed the sea to flood the area, the Germans attempted to break through Allied defensive lines east of Ypres. The Germans threw newly formed divisions—consisting primarily of 17-to-20-year-olds—into the battle, but these poorly trained but enthusiastic youth suffered such horrendous casualties that the Germans used the phrase "The Massacre of the Innocents at Ypres" to describe the action.

Despite the initial failures, both sides continued to seek a breakthrough. They believed that if they could reach the open fields behind the trenches and barbed wire, a decisive battle could be fought and victory attained. The attacks, however, invariably failed. The length of the opposing lines and the strength of the defensive positions seriously limited the combatants' ability to maneuver. With no open flanks and with barbed wire, entrenchments, machine guns, and artillery creating a significant barrier, most attacks quickly ground down to muddy and bloody halts. On those rare occasions when an attack managed to break through the enemy's position, sufficient forces could not move quickly enough through the opened gap to take advantage of the momentary opportunity. Both sides quickly recognized the advantages of using heavy concentrations of artillery fire to blast their way through the enemy's lines. Reliance on massive amounts of artillery, however, increased the demand for munitions and complicated coordination of infantry and artillery actions.

After the first battle of Ypres ended in the middle of November 1914, the Allies launched several attacks. In December, Joffre attacked unsuccessfully north of Arras and supported this attack with another one in Champagne, but neither attack yielded important results. The French blamed their failures on the absence of sufficient artillery preparation and on inadequate coordination between the artillery and the infantry. In February 1915 the French again attacked in Champagne, and in April they attempted to reduce the German-held salient around St. Mihiel. Both attacks failed despite the improved use of artillery.

The Germans initially had the upper hand in artillery exchanges, for they had considerably more heavy artillery than the Allies. Each German corps had 16 150-mm howitzers, 18 105-mm howitzers, and 126 77-mm field guns, a total of 160 tubes, while a French corps had only 120 75-mm guns. Though the British had fewer artillery pieces than the French, each of their infantry divisions did have four 60-pounders that could reach the Germans' 150-mm howitzers. For months the Germans skillfully used their more numerous and longer-range artillery to shatter Allied attacks, disrupt their artillery, and inflict large numbers of casualties.

In March 1915 the British attacked at Neuve Chapelle in their first serious attempt to break through the German trench system. To make a penetration, the British concentrated 40,000 men and sixty-two light artillery batteries along a front of about 2,000 yards. Their objective was to seize Aubers Ridge, which was behind the German line and being used to observe their positions. Hoping to surprise the Germans, the British moved their guns forward at night and registered them surreptitiously by firing only a few rounds. This provided sufficient firing data for all the guns to fire more accurately and effectively. Relying heavily on aerial photographs to identify targets, they intended to fire an intense, thirty-five-minute preparatory bombardment which would also include cutting the barbed wire with shrapnel from 18-pounders. When the attack began, the British made some advances but could not exploit their advantage before the attack bogged down because of inadequate coordination between the artillery and the infantry. As the British advance slowed, the Germans moved reinforcements into the gap and halted the attack. Future attacks usually relied on much more extensive and longer artillery preparation.

A momentary advantage appeared for the Germans in April 1915 when they employed chlorine gas on the Western Front. The use of poisonous gasses had been proposed during the Crimean War and the American Civil War, but none had been used. As early as 1899 at the Hague Conference, the international community passed a declaration prohibiting the use of shells filled with asphyxiating gasses. By 1915, the desire to overcome the

Operations on the Western Front, 1915–1916

Allied attack
German attack
Western Front
Areas seized:
Allies
Germans

GERMANY

Rhine R.

ALSACE

Lorraine
Jan. 1915

Moselle R.

LUX.

Verdun
Feb.–Aug. 1916

LORRAINE

St. Mihiel

Meuse R.

Champagne
Feb.–Mar. 1915
Sept.–Nov. 1915

CHAMPAGNE

Antwerp

Lys R.

BELGIUM

Reims

Soissons
Jan. 1915

Soissons

FRANCE

Yser
Jan. 1915

Ypres
Apr. 1915

Yser R.

FLANDERS

March 1915
May 1915
Sept. 1915
May–June 1915
Sept.–Oct. 1915

Vimy
Arras

ARTOIS

Somme
June–Nov. 1916

Marne R.

Paris

Seine R.

ENGLISH CHANNEL

0   20   40 mi
0   20   40 km

bloody tactical stalemate had led both sides to employ tear gas. On January 31, 1915, the Germans fired over 18,000 artillery rounds filled with asphyxiating gas at the Russians, but the rounds had little or no effect because of the cold weather.

On the morning of April 15, 1915, the Germans released a cloud of yellowish-green chlorine gas against French positions about three miles north of Ypres. Though the equipment consisted of little more than commercial cylindrical containers, the unexpected appearance of gas in the trenches led to panic and the French troops ran away, leaving a huge hole in their defensive line. The Germans, protected only by cotton wadding tied over their faces, moved forward into the opening, but were soon stopped by their own gas and then by the heroic fighting of the Canadians and French. The Allies reestablished their defensive lines, but the Germans had made significant gains.

Poisonous gasses were used throughout the war, but they never again came so close to providing a decisive edge for victory. In fact, very few soldiers actually died from poisonous gasses. Thus chemical warfare added to the terror and casualties of the war but did little to shorten it. One of the interesting byproducts of the use of gasses was the introduction of smoke-making devices to simulate gas. These soon provided the smoke screens that would be used in attacks for the remainder of the war.

Despite the use of chemicals and despite extremely high casualties, the Allies continued to attack and to seek a breakthrough of the enemy's defensive lines. On May 9, 1915, a combined Franco-British attack began in Artois between Neuve Chapelle and Arras. The main objective was to seize Vimy Ridge, which dominated the entire region, but neither the French nor the British came close to breaking through the enemy's defenses.

The opposing armies quickly recognized the difficulty of moving across terrain where massive artillery barrages had fallen. The heavily churned and broken ground slowed the advance of follow-on forces and in particular delayed the forward displacement of artillery batteries. An attacker sometimes had to build roads through positions previously held by the enemy before heavy artillery pieces could be advanced. Since the infantry could hardly move without the protection of artillery, the depth and pace of penetrations were severely limited by the moving of artillery across the devastated ground. The Germans learned that they could rush reinforcements by light railway to a threatened sector faster than the Allies could push through devastated terrain. As a consequence, attacks rarely advanced more than a mile or two, and thousands of Allied soldiers lost their lives in vain attempts to achieve the much-desired breakthrough.

After a summer of recuperation and accumulation of supplies and equipment, the Allies attacked in Artois and Champagne in September. In Artois, the British attacked toward Loos, while the French again attacked toward Vimy Ridge. In Champagne, the French attacked midway between Reims and Verdun. The Allies were particularly optimistic about the attack in Champagne, for they attacked with two armies against twelve German divisions along a front of fifteen miles. With gasses being used, with follow-on infantry ready to move, with cavalry available for the exploitation, and with a violent artillery preparation from 2,500 guns lasting three days, the Champagne attack seemed a sure success. But like the attacks in Artois, it too failed, even though it initially made significant gains. For the first time in the war, the Germans had prepared a second belt of defenses and withdrew part of their artillery behind this belt before the French attacked. Though the German defenders were shaken and Falkenhayn feared a breakthrough, the second belt managed to hold. The French had made extensive preparations and suffered huge losses, but they had nevertheless failed.

The year of costly Allied attacks came to a close with the failure of the Champagne offensive. Despite numerous attacks and the loss of thousands of lives, the defensive lines on the Western Front never moved more than three miles in either direction. Hoping a new commander would bring an end to the slaughter, the British replaced General Sir John French with General Sir Douglas Haig at the end of 1915. The French also sought to reduce their casualties. During the sixteen months from August 1, 1914, to November 30, 1915, 664,000 French soldiers had died; during the thirty-five months from December 1915 until the armistice another 683,000 would die. Instead of replacing Joffre in 1915, however, the French intensified their efforts to devise operational methods that would save French lives.

From the Allies' viewpoint, the only positive development in the first year of fighting was some progress in improving cooperation between the British and French armies. The Allies, however, did not establish a clear chain of command; with neither a supreme war council nor a supreme commander, the best the Allies could do was to coordinate their strategy and operations.

Life and Death in the Trenches

More so on the Western than on the Eastern Front, the trench came to symbolize the new type of warfare now facing the participants. Its appearance and use changed greatly during the first two years of the war. The first trenches to appear on the Western Front were little more than long, shallow ditches about waist deep; but after the Western Front stabilized, they became much deeper and much more extensive. Initially consisting of only one or two lines, trenches eventually consisted of two or three lines and in some cases two or three belts, each with multiple lines of trenches. As the terrifying effects of artillery became apparent, the trenches became deeper and much more elaborate. Except for those areas where high water tables prevented deep digging, most trenches became deeper than a man's head and one or two yards wide. Instead of being straight lines, trenches quickly assumed a zigzag appearance. Turns and bends in a trench prevented an enemy from using enfilading fire down the entire length of a trench if a small portion of it was captured. Between the opposing lines of trenches and thousands of rolls of barbed wire, a "no-man's-land" quickly appeared. Depending on the terrain, the separation between the opposing trenches varied from a few dozen to several hundred yards.

Trenches running perpendicular to the main lines were also used. These zigzag-shaped trenches, known as communication trenches, connected one line of trenches to another and enabled troops to move back and forth between lines in relative safety. Messengers and reserves frequently

An extensive network of trenches quickly appeared on the Western Front. Those who lived in the trenches used boardwalks to keep their feet dry and sand bags to keep the walls of the trenches stable. Signs provided directions to the front lines as well as to other points.

moved back and forth between the connecting trenches. Shallow trenches were also placed ahead of the front lines. These trenches extended to observation posts or early warning positions.

As the effects of firepower became more apparent in the second and third years of fighting, the opposing armies often used strong points, rather than continuous lines of trenches. Scattered in depth, the strong points were usually organized for all-around defense and strengthened by numerous machine guns. With enormous amounts of artillery churning and plowing the ground, neat lines of entrenchments quickly disappeared in a moonscape of shell holes and mine craters. Though entrenchments remained important, defensive positions came to resemble a checkerboard, rather than a system of lines. The use of strong points was particularly prevalent after late 1916.

Commanders found it extremely difficult to feed and care for their soldiers in the trenches; indeed, providing a hot meal to soldiers in the trenches proved to be a most arduous task. The Germans made special efforts to shelter their soldiers when they were not occupying the front line and often prepared deep dugouts that could protect platoons and companies from Allied artillery fire. By Allied standards, many of their dugouts were almost luxurious—some even included beds and electric light systems. The Germans also made wide use of concrete pillboxes, often camouflaged and hidden from artillery fire. One can still often identify the location of German positions by the presence of these rudimentary but effective concrete bunkers.

Life in the trenches was grisly—the overpowering stench of decaying bodies of men and animals, of human excrement, and of chloride of lime to combat odors and disease could not be escaped. Soldiers had to coexist with huge rats feeding off the dead. The constant threat of death also weighed against the trench occupants. In addition to the danger of an attack or raid, random artillery rounds sometimes fell among soldiers who had to endure incessant sniper fire. A simple hot meal and cool beverage in a place safely to the rear must have seemed like heaven to a soldier who had survived a long stretch in the trenches.

Peripheral Operations

From the earliest days, it was clear that the Great War would not be confined to the European continent. As early as August 7, 1914, British and French troops invaded German Togoland on the coast of west-central Africa. Other German possessions in Africa, including Southwest Africa and the Cameroons, soon came under pressure. By November 1914, German possessions in the Pacific had been seized by Australia, New Zealand, and Japan. A notable exception to the relatively rapid defeat of Germany's forces in its colonial possessions occurred in East Africa, where a small detachment managed to resist Allied forces until the end of the war.

The entry of the Ottoman Empire into the war on the side of the Central Powers, as well as growing discontent—particularly among the British—with the deadlock on the Western Front, however, prompted the Allies to launch operations on the periphery of Europe. To some, the Ottoman Empire appeared easier to break than the German defenses on the Western Front. The British split into two schools of thought—one seeing western Europe as the decisive theater and the other calling for attacks on the enemy's strategic flanks. Joffre strongly objected to attacks on the periphery of Europe, for he believed that victory could be achieved only on the Western Front and that the diversion of resources to other theaters would delay a decision. Nevertheless, between 1915 and 1916 the Allies sought gains in peripheral operations while simultaneously seeking a breakthrough on the Western Front. Whether one views the peripheral operations as B. H. Liddell Hart did as a "Strategy of the Indirect Approach," or as J. F. C. Fuller did as a "Strategy of Evasion," significant forces became involved in campaigns in the Middle East and on the periphery of Europe.

In January 1915 the British defended Egypt against a Turkish invasion, and over the next three years of fighting gradually moved into Palestine with British forces eventually fighting under the command of General Sir Edmund Allenby. In March 1915 the British began the Dardanelles campaign in an abortive attempt to open the narrow straits between the Aegean and Black seas. In the spring of 1915, British forces expanded their control over Mesopotamia and moved courageously up the Tigris River against overwhelmingly larger Turkish forces. In October, British and French forces launched the Salonika campaign into Macedonia in an attempt to aid the Serbian army.

Of these campaigns, the Gallipoli campaign in the Dardanelles was the most poorly conducted. The objective of the operation was to seize the Straits of the Dardanelles. In doing so, the Allies could expand seaborne lines of communications with Russia and sever links between the Central Powers and most of the Ottoman Empire. Although the Turks had managed to block the Straits with minefields, shore batteries, and two German ships, the Allies expected the Turkish defenses to crumble under only light pressure. The Allies initially dispatched a sizable naval squadron with orders to seize the Gallipoli peninsula and Constantinople, but after three of the eighteen Allied battleships were sunk and three others badly damaged, the naval forces pulled back and awaited the arrival of ground forces. During this delay, the Turks formed a separate army for the defense of the Dardanelles and placed it under the command of General Otto Liman von Sanders, the head of the German military mission. The new commander quickly located his forces in central positions where they could react rapidly to any Allied landings.

When an Allied force consisting of British, French, and Australian–New Zealand (ANZAC) troops attacked on April 25, 1915, the operation began as planned but soon degenerated into a disaster. The Allies landed at several different points near the southwestern tip of the long Gallipoli peninsula. With troops disembarking from barges towed by rowboats and from colliers that had been converted into infantry landing craft, the British and ANZAC forces encountered strong opposition and were prevented from moving inland. The British landing at Cape Helles at the tip of the peninsula met particularly strong resistance; on one beach 70 percent of the first 1,000

Gallipoli, 1915

0   1.5   3 mi
0   1.5   3 km

SUVLA
BAY

Limit of Allied
Advance

Aug. 6

Apr. 25

AEGEAN
SEA

Limit of Allied
Advance

CAPE
HELLES

DARDANELLES

Apr. 25

○—○ Mines
☒ Fortifications
Aug. 6 Allied landings

troops to land became casualties. Attacks on subsequent days made only minimal gains and within two weeks of the first landings, Gallipoli resembled the Western Front with its entrenchments and fortified positions.

On August 6, the British landed additional forces at Suvla Bay, about fifteen miles north of Cape Helles, and attempted to outflank the Turkish defenders to the south. Despite being unopposed initially, the slow advance of the British and the rapid reaction of the Turks soon resulted in another stalemate. The Allied operation suffered from numerous deficiencies including lack of experience in amphibious operations, water shortages, poor fire support, misused communications, and muddled commanders. In December 1915 the Allies abandoned the Suvla Bay beaches, and in January 1916 the last Allied soldiers withdrew from Cape Helles and thereby from the Dardanelles peninsula. The British alone had suffered more than 200,000 casualties. Neither the Gallipoli campaign nor the other peripheral operations contributed significantly to shortening the war.

The Eastern Front

After the failure of the Schlieffen Plan in 1914, the Germans reconsidered their strategic alternatives. For a short time in November–December 1914 they temporarily relied on a defensive strategy, later described by Falkenhayn as a "transition to trench warfare." Emphasis on the defense enabled the Germans to protect their frontiers, increase the manufacture and supply of matériel, expand the capacity of their railways, take advantage of interior lines, and rest, train, and reequip their troops. As the Germans analyzed their alternatives, the military hierarchy was split by a debate between the "Westerners" (led by Falkenhayn) and the "Easterners" (led by Hindenburg and Ludendorff) about whether the German effort should be focused in the east or the west. Hindenburg and Ludendorff believed the shifting of divisions from the west to the east would enable the Central Powers to defeat Russia and induce the other Allied powers to end the war. Insisting the war could be won only in the west, Falkenhayn rejected this argument.

Friction between the Germans and the Austrians complicated Falkenhayn's dilemma. Much like the Allies, the Central Powers had no supreme command. Though the Germans slowly assumed the role of "senior partner" in the alliance, the Austrians did not enter into a clearly secondary role until late 1916. Despite the better performance of the German military and the need to use German forces to stiffen the Austrians, Conrad von Hötzendorf, the chief of the general staff, refused to relinquish Austria-Hungary's freedom of action in making strategy or conducting military operations. Relations between Falkenhayn and Conrad became particularly strained in early 1915 when the Germans pressured the Austrians to yield territory to the Italians in order to keep them from entering the war on the side of the Allies. Conrad, nevertheless, continued to demand additional support from Germany.

Despite his desire to focus German efforts in the west, Falkenhayn soon found himself compelled to come to the aid of the Austrians. In January 1915, he gave four corps to Hindenburg for an attack from East Prussia that would force the Russians to divert forces to the north and provide the Austrians in the south some relief. Meanwhile, Conrad launched an attack from the Carpathian Mountains, but the Austrians suffered heavy casualties and made no progress. On February 7, Hindenburg's Eighth Army defeated the Russian Tenth Army in the second Masurian Lakes campaign, but most of the Russians escaped and established new defensive positions to the east. On February 27, Conrad launched another attack and failed again. About one month later, about 120,000 Austrians surrendered at the fortress of Przemysl, which had been surrounded for months. In April, the Russians began a new offensive and seized the important Dukla Pass, thereby threatening to break through the mountains into the heart of Austria-Hungary.

As the Austrian situation deteriorated, Falkenhayn concluded that the Central Powers had to cripple Russia's offensive capability. After Allied offensives on the Western Front failed in February–March 1915, he believed that the Allies could not yet force a decision on that front and that he had the freedom to focus on the east. Instead of allowing Hindenburg to attack from the north, however, he decided to strike the Russian center. After initiating preparations, he contacted Conrad in the middle of April and coordinated the upcoming attack.

The Gorlice-Tarnow Breakthrough and Russian Withdrawal

To increase the chances of success against the Russians, Falkenhayn directed the formation of Eleventh Army and appointed General August von Mackensen as its commander. Mackensen chose Colonel Hans von Seeckt as his chief of staff. Consisting of eight German and three Austrian divisions, Eleventh Army moved into position north of the Carpathian mountains between the Austrian Third and Fourth armies. Conrad refused to give the Germans overall command of the operation. Though Mackensen also controlled the operations of the Austrian Fourth Army, the German and Austrian high commands jointly approved all major directives, and the Austrians issued them.

Most of the German divisions in Eleventh Army had recently served on the Western Front, as had Colonel von Seeckt, one of the most outstanding officers in the German army. Von Seeckt had played a key role in the January 1915 attack at Soissons and had learned important lessons about the need to modify infantry tactics and achieve better cooperation between infantry and artillery. He now applied some of these ideas on the Eastern Front. The subsequent German success, however, was due less to the introduction of fundamentally new methods than it was to Russia's shortage of machine guns and the inability of its artillery to work closely with its infantry. That the Germans had not yet solved the riddle of breaking through an enemy's defensive position is best illustrated by several of the regiments in the Gorlice-Tarnow attack taking casualties at the same rate as in the disastrous Ypres offensive of the previous fall.

Gorlice-Tarnow Breakthrough, May–September 1915

BALTIC SEA

• Riga

• Dvinsk

July 13

May 2

Aug. 15

• Königsberg

RUSSIA

EAST PRUSSIA

Vistula R.

Bug R.

Aug. 15

PRIPET MARSHES

• Warsaw

Pinsk •

• Brest-Litovsk

Lodz •

July 13

• Lublin

POLAND

San R.

Sept. 30

• Tarnow

Lemberg •

Przemysl •

XXXX
Eleventh

• Gorlice

June 1

July 13

GALICIA

May 2

~~~~~ Central Powers' lines

| 0 | 50 | 100 mi |
| 0 | 50 | 100 km |

The two Russian corps opposing Eleventh Army between Gorlice and Tarnow were not prepared for the onslaught that struck them on May 2, 1915. Four hours of preparatory fire from German artillery reduced their trenches, opened holes in their sparse barbed wire, cut communications lines, and disrupted their artillery. Pushing forward rapidly and advancing almost eight miles in the first two days, the Germans quickly punched through the shallow defenses of the Russian Third Army. With few Russian reserves available, the Germans continued moving forward rapidly, but the Russian *Stavka* refused to give General Ivanov, the commander of the Southwest Front, permission to withdraw; Russian leaders feared the Germans would outflank their forces as they pulled out of the Carpathian Mountains. This refusal condemned Third Army to staggering losses. On May 10, Third Army finally received permission to withdraw to the San River, which was about seventy-five miles east of their original position.

After arriving at the San River, the Russians found themselves in an extremely weak position; they had lost 80 percent of Third Army. Almost no defensive positions had been prepared, and much of the barbed wire and timber seized from the Austrians that could have been used to strengthen their positions had been sold to the local population. Supplies of artillery ammunition were extremely limited; the Russians had only 100,000 rounds in reserve while the German Eleventh Army alone had more than one million. To add to the Russians' difficulties, German positions on the western bank of the narrow river completely dominated the eastern bank in several key areas.

The battles along the San River followed the Gorlice-Tarnow pattern with the Germans establishing a large bridgehead across the river between May 16 and 19. Meanwhile, the Russians pushed back the Austrians, and the Germans had to rush to their assistance. In mid-June, the German offensive began anew, and on June 22 Austro-German forces captured Lemberg, fifty miles east of the San River. The Russians began a full-scale retreat and fell back; by the time they stopped some units were seventy-five miles east of the San River and 150 miles east of Gorlice-Tarnow. The Central Powers once again controlled most of Galicia.

Between June 3 and July 1, a debate occurred between Falkenhayn, Conrad, and Hindenburg over the Central Powers' strategy. With Italy entering the war on May 23 on the Allied side, Conrad wanted to concentrate against Italy, but Falkenhayn preferred to concentrate against the Allies in France. He believed that the offensive against the Russians had achieved its purpose and had neutralized Russian military power. Hindenburg and Ludendorff aggressively opposed the movement of divisions away from the Eastern Front and argued for a continuation of the attack in the east. Conrad and Falkenhayn finally agreed that the best course of action was to continue the offensive against Russia.

As the Central Powers pressed the Russians, they shifted the direction of their attack in Galicia from the east to the northeast toward Brest-Litovsk. In a gigantic pincer movement, other forces attacked toward Brest-Litovsk from the north. With pressure coming from the south and the north, the Polish salient was quickly overrun. Lublin fell on July 30, Warsaw on August 4. By August 30 the Russians had withdrawn east of the Bug River and Brest-Litovsk, and the Central Powers had established a vast front across the base of the Polish sálient.

The Russian withdrawal continued. By September 30, the Central Powers had moved deep into Russia. They occupied a line running from Riga on the Baltic Sea, to Dvinsk, to Pinsk, to the Romanian border. This line was about 200 miles east of Gorlice-Tarnow where Mackensen's forces had made the first breakthrough in May 1915. Except for the moves associated with Brusilov's offensive in 1916 and the Russian collapse in 1917, the opposing forces on the Eastern Front remained generally along this line for the remainder of the war.

The Central Powers had gained a victory of immense proportions and had inflicted more than 2 million casualties on the Russians. Their success was due as much to the ineptitude of the Russian army as it was to the professionalism and preparedness of the German army. With more advanced techniques of artillery and infantry coordination, a more effective command and staff structure, and more supplies, the Central Powers had significant advantages. The Russians were hampered by an inefficient and fragmented high command and were outnumbered in machine guns and artillery pieces. Nevertheless, the Russians did not quit fighting, and thousands of them lost their lives.

The disaster provoked an immediate outcry in Russia, and complaints focused on crippling shortages in rifles and in artillery shells. In reality, however, the Russians needed more than an increase in the number of weapons and shells. Russian leaders recognized the poor organization of the army and the ineptitude of some of the commanders; they soon began streamlining their command structure and replacing weak commanders. Having reduced the Russian threat, Falkenhayn shifted forces to the west where the buildup of Allied troops posed a greater threat.

1916: The Battles of Attrition

Even though the Allies had the common goal of defeating Austria-Hungary and Germany, they had no common, agreed-upon strategy for achieving this goal. The first meeting of Allied military leaders occurred in July 1915, but no supreme command or common staff structure emerged, and almost no agreements—except for a call for future meetings—were reached on the conduct of coalition warfare. In December 1915, military leaders of France, Great Britain, Belgium, and Italy and representatives from Russia and Japan met at Joffre's headquarters.

This was the first and only time that the major Allies formulated and attempted to carry out a coordinated strategy; but the strategy was neither detailed nor tightly coordinated. To regain the initiative from the Germans, which they had seized in the west in 1914 and on the Eastern Front in 1915, the Allies agreed to launch offensives on the principal fronts in France,

Russia, and Italy, but they did not establish formal mechanisms for coordinating strategy and operations. The Allies preferred personal meetings and coordination among the military leaders rather than a formal command and staff structure that could have impinged on their sovereignty.

Of all the Allies, the French and British cooperated the best, but the British were reluctant to subordinate their small and still expanding army to the French. They preferred to make their main effort in Flanders, close to the Belgian coast, which they believed to be "an objective of great political and naval as well as military importance." In February 1916, the French and British finally agreed to conduct a combined offensive on both sides of the Somme River and tentatively scheduled the offensive for the late summer of 1916. This agreement was overcome by events when the Germans launched an offensive on February 21 at Verdun.

While the Allies reconsidered their strategy, Falkenhayn shifted his main effort from east to west. By late 1915, the Central Powers had successfully reoccupied Poland and Galicia and had seriously weakened the Russians. Similarly, the Allied attack in the Balkans through Salonika had been stymied, and the Allies were withdrawing from Gallipoli after the failure of their attempted invasion. The only area in which the war was not going well for the Central Powers was on the sea, for the naval blockade was beginning

General Erich von Falkenhayn became Germany's chief of the general staff in September 1914. He presided over the shifting of German strategic focus from the Western to the Eastern Front in 1915 and back to the Western Front in 1916.

to cause shortages (particularly of food) and to affect military operations. The sea power of the Allies also enabled them to add to the men and matériel on the Western Front. If the Central Powers did not act quickly, the buildup of Allied troops and matériel would soon provide them an important advantage in what clearly had become a war of attrition.

The Battle of Verdun

In Falkenhayn's analysis of his options on the Western Front, which he completed in December 1915, he described England as Germany's "arch enemy" and the war on the Continent as a "sideshow" for the English. If the Germans defeated France, he said, England's "best sword" would be removed from its hand, and the "strong probability" existed that it would "give up." He also argued that France was "almost exhausted" and that an attack on Verdun would force France to "commit every man available" since Verdun anchored the center of the entire Allied line. Given the closeness of Verdun to German railway connections (only twelve miles), the Germans could, theoretically, make a "relatively small effort" in which the forces of France could be "bled white." Thus Falkenhayn consciously chose a battle

Battle of Verdun, 1916

0   3   6 mi
0   3   6 km

Meuse R.

Front line
Feb. 21

Ft. Douaumont
Ft. Vaux

Front line
Aug. 8
Limit of German advance

Verdun

Voie Sacrée

Meuse R.

¤ Major fortifications

of attrition; he intended to weaken French morale significantly and to force them to the breaking point. In believing Germany had to make only a relatively small effort, however, Falkenhayn forgot that attrition is a two-edged sword. France and Germany were about to become embroiled in a gigantic battle that would consume hundreds of thousands of lives.

When the Germans attacked on February 21, 1916, Falkenhayn ordered the German crown prince, William, whose Fifth Army had the mission of making the assault on Verdun, to confine his attack to the eastern side of the Meuse River. This river split the fortress system around Verdun through its center. With the city in the center, the fortress system consisted of more than twenty smaller forts arranged in a circle with a radius of about four to five miles. By insisting that the crown prince not attack on both sides of the Meuse, Falkenhayn intended to minimize casualties by attacking on a narrow front. Unfortunately for the German infantry, his order sent them forward into the roughest terrain around Verdun.

The German attack on February 21 began with a twelve-hour bombardment from 1,400 guns firing about 100,000 shells per hour into the small area. Late in the afternoon the infantry moved forward with scouts in the forefront; they located areas not destroyed by artillery fire and directed further fire against them. If they encountered a strong point, they bypassed or encircled it. Centers of resistance fell one by one, but the Germans succeeded in advancing only three miles after two days of fighting. Despite the Germans' overwhelming advantage in infantry and artillery, the French delayed their advance by a heroic defense and by highly effective artillery fire from across the river into the German flanks.

The Germans continued to attack over the next several days, and in one of the greatest coups of the war managed to capture Fort Douaumont, the most important fortification in the fortress system, without firing a shot. In the heat and confusion of battle, French commanders on both flanks of the fort assumed that a permanent garrison was holding it, but in fact only a few soldiers were manning it. A handful of Germans surprised the few occupants and captured the fort easily. The fall of Fort Douaumont was one of the most tragic blunders of the war and cost France thousands of lives as it attempted to regain the fort.

To ensure Verdun did not fall, Joffre placed General Henri-Philippe Pétain in charge of its defense. Though hampered by a severe bout of double pneumonia, Pétain managed to strengthen Verdun's defenses and to reoccupy and rearm the forts still in French hands. Early in the war, the French had removed much of the artillery from the forts when they were desperately seeking longer-range artillery. Pétain assigned garrisons to the forts and ordered them to fight to the last man. Simultaneously, he began improving transportation links to the threatened sector. The two main rail lines to Verdun were unusable, for one was cut off by German forces in the St. Mihiel salient and the other by enemy artillery fire a dozen miles west of Verdun. Almost all the supplies for Verdun had to move along the narrow road from Bar-le-Duc. Soon an almost endless stream of trucks moved constantly up the important road that became known as the *Voie Sacré*, or Sacred Way.

Pétain also reorganized his defenses, breaking down his sector into four corps areas, each with its own artillery support. Part of this effort included the strengthening of the western bank of the Meuse. Recognizing the awesome power of the German artillery, he modified the defensive scheme by placing an advanced line of resistance in front of the principal line of resistance. The forward line did not have to be held at all costs and provided some elasticity for the defense; it also limited the number of soldiers coming directly under enemy fire.

By the end of February, the German Fifth Army's attack on the eastern bank had ground to a halt, so Falkenhayn approved expanding the fight to the western bank. On March 6, the Germans launched a powerful attack on the western bank and made their largest gains along the Meuse. Another attack began on March 20, followed by another on March 28 after fresh reserves were brought up. Despite the huge concentration of men and matériel, the Germans advanced only two miles.

On April 9 the Germans launched attacks on both sides of the Meuse, but again the French somehow managed to stop them. The next two months witnessed several bitter battles that resulted in only small changes in the location of the lines. After one final attempt to break through French lines on the western bank, which witnessed a huge expenditure of ammunition and lives, the Germans shifted away from the western bank and for the remainder of the battle concentrated on the eastern bank.

The bloody attacks and counterattacks continued through August when Falkenhayn was relieved as chief of staff of the German army. Hindenburg replaced him, and one of his first orders halted the attacks at Verdun. During the next three months the French launched several carefully controlled attacks with the infantry advancing by bounds as enormous artillery concentrations flattened German defenses to their front. These methodical attacks with limited objectives succeeded in pushing the Germans back slowly from their expensively gained terrain.

Though some innovations occurred in artillery and infantry tactics, the bulk of the fighting at Verdun was characterized more by its brutality than by its sophistication or subtlety. With hundreds of thousands of men jammed into a relatively small area and with the skies constantly filled with falling artillery shells, the Germans called Verdun the "sausage grinder" and the French called it the "furnace." A typical battle began with an artillery bombardment to obliterate the enemy's forward defenses. As reinforcements rushed forward to strengthen the defenses, many died under enemy artillery barrages before they could reach the forward positions. The survivors in forward positions, as well as the reinforcements, often fought desperately from destroyed shell-holes and trenches until friendly artillery and machine-gun fire repulsed the attackers.

By the time the fighting ended, the struggle had indelibly marked both armies. No one knows the exact number of casualties, but the French acknowledged having 377,231 casualties, with 162,308 soldiers killed or missing. Although the Germans probably suffered fewer casualties than the French, the combined losses of both countries may have been over 700,000.

Despite the sufferings of hundreds of thousands of soldiers, the front lines had barely moved.

The Battle of the Somme

Just prior to the attack on Verdun, the French and British had agreed to make a combined attack on the Somme, but the German attack derailed Allied plans. As enemy pressure on Verdun increased, Joffre asked the British to launch a diversionary attack in the Somme region and thereby relieve some of the pressure on Verdun. Haig delayed the attack, however, so he could complete the training of newly arrived divisions. He also recognized the considerable strength of the German defenses to his front and wanted his units as well prepared as possible.

Although the plan for the Somme attack was ambitious, it was fairly simple. Along a front of about twenty miles, the Allies intended to attack with the British Fourth Army in the north making the main attack and the French Fifth Army in the south making a supporting attack. After reaching the high ground between Bapaume and Péronne, the Allies would expand the gap by having the British turn north and northeast and the French east. Large cavalry forces would exploit the breakthrough by moving northeast in the direction of Cambrai.

British infantry leaving a forward trench on the first day of the Battle of the Somme. Many of the British never made it through their own barbed wire even though nearly 250,000 artillery shells exploded on German trenches in the hour just prior to the assault.

The key to the British attack was the overwhelming use of artillery. Massive preparatory fires rained on the German positions from June 24 until the attack on July 1. With 1,437 guns firing, the British sent 1,508,652 shells into the German lines. British leaders confidently believed the artillery would destroy the wire entanglements to the infantry's front and annihilate the German defenders. To ensure control by their officers, the heavily burdened British infantrymen were told to march slowly and steadily toward the enemy's lines; no one expected any serious opposition. Tragically for the British, the 1.5 million rounds of artillery did not obliterate German defenses. After the preparatory fire had ceased and the barrages had shifted from the front lines to the rear, German infantry emerged from their dugouts and delivered withering fire against the surprised and helpless British. Hurrying forward to join the attack on time, many British soldiers never even made it to the front lines of their own position.

Within the first hour of the attack, the British suffered 30,000 casualties; by the end of the day they lost 57,400—the highest rate of casualties ever experienced by the British army. The losses exceeded the total British combat casualties in the Crimean, Boer, and Korean wars combined. But despite these tremendous losses, General Haig continued to attack. Remaining optimistic about the possibility of making a breakthrough and determined to divert the Germans from Verdun, he pressed forward. With his forces taking large numbers of casualties at Verdun and the Somme, Falkenhayn ordered his commanders not to give up any terrain. German casualties also mounted alarmingly.

In mid-November the offensive on the Somme finally ended. Ludendorff noted in his memoirs that both sides were "utterly exhausted." The Allied blockade that prevented trade between the Central Powers and the rest of the world had weakened Germany. The effect of so many losses in 1916 and of large shortages of foodstuffs and other important goods greatly complicated Germany's continuing to press for a military victory in the war.

The Brusilov Offensive

The situation also became increasingly difficult in Russia. To support the offensives that were supposed to be launched by the Allies in the late summer of 1916 on the Western Front, Tsar Nicholas II agreed to launch an offensive on the Eastern Front. That he would do so is more an indication of his loyalty to his allies than of his army's preparedness. Nevertheless, the Russians had worked hard to improve their army following the disasters of 1915. In addition to greatly expanding the army's size, military leaders made the supply system more efficient and issued additional rifles, machine guns, field artillery pieces, and ammunition. Despite the increased supplies of ammunition, the number of rounds available per artillery piece remained significantly lower than that of the Allies on the Western Front.

As part of the effort to reinvigorate the Russian army, the tsar dismissed his uncle, Grand Duke Nicholas, as commander-in-chief, and on September 18, 1915, he personally assumed command of the entire front. While this caused some distress among the officers who admired the Grand

Duke, the tsar also appointed General Michael V. Alexeyev as his chief of staff, the officer who actually ran the army. Alexeyev was neither brilliant nor extremely talented, but he brought in additional officers to the *Stavka* and improved its functioning. Despite improvements in military effectiveness, the domestic situation deteriorated, for with Tsar Nicholas deeply involved in military operations, the direction of the government was left in the hands of Tsarina Alexandra and the mysterious holy man, Gregory Novykh, better known as Rasputin, who had a great deal of influence over the tsarina.

As part of the tsar's reforms, General Aleksei A. Brusilov replaced General Ivanov as commander of the Southwest Front. From the beginning, Brusilov recognized the necessity to resume the offensive and make numerous changes in techniques and organization so attacks could succeed. More than other Russian leaders, he tried to learn from the experience and methods of the Germans and the Allies. Among the points he emphasized were the use of surprise, the need to move reserves forward secretly and to protect them in deep dugouts, the need to coordinate artillery and infantry more closely, and the importance of improving front-line trenches and moving them closer to enemy lines. Brusilov also believed the Russians should attack on multiple axes—rather than mass in one sector—to prevent the enemy from concentrating all his reserves in a single sector.

What mattered most, however, was the diversion of German troops from the Eastern to the Western Front for the Verdun offensive. The Austrians also diverted some nine divisions to the Italian front for an offensive in Trentino. By May the inferno at Verdun was in full blaze, and the Austrians were making gains against the Italians.

An initial offensive in the north by the Russians on March 18, 1916, failed, but after Joffre pleaded for the Russians to launch their promised attack, the tsar asked Brusilov to attack in the south. Along a front of more than 175 miles, Brusilov's offensive began on June 4 with a one-day artillery preparation, followed by an infantry assault by his four field armies. The attack was a huge success. By June 12 Brusilov's forces had captured more than 190,000 Austrians, 216 guns, and 645 machine guns. Counting other casualties, the Austrians lost more than half their forces facing the Russians. On July 2 the commander of the northern Russian front began his attack, supported by far more artillery than had been available to Brusilov's forces. Though the northern front made only small gains, Brusilov continued advancing, and the Central Powers began rushing in reinforcements to halt him. As Germans and Austrians poured into the Galician area, Brusilov slowly lost the momentum of his attack since he had no reserves. Nevertheless, his forces captured more than 390,000 prisoners by the end of July and advanced more than fifty miles at their deepest point of penetration. But his advance did not sever the important railway line from Kowel to Lemberg that provided lateral communications for the Germans and the Austrians, and the offensive ended toward the end of September. Russian casualties for the year approached one million.

Along with the casualties and losses suffered by Germans on the Western Front at Verdun and the Somme, Brusilov's offensive had far-reaching

Brusilov Offensive, June–September 1916

PRIPET MARSHES

Brest-Litovsk

Pinsk

Kowel

RUSSIA

Lemberg

Russian line June 4

✕✕✕✕✕
Southwest

Przemysl

GALICIA

Russian line Sept. 20

0   40   80 mi
0   40   80 km

ROMANIA

effects. The Austrian attack into Italy and the German attack against Verdun had been weakened. Falkenhayn's position as chief of staff had also eroded; and not surprisingly Hindenburg's position had strengthened since the Russians had achieved little or no gains in the north. In August 1916, Hindenburg replaced Falkenhayn; Ludendorff accompanied him to Berlin. The Russians' success against the Austrians also encouraged the Romanians to join the Allies, but a German army under General Falkenhayn, who had been demoted to commanding the combined forces of the Central Powers in Romania, quickly crushed the Romanian army. German and Austrian forces entered Bucharest on December 6, 1916. Although Brusilov's offensive was Russia's greatest victory of the war, its huge casualties contributed to the Russian people's growing disillusionment with the war and ultimately to the outbreak of revolution in Russia.

Tactical and Technological Innovations

Throughout the disastrous early years of the war, the participants continued to seek better methods of attacking or defending. Some advances came from improvements in tactical methods. For example, one of the most important innovations of 1916 was the "rolling barrage," or "creeping barrage." Both the French and British have claimed they introduced it. Whatever its origins, previous methods of artillery support for attacking infantry consisted essentially of a barrage of fire falling on the infantry's successive objectives. As communications and fire-control techniques improved, artillerymen devised methods for keeping a barrage moving forward about one hundred yards in front of advancing infantry. With the artillery barrage and the infantry moving about one hundred yards every three to five minutes, attacking infantrymen could move into an enemy's trench line before the defenders could come out of their shelters and occupy their firing positions. Despite the significant advantages the rolling barrages provided an attacker, the new methods did not enable anyone to achieve a breakthrough on the Western Front in 1916.

Innovations in defensive techniques nullified innovations in offensive techniques. Indeed, the French finally learned at Verdun the importance of adopting a more flexible defense. The Germans made the most important innovation in defensive tactics, however, when they adopted the "elastic defense" on December 1, 1916. The keys to this new German defensive tactic were fewer soldiers in the front line, a willingness to yield terrain, and a reliance on counterattacks. When an attacker was extended and vulnerable, a timely counterattack could destroy him when he was most off balance and before he consolidated his gains. To launch local counterattacks, the Germans placed small units behind the front lines and worked hard to develop the initiative and judgment of the small-unit leaders upon whom the success

Even more than the machine gun, artillery dominated the World War I battlefield. The French estimated that three quarters of their casualties in the first three years of the war resulted from enemy artillery.

of the counterattacks depended. Commanders of much larger units, such as corps and field armies, also designated units for counterattacks. By the time the Allies launched their offensives in 1917, the Germans had this new defensive system in place.

As the opposing sides sought methods of breaking through their opponents' defenses and achieving a decisive victory, they devoted considerable resources and time to developing new technologies. Soldiers hoped some new weapons would give them an edge and provide them a means of ending the stalemate that gripped the battlefield, particularly on the Western Front. Of the many types of new technologies that were tried and developed by the military, one of the earliest was gas. Both sides on the Western Front frequently used it, but it became clear that gas could only add to the terror of a stalemate not end it. Other innovations included the flamethrower, trench mortar, bangalore torpedo, and light machine gun.

The Airplane

One weapon that exercised an important influence over the fighting and whose use increased dramatically during the war was the airplane. Although airplanes had been used in combat in Libya and in the Balkans before World War I, most armies had reservations in 1914 about the utility of flying machines, and some believed the airship (the dirigible) had more potential than the airplane. Officers argued that the dirigible had greater range, speed, and load-carrying ability than the fragile airplane, which could not carry a large military load. By January 1915 German Zeppelins, which could carry about 5,000 pounds of bombs, were flying out of Belgium and dropping their bombs on London.

Though dirigibles and balloons remained in use, the airplane proved more useful and was enthusiastically developed by most participants in the war. During the first battle of the Marne, both sides relied on airplanes to provide them information about the enemy, and by late 1914, aerial photography was widely used on the Western Front. Problems with communications continued, for until the planes were equipped with the Marconi wireless, the pilot had to land and pass on important information personally or had to drop handwritten messages. Nevertheless, constant reconnaissance flights made it extremely difficult to conceal preparations for a major offensive, and by the end of 1914, no ground commander would consider an operation without aerial assistance.

To prevent the enemy from acquiring damaging information, both sides devoted considerable effort to destroying enemy reconnaissance planes. The first weapons used in aerial combat were pistols and rifles, but within weeks after the beginning of the war, observers in two-seater airplanes were firing crudely mounted machine guns. After the introduction of the interrupter gear, which synchronized the firing of a machine gun with the spinning of a propeller, machine guns were mounted on the front of airplanes and fired directly at the enemy. Huge "dogfights" quickly became common over the Western Front.

During the four years of the war, numerous technical advances provided the airplane with greater speed, range, climbing power, maneuverability, and structural strength. The British launched bombers against Zeppelin hangars in Germany in September 1914. When the war began, none of the participants had a mechanism that would release a bomb from an airplane,

Use and control of the air remained a high priority for the combatants of World War I. The value of the airplane is evident in the British producing 25,685 airplanes in 1918, the French 24,652, and the Germans 17,000.

but by the end of the war, the British had produced a bomb weighing 3,360 pounds and a mechanism for releasing it.

Of all the nations involved in the war, the British—under the prodding of General Sir Hugh Trenchard—placed the strongest emphasis on strategic bombing directed at the enemy's civilian population, industrial capacity, and lines of communication. Trenchard believed airplanes could do more than serve as fighters or support ground operations; he believed long-range, high-payload bombers could blast Germany out of the war. The Germans also developed strategic bombers, which carried out their first raid on Great Britain in June 1917, but the war ended before ideas about strategic bombing could be fully tested.

Aircraft also played an important role in naval warfare, where they provided important advantages in aerial spotting and reconnaissance. Prior to World War I, navies often floated airships high above their fleets, and they quickly developed the ability to hoist seaplanes over the sides of ships, where they could land and take off from the water. The first flight of an airplane from a ship occurred in November 1910 off the USS *Birmingham*. In December 1914, the British launched a seaplane carrier raid on the German North Sea base of Cuxhaven but inflicted little or no damage. In late 1914 and early 1915 the British placed long, downward sloping ramps on several ships and thereby enabled seaplanes to take off without being hoisted over the side. The seaplanes could not land on the ships, however, and had to land on the sea before being hoisted back on the ships. In 1918 the British added a landing deck on the rear of a ship, permitting planes to take off and land on the same ship. Numerous accidents, however, limited the use of the landing deck; the new ships would make much more significant contributions in World War II.

The Tank

Another weapon introduced during World War I was the tank. In October 1914, Lieutenant Colonel Ernest D. Swinton began British efforts to develop an armored vehicle, but he failed to generate any enthusiasm for his idea among British military leaders. After Winston Churchill, First Lord of the Admiralty, encouraged the British army to investigate the idea, the British began working energetically in 1915 to create an armored fighting vehicle. The French effort was led by General Jean B. Estienne who had an idea similar to Swinton's. After the two nations became aware of each other's efforts, they agreed to delay using the new weapon until enough were available for a mass assault. Both recognized the tank's ability to move across the devastated and deadly battlefield and hoped for a surprise introduction of the new weapon.

Despite the agreement between the two nations, the British threw their small number of tanks into an offensive on the Somme on September 15, 1916, and achieved very little. The French used their tanks for the first time on April 16, 1917, as part of the ill-fated Nivelle offensive in Champagne, but they were hardly more successful than the British. The Germans

Mark IV tank stuck in a trench. Tanks helped the infantry advance across no-man's-land, but they failed to live up to their proponents' exaggerated claims because of their slow speed, low power, and inexperienced crews.

did not begin developing tanks until the British and French had used tanks against them. After the dismal failure of the French tanks in Nivelle's offensive, Ludendorff dismissed tanks as being almost useless. Not until November 20, 1917, did the British at Cambrai make the first successful attack with tanks in large numbers.

*   *   *   *

From late 1914 to 1916, the combatants expended thousands of lives and enormous resources trying new methods, technologies, and strategies in desperate attempts to end the war. Along with the appearance of tanks, planes, and gasses came better methods for attacking and defending, such as the Germans' use of the elastic defense. And all the combatants gradually improved their methods of coordinating infantry and artillery actions. While the Allies simultaneously sought a breakthrough on the Western Front and success on the periphery of Europe, Germany changed its strategy from a focus on the west in 1914, to the east in 1915, and back to the west in 1916. By 1916, Falkenhayn had abandoned hopes of a breakthrough in the Western Front and unwisely hoped a gigantic battle of attrition would force the Allies to yield.

By the end of 1916, the strains, disruptions, and costs of total warfare had seriously affected all the participants. In the waning days of 1916 hopes for peace flickered but soon faded. As the new year began, the belligerents renewed their efforts to achieve victory. Much as if the exhausted combatants were tied to death itself, none chose to leave the struggle. To surrender was unthinkable; to withdraw without victory after the loss of so many lives was impossible.

SUGGESTED READINGS

Ashworth, Tony. *Trench Warfare 1914–1918: The Live and Let Live System* (New York: Holmes & Meier, 1980).

Bidwell, Shelford, and Dominick Graham. *Fire-Power: British Army Weapons and Theories of War, 1904–1945* (London: George Allen & Unwin, 1982).

Clark, Alan. *The Donkeys* (New York: William Morrow and Company, 1962).

Heller, Charles E. *Chemical Warfare in World War I: The American Experience, 1917–1918* (Fort Leavenworth, Kans.: Combat Studies Institute, 1984).

Horne, Alistair. *The Price of Glory: Verdun, 1916* (New York: Macmillan Co., 1962).

Keegan, John. *The Face of Battle* (New York: Viking Press, 1976).

King, Jere C. *Generals and Politicians: Conflict Between France's High Command, Parliament, and Government, 1914-1918* (Berkeley: University of California Press, 1951).

Leed, Eric J. *No Man's Land: Combat and Identity in World War I* (Cambridge: Cambridge University Press, 1981).

Middlebrook, Martin. *The First Day on the Somme: 1 July 1916* (New York: W. W. Norton & Company, 1972).

Moran, Charles M. W. *The Anatomy of Courage* (London: Constable, 1945).

Remarque, Erich Maria. *All Quiet on the Western Front*, trans. A. W. Wheen (Boston, Mass.: Little Brown, 1929).

Siney, Marion. *Allied Blockade of Germany, 1914–1916* (Ann Arbor: University of Michigan Press, 1957).

Stone, Norman. *The Eastern Front, 1914–1917* (New York: Charles Scribner's Sons, 1975).

Terraine, John. *Douglas Haig: The Educated Soldier* (London: Hutchinson, 1963).

Travers, Tim. *The Killing Ground: The British Army, the Western Front, and the Emergence of Modern Warfare* (London: Allen & Unwin, 1987).

19

1917: THE YEAR OF DESPERATION AND ANTICIPATION

Unrestricted Submarine
Warfare

The Disastrous Allied
Offensives of 1917

Creating the American
Expeditionary Force

Cambrai: The Final Allied
Offensive of 1917

For both the Allies and the Central Powers, 1917 was a crucial year in the war. The Central Powers faced a particularly serious situation at the end of 1916 as discontent increased in the civilian populace and food shortages and health problems worsened. After Woodrow Wilson was reelected President of the United States in 1916, he attempted to mediate peace by asking the belligerents to make public the conditions under which they would conclude peace. The Germans finally provided the conditions under which they would accept peace, but their response was accompanied by notification of their intent to resume unrestricted submarine warfare on February 1, 1917. As German submarines began sinking hundreds of thousands of tons of Allied shipping, France launched an offensive in April 1917. This offensive failed miserably and led to the outbreak of mutinies in the French army. Thereafter, France concentrated on rebuilding the morale of its shattered army, while Great Britain assumed an increasingly larger role in the land war. The British attack at Passchendaele in the summer and fall of 1917, however, did little to end the war. Amidst the growing sense of desperation in Europe, the overthrow of Tsar Nicholas in March 1917 and the seizure of power by the Bolsheviks in November contributed to the Russians' eventually leaving the war. Though the entry in April 1917 of the United States into the war renewed hope among the Allies for winning the war, the task of organizing, equipping, and transporting more than 2 million soldiers to Europe proved to be one of the most difficult and significant accomplishments of the entire war.

While sweeping changes altered the list of participants in the war, some innovations occurred in the waging of war. The disastrous offensives of 1917 drove the Allies to rely more and more on limited offensives, rather than to seek a complete breakthrough of German defenses. And at Cambrai the British launched a large armored attack supported by aircraft in November 1917. The year ended with the belligerents anticipating the entry of a massive American force into battle and the launching of a major German offensive in 1918.

Unrestricted Submarine Warfare

The German decision to resume unrestricted submarine warfare greatly affected the conduct of the war. Though the decision did not bring immediate disaster for the Germans, it resulted in the United States' entering the war at a time when Russia was forced to withdraw. The Americans began arriving in substantial numbers about the same time the Russo-German armistice of Brest-Litovsk ended active operations on the Eastern Front. Although the Americans did not win the war for the Allies, their entry ensured that the Allies would not lose.

The decision by Germany in early 1917 to resume unrestricted submarine warfare came after several years of discussions about the relationship between naval and land operations. In the first days of August 1914, German military leaders considered using sea and aerial forces to end Great Britain's participation in the war. Most plans on the subject lacked substance, for despite Germany's monopoly of the Zeppelin, it lacked the forces to make continuous, effective attacks against the British. About all it could do was lay some minefields and send out some light ships to bombard a few coastal towns. Great Britain effectively used its superior sea power to deliver supplies to its armies and those of its allies while denying seaborne supplies to the Central Powers. By the end of 1914 British naval forces cut Germany off from the high seas and imposed a blockade that severely restricted their supply of war matériel. In March 1915, the Allies added foodstuffs to the list of contraband, making the blockade total.

Since Great Britain had almost twice as many capital ships available in the North Sea, Germany was hesitant to challenge British sea power, and its High Seas Fleet remained bottled-up along the short coastline between the Netherlands and Denmark. Not until May 31, 1916, did the German fleet venture out of its heavily mined and fortified bases and engage the British Grand Fleet in the Battle of Jutland. Although the battle involved 254 ships and was the largest naval battle ever fought up to this time, the strategic situation did not change, for the German fleet escaped without being annihilated and the blockade of Germany continued.

More than one year before the Battle of Jutland, Germany declared the waters around Great Britain and Ireland to be a "war zone." On February 4, 1915, it published a notice about the establishment of the war zone and warned of the destruction of enemy merchant vessels within it even though it would not always be possible "to avert danger . . . to the crew and passengers." The same notice also warned of possible unintentional attacks on neutral ships. Germany's main weapon for attacking Allied shipping was the submarine, or the U-boat, which most navies previously had ignored.

When Germany established the war zone, it had only twenty-one submarines in the North Sea. The actual number at sea at any one time was usually no more than one third of its fleet. Despite complaints from neutral nations, particularly the United States, and despite a widespread belief that the Germans could not actually establish a war zone, submarines began sinking an average of more than one ship a day for the remainder of 1915.

The sinking of the *Lusitania* on May 7, 1915, and the death of more than one hundred American citizens on the British ship created a great stir in the United States, but the Germans insisted that the vessel was carrying munitions and was therefore a legitimate target. After the sinking of another British ship, *Arabic,* in which two Americans lost their lives, American protests became more vehement. Unwilling to face war with the United States, Germany retreated and abandoned unrestricted submarine warfare on September 20, 1915. It shifted the focus of its submarine operations to the Mediterranean.

But at the end of 1915, the German army and navy joined forces to place renewed pressure on the German chancellor, Theobald von Bethmann Hollweg, to resume unrestricted submarine warfare. Bethmann Hollweg feared an expansion of submarine warfare would bring the United States into the war on the side of the Allies. When Kaiser William II supported the chancellor, the secretary of state for naval affairs, Admiral Alfred von Tirpitz, resigned in protest. He and other naval officials had argued that unrestricted submarine warfare would force Britain to surrender in two to four months. At last yielding to the pressure, the kaiser decided to resume submarine attacks but not in an unrestricted manner. Attacks would be launched only within the war zone and only against merchant ships carrying weapons for protection against submarines.

In late 1916 the question of using unrestricted submarine warfare rose again. Except for its narrow North Sea coast, Germany remained confined within central Europe, cut off from the world's markets by Allied armies and navies. The British blockade had wrecked Germany's export trade, had denied it essential raw materials, and was affecting its citizens' morale. The shortage of foodstuffs made Germans go hungry and raised the death rate of the elderly and of infants. Moreover, the heavy losses at Verdun, on the Somme, and in the Brusilov offensive convinced the army's new leaders, Hindenburg and Ludendorff, that Germany could not endure the military stalemate much longer.

When the Germans began their unrestricted submarine warfare campaign in 1917, they had about 150 U-boats but kept only 30 to 35 operating in the Atlantic at any one time. This small number of U-boats nevertheless sank more than 3 million tons of shipping in the first five months of the campaign.

Over Bethmann Hollweg's objections, Hindenburg and Ludendorff convinced the kaiser to resume unrestricted submarine warfare. They determined that Great Britain could be forced out of the war before the United States could intervene decisively on the continent of Europe. The kaiser's decision rested on the navy's promise of a war of attrition at sea in which German submarines would sink an average of 600,000 tons of shipping each month and would force Britain to come to terms in five months. Although Germany's submarines managed to sink an even larger amount of shipping for a short period, its military analysts had woefully miscalculated British self-sufficiency and resilience; they also underestimated the effect that the United States' entering the war would have on the Allies.

On January 31, 1917, Germany notified the United States of its resumption of unrestricted submarine attacks. President Woodrow Wilson broke off diplomatic relations and ordered the arming of American merchant ships. Meanwhile, the publication of the infamous Zimmermann telegram appalled most Americans. Germany's foreign secretary, Arthur Zimmermann, sent instructions to the German ambassador in Mexico to work toward an alliance with Mexico and Japan in the event of war with the United States. In return, Germany would restore to Mexico the states of New Mexico, Arizona, and Texas. After German submarines sank several U.S. ships in February and March, Wilson concluded that war was unavoidable and he obtained a declaration of war from Congress on April 6, 1917.

The Disastrous Allied Offensives of 1917

In late 1916 and early 1917, the Allies continued their efforts to break through German lines and win the war with an offensive strategy. Despite the losses at Verdun and the Somme in 1916, the debate between France and Great Britain focused less on strategy than on command relationships. Although the role of the British forces on the continent gradually expanded between 1914 and 1917 and by the summer of 1917 rivaled those of France, no centralized command structure for controlling British and French operations emerged, primarily because the British refused to play the subordinate. Consequently, many aspects of military operations and strategy on the Western Front remained loosely coordinated. A similar situation existed among the other allies as well.

Soon after David Lloyd George became prime minister of Britain in December 1916, however, he succumbed to French persuasion and agreed to place the entire BEF at France's disposal for offensives on the Western Front in 1917. Lloyd George did this reluctantly, for he strongly believed the Allies should concentrate against the weaker of the Central Powers, Austria-Hungary, and make their main attack along the Italian front. General Douglas Haig, who had replaced Field Marshal Sir John French as commander of the BEF in December 1915, strenuously objected to his forces being controlled by the French, but he finally agreed to tailor the conduct of his operations to those of the French—but only during the upcoming campaign.

The Allied plans for 1917 were greatly influenced by the appointment on December 12, 1916, of a new commander for French forces. Joffre was promoted to the rank of marshal of France and appointed as an advisor to the government, and General Robert G. Nivelle became commander of the French armies on the Western Front. In essence, Joffre was promoted out of his position, so a younger, more vigorous leader with new ideas could take charge. Nivelle was appointed commander only of those forces in northern and northeastern France, not all French forces, but his political masters expected much from the new commander who promised a major breakthrough.

When Nivelle and Haig coordinated the operations that would take place in 1917, the British commander agreed to launch a limited offensive near Arras to divert enemy attention and forces from the main French attack on the Chemin des Dames between Soissons and Reims. The French attack would occur after the British attack. The idea was to draw the German reserves toward the northwest so they could not be used against the attempted breakthrough by the French. Following the attacks at Arras and the Chemin des Dames, Haig intended to launch an attack on Messines Ridge, the high ground occupied by the Germans in the salient south of Ypres.

The British had to capture this high ground before they could launch Haig's main effort, an attack around Ypres. Haig did not want the attack at Arras or Messines Ridge to drag on for too long, for his main goal in the Ypres attack was to push the German lines back and capture the key submarine bases at Ostend and Zeebrugge in Belgium. He also hoped to drive the German flank farther along the Belgian coast, thereby opening it to further attacks. Thus Haig and Nivelle envisaged a series of attacks: Arras, Chemin des Dames, Messines Ridge, and then Ypres.

The Germans did not docilely await the Allied attack. Since Hindenburg and Ludendorff anticipated large Allied offensives in 1917, they decided to retire from the huge Noyon salient and occupy a shorter, stronger position to its rear. The newly fortified zone was named the "*Siegfried Stellung*" but was soon tagged the "Hindenburg Line" by the Allies. A key aspect of the Hindenburg Line was the establishment of reverse slope positions and the use of elastic defenses. The elastic defense sought to prevent a breakthrough and to inflict maximum casualties on the enemy by bending but not breaking in the face of an attack. Establishing defensive positions in depth, the Germans placed small forces forward to avoid heavy losses from enemy artillery fire and relied on a network of mutually supporting strong points to halt the enemy. Large numbers of machine guns and carefully planned artillery fires strengthened the defenders. The construction of the Hindenburg Line enabled the Germans to shorten their defensive lines and to increase the size of their reserves. Commanders at all levels prepared to use counterattacks to disrupt the enemy's advance or to push him back before he could consolidate his hard-won gains.

The British launched their limited offensive near Arras on April 9. After five days of preparatory artillery fire, First and Third armies met great success. Most notable was the Canadian seizure of Vimy Ridge, an important piece of terrain that the Germans had held for more than two and a half years. Because of the nature of the terrain, the German commander had not organized an elastic defense but instead had placed strong defenses along the heights of the ridge and held large reserves to its rear. Though fighting under unfavorable circumstances, the Canadians finally captured the much-contested ridge.

General Edmund Allenby, who commanded Third Army, ordered his cavalry forward so the gains could be exploited, but the efforts to parlay the gains into a breakthrough and exploitation failed. From April 12–17, the British Fourth Army attacked south of Arras, and then from April 23–28 and May 3–5, First and Third armies continued attacking. Although the later battles captured far less terrain than the first battle, the British inflicted heavy casualties on the Germans and managed to divert some units and matériel from the main French effort at the Chemin des Dames.

The Nivelle Offensive

Ten days after the Americans entered the war, the French launched their disastrous offensive at the Chemin des Dames. Instead of waiting for the arrival of large numbers of American troops, the French were persuaded by false promises from Nivelle that a breakthrough could be made. Unfortunately for France, Nivelle's "formula" for success proved to be a formula for disaster.

Nivelle was an excellent officer who quickly rose from the rank of colonel in 1914 to a corps and then a field army commander. An innovative artillery officer, he had made his reputation by being the inventor—according to the French—of the rolling barrage and had coined the slogan "The artillery conquers; the infantry occupies." Nivelle had added to his reputation by successfully launching an attack at Verdun in October 1916. After detailed rehearsals and eight days of preparatory artillery fire, he had used seven divisions along a four-mile front to capture Fort Douaumont. His forces penetrated no more than two miles, but the advance seemed spectacularly deep by the standards of the day. Two months later he launched another successful attack which managed to penetrate four to five miles. After more than three years of terrible losses, Nivelle had apparently found the formula for unlocking the riddle of trench warfare, the main feature of which was reliance on tightly controlled infantry attacks, supported by vast amounts of artillery. In his December attack at Verdun, Nivelle used more than one million rounds of artillery against German positions before beginning the rolling barrage of artillery fire in front of the advancing infantry.

After Nivelle became commander of the northeastern front in December 1916, he began work on a plan to smash through the German defenses in the Champagne sector between Soissons and Reims. His objective was the heights of the Chemin des Dames to the north of the small Aisne River. To the detriment of Nivelle's grand scheme, the Germans obtained information about his plan and reorganized their positions in preparation for his attack. One of their key changes was the use of an elastic defense that placed only a minimum number of infantrymen in forward trenches. They placed most of their troops on the reverse slope of the Chemin des Dames so they could be protected from the direct fire of the Allies, and they reinforced the threatened sector with an additional field army.

Despite indications that the Germans expected an attack on the Chemin des Dames, Nivelle remained confident of achieving a breakthrough and insisted on launching his offensive. In comparison to some attacks of the past, he had a huge force. He massed two armies along a front of approximately forty miles and kept two armies in reserve, totaling approximately 1,400,000 men in fifty-two divisions. To support the four armies, he had approximately 1,800 75-mm guns, 1,700 heavy artillery pieces, and 1,650 mortars and accompanying guns. Stocks of ammunition included 24 million rounds of 75-mm shells and 9 million rounds of heavy artillery ammunition.

Nivelle's plan was relatively simple. On the right-front of his four field armies, Fifth Army had fourteen infantry divisions, ten of which were in the front line. On the left-front, Sixth Army had fourteen infantry divisions, eight of which were in the front line. After the two armies attacked and broke through the German defenses, Sixth Army was supposed to turn

Nivelle's Plan, April 1917

Actual gains
X X X X French armies

Laon
Ailette R.
Aisne R.
Aisne R.
Soissons
X X X X
Sixth
X X X X
Tenth
X X X X
Fifth
Reims
X X X X
Fourth

0   5   10 mi
0   5   10 km

toward the west and Fifth Army toward the east. This would enable Tenth Army to pass through the two leading armies and advance toward the north. Despite increasing indications of German preparations, Nivelle confidently expected Tenth Army to advance fifteen miles by the end of the second day's attack. First Army remained in reserve.

Before the attack began on April 16, the French pounded the German positions with nine days of artillery preparation. After this lengthy preparation, the first wave of infantry easily occupied the initial enemy positions, which were only lightly occupied because of the elastic defense. The French soldiers also reached the geographic crest of the heights without difficulty, but as they moved over the crest of the Chemin des Dames and began descending the slope, heavy enemy fire halted their advance. The Germans had located their main positions on the reverse side of the slope, out of sight of French artillery observers. They had also placed many of their machine guns in concrete shelters or bunkers and thus had protected them from the massive French artillery concentrations.

Some of the French infantry managed to advance down the slope to their front, but German fire halted almost all of them. The following waves of infantry did not fare any better. All attempts to regain forward movement collapsed as soon as the French infantry arrived on the line covered by enemy machine guns. The only possible movement was through trenches using grenades, but this was soon stopped by the Germans.

For the remainder of the first day and for the two following days, combat atop the Chemin des Dames assumed the form of a series of limited attacks, preceded as much as possible by artillery bombardment of the enemy's positions and executed under the control of local commanders according to the availability of munitions and grenades. Many of the units who participated in the initial attacks were pulled out of the lines during the night of April 18–19.

After three days of heavy losses, Nivelle concluded that the French could not break through the strong German defenses and modified his plan. Believing that the Germans had weakened their defenses on his right so they could concentrate sufficient forces in front of his attack, he launched a limited offensive to slice off the shallow German salient above Reims. He ordered Fifth Army, which was on the right-front in the attack against the Chemin des Dames, to attack in a northeasterly direction, while Fourth Army, which was to its right and which had made some gains against the Germans, continued its attack toward the northwest. But the French had lost the initiative, and this limited offensive fared no better than the first attack.

Although the fighting continued until May 7, it was obvious within a week that the Nivelle offensive had failed dismally, particularly when compared to the successful British attack at Arras. The casualties during the first week were approximately 117,000, including 32,000 dead. Perhaps more importantly, the senseless losses plunged much of France into despair. Exhaustion, indiscipline, and low morale had replaced the exhilaration and optimism that Nivelle had engendered in the French army.

An aerial view of a battlefield in France. By 1917 thousands of artillery rounds had devastated the once-pastoral countryside and obliterated the previously neat lines of trenches.

As a consequence of his failure, the French government relieved Nivelle and named Pétain to command the armies on the Western Front. This relief signaled the end of France's efforts to break through German defenses, for Pétain would employ only limited offensives that sought mainly to capture key terrain and force the Germans back. The relief of Nivelle also signaled the end of military leaders operating without the guidance and occasional interference of political leaders. Disgusted political leaders began exercising greater control over military operations, and the assumption of power by Georges Clemenceau, who became premier of France in November 1917, symbolized the opening of a new era. He expressed its theme when he said, "War is too important to be left to the generals."

The major task confronting Pétain as commander of the French army in northern France, however, was restoring the fighting spirit of his soldiers. After more than one million soldiers had died in battle and many more were wounded, the French army seemed to be on the verge of complete collapse. Mutinies in May and June affected fifty-four divisions, more than half of the French army. Although the French had agreed to launch an offensive during the summer to support a British offensive in Flanders, Pétain reluctantly informed Field Marshal Haig's headquarters that such an offensive was impossible. To end the mutinies, Pétain initiated a program of swift and severe punishment. He also visited many of the French divisions and appealed to the soldiers' pride and patriotism. To restore the faith of the French troops in their higher-level commanders, he took steps to improve living conditions by modifying the furlough system and providing better food in the trenches. Finally, he established rest camps to provide exhausted soldiers a break from the fighting in the trenches. By the end of July most of the mutinies had ended, and in September only one act of collective disobedience occurred. Though the French army remained fragile, Pétain's efforts had succeeded in restoring discipline.

On August 20, Pétain launched a limited offensive at Verdun and achieved moderate success. As soon as the Germans brought reserves into the area and offered stiff resistance, he halted the attack. At La Malmaison at the end of October, he launched a more elaborate offensive, attacking with Tenth Army along a front of about seven miles. The objective of the attack was the high ground anchoring the German right flank along the Chemin des Dames. The attack was supported by fourteen tank companies and approximately 1,850 artillery tubes, which provided three days of preparatory fire. After advancing about three miles, the French outflanked the Germans on the Chemin des Dames and forced them to withdraw.

Pétain's gains on the much-contested terrain demonstrated that limited offensives could achieve important gains and that his reforms for reviving the morale of the French had at least partially succeeded. Instead of continuing forward in an attempt to break through the German defenses completely or beginning another major offensive elsewhere, however, he preferred to await the arrival of "the Americans and the tanks."

Messines Ridge and Passchendaele

During the period of the French mutinies, the British maintained pressure on the Germans, thereby providing the French time to rebuild their army. The British also prepared for an offensive at Ypres that would push the Germans back and permit the capture of the submarine bases at Ostend and Zeebrugge. The desire to capture these bases intensified when Admiral Sir John R. Jellicoe warned that the war could not be continued through 1918 if shipping losses persisted at such a high rate. To reach the submarine bases, however, the British had to push back or break through the German defenses, a task they had not been able to accomplish during the past three years.

Before attacking at Ypres, Haig launched a limited offensive against Messines Ridge, which dominated the plain around Ypres. Although having to contend with German countermining, British tunneling companies dug shafts deep under the ridge for more than a year and packed them with 500 tons of explosives. After a seventeen-day artillery preparation, nineteen huge mines exploded simultaneously under the ridge on the morning of June 7.

Operations in Flanders, June – December 1917

FLANDERS

Dec. 7

Passchendaele

July 30

July 31

Sept. 20

Canal

X X X X
Fifth

Ypres

June 7

June 15

Canal

Messines

X X X X
Second

July 31

Lys R.

	June 7
	June 15
	July 31
	Sept. 20
	Dec. 7

0   2.5   5 mi

0   2.5   5 km

With an unfavorable wind disrupting the British use of gas, a heavy artillery barrage began falling on German positions immediately after the explosion. Just behind the artillery barrage, nine infantry divisions advanced in an assault, and within twelve hours, they captured almost the entire objective, which included one of the most devastated areas ever encountered in the history of warfare.

The swift and easy success at Messines Ridge was not a portent for the future, for the British now entered one of the bloodiest and most futile campaigns of the entire war. Although the subsequent campaign was the Third Battle of Ypres, it became known as "Passchendaele," a word that has become synonymous in military history with suffering and disappointment. During the first part of the war the British had relied on volunteers to expand the size of their forces and replenish their losses. Because of severe manpower shortages, however, they adopted conscription in January 1916, but only after much debate. Many of these conscripts subsequently became casualties under the terrible conditions of Passchendaele.

With little or no thought being given to the effect on the terrain, the British began in July 1917 with one of the heaviest bombardments of the entire war. More than 3,000 guns fired more than 65,000 tons of artillery shells for almost two weeks prior to the launching of the attack on July 31. The British quickly captured their initial objectives and then prepared to move toward their main objective, the village of Passchendaele, which lay less than four miles to their front.

Then rain began to fall. Although the Ypres area in peacetime consisted of many idyllic pastures that centuries of labor had reclaimed from marshes, heavy bombardment disrupted the drainage system, and unusually heavy rains turned the area into a vast swamp. To facilitate movement, the British constructed plank roads and laid many miles of boards across the quagmire. The mud was bad enough, but the introduction and use by the Germans of mustard gas during the campaign made living conditions even more difficult to endure. On August 16 the attack began again. Except for units in the center, however, the British captured very little terrain.

Believing a change in commanders would improve British fortunes, Haig replaced Fifth Army commander, General Sir Hubert Gough, with General Sir Herbert Plumer. The new British commander began a series of attacks with limited objectives. Fortunately for his soldiers, the weather turned favorable, and several attacks occurred in huge dust clouds. The weather did not last long, and the terrain once again turned into mud. The next phase of the offensive, which began on September 20 and continued on September 26 and October 4, also yielded some success. As the British attacks continued pushing forward, the Germans stopped using an elastic defense and began placing larger numbers of troops in forward trenches. This caused them to suffer high casualties because the British used massive amounts of artillery in their carefully controlled attacks. The Germans also began taking higher casualties in their counterattacks. Close coordination between the Royal Flying Corps and the infantry and artillery often enabled the British to disrupt the frequent enemy counterattacks.

In December 1915, Sir Douglas Haig succeeded Sir John French as commander of the British Expeditionary Force. In late 1917, Haig remained confident that he could achieve a breakthrough at Passchendaele even though he had failed to break German defensive lines on the Somme a year earlier.

Finally, on November 6, two divisions managed to occupy the ruin of Passchendaele village. By November 10, the British had expanded their control over the ridge on which the ruins of the village sat; then Haig ordered a halt to the offensive. Both the British and the Germans had lost about 240,000 men. Despite their optimism at the beginning of the campaign, the British had not been able to break through the German lines, and the goal of seizing the submarine bases along the Belgian coast had long since been forgotten.

As the Allies awaited the arrival of large American forces, the situation became even bleaker on the Eastern Front. After the overthrow of Tsar Nicholas in March 1917 and the establishment of a provisional government, Russia attempted to remain in the war. In July the Russians attacked into Galicia. Though they made some gains, the Germans and Austrians counterattacked and drove them back. In subsequent weeks the Russian army began to disintegrate completely; soldiers on the front did little or no fighting, while soldiers in the rear joined the revolutionary forces. In September the Germans launched the last campaign of World War I on the Eastern Front. Against only slight resistance, they crossed the Dvina River and seized Riga. Two months later, the Bolsheviks seized power and almost immediately called for an ending of the war.

Creating the American Expeditionary Force

When the German high command assessed the dangers of resuming unrestricted submarine warfare in late 1916, it dismissed the possibility of the United States' entering the war quickly and playing a significant role. The Germans recognized that the United States had more than 100 million citizens, one of the world's richest and largest economies, and a first-class fleet that rivaled that of the British. But they also recognized that the United States faced enormous difficulties in vastly increasing the size of its small army and in transporting its forces to Europe. In the end, the Germans took a calculated risk and lost, for they failed to end the war before American soldiers and supplies helped halt their final drives and push them back to defeat.

In April 1917, the United States faced enormous challenges if it were to participate in the European conflict. Despite the reforms following the Spanish-American War, the U.S. Army had no large tactical units, few weapons, an extreme shortage of officers, and little or no training. On April 6, 1917, the War Department had only 213,557 troops at its disposal, including 127,588 active, 5,523 Philippine Scouts, and 80,446 National Guard troops. No active units larger than a regiment existed. In a matter of months, the Americans not only had to expand the size of their army but also equip and supply it, train it for modern warfare, and transport it to Europe. Rarely has any military force faced such a huge challenge.

The first challenge faced by the small American army was the induction and training of millions of recruits. After six weeks of spirited debate, the United States passed the Selective Service Act of May 18, 1917, that provided for the conscription of males. Meanwhile, a wave of volunteers enlisted in May and June. The first draft did not occur until July 20, and the first large contingent of conscripted soldiers did not arrive until September. Thereafter, a steady stream of inductions and voluntary enlistments swelled the size of the American armed forces. At the time of the Armistice in November 1918, the United States Army consisted of 3,685,458 soldiers, an increase of more than seventeen times the number of soldiers available in April 1917.

Amidst a great outpouring of public support for the war, waiting for the manufacture and delivery of weapons and equipment severely constrained the rapid expansion of the army. Prior to the declaration of war, no one recognized the complexity of mobilizing sufficient assets to equip, train, and transport 2 million Americans overseas. As early as July 1917, the shortage of clothing, for example, was so severe that the army's quartermaster general recommended that the first induction of personnel be postponed from September to October. More severe shortages existed in weapons and ammunition. Consequently, matériel needed for expanding the army to more than seventeen times its previous size could not be met as quickly as individual soldiers could be inducted and trained. On numerous installations, combat units did not have uniforms, modern rifles, or field artillery pieces. Some newly inducted soldiers trained in coveralls and used wooden sticks to simulate weapons, while the War Department and American industry exerted a Herculean effort to overcome critical shortages.

To facilitate coordination and to enhance the effectiveness of the nation's mobilization, President Wilson created a number of boards, including the War Industries Board, the Food Administration, the Fuel Administration, and the Railroad Administration. These boards coordinated the mobilization effort, accelerated production, and contributed significantly to the eventual Allied victory. Nonetheless, some shortages proved impossible to overcome; for example, the army modified and issued its soldiers British Enfield rifles that were already being manufactured in the United States, as well as Allied machine guns and mortars. French factories produced much of the heavier weapons and equipment for the Americans.

Additional challenges appeared in distributing goods to appropriate units. Even after weapons and equipment were manufactured, the logistics apparatus for controlling their distribution suffered serious flaws. Every conceivable problem appeared, from the provision of wrong supplies, to the frequent arrival of defective or useless equipment, to the loss of badly needed equipment. Among complaints about the logistics system, commanders in Europe sharply criticized the arrival of lawn mowers, cuspidors, and floor wax when other critical supplies were needed. In October 1917 when soldiers of the 1st Infantry Division entered the trenches, severe shortages of winter clothing and blankets kept them in their summer uniforms. Despite complaints in Congress about the supply system having "almost stopped functioning," sufficient equipment and supplies somehow did find their way to the right units. Considering the tremendous increase in the size of the army and the huge requirements associated with transporting and supplying the AEF in Europe, one should perhaps marvel that the system managed to function as well as it did.

Transporting the AEF to Europe

Although significant challenges continued to exist in inducting and training military personnel and in providing them with adequate equipment, American soldiers could contribute to the war effort only if they traversed the Atlantic Ocean. Unfortunately for the Americans, the U.S. merchant marine lacked sufficient ships to carry the entire AEF across the Atlantic. This problem existed before German submarines began destroying shipping faster than it could be replaced. One historian has observed that the Norwegians had a larger capability in 1917 for transporting an army overseas than the Americans. To overcome this serious deficiency, the United States took extraordinary steps to add ships to its fleet, including using seized German ships. Nonetheless, more than half the AEF eventually traveled to Europe on British troop transports. To ensure the best utilization of existing shipping, the United States set up a Shipping Board to acquire the necessary ships, a Shipping Control Committee to coordinate the use of shipping, and an Embarkation Service to supervise the shipment of munitions, supplies, and personnel. Though some persistent problems continued, most were solved by the end of the war.

The entry of the United States coincided with the highest rate of shipping loss experienced by the Allies during the war. While losses on short voyages such as across the English Channel were low, losses in long-distance ocean shipping amounted to about one-fifth of all ships undertaking such voyages. After the Americans entered the war, the possibility of a large engagement between fleets remained extremely small, for the only large-scale engagement of opposing fleets during the war had occurred at Jutland in May 1916 with indecisive results. It quickly became apparent that the mission confronting the U.S. Navy differed significantly from the task for which it had been prepared. Instead of relying on battleships and battle cruisers to fight enemy vessels, the navy found itself needing more destroyers and anti-submarine craft to protect and assist the movement of forces to Europe.

When Rear Admiral William S. Sims, who was commander of U.S. naval forces operating in European waters, arrived in Great Britain in early April 1917 to discuss the employment of the American navy, he was surprised at the high rate of loss for ocean shipping and disturbed by pessimistic assessments from British authorities who considered the situation "hopeless." As a younger officer, Sims had impressed his superiors with his ability and willingness to adopt new ideas, and he soon demonstrated those same creative qualities by recognizing the requirement to establish a convoy system. British admirals had long before rejected convoys; they believed convoys served merely to group ships as targets, increased the chances of collisions, and reduced the efficiency of ocean transport. After convincing the British to study more systematically the advantages of convoys, he urged his superiors in the United States to send as many antisubmarine vessels as possible to Europe. The Department of the Navy reluctantly accepted the use of convoys on July 2, for it favored defending specific ocean routes—preferably by offensive action—rather than concentrating defenses around slow-moving and difficult-to-control convoys. As the use of convoys became common, the rate of losses began to decline immediately and by the end of the year was only one-fifth of what it had been in April 1917.

Except for extremely fast ships that continued to sail independently, most ocean convoys had twenty or thirty ships, moving in four to six columns. Naval escorts patrolled the flanks of these convoys, as well as the front of especially slow convoys. Heavily escorted troop convoys regularly made the transatlantic run, and by the summer of 1917, about 50,000 troops a month began reaching Europe. By 1918 about one-quarter of a million troops were arriving each month. Many of those who made the passage safely owed their lives to the wisdom and energy of Admiral Sims and to the professional skills of the U.S. Navy.

The Issue of Amalgamation

On June 13, General John J. Pershing, the commander of the AEF, arrived in France. Within days he and his staff began preparing for the arrival of a huge American force. They faced a formidable task, for neither Pershing nor any other living American had any experience in employing the large number of troops that would eventually comprise the AEF. A veteran of the Indian wars and the Spanish-American War, Pershing had commanded the punitive expedition against Mexico in 1916 and had the personal qualities to meet the challenges confronting him, but he had never participated in a major war and naively believed American attacks could break the deadlock on the Western Front. In future months he would emphasize open rather than trench warfare and would impose high standards of marksmanship, drill, and discipline on his soldiers.

While attempting to come to grips with the difficulties of transporting a huge American army across the Atlantic, Pershing had to face the sensitive issue of Great Britain and France's request to attach American units to the armies of other nations. Instead of awaiting the organizing, transporting, and training of American divisions and corps, the Allies wanted to rush Americans into combat as small units; such use of American troops would enable them to participate in the fighting much more quickly. Since the

General John J. Pershing (seated, second from the left) and the staff of the American Expeditionary Force in June 1917. Pershing faced the twin challenges of preparing the AEF for combat and keeping it autonomous from the French and British.

Allies had suffered the great bulk of their casualties in infantry squads, platoons, companies, and battalions, it made sense in their eyes to "amalgamate" small American units into already existing command and support structures in Allied regiments and divisions. Considerations of timing, efficiency, and logistics also strongly argued against their awaiting the organization of an independent American army. Some Allied officers insisted it was a foolish expenditure of lives to train division and corps commanders instead of using already experienced Allied commanders; one argued that a division commander had to lose 12,000 casualties before he became sufficiently proficient at his job.

Despite grave problems in transporting and preparing his large force, Pershing adamantly refused to accept amalgamation. President Wilson's desire for the United States to play an independent and important role at the postwar peace conference buttressed his position. Pershing frequently pointed out the strong disadvantages of amalgamation: language problems with the French, Irish-American dislike of the British, effect on the subsequent peace negotiations, and potentially disruptive resentment against Allied commanders responsible for high American casualties. He also recognized the sensitivity of national pride and the significance of having a separate American army contribute to Allied victory in the Great War.

After Prime Minister Lloyd George exerted diplomatic pressure on President Wilson to accept amalgamation, Pershing found himself almost alone in resisting Allied pressure for sending Americans directly to the trenches. He bent only once under the pressure when he assigned the four African-American regiments of the 93rd Division to the French. Although Pershing stipulated that the regiments were to be returned when he asked for them, they remained with the French throughout the war. After receiving French weapons and uniforms, one of the regiments, the 369th, spent 191 days in the front lines

The Americans Enter the Trenches

Despite the vast industrial capability and military potential of the United States, it had to act as a junior partner in its efforts to contribute to the war. The fighting had been in progress for thirty-two months, and the Americans had to construct their plans and commit their forces within the framework of already existing Allied plans and dispositions. One of the most important strategic questions was the placement of the American forces in France. Though Pershing had his choice on the location of the American front, his options were limited by the British desire to cover the channel ports and by the French being reluctant to have any army but their own defend Paris. Consequently, the main area available to him was in Lorraine near the St. Mihiel salient. Placing the Americans in Lorraine also had the advantage of enabling them to route their supply lines away from the channel ports being used by the British and around the potential bottleneck of Paris. Moreover, an offensive toward the north by the Americans could sever the important railway line through Metz (which the Germans used to support the western extension of its front across France) and capture the huge iron mines of the Briey Basin and the coal mines near Saarbrücken. Thus, when offered a choice of sectors, Pershing chose for logistical and strategic reasons the area the Allies wanted him to take.

Before American troops began arriving in large numbers, their logistics system began to take shape. Known as "Services of Supply," the system proudly trumpeted its mission of relieving "the combatant field force from every consideration except that of defeating the enemy." To accomplish this mission, about 670,000 men eventually became involved in the myriad tasks associated with supporting a large army in the field; everything from hospitals, to schools, to replacement centers, to maintenance shops, to storage depots came under the large thumb of the Services of Supply.

To demonstrate its resolve, the United States hurriedly dispatched a combat division to Europe. Since no organic divisions existed, the U.S. Army brought the 16th, 18th, 26th, and 28th infantry regiments from the Mexican border, formed them into the 1st Infantry Division, and promptly shipped them to Europe. Shortly before departing, a period of disruptive personnel turbulence occurred when many of the regular soldiers from the four regiments were transferred to training camps and replaced by raw recruits. By the time the regiments steamed for France, more than half the personnel were recruits. After arriving in the port of St. Nazaire in late June 1917 and having a detachment march through Paris on the Fourth of July, the division rode boxcars to Lorraine and began intensive training.

Though assisted in its training by the French 47th Division, the 1st Division was not ready to enter the trenches until October 21. Beginning that day individual battalions began moving into a quiet sector of the trench line for ten days. Early on the morning of November 3, three American soldiers from Company F, 16th Infantry Regiment, died during a German raid on their trenches. These were the first soldiers in American units to die in the Great War. By November the AEF had four divisions in France (the 1st, 2nd, 26th, and 42nd), but they were not yet ready to play a large role in the fighting. At the end of November, the 1st Division began further training, but not until January 18, 1918, six months after its arrival in France, did it assume responsibility for a sector on its own.

One month later the 26th Division occupied a sector at Soissons and the 42nd moved into the trenches near Lunéville. The following month the 2nd Division occupied part of the line near Verdun. By the middle of March 1918, the Americans had made no significant contribution to the actual fighting, and Allied disappointment and resentment reached a peak. The Allies were particularly concerned, because they were convinced—correctly—that the Germans were shifting forces and preparing for a major offensive on the Western Front. Nevertheless, from June 1917 until May 1918, American combat units in France concentrated on training. Pershing refused to allow them to enter the trenches in large numbers until their training was complete and until sufficient combat units and support had arrived for the Americans to operate independently.

The Air Service of the AEF

The challenge of creating an air service to support the AEF was as difficult as any faced by Pershing. Among the reasons for this, as Pershing explained to King George V on June 9, 1917, was that the United States had only fifty-five military planes, almost all of which were obsolescent when it entered the war. Yet during the punitive expedition to Mexico, the new American commander had recognized the importance of aviation. He soon acted to improve American aviation in Europe and appointed Colonel Billy Mitchell as the aviation officer of the AEF.

Before the United States declared war, Mitchell had been in Europe for almost two months, studying the role of aviation in the war. For a time he had used his own money for setting up an official aviation office. He quickly recognized that American aircraft were decidedly inferior to European models because three years of warfare had accelerated the development of aviation far beyond the models available to the American military, most of which were similar to the ones available in Europe in 1914. Despite the best efforts to produce modern aircraft in the United States, organization and technical problems hampered production, and the Americans soon turned to the Europeans for delivery of aviation equipment.

As months passed, very little equipment arrived for American aviators. The failure to produce adequate aircraft in the United States was compounded by the failure of French industry to meet promised delivery dates. Moreover, the number of aviation personnel increased very slowly. The shortage of shipping and the according of a higher priority to the shipment of infantry in the spring of 1918 resulted in no aviation personnel arriving in May and June. Of the small number of airplanes received by the air service, almost all were French fighters.

A year after the declaration of war, the first air squadron was formed in April 1918 with American pilots who had served with the Allies. Soon, the number of American-trained pilots began to increase slowly. After Major General Mason Patrick arrived in France and became chief of the air service, Mitchell found himself directing the American planes in combat. Though the number of aircraft slowly increased until there were forty-five squadrons at the front at the time of the armistice, Mitchell never had more than 650 planes, almost all of which were fighters. The American aerial forces never had the capability for strategic bombing and remained primarily concerned with supporting the land battle or fighting against enemy aircraft.

Cambrai: The Final Allied Offensive of 1917

As the Americans slowly built up and transported their forces to the European continent, the bloodbath continued. Following the French disaster at Chemin des Dames and the British losses at Passchendaele, the Allies were in no shape to deliver a knockout blow to the Germans, but they became concerned in late 1917 that the balance would tilt in favor of the Germans before the Americans arrived. Believing that the position of the Provisional Government in Russia (which had seized power in March 1917) had become increasingly precarious, the Allies foresaw the complete collapse of Russia and feared a flood of German divisions moving from the Eastern to the Western Front.

Allied fears were heightened when Austro-German forces won a brilliant victory over the Italians in the Battle of Caporetto during October–November 1917. The Italians lost more than 3,000 guns and about a million soldiers killed, wounded, or captured. Although the assistance of six French and five British divisions seemed momentarily to hold off disaster, the Allies faced the disconcerting specter of complete collapse on the Eastern and Italian fronts and the subsequent concentration of all the Central Powers' forces on the Western Front. Meanwhile, German submarines continued to gnaw at the lifeline of Allied shipping.

While fighting was still going on at Arras and the Chemin des Dames, Haig and Nivelle agreed that the Allies had to clear the submarine bases in Belgium either by advancing directly from Ypres or "indirectly" by attacking toward Charleroi-Liège. Haig soon directed the completion of a study on breaking through the Hindenburg Line in the vicinity of Cambrai. Since the firm, rolling terrain around Cambrai was ideal tank country, Lieutenant Colonel J. F. C. Fuller of the Royal Tank Corps drew up a scheme for a quick armored raid that would plunge through German lines, capture and destroy enemy personnel and equipment, and then return to friendly lines. British commanders, however, quickly decided on a full-scale battle in which the tanks were tied to the infantry and artillery. In the middle of October, Haig approved a plan for an attack at Cambrai.

The British Third Army, which was given responsibility for the attack, concentrated its forces along a six-mile front. The attack began with five divisions on line, one division following, and three divisions in reserve. To their rear, five cavalry divisions were set to race toward Cambrai. The Royal Tank Corps of the British army, which was commanded by Brigadier General Hugh Elles and which had Fuller as chief of staff, supported the attack with three tank brigades. Of 476 available tanks, 374 were combat tanks and 98 were administrative tanks, including those specially equipped for clearing wire, communicating, or carrying bridging material. The tanks were Mark IVs, which were huge, rhomboidal-shaped fighting vehicles carrying four 6-pounder guns and four machine guns.

Though one division commander refused to use the methods devised by the Royal Tank Corps, the other divisions practiced an intricate procedure for coordinating the actions of tanks and infantry. The main feature of this procedure was to have a section of three tanks lead an infantry company across no-man's-land and through enemy wire. With one tank leading and two tanks following in echelon on both sides, the infantry company advanced under the protection of the tanks. An infantry platoon moved in a flexible column formation behind each of the following tanks. When the leading tank reached the enemy's trenches, it swept them with fire, dropped its fascines—which were rolled bundles of sticks—into the trenches, and then crossed. After reaching the enemy trenches, the two leading infantry platoons cleared out the enemy. The two rear platoons then moved forward, sealed off the captured trench, and worked on improving paths through the wire. Meanwhile, the tanks continued forward to the next trench, and the infantry quickly followed. Since each of the tanks carried a fascine, the force could cross three trenches before being halted.

The British tried several new techniques in the attack. Fourteen squadrons of the Royal Flying Corps provided air support, which included not only flying the normal observation missions and attacks on German aircraft and headquarters but also providing direct support to ground units. The flying squadrons prepared to move forward with the first wave and to fire directly into the enemy's trenches. Also the British, preferring the advantage of surprise, decided to attack without the usual prolonged artillery preparation. The bombardment was supposed to begin at the same time as the assault, without preliminary registration that might have compromised

Battle of Cambrai, November–December 1917

the plan. Although the technique of using maps (rather than visual sight-ings) to control the firing of artillery had not been used extensively up to this point, the use of maps and what came to be known as "predicted fire" proved to be extremely successful.

The attack began early on the morning of November 20, 1917. Ludendorff noted in his memoirs that the Germans expected the Allies to continue the attacks in Flanders and on the French front and did not expect them to begin an attack at Cambrai. By the end of the first day, the British had advanced about three miles and punched through the main defenses and support line of the Hindenburg Line. This was the deepest penetration into German lines on the Western Front since the beginning of trench warfare. Of the 374 combat tanks that took part in the fighting, 179 were out of action, but only sixty-five because of enemy fire. On the second day, the British made additional gains, but the Germans brought four more divisions into the area. On the third day, very little was accomplished. In the face of determined German resistance, those battalions that made any gains at all soon lost them. For the next several days, bitter fighting swirled around the high ground in the area.

By November 30, the British Third Army was crammed into a salient about seven miles deep and eight miles wide. Having brought forward significant artillery and reserves, the Germans struck after an all-night bombardment. The strong German attack pushed the British behind their original starting point. Some sharp fighting continued, but the offensive and the counterattack were over. Of the 474 tanks that entered the battle, less than one-third returned from Cambrai. Most of them required extensive repairs, and very few ever participated in a battle again. The Battle of Cambrai was the last major battle fought by the Allies on the Western Front in 1917.

*   *   *   *

As 1917 came to a close, the hopes of the Allies rested on the "Americans and the tanks." The French and British had suffered terribly at the Chemin des Dames and at Passchendaele. Their losses provided vivid evidence about the high price an attacker could pay and underlined the wisdom of using limited offensives to help reduce casualties. Limited offensives, however, held little promise for ending the war other than through attrition. Despite the introduction of the tank, the experience of Cambrai confirmed that much remained to be done before the tank could alter the nature of the battlefield. The British high command began developing a plan for 1919, but its success rested upon efforts to improve and manufacture tanks by the thousands. The most fervent Allied hope, however, was that large numbers of Americans would arrive on the Western Front before the Germans shifted forces from the east and launched a final desperate offensive.

Despite widespread starvation and shortages, the year did not end on an entirely negative note for the Central Powers. The victory against the Italians at Caporetto in October–November 1917 and against the Russians at Riga in September 1917 suggested that the Central Powers had made important steps in breaking the deadlock of trench warfare. Additionally, peace discussions had begun on December 22 at Brest-Litovsk, and on March 3, 1918, the Bolsheviks signed a treaty that yielded vast areas and important resources to the Germans. The treaty accelerated the shifting of German forces to the west and the German army's preparation for what Ludendorff called the "biggest task in its history"—the launching of the final offensives in the spring of 1918.

SUGGESTED READINGS

Braim, Paul F. *The Test of Battle: The American Expeditionary Forces in the Meuse-Argonne Campaign* (Newark, N.J.: University of Delaware Press, 1987).

Coffman, Edward M. *The War to End All Wars: The American Military Experience in World War I* (Madison, Wisc.: The University of Wisconsin Press, 1968).

Cooper, Bryan. *The Battle of Cambrai* (New York: Stein and Day, 1968).

Halperin, Paul G. *A Naval History of World War I* (Annapolis, Md.: Naval Institute Press, 1994).

Legg, Stuart. *Jutland* (New York: John Day Co., 1967).

Macdonald, Lyn. *They Called It Passchendaele* (London: Michael Joseph, 1978).

McKee, Alexander. *Vimy Ridge* (Toronto: The Ryerson Press, 1966).

Millet, Allan R. *The General: Robert L. Bullard and Officership in the United States Army, 1881–1925* (Westport, Conn.: Greenwood Press, 1975).

Ryan, Stephen. *Pétain the Soldier* (New York: A. S. Barnes and Company, 1969).

Smythe, Donald. *Pershing: General of the Armies* (Bloomington, Ind.: Indiana University Press, 1986).

Trask, David F. *The United States in the Supreme War Council* (Middleton, Conn.: Wesleyan University Press, 1961).

Watt, Richard M. *Dare Call It Treason* (New York: Simon and Schuster, 1963).

Wolff, Leon. *In Flanders Field, the 1917 Campaign* (New York: Viking Press, 1958).

Woollcombe, Robert. *The First Tank Battle: Cambrai, 1917* (London: Arthur Barker Limited, 1967).

20

BREAKING THE HOLD OF THE
TRENCHES, 1918

Infiltration Tactics and the
Failure of the German
Offensives, March–July 1918

Overwhelming the Germans
with Men and Machines

The Great War

As the bloody months of 1917 drew
to a close, some military leaders believed the strategic situation momentarily
favored the Central Powers more than the Allies. With the Russian army collapsing in the east, with the defeat of the Italian army at Caporetto, and with
the British weakened by the unrestricted submarine warfare campaign, some
leaders believed Germany had an opportunity to gain military superiority on
the Western Front. They also believed the German army had demonstrated
during the breakthroughs at Caporetto and Riga that it could break the
deadlock of trench warfare on the Western Front. With the introduction of
infiltration tactics, the Germans seemed to have developed a new method for
restoring mobility to the battlefield.

Despite these promising indications, long-term prospects were not
favorable to the Central Powers. The German people were obviously growing more and more discontented with the war, and Americans were entering
Europe by the thousands. Clearly, decisive action had to be taken quickly if
Germany was to win the war militarily. In a race against time, the Germans
began preparing for a huge offensive, while the Allies did all they could to
accelerate the arrival and preparation of the Americans.

Infiltration Tactics and the Failure of the German Offensives, March–July 1918

The overthrow of Russia's tsarist government in March 1917 by a provisional government and the seizure of power by the Bolsheviks in November created new hope in Germany. For the military, the ending of the war in the east meant troops and equipment could be shipped from the east, but for the civilians the collapse of Russia suggested the possibility of greater food supplies and other necessities. Throughout 1916–1917, the effects of the Allied blockade reached their peak as distress and discontent caused by food shortages increased among the civilian population. Families became especially concerned about the undernourishment of their children, and misery became particularly acute among the poor. The winter of 1916–1917 was known as the "turnip winter," when German citizens were forced to eat turnips, which were usually fed to cattle.

In the army and navy, resentment grew among the enlisted men, for they were angered by a system that provided better food for officers. Also, being bottled up in ports for years with little to do made sailors discontented and vulnerable to propaganda. Dissatisfaction became most obvious when the crew of the *Prinzregent Luitpold* mutinied on June 6, 1917, and went on a hunger strike.

Opposition to the war also grew rapidly in organized labor. In January 1918, the first outbreak of widespread political strikes occurred. On January 28, some 400,000 workers in Berlin went on strike, seeking food and higher wages and demanding an end to the war. The movement spread to most of the larger industrial cities and involved more than one million workers. This growing evidence of mounting civilian discontent heightened the German military's interest in bringing the war to a close.

For some leaders, the prospect of Russia's withdrawal from the war offered the best chance of reviving flagging German morale. Leaders in German industry and commerce believed the Treaty of Brest-Litovsk would open vast areas in eastern Europe to economic exploitation. By the treaty of March 3, 1918, Russia lost one-fourth of its territory—44 percent of its population, 73 percent of its iron ore, and 75 percent of its coal. Before the treaty was signed, German leaders received optimistic projections of food shipments from the Ukraine, but actual shipments always remained below expectations. This environment of disappointment intensified German interest in a rapid victory.

Throughout this period, the German high command greatly expanded its power, and by the end of 1917, the high command—particularly Ludendorff—dominated the German government. The extent of Ludendorff's power can be seen in a meeting held on November 11, 1917, in Mons, Belgium, to discuss German strategy for 1918. Neither Kaiser William II, the chancellor, nor Hindenburg was present. Although Ludendorff later lamented the absence of a strong political figure in Berlin, he would never have tolerated the emergence of a German Clemenceau who would have argued, "War is too important to be left to the generals." Instead of military policy being subordinate to political power and objectives, the German government had become the servant of the high command.

When Ludendorff arrived at the meeting at Mons in November 1917, he did not believe that unrestricted submarine warfare had failed, but he knew that the Americans were beginning to pour into Europe and that the Allies were once again building up enormous quantities of matériel. He had already made up his mind that Germany had to achieve a major victory and force the Allied powers to recognize that continuing the war offered no chance of success, despite the involvement of the Americans. Moreover, launching a final desperate offensive would, he hoped, end the general despair in Germany about the hopelessness of the struggle as well as revive the fighting spirit of Austria-Hungary, Bulgaria, and Turkey. The key decision in the November 1917 meeting thus concerned the launching of an offensive on the Western Front in the spring of 1918. The Germans believed a series of offensives, delivered at intervals and at several different points, would restore mobility to the battlefield and end the long stalemate that had lasted for four years on the Western Front.

The Germans focused on the British front (Flanders, Arras, and the Somme); they believed Great Britain might be more eager for peace once its

Kaiser Wilhelm II with Hindenburg on his right and Ludendorff on his left. Despite the Kaiser's constitutional authority as Supreme War Lord, he was disregarded almost entirely by the real makers of policy, Hindenburg and Ludendorff.

soldiers suffered terribly. With the heavily used Channel ports to its rear, Flanders appeared to be the most favorable area for an attack, since a breakthrough could sever the BEF's communications lines to Great Britain. The possibility of rains soaking the soft terrain in Flanders, however, ruled out any offensive before May. An offensive in Arras (south of Flanders and north of the Somme) also seemed unwise because of strong British defenses.

The most vulnerable area appeared to be the Somme, where the British seemed to be overextended and their defenses the weakest. An offensive there, near St. Quentin and Cambrai, offered the possibility of splitting the British and French forces. If an advance deep into the Allied positions were made, the Germans would push the British toward the Channel coast. Ludendorff believed that the defeat of the British forces would drive them out of the war and ultimately provide a favorable peace for the Central Powers. Nevertheless, tactical considerations dominated his thinking, and he later explained, "A strategic plan which ignores tactical factors is doomed to failure."

On January 21, Ludendorff ordered preparations to begin for an offensive, code named "Michael," to be launched in the Somme area. In October 1917, the Germans had only 150 divisions on the Western Front, but by the spring offensive of 1918, they would have 192.

Infiltration Tactics

Although Ludendorff warned the kaiser that the impending struggle would be "immense" and take a "long time" and that the battle would flow from one point to another, he was confident that the German army would succeed. Since the "Massacre of the Innocents" at Ypres, the Germans had devoted considerable efforts to solving the riddle of trench warfare, and they had improved their tactical methods through a process of incremental change. German leaders recognized the unfavorable strategic situation facing them and were more willing than the Allies to take risks or consider new methods. The general staff also encouraged innovation and circulated information among units about successful methods such as the elastic defense. In Ludendorff's judgment, successful attacks in late 1917 on the Italian front and the Eastern Front had demonstrated the Germans' ability to break the deadlock of trench warfare. He recognized the difficulties, however, of changing the entire thinking of the army from trench warfare back to the offensive.

Between November 11, 1917, when the Germans decided to attack, and March 21, 1918, when the attack began, the German army worked diligently to improve its offensive doctrine and to prepare its units for the attack. After careful reexamination of their own experience with the offensive, the Germans published on January 26, 1918, the basics of their new doctrine in a pamphlet entitled *The Attack in Position Warfare*. Contained within the pamphlet was the outline of new tactics (which were not completely new) which later became known as "infiltration tactics."

The tactics emphasized bypassing enemy resistance and pushing forward as far as possible. Using specially trained assault troops, armed with light machine guns, the Germans expected small units to exploit success at weak points and to advance as far and as quickly as possible into enemy defenses. Instead of clearing pockets of enemy resistance as they advanced, the assault troops were expected to continue to advance and to reach the enemy's artillery. The January 1918 pamphlet explained, "The aim of the breakthrough should be the enemy's artillery." Follow-on units were expected to neutralize bypassed enemy strong points. If the reserves were committed, they would reinforce success, not push their way through unbroken enemy defenses.

The new tactics relied strongly on effective artillery support. Using techniques devised by Colonel Georg Bruchmüller, the Germans prepared to fire artillery in depth through the enemy's positions. They also practiced using a rolling barrage in front of the advancing infantry. Despite reservations from infantrymen who feared being fired upon accidentally and from artillerymen who wanted greater precision, the Germans adopted in January 1918 a system of predicted fire known as the "Pulkowski method." With this method of fire, an artillery unit could support infantry attacks without pre-registering and without losing the element of surprise. Technical firing tables and coordinates from improved maps provided data that could be modified for deviations caused by weather conditions or wear on an artillery tube. These methods shortened the time needed for artillery preparation before an offensive and encouraged the use of "hurricanes" of fire—short, intense, surprise bombardments immediately before an attack began. For their attacks on March 21 and April 9, 1918, the Germans used some pre-registration, but they engaged most targets using the predicted fire method. After April 9, they supported almost all attacks with the new method.

In addition to changes in infantry tactics and in coordination between infantry and artillery, the Germans recognized the error of trying to command from the rear by using a telephone. In the spring of 1918, Ludendorff ordered all division commanders in the coming offensives to command from the front lines on horseback. He recognized the importance of their presence and their personal example in motivating soldiers to continue moving forward.

To ensure the highest levels of performance, the Germans strongly emphasized training and physical fitness before the battle. Companies, battalions, and regiments followed detailed training guidelines on the conduct of assaults. As smaller units finished their training, complete divisions began conducting practice assaults. Many of the exercises included live fire, as well as the employment of rockets and flares to control artillery. Of their 192 divisions on the Western Front, the Germans trained and equipped only fifty-six in the new tactics. The remainder concentrated on holding the German line and had a lower priority for replacements, training, and equipment.

The Spring Offensive

At 0440 hours on March 21, 1918, the long-awaited spring offensive began. The Germans launched their attack in the area of the Somme with three armies: the Seventeenth Army on the right, the Second Army in the center, and the Eighteenth Army on the left. The Seventeenth and Second armies belonged to the army group commanded by Crown Prince Rupprecht of Bavaria, and the Eighteenth Army belonged to the army group commanded by German Crown Prince William. Ludendorff had decided to split the attack between two army groups so he, as he later explained, "could exercise a far-reaching influence on the course of the battle."

The German attack on March 21 struck the British Fifth Army and the Third Army to its north. For some time the Allies had expected the Germans to begin an offensive, and Haig had anticipated a strong attack on the front of Fifth Army, commanded by General Sir Hubert Gough, which faced St. Quentin in the Somme area. Nevertheless, Gough's army was spread across a forty-mile front, had done little to establish a defense in depth, and was not fully prepared to ward off a major attack. British defenses were particularly weak in the southern part of Fifth Army's front, for this area had recently been turned over to the British by the French. This was to be the area where the German Eighteenth Army made its largest advances.

From 0440 until 0940 hours, the Germans fired an artillery bombardment that consisted of gas, smoke, and high-explosive shells. At 0940, the Germans advanced with thirty-two infantry divisions, closely followed by an additional twenty-eight. A heavy rolling barrage preceded the infantry. The Germans wanted their infantry to penetrate about five miles, the distance between the front line and the British artillery. By nightfall, Second and Eighteenth armies in the German center and left had pushed through most of the forward zone of the British Fifth Army, but Seventeenth Army on the right encountered a more stubborn resistance from the British Third Army. Ludendorff had expected Seventeenth and Second armies on the center and right to make the most progress and planned on their turning to the right and enveloping the British forces. Since Seventeenth Army was advancing slowly and Eighteenth Army on the left was advancing rapidly, however, Ludendorff decided to reinforce the Eighteenth Army's success and began sending it additional forces and supplies.

In subsequent days, the German advance continued, particularly in the center and left sectors. Pétain and Haig had earlier agreed that France would send reinforcements if a major offensive were launched against the British, and so on March 23, Pétain agreed to send sufficient forces to prevent the Germans from splitting the French and British. Pétain remained concerned, however, about the possibility of an offensive on his own front between Soissons and Reims, and he did not send reinforcements as rapidly as Haig desired.

By the morning of March 25, the fourth day of the offensive, the French Third Army with seven divisions was deployed on the southern flank of the expanding German salient, and the French First Army with six divisions was on its way. General Émile Fayolle assumed command of a provisional army group that included French and British units south of the Somme River. On March 27, the German Eighteenth Army captured Montdidier, but its forces were exhausted and running out of supplies. To the north of Eighteenth Army, the Germans made several other assaults, attempting to capture the railhead of Amiens, but on April 4, Ludendorff halted the offensive.

The first attempt to break through Allied lines had failed. This failure resulted from a variety of factors, including the Allies' successful reinforcement of the threatened area. The Germans were also stymied by the difficulties of transporting troops and artillery across the destroyed terrain of the attack, the inability of reserves and supporting units to keep up with the leading forces, and the lack of discipline among some German units. Though the Germans had made numerous tactical innovations, problems that had existed from the beginning of the war continued to limit their ability to make a breakthrough. Most notably, the Germans had not been able to prevent the enemy from moving in fresh troops by railway and roads into the endangered area. Nevertheless, the German army had advanced some thirty-five miles, the largest advance by far of any army on the Western Front since 1914.

Allied Unity of Command

Throughout the first three years of the war, the Allies had made some attempts to coordinate their strategy and operations, but concerns about relinquishing their sovereignty made them reluctant to adopt a unified command system. In early 1917, Lloyd George had agreed to (and Haig had reluctantly accepted) the British forces in France being subject to the orders of Nivelle for the 1917 offensives. The failure of these attacks ended this arrangement. Not until after the collapse of Russia and the defeat of Italy at Caporetto in late 1917 did the Allies take steps to establish a formal system of coordinating their strategies.

As French and British divisions moved into Italy to bolster their ally, Allied heads of government met at Rapallo, Italy, in November 1917 and agreed to form the Supreme War Council. Focused on the Western Front, the council consisted of each nation's head of government and one other high-ranking member of the government. The council also had a board of permanent military representatives that met at Versailles. According to the council's charter, the military representatives were supposed to "watch day by day the situation of the forces and of the means of all kinds of which the Allied armies and the enemy armies dispose." Thus, no hint of real command authority existed. The weakness of the Supreme War Council became very evident when an attempt to form a general reserve in January 1918

When General Ferdinand Foch was charged with coordinating the actions of the Allied armies on the Western Front, he responded with enthusiasm and energy. Never losing his faith in the offensive despite years of losses, he successfully coordinated the final drives that defeated the Germans.

foundered: only days before the German spring offensive, the executive committee of the Supreme War Council concluded that it was "impossible" to organize an Allied general reserve.

The crisis engendered by Germany's success along the Somme led Allied leaders to assemble in late March 1918 at Doullens, France, to consider alternatives for strengthening coordination among their military forces. After much wrangling, Foch was charged "with coordinating the action of the Allied armies on the Western Front." Although his responsibilities were only for the duration of the crisis, the Allies—including the Americans—agreed on April 3, 1918, to an extension of Foch's powers. The agreement stated, "The British, French and American governments . . . entrust to General Foch the strategic direction of military operations."

For the first time in the war, some semblance of a unity of command existed among the Allies. Upon the insistence of the British, however, the commander of each national army would have the right to appeal to his government if he thought Foch's orders endangered his army.

The Germans Continue Their Offensive

As the tactically impressive but strategically unsuccessful March offensive came to a halt, Ludendorff launched another attack, striking the Allies in Flanders, with the main attack hitting twenty miles south of Ypres, near the Lys River. This area was more than sixty miles northwest of the area in which the Somme operation occurred. Though Ludendorff's strategic objectives are not completely clear, he evidently aimed to strike a weaker portion of the British front and perhaps to capture the vital rail junction of Hazebrouck.

On April 9, the second offensive began, its main attack striking the Portuguese II Corps. By April 12, the Germans had made significant gains, and Haig desperately sought assistance from Foch. Foch sent only token forces to reinforce the British; he hoped to retain sufficient forces to create a reserve capable of responding to a larger German attack that he expected to strike in the Somme region. Haig responded with a "backs to the wall" order, and British soldiers responded with some of the most gallant and tenacious fighting of the war. The battle continued until April 29 when the German attack ground to a halt. During the fighting German operations were affected by a breakdown in discipline, particularly when the troops captured well-stocked British supply dumps. This was an early indication that the German army was beginning to deteriorate. In another ominous development for the Central Powers, the Allies began launching new ships in April at a faster rate than German submarines could destroy them.

Ludendorff launched his next blow on May 27 near Soissons against the Chemin des Dames, the scene of Nivelle's disastrous attack of 1917, which had remained quiet for more than a year. The third offensive was a diversionary attack, for the Germans sought to divert Allied reserves from Flanders and then to resume their attacks against the British. Even though the terrain on the Chemin des Dames favored the defenders, the Germans achieved surprising success. The defending forces in this region included a British corps that had been mauled in the first two German offensives and sent to recuperate in what was supposedly a quiet sector. The commander of the French forces, General Denis A. Duchêne, had refused to establish a defense in depth and had placed his meager forces along the high ground. The attackers swept through the thinly held front easily and advanced more than twelve miles on the first day of their attack. This was the largest advance made in a single day on the Western Front since the early months of the war, and Duchêne paid the penalty for his unpreparedness by being relieved of his command. As with other German attacks, the Allies moved reserves into the endangered area. This time, however, some of the reserves were Americans whose hard fighting at Château Thierry and Belleau Wood helped stop the German attack by June 4. The Germans were not prepared to exploit their gains, but they established a large salient near the Marne.

With the ending of this attack, Ludendorff's offensives had accomplished little more than the creation of three large salients (Somme, Lys, and Marne) and the depletion of the German army. Still seeking to draw Allied reserves away from Flanders, he decided to launch an attack between the Somme and Marne salients. By attacking from the neighboring flanks of the Somme and Marne salients between Montdidier and Noyon, he planned on expanding the two salients into a single larger salient and threatening Paris. Unbeknownst to the Germans, the Allies had detected preparations for the attack and had prepared strong defenses in depth. Just prior to the Germans beginning their artillery preparation for the attack on June 8, the French began counterbattery artillery fire. Although the attackers made limited gains, a French counterattack with tank support stopped them. By June 13 the fourth offensive was over.

During the month of comparative quiet that followed, Ludendorff prepared two great attacks that would comprise his fifth and final offensive: the first was an attack in the Champagne-Marne area on both sides of Reims; the second was the long-awaited offensive in Flanders. Just as had occurred in June, the Allies detected preparations for an attack in the Reims area, with much of the information coming from an ever-expanding flow of German deserters. Consequently the Allies strengthened their defenses in this area. Before the German attack began, Allied counterbattery fire disrupted their efforts. With one of the most spirited defenses coming from the U.S. 3rd Division along the Marne River, the Germans made only limited gains in their attack, which began on July 15 but ended by July 17. The final, great offensive in Flanders never occurred.

The Americans Enter the Battle

Without the moral and matériel support of the Americans, the French and British might not have survived the German spring offensive. Large numbers of Americans did not fight the Germans until the summer of 1918, but their entry into battle helped blunt the German attack. Not surprisingly, given Pershing's faith in the offense, the first important action was an attack conducted by the 1st Infantry Division at Cantigny near the tip of the Noyon-Montdidier salient, created during the first German offensive. The Americans staged a limited attack on the ruined village of Cantigny as part of a French attempt to retake Montdidier. Beginning at 0545 hours on May 28, the 1st Division attacked with its 28th Infantry Regiment and reached its objective by 0730 hours. The Germans launched six or seven counterattacks, but they failed to coordinate their artillery support with their infantry attacks and thus failed to push the Americans back. For the next several days, the men of the 28th and 16th regiments endured continued shelling and machine-gun fire. The attack was not significant strategically, but its success did bolster American confidence.

Following Pétain's appeal for assistance in halting the third German offensive at the Chemin des Dames, Pershing dispatched the U.S. 2nd and 3rd Divisions toward the Marne near Château Thierry. One of the two brigades of 2nd Division was a U.S. Marine brigade. The arrival of 3rd Division at Château Thierry on May 31 and 2nd Division at Belleau Wood-Bouresches-Vaux on June 1 demonstrated the willingness and ability of the Americans to fight. Their contributions were more important strategically than the fight at Cantigny, for their strong defenses and counterattacks played a key role in halting the third German offensive. Some French officers credited the Americans with having saved Paris.

On July 15 the fifth German offensive struck along the Marne River east of Château Thierry. Though the Germans crossed the Marne and established a sizeable bridgehead, the U.S. 3rd Division held firm, fighting in three directions. On the division's right flank, 30th Regiment was forced

An American column moving across a cratered battlefield. Throughout the war, armies on the offensive faced considerable difficulties moving across terrain that had been softened and churned by thousands of artillery rounds.

back under the German attack, but 38th Regiment on its left held firm. In an action Pershing later described as "one of the most brilliant pages in our military annals," Colonel Ulysses Grant McAlexander's regiment withstood the attack of two German divisions. The actions of 38th Regiment sealed the end of the fifth German offensive and contributed significantly to 3rd Division becoming known as "The Rock of the Marne."

Although Ludendorff still clung to his hope for a final offensive in the Flanders sector, the opportunity for decisive action had slipped away. His forces had suffered terrible losses, his reserves and supplies were depleted, and the morale of his soldiers was sinking rapidly.

Overwhelming the Germans with Men and Machines

As the fifth and final German offensive ground to a halt, the Allies accelerated their efforts to seize the initiative with strong counterattacks. Foch's initial efforts focused on three salients held by the Germans (Marne, Somme, and St. Mihiel). Since the middle of April, he had worked energetically to assemble forces for a counterstroke, and on July 18, after concentrating his forces around the Marne salient, he launched the Second Battle of the Marne. This was the first of a series of great drives that would roll back the German army.

Beginning at 0435 hours on July 18, the French Tenth Army made the main attack into the western neck of the Marne salient near Soissons, while Sixth, Ninth, and Fifth armies pushed against the salient on its other sides. Nine American divisions participated in the Allied attempt to push the Germans out of their positions. The American divisions attacked as part of three French field armies and did not operate as an independent force. The actions of 1st and 2nd divisions as part of the French Tenth Army were particularly important, for when their attacks threatened Soissons and the main German supply line running through it, the Germans had no choice but to withdraw. Though the Germans were forced out of the salient, their withdrawal was conducted skillfully and orderly. Nonetheless, the success at driving the Germans out of their Marne position clearly demonstrated that the initiative had passed to the Allies.

Foch's next attack struck the northern part of the Somme salient and is sometimes called the Battle of Amiens. The date of its launching was later described by Ludendorff as the "black day of the German army." The attack marked a turning point in the conduct of Allied operations and inaugurated the form of relatively open warfare that characterized the last months of the war.

The attacking forces consisted of the British Fourth Army under General Henry Rawlinson and the French First Army under General M. Eugène Debeney. The British Fourth Army was responsible for the main attack, and Rawlinson had the Canadian Corps of four divisions and the Australian Corps of five divisions lead it. Both corps were renowned for their fighting abilities. As one indication of how the war was changing, Rawlinson's army was reinforced by twelve battalions of tanks (414 combat tanks and 120 administrative tanks).

After a concerted effort to prevent the Germans from detecting the Allied preparations, the British attack began at 0420 hours on August 8 without any preparatory fire and with almost no prior registration of the artillery. Since the French had only two battalions of tanks (seventy-two tanks) to support their attack, they began their artillery preparation at the same time as the British began their attack, and then sent their infantry forward forty-five minutes later. They had delayed their artillery preparation and infantry attack to avoid warning the Germans of the impending Allied attack.

The attackers, particularly the Canadians, advanced swiftly. By noon they had advanced up to ten miles and captured some 16,000 prisoners. Though the French advance was slower, they also captured many prisoners and weapons. For the remainder of the month, Haig continued pressing on the Somme salient. For a short time he shifted the main attack to the British Third Army on the left of Rawlinson's Fourth Army, but then ordered an advance by both field armies. By the end of the month the Germans began pulling back to the Hindenburg Line, where they had started their Somme offensive in March.

The counterattack by the French and Americans on July 18 against the Marne salient had been a rude shock to the Germans, but the success of the Allies against the Somme salient was the beginning of the end. German losses on the Marne and on the Somme had not been large, but the Allied victories had sent a clear signal that Germany's power could only get weaker while that of the Allies could only get stronger. The kaiser held a conference at Spa on August 14, and German military leaders acknowledged that the war no longer could be won militarily. They concluded, "We have reached the limits of our endurance."

Reduction of the St. Mihiel Salient

The swiftly changing situation was as much a surprise to the Allies as it was to the Germans. Most Allied leaders had anticipated some gains in the campaigns of 1918 but expected the final blow to occur in 1919. In June, Marshal Foch had encouraged the British and Americans to prepare their forces for the final effort in 1919. And when Haig launched the offensive against the Somme salient on August 8, he planned only on conducting a limited offensive and did not expect to make dramatic gains. He too had expected the decisive battles to occur in 1919.

As the deterioration of the Germans became apparent to the Allies, Foch recognized the importance of continuing pressure on the enemy. If the Germans succeeded in making an orderly withdrawal to their own frontiers, they could destroy roads, bridges, and railways and thereby force the Allies to rebuild lines of communication before they advanced. The Germans could also carry much of their supplies and equipment with them and perhaps reestablish their defenses near their own border. Consequently, Foch began preparations for two simultaneous attacks that would advance and then turn inward as if they were giant pincers. A combined Franco-British force would advance in the west toward Cambrai, Le Cateau, and the railway junction at Aulnoye, while a Franco-American force would advance in the east toward the railway junction at Mézières. While these attacks drove forward, Foch would launch a series of staggered attacks along the entire front to confuse the Germans and prevent them from concentrating their reserves against the two pincers. What was eventually to be the American Meuse-Argonne offensive would be the main component of the eastern pincer.

As events accelerated on the Western Front, the Americans had to change some of their long-standing plans. In June 1917, Pershing and Pétain had agreed that once an American army was formed, its first mission would be the reduction of the St. Mihiel salient. In the following months many of the recently formed American divisions served in that sector so they could familiarize themselves with the terrain. By July 1918, Pershing had sufficient forces to form First Army officially; he then named himself its first commander. Amidst the important changes of August 1918, Foch told Pershing that he wanted to split the American forces and to commit substantially fewer forces against the St. Mihiel salient, which he considered less important than the launching of an offensive toward Mézières in the

Meuse-Argonne area. But as before, Pershing strongly objected to dividing his forces.

The two leaders finally compromised by agreeing that First Army would attack the St. Mihiel salient but would then participate in a major offensive farther west in the Meuse-Argonne area. This plan was extremely ambitious, for it called upon the American First Army, whose staff had no experience in large operations, to engage in a major battle and then to disengage and move about thirty miles west for another major battle. Such a task would have been difficult for an experienced army; for the untested First Army, it was a superhuman task.

The offensive against the St. Mihiel salient began at 0500 hours on September 12 after a four-hour artillery preparation. Pershing attacked with four corps, composed of four French and eight-and-one-half American divisions. Seven of the American divisions were on the southern face of the salient; the other one-and-one-half divisions were on the western face. The

St. Mihiel and Meuse-Argonne Offensives, September–November 1918

French divisions concentrated against the high ground at the southwestern tip of the salient. To support the attack, there were 3,010 artillery tubes and 267 light tanks, almost half of which were manned by French soldiers. The attack on St. Mihiel was the first on the European continent by an entire American field army, and it relied heavily on Allied assistance.

Above the battlefield, Colonel Billy Mitchell achieved the greatest concentration of aircraft during the war. The 1,481 Allied airplanes, not one of which was American built and many of which were flown by British, French, and Italian pilots, overwhelmed the German force of 283 planes. Colonel Mitchell, who had only loose control over the planes flown by Allied pilots, wanted to attack the lines of communication and supply system deep in the Germans' rear, but Pershing insisted that the huge armada of planes be subordinated to the needs of the ground battle. The performance of Mitchell and his pilots in the subsequent fighting delighted Pershing and resulted in Mitchell's promotion to brigadier general.

Despite heavy rains that made the soldiers miserable, movement over muddy terrain dificult, and aerial operations risky, the attack went as planned. Fortunately for the Americans, the Germans were in the process of evacuating the salient, and the advance went forward much more easily than expected and without heavy casualties. By the time First Army stopped on a line at the base of the salient, it had captured 450 guns and 16,000 prisoners, while taking 7,000 casualties. Flushed with success from having reduced the salient in two days, the Americans could have continued to attack and perhaps reached Metz, but Pershing had agreed with Foch to halt the attack at the base of the salient and begin preparations for the offensive farther west. Several high-ranking officers within the AEF, including Brigadier General Douglas MacArthur, complained that a marvelous opportunity for an important advance and perhaps even a breakthrough had been missed.

The Meuse-Argonne Offensive

For the Meuse-Argonne offensive, Foch ordered the American First Army to relieve the French Second Army in its sector, which included the Argonne Forest and the area east to the Meuse River. He also assigned the French Fourth Army to a sector west of the Argonne Forest. The French Fourth and the American First armies were to attack northwest and either cut or interdict the railway line that ran east–west through Sedan and Mézières. The railway line had great strategic importance, for by cutting it the Allies not only could prevent the Germans from moving laterally along the Western Front, but also prevent the Germans from carrying many of their supplies with them as they withdrew in the face of Allied pressure. The loss of many tons of supplies would greatly weaken the Germans' ability to continue their resistance until 1919.

After relieving the French Second Army and occupying the Meuse-Argonne sector, the American front extended some ninety miles from the eastern edge of the St. Mihiel sector to the western edge of the Argonne Forest. For the headquarters of First Army, the requirement to concentrate the huge American force in the Meuse-Argonne sector was doubly difficult, because it had to direct the St. Mihiel operation while simultaneously beginning the concentration of other forces to the west. Inexperienced commanders and staffs at army, corps, and division levels had to control the complicated operation of replacing the French Second Army in the Meuse-Argonne area before the attack began. None had any experience with such a huge and complex operation. The staff officer in First Army headquarters who planned the vast movement of Americans and their supplies was Colonel George C. Marshall Jr. Working unbelievably hard and with rare attention to detail, Marshall handled the difficult task brilliantly. Beyond a doubt, it was one of the most difficult staff operations of the war.

The fact that most of those who participated in the battle had very little combat experience complicated First Army's task. Having used the most experienced divisions in the St. Mihiel offensive, the Americans had to commit a number of untried divisions in the Meuse-Argonne offensive. Of the nine divisions scheduled for the Meuse-Argonne offensive, only four had participated in combat operations, and the other five had had almost no combat experience. Moreover, the experienced divisions contained large numbers of recent replacements, some of whom had been in the army for only six weeks and had never fired their rifles.

Using only three small roads, the French pulled back eleven divisions, plus support units and headquarters, while the Americans moved in fifteen divisions, plus support units and headquarters. To make the operation even more difficult, most of the moves occurred at night. The transfer of the American forces to the Meuse-Argonne area required the movement of more than 600,000 soldiers and many hundreds of tons of equipment and supplies over a long distance. Some troops and equipment began moving toward the Meuse-Argonne area ten days before the beginning of the St. Mihiel offensive.

Once the offensive began, the Americans faced extremely strong enemy defenses. The Germans recognized the strategic importance of the railway to their rear and had worked diligently for more than three years to create a strong defensive zone in the Meuse-Argonne sector. Beginning with terrain that was strongly defensible because of many hills and thick woods, the Germans built three major belts of fortifications and established a lightly manned defensive position to their front. The belts of fortifications included numerous trenches, concrete dugouts, concrete machine-gun emplacements, and strong points. Miles of barbed wire reinforced these defenses, and the thick vines and brush that had grown up during the four years of German occupation concealed them from the attackers until the Allies were on top of them.

As the first part of the multistaged operation, Pershing planned on moving forward ten miles with a quick thrust. While a French and an American corps made a feint with artillery fire and raids in the old St. Mihiel sector to the east, the main American attack would be made by three corps (nine divisions) moving on line across a front of about twenty miles. Since Pershing's forces initially faced only five under-strength German divisions, he counted on the element of surprise to increase his advantage of attacking

with superior numbers. However, German commanders learned of the up
coming attack and began reorganizing their front-line troops and movin
reinforcements forward before the Americans launched their attack.

After a six-hour preparation fired by some 4,000 artillery piece
American infantry and 189 light tanks moved forward rapidly at 0530 hour
on September 26; they overwhelmed the forward defenses of the German
easily, with a few units advancing as much as four miles. But from then or
things became disorganized and confused. Because of the Americans' inex
perience, numerous problems appeared: officers failed to coordinate prop
erly the infantry and artillery, soldiers tended to attack and die in bunches
and tanks lagged behind. As traffic-control problems increased, march disci
pline disappeared, and convoys got mixed together on the heavily travele
roads. The Americans continued to attack on September 27, but they suf
fered frightful casualties. In contrast to the other Allied offensives farthe
west, the American offensive achieved disappointing results.

On October 4, after regrouping, First Army attacked again, seekin
the same objective as the September 26 attack. As in the previous attack, th
infantry charged ahead bravely, performing many heroic acts, but thei
courage did not deflect the bullets and artillery fire of the well-prepared Ger
mans. On October 8, First Army attacked east of the Meuse River, but thi
attack also ground to a halt.

On October 12, Pershing split First Army, which was becoming to
unwieldy, into two armies. He appointed Major General Hunter Liggett a

Not having experienced three years of trench warfare, the Americans had an almost naive
faith in the offensive. Pershing insisted that American soldiers wear their uniforms correctly
and train for mobile operations.

the commander of First Army and Major General Robert L. Bullard as commander of Second Army. Pershing became an army group commander. While First Army focused on the Meuse-Argonne area, Second Army focused on the base of the old St. Mihiel salient.

From October 14–19, First Army attacked again but soon halted because of high losses. After three weeks of heavy fighting, the Americans had suffered about 55,000 casualties and had advanced no farther than where they had hoped to be on the first day's attack. Criticism against Pershing from Clemenceau, the French premier, became particularly sharp after the American attack had halted. In his characteristically blunt fashion, Clemenceau spoke of a "crisis" in the AEF and complained of many excellent American troops being "unused." Foch reacted to these criticisms by defending Pershing. He explained that the Americans problems were not due solely to Pershing but to the inexperience of lower-level commanders and staffs.

Using the latter part of October to reorganize the forces of First Army, Liggett attacked again on November 1 with seven veteran divisions. After a two-hour artillery preparation, the attack began at 0530 hours with only eighteen tanks accompanying the infantry. The attack proceeded much more smoothly than previous attempts, and most divisions quickly reached their first objectives. As the demoralized Germans began withdrawing, the rate of advance by the Americans increased. The German commander attempted to withdraw behind the Meuse River, but on November 3–5, the U.S. 5th Division fought its way across before the Germans could reestablish their defenses. The end of the war was clearly near.

The armistice on November 11 finally ended the Meuse-Argonne offensive in which more than 850,000 Americans had participated. During the forty-seven-day campaign, First Army suffered about 117,000 casualties while capturing 26,000 prisoners, 875 cannon, and 3,000 machine guns and inflicting about 100,000 casualties.

The Final Allied Offensives

While the Americans delivered their attacks in the St. Mihiel and Meuse-Argonne sectors, the other allies were also making several important attacks. To the north, Belgian, British, and French units attacked in Flanders in late September and eventually seized the Ypres ridge. As German resistance dwindled, rain and mud delayed the Allies' continued advance. In perhaps the most important attack along the front, one French and three British field armies attacked in the Somme sector. By the first week in October, these armies had fought their way through the Hindenburg Line and forced the Germans to withdraw. To their right, three French armies advanced slowly in the Allied center and maintained pressure on the Germans.

As the Allies advanced, the situation of the Central Powers became hopeless. While American moral and matériel support strengthened Allied resolve, the morale of the Central Powers was drained by four years of bloody losses and weakened by the Allied blockade; their will to fight had collapsed after the failure of the spring offensives. On September 29, Hindenburg and Ludendorff told Kaiser William II that Germany had to request an armistice; and they urged that a new democratic government be formed in Berlin. Several days later, the German and Austrian governments appealed to President Wilson for an armistice based on his Fourteen Points, but the Allies had not yet agreed on the particulars of a peace settlement. In late October, Austrian defenses along the Piave River collapsed completely; the Italians advanced quickly and captured several hundred thousand prisoners. Recognizing the inevitable, the Austrians notified President Wilson that they were willing to conclude a separate peace. On October 26, when Ludendorff showed signs of wanting to continue the war, the kaiser dismissed him.

By November 1, the Allied armies were prepared for their final offensive against the Germans. Foch's plans for continuing the attack were similar to his original concept. With the major thrusts coming from British-French forces in the west and American-French forces in the east, and with French forces maintaining pressure in the center, he intended to prevent the Germans from conducting an orderly withdrawal. As the Allies resumed their attack and as their rate of advance accelerated, German interest in concluding the war intensified.

On the evening of November 7, members of a German armistice commission departed for France and drove toward a secluded forest near Compiègne, forty miles north of Paris. The following morning they met Foch in a railway car. He had been granted authority to offer the terms of an armistice. The German commission was dismayed to find that the terms bore little resemblance to Wilson's Fourteen Points. But when they complained to Foch, he informed them that hostilities would not cease until an armistice was concluded. The next few days were a whirlwind of activity; revolution broke out in various German cities, the kaiser abdicated and fled to Holland, and the German delegates finally received permission to sign the armistice. The Great War ended at 1100 hours on November 11, 1918.

The Great War

In terms of military developments, the events of World War I had corroborated many of Ivan Bloch's pessimistic predictions. The nations of Europe—both the winners and the losers—had paid remarkably high prices. The chief combatants had lost 8.5 million soldiers killed and 20 million wounded. As Bloch had predicted, the providing of unlimited resources to the military and the introduction of new weaponry had transformed war into an endless cycle of attrition. The huge costs and terrible sacrifices eventually brought on revolution and ruin. Bloch had been mistaken, though, in his underestimation of the willingness of belligerents to commit their resources and the lives of their people to the demands of total war.

Though all changes were not yet evident by 1918, it soon became apparent that the Great War was a turning point in the history of the world. The German, Austro-Hungarian, Russian, and Ottoman empires were among the victims of the war, and the structure of the European state system was fundamentally altered. With Europe distracted by four years of war, the rest of the world speeded up its industrialization and modernization and brought the age of European economic supremacy closer to its end. Among other changes, the necessity for governments to plan and direct the activities of their people cast them into arenas from which they would not depart. With so many men in military service, women worked in jobs that previously had been closed to them and in doing so took an important step in modifying their role in society.

The Great War added new meaning to the term "total war," as entire societies were mobilized and committed to the war effort. The major belligerents used conscription to provide millions of men for their armies, but many other men and women contributed to the war effort in factories, fields, mines, and offices. Almost the entire resources of states were committed to the war effort, particularly those of industry. Factories poured out thousands of rifles, mortars, trucks, airplanes, typewriters, telephones, and other items, as well as millions of artillery and rifle rounds and millions of uniforms, blankets, helmets, and boots. Huge logistical systems had to be organized to obtain, allocate, and deliver these products. The "nation in arms" had become a reality.

The war also fundamentally altered the nature of land warfare. Nineteenth-century battles, which sometimes appear almost quaint in comparison to those of 1914–1918, were a thing of the past. As military leaders confronted the unexpected challenges of the Great War, much of their thinking and many of their long-established practices had to change. New methods for organizing, equipping, supplying, and moving huge armies had to be devised. Nonetheless, most armies adapted slowly to the new conditions of the battlefield, and thousands of soldiers died in vain attempts to apply methods that might have worked in the past but that were no longer sufficient for the new conditions. As is all too often the case, the tragedy of huge casualty lists forced most armies to adapt.

As armies adjusted to the new conditions, numerous innovations occurred. New weapons, such as the tank, flamethrower, and light machine gun, provided means for punching through strong defenses. And for the first time, war became truly three-dimensional because of the airplane. From the first battle to the last, commanders on both sides depended on aircraft to provide information about the enemy, adjust artillery fires, attack enemy targets, and control the air above the ground forces. The war also affected naval forces. Though rudimentary, the aircraft carrier became a reality, and the submarine proved deadly against surface shipping.

Conceptual changes also occurred. Gradual improvements in coordination between artillery and infantry enabled attacks to succeed with fewer

Artillery, machine guns, and poison gas transformed the battlefield of World War I into a moonscape of destruction and carnage.

casualties, and new techniques, such as rolling barrages and predicted artillery fire, enhanced the performance of artillery. Similarly, the use of the elastic defense and infiltration tactics provided new methods for attacking and defending. The development of new tactical methods and the use of limited offensives provided advantages that were not foreseen in the early days of the war. By 1918, soldiers had uniforms, weapons, equipment, and methods that differed significantly from those of 1914.

Despite intense efforts by most belligerents, some military questions had not been resolved by November 1918, particularly those relating to breaking through soundly prepared defensive positions—as the failure of the Germans in 1918 demonstrated. Nevertheless, the Great War had witnessed the introduction of many concepts and weapons that would dominate twentieth-century warfare.

SUGGESTED READINGS

Asprey, Robert B. *At Belleau Wood* (New York: Putnam, 1965).

Braim, Paul F. *The Test of Battle: The American Expeditionary Forces in the Meuse-Argonne Campaign* (Newark, N.J.: University of Delaware Press, 1987).

Coffman, Edward M. *The War to End All Wars: The American Military Experience in World War I* (Madison, Wisc.: The University of Wisconsin Press, 1968).

De Groot, Gerard J. *Douglas Haig, 1861–1928* (London: Unwin Hyman, 1988).

Fischer, Fritz. *Germany's Aims in the First World War* (New York: W. W. Norton & Company, 1967).

Goodspeed, D. J. *Ludendorff, Genius of World War I* (Boston: Houghton Mifflin Co., 1966).

Gudmundsson, Bruce I. *Stormtroop Tactics: Innovation in the German Army, 1914–1918* (New York: Praeger, 1989).

Hurley, Alfred F. *Billy Mitchell: Crusader for Air Power* (New York: F. Watts, 1964).

Lupfer, Timothy P. *The Dynamics of Doctrine: The Changes in German Tactical Doctrine During the First World War* (Fort Leavenworth, Kans.: Combat Studies Institute, 1981).

Middlebrook, Martin. *The Kaiser's Battle, 21 March 1918: The First Day of the German Offensive* (London: Allen Lane, 1978).

Millet, Allan R. *The General: Robert L. Bullard and Officership in the United States Army, 1881–1925* (Westport, Conn.: Greenwood Press, 1975).

_____. "Cantigny, 28–31 May 1918," in Charles E. Heller and William A. Stofft, *America's First Battles, 1776-1965* (Lawrence, Kans.: University Press of Kansas, 1986), pp. 149–185.

Pitt, Barrie. *1918, The Last Act* (New York: W. W. Norton & Company, 1963).

Prior, Robin, and Trevor Wilson. *Command on the Western Front: The Military Career of Sir Henry Rawlinson, 1914–1918* (Oxford: Blackwell Publishers, 1992).

Samuels, Martin. *Doctrine and Dogma: German and British Infantry Tactics in the First World War* (Westport, Conn.: Greenwood Press, 1992).

Smythe, Donald. *Pershing: General of the Armies* (Bloomington, Ind.: Indiana University Press, 1986).

★ ★ ★ ★

Total War
Around the
World

21

GERMANY TRIUMPHANT: RESTORING MOBILITY TO WAR

Military Developments
Between the Wars

The Outbreak of
World War II

Poland

The Scandinavian
Campaign

The French Campaign

World War II was the largest and most costly conflict in human history. It began with the German invasion of Poland on September 1, 1939; it ended on the decks of the battleship *Missouri* on September 2, 1945. By its conclusion the war in Europe had killed approximately 15 million military and 35 million civilians. The Nazis had exterminated 6 million Jews and countless others; 25 million Soviets were homeless; and Allied strategic bombing had wrecked every major German city. In Asia the casualty bill was equally horrendous. No one knows how many died as a result of the Sino-Japanese war; famine, military actions, disease—all combined to raise the Chinese losses to tens of millions. The fire-bombing of Tokyo and the dropping of the atomic bomb on Hiroshima, *each* killed well over 100,000 Japanese.

In a real sense World War II resulted from the desire of three of the major powers to overturn the legacy of the nineteenth century. Germany, Japan, and Italy had come late to the division of the world; World War I served only to exacerbate their frustrations. In the case of all three nations, ferocious ideologies emerged out of national historical experiences and economic collapse in the depression, and extreme ideological nationalism led them to wage merciless war against their enemies. Though initially hesitant to mobilize all its resources, Nazi Germany defined the terms within which it would fight World War II as a total war. In reply, the democracies had to go to equal extremes in order to survive. The cost was terrifyingly high, and if the world that emerged in 1945 was less than perfect, at least it was a world in which the three great tyrannies of Germany, Japan, and Italy no longer existed.

Perhaps the best way to understand warfare during World War II is to think of the period 1914–1945 as a single continuum, for the battlefields of 1939 to 1945 represented a continuation and an amplification of the developments that had occurred in World War I. Except for the final explosion of the atomic bomb, there was little that was revolutionary about World War II. Even the seemingly revolutionary operational employment of tanks by the Germans in 1940 represented the fruition of tactical and operational concepts the Germans had developed in the latter part of World War I. Technological developments largely followed the paths laid out by the last conflict, even though advances in communications, radar, sonar, jet power, proximity fuses, rockets, and other equipment raised technology to new levels. The mobilization of men, women, machines, and raw materials also largely followed the paths laid out in the last conflict. What was different was the harnessing of all resources to the war effort at unprecedented levels and the unparalleled destruction, particularly of civilians and their possessions, in the course of the war. It was not revolutionary tactics or exotic weapons but rather the greater industrial potential and economic strength that won the war. God, as Napoleon had suggested, was indeed on the side with the biggest battalions.

Military Developments Between the Wars

Ground War

With the end of World War I, Europe and the world settled into an uneasy period of peace lasting barely twenty years. With huge arsenals remaining from the Great War, the thinking of most armies remained constrained by the capabilities of weapons left over from the war. As weapons like the tank became more capable, most military leaders simply integrated the improved weapons into old concepts and prepared to fight tightly controlled and relatively static battles reminiscent of the Great War. The Germans, however, prepared to fight mobile battles. By carefully studying the experiences of World War I (particularly the doctrinal developments of the war's last years), they identified the most important innovations of that war and concluded that those innovations provided the conceptual framework for restoring mobility to the battlefield. They also recognized how improved tanks and airplanes could magnify the effect of infiltration tactics and make them even more dramatic. Thus the Germans adapted more successfully than their opponents, devised concepts for mobile warfare, and inflicted crushing defeats on their enemies in the early years of World War II.

Historians have often pictured development of the *Blitzkrieg* as a revolutionary step that took place in the late 1930s; it was not. Almost immediately after the Weimar Republic had settled down, the *Truppenamt* (the title of the disguised general staff) finished a doctrinal manual that crystalized the World War I experience. Completed in 1924, *Die Truppenführung* expertly distilled the tactical and operational methods of World War I and provided the basis of the German "way of war." The doctrine emphasized a number of crucial ideas: (1) the nature of the modern battlefield demands decentralized, mission-oriented orders; (2) speed and exploitation of enemy weaknesses demand that whether on the offensive or defensive, troop commanders use initiative and take advantage of developing situations without waiting for orders; (3) modern warfare demands a close integration and cooperation between combat branches; and (4) commanders must exercise leadership from the front.

The German success in preparing for the next conflict reflected personal as well as intellectual factors. The first commander-in-chief of the *Reichswehr* (the German army during the Weimar Republic), General Hans von Seeckt, was a general staff officer. When the Western Powers dictated a reduction of the German army to 5,000 officers and 100,000 men after World War I, Seeckt confronted the necessity of drastically reducing the officer corps. In so doing he insured that members of the general staff controlled all key positions. This was a crucial step because general staff officers had developed the offensive and defensive doctrine in 1917–1918 that had

Despite the constraints imposed by the Treaty of Versailles, General Hans von Seeckt prepared the German army for highly mobile, offensive operations.

altered the World War I battlefield. Seeckt also focused the army on the offensive. With only 100,000 soldiers, the Germans could not wage a long defensive campaign; instead, the army would become a powerful striking force relying on mobility and surprise, rather than enormous amounts of firepower. In essence, Seeckt shaped the army for what came to be known as the *Blitzkrieg*, and he did this before the Germans had panzer divisions.

Shortly after Adolf Hitler came to power on January 30, 1933, the German military began a massive rearmament program. Given Hitler's program for extensive conquests on the European continent, the army was the centerpiece of German rearmament. In particular, the army's commander-in-chief, Colonel General Werner von Fritsch, and the chief of the general staff, General Ludwig Beck, set the tone and direction of the army effort. They aimed at creating a modern military force and incorporating the experience of World War I in its doctrine, training, and preparation. In no sense was their approach revolutionary. The focus of the buildup emphasized traditional combat branches, infantry and artillery. But their doctrine concentrated on decentralized authority, flexibility, speed, and exploitation, a framework that eventually translated into the basis of modern mechanized warfare.

Between 1933 and 1939, the Germans greatly expanded the size of their army and armored forces. Beck backed the establishment of the first three panzer divisions in 1935, and during the same period he ordered the general staff to conduct a war game on the employment of panzer corps. By 1936 the Germans were studying the employment of a panzer army and in 1938 began forming two more panzer divisions. By the start of the war in September 1939, they had fifty-four active divisions, six of which were armored. But for economic reasons as well as the shortage of petroleum available to the Third Reich, the *Wehrmacht* remained a traditional infantry-dominated army. Nevertheless, its leaders had shaped it into a highly mobile and capable force, the perfect tool for Hitler's aggressive policies.

On the basis of their experiences in Poland, the Germans converted four light divisions into panzer divisions, with motorized infantry divisions backing them up. Still, the army that invaded France in May 1940 consisted of less than twenty motorized and mechanized divisions and over one hundred regular infantry divisions. Nevertheless, all these divisions, including the armored, possessed a common doctrinal conception, and all were prepared to fight highly mobile battles.

German preparation went beyond developing a doctrine for mobile warfare and forming panzer units. The Germans expected all officers to be thoroughly familiar with doctrinal and tactical concepts. Whether in exercises or on the battlefield, units had to live up to the spirit of doctrine. When they did not, commanders instituted rigorous training programs to ensure that standards rose. German officers, however, did not learn to apply doctrine blindly; rather they learned to solve tactical and operational problems by using doctrine as a framework or guide, not as a formula. In accordance with their tradition of *Auftragstaktik*, or mission-oriented tactics, commanders were expected to understand the *intent* of their leaders and to take initiative when necessary to accomplish the mission. Thus in an environment that emphasized decentralization and initiative, the Germans prepared their officers and units to function smoothly on a mobile battlefield.

In Britain the educated elite rejected the possibility that their army might ever again fight on the European continent. Nevertheless, Britain produced two of the more original military thinkers during this period: J. F. C. Fuller and B. H. Liddell Hart. Fuller, a tank officer in World War I, wrote extensively on the potential of the tank. Liddell Hart, an infantry officer in the war, extended Fuller's ideas to suggest the possibility of using tanks not only to break through enemy lines but also to drive deep into enemy rear areas as an exploitation force and disrupt its command and control. Under these two men's influence in the 1920s and early 1930s, the British army carried out experiments with armored test forces. Limited defense budgets, however, made it difficult to fund extensive experiments or form armored units. Additionally, the general unwillingness of the British even to consider another war in Europe made the formation of armored units unnecessary and unlikely. It was difficult to see what armored divisions would do for an army that was going to fight only colonial wars. In the end even Liddell Hart abandoned his advocacy of mechanization and argued for an army that would have no continental role.

Nevertheless, the problems confronting the British army resulted from more than a lack of public interest or funds; some were of its own doing. Not until 1932 did the army establish a committee to study the lessons of World War I. When that committee presented its findings, the chief of the imperial general staff prevented the report from circulating in the army. Throughout the interwar period, the officer corps reflected the stratification of British society; social standing contributed more to advancement than did professional competence and tactical proficiency. The army had no common doctrinal framework within which it prepared for war, and the combat branches went their own separate ways.

The British army did conduct a series of remarkable experiments in the late 1920s and early 1930s to examine the potential of armored warfare. Those tests underlined the potential that tanks offered as well as some of the limiting factors. The British failed, however, to incorporate the lessons of these experiments into the development of their armored forces. Ironically, the Germans learned the most from these efforts and began their armored forces in 1933 based on much of what they had learned from observing the British experiments.

The French developed forces and doctrine very different from those of Germany. Facing a potential enemy with nearly twice the population and much greater economic means, they devoted considerable efforts and resources in the interwar period to ensuring their security. Most noteworthy among their accomplishments was the building of the Maginot Line along the northeastern frontier of France. Composed of huge underground fortresses with elaborate electrical, ventilation, and communications systems, the Maginot Line protected key natural resources and large industrial and population centers along the frontier. Though historians have sometimes blamed the disaster of 1940 on a "Maginot Line" mentality, the defensive line accomplished its strategic purpose of shielding vulnerable areas and permitting the concentration of forces along other parts of the frontier.

The French also spent considerable sums on the development of armored forces; by 1940 they had approximately the same number of tanks as Germany. Instead of concentrating their tanks in large armored formations, however, they spread them thinly across the army. They developed large cavalry divisions that resembled German panzer divisions, but they did not form their first armored division until after the Germans overran Poland in September 1939. After devoting years to careful analysis and experimentation, the French prepared to fight methodical battles in which infantry, artillery, and tanks remained under the tight control of higher commanders and moved short distances from phase line to phase line. Thus the French tried to control the battlefield and their troops in a fashion that the battles of

1918 had already proven unrealistic. Their excessive emphasis on firepower robbed subordinate commanders of initiative and flexibility and ruled out the possibility of any grand maneuvers.

The Soviets provide an interesting and tragic contrast. Arising out of the collapse of 1917, the Red Army, largely created by Leon Trotsky, had beaten back both its Russian opponents and invading Poles in 1919–1921. The Soviets then had to create a military organization loyal to the revolutionary regime. Even within the Red Army, serious disagreements existed as to what kind of forces the Soviet Union required for its defense in a hostile world. A substantial group, centered around former tsarist officer Mikhail N. Tukhachevskii, pushed for creation of an elite force on the leading edge of emerging technology and military thinking. Under Tukhachevskii's leadership the Red Army created its first armored divisions in 1931 (four years before the Germans) and organized large-scale paratrooper drops for the 1935 and 1936 maneuvers.

But the idea of a mass conscript army still appealed to many; as a result, the Soviets vacillated and followed both paths. A series of five-year plans, launched by Stalin in 1927, forced the industrialization of Russia and aimed at providing an economic base to support great military forces. But in May 1937, Stalin loosed his secret police on the Soviet military. A devastating purge savaged the army; Tukhachevskii and virtually all of the modernizers died in front of firing squads. The doctrine developed by these "traitors" also had to go; 1939 found the Soviets busily dismantling the Red Army's armored divisions at the moment that the Nazi panzer divisions were winning their first successes.

In many ways the experiences of the U.S. Army in the interwar period reflected those of the British army. In the early 1920s, Congress had passed the National Defense Act which, had it been implemented, would have provided a framework for developing coherent military forces. But it was not implemented. Instead, as "normalcy" tightened its grip on the American public, defense budgets steadily declined in the 1920s; the arrival of the depression in 1929 further decreased funding available to the military. In the 1920s, with a relatively benign international climate, there was some justification in the disinterest that politicians and public displayed toward the military. But the continuing disinterest in the 1930s as war approached is indeed difficult to explain.

The army in the interwar years confronted no opponents. The Indian wars had ended years earlier, and the Filipinos awaited independence. In small, isolated posts scattered around the United States and its possessions, the interwar army possessed neither equipment, nor funding, nor force levels to prepare seriously for war. As one historian of the army has suggested, "The Army during the 1920s and early 1930s may have been less ready to function as a fighting force than at any time in its history."*

---

*Russell F. Weigley, *History of the United States Army* (New York: Macmillan, 1967), p. 402.

So parsimonious was Congress that the army's annual report for 1934 indicated that it possessed only *fourteen* post–World War I tanks.

Nevertheless, if the army had little chance to experiment with new ways of war, it did develop extraordinary officers who emerged in World War II to lead great citizen armies. Its educational system also provided a framework within which to think about the next war. If its intellectual preparations were weaker than those in Germany on the tactical and operational levels, it is clear that American officers developed an understanding of strategy and logistics that the German officer corps never possessed. Virtually all the important commanders of World War II served lengthy terms in the army's various schools. That intellectual preparation paid enormous dividends when war arrived.

Air War

All of the missions that make up the employment of air power had appeared by 1918. Strategic bombing, interdiction, close air support, reconnaissance, air defense, and air superiority had all played roles in aerial combat during World War I. Yet the full potential of air power, as well as its limitations, remained unclear. Despite the ambiguities that existed within the body of military experience, advocates of air power argued that air forces would be the dominant military force in future wars and that armies and navies would be of little significance. They believed that air power offered a cheap and easy path to victory and an alternative to the costly attrition of the trenches, but only if nations employed air power as a unified force to break the enemy's will. Air forces, in the view of theorists, must not fritter away their strength in supporting ground forces in defending one's own territory, or even in gaining air superiority; instead of "tactical" missions to support the army (or navy), the single proper role for air power must be "strategic" bombing.

Yet within this dogmatic framework, British and American views diverged significantly on the choice of targets. Like Guilio Douhet (the Italian air power theorist), Sir Hugh Trenchard (the first commander of the Royal Air Force after World War I) argued that the most vulnerable target to air attack was the enemy's civilian population. Trenchard believed that the working class could not stand up to the pressures of bombing; under air attack civilians would rebel and demand peace.

In the United States, Brigadier General Billy Mitchell shaped the tone of relations between airmen and the traditional services. That tone was intolerant and uncompromising. Mitchell and fellow enthusiasts denied that the older services would have a role in future conflicts. Unlike other air-power theorists, however, Mitchell recognized that enemy air forces represented a significant hindrance that an air force would have to defeat *before* it could execute successful bombing operations.

In the 1930s, that basic principle disappeared from the American Air Corps Tactical School. The army school was a hotbed of theoretical musings that created an American strategic bombing doctrine. Its approach did not

Father of the Royal Air Force in Britain, Sir
Hugh Trenchard believed civilians were a
legitimate target of bombers. Destruction of
civilian lives and property, according to
Trenchard, would destroy civilian morale
and alter the entire course of a war.

seek attacks on enemy population centers, but rather on vulnerable sectors of
what planners called the enemy's industrial web. Its argument rested on the
premise that large formations of bombers, unescorted by defensive fighters,
could fly deep into enemy territory and drop their bombs on key industrial
targets (such as ball-bearing plants or oil refineries), the destruction of which
would cause the collapse of the enemy economy. The problem with this
argument lay in the difficulty of carrying out the missions. Could bombers
find their targets (particularly in bad weather conditions) and destroy them;
could they fight their way through enemy air-defense systems without cover
from long-range escort fighters? But the greatest fallacies lay in the arguments that the economies of modern industrialized states were fragile and
easily damaged and that the bomber would always get through.

    In Germany the new leader of the Luftwaffe was Hitler's ruthless
and thoroughly corrupt subordinate, the World War I ace, Hermann Göring,
who aimed to make his air force the most formidable in Europe. The idea of
strategic bombing appealed both to Göring and to the Luftwaffe's senior
leadership. In 1936, however, the Luftwaffe canceled two prototype four-
engine bombers because both aircraft designs were already obsolete. Design
work continued throughout the 1930s on the four-engine He 177, which the
Germans regarded as their future strategic bomber, but a variety of engineering mistakes and technological problems rendered that program a disastrous failure. Thus the Luftwaffe continued to have problems in developing a strategic bombing capability.

    Nevertheless, more so than the British and American air forces, the
Luftwaffe developed a realistic and balanced air doctrine. Partially as a

result of experiences in the Spanish Civil War, the Germans discovered that it was difficult to place bombs accurately on target and that bombing civilians did not necessarily lead to the collapse of morale. In addition, they placed considerable emphasis in their air doctrine on supporting the army. The Luftwaffe preferred the interdiction mission to close air support, but after Spain it also developed the capability to support the army in breakthrough battles. However, through 1940 the Luftwaffe could not support the army's tanks once the exploitation phase had begun.

Naval War

Navies provide an interesting contrast. Their great prophet, the American theorist, Alfred Thayer Mahan, appeared before World War I; by and large navies saw no reason to change their operational approach because of wartime experience. Having developed sonar (called "asdic" by the British—a device that used sound waves to detect submerged submarines out to a range of about 1,500 yards) at the end of World War I, the Royal Navy believed that it had solved the submarine menace and proceeded on that assumption in its planning and preparations for a future war. In 1938, believing convoys would no longer be necessary, it quietly acquiesced to the surrender of western Irish ports essential to convoys in the eastern Atlantic. Ironically, the German navy, having read British pronouncements about ending the submarine menace, believed those reports. Despite their great success with the submarine in World War I, the Germans displayed minimal interest in the U-boat as they rearmed. Also, neither the British nor the German navy paid much attention to air power. British naval air power remained hobbled by the surrender of its assets to the Royal Air Force (RAF) in 1918. Nor did the German navy show much interest in naval air power, and squabbling with Göring's Luftwaffe ensured that the navy received little air support. In both fleets the emphasis remained firmly on the battleship and big gun.

The interesting developments in naval operations came in the Pacific. Both the United States and Japan sensed a great naval clash in the offing. In America, naval airmen, led by Rear Admiral William A. Moffett and helped by Billy Mitchell's wild attacks, convinced more conservative admirals that naval air power represented a significant supplement to fleet capabilities. Much the same thing happened in Japan; by the mid-1930s both navies had developed sophisticated concepts for carrier operations that would soon change the face of naval war.

The Japanese and Americans made significant advances in other areas as well. Both developed amphibious capabilities to seize bases in the wide expanses of the central Pacific. U.S. Marine Corps doctrine provided the departing point for solving the basic problems associated with amphibious war. The willingness to recognize the threat of the submarine was, however, less obvious. The Japanese expended great resources in the 1930s in building up their merchant marine to supply the home islands in case of war; however, they made *no* preparations to defend that merchant marine against

U.S. submarines. The Americans did no better in preparing themselves to meet the threat of U-boats in the Atlantic, even after watching the Germans savage the sea lines of communication to Britain in World War I.

Historians often berate military leaders for preparing for the last war. In fact they would fare better if they prepared for the next war on the basis of what had happened in the last. Unfortunately, they generally do not. Disinterested in the uncomfortable experiences of World War I, military leaders in the 1920s and 1930s preferred for the most part to study what was agreeable and what supported preconceived notions. The results would show all too clearly in the next war.

The Outbreak of World War II

World War I had not solved the German problem, even though defeat in 1918 and the Versailles Treaty hobbled the Germans in the short term. The results of World War I did not limit Germany's long-range potential, for the Reich was still the most powerful nation in Europe. To the east and south, Russia's and Austria-Hungary's collapse had left weak and politically divided states—a region open to German penetration and domination. Only in the west did the Germans have a frontier with a major power, a France weakened by the blood-letting of four years of war.

The Treaty of Versailles did attempt to shackle German potential, but in strategic terms the treaty failed before its signing. Angered by the provisions and burden of the treaty, most Germans refused the obvious explanation for the defeat of 1918 that the Reich had fought the whole world and lost; rather, they believed, erroneously, that their army had remained unbeaten in the field and that defeat had come as a result of traitorous actions by Jews and Communists who had stabbed the front-line soldiers in the back. In the early 1930s the troubles of the newly established Weimar Republic combined with a worldwide depression to destabilize German political life. In the hour of political despair, Adolf Hitler and his evil cohorts grasped the mantle of power.

Hitler brought to office a coherent and consistent ideology. Unlike Marx, Lenin, and Stalin who defined the Left's enemies on the basis of class, Hitler defined evil along racial lines. He believed the Aryan race solely responsible for creating the world's great civilizations and the Jews responsible for subverting and undermining human progress. Moreover, he argued that Germany must acquire a great European empire to provide the living space and resources for the German people; the Reich must acquire land in the east at the expense of the inferior Slavic races, particularly the Russians. In Hitler's vision, the new German empire, free of Jews, would control Europe from the Urals to Gibraltar and from the North Cape to the Alps. This ideologic vision provided the motivation behind the most catastrophic war in human history.

After becoming chancellor in January 1933, Hitler had to consolidate his power and mitigate the depression's economic and social dislocations. Despite the weakness of Germany's position, he embarked on a risky diplomatic course. In 1933, Germany withdrew from the League of Nations; in 1935 it declared conscription and creation of the Luftwaffe; and in 1936 it remilitarized the Rhineland. Hitler also provided the military services with funds to undertake a massive program of rearmament. After all, as he made clear, he was not interested in reestablishing Germany's World War I frontier, but rather in destroying the entire European balance of power.

The rearmament program, however, brought with it considerable economic dislocation. Nazi Germany was a resource-poor nation with few raw materials and limited access to foreign exchange. Consequently the rearmament program ran into trouble almost immediately. In a conference with his military and diplomatic advisors in November 1937, Hitler announced that Germany would have to take greater risks in foreign policy to escape its economic and strategic difficulties; however, he ran into substantial opposition from his ministers of defense and foreign policy and the army's commander-in-chief. Within three months he had dispensed with all three. In the resulting political storm, Hitler doubled the stakes and deliberately manufactured a crisis with Austria. In March 1938, the *Wehrmacht* marched into Austria with no opposition from the French or British. The *Anschluss* (occupation of Austria) brought the Third Reich a number of advantages. Austria possessed foreign exchange, a large untapped labor force, and a geographic stranglehold over Czechoslovakia. Hitler's triumph reduced the political crisis within Germany.

Scarcely had the dust settled on Austria before Hitler turned his attention to Czechoslovakia. Again he courted a crisis, this time to isolate the Czechs, so that the *Wehrmacht* could execute a quick campaign. Hitler's actions alarmed Germany's generals and created strong military opposition to his plans. Throughout spring and summer 1938, the chief of the general staff, Ludwig Beck, wrote a series of memoranda arguing that Germany's strategic situation was desperate; then in late August he resigned in protest. The British prime minister, Neville Chamberlain, resolved to prevent the outbreak of war; he eventually persuaded Hitler to accept the Sudetenland, the German-speaking districts of Czechoslovakia where most Czech fortifications were located. Few in England or France voiced opposition to the Munich settlement at the end of September 1938. Although Winston Churchill strongly criticized the government's policies in the House of Commons, many believed Churchill was a foolish old man for still believing in military power and strategic issues.

The nature of Germany's aims became clear in March 1939, when Hitler ordered his troops to occupy the remainder of Czechoslovakia. Germany's continued economic difficulties lay at the heart of his decision; Czechoslovakia with its foreign exchange holdings and industrial resources offered a tempting target. While the Germans gained much equipment and matériel from their seizure of the remainder of Czechoslovakia (enough to equip eight infantry and three panzer divisions), their actions prodded the

Western Powers into taking action. Hitler's move so outraged the British public that Chamberlain finally embarked on a massive effort to repair Britain's dilapidated defenses and to challenge Germany's expansionary policies. It was too little, too late.

At the end of March 1939, the British precipitously guaranteed Poland's independence. Outraged by this action, Hitler ordered his generals to draw up plans to invade Poland by September 1, 1939. Unlike the year before, the German military fell into line behind Hitler; they raised no objections about the strategic wisdom of invading Poland and unleashing a major war. On his part, Hitler seems not to have taken British and French intervention seriously. As he told his entourage, he had seen his "enemies at Munich and they were worms."

Nevertheless, at the end of August he engineered a pact with Stalin. That deal, the infamous Nazi-Soviet Non-Aggression Pact, divided eastern Europe between the two powers. Germany gained the right to destroy Poland without interference from the Soviet Union; and in return Stalin received eastern Poland, while Finland, Latvia, Estonia, Lithuania and the province of Bessarabia (in Romania) all fell within the Soviet sphere. Stalin also committed his regime to remaining neutral and removed the threat of a two-front war; the Soviet Union would soon send massive quantities of raw materials (grain, oil, manganese, etc.) to prop up a seriously strained German war economy. Stalin clearly hoped that a German-Allied conflict would result in a stalemate, as had occurred in World War I, in which the contending capitalistic powers would fight themselves to exhaustion. The Soviet Union would then be able to step in and dominate what was left of Europe. As for Hitler, the deal promised him peace in the east after he had conquered Poland and enabled him to face the Western Powers with his full strength if they intervened on Poland's behalf.

By August 1939, circumstances had set the stage for another great European war unleashed by German actions, this time motivated by Nazi ideology. Hitler had determined to create a Nazi hegemony from the Urals to Spain. The Germans, along with various lesser Aryan nations, would rule the Reich and exterminate other "subhuman" races such as the Jews and Gypsies. There would be no pity and no quarter; the racial crusade began the moment the Germans crossed the border into Poland.

Poland

On September 1, 1939, the *Wehrmacht* precipitated World War II by attacking Poland. Vigorous German offensive action broke the Polish defenses, while the Luftwaffe struck Polish air bases. Heavy air attacks also occurred against military targets in Warsaw; these attacks were accompanied by considerable collateral damage and casualties among the civilian populace—not surprising given the current technology. On September 3, the governments of Britain and France honored their obligations to the Poles and declared war on Germany. Hitler's gamble that swift military action, the Nazi-Soviet Pact, and the Western Powers' own reluctance to go to war would deter a larger war had failed.

Planning for the attack on Poland had begun in April 1939 in response to Britain's guarantee of Polish independence. Given Germany's great advantages (among others the Reich bounded Poland on three sides), operational planning did not require military genius. The OKH (*Oberkommando des Heeres*, army high command) created two army groups, North and South, to break into central Poland. Army Group North, under Colonel General Fedor von Bock, consisted of the Third and Fourth armies; its assignment was to cut the Polish Corridor—the sliver of Polish territory separating East Prussia from the rest of Germany—and threaten Warsaw from the north. Bock's army group held the 10th Panzer Division in reserve and General Heinz Guderian's XIX Panzer Corps (one panzer and two motorized infantry divisions) for its mobile operations.

The main attack came from Army Group South, commanded by Colonel General Gerd von Rundstedt; it consisted of Eighth, Fourteenth,

Campaign in Poland, September 1939

and Tenth armies. The first two would protect the flanks of the main drive launched by Tenth Army against Warsaw in the heart of Poland. Of the fifty-five German divisions, Army Group South had twenty-eight, including thirteen in Tenth Army and eleven in Fourteenth Army. The seven panzer divisions were spread among the five German armies.

The Poles were in an impossible strategic situation; their whole country was a flat plain. The only defensible feature was the Bug River, but it lay so far to the east that a defense along it would have forced the Poles to surrender everything of political and economic value before the fighting even began. Unwilling to surrender their territory, Polish leaders chose a forward defense, thereby allowing the Germans to divide the Polish army and defeat it in piecemeal fashion.

Not fully mobilized and spread thinly across a lengthy frontier, the Poles put up a stout resistance. Nevertheless, German armored and motorized units soon broke through. Army Group South achieved the greatest success. By the end of the first day several of its forward units had advanced fifteen miles, and within the first days, its tanks had breached frontier defenses and gained operational freedom. By September 6, its panzer units were halfway to Warsaw and had isolated Polish forces in the Posen sector. Meanwhile, Army Group North sliced across the Polish Corridor. While some elements drove toward Warsaw, Guderian's panzer corps moved across East Prussia and advanced deep behind the Polish capital; this move destroyed the possibility of a sustained resistance behind the Vistula River.

From the air, the Luftwaffe hammered enemy ground forces. In the air-to-air battle, superior numbers quickly told. Along with winning air superiority, the Luftwaffe interdicted the Polish railroad system and severely restricted frantic Polish efforts to complete their mobilization, while close air-support strikes helped the army in its efforts to penetrate Polish defenses. Thereafter, the Luftwaffe found it difficult to provide close air support in the mobile environment, largely because communications between ground and air forces were completely inadequate. Yet air strikes against Polish troops attempting to concentrate west of Warsaw were so effective that the Poles collapsed entirely in that sector.

German breakthroughs and relentless exploitation broke Polish resistance within one week. When the Polish high command moved from Warsaw on September 7, it completely lost control of its military forces. Eager to participate in the victory, the Soviet Union moved into eastern Poland on September 17 to "protect" the local population. By the end of the month Polish resistance had ceased; the Poles had lost 70,000 killed, 133,000 wounded, and 700,000 prisoners. German losses were only 11,000 dead, 30,000 wounded, and 3,400 missing.

The process by which the German army examined its performance after the Polish campaign suggests why it did so well on the battlefields of World War II. By early October, the OKH had gathered "after action" reports from the army groups down to the regimental level; it then established a rigorous training program throughout the entire army to correct the deficiencies and doctrinal weaknesses that after-action reports had highlighted. Over the next six months the OKH ensured that subordinate commands executed that program rigorously. From October 1939 through April 1940 the army trained ruthlessly and endlessly (sixteen hours a day, six to seven days a week), and when the *Wehrmacht* came west in May 1940, few armies in the twentieth century have been as well trained or highly disciplined.

German success did not come from a revolutionary secret developed in the interwar years; rather, it rested on the firm foundation of a coherent, modern doctrine emphasizing speed, exploitation, combined arms, and decentralized command and control. Nonetheless, the Germans had many improvements to make in both their doctrine and their battlefield performance. For example, they emphasized combined arms by including infantry and tank regiments in their panzer divisions, but they did not perfect the combining of those arms until the 1940 campaign in France.

From the beginning, the invaders embarked on Hitler's ideological crusade. Atrocities, unseen by Europeans for centuries, fell on Jews and Poles alike; Hitler demanded the liquidation of Poland's ruling and intellectual elite, an effort that Stalin's NKVD (secret police) pursued with equal enthusiasm in the east. Senior generals had full knowledge of what the Nazis were doing. The chief of the general staff, Franz Halder, noted in his diary after a speech by Hitler: "Poland is to have its own administration. It is not to be turned into a model state by German standards. Polish intelligentsia must be prevented from establishing itself as a new governing class. Low

The Panzerkampfwagen IV had a short-barreled 75-mm gun, weighed about twenty tons, and had a range of about 125 miles. It was the best German tank in the Polish and French campaigns. Throughout the war the Germans considered it a useful tank.

standards of living must be established. Cheap slaves." An even darker fate awaited the Jews.

The Allied Powers did almost nothing as Poland went down to defeat. They never intended to launch a major offensive into Germany this early in the war. Instead, they concentrated on mobilizing and preparing their forces and hoped to halt the Germans when they turned toward the west. A major offensive would occur only after they had halted the German attack in the west. In the meantime, the French sent out patrols that did not even reach the outpost line of the West Wall, despite the fact that one of Germany's key economic districts, the Saar, lay on the other side of the frontier. This lack of action allowed the German war economy to utilize the Saar's industries unhindered for the first nine months of the war. Similarly, Allied politicians and military leaders refused to undertake any action against German imports of Scandinavian iron ore, and they found numerous reasons to allow the Italians to escape into neutrality. Quite rightly the Western media dubbed the period between the defeat of Poland and the following spring as the "phony war." Failure to exert any pressure on the Germans allowed the Nazis to husband their military strength and mitigate their serious economic problems until the great throw of the dice in spring 1940.

The Scandinavian Campaign

While the Germans and the Western Powers faced off inconclusively in central Europe, the Soviets moved against the Baltic states. In fall 1939 they demanded that the Baltic republics allow Red Army garrisons on their territory. Lithuania, Latvia, and Estonia acceded. The Soviets then demanded that Finland cede territory and make similar concessions. The Finns agreed to the cession of territory but refused any terms that compromised their independence. A furious Stalin ordered the invasion of Finland; the time of year (late November) speaks volumes for Stalin's arrogance as well as a misplaced belief that the Finns could hardly wait to join his "workers and peasants' paradise."

Instead of an easy victory, the Red Army suffered humiliating defeat. From December 1939 through March 1940, the Soviets hurled tens of thousands of troops against the Finns. Relying on massive amounts of artillery and human wave attacks, the Soviets finally broke Finnish resistance. The poor performance of the Red Army in the Winter War underlined its weaknesses, particularly in terms of leadership and initiative, direct results of the purges from 1937 to 1939. Soviet troubles in Finland also reflected a hasty mobilization, lack of preparations, and the difficult conditions in the theater. The Red Army's performance in Finland misled the Germans who overlooked the skillfully executed operations of the Soviets against the Japanese at Nomonhan in August 1939.

The Winter War focused attention on Scandinavia. In February 1940, British destroyers sailed into a Norwegian fiord to rescue Allied merchant sailors imprisoned on a German supply ship. The commander-in-chief of the German navy, Admiral Erich Raeder, had been pressing for a campaign to seize Denmark or Norway to outflank Britain and provide U-boat bases to strike deeper into the Atlantic. Hitler now gave his enthusiastic approval for an attack on Scandinavia in early spring.

Denmark represented no significant problem because of its proximity to the Reich; the attack on Norway, however, required an intricately coordinated operation. The Germans had to capture the major harbors and airfields in Norway before the Royal Navy could react. Supply ships and oilers had to move out in advance of attacking forces—transported by warship—and arrive concurrently with naval units. For one of the few times in the war the Germans placed a joint operation under control of the OKW (*Oberkommando der Wehrmacht*—armed forces high command). General Nikolaus von Falkenhorst commanded the landing and ground operations.

All in all, *Weserübung* (code name for the attack) was a risky operation. On D-1 the Norwegians and British possessed clear intelligence that the Germans were launching a major operation in the North Sea. The former, however, failed to mobilize despite the fact that German soldiers had washed ashore on a beach in northern Norway from a supply ship sunk by a Polish submarine. The Royal Navy picked up the German navy's movement into the North Sea but interpreted the intelligence as indicating that the Germans were breaking out into the Atlantic.

Denmark fell with hardly a shot—not so for Norway. Even before the operation began, a British destroyer had rammed and seriously damaged the heavy cruiser, *Hipper*. The naval force running the Oslo fiord met unexpected opposition from the ancient forts guarding the passage and had to retreat and land its remaining troops at the mouth of the fiord after losing the new heavy cruiser, *Blücher*. The Norwegians failed to utilize the respite. Their cabinet ordered a mobilization by mail; and no one thought to block Oslo's airport. By mid-morning German paratroopers had seized the Oslo airfield and the Luftwaffe rushed in troops by Ju 52s (the German transport aircraft); within five or six hours the Germans had bluffed their way into the capital. By that time, the Norwegian government had fled and resistance had begun throughout the country. The Germans achieved greater success elsewhere in Norway. Luftwaffe strikes silenced coastal defenses, paratroopers seized major airports, and the navy grabbed other ports without serious losses.

In the early morning hours of April 10, however, a small force of British destroyers followed the German picket destroyers up the Narvik fiord; in a fierce gun duel they sank four out of ten of the enemy destroyers and all the German tankers. The surviving ships were trapped. Within the week, the battleship *Warspite* sank the remaining German destroyers in Narvik, a force that contained half the destroyers in the German navy.

Despite these losses, the Germans held all the cards, for they controlled the major ports and airfields. The Allies launched two unsuccessful expeditions to drive the Germans from northern Norway. Near Trondheim 240 miles from Oslo, British troops landed but accomplished little. Farther north, an Anglo-French expedition enjoyed more success against German

Scandinavia, April 1940

0   200   400 mi
0   200   400 km

ATLANTIC

OCEAN

Narvik

Bodo

Trondheim

NORWAY

Bergen

Oslo

SWEDEN

Stockholm

Sola

Kristiansand

North
Sea

DENMARK
Copenhagen

Baltic
Sea

FINLAND

ESTONIA

LATVIA

LITHUANIA

East
Prussia

GREAT
BRITAIN

London

NETHER-
LANDS

BELGIUM

Berlin

GERMANY

POLAND

mountain troops in Narvik, but by the time the Allies took the port (early June) disasters in Western Europe had led to the collapse of the entire effort in Scandinavia.

Meanwhile in early June, despite intimations that an invasion of Britain might be necessary, the German navy launched its two battle cruisers, the *Gneisenau* and *Scharnhorst*, to influence what it regarded as the coming postwar budget debates. They did sink the British aircraft carrier *Glorious*, but both received such extensive damage that they remained in dry dock until December 1940. Whatever its success in Norway, the German navy had suffered irreplaceable losses. At the end of June 1940, it had only one heavy cruiser and four destroyers operationally ready, a force totally inadequate to support a successful landing on the British Isles.

Norway provided few strategic gains for Germany. In the short run the campaign ruled out an amphibious operation against the British Isles; in the long run, it represented a drain on resources that the Germans could have better utilized elsewhere. By 1943, Norway was tying down hundreds of thousands of troops to no useful purpose. After the fall of France, neither the submarine bases nor the secure route for Swedish ore proved to be of crucial strategic importance in the unfolding war.

The French Campaign

Victory over Poland confronted the Reich with serious economic and strategic difficulties. Underlining the Germans' predicament was the fact that the military had done little contingency planning for a campaign in the west. Therefore, Hitler's demand that the *Wehrmacht* launch a fall campaign against the Western Powers caught his senior military advisors with no operational plans and an army unprepared for a major campaign. Consequently, German military leaders argued furiously with their Führer to delay the fall campaign until the following spring; they did not, however, dispute Hitler's strategic or political assumptions. Instead they argued their case entirely on operational and tactical grounds.

Hitler had no clear conception or objective for a campaign in the west; rather, he believed that the Western Powers lacked the political stomach for a great war. Thus he directed the OKH to seize the Low Countries and northern France to the Somme River so that the Luftwaffe and navy could attack the British Isles. Hitler obviously hoped that such a strategy would drive Britain, led by Chamberlain, from the war. Once Britain withdrew from the war, Hitler believed France would not continue the fight alone. In no respect did the initial directive aim to destroy Allied ground power on the Continent; nor was it a replay of the Schlieffen Plan.

When the OKH completed its plan for taking the Low Countries and driving the French back to the Somme, no one concerned, neither Hitler nor the generals, was happy with it. Nevertheless, arguments between Hitler and his generals focused on the readiness of the army for a campaign in the west rather than on German strategy. German military leaders, on the basis of after-action reports from the Polish campaign, remained extremely concerned about the readiness of their forces, particularly the infantry. Despite their objections, Hitler insisted on the launching of an immediate offensive, and on a number of occasions the *Wehrmacht* rolled up on the frontier and prepared to attack with a fundamentally flawed strategy. Only bad weather prevented the Germans from making a serious mistake. Arguments in the high command continued into January, when a courier aircraft, carrying a staff officer and the German plan, went astray and crash-landed in neutral Belgium. The operational details consequently fell into Allied hands. Only at this juncture did the generals persuade Hitler to call off the attack until spring, and a fundamental operational reassessment began.

By January, Hitler had already conceived of launching a major attack through the Ardennes, the heavily forested and rolling countryside between the Maginot Line in northeast France and the flat countryside of western Belgium. His intuition received support from Army Group A's chief of staff, General Erich von Manstein, who independently concluded that a drive through the Ardennes with armored forces could split the Allied front and offer enticing operational prospects. But such a plan possessed considerable risks; if the Allies reinforced the Ardennes quickly, the Germans would not be able to fight their way into the open beyond the Meuse River.

The OKH found Manstein's proposal, supported by his commander, Rundstedt, both self-serving and risky. But after a series of debates with Hitler, a number of war games, and serious reconsiderations within the OKH, the Germans expanded the Ardennes conception to include nearly all the panzer and motorized forces. In the north, Army Group B, under Bock, would seize Holland and advance into western Belgium in order to fix Allied attention on that area. Meanwhile, Army Group A would push its panzers through eastern Belgium and the Ardennes as rapidly as possible; if all went well they would break into the open on the west bank of the Meuse River before the Allies could react. The success of the daring strategy rested on the Germans' moving large armored forces through the Ardennes and over the Meuse before the Allies could concentrate additional forces along the Meuse and trap the Germans in the Ardennes.

While the Germans hammered out their plans, British and French commanders also prepared for the coming battle. They carefully coordinated their strategy and prepared for French forces to hold along the Maginot Line while a combined French and British force rushed forward into Belgium. The Allies, expecting the Germans to launch their attack through central Belgium, much as they had done in 1914, placed few forces along the Ardennes. It was not that the French failed to see that the Germans might attempt a breakthrough in the Ardennes; rather, they believed they could concentrate reinforcements along the Meuse before the Germans could move large forces through the Ardennes and achieve a breakthrough. As the French prepared to fight a methodical battle with a highly centralized command and control system, they failed to recognize the effect that mechanized forces would have on the tempo of operations. Nothing underlines more clearly their misunderstanding of German mobility than General Maurice Gamelin's decision to move his Seventh Army (the only large reserve force available to him and consisting of some of the best mechanized and motorized units in the French army) from its central location near Reims to the far left of the Allied front. Its task now was to move forward to link up with the Dutch. Thus, for strategic reasons of dubious merit, Gamelin dispersed the French operational reserves.

The armies that clashed in 1940 disposed of relatively equal numbers of troops; the Allies, in fact, possessed more tanks, the Germans more

Disposition of Forces and Plans, May 10, 1940

aircraft. But equivalency in forces hid a number of German advantages. On the Allied side, British and French armies had begun to work together only in 1939. The Belgians and Dutch entered the war only after the Germans began their offensive; little or no consultation on either strategic or operational matters had occurred before the Germans struck. Consequently, under the pressure exerted by the German advance the Allied high command never operated effectively or efficiently. On the other hand, the Germans came west with a coherent operational doctrine and conception, executed with ruthless efficiency. The results reflected the thorough intellectual preparations that the German military had made since World War I.

The Opening Moves

The German attack began on May 10, 1940. The Luftwaffe struck across the length and breadth of western Europe. It aimed first to achieve general air superiority; therefore most of its first strikes hit Allied air bases. These raids achieved some successes but met ferocious resistance, resulting in heavy losses. On the first day the Luftwaffe lost more aircraft than on any other day in 1940 (including the Battle of Britain). Some strikes hit the Allied transportation system to delay movement of reserves; significantly, few attacks struck Allied forces moving forward into Belgium and Holland.

Despite heavy losses, the Luftwaffe not only gained air superiority in the first days but also provided strong support to German ground forces. At dawn on May 10, Ju 52s dropped German paratroopers on a series of major targets; the Germans attempted to seize the main airfield near the Hague and capture the government, thus ending Dutch resistance. The sudden descent failed, however, as the Dutch army responded and drove the paratroopers off the airfield. Nevertheless, the strike at the Hague thoroughly distracted the Dutch. Meanwhile other paratroopers seized the major bridges leading into fortress Holland, so that the 9th Panzer Division could sweep through Dutch defenses and into the middle of the country. By May 15, the Dutch position was hopeless. After the Luftwaffe destroyed the center of Rotterdam, the Dutch, fearing that the Germans would repeat such attacks, surrendered. At the time German propaganda was not slow to draw a connection between terror bombing and the Dutch collapse. But the real credit for the success in Holland rested on the courage and operational imagination with which fewer than 5,000 German paratroopers seized crucial communication points in Holland.

To the south of Holland, Army Group B rolled swiftly into Belgium. Airborne forces aided its advance. In one particularly daring and important operation, 180 German troopers landed by glider on top of Eben Emael, the large fortress in the center of the major avenue of approach into central Belgium. Within hours, they had blinded the fort and opened the way for Army Group B, which consisted almost entirely of infantry divisions. The swift collapse of the Dutch and of Eben Emael, as well as the hammering advance of Bock's infantry in central Belgium, captivated the attention of the French high command and convinced the Allies that the Germans were attacking as they had expected.

The drive through the Ardennes proceeded flawlessly. Because of Belgian neutrality, the French could do little to hinder a German move through the difficult Ardennes terrain. By the evening of May 12, the three panzer corps had arrived on the Meuse; in the north Hoth's XV Panzer Corps reached the river south of Dinant; Reinhardt's XLI Panzer Corps arrived at the mid-point of the panzer fist; and in the south Guderian's XIX Panzer Corps reached the Meuse near Sedan. The first to cross was Hoth's corps. The 7th Panzer Division, driven by its commander, Erwin Rommel, achieved the first lodgement on the west bank of the Meuse. At great cost to its infantry, 7th Panzer battered the French back and began building a bridge for its tanks to cross. Rommel's success opened the way for Hoth's other division, 5th Panzer, to cross; consequently the northern flank of French forces holding the Ardennes began to dissolve. In the center, tenacious resistance savaged the infantry of Reinhardt's panzer divisions; they made a small lodgement but could not get their tanks across.

In the south, Guderian crossed late on the afternoon of May 13 as sustained, heavy air attacks punished French defenders. Of the three attacking divisions, 10th Panzer Division on the left got less than a company across and lost forty-eight out of fifty of its assault boats. On the right 2nd Panzer ran into equal difficulties; only 1st Panzer Division in the center, led by the 1st Infantry Regiment and the army's *Grossdeutschland* Infantry Regiment,

General Heinz Guderian strongly and enthusiastically supported the Nazis. Though his influence over the development of German armored forces is often exaggerated, he possessed a sophisticated understanding of mobile warfare.

fought its way across and onto the heights overlooking the Meuse and Sedan. This gain allowed German engineers to build pontoon bridges, and in the early morning hours of May 14, 1st Panzer began moving its tanks across the river. The 1st Panzer Division's success opened the way for both the 10th and 2nd Panzer divisions to cross.

The French response to Guderian's crossing was late and uncoordinated. Although some infantry units fought with considerable bravery, others offered only token resistance. French artillery units, whose morale had been eroded by Luftwaffe attacks, panicked and ran; reserves in the area, a few battalions of infantry, dissolved. By the time French commanders launched a halfhearted counterattack, units from the XIX Panzer Corps were across in strength. Several divisions, including the 3rd Armored and 3rd Motorized, were available to the French. The corps commander of these two divisions, General Jean Flavigny, ironically a proponent of tanks in the interwar period, failed to launch a counterattack; instead he parceled his forces out along the disintegrating front, where the growing German tide swamped them. On May 14, Allied air launched a massive effort to knock out the pontoon bridges across the Meuse at Sedan; they met tenacious opposition from German fighters and antiaircraft batteries. The RAF lost forty out of seventy-one obsolete "Battle" bombers attacking the bridges; French losses were as heavy. By now Guderian's forces were rolling west in full flood.

The German leadership suffered several cases of bad nerves. On the evening of May 15–16, Colonel General Ewald von Kleist, commander of Reinhardt and Guderian's panzer corps, intervened to stop the exploitation to the west. Kleist was clearly acting at the behest of the OKW, which feared an attack against the flank of the advancing German forces. Guderian objected strongly and received permission to continue his advance. By evening on the 16th, XIX Panzer Corps had reached Marle, fifty-five miles from Sedan (traveling forty miles on that day alone). That evening Guderian received a peremptory order to halt; infuriated, he reported that he was resigning from command of XIX Corps. At that point, Rundstedt stepped in and worked out a compromise that ordered the corps' headquarters to remain in place while Guderian's panzer divisions continued a "reconnaissance in force"—in effect a license to steal.

The French Collapse

Guderian's breakthrough in the south combined with Hoth's success near Dinant to uncork Reinhardt's panzer corps. Once Reinhardt had crossed near Monthermé, the Germans had achieved a breakthrough of massive proportions, one that ran from Dinant to Sedan, a distance of almost forty miles. A giant fist of seven armored divisions then pushed toward the Channel. Throughout the drive to the Channel, Hitler, OKW, and OKH worried that everything had gone too well. Meanwhile small Allied counterattacks on the flanks of the panzer wedge exacerbated German worries. On May 19, Charles de Gaulle's 4th Armored Division caused some temporary dislocation on the southern flank. On the 21st a more substantial strike by British armor hit 7th Panzer and SS *Totenkoph* divisions, but the intrepid Rommel soon restored the situation. In reality the flanks were solidifying faster than the Allies could respond. Behind the armored advance, German infantry divisions pounded down the roads at over twenty miles per day to relieve the screening forces on the flanks. On May 19, 1st Panzer Division reached Péronne on the old Somme battlefield; the next day 2nd Panzer reached the coast near Abbeville. Ecstatic over reaching Abbeville, neither OKW, OKH, nor Army Group A thought to order Guderian to capture the Channel ports. But the Germans had cut off the whole Allied left wing.

Not until after the Germans crossed the Meuse did the French recognize the location of the main attack. But as Gamelin admitted to Churchill on May 15, they had no reserves. In this desperate hour paralysis gripped French leaders. Unable to deal with the speed of German moves, the French high command collapsed. Thus, there was no effective response as the panzer divisions drove relentlessly toward the Channel. Gamelin's failure to halt the Germans resulted in his removal. His replacement, General Maxime Weygand, arrived from Syria tired and incapable of wresting the initiative from the Germans.

By May 23, Guderian was moving up the Channel coast supported by Reinhardt's panzers to the east. The next day both threatened Dunkirk, the last port through which an Allied evacuation could take place. At that point, the OKW issued one of the most controversial orders of the war—its infamous "stop order," halting German armor. After the war German generals singled Hitler out as responsible for the failure to finish off the Allied left wing. In fact, besides the Führer, a number of senior generals, including Rundstedt and Guderian, shared the blame. The German senior leadership worried that the campaign thus far had proceeded too flawlessly and that their armor had suffered heavy losses; consequently it seemed best

to preserve the panzer divisions for the final task of destroying France. A·
the time there was much that supported the decision: the panzer forces were
a strategic weapon of decision, not a siege force, that had suffered heavy
losses; much of France had yet to be conquered; and the panzer divisions
would have to change their axis of advance substantially for the upcoming
campaign.

The halt, however, allowed the British and French to establish a
defense line around Dunkirk and provided the commander of the British
Expeditionary Force (BEF), Lord Gort, time to save the British army. As
early as May 19, Gort had warned London that his forces might have to
withdraw from the Continent. Hardly happy with that communication, the
War Cabinet instructed the navy's command at Dover to gather vessels for a
possible evacuation.

For the next four days Gort maintained the position of a loyal army
commander faithfully executing the orders of the French high command.
On the evening of May 23–24, however, he broke with that role without fully
informing the French and ordered his 5th and 50th divisions (nearly surrounded at Arras) to pull back to the coast. On the next day he used those
two divisions to bolster his left flank, where the Belgians were collapsing.
Gort's decision ended the prospect of an Allied counterattack from the
pocket—an action that French leaders sharply criticized. Despite the con-

troversy surrounding his decision, Gort managed to cover his northern flank and make the Dunkirk evacuation possible.

As Allied forces streamed into the pocket, the British set in motion a full-scale evacuation, Operation "Dynamo." They had already evacuated 28,000 noncombat troops. Evacuation proceeded at full speed, but the British at first failed to extend a helping hand to the French. The French high command exacerbated the situation by refusing to authorize its commanders to participate in the evacuation; nor did it alert the French navy that such an operation was imminent. By afternoon May 29, the British had evacuated a large number of troops, the French none. At this point Churchill stepped in and ordered that British ships share space on a one-to-one basis with the French; but the damage had already been done.

Fortunately for the Allies, things began to go wrong for the Germans. By May 26, no less than two army groups and four army headquarters were controlling attacks on the Dunkirk perimeter. Not until May 30 did the Germans reorganize their command structure and place Eighteenth Army in control of the Dunkirk perimeter. And it was only on that day that they realized the British were getting away. On May 31, 68,000 Allied troops escaped, raising the total evacuated to 194,000. On June 1 a further 64,000 came out; by now virtually all the BEF had escaped. By the time Operation Dynamo ended on June 3, no less than 340,000 Allied troops had evacuated Dunkirk.

The German failure at Dunkirk was also a Luftwaffe failure. Most of its aircraft were still operating from bases in western Germany; as a result they were farther from Dunkirk than British fighters operating from the British Isles. Spitfire and Hurricane attacks were a nasty surprise to the Luftwaffe, which had had pretty much its own way in the campaign. Altogether the RAF lost 177 aircraft during the air battles over Dunkirk, the Luftwaffe 240. The successful withdrawal should not, however, obscure the extent of the catastrophe. As Churchill commented: "Wars are not won by evacuation." While the evacuation spared the British army and permitted it to fight again, the Germans had completely destroyed the balance of power in Europe.

One should not lose sight of the moral parameters of the Nazi conquest in the west. On May 27 a company of the SS *Totenkoph* Division captured one hundred men of the British Royal Norfolk Regiment. They lined the British soldiers up against a barn wall and machine-gunned them; afterward they bayoneted the wounded. German military authorities brought no charges against the soldiers involved in the incident. Along with the destruction of Rotterdam, this murder of British prisoners suggests the brutality of Nazi conquest.

The End in France

By now a deep malaise had spread throughout the French high command and the government. Premier Paul Reynaud had relieved Gamelin, appointed Weygand as his successor, and brought the aged Marshal Pétain back from Spain. But the change in leadership could not halt the expanding disaster, as the *Wehrmacht* turned to deal with the remainder of France. Its panzer divisions, extricated from Dunkirk, redeployed to jump off positions in north central France. Three army groups (Rundstedt's Army Group A, forty-five divisions; Bock's Army Group B, fifty divisions); and Wilhelm Ritter von Leeb's Army Group C, twenty-four divisions; plus twenty-three divisions in OKH reserve fell on a French army of barely fifty divisions.

Army Group B jumped off on June 5. The French had improved their methods of fighting and, despite overwhelming German superiority, put up tenacious resistance. So tough were the defenses in front of Kleist's panzer group that the OKH pulled the entire group out on June 7 and moved it farther east. Not surprisingly, Rommel's 7th Panzer Division captured two railroad bridges on the lower Somme and in a matter of hours was hustling down French roads toward the Seine River. By the end of the campaign, Rommel's forces had swept to Rouen, sidestepped to the coast to put the French IX Corps (including the British 51st Division) in the bag, and then driven on to Cherbourg. In six weeks 7th Panzer Division captured 97,648 prisoners, 277 guns, 458 armored vehicles, and 400 tanks. Rundstedt's Army Group A attacked on June 9 and rapidly swept the French off the battlefield. Guderian drove to the Swiss frontier, while Paris fell on June 14.

The Anglo-French alliance, barely patched together in the late 1930s, collapsed under the weight of defeat. Late on June 16, Reynaud resigned, and Pétain assumed power. Within two hours he asked for an

The British used more than 850 ships of all shapes and sizes to evacuate Allied troops from Dunkirk. They had hoped to rescue 45,000 men but managed to evacuate 340,000.

armistice. A few days later in the forest of Compiègne, representatives of France signed an armistice in the same railroad car in which the Germans had capitulated in November 1918.

*   *   *   *

In the campaigns of 1939 and 1940, the Germans restored mobility to the battlefield and swiftly defeated Poland, Norway, and France. Their success rested less on a revolutionary idea than on an evolutionary process that had begun in 1917–1918. Through intelligent, careful analysis of the experience of World War I and of the possibilities of improved technology, they developed a doctrine for mobile warfare that rested as much on artillery and infantry as it did on tanks. Placing a greater value on maneuver than on firepower, the Germans shaped their army for mobile operations. Unlike the British and French forces, the armor, artillery, and infantry in the German army spoke the same language—one of speed, exploitation, decentralized authority, and ruthless, aggressive leadership.

Yet, the victory over France did not solve Germany's problems. Despite the doctrinal coherence and effectiveness of the German way of war, the *Wehrmacht* remained a hybrid military organization. Of the divisions that invaded France in May 1940, only eighteen were modern motorized and mechanized units; the remainder, over 80 percent of the force, were World War I–style infantry who marched on foot and depended on horse-drawn transport to bring up their artillery, supplies, and baggage. Additionally, German units possessed diverse equipment, most clearly demonstrated by three panzer divisions' being equipped primarily with Czech tanks. And there was scant prospect that the armament industry would be able to replace horse-drawn wagons with trucks or foreign equipment with German-made matériel. German logistics remained weak at best; the devastating nature of their victory in 1940 hid the sloppiness with which the support structure was able to move supplies forward. Some of Guderian's units, for example, had to depend on French gas stations for their fuel in the drive to the Channel.

Nevertheless, the Germans had achieved an important victory that allowed them to escape the economic constraints under which they had operated thus far. To maintain Germany's newly won position in the world, the Germans would have to recognize how vulnerable they remained in the center of Europe. But they did not; instead Hitler, his generals, and many of the German people drew the conclusion that nothing was impossible for the Third Reich. Instead of using caution, they would now reach out to expand the boundaries of greater Germany to the limits of their dreams.

SUGGESTED READINGS

Bond, Brian. *British Military Policy between the Two World Wars* (Oxford: Clarendon Press, 1980).

Corum, James S. *The Roots of Blitzkrieg: Hans von Seeckt and the German Military Reform* (Lawrence: University Press of Kansas, 1992).

Deist, Wilhelm. *The Wehrmacht and German Rearmament* (Toronto: University of Toronto Press, 1981).

Dennis, Peter. *Decision by Default: Peacetime Conscription and British Defense, 1919–1939* (Durham, N.C.: Duke University Press, 1972).

Doughty, Robert A. *The Seeds of Disaster: The Development of French Army Doctrine, 1919–1939* (Hamden, Conn.: Archon Books, 1985).

———. *The Breaking Point: Sedan and the Fall of France, 1940* (Hamden, Conn.: Archon Books, 1990).

Erickson, John. *The Soviet High Command: A Military-Political History, 1918–1941* (Boulder, Col.: Westview Press, 1984).

Glantz, David M. *Soviet Military Operational Art: In Pursuit of Deep Battle* (London: Frank Cass, 1991).

Hurley, Alfred F. *Billy Mitchell: Crusader for Air Power* (Bloomington: Indiana University Press, 1975).

Knox, MacGregor. *Mussolini Unleashed: Politics and Strategy in Fascist Italy's Last War* (Cambridge: Cambridge University Press, 1982).

Liddell Hart, B. H. *History of the Second World War* (New York: G. P. Putnam's, 1978).

Millett, Allan R., and Williamson Murray, eds. *Military Effectiveness*, Vol. II, *The Inter War Period* (London: Allen and Unwin, 1988).

Murray, Williamson. *The Change in the European Balance of Power, 1938–1939: The Path to Ruin* (Princeton: Princeton University Press, 1984).

———. *Luftwaffe* (Baltimore: Nautical and Aviation Publishing Co., 1985).

Murray, Williamson, and Allan R. Millett. *Calculations: Net Assessment and the Coming of World War II* (New York: The Free Press, 1992).

Taylor, Telford. *The March of Conquest: The German Victories in Western Europe, 1940* (New York: Simon and Schuster, 1958).

Trythall, Anthony J. *"Boney" Fuller: The Intellectual General, 1878–1966* (London: Cassell, 1977).

Winton, Harold R. *To Change an Army: General Sir John Burnett-Stuart and British Armored Doctrine, 1927–1938* (Lawrence: University Press of Kansas, 1988).

22

GERMANY ARRESTED: THE LIMITS OF EXPANSION

The Battle of Britain

The War in the
Mediterranean, 1940–1942

Libya and Egypt, 1941–1942

Operation "Barbarossa"

The conquest of France in the stunningly short period of six weeks capped seven years of diplomatic, strategic, and military successes for Adolf Hitler's regime. Though nothing seemed impossible to the victorious Germans, the Third Reich could not strike decisive blows at any of its potential future opponents. Indeed, a careful assessment of Nazi Germany's political and strategic position in summer 1940 would have left cause for sobering doubts; at a minimum it would have concluded that preparations for a long world war, utilizing the entire economic structure of central and western Europe, must begin at once. Instead, the Germans first made a halfhearted stab at solving the British problem by aerial assault, then struck at the Soviet Union, and finally foolishly declared war on the United States. Italian failures also drew the Germans into expensive campaigns in North Africa and the Balkans.

The Germans encountered substantial difficulties in the campaigns against Britain and the Soviet Union. Despite aerial attacks of unparalleled intensity and size, the British proved resilient to air attack and the campaign proved expensive for the Germans in terms of aircrews, aircraft, and industrial resources. In the Mediterranean the British initially met success against the Italians; when more capable German forces and commanders arrived, the opposing forces raced back and forth across the 400-mile North African coastline in seesaw campaigns, but the Afrika Korps failed to drive the British out of Egypt. After the Italians blundered miserably in the Balkans, the Germans intervened and rapidly overran Yugoslavia and Greece, but they failed to extinguish resistance in remote areas. The German airborne attack against Crete also achieved success, but difficulties in the campaign made the Wehrmacht and Hitler leery of such operations in the future. In the east, the invasion of Russia propelled the war to a higher level in terms of numbers of soldiers and equipment involved. Despite initial German successes, the Soviets managed to escape defeat and to bring vast forces to bear against the invaders. As Soviet resistance continued, the Wehrmacht suffered mounting losses and encountered severe logistic problems. By spring 1942 the Germans had won impressive military victories on the ground and in the air, but they had fashioned a noose firmly around their own necks.

The Battle of Britain

Before the House of Commons on June 18, 1940, Winston Churchill warned his fellow countrymen: "What General Weygand called the Battle of France is over. I expect that the Battle of Britain is about to begin." Though most military analysts concluded that it would be a short battle, Churchill did not believe that the war was over. He concluded that crossing the English Channel represented a complex operational problem, which the Germans probably could not solve. Moreover, he recognized that neither the United States nor the Soviet Union could allow a Nazi hegemony over Europe and that Germany's newly won position carried with it inevitable frictions that would result in conflict between the Reich and those two great neutral powers.

Not surprisingly, the British made approaches to both governments. The Soviets, busily engaged in gobbling up the Baltic Republics, in stealing the provinces of Bessarabia and Bukovina from Romania, and in congratulating the Nazis on their successes, exhibited little interest in cooperating with Britain. The United States was another matter. Franklin D. Roosevelt, making an unprecedented bid for a third term with an American people deeply divided over foreign policy, nevertheless made clear over summer 1940 that America was deeply committed to Britain.

By early July, Churchill felt sure enough of Roosevelt to move. With Italy's entrance into the war, the naval balance in the Mediterranean was tipping against the British; not only had the French withdrawn from the alliance, but the British feared that the new regime in France and its fleet might join the Axis Powers. On July 5 the British acted: the Royal Navy seized French ships in British ports; in Alexandria it demobilized and disarmed units of the French navy. Finally, Force H, operating out of Gibraltar and led by battle cruiser *Hood*, appeared off Mers el Kébir in North Africa. The British issued an ultimatum with three options: sink or abandon their ships, join Britain, or be destroyed. The French refused negotiations and were building up steam when the ultimatum expired; Force H opened fire and a deluge of 15-inch shells fell on the French fleet. The attack sank battle cruiser *Dunkerque* and three older battleships and killed 1,250 French sailors. Ironically only two weeks before, French and British troops had been fighting against the Germans.

The attack underlined Churchill's resolve. Not until the end of July, however, did the German high command take the British problem seriously. They then prepared two approaches: first, "Sea Lion," a joint-service, amphibious landing on the British coast; and second, a great air offensive to gain air superiority and wreck Britain's industrial infrastructure. One wonders how seriously Hitler considered the landing in Britain. The Luftwaffe hardly participated in Sea Lion's planning, while the army planned for an invasion the navy could not have supported, even at full strength. The navy, left with only one heavy cruiser and four destroyers after Norway, proposed a landing the breadth of which would not have supported a brigade. Rhine river barges would have transported the landing force. The whole planning process also involved considerable interservice bickering and gross misjudgments. Army planners proceeded as if a Channel crossing were just another river crossing!

None of this bothered the Luftwaffe; Hermann Göring and his commanders planned to win the war against Britain by themselves. At the end of June the Luftwaffe turned to the problem of winning air superiority over the

British Isles. On June 30, 1940, Göring issued general instructions. After redeployment, the Luftwaffe would begin a sustained effort to achieve air superiority. Initial targets would be Fighter and Bomber commands, ground-support echelons, and the aircraft industry. Above all, Göring underlined, the Luftwaffe must attack the RAF ceaselessly.

Unfortunately for the Luftwaffe, it entered battle with an intelligence picture that was faulty in every respect. German intelligence calculated that the Spitfire and Hurricane were inferior to German fighters and that British fighter production was between 150 to 300 machines per month. In fact the Spitfire was equal to the Bf 109, and both British fighters were superior to the Bf 110. British fighter production had also reached nearly 500 machines per month by late summer 1940. Moreover, the Germans failed to recognize the importance of British radar and ground control systems.

Building on faulty intelligence, Luftwaffe operational estimates forecast that four days' fighting would break Fighter Command, and that four weeks would destroy the rest of the RAF and the factories on which British air strength rested. Then the Luftwaffe, bombing enemy cities day and night, could protect Sea Lion, if the British still refused to surrender.

Two German *Luftflotte*, Second and Third, deployed in northern France with 2,600 bombers, dive bombers, and fighters; *Luftflotte* Five with 300 bombers and fighters in Norway would strike at northern Britain. One significant weakness affected German strategy from the start: the Bf 109 could barely reach London, while the Bf 110, a long-range escort, could not face RAF fighters in air-to-air combat. Consequently, the Germans could mount daylight strikes only to London; beyond the capital German bombers could fly only under cover of night.

The British victory in the Battle of Britain resulted from years of thought and scientific preparation. Air Marshal Sir Hugh Dowding deserves credit for much of that preparation.

The fact that the Germans confronted a well-prepared opponent was due almost completely to the foresight of Air Marshal Sir Hugh Dowding. As the RAF's head of research and development in the mid-1930s, Dowding supported development of radar; he also put together the specifications and contracts that resulted in procurement of Spitfires and Hurricanes. In 1937 he took over Fighter Command and in that position created a doctrine and force structure to defend Britain from attack. Thus Dowding fought and won the Battle of Britain with a force whose development he had overseen and whose doctrine and organization he had developed—surely one of the most impressive achievements in twentieth-century military history.

Both air forces had suffered heavily in the Battle of France; the Luftwaffe had lost 30 percent of its bomber force, while the RAF had lost nearly 20 percent of its fighter pilots. But the British enjoyed important advantages. They were defending their homeland; since most air battles would occur over Britain, many British pilots who parachuted would return to operations. Moreover, Fighter Command needed only to hold on until fall when bad weather arrived. To succeed the Germans had to win a decisive victory; even then it was doubtful whether Sea Lion could achieve a successful lodgement across the Channel.

To oppose the Luftwaffe, Dowding possessed approximately 900 fighters, between 500 and 600 aircraft serviceable on any given day. Nevertheless, the disparity between Fighter Command and the Luftwaffe was not as great as it might seem; the Luftwaffe possessed a bare equivalency in Bf 109s and the success or failure of air superiority fighters would determine the outcome. Dowding aimed: (1) to keep his command in being; (2) to fight a sustained battle of attrition; and (3) to prevent the Luftwaffe from impairing Britain either economically or militarily. Half of his fighters defended southern England; a substantial number remained north of London. Throughout the battle Dowding could feed in fresh squadrons and pull back the exhausted.

Over July and early August the Germans built up their tempo of operations. They hoped to clear the Channel and achieve a measure of psychological superiority. They succeeded in the former but failed in the latter. Dowding eventually concluded that committing fighters to cover convoys was too costly; in the meantime Fighter Command achieved valuable experience in how German raids built up and how its own system would react.

On July 21, Göring advised his commanders that the objectives of Luftwaffe attacks should be the RAF and its production base. He also underlined that they should strike Fighter Command's morale and urged that the German fighters possess maximum latitude in protecting bombers. Thus bomber raids would bring up enemy fighters, while Bf 109 sweeps sought out and attacked those fighters. Three days later *Fliegerkorps* I mapped out four distinct missions for the campaign. First would be attacks on Fighter Command. But it also singled out Bomber Command and attacks on imports; finally, independent of the first three missions, it urged ruthless "retaliatory" terror raids against British cities.

Officially the Battle of Britain began on August 13, although the RAF noted a sharp increase in operations on the preceding day. On "Eagle

Day" the Germans directly attacked Fighter Command. The most dangerous attacks struck at radar sites along the coast, but the Germans soon abandoned this avenue as unproductive. By mid-August the British had lost 148 fighters to 286 aircraft for the Luftwaffe (only 105 Bf 109s). German intelligence, however, failed to perceive how British defenses were working. The early air battles should also have alerted the Germans to the weaknesses of their own intelligence; *Luftflotte* Five from Norway received a savage beating from fighters that its intelligence had described as nonexistent.

Adding to Luftwaffe discomfort was a consistent lack of focus and direction. Göring finally recognized the vulnerability of the *Stuka*, a dive-bomber whose lack of speed made it an easy target for British fighters. He made, however, the crucial mistake of tying Bf 109s more closely to the bombers, thus robbing the fighters of their flexibility. Finally, Göring concentrated Bf 109s under Field Marshal Albert Kesselring's command near Pas de Calais. While this shift enabled the Luftwaffe to pressure RAF bases in front of London, it also relieved the pressure on Fighter Command's structure over the rest of southern England.

As the air campaign developed, Dowding altered his operational conceptions. British fighters no longer pursued enemy aircraft over the Channel but now concentrated exclusively on attacking bombers. In the ten days after Eagle Day, Fighter Command lost 126 fighter pilots killed, wounded, or missing, a 14 percent loss. But enemy fighters and bombers were scarcely in better shape. Throughout the last week of August and into early September, the Germans severely damaged British airbases and sector stations in southern England. Fighter Command struggled desperately to maintain its equilibrium despite mounting losses.

The Germans broke first. Discouraged by British resistance, Hitler and Göring, with Kesselring's wholehearted support, switched from an air superiority strategy to strategic bombing in the hope that it would destroy London and sap British morale. The shift came suddenly. On September 7, Kesselring launched nearly 1,000 aircraft on London (348 bombers and 617 fighters). The raid caught British defenses by surprise; Fighter Command's response was ragged; controllers at sector stations initially concluded the Luftwaffe was striking at southern England. As a result, British fighters failed to attack until enemy bombers were on the way back. In swirling dogfights, Fighter Command lost twenty-two more fighter pilots, but the Germans lost the same number along with numerous bombers. Damage in London was frightful, and night raids worsened the loss. But the respite allowed Fighter Command to recover.

One week later, Kesselring launched a second blow at London. This time he ran into a well-prepared and rested enemy, eager to attack the raiders. From the moment the Germans crossed the coastline, British fighters slashed into Luftwaffe formations. Both sides lost equivalent numbers of fighters; the Germans, however, lost forty-one bombers. What made September 15 decisive was the fact that many Luftwaffe bomber crews cut and ran, dropping bomb loads all over Kent. Deceived again by intelligence experts who had erroneously concluded that Fighter Command was beaten, and having suffered heavy losses since May, Luftwaffe crews had had

The British were outraged by the bombing in November 1940 of the cathedral at Coventry and the killing of 554 civilians. Three years later in July 1943, 30,000-40,000 German civilians died under Allied bombs in Hamburg.

enough. Though air attacks would continue, the Battle of Britain was over. The Luftwaffe had not won anything approaching air superiority, and Hitler postponed Sea Lion on September 17. Winston Churchill eloquently expressed the triumph: "Never in the field of human conflict was so much owed by so many to so few."

In retrospect it is hard to see how the Germans might have made a success of Sea Lion, considering the state of their navy and the problems besetting the Luftwaffe. That should not, however, diminish Dowding's accomplishments or the psychological importance of the British victory. Those responsible for Munich and appeasement in the 1930s possessed neither the strategic understanding nor the toughness of spirit needed to make the frightening decisions necessary for the defense of Britain in summer

1940. Only Churchill, called to be the prime minister on May 10, 1940, as German spearheads slashed into western Europe, possessed those qualities. His monumental eloquence and driving leadership imbued the British with the belief that they could win. On the other hand, Dowding's solid, professional leadership ensured that British air defenses made few mistakes. Britain's success made it clear to the world that the Nazis were not omnipotent—a factor of immense importance.

Though the Germans had lost the Battle of Britain, their efforts to cow Britain by terror attacks did not cease; rather, they shifted their emphasis to night bombing. Of all the world's air forces only the Luftwaffe had actually developed the navigational means to bomb in bad weather or at night. Luckily British intelligence provided warning that the Germans possessed such a capability. Through examination of crashed bombers, decryption of German message traffic, and imaginative analysis by a young scientist, R. V. Jones, the British unraveled the German system. Jones convinced his superiors and eventually Churchill of the danger, and as a result British scientists developed effective countermeasures that warped the radio beams on which German navigational systems operated. All this was of enormous importance because British defenses were blind. Air defenses could scramble single-engine fighters in the general direction of incoming bombers, but once airborne the fighters could not intercept their opponents at night. By late 1940 the first experiments with airborne radar were underway, but the sets on which interception depended were unreliable, bulky, and often inaccurate.

The problem confronting German planners in the nighttime offensive was target priority: should the Luftwaffe attack specific segments of British industry such as aircraft factories, or systems of interrelated industries such as imports and distribution, or even popular morale? The nighttime bombing offensive attempted all three strategic aims; not surprisingly it failed. As with daylight attacks, the Luftwaffe lacked either the strength or capability to achieve such wide-ranging objectives, and direct attacks on the British population only spurred the British to pay the Germans back in kind.

The *Blitz* underscored a number of important points. First, the resilience of modern economies and states allowed them to absorb great punishment. Second, the air weapon was a difficult one to wield with precision; achieving accuracy or sustained levels of damage was not easy. Finally, despite claims by airmen that air power would provide an easy solution to the costs of modern war, it was in fact extraordinarily expensive in terms of aircrews, aircraft, and industrial resources.

The War in the Mediterranean, 1940–1942

The focus now shifted to the Mediterranean. For the British the Suez Canal and Gibraltar held the key to their empire in India and the Far East. But

Italy's increasing hostility in the late 1930s forced the British to turn to the route around the Cape of Good Hope. Nevertheless, the greatly increased distances that British shipping had to travel with Italy's entrance into the war gave the British considerable incentive to open the Mediterranean.

The Italians viewed the Mediterranean as *mare nostrum* (our sea) and as the basis for the restoration of the Roman Empire. As such, Benito Mussolini recognized that he would have to expel Britain from Gibraltar and Suez. But fearful of German ambition, he hesitated to request Hitler's aid. Italy would, therefore, begin by fighting its own "parallel war." On the other hand, the Germans, with Hitler's dreams of living space in eastern Europe, had little inclination to look to the Mediterranean for strategic advantage.

Mussolini's Parallel War

On June 10, 1940, Mussolini declared war on the hard-pressed Western Powers. This was a popular move for most Italians, who believed that the British and French had robbed them of the fruits of their victory in 1918. Mussolini's conceptions, as with those of Hitler, were revolutionary. He aimed to use foreign conquest to create a Mediterranean empire and in turn to exploit that "success" to revolutionize Italian society. Mussolini's wars were murderously effective against poorly armed African peoples, but the Italians made only superficial preparations to meet their better armed and prepared opponents. The army focused on defending the Alps rather than preparing for an ambitious and difficult campaign; the air force dreamed of strategic bombing but possessed no ability to intervene in a naval war in the Mediterranean; and the navy felt thoroughly inferior to the Royal Navy.

Because of a lack of strategic and operational planning, the Italians floundered despite opportunities created by the French collapse and British weaknesses. The army's inadequate planning and preparations were symptomatic of all services: Marshal Rodolfo Graziani, army chief of staff, proclaimed in the last prewar conference that "when the cannon sounds everything will fall into place." Such wishful thinking did not make up for inadequate preparation. In the last desperate days of French resistance, the Italians launched a series of ill-prepared attacks on France; lack of success prevented them from taking advantage of the armistice with Vichy France. In early July a force of Italian battleships escorting a convoy to Libya ran into the British eastern Mediterranean fleet escorting a convoy to Malta. Despite advanced warning, greater numbers, and air superiority, the Italians fled in disarray. Arriving late, the Italian air force bombed both fleets indiscriminately but damaged nothing seriously since it possessed no armor-piercing bombs or aerial torpedoes. In September the Italian commander in Libya, Graziani, finally moved on Egypt. A lackadaisical advance got his forces to Sidi el Barrani, fifty miles from his starting point.

Meanwhile, events in the Balkans picked up momentum. Emboldened by the collapse of Europe's equilibrium, the Hungarians determined to regain Transylvania, lost to Romania in 1918. The Germans, given their dependence on Romanian oil, had no desire to see a conflict break out

The Mediterranean Theater

FRANCE

SPAIN
• Madrid

PORTUGAL

Lisbon

Gibraltar

MOROCCO

Casablanca

Oran

Algiers

ALGERIA

CORSICA

SARDINIA

Toulon

ITALY

Rome

Naples
Taranto

SICILY

TUNISIA

Tunis

Tripoli

MALTA

YUGOSLAVIA

BULGARIA

ALBANIA

GREECE

Athens

Cape
Matapan

CRETE

MEDITERRANEAN SEA

LIBYA

Benghazi

El Agheila

CYRENAICA

Tobruk

Bardia

Sidi el
Barrani

El
Alamein

TURKEY

Constantinople

Alexandria

Suez
Canal

Nile R.

EGYPT

QATTARA
DEPRESSION

0   150   300 km
0   150   300 mi

between those two states. Therefore, with help from the Italians, they imposed a settlement that returned most of Transylvania to Hungary. Rebellion resulted in Romania; the king abdicated and General Ion Antonescu established a military dictatorship. The Germans, confronting a possible Romanian collapse, stepped in to stabilize the situation. At Romania's request, Hitler sent a military mission—one that by December consisted of no less than a panzer division, a motorized infantry division, two flak regiments, and two fighter squadrons. Ostensibly the German "advisors" were there to help the Romanian military; in fact they were there to guard the oil and warn the Soviets against fishing in troubled waters.

The Italian Collapse

Whatever the positive benefits from the move into Romania, it backfired on the Germans, for Mussolini viewed it as a cavalier disregard of Italian interests. As he told his foreign minister Count Galeazzo Ciano, "Hitler always confronts me with a fait accompli. This time I am going to pay him back in his own coin. He will find out that I have occupied Greece." Mussolini then ordered hurried preparations for an attack despite the lateness of the season.

Launched into northern Greece in early November 1940 from Italian-occupied Albania with little logistical support, in most cases with no winter clothing, and with numerical inferiority, the Italians marched straight into defeat. After initial successes, a combination of bad weather and Greek numerical superiority led to a general collapse. The Italian air force, with neither the inclination nor the preparation to support the army, confined its efforts to terror attacks on Greek cities. A string of incompetent commanders, including General Uboldo Soddu—who whiled away evenings in Albania by writing musical scores for movies—failed to rectify the situation. Not only had Mussolini upset the delicate balance in the Balkans, but he also had made British, and perhaps Soviet, intervention possible. The threat to Romanian oil was obvious; given winter conditions, Germany could do little.

Mussolini's run of troubles, however, had barely begun. On the evening of November 11–12 British torpedo aircraft from the carrier *Illustrious* struck the naval base at Taranto and sank half the Italian battle fleet. With this stroke the balance in the Mediterranean swung permanently in Britain's favor. One month later the British army attacked in North Africa. What the theater commander, General Sir Archibald Wavell, intended as a mere raid resulted in a complete rout of Italian forces. Mutually unsupporting positions around Sidi el Barrani collapsed before the onrush of the British 7th Armored and 4th Indian Divisions driving rapidly westward. Though Italian forces were on the run, Wavell pulled 4th Indian out of the line and transferred it to the strategically useless campaign in Ethiopia. The two-week period during which British forces reorganized was not enough for the Italians to recover; but it did, however, allow the Germans to get across the Mediterranean to Tripoli.

In early January British forces resumed their advance into Libya. Tobruk fell with startling suddenness. As the Italians hustled down the coastal road past Benghazi in a desperate retreat toward Tripoli, the 7th Armored Division sliced across the desert, caught the Italians at Beda Fomm, and destroyed what was left of Mussolini's African army. British forces advanced to El Agheila, where they halted; they had advanced more than 400 miles. There Wavell helped others persuade Churchill that his troops could not reach Tripoli and that the British should aid Greece as quickly as possible. Nevertheless, the British, for a loss of only 2,000 men, had captured 130,000 Italians and stripped the last pretensions of competence from Mussolini's military forces.

The Germans Arrive in the Mediterranean

Italy's disasters in early 1941 threatened to undermine the Axis position in the Balkans and Mediterranean. In response, Hitler's strategy had strictly limited aims: restore a collapsing situation in the Mediterranean; prevent Italy's collapse; and protect the southern flank of German forces gathering for the invasion of the Soviet Union. Since conquering the Soviets represented the heart of Hitler's revolutionary goals, there was no serious consideration among the Germans of alternatives to the eastern campaign.

The commander of the forces deployed to North Africa in early 1941, soon called the Afrika Korps, was a newly promoted lieutenant general, Erwin Rommel. Rommel had had a spectacular career in World War I. In the interwar period he remained in the infantry, but after the Polish Campaign, assumed command of 7th Panzer Division. In the French campaign, Rommel played a crucial role in the breakthrough along the Meuse River. As a reward, he received command of the corps-sized force deploying to aid the Italians. Rommel's orders were defensive; he was to protect Tripoli and support the remnants of the Italian army in North Africa. But Rommel believed that he must strike or be destroyed; he would soon emerge as the war's premier field commander.

Characteristically, Rommel disregarded his instructions and attacked even though only one division had arrived. Coordination between British units new to the theater collapsed in confusion, and Rommel surged east across Libya. By the end of April the Germans had chased Commonwealth forces almost 400 miles and driven them out of Libya except Tobruk. By holding that port, the British complicated the Germans' logistical problems; for the next six months Rommel found himself caught between Egypt's frontier defenses and Tobruk; he was unable to deal with either satisfactorily. Nevertheless, with only one motorized division he had restored the Axis position in North Africa and rocked the British; he had driven his opponents back to where they had begun.

In the Balkans geography constrained Axis actions. Given the limited logistic capacity of Albania, the Italians could not funnel sufficient troops and equipment directly to the front facing the Greeks. To advance against the Greeks, the Germans had to move through Yugoslavia or Bulgaria. The need for action became more critical in March 1941 when British troops arrived at Athens to reinforce the Greeks.

After Erwin Rommel arrived in North Africa in February 1941, he demonstrated a remarkable mastery of mobile operations, but he could not overcome the greater numbers of the Allies and his own shortages of supplies and fuel.

As the Germans built up Field Marshal Sigmund Wilhelm List's Twelfth Army in Bulgaria for its April attack, German diplomats assuaged Turkish fears and intimidated the Yugoslavs into joining the Axis on March 25. But on the evening Yugoslav negotiators returned to Belgrade, Serbian officers overthrew the government. Wildly cheering crowds in Belgrade, bedecked with French and British flags, underlined the mood. Within hours, Hitler ordered the OKW, the armed forces high command, to "smash Yugoslavia." By evening, after conferences with Field Marshal Walther von Brauchitsch (the army's commander-in-chief) and Göring, the Führer signed Directive 25 requiring that Yugoslavia be "beaten down as quickly as possible." Hitler also ordered the Luftwaffe to destroy Belgrade.

German planning rapidly adapted to changing circumstances. Within one week, OKH, the army high command, had altered Twelfth Army objectives to include southern Yugoslavia. Meanwhile, Second Army established itself in Austria and Hungary so it could execute a major attack from the north. As panzer forces from the two armies concentrated their thrusts from the south and north on Belgrade, German infantry would overrun the remainder of Yugoslavia. Along with ground deployments came extensive Luftwaffe redeployments. The code name for the aerial assault on Yugoslavia was "Punishment," an accurate reflection of Hitler's fury. By the time the Luftwaffe had completed attacks on Belgrade, 17,000 people had died.

From the onset the Balkan campaign split into two separate operations: the conquest of Yugoslavia and that of Greece. Fortunately for the Germans, the Yugoslavs failed to mobilize; the ferocious air attacks on Belgrade shattered the government; and the Yugoslavs attempted to defend their

Messerschmitt Bf 110 fighters supporting German operations in Yugoslavia in March 1941. The Germans had great hopes for the Bf 110 as a multi-role "strategic" fighter, but numerous design flaws limited its effectiveness except as a night fighter.

entire country. But Nazi forces easily broke through their defenses. Within five days the Germans had seized Belgrade as the Yugoslav army collapsed in disarray. Ironically the extent of the success contributed to the undoing of long-range Nazi interests in Yugoslavia; almost immediately, the OKH began recalling units for the operations against the Soviet Union. That process left substantial numbers of armed Yugoslavs in mountains and remote areas. Though the government had ceased to exist, the German victory did not extinguish resistance.

The campaign against Greece was a replica of Yugoslavia; XXXX Panzer Corps outflanked Greek defenses and sent Allied forces pell-mell to the south. The Greek army collapsed, and the British withdrew by sea in the face of the Luftwaffe's overwhelming air superiority. Nevertheless, at the end of April the Royal Navy managed to evacuate nearly 51,000 of the 62,000 British soldiers in Greece.

The Fall of Crete

In retrospect, the strategic prize in the Mediterranean was not Greece but Crete. Possession of that island would have provided a base for RAF raids on Romanian oil fields, as well as a base from which to supply partisan movements throughout the Balkans. The Germans recognized the threat, and as their forces pushed the British and Greeks southward, German planners under paratroop general Kurt Student were already preparing a strike at Crete. Student envisioned an airborne attack on Crete's airfields, supported by coastal landings. But the Italian naval disaster at Cape Matapan at the end of March, where the British sank three heavy cruisers, indicated that any attack on Crete must rely almost exclusively on airborne forces. The final plan was simple: seize the airfields at Maleme, Rhethymnon, and Herakleion with the Luftwaffe's 7th Airborne Division and then reinforce as rapidly as

Crete and Surrounding Region, May 1941

possible with the 5th Mountain Division by using Ju 52 transport aircraft. But there were obstacles: the Allies had more troops on Crete than German intelligence reported; the local population proved distinctly hostile; and "Ultra" intelligence informed the British as to the coming attack.

The British had their own problems: many defenders had just been evacuated from Greece; they were short of equipment; and their morale was hardly solid. And despite signals from intelligence indicating that the Germans would launch an airborne assault on the airfields, Major General Bernard Freyberg, commander of Commonwealth forces, emphasized a defense of Crete's shores from the sea rather than from the air. Nevertheless, the attack on Crete, starting on May 20, almost failed. After its towrope parted, the glider carrying the 7th Airborne's commander crashed well before reaching the island. New Zealand troops at Maleme inflicted prohibitive casualties on the paratroops and retained control of the airfield. Without radios, the Germans at Maleme could not notify Student of their desperate situation. Airborne drops at Herakleion and Rhethymnon that afternoon resulted in an even greater disaster. Finally, Italian naval forces, escorting two convoys of reinforcements, ran into the Royal Navy and lost the troop ships they were convoying.

But the British lost the battle for Crete as a result of decisions taken at the end of the first day. The battalion holding the hill overlooking Maleme retreated, despite the fact that it had suffered no more heavily than its opponents. Freyberg's attention remained fixed on the sea, and few reinforcements reached the airfield's defenders—a period during which German paratroopers were particularly vulnerable to counterattack. Once the paratroopers controlled Maleme, however, they could receive reinforcements and heavier weapons; then the balance slowly but inexorably tilted against Commonwealth forces. Despite ferocious Luftwaffe attacks, the Royal Navy eventually evacuated most of Crete's defenders, but the British had lost a crucial geographical position in the Mediterranean. Romanian oil flowed to the Reich throughout spring 1944, hindered by nothing more than a smattering of air raids.

The German victory cost the paratroopers heavily. Nearly 60 percent of the transport aircraft were destroyed or badly damaged in the attack. Attacking airborne forces suffered such heavy losses that Hitler refused to employ them again as airborne forces until 1944. Ironically the allies reaped the lessons of Crete. On the receiving end of the aerial assault, they were far more impressed by the attack than were the Germans. As a result, much of the doctrine and concepts for British and American paratroop forces were derived from German airborne operations against Crete.

Libya and Egypt, 1941–1942

By late spring 1941 the Germans had achieved their short-term strategic goals in the Mediterranean. Rommel had restored the situation in Libya; intervention in the Balkans had repaired the damage done by Mussolini's invasion of Greece; seizure of Crete had driven the Royal Navy out of the Aegean Sea. But there were long-range drawbacks to these successes. While the Nazis had smashed the Greek and Yugoslav governments, they failed to achieve control of the countryside as the withdrawal to support Operation "Barbarossa" began, nor had they disarmed substantial numbers of the troops in remote Balkan areas—precisely the areas most likely to support guerrillas. On the strategic side, the Germans could not exploit their successes in the Mediterranean because they had already decided to invade the Soviet Union.

As Germany turned from the Mediterranean, the Middle East became a strategic backwater. Hitler now aimed to ensure that Italy remained in the war and to prevent the British from achieving a success that might threaten the Reich's southern flank. Rommel was chiefly responsible for meeting these objectives. Despite confronting considerable odds and having to operate at the end of long, tenuous supply lines, he emasculated much of the British military effort and by early summer 1942 even threatened to destroy Britain's position in the eastern Mediterranean.

Rommel on the Defensive

The British enjoyed a number of advantages that make Rommel's success even more remarkable. With the help of Polish cryptanalysts, they broke into the high-grade cipher transmissions of the German armed forces, particu-

The Western Desert

MEDITERRANEAN SEA

Tripoli

TUNISIA

Benghazi

CYRENAICA

Beda
Fomm

El Agheila

LIBYA

Gazala
Tobruk
Bardia
Sidi el Barrani

Alexandria

El Alamein

QATTARA
DEPRESSION

Cairo

Suez
Canal

Nile R.

EGYPT

| 0 | 150 | 300 mi |
| 0 | 150 | 300 km |

larly those of the air force, in 1940. This message traffic contained information about the plans, combat readiness, and intentions of the German high command, Hitler, and senior commanders in the field. The breaking of German codes for much of the war thus provided the British with clear insights into German strengths and weaknesses. "Ultra" (the code name for decrypted messages from the German "Enigma" cipher machine) often provided the British with pinpoint information on the timing and tracking of supply convoys from Italy to Libya, thus allowing the British to intercept and destroy them. The losses kept the Axis forces desperately short of supplies. Sometimes, however, intelligence from Ultra could be misleading because Rommel frequently disobeyed orders from Italian as well as German high commands. The second British advantage lay in air power. Not only did the RAF posses numerical superiority, but its doctrine, developed by open-minded airmen like Sir Arthur Tedder, enabled the RAF to render effective close air support. Unfortunately, that air support could not rectify the weaknesses of British ground forces.

In June 1941, the British held the port of Tobruk in Libya and a front-line position just inside the Egyptian border. British armored forces held a four-to-one superiority in tanks over the Germans, whose armor was split between Tobruk and the Egyptian-Libyan frontier. Rommel, however, had created a number of tank traps, using 88-mm guns, and German defenses were carefully and skillfully sited. On June 15, Wavell launched "Battleaxe," an operation characterized by caution and inflexibility. Hoping to achieve a breakthrough before Rommel could concentrate his forces, the British attacked along the coastal road to drive straight on to Tobruk. Rommel's shrewdly prepared defenses, however, wrecked the attackers' momentum. By nightfall the British had lost half their tanks, while Rommel's armor, still shielded by antitank guns, had not come into play. A sweeping German counterattack around the British flank then drove British armor back in headlong retreat to its starting positions in Egypt. Battleaxe cost the

British ninety-one tanks, while the Germans lost only twelve (most of which they recovered and repaired).

The failure led to Wavell's removal. His replacement as Middle East commander-in-chief was General Sir Claude Auchinleck whose experience had been with the Indian army. From June through November 1941, Auchinleck prepared for another go at the Afrika Korps. For the first time, the British received substantial American aid to supplement their own equipment. Meanwhile Rommel had received barely sufficient supplies to keep his forces going. The German high command gave highest priority for supplies and reinforcements to the battles in Russia, and British air and naval attacks, aided by Ultra intelligence, proved deadly to Axis sea lines of communication. By mid-fall 1941 the British had established a considerable superiority in weapons and divisions in Africa; the RAF had nearly 700 air-craft against 120 for the Luftwaffe and 200 for the Italians; in tank strength the British had 710 against 174 German and 146 Italian vehicles. British weaknesses had more to do, however, with the intangibles of battle, and those came close to causing another defeat.

Operation "Crusader" began on November 11, 1941. One of Eighth Army's two corps, XIII, was to pin the Germans along the frontier, while XXX Corps swept around Rommel's flank to link up with Tobruk. The plan appeared clever, but in reality it split British armor, already weakened by diversion of a brigade of heavy tanks to support XIII Corps' infantry.

The attack got off to a slow start—so slow in fact that Rommel missed what was happening. When he reacted, he moved with usual dis-patch; he screened off XXX Corps with antitank guns. Meanwhile, the British committed their armor piecemeal, and the Germans mauled it badly. In one action, Italian forces, showing considerable improvement, imposed a heavy toll on 22nd Armored Brigade, which lost 40 out of its 160 tanks. On November 24, Rommel pulled most of his tanks out of the main battle and dashed for the Egyptian frontier.

The balance on the swirling battlefield, however, slowly tilted to the British. Once Rommel's strike at British rear areas had failed to shake his opponents, he had to withdraw. Moreover, pressure exerted by the British from Malta placed extraordinary strains on the Afrika Korps: air and naval attacks sank nearly 80 percent of Axis supply ships crossing in October and November. Rommel's retreat took his forces back all the way across eastern Libya to El Agheila. Though Crusader appeared to represent a considerable turn in the desert war, the success rested on numerical superiority and German logistical difficulties, not from equality in tactics or battlefield performance.

As German forces retreated through Libya, the balance shifted back in their favor. *Luftflotte* Two (Second Air Force) transferred to the Mediter-ranean from Russia and launched a massive aerial assault on Malta. Conse-quently Rommel's forces now received most of the supplies dispatched from Italy. Retreat through Libya also enabled the Germans to fall back on sup-ply dumps and restore their strength while it stretched British supply lines. Finally, Crusader resulted in heavier losses among combat veterans in Eighth Army than in the Afrika Korps.

Rommel Counterattacks

As the British halted near El Agheila in late 1941, having advanced some 400 miles, they repeated their mistake of February 1941: they pulled experienced forces back for rest and refit and pushed brand-new units to the front. Strengthened with new tanks and quick to take advantage, the Afrika Korps came boiling out of its defensive positions in January 1942 and struck the newly arrived 1st Armored Division. That division's three cavalry regiments, newly converted to tanks, knew little about armored operations and less about desert combat; the three British regiments came into play separately and were destroyed separately. The deadly combination of German panzers and 88-mm antitank guns leapfrogging from position to position ruled the battlefield. Rommel's thrust pushed the British back to Gazala, just west of Tobruk, and allowed his troops to reoccupy Benghazi, where both sides, exhausted by two months of combat and movement, settled down to build up for another battle.

In spring 1942, Churchill vociferously pressured his commanders in Libya to attack; Ultra indicated an enormous British superiority in every category of weapon. What intelligence failed to reveal, however, were enemy advantages in leadership, doctrinal coherence, and tactical proficiency. British generals resisted Churchill's urgings and set the date for their offensive in early June; it was too late. On the evening of May 26, Rommel moved, hooking around the British left flank and piling directly into the middle of the Eighth Army.

The British deployment possessed a number of weaknesses. The Gazala Line, approximately forty miles west of Tobruk and held by XXX Corps, reached deep into the desert with its infantry concentrated in strong points, called boxes, protected by minefields and barbed wire. The Bir Hacheim fortress anchored the southern tip of the line. Eighth Army commander, General Neil Ritchie, mistakenly believing that a German attack would come against his center, dispersed his armor to cover both his flank and the expected attack on his center. Auchinleck did suggest a concentration of armor, but Ritchie disregarded the suggestion.

Rommel's move underlines the extraordinary risks he was willing to run; he aimed to encircle the entire Gazala Line and Eighth Army. But things failed to work as he expected. The Germans began on May 26 with a diversionary attack on the center of the Gazala Line where Allied commanders expected an attack; that night the main body of the Afrika Korps moved around the Allies' southern flank. As he moved deep into the Allied rear, Rommel ran into heavy opposition; American M-3 Grant tanks had arrived in quantity and provided a nasty surprise. By the second day, the Germans were in serious trouble. Having moved around the British flank, the Afrika Korps found itself trapped against the Gazala Line with no route through which its supplies could flow; and it was rapidly running out of food, water, and ammunition. Fortunately for the Germans, the British launched a series of piecemeal attacks. Rommel's screen of antitank guns once again devastated British armor, while the panzers remained skillfully camouflaged in hull-down positions. Finally, the Afrika Korps overwhelmed Bir Hacheim

Rommel's operations in the desert relied on the mobility of his tanks, such as the Panzerkampfwagen III. He often massed his armored forces and delivered lightning-like blows against the more numerous but less flexible British forces.

and cleared a passage for supplies. The British had turned a promising situation into a catastrophe after two weeks of fighting.

On June 11, Rommel attacked eastward; on the next day his armor trapped two British armored brigades and destroyed them. A third armored brigade intervened to help its comrades, but again it ran into well-sited German defenses and was also destroyed. Such heavy losses cost the British their advantage in tanks; the Germans now had numerical superiority. Rommel turned north toward the coast and attempted to cut off British infantry withdrawing from the Gazala Line. Though most escaped, their retreat carried them straight to and over the Egyptian frontier in headlong flight.

Chewing its way through the collapsing British, the Afrika Korps headed eastward. On June 19 German forces brushed past Tobruk in pursuit of Ritchie's troops. The port's defenders consisted of 2nd South African Division, the Guards Brigade, and 32nd Tank Brigade with seventy tanks; confident that Rommel was going elsewhere, the defenders settled down. At dawn on June 20 a massive artillery bombardment hit the southeast side of the fortress, followed by the Afrika Korps, which had doubled back overnight. By mid-morning the garrison commander had decided the situation was hopeless and surrendered himself and 35,000 troops.

The Germans confronted the question of what to do next. Luftwaffe air attacks had severely battered Malta, and German paratroopers were preparing to give the coup de grâce. Given Rommel's extraordinary successes, however, did it make sense to stop just as the Afrika Korps rolled up on the frontier with the British in a state of complete demoralization? Rommel argued that he had an opportunity to drive the British from Egypt. Moreover, casualties on Crete, strong British defenses on Malta, and doubts about Italian reliability made an attack on the island a risky affair. Hitler sided with Rommel.

Rommel's pursuit carried him deep into Egypt. Yet his attempt to drive the British out of Egypt ultimately failed. Auchinleck relieved Ritchie and assumed command of Eighth Army. Halting his forces at El Alamein, he established a defensive position between the Mediterranean and the Qattara depression. The new position had no open flank because the Qattara depression, located thirty-five miles south of the coast, was a great salt sea impassable to heavy vehicles. Distances from Libya also complicated the German logistical situation. There at El Alamein in early July 1942 the British held, only sixty miles from Alexandria, and Rommel's slim chances of conquering Egypt faded.

Operation "Barbarossa"

At the end of July 1940, Hitler determined to destroy the Soviet Union. Strategic and ideological reasons lay behind his decision. On the one hand, he recognized that the United States and the Soviet Union represented significant strategic factors that explained British intransigence. But ideology underlay Hitler's decision as well; to him the Soviet Union represented an amalgamation of his greatest enemies, the Jews and Slavs. Not until he had destroyed Stalin's "Jewish-Bolshevik" regime would the biological revolution of Nazi Germany be safe. Finally, according to the Führer's *Weltanschauung*, the Third Reich desperately needed the agricultural and raw material resources of European Russia so that it would no longer have to depend on maritime trade for raw materials and foodstuffs. Without land and space, the German nation, Hitler believed, would never realize its full potential.

Because ideology played a crucial role in "Barbarossa" (the invasion's code name), the Germans came as conquerors, not as liberators; their conquest would bring slavery for Slavs and extermination for Jews. In its wake "special action" task forces of the Waffen SS accompanied each invading army group (three in number) to liquidate Jews, Communists, and other undesirables; these SS units received the wholehearted cooperation of most army commanders. Moreover, the army made its own contribution to the hideousness of war in the east; out of the approximately 3 million Soviet soldiers captured in summer and fall 1941, barely 100,000 survived the war—virtually all were under Wehrmacht, not SS, jurisdiction. The fanatical resistance of the Soviet population in defense of Stalin's malevolent regime largely resulted from the criminal behavior that marked German actions from the onset of Barbarossa.

Planning

By fall 1940 the Germans were deep into planning. The general staff accepted Hitler's assumption that the Wehrmacht could destroy the Soviet Union within one year. Basic to the Nazi approach was a belief that an invasion would catch and destroy the Red Army in the border areas. If that did not occur, several factors would have a negative effect on the course of subsequent operations. The theater itself broadened almost immediately, which would spread out the invaders; moreover, the depths of European Russia would allow the Soviets to trade space for time, while the campaign season itself would be short. Logistic war games gave clear warning that the Wehrmacht would face difficulties in supplying forces beyond a line running from Estonia to Smolensk and into the central Ukraine.

Operational planning by the OKH focused on Moscow as the strategic goal. However, the OKW emphasized that an advance on Moscow would depend on successes on the flanks—clearing the Baltic states to Leningrad and occupying the Ukraine. While differences between OKW and OKH conceptions remained relatively small, Hitler opposed the suggestions of his military advisors. He minimized Moscow's importance and argued that the invasion must achieve success on the flanks: in the north, Leningrad, cradle of the Bolshevik revolution; and in the south, the Ukraine, heartland of Soviet agriculture. To avoid Hitler's ordering a focus on the flanks, Colonel General Franz Halder (chief of the army's general staff) completed the final plan for Barbarossa without addressing this fundamental divergence of views. He obviously hoped that after the first stage of the invasion, the army leadership could persuade Hitler to go for Moscow. Consequently, German conceptions for the invasion contained a significant divergence that the high command refused to resolve until the campaign's mid-point. All of the planning also assumed that the Germans would destroy the Red Army in the border areas.

For the invasion the Germans deployed three army groups. Army Group North, under Field Marshal von Leeb, consisted of Fourth Panzer Group and Sixteenth and Eighteenth armies (three panzer, three motorized infantry, nineteen infantry, and four security divisions). Army Group Center, under Field Marshal Fedor von Bock, contained Second and Third Panzer groups as well as Fourth and Ninth armies (nine panzer, six and one-half motorized infantry, thirty-seven infantry, and one cavalry divisions). Finally, Army Group South, under Field Marshal Gerd von Rundstedt, consisted of First Panzer Group and Sixth, Eleventh, and Seventeenth armies (five panzer, four motorized infantry, twenty-eight infantry, two mountain, four light, and three security divisions). The OKH held two panzer, one motorized infantry, and eleven infantry divisions in reserve.

The objectives for the army groups reflected the planning: Army Group North was to clear the Baltic states; Army Group Center was to advance to Smolensk; and Army Group South was to push toward Kiev and then down the Dnieper bend, while Eleventh Army covered Romania and its oil. Consequently, Leningrad, the Ukraine, and Moscow were all objectives, but there were no clear priorities, no alternatives, and no examination of what the Wehrmacht would do should the Soviet Union not collapse. Even at the operational level, German field commanders were unsure whether the first objective of Army Group Center was encirclement of Soviet forces around Minsk or those farther east at Smolensk.

The German army that invaded the Soviet Union was an extraordinary military instrument. It was thoroughly trained; its doctrine was balanced and realistic; it had honed its battlefield skills by two years of campaigning; and its officer corps was flexible, adaptive, and professional. Nevertheless, its successes hid significant weaknesses. The inadequacies of rearmament in the 1930s forced the army to equip many units with foreign and obsolete weapons. Its panzer and motorized infantry divisions acquired many of their support vehicles by stripping western Europe of civilian trucks—vehicles that were neither designed nor built for the rigors of primitive Soviet roads. Moreover, the Germans were unprepared for the logistic demands of a theater that possessed continental dimensions. Finally, German intelligence did as bad a job in judging Soviet capabilities as it had done in judging the RAF. It underestimated the Red Army and its reserves considerably, miscalculated the recuperative powers of Soviet industry and military organizations, and underestimated the technological sophistication of Soviet weaponry.

The Soviet Union had its own weaknesses. Stalin understood the political vulnerability of his own regime only too well and consequently refused to trade space for time. He moved much of the regular army to the frontier to prevent the Germans from driving into the interior and then refused military commanders permission to make defensive preparations for fear of provoking the Germans. Using estimates more in tune with the tempo of the French army of 1940 than of the Wehrmacht, the Red Army calculated that it could hold the Germans close to the frontier and then counterattack.

Even more disastrously, Stalin's murderous purges of the Red Army had created a legacy of timidity, fear, and incompetence. The Soviet high command was incapable of understanding the German system of warfare or reacting to it. Any Soviet officer who dared to question the great leader's assumptions ran the risk of being accused of defeatism. In June 1941 the Soviet Union and its Red Army awaited the German invasion almost totally unprepared for what was to come.

The First Weeks of Barbarossa

At 0330 hours on June 22, 1941, German artillery from the Baltic Sea to the Black Sea opened fire; large numbers of Luftwaffe aircraft had already crossed the frontier to attack the Red Air Force. The Germans found Soviet aircraft parked wing tip to wing tip. By noon Soviet aircraft losses on the ground and in the air had reached 1,200. Field Marshal Erhard Milch, the Luftwaffe's chief logistics officer, recorded that the Soviets lost 1,000 aircraft on the 22nd, 800 on the 23rd, 557 on the 24th, 351 on the 25th, and 300 on the 26th. German air successes came at the expense of ill-trained and

German Invasion of USSR,
June 22 – December 5, 1941

ill-equipped Soviet aircrews, floundering in impossible tactical formations. Within the first week, the Luftwaffe had gained such a degree of air superiority that for the next five months it could support the army's advance with interdiction and unhindered close air support.

On the ground the Germans were equally successful. Stalin's obdurate refusal to allow his forces to make defensive preparations or to raise their alert status resulted in much of the Red Army's being surprised in indefensible positions. The warning that an invasion was imminent did not go out from Moscow until midnight. Thus few front-line units received any kind of warning. Across the Eastern Front the Red Army, staggered by the ferocity of the blow, struggled to adjust as communications collapsed, rear-area headquarters lost control, and chaos and confusion reigned.

German armor quickly clawed its way into the open; behind it German infantry pounded down the lanes of western Russia sometimes at the rate of thirty miles per day. Manstein's LXVI Panzer Corps, assigned to Army Group North and attacking from East Prussia into Lithuania, broke loose and in four days drove two hundred miles to seize the bridges across

The Germans used self-propelled guns, such as this Sturmgeschütz, to support infantry attacks. They manufactured about 10,500 throughout the war.

the Dvina River at Dvinsk. Manstein then urged commander of Fourth Panzer Group, Colonel General Erich Hoeppner, to push the other panzer corps forward, while LXVI Panzer Corps moved deeper into Latvia. Hoeppner was not sure, however, whether his mission was to sweep the Red Army out of the Baltic states or to guard the flank of the advance on Moscow. Leeb, commander of Army Group North, also remained in the dark as to his next objective but settled on a conservative broad-front advance that allowed Soviet forces to recover their balance and escape from Lithuania and Latvia.

By mid-July, Army Group North had advanced three-quarters of the way to Leningrad, but serious difficulties had emerged. While it had smashed Soviet resistance and driven the Red Army from the Baltic States, the advance of its mechanized units had split into two separate axes: the first to protect the advance on Moscow, the second to push toward Leningrad. Furthermore, spearhead units were at the end of long and tenuous lines of communication, while supporting infantry were far behind and food, fuel, and ammunition were in short supply at the front.

Army Group South ran into serious difficulties from the start. Part of the problem was the fact that many of its formations had fought in the Balkans and had not had time to recuperate. Moreover, the Soviets deployed a high percentage of their forces and best units in the Ukraine, and their commander largely ignored Stalin's order not to undertake preparatory measures. As a result, Soviet troops delayed First Panzer Group's advance.

The Germans did succeed in battering Soviet defenders back to Kiev, but Hitler ordered Rundstedt, the commander of Army Group South, not to attack the city. Not until early August did First Panzer Group break clear and encircle twenty Soviet divisions near Uman. That victory resulted in the capture of 103,054 prisoners and the destruction of three Russian armies, 858 artillery pieces, and 317 tanks.

If advances by Army Group North and Army Group South failed to achieve complete success, Army Group Center's Second and Third Panzer Groups won stunning victories. Here one of the worst sycophants in Stalin's military system, General Dmitrii G. Pavlov, played a major role in the collapse. After service in the Spanish Civil War, Pavlov had persuaded Stalin that mechanized warfare represented a dead end. Consequently, Stalin directed the Red Army to disband its armored formations in late 1939. Despite the fact that German panzer groups had achieved operational freedom at the end of the first day, Pavlov, echoing orders from the *Stavka* (Soviet high command), persisted in shoveling Soviet forces forward to deliver hopeless, pointless counterattacks. Communications between his units died as the Germans rushed forward. The Red Army stood in place, moved forward deeper into the encircling pincers, or simply collapsed. Second and Third Panzer groups swung in and met at Minsk on June 28 to complete the first encirclement. Within the larger Minsk encirclement, Fourth and Ninth armies completed a smaller one around Bialystok. Somewhere around 324,000 prisoners fell into German hands; along with the prisoners went heavy Soviet casualties with 3,300 tanks and 1,800 artillery pieces knocked out or captured.

In early July German successes led Halder to note in his diary:

> On the whole, one can already say that the task of destroying the mass of the Russian army in front of the Dvina and Dnieper has been fulfilled. I believe the assertion of a captured Russian general to be correct that we can calculate on meeting east of the Dvina and Dnieper only disjointed forces which alone do not possess the strength to hinder German operations substantially. It is, therefore, truly not claiming too much when I assert that the campaign against Russia has been won in fourteen days.

In early July Army Group Center's panzer groups renewed their drive. By late July the Germans had completed encirclement of Smolensk despite desperate and often successful Soviet efforts to break out. Waves of Soviet counterattacks from the outside attempted to loosen the German hold on the pocket. Only by August 5 did the Germans complete destruction of the Smolensk cauldron; another 300,000 prisoners fell into their hands, with 3,205 tanks and 3,000 artillery pieces destroyed or captured.

Difficulties

But the German advance came to a halt. At this point the extent of Nazi miscalculations and Halder's overoptimism emerged. Neither the Soviet state nor its military institutions had collapsed, and the logistic realities of

Russian distances exacted a high price on the invaders. Armored spearheads were at the end of over-extended lines of communication. Supplies of ammunition and fuel barely made it to the front, while virtually no rations arrived. Finally a series of savage Soviet counterattacks struck the German spearheads. Though these attacks were uncoordinated and often badly led, they imposed a heavy toll.

Exacerbating German problems was the fact that the Soviets mobilized far more troops than German intelligence had calculated. By July 1, as a result of mobilizing all reservists between the ages of twenty-three and thirty-seven, the Red Army possessed 5,300,000 additional soldiers. The reserve formations these men joined were desperately short of equipment, lacked experienced officers and noncommissioned officers, and were often ill-trained and ill-prepared. They represented, however, a numerically formidable force whose counterattacks fell on the German mechanized spearheads—units already exhausted by the advance, short of ammunition and fuel, and separated by wide distances from supporting infantry units.

The heaviest fighting occurred against Army Group Center. In mid-July, Second Panzer Group had seized the high ground around Yelnya, fifty miles east of Smolensk, as a jumping off point for the attack on Moscow. Eleven Soviet armies attacked across the entire front of Army Group Center, but the nastiest fighting occurred around Yelnya, where no less than six Soviet armies attacked in efforts to break the Smolensk encirclement. Despite considerable doubts as to whether Moscow would be the next objective, the Germans decided to hold the salient. Nevertheless, by early September the Soviets had forced the Germans to abandon Yelnya, inflicted over 40,000 casualties, and wrecked five infantry divisions. The Soviet attacks had an effect beyond the casualties inflicted; heavy, unrelenting attacks forced the Germans to expend virtually all ammunition and fuel that the overextended logistic system brought forward. Consequently the Germans failed to establish the supply dumps necessary for resumption of the advance; nor could they refit the panzer and motorized infantry divisions for the next stage of the campaign.

Despite prodigious marches (in some cases twenty to twenty-five miles per day), German infantry were still far to the rear, and armored and motorized infantry received the brunt of Soviet attacks. Fighting in August increased losses among those units that had borne the brunt of fighting and on whose shoulders further advances depended. Halder's diary entry for August 11 underscores the shifting mood within the German high command:

> The whole situation shows more and more clearly that we have underestimated the colossus of Russia—a Russia that had consciously prepared for the coming war with the whole unrestrained power of which a totalitarian state is capable. This conclusion is shown both on the organization as well as the economic levels, in the transportation, and above all in the infantry divisions. We have already identified 360. The divisions are admittedly not armed and equipped in our sense, and tactically they are badly led. But there

they are; and when we destroy a dozen the Russians simply establish another dozen.

Moreover, Stalin's hand remained firmly on the helm of what had become a ruthless, desperate effort to survive. In mid-July he reimposed the commissar system and turned his NKVD—the secret police—loose on "slackers and defeatists." Nevertheless, the defects that had caused the early defeats continued to permeate the system. The Soviet military style did not tolerate failure and rewarded initiative with savage punishment. In the north tens of thousands of Leningrad civilians dug anti-tank ditches and bunkers to protect the city, but local authorities refused to stockpile foodstuffs for a siege or to allow evacuation of the old or even the young. To do so smacked of defeatism.

Along with a darkening operational situation and supply difficulties, the Germans magnified their problems by engaging in debate over the campaign's next objectives. Halder and Brauchitsch (commander-in-chief of the army) argued for a resumption of the advance on Moscow as soon as sufficient supplies arrived. Hitler in turn pressed for an advance on Leningrad and the Ukraine; nevertheless it was not until the end of August that the Führer finally forced the military to accept his decision. Only at that point were German forces in a position to resume their advance. But as the Wehrmacht entered the final stages of the campaigning season, there were dangerous signs. By September 1, it had suffered 409,998 casualties out of an average strength of 3.78 million. Moreover, the eastern army was short 200,000 replacements; OKH had committed twenty-one out of the twenty-four divisions in its reserve and virtually nothing remained, while only 47 percent of the armored force remained "in commission."

In accord with Hitler's decision to advance on the Ukraine, Guderian's Second Panzer Group turned south to slice behind Soviet forces near Kiev. At the same time Kleist's First Panzer Group, which had advanced down the Dnieper bend, crossed that river and swung north. As the German drives gathered steam, Russian commanders desperately appealed to *Stavka* for permission to abandon Kiev. Stalin still refused to countenance withdrawals. On September 16, German spearheads met at Lokhvitsa in the eastern Ukraine, one hundred miles east of Kiev; the encirclement encompassed four Soviet armies. By month's end after final destruction of the pocket, the Germans claimed 665,000 prisoners, 824 tanks, 3,018 artillery pieces, and 418 antitank guns.

While Army Group South completed destruction of the Kiev pocket, Army Group North advanced to the gates of Leningrad and almost entirely encircled the city; only a tenuous lifeline remained across Lake Ladoga. The siege of Leningrad fell on a city that possessed a peacetime population and minimal supplies of food and fuel; in the first winter over one million of its citizens would die of starvation.

The Battle of Moscow

With successes in the north and south, Hitler concluded that Stalin's regime was about to collapse. He therefore authorized an advance on Moscow before the onset of winter. With Army Group Center launching the main effort, the objectives for Operation "Typhoon" were to destroy the rest of the Red Army and capture Moscow. Hitler and his army commanders expected that Typhoon's success would result in the long-awaited collapse of the communist regime.

Combined with the lateness of the season and the failure to make up for losses suffered over the summer, the supply situation should have caused the Germans great worry. On September 13, commander of Fourteenth Army reported: "at the moment [the supply system meets] current consumption only. The transport situation [has] not thus far allowed establishment of depots sufficiently large to enable the troops to receive what they need in accordance with the tactical situation. The army lives hand to mouth, especially as regards the fuel situation." In effect Wehrmacht units were not in a position to build up crucial supply dumps (including supplies required for winter weather) because the logistical system could barely supply sufficient ammunition and fuel to meet current demands.

In the last half of September, the Germans regrouped for Typhoon, the final push. Second and Third Panzer groups rejoined Army Group Center, along with much of Fourth Panzer Group. To unhinge the Soviets before the other panzer groups moved out, Guderian began Second Panzer Group's offensive two days early and advanced rapidly. Soon after, the other panzer groups also blasted their way into the open. *Stavka* appears to have believed that the lateness of the season precluded further German advances on Moscow. Stalin's demand that the Red Army defend every square inch of Soviet soil spread the defenders out, and there were few reserves to counterattack German breakthroughs. Not until October 5 did Stalin and his advisors recognize that major operations were occurring on the central front. Ironically the Soviets awoke to the danger only through a speech by Hitler in Berlin declaring that a great offensive had begun. Within one week the Germans had ripped open Soviet front lines and encircled two enormous groups of Soviet armies. West of Moscow, near Vyazma, they encircled six armies; near Bryansk, about 150 miles to the south, they encircled three more. When the battle was over, the Germans claimed another 600,000 prisoners. The German advances caused outbreaks of panic and looting in Moscow as the Red Army seemed on the brink of collapse. So great was the booty in material and prisoners that Goebbel's Propaganda Ministry announced that the Wehrmacht had won the war in the east.

At this point the weather broke. Autumn rains arrived to turn roads and countryside into seas of mud. The German advance halted in its tracks, while the *Stavka* desperately hurried forward reinforcements from the interior. The German situation became increasingly desperate. The farther forward the Wehrmacht advanced, the greater the strain on its logistics. The demands of Typhoon and subsequent advances consumed forward stockpiles as well as the ammunition and fuel that arrived through the supply system. That consumption in turn meant that the Germans possessed virtually no stockpiles of fuel, ammunition, or winter clothing.

Despite dropping temperatures, Halder, Brauchitsch, and Bock supported continuing the Moscow drive. German intelligence estimated that

Georgi Zhukov was the Soviet Union's premier expert in mass mechanized warfare. Victor at Moscow, Leningrad, Stalingrad, and Kursk and "liberator" of Berlin, he usually commanded over one million soldiers organized into more than a dozen armies.

the victories at Bryansk and Vyazma had exhausted Soviet reserves. Bock concluded that "the Germans could now afford to take risks." In early November, Halder expressed the pious hope that it would not snow until January so that the advance could continue. Colder weather did in fact allow the advance to begin again, but worsening conditions took a terrible toll on troops, still dressed in summer uniforms. As the weather turned cold, conditions reduced the German soldiers to desperate expedients such as lighting gasoline fires under the crankcases of tanks to warm engines sufficiently to turn over.

The Soviet Counterattack

As the Soviet situation deteriorated, Stalin rushed his most competent commander, Georgi Zhukov, to defend Moscow. Zhukov was as ruthless and effective a practitioner of the operational art as World War II produced; he was one of the few competent Soviet officers to survive the purges. Now in front of Moscow, he waged a delaying defense and for the first time effectively traded space for time. Meanwhile he built up a substantial reserve from reinforcements arriving to defend Moscow (some from as far away as Siberia). Zhukov believed that the Soviets could go over to the offensive once the Germans had exhausted themselves. Not surprisingly, German intelligence picked up little of this threatening situation. By December 4 the Germans had clawed their way to Moscow's outskirts, but they possessed neither the strength nor will to continue. That night temperatures fell to −25° Fahrenheit; one infantry regiment suffered 300 frostbite casualties. On December 6 the Soviets counterattacked.

The Germans had already lost the initiative elsewhere in the east. In the north, savage Soviet attacks kept open their fragile supply line across Lake Ladoga to Leningrad. In the south the Germans had taken Rostov at the end of November; however, Soviet counterattacks threatened to envelop the German spearheads. Rundstedt, the commander of Army Group South, ordered a withdrawal to the Mius River, but Hitler countermanded the retreat, fired the field marshal, and appointed Field Marshal Walther von Reichenau as his replacement. The new commander reaffirmed Rundstedt's retreat order and then suffered a heart attack. Events in the south presaged a crisis throughout the German high command and the collapse of Hitler's confidence in his generals.

As German forces teetered, Hitler made a crucial decision that sealed the Reich's fate. On December 7, 1941, the Japanese struck both British and Americans in the Pacific. Despite his own troubles in the east, Hitler decided to support his ally by declaring war on the United States. In so doing, he enabled Roosevelt to picture the Japanese attack on Pearl Harbor as part of a larger Axis plot; consequently American strategy, developed in consultation with the British in early 1941, identified the Third Reich as the greatest danger. Hitler's decision sprang from several factors: frustration at the desperate situation in the east, anger at Roosevelt's aggressive actions over summer 1941, and a contempt for the United States and its "mongrelized," racially mixed population. Hitler, as with most German leaders, ignored America's economic potential and encountered no objections to his decision. The army, desperately concerned over its situation in Russia, hardly cared about the consequences of America's entry; the navy on the other hand had actively pushed Hitler for a declaration of war on the United States throughout summer 1941 because such a declaration would increase operational possibilities for its U-boats. The Luftwaffe expressed no opinion.

Soviet forces that counterattacked the Germans in front of Moscow on December 6 were well prepared for the harsh conditions of winter. Nevertheless, Zhukov recommended limited objectives for the offensive: namely the destruction of one or two German armies lying in front of Moscow. Stalin, however, ordered a general offensive to destroy German forces across the whole breadth of the Eastern Front. For a period in December and January it appeared that Stalin was right. The headquarters war diary of one German unit recorded the desperate conditions of its troops:

> Discipline is breaking down. More and more soldiers are heading west on foot without weapons, leading a calf on a rope or pulling a sled loaded with potatoes. The road is under constant air attack. Those killed by the bombs are no longer being buried. All the hangers on (cargo troops, Luftwaffe, supply trains) are pouring to the rear in full flight. Without rations, fleeing irrationally, they are

pushing back. Vehicle crews that do not want to wait out the traffic jams in the open are drifting off the roads and into the villages. Ice, inclines, and bridges create horrendous blockages.

The desperate situation resulted in a crisis between Hitler and his generals, with the latter arguing for sweeping withdrawals to more defensible positions. Hitler believed that any retreats could turn into a rout that would repeat the fate of Napoleon's Grand Army in 1812. The Führer, therefore, demanded the army stand firm. Those who ordered retreats found themselves relieved from command or court-martialed. Brauchitsch (commander-in-chief of the army), Bock (commander of Army Group Center), Leeb (commander of Army Group North), Rundstedt (commander of Army Group South), Hoeppner (commander of Fourth Panzer Group), and Guderian (commander of Second Panzer Group) all found themselves summarily relieved. Hitler named himself commander-in-chief of the army. From this point, the German military functioned with the OKH in charge of the east, the OKW in charge of the Mediterranean and west, the Luftwaffe high command in charge of the air war, and the naval high command in charge of the U-boat war. Nowhere except in Hitler's mind did the threads of German strategy come together.

Halder's diary suggests the difficulties that German troops encountered on the Eastern Front:

> 25 December: A very bad day . . . ; 27 December: desperate attempts to check the enemy east of Sukhinichi . . . ; 29 December: *Very bad day!* . . . ; 31 December: *Again an arduous day* . . . ; 3 January: Another dramatic scene with the Führer, who calls in question the generals' courage to make hard decision . . . ; 8 January: *Very grave day.*

By early January Zhukov had driven back both flanks of Army Group Center, but the Germans hung on desperately. In retrospect, Hitler's demand to stand fast saved the Wehrmacht from collapse. The Soviets on their part attempted too much, and their advance flowed into areas possessing little operational or strategic significance. At times their forces cut lines of communication on which the German front depended, but the Germans held the crucial roads and supply centers. Slowly they recovered their equilibrium, while the Red Army, bled white from the fighting of the summer of 1941, found it difficult to maintain momentum. Unlike the German advances over the summer and fall, the Soviet winter offensive failed to gain any significant operational success except to batter the Germans back from Moscow. Yet when the winter was over, the Germans had suffered losses from which their army never recovered. By mid-March the fighting died down as the spring thaw arrived; the two armies began preparations for the summer battles of 1942.

✳   ✳   ✳   ✳

The fall of France in 1940 had not translated into an immediate strategic success for the Germans. The British had possessed an effective and competent air defense system, while the Wehrmacht had possessed neither doctrine, nor training, nor the understanding to make an amphibious assault on the British Isles. Sea Lion was stillborn from its conception. Britain's successful defense raised a number of intractable problems the Germans were incapable of addressing, problems that Italian incompetence only exacerbated. Forced by Italian defeats to move in strength into the Balkans and to support Libya, the Germans repaired the damage for the short run. But since they had little interest in the area, they failed to turn British defeats into a strategic rout.

1941 was the crucial year on which the fate of the world turned. In this year the Germans made a number of crucial mistakes. They failed to mobilize the European continent for the long haul. Then they embarked on an ill-prepared and poorly conceived crusade against the Soviet Union, one in which their operational and tactical excellence could not redress the political and strategic mistakes inherent in their approach to war against the Soviets. Finally, in desperation because of difficulties in the east, they declared war on the United States. Even more quickly than they had in World War I, the Germans had turned the war into a conflict in which everyone was against the Reich.

For Germany's opponents in 1941 the problem was quite different. For them it was a matter of hanging on until their superior resources changed the course of the war. The enormous logistical shortcomings displayed by the Wehrmacht in its invasion of Russia underlined German vulnerabilities. While the Germans could fight battles extraordinarily well, they were less capable of fighting a war of prolonged duration. Unfortunately for them, the outcome of the war ultimately would rest on the capacity to mobilize and project military power over an extended period and over extreme distances. With Nazi expansion halted, the Allies at last possessed the reason, time, and energy to mobilize fully their popular and economic resources. The war that now emerged would increasingly become a clash of economic strength, in which the Allied powers enjoyed significant advantages.

SUGGESTED READINGS

Barnett, Correlli. *The Desert Generals* (Bloomington: Indiana University Press, 1982).

Bartov, Omer. *Hitler's Army: Soldiers, Nazis, and War in the Third Reich* (New York: Oxford University Press, 1991).

Erickson, John. *The Road to Stalingrad* (New York: Harper & Row, 1975).

Fugate, Bryan. *Operation Barbarossa* (Novato, Calif.: Presidio Press, 1984).

Howard, Michael E. *The Mediterranean Strategy in the Second World War* (New York: Praeger, 1968).

Irving, David. *The Trail of the Fox* (New York: E. P. Dutton, 1977).

Knox, MacGregor. *Mussolini Unleashed, 1939–1941: Politics and Strategy in Fascist Italy's Last War* (Cambridge: Cambridge University Press, 1982).

von Manstein, Erich. *Lost Victories*, ed. and trans. by Anthony G. Powell (Chicago: H. Regnery, 1958).

Millett, Allan, and Williamson Murray. *Military Effectiveness*, vol. 3 (London: Allen and Unwin, 1988).

Murray, Williamson. *Luftwaffe* (Baltimore: Nautical and Aviation Press, 1985).

Overy, R. J. *The Air War, 1939–1945* (New York: Stein and Day, 1980).

Pogue, Forrest. *George C. Marshall* (New York: Viking Press, 1963–1987), 4 Vols.

Taylor, Telford. *The Breaking Wave: The Second World War in the Summer of 1940* (New York: Simon and Schuster, 1967).

Ziemke, Earl F., and Magna E. Bauer. *Moscow to Stalingrad: Decision in the East* (Washington: Office of the Chief of Military History, 1987).

23

THE ATLANTIC AND THE PACIFIC: PRODUCING AND PROJECTING MILITARY POWER

The Pacific War, 1941–1942

Mobilizing and Projecting
Military Power

The European War at Sea,
1939–1945

The Air War

$\mathbb{W}$ith the entry of the United States
and the Soviet Union, the war became a conflict of global dimensions and
unprecedented scale. The process of defeating the Axis involved not only
translating large populations and economic resources into military means
and combining complex technologies into effective production of weapons
but also—particularly for the Americans and British—protecting long and
vulnerable lines of communication and projecting military power across
great oceans. Throughout 1941 and 1942 German U-boats threatened the
entire Allied war effort. With forces scattered across the face of the earth, the
Allies halted the Japanese, mobilized the resources to fight massive battles,
overcame the U-boat threat, and finally began projecting the military power
on which victory rested. As the battle of the Atlantic escalated, the British,
later joined by the Americans, waged a great air offensive against the Reich.
Until the means for a successful assault on Fortress Europe became available, strategic bombing remained the primary means for the United States
and Britain to strike Germany.

The naval wars in the Atlantic and Pacific differed greatly. Except
for a few unsuccessful raids by surface ships, the battles in the Atlantic
revolved around attacks by or attacks on German submarines. In the Pacific
numerous large engagements of surface ships, supported by aircraft,
occurred. Early in the war, however, it became apparent that the Pacific

required a balance of land, air, and sea forces; geography dictated a solution different from that in the Atlantic. Though accepting the Allied strategy of "Germany first," the Americans found themselves shifting more and more resources into the Pacific, and with the attacks on Guadalcanal and New Guinea, they made the first tentative steps in what would become a massive assault across the Pacific. Nonetheless, many dark days remained before the Allies could translate their manpower and industrial advantages into sufficient military power to push the Japanese back in the Pacific and assault Fortress Europe.

The Pacific War, 1941–1942

Origins of the Pacific War

The origins of the Pacific war lay in the deeply rooted expansionist desires of Japan. When Western traders first reached the Home Islands in the mid-sixteenth century, the Japanese proved receptive to European ideas and permitted trade to occur for much of the next century. Beginning in the mid-seventeenth century and continuing for the next two centuries, however, they drove most foreigners out and isolated themselves from the West. But by the mid-nineteenth century they could no longer maintain their isolation and undertook a remarkable transformation to remake Japan. Using the British as models for their navy and the Prussians for their army, they built up effective and efficient military institutions, which defeated the Chinese in 1895 and tsarist Russia in 1905. Those wars gave the Japanese hegemony over Korea, which they annexed in 1910.

A lack of natural resources constrained the Japanese economy as it modernized and expanded, and imports became dependent upon the foreign exchange that exports earned. Until 1929 trade and industry prospered due to the upswing in the world economy. But the burden of industrialization rested on the back of Japanese peasants, and that burden was heavy, especially considering the poverty of the countryside. In 1929, when the world market collapsed and the Great Depression began, all the industrial nations, especially Japan, were hit hard. The reaction of an already xenophobic and nationalistic elite was extreme. The army's officer corps, which drew many officers from the countryside, found the idea that Japan must conquer larger markets most attractive.

Since the Russo-Japanese War, nationalists had considered China an obvious area for Japanese expansion. In 1931, the Japanese army in Korea took matters into its own hands and seized Manchuria, which it then renamed Manchukuo. The League of Nations condemned the action, as did the United States, but no one undertook serious reprisal. For the next six years intermittent military action and political intrigue continued in north China. An army memo explained: "The natural resources of Manchuria are far exceeded by those in North China. There are limitless deposits of iron

The Far East

USSR

Nomonhan

MONGOLIA

MANCHURIA

Vladivostok

Beijing

Port
Arthur   KOREA

Sea of
Japan

Tokyo

CHINA

Yellow
Sea

Tsushima Strait

JAPAN

East
China
Sea

Okinawa

PACIFIC
OCEAN

Iwo Jima

Hong Kong   Formosa

| 0 | 225 | 450 mi |
| 0 | 225 | 450 km |

PHILIPPINES

and coal in Shansi province. If we are careless, these resources will end up in English or American hands."*

In summer 1937, the army manufactured an incident at the Marco Polo bridge (near Beijing) between Manchuria and China and initiated major military operations against the Chinese. The home government had no advance warning but approved the operation due to fear of radical nationalists. Thus without addressing the political or strategic ramifications, the Japanese engaged in a full-scale yet undeclared war in northern China. The Chinese factions could not withstand ruthless Japanese assaults, but the

---

*Ienaga Saburo, *The Pacific War, World War II and the Japanese, 1931-1945* (New York: Pantheon Books, 1978), p. 68.

A Japanese infantry squad advances in China. Japanese soldiers distinguished themselves by their stamina, aggressiveness, and obedience. A British field marshal said, "We talk a lot about fighting to the last man and the last round, but only the Japanese soldier actually does it."

Japanese never possessed the strength to occupy all of China. While they occupied major ports and cities along the coast, much of the countryside remained beyond their control. Chinese guerrillas, especially Mao Zedong's Communists, made life miserable for the occupiers.

As if the "China incident"—the Japanese euphemism for their war against China—were not enough, the Japanese army courted several direct confrontations with the Red Army in Manchuria. In summer 1939 the Japanese seized a disputed area in western Manchuria; in late August the Red Army, under the future marshal Zhukov, counterattacked and destroyed a reinforced Japanese division at Nomonhan. Not surprisingly, after that defeat the Japanese army exhibited less interest in fighting the Soviet Union—at least until it had dealt with its China problem.

Americans watched Japanese behavior in China with growing outrage, but even the direct attack by Japanese aircraft on a clearly marked U.S. gunboat in China in December 1937 failed to elicit any American commitment to the Chinese. Moreover, American defense expenditures in Asia remained minimal: the Philippines received little funding, and none of the Pacific islands, on which a naval war depended, received sufficient resources from Congress to defend themselves.

The collapse of the Western Powers in spring 1940 turned Japanese attention toward the colonial empires of Southeast Asia. In June 1940 their foreign minister advocated inclusion of portions of Southeast Asia in a "New

Order in East Asia." The Japanese subsequently pressured the French to permit the stationing of troops in northern Indochina, and in July 1941 they occupied southern Indochina. This move placed them in a position to advance against British and Dutch colonial possessions in Southeast Asia and the Southwest Pacific. Viewing the Japanese move southward as a threat to the Philippines, the Americans finally reacted by embargoing exports to Japan, including oil, and by freezing Japanese assets in the United States. Oil was the essential element in the embargo, for without oil the Japanese economy and military machine would collapse. In October General Tojo Hideki became premier and one month later called for the elimination of British and American influence from the Orient.

Strategy and Plans

American strategy for a war in the Pacific changed dramatically in the interwar period. Planning initially rested on the "Orange" plan, which the U.S. military developed before World War I as one of the "color" plans (black for Germany, red for Great Britain, green for Mexico, orange for Japan). The "Orange" plan resurfaced after 1918 and called for an "offensive war primarily naval in character" in the Pacific. It emphasized a naval drive through the central Pacific and a great clash of battle fleets. Throughout the 1920s and 1930s, students and faculty at the Naval War College tested and refined aspects of the American plan for the Pacific. In the late 1930s, as international tensions increased, the Americans began modifying these war plans. Designated "Rainbow" to distinguish them from the "color" plans, the new plans faced the possibility of the United States' having to meet the combined threat of Germany, Italy, and Japan. At a meeting of British and American staffs in January 1941, the future allies agreed that the main effort had to be made in the Atlantic, not in the Pacific, and that Germany and Italy had to be defeated first, not Japan. The new plan, "Rainbow 5," provided the main outline of strategy for World War II, but it changed Pacific strategy at the onset of a war from offensive to defensive.

American strategy changed because the combination of German, Japanese, and Italian power confronted the United States with significant threats from both east and west. President Franklin Roosevelt seems to have recognized the danger far earlier than most other Americans including his advisors. The problem then for him was how to push the buildup of U.S. forces to meet the threat without occasioning a political revolt from a population still drunk on isolationism. The fall of France made the danger greater, exacerbating American vulnerabilities in both the Atlantic and Pac-ific. In summer 1940 the president took the extraordinarily courageous dec-ision in an election year to support Britain; but that support could only re-tard the American buildup in the Pacific. Moreover, Roosevelt also 16determined that the United States would pursue a Germany-first strategy, given that nation's potential—a decision he maintained even after war began. But the problem for American planners lay in the fact that at least until 1943, when American industry would finally be producing vast quantities of weapons, equipment, and munitions, they would possess scant military means to deal with immensely complex logistic demands, not to mention opponents far better prepared to fight in the immediate future.

Defense of the Pacific proved difficult. The United States refused to send naval forces to help defend Singapore, which the British viewed as the "Gibraltar" of the Far East. With Japanese-held islands lying across the central Pacific, the Philippines seemed surrounded. Though planners anticipated problems maintaining contact with the Philippines, the United States began pouring units and resources into the islands. After the arrival of additional air and ground units, American strategists hoped to continue fleet operations from Manila and placed great faith in the buildup of heavy bombers in the Philippines both for their deterrent as well as their combat value. Nevertheless, planners did not expect the outbreak of war before spring 1942 and did not anticipate a swing in the balance in the Pacific toward the United States until 1943 when ships authorized in the 1938 building program came into service. Despite heightened tensions and extensive preparations, American commanders refused to believe that the Japanese would actually launch a surprise attack against the United States, particularly against the Pacific fleet at Pearl Harbor in the Hawaiian Islands.

In Japan the army and navy had developed substantially different strategic visions. The army looked toward Asia for expansion; as the dominant service, it had acquired a peculiarly parochial viewpoint, largely ignorant of the outside world. The Imperial navy, however, looked to Southeast Asia; it had acquired a better appreciation for Japan's vulnerability and for the most part urged greater caution in national strategy. Tied down in China, with major commitments in Manchuria on the Soviet frontier, the army could put only a small portion of its forces into the drive that overwhelmed the Western colonial empires in Asia. The navy would have to carry the bulk of the burden.

For decades the Japanese navy had planned for a war in the Pacific against the United States. Even before World War I, the Japanese planned on seizing control of the Philippines and Guam and intercepting and destroying the U.S. fleet when it crossed the Pacific and attempted to protect American possessions. Expectations of a decisive naval battle required highly proficient forces, and the Imperial navy became one of the best peacetime navies in history. It trained long and hard under the most strenuous of conditions; its pilots were outstanding. No other navy was as well-trained to fight at night. As for its technological capabilities, the "long-lance" torpedo was by far the best in the world, while its super battleships, *Yamato* and *Musashi*, were truly awesome representatives of a dying age. Finally, its conception and preparation for carrier warfare fully equalled that of the U.S. Navy, and its aircraft and pilots were initially superior to their American counterparts.

In late 1941 the army and navy established the broad outlines of Japanese war plans. They would attack Malaya and the Philippines simultaneously, seize the Dutch East Indies, and then launch a major offensive into Burma. After capturing Wake and Guam and thereby cutting America's lines of communication across the Pacific, they would establish a defensive perimeter extending west to Burma, east through the Dutch East Indies and

The Japanese Advance, 1941–1942

Japanese advance

New Guinea to the Gilbert Islands, and north to Wake and the Kurile Islands. The Japanese initially hoped to lure the U.S. fleet into the central Pacific where submarines and aircraft could reduce its strength; their main fleet would administer the coup de grâce in the seas near Japan. But the commander of the Japanese fleet, Admiral Yamamoto Isoroku, unveiled a daring operational plan; his carriers would cross the northern Pacific and attack the American fleet at Pearl Harbor. Yamamoto hoped that the strike at Pearl Harbor would destroy or immobilize the American fleet and allow time for his forces to seize the resources that Japan's war economy needed and to construct an island barrier against an American counterattack. Then, he assumed, the United States would sue for peace, as tsarist Russia had done in 1905. Nevertheless, Yamamoto had had extensive exposure to America, including a year at Harvard University, and recognized the dangers that Japan would run in fighting a long war with the United States.

American intelligence picked up much of the Japanese movement in the weeks before war; historians have pointed to intercepts and other signals that suggested Pearl Harbor as a possible target. As in Europe, decrypts of Japanese signals (in the Pacific called "Magic") would play a crucial role in the eventual Allied victory. But no intercepts or other intelligence could overcome American perceptions of the Japanese as having an inferior military; the subsequent disaster at Pearl Harbor resulted more from this attitude than from poor or mishandled intelligence.

The Japanese Triumphant

In the morning hours of Sunday, December 7, 1941, American peacetime assumptions collapsed. The Japanese carriers had crossed the northern Pacific unobserved. From a point north of the Hawaiian Islands, they launched two waves of aircraft. The attackers reached Pearl Harbor at 0800 hours to discover the American battle fleet at anchor and the defenses at a minimal level of readiness. Japanese torpedoes and bombs found inviting targets, while their fighters destroyed the American aircraft parked wing tip to wing tip on Hickam Field. U.S. opposition was light, and Japanese losses were minimal. By the time it was over, the battleship *Arizona* had blown up; *Oklahoma* had capsized; *West Virginia* and *California* lay buried in mud; and *Nevada* got underway but had to be beached because of extensive damage. Japanese bombs damaged the *Pennsylvania* in dry dock and exploded destroyers *Cassin* and *Downes*. American casualties totaled 2,403 dead and more than 1,000 wounded.

Despite its results, the attack on Pearl Harbor proved to be an operational failure and strategic disaster for the Japanese. On the strategic level, the "sneak" attack united American support to enter the war. On the operational level, the Japanese sank an obsolete battle fleet but failed to destroy either fleet repair facilities or the gigantic fuel reserves, over one million tons. That fuel supply supported U.S. fleet movements for most of 1942; had the Japanese destroyed it, the Americans would have been forced to operate from the West Coast for the next year. Furthermore, American carriers were not in the harbor at the time of attack and thus escaped to fight another day.

Worse disasters soon befell the Allies; Japanese air attacks in the Philippines caught the Far Eastern Air Force deployed in peacetime fashion on Clark airfield. American air strength in the Philippines went up in smoke, even though eight hours had passed since Pearl Harbor. Two days later Japanese aircraft operating from southern Indochina caught and sank the British battleship *Prince of Wales* and battle cruiser *Repulse*. That success, even more than the attack on the American battle fleet, underlined the vulnerability of ships to air attack; the day of the battleship was over. Coupled with losses at Pearl Harbor, the loss of two British capital ships shifted the balance of naval power in the Pacific decidedly in favor of the Japanese.

Another disaster occurred in Malaya where nearly 200,000 British and Commonwealth troops defended the peninsula and Singapore. Despite nearly a two-to-one superiority, the British found the enemy skillful at infiltration and exploitation; the Japanese had little experience in jungle fighting but their tactical skills were outstanding. Under command of General Yamashita Tomoyuki, they outflanked the British from one position to another; by early February they had reached Singapore. On February 15, 1942, barely two months after Japanese landings, Lieutenant General A. E. Percival surrendered the city and its garrison in one of the most humiliating defeats ever suffered by British arms. That defeat reflected the gross overconfidence of British leaders and their failure to prepare their troops to fight in the jungle. It also demonstrated superb leadership and performance by the Japanese.

In the Philippines, American defensive efforts were no more successful, although they lasted longer. When General Douglas MacArthur assumed command of Philippine defenses, he convinced Washington that he could do more than simply defend Manila Bay. With additional reinforcements and supplies, he planned on meeting the invaders on the beaches and driving them into the sea. Shortly after the attack on Pearl Harbor, the Japanese made initial landings on the northern and southern tips of the main island of Luzon; then on December 22 they made their main landings in Lingayen Gulf about 125 miles north of Manila. They easily drove the defenders back, and on December 24, MacArthur ordered his forces to withdraw to the Bataan Peninsula. Abandoning much of their ammunition, equipment, and rations, which had been stockpiled forward near the beaches, the combined American and Philippine force established a twenty-mile defensive line on the northern part of the peninsula, while MacArthur's headquarters and the Philippine government moved to the island of Corregidor in Manila Bay.

By the time MacArthur's forces reached Bataan, they were on half rations; within a few weeks they were receiving less than one thousand calories per day. This inadequate diet largely resulted from MacArthur's faulty prewar strategy that had attempted to defend all of Luzon. By April, Bataan was finished, and in early May, Corregidor surrendered. In the meantime Roosevelt, realizing that he would have a public relations disaster on his

Seizure of Luzon, December 10, 1941 – May 6, 1942

hands if MacArthur fell into Japanese hands, ordered the general to relinquish command to Lieutenant General Jonathan M. Wainwright and move to Australia. There MacArthur assumed command of American and Australian forces in the Southwest Pacific.

Meanwhile, as Japanese forces reduced the Americans in Bataan, they continued their rampage in Southeast Asia and the Southwest Pacific. On January 21 they attacked Borneo with its rich oil resources. At the end of February they destroyed Allied naval forces in the East Indies (present-day Indonesia) in the battle of the Java Sea. On March 1 the Japanese landed successfully on Java, and the collapse of the Dutch colonial empire followed shortly thereafter. The Imperial navy moved at will through the waters in the Southwest Pacific. In late March, Japanese carriers struck into the Indian Ocean; in a one-week operation their forces chased the Royal Navy to Madagascar, while sinking a light carrier and two heavy cruisers.

The Japanese Checked

In spring 1942, the Japanese decided not to halt and erect a defensive perimeter, as their previous strategy suggested, but to use their fleet more aggressively and extend control over the Pacific. To this end they planned two major operations: against Australian forces in New Guinea near Port Moresby and against Midway (1,300 miles northwest of Honolulu) with the hope of destroying the remainder of the American fleet. Both Japanese operations aimed to extend the defense ring of island bases around their conquests and the Home Islands. American fleet intelligence from Magic, however, warned Admiral Chester W. Nimitz, Commander-in-Chief, Pacific (CINCPAC) and allowed him to deploy his weaker American forces against both threats.

To meet the strike against Port Moresby, Nimitz concentrated carriers *Lexington* and *Yorktown* in the Coral Sea off the eastern tip of New Guinea against an enemy force of two fleet carriers and one light carrier. The subsequent battle of the Coral Sea on May 4–8, 1942, was a new type of sea battle, waged by exchanges of air strikes, without the opposing surface ships ever making direct contact. American air attacks sank light carrier *Shoho* and damaged the larger *Shokaku*; even more significantly the air battles severely weakened the air components of both Japanese carriers so that neither would be available for operations in the immediate future. Japanese air attacks lightly damaged the American carriers; both, however, continued launching and recovering aircraft. But, a series of massive internal explosions wracked the *Lexington*. The ship's position was soon hopeless, and it had to be sunk by escorts. With the *Yorktown* also damaged, American losses in the Coral Sea were heavier, but the Japanese called off the amphibious attack on Port Moresby.

Approximately three weeks earlier, the Americans had launched an audacious raid against the Japanese Home Islands by flying B-25 bombers off the carrier *Hornet*. The operation was the brainchild of navy and army planners; it soon received the support of General Henry H. "Hap" Arnold, chief of army air forces. A relatively junior air reserve officer, Lieutenant Colonel James H. Doolittle, who had a reputation as one of the great flyers in the interwar period, put the force together. The navy provided the *Hornet*, and by the end of April 1942 the force was at sea ready to launch its aircraft. The plan was to launch the bombers close enough to the Home Islands so that the B-25s could reach China and reinforce the Chinese air force. However, the task force ran into a Japanese picket line of fishing vessels. Fearing compromise, the attackers launched early. Although they surprised the Japanese, they did not have the range to reach friendly airfields, and most crashed in China. The damage caused by Doolittle's bombers was minimal; however, an outraged and humiliated Japanese high command advanced the date for the Midway operation and set in motion the crucial confrontation in the Pacific war.

The Japanese designed an excessively complex plan to lure the American fleet to its destruction and to seize Midway by amphibious assault. No less than six different divisions of the Imperial fleet had separate responsibilities. In a diversionary operation, a strike force of two light carriers would attack American bases in Alaska and occupy two islands in the Aleutian chain, Attu and Kiska. Four battleships would provide a screening force to cover that raid. On the next day, the main carriers under Admiral Nagumo Chuichi would pound Midway, while behind them Admiral Yamamoto with superbattleships *Musashi* and *Yamato* would move up to destroy the American fleet, if it intervened. Finally another fleet moving from the southwest with two battleships, six heavy cruisers, and a small aircraft carrier would protect amphibious forces on their way to Midway.

The Japanese plan, even given its excessive complexity, might have worked. Intelligence from Magic, however, gave the game away even before the enemy left port. As a result, the feint at Alaska failed to fool Nimitz; the Midway garrison received extensive reinforcements of air and ground forces; and the American fleet, including the carriers *Yorktown*, *Hornet*, and *Enterprise*, was at sea ready to intercept the Japanese carrier force. The American battleships remained in San Francisco because they were not fast enough to keep up with the carriers—an indication of how rapidly the battleship had declined in American naval eyes. The *Yorktown*'s presence underlines the importance of Magic; the carrier returned to Pearl at full speed from the Coral Sea. Initial estimates were that it would take ninety days to repair damage it had suffered in battle; however, given the emergency, the *Yorktown* steamed out of Pearl Harbor forty-eight hours later after desperate emergency repairs.

The Japanese suspected nothing about these preparations. For the first time in the Pacific, luck turned against them. On June 4, their carriers and supporting vessels arrived north of Midway; all of the scouting aircraft took off on time except for the aircraft scheduled to search the sector where the American fleet lay waiting. Nagumo launched half of his aircraft for an attack on Midway, while the other half, armed with torpedoes and armor piercing bombs, remained on the carrier decks. Two hours later with no hostile reports from search aircraft, he ordered these weapons changed to high-explosive bombs to execute a second strike on Midway. As rearming proceeded, the search aircraft suddenly reported American fleet units. Additional moments passed until the aircraft reported one American carrier; with this warning, Nagumo decided to rearm the aircraft on the decks with the weapons needed to strike the American fleet. Meanwhile, heavy air attacks from Midway-based aircraft exacerbated Japanese problems. The attacks did no damage, but they made the task of rearming more difficult, as Japanese ships maneuvered at full speed.

Here again luck intervened. The first American carrier aircraft to find the Japanese were torpedo bombers, first from the *Hornet*, then from the *Enterprise* and *Yorktown*. Japanese fighters and antiaircraft guns slaughtered the American aircraft, which failed to achieve any hits; but low-flying torpedo bombers pulled Japanese fighters down to sea level. Shortly after the last torpedo bomber had gone in and just as the Japanese carriers turned into the wind to launch aircraft, the dive bombers from *Yorktown* and *Enterprise* arrived overhead. With no interference, they attacked the Japanese carriers, whose decks remained full of armed and fueled aircraft, high-explosive bombs, and ammunition for land targets (the munition handlers had not yet returned the downloaded weapons to the magazines). In a remarkably brief period they wrecked three carriers (*Akagi*, *Kaga*, and *Soryu*). Shielded by a rain squall, the last carrier, *Hiryu*, escaped damage for the moment and then launched aircraft against *Yorktown*, achieving a measure of revenge; three bombs and two torpedoes from the *Hiryu*'s aircraft severely damaged the American carrier and eventually contributed to its loss. Later that afternoon, pilots from the three U.S. carriers (those from the *Yorktown* were flying off other carriers) found the *Hiryu* and left it sinking as well. In early evening, the U.S. fleet pulled off to the east to avoid a night surface engagement.

Midway was a major success for the U.S. Navy; American aircraft had destroyed four Japanese carriers. Even more important the Japanese lost most of their flight crews—the best trained in the world—in the flaming wreckage. The threat to Midway was gone, and initiative in the Pacific now swung tentatively to the Americans.

The Counteroffensive

By this point, command relations in the Pacific had solidified. The size of the theater—the entire expanse of the Pacific and Indian oceans—made some division inevitable. But interservice as well as political realities resulted in the creation of two distinct American efforts. There was some irony in this state of affairs, because in Europe the Americans were preaching to their British allies about the need for a single, united command against the Germans. In the Pacific, however, they waged anything but a unified effort.

The division of responsibility resulted as much from personalities as from strategic necessity. MacArthur's escape from Bataan presented

After World War II Douglas MacArthur complained in a somewhat self-serving fashion, "[F]ailure to unify the command in the Pacific . . . resulted in divided effort, the waste, diffusion, and duplication of force, and the consequent extension of the war with added casualties and cost."

Roosevelt with a difficult decision. To bring him back to America would have caused considerable pressure to place him in a high military position; if left in a united Pacific command, his date of rank made him superior to any American officer, a state of affairs unacceptable to the navy, particularly since the Pacific was an ocean and MacArthur was a soldier. As a compromise, the Joint Chiefs of Staff (JCS) divided the Pacific in half and gave MacArthur command of the Southwest Pacific and Admiral Nimitz the Central Pacific. The two separate commands would cooperate as necessary.

Immediately after Midway, MacArthur proposed to attack the main Japanese base at Rabaul on New Britain; to achieve that goal, he argued that he needed two carriers and an amphibious division (marines). This self-seeking proposal met a self-seeking response. Admiral Ernest King, the chief of naval operations, proposed that Nimitz take command of all MacArthur's ships and aircraft; the army would merely provide forces to garrison islands that the navy and marines captured. After a week of acrimonious debate, the JCS hammered out a compromise that it published in a directive on July 2, 1942. The decision represented a less risky approach and reflected the real balance of American and Japanese forces in the Pacific. An advance on Rabaul would take place, but in three stages. The first included a landing in the southern Solomons on the islands of Guadalcanal and Tulagi (a tiny island twenty miles off the northern coast of Guadalcanal). Seizing them would protect communications to Australia. Stage two would involve an advance along the northeast coast of New Guinea and culminate in the third stage, a direct assault on Rabaul.

The Tulagi-Guadalcanal operation in August 1942 opened the American counteroffensive. When marines landed at Red Beach on Guadalcanal on August 7, they encountered little resistance because Japanese construction crews had no protecting troops. Outside of the initial landings and seizure of the airfield, nothing else went right. The lack of beach personnel and suitable landing craft resulted in supplies being unloaded on the beach haphazardly; congestion also prevented some landing craft from discharging their cargo. Then the commander of the naval task force, Vice Admiral Frank J. Fletcher, pulled his carriers out of the area almost immediately after the landing.

Disaster followed. An Allied force of heavy cruisers and destroyers under command of Rear Admiral V. A. Crutchley of the Royal Navy guarded the landings. As Fletcher's carriers exited the area, an Australian patrol aircraft spotted Japanese warships heading south from Rabaul into "The Slot" which was formed by the parallel lines of islands making up the Solomons. However, the pilot failed to report his sighting immediately. Moreover, he described the enemy force as three cruisers, three destroyers, and two sea plane tenders. In fact it consisted of five heavy cruisers, two light cruisers, and a destroyer, all of which were heading at full speed towards Guadalcanal. The report did not get to Allied fleet commanders until 1700 hours, even though the initial sighting had occurred at 1030.

Five Allied heavy cruisers and five destroyers protected the anchorage near Guadalcanal where the merchant ships were still unloading sup-

The Solomon Islands and Guadalcanal, August 1942

plies. Around 0130 hours, the attackers struck. None of the Allied vessels spotted the Japanese until it was too late. Though one lucky American shot caused minor damage on an enemy cruiser, the Japanese sank four cruisers and damaged two destroyers and one heavy cruiser. Fearing Allied aerial attacks at dawn, the Japanese admiral broke off the action and retreated; by so doing he permitted the invasion to continue.

The battle of Savo Island was a disaster for the U.S. Navy. It was even more humiliating than Pearl Harbor, for at least in December 1941 the United States had been at peace. The next morning after dumping some supplies on the beach, the support vessels weighed anchor and abandoned the marines who consequently had no barbed wire, no construction equipment, and only minimal supplies of ammunition and food. They were at the end of long and tenuous lines of supply, but they enjoyed one priceless asset: Japanese engineers had almost completed construction of Guadalcanal's airfield. On August 15, four U.S. destroyers slipped into Guadalcanal with aviation fuel, ammunition, and ground crews. Five days later, twelve dive bombers and nineteen fighters arrived at the newly named Henderson Airfield. Possession of the airbase gave marines a crucial advantage in coming weeks.

The Pacific war had exploded on the United States and the colonial empires of Southeast Asia. Now with Hitler's declaration of war, the Americans were in a two-front war. Given the reaction of the American people to Pearl Harbor, the Pacific theater represented a strong and continuing area of interest to American military planners. Yet in the long run, Germany was the greater danger. For Roosevelt and the JCS, strategy became a delicate balancing act between the requirements of a "Germany first" strategy and the political realities of public demands that U.S. forces avenge Pearl Harbor. In early 1942, the Japanese sweep through Southeast Asia and the Southwest Pacific had threatened the entire theater; only the Coral Sea and Midway provided a breathing spell. Now with the commitment to Guadalcanal and New Guinea the Americans had made the first tentative steps forward. But shortages of resources and heavy demands of a two-front war represented strategic and logistical problems that the Americans could not fully solve until 1944.

Mobilizing and Projecting Military Power

The United States

The Japanese attack on Pearl Harbor caught the United States in the first stages of a massive mobilization of its industrial and manpower resources. In no sense was the nation or its military prepared for war. In the 1920s and 1930s the United States had spent less than 2 percent of its gross national product on defense; even with the start of World War II, U.S. defense expenditures were less than five billion dollars. In 1940 those expenditures ballooned to nearly twenty billion, while the peacetime proposals of both army (which included the air force) and navy for expansion reached over one hundred billion dollars. In summer 1940, the fall of France led Congress to pass the first peacetime draft in American history. But the draft and buildup of American military power met strong opposition from many. In summer 1941 with Britain still isolated in western Europe, with the Japanese pursuing an evermore threatening policy in the Pacific, and with Nazi armies slicing through the Soviet Union, the Congress of the United States renewed the peacetime draft by *one* vote. Those drafted were hardly much happier; a movement among draftees called themselves the "Ohio" gang—"over the hill in October."

Anger over Pearl Harbor dissolved opposition to American involvement in the war; Americans rallied behind the president and the military in support of the war effort in a fashion that has never been seen, before or after, in U.S. history. The problem was how to translate economic strength and popular enthusiasm into military power. American leaders, political as well as military, had the experience of U.S. mobilization in World War I to use as a model and therefore avoided some of the mistakes that had beset mobilization in that conflict. Economic mobilization began in August 1939 when Roosevelt created several boards to plan for conversion of industry to war production, to control consumer prices, and to coordinate use of scarce materials. Prewar efforts functioned poorly, but by early 1943 the nation's economy had converted to a wartime footing and functioned relatively smoothly. Though the United States relied on numerous controls and boards, the many voluntary measures of its mobilization contrasted sharply to the mandatory approach of the Soviet Union, Britain, Germany, and Japan.

In May 1943, the Office of War Mobilization under James F. Byrnes, a former Supreme Court justice, received complete control over establishing priorities and prices. Strict regulation of rents, food prices, and wages went into effect, as did rationing of items such as meat, shoes, sugar, and gasoline. The combined effects of conscription and expanded industrial production produced a labor shortage and increased bargaining power for workers. The National War Labor Board, created after Pearl Harbor, served to arbitrate disputes and hold wage rates down. As a result, prices and wages soared during 1942, but they leveled off in 1943 and remained steady until the end of the war.

The labor shortage also encouraged large numbers of American women to join the work force. In addition to those serving in the military, many women found jobs in hospitals, factories, transportation, offices, and farms. Though most withdrew from the labor market after 1945, their participation during the war contributed to significant changes in the economic status of women in American society. African-Americans also benefited from the labor shortage; many found previously closed jobs open to them. They also found more opportunities in the military; one (Benjamin O. Davis) became an army general for the first time and more than 600 became pilots. Though treated somewhat better than they had been in World War I, they continued to suffer from prejudice and mistreatment, and the practice of segregating blacks from whites continued.

When the Japanese struck Pearl Harbor, American mobilization had been underway for about a year and a half. As U.S. industry strained to meet the needs of its allies and its own rapidly expanding forces, severe shortages appeared. By 1943, however, the dividends of the economic mobilization and the strengths of American industry became apparent. The results of that effort were truly awesome. In 1944 alone the U.S. aircraft industry produced 73,876 combat aircraft. In *all* of World War II the Germans produced only 86,311. In 1941, two years *after* Nazi Germany had started World War II, its factories produced 3,256 tanks for the entire year, including 698 made in Czechoslovakia. In 1943, two years after it entered the war, Soviet industry was producing over 1,300 tanks per month; American production that same year was over 2,400 per month. Similarly, the naval buildup in the Pacific reached extraordinary levels; by 1944 a new *Essex* class fleet carrier or an *Independence* light carrier was arriving in Pearl Harbor every month, and in some months one of each. By the battle of Leyte Gulf in October 1944, the attacking U.S. fleet possessed no less than seventeen fleet carriers. One also needs to recognize that in addition to

M-3 Grant tanks being produced in Chrysler Corporation's Tank Arsenal in Detroit, Michigan. During the war, the Detroit Tank Arsenal produced 22,234 tanks, or about 25 percent of all tanks produced in the United States.

projecting power around the world and supplying huge quantities of weapons to Allies, Americans also grew, processed, and transported large amounts of food and foodstuffs that prevented their allies from starving. Finally, the United States bore the immense financial and economic costs involved in the Manhattan project, which resulted in production of the atomic bomb. No other nation or economic system could have financed such a development during the war.

But there were difficulties in the early years of American mobilization. The shipment of military equipment to Britain and then the Soviet Union in 1940 and 1941 provided a shield for American preparations. Such shipments, however, also deprived U.S. military forces of equipment that was vital to preparations for war. Even in 1943, lend-lease shipments were a significant drain on equipment stocks. Other difficulties included priorities. In 1942 German successes in the battle of the Atlantic threatened to cut the sea lines of communication between Britain and the United States by sinking many merchant vessels. That same year, the American shipbuilding industry produced three million tons of merchant vessels; in response to Britain's desperate plight as well as the demands of military forces deployed around the world, industry increased production to nine million tons in 1943. Nevertheless there was a cost: production of such large numbers of merchant vessels adversely affected the production of landing craft essential for Allied amphibious attacks on Fortress Europe *and* the Japanese island empire in the Pacific.

The production of weapons represented only part of the problem; turning millions of young men into efficient and effective combat units was another. Critics of the tactical and operational competence of American forces in World War II often use as their model of comparison the performance of German soldiers. Such a comparison is fundamentally false. German rearmament began in 1933; it represented an effort that government as well as the officer corps knew would lead to a major conflict. The Germans had six years of peace and one and a half more of relatively light combat to prepare their ground forces. Moreover, they usually were on the defensive when they faced the Americans.

But the Americans, beginning the mobilization of their economy and their military in September 1939, found themselves in heavy combat on land, sea, and in the air within two years of the initiation of their effort. On the day that Germany invaded Poland, the U.S. Army possessed 14,486 officers and 175,353 enlisted men. Six years later at the end of World War II, the army possessed 891,663 officers and 7,376,295 enlisted personnel. Over those six years, the performance of American ground forces steadily improved as commanders and units gained combat experience. And there is no doubt that American naval and air forces were distinctly superior in qualitative as well as quantitative terms to their enemies by 1943. Though the ground forces may have lagged qualitatively behind their naval and air contemporaries, particularly in the early part of war, there were exceptions. The 88th Infantry Division in the Italian campaign consistently proved itself superior to its German opponents, as did the American airborne divisions. Nevertheless, there is considerable evidence that many American combat units did not match their German opponents on the ground.

A number of reasons explain this state of affairs. On the negative side, U.S. forces initially relied on the M-3 Grant but then in 1942–1943 replaced it with the M-4 Sherman tank, which was more mobile and mechanically reliable than German tanks, but which could not match German Panthers or Tigers in killing power. Recognizing the need for a heavier tank, the Americans built the M-26 Pershing but manufactured only 700 before Germany surrendered. Consequently, American armored-fighting vehicles remained qualitatively inferior to those of their opponents. Additionally, the system of manpower allocation to the armed forces sifted out too many of those who scored highly on intelligence tests into the army air forces, the navy, and innumerable technical positions and left too few among those who had to do the fighting on the ground. To make matters worse, the army all too often regarded soldiers as interchangeable parts that it could shift from one unit to another with little regard for unit cohesion.

Manpower demands on the U.S. population limited the options of military leaders. The war required that millions of Americans be involved in the manufacture of military matériel. Then the services needed millions more; at the war's end the army possessed 5.9 million men and women, the army air forces 2.3 million, the navy 3.4 million and the marine corps nearly half a million. All these military forces required enormous support to get overseas and then to fight a massive *two-front* war over distances that no other combatant had to consider. Originally army planners had foreseen the need for ground forces in excess of two hundred divisions. The realities of fighting the war in the Pacific and the air assault on the Reich forced the Army's chief of staff, General George C. Marshall, to scale back the program to ninety divisions.

That decision resulted in serious but unavoidable consequences. By the end of the war eighty-nine out of those ninety divisions had been committed to combat—scarcely much margin of security. In Europe the fighting forced American commanders to commit infantry and armored divisions to sustained combat, often beginning with Normandy and continuing through Nazi Germany's collapse. Consequently, there was little opportunity (with the exception of airborne divisions) to pull divisions out of the line to rest, refit, and retrain and to give combat units a chance to absorb replacements outside the front lines. In the Battle of the Bulge, this situation had the serious consequence of leaving General Dwight D. Eisenhower, the Allied supreme commander, with a reserve pool of two airborne divisions for the *entire* front—from Holland to Switzerland—on which American troops were fighting. Nevertheless, the main concern for American planners was balancing between the requirements for manpower in the work force and the military in order to sustain the economy as well as operations in the field. Whatever the drawbacks of having only ninety army divisions, it reflected serious choices with which American leaders for the most part grappled more effectively than did their German counterparts.

Great Britain

No country mobilized more extensively than did the British. The nature of the German threat, which lay across the straits of Dover, barely twenty miles away, underlined the desperate situation confronting Britain in June 1940. In 1939 the British had devoted 2.8 percent of their labor force to military service; by 1944 that number had grown to 24.1 percent. Similarly in 1939, 6.4 percent of the labor force worked in defense-related industries; by 1944 the number had grown to 17.7 percent. The hardship and pressures that this unprecedented mobilization placed on the British is captured by a 1944 report.

> The British civilian has had five years of blackout and four years of intermittent blitz. The privacy of his home has been periodically invaded by soldiers and evacuees. In five years of drastic labor mobilization, nearly every man and every woman under fifty without young children has been subject to direction to work, often far from home. The hours of work average fifty-three for men and fifty overall; when work is done, every citizen who is not excused for reasons of family circumstances, work, etc., has had to do forty-eight hours a month duty in the Home Guard or Civil Defense.

Supplies of all kinds have been progressively limited by shipping and manpower shortage; the queue is part of normal life. Taxation is probably the severest in the world, and is coupled with continuous pressure to save. The scarce supplies, both of goods and services, must be shared with hundreds of thousands of United States, Dominion, and Allied Troops; in the preparation of Britain first as a base and then as a bridgehead, the civilian has inevitably suffered hardships spread over almost every aspect of his daily life.

The war effort raised enormous problems. Britain's industrial plant and processes were antiquated and out of date. Yet on a relatively weak economic base the British produced almost as many aircraft as did Nazi Germany, which had all of western and central Europe upon which to draw. In armored fighting vehicles the British produced 27,896 to 46,837 for the Reich. When one considers that the Americans produced 88,410 armored fighting vehicles, and the Soviets 105,251, one gets a sense of how extraordinarily outnumbered the Germans were. But no matter how extensive Britain's mobilization, there were factors they could not overcome. Weaknesses in the industrial base placed limitations on what they could do; the antiquated nature of British industries, particularly the motor industry, had serious consequences. The inadequacy of British tanks throughout the war was one glaring example; the failure of much of the truck fleet on which General Sir Bernard Montgomery's advance in 1944 depended was another.

Germany

Of all the national economic performances, however, it was that of Nazi Germany that left the most to be desired. Hitler's Reich had launched World War II on a most inadequate economic base, one that had contributed to Hitler's belief that the Third Reich must expand to gain the economic resources required for its long-term security. Through the fall of France in spring 1940, Germany lived a precarious economic existence; only the incorporation of Austria in March 1938 and the seizure of Czechoslovakia in September 1938 and March 1939 prevented economic collapse and allowed rearmament programs to proceed. By 1938 the Reich was devoting 18 percent of Germany's gross national product to military spending.

The conquests of Poland, Scandinavia, the Low Countries, and France placed their economic and industrial resources at the disposal of the Reich and brought the Balkans and neutrals like Switzerland, Sweden, and Spain within the Nazi economic orbit. Germany possessed economic resources and industrial capacity the likes of which the Reich had never had before. But Hitler and his senior leadership drew the inaccurate conclusion that the existing production levels in Germany were sufficient to win the war. Moreover, fearful of Nazi Germany's political stability, they hesitated to bring into effect the kind of complete mobilization that Churchill instituted in Britain from 1940 until 1943. Consequently the Germans refused to introduce measures that would have mobilized their population and manpower for total war. At the precise moment that their actual (Britain) and potential (the United States and the Soviet Union) opponents were setting in motion massive mobilization and rearmament programs, the Germans continued business as usual with eight-hour shifts and six-day work weeks. Neither aircraft nor tank production, nor any other crucial indicators showed significant upward movement. Even more important was the fact that the Germans made few efforts to draw on the European economy to expand future production; instead they busily stripped factories in western Europe of machine tools and shipped them back to industrial plants in the Reich that were still working only single shifts.

This short-sighted approach continued through December 1941. However, defeat in front of Moscow, accompanied by loss of much of the army's equipment, and collapse of the Luftwaffe's logistic system (exacerbated by the brutal Russian winter) finally awoke German leaders to the fact that they needed to undertake desperate measures to fight a world war. The death of the armaments minister, Fritz Todt, in February 1942, led Hitler to make one of his more inspired decisions: the appointment of his personal architect, Albert Speer, as Todt's replacement. The thirty-six-year-old Speer possessed extraordinary managerial and leadership skills, as well as keen commonsense. He set about to allow Germany's industrial magnates and firms maximum latitude to expand production. Nevertheless, severe constraints limited options in the economic sphere. Despite the seriousness of the situation, Hitler refused to allow total mobilization of Germany's resources. For ideological reasons, he forbade mobilization of German women to support the war effort; consequently a substantial labor source remained untapped throughout the war in stark contrast to what was occurring elsewhere in the world.

Hitler's decision limiting economic mobilization also reflected his misreading of the lessons of World War I. He believed that the severe pressure in 1918 for armaments production had resulted in the collapse of morale and revolution in Germany. Nevertheless, the Nazi regime undertook extraordinary measures to stoke the war economy; it mobilized slave labor from across Europe; and Nazi authorities soon dragooned millions of French, Russians, Italians, Poles, and other nationalities into German factories.

From spring 1942 a steady and impressive upswing of weapons and munitions production occurred. That growth proceeded through summer 1944 despite Allied strategic bombing attacks. Nonetheless, increases in German production from 1942 to 1944 remained substantially behind those occurring in the United States, the Soviet Union, and Britain. The lost years of 1940 and 1941 were years that the Germans could not make up.

Equally important was the fact that Allied strategic bombing severely retarded German production. Across the Atlantic the Americans increased aircraft production by use of mass-production techniques; the Willow Run aircraft plant of Ford in Michigan possessed a factory floor over two miles long. B-24s began at one end as a tail assembly and rolled out the other as completed aircraft. In Germany the exact opposite occurred as air attacks forced the Germans to decentralize aircraft production into small, inefficient manufacturing operations. Moreover, the quality of the work significantly declined over the course of the war as more slave workers occupied crucial production positions. These unwilling slaves, undernourished and subjected to horrendous treatment, were hardly eager to turn out first-class products for their rulers. The result was a significant decline in quality of weapons produced by German industry.

Defeat at Stalingrad in February 1943, followed shortly thereafter by collapse in North Africa, finally persuaded Hitler to allow Joseph Goebbels and Speer latitude to extend war and mobilization measures throughout German society. But the Führer still held back on some measures, particularly regarding the wider employment of women in German industry. Meanwhile, strategic bombing attacks destroyed German cities and disrupted industries. By 1944 the impact of enemy bombing caused serious consequences in oil, aircraft, and transportation. Desperate efforts to squeeze the last products out of the German economy prolonged, but could not alter, the final result: catastrophic national defeat.

The European War at Sea, 1939–1945

While the opening campaigns of the war were unfolding on land, the crucial campaign of World War II had already begun in the North Atlantic. From the outbreak of war, German U-boats waged a tenacious struggle to sever lifelines between the British Isles and the rest of the world. Had they succeeded, there would have been no second front, no air campaign against the Third Reich, and few supplies for the hard-pressed Soviets; and Britain itself, confronted with starvation, might well have sued for peace. As Churchill commented: "The only thing that ever really frightened me during the war was the U-boat peril."

First Battles

Neither the British nor the Germans had prepared for the battle of the Atlantic. Having developed sonar (called asdic by the British) at the end of World War I, the Royal Navy comfortably assumed that it had solved the submarine menace. During the interwar period it did little serious preparation for protecting convoys; and it constructed few antisubmarine vessels. With the outbreak of war, it could protect only the most important shipping routes.

The Germans for their part displayed no more foresight. Before the war, the commander-in-chief of the navy, Admiral Erich Raeder, emphasized creation of a great battle fleet that would eventually be capable of challenging Britain on the seas. When the war began, the Germans had two battleships and two near completion, three pocket battleships, three heavy cruisers, and five light cruisers. They also had fifty-seven submarines, about half of which were capable of sustained operations at sea. With the outbreak of war in September 1939, Raeder recognized that since war had come early, the navy could not challenge Britain on the surface; it had to use its ships as raiders, while its submarines executed attacks on British commerce.

In fall 1939 German submarines achieved some notable successes; they sank the aircraft carrier *Courageous* and battleship *Royal Oak*. But their number was so small that after an initial wave of attacks, they inflicted minimal damage. The picture was not much rosier for the surface navy. The Scandinavian campaign cost it virtually all its strength, either sunk or damaged. Nevertheless, German successes in spring 1940 altered the Reich's strategic position. The commander of the U-boats, Admiral Karl Dönitz, moved submarine bases to the west coast of France and then launched an energetic anticommerce campaign.

By fall 1940 the U-boat force, while not significantly larger, had achieved a high level of effectiveness. Dönitz spread the submarines in patrol lines across the most likely lanes approaching the British Isles. When one made contact, it reported by radio the location, size, and direction of movement to Dönitz, who then concentrated his submarines in wolf packs against the enemy. Eventually, overcontrol by radio would cost the Germans dearly, but now it worked.

On October 5, 1940, Convoy SC-7 departed Canada with thirty-four slow merchant vessels. Its escort for much of the journey was a single sloop; its opponents were some of the great U-boat aces of the war. In mid-ocean another sloop and a corvette joined up. Eventually two more corvettes arrived. None of the escorts possessed radar; they had not trained together; and the sonar on some of the corvettes was obsolete. The result was a slaughter; SC-7 lost twenty ships with two others damaged. At the same time that U-boats were savaging SC-7, the fast convoy HX-79 departed Halifax for Britain. This convoy had a larger escort, including two armed merchant cruisers, two destroyers, four corvettes, a minesweeper, and three trawlers. But the escort fleet was no better trained. Attacking U-boats sank nearly 25 percent of HX-79's merchant vessels.

The arrival of winter provided a covering blanket over convoys. But in spring 1941 shipping losses in the Atlantic began an ominous upswing. In March losses were 243,020 tons; in April 249,375 tons; in May 325,492 tons; and in June 310,143 tons.

While British losses mounted in the U-boat war, the Germans moved to change the surface equation. Raeder hoped to make a great raid against British shipping by uniting the new battleship *Bismarck* and heavy cruiser *Prinz Eugen* (in the Baltic) with battle cruisers *Scharnhorst* and *Gneisenau* (in Brest). But *Scharnhorst* needed repairs, and an RAF Coastal Command aircraft torpedoed *Gneisenau*. Nevertheless, the Germans launched *Bismarck* and *Prinz Eugen*, as well as a number of supply ships and weather ships, on the raid. As the heavy German ships approached the Denmark Straits, British cruisers picked them up and began shadowing. On May 24 battle cruiser *Hood* and the new battleship *Prince of Wales* attacked, but the Germans destroyed *Hood*, while mechanical problems forced *Prince* of *Wales* to break off action. *Prinz Eugen* escaped to the south and eventually entered Brest. Crippled by a rudder jammed by British attacks, the *Bismarck* did not get away and on May 27 was finally sunk by the British battle fleet. This ended German attempts to challenge British dominance of the ocean.

Intelligence Intervenes

As a consequence of the *Bismarck* breakout, the intelligence equation in the Atlantic underwent a drastic change. On May 8, 1941, escorts of convoy OB-318 damaged a U-boat and forced it to the surface. After capturing the crew, British sailors boarded the badly damaged submarine and extracted the Enigma enciphering machine and its settings for the next seven weeks. Seizure of a weather trawler at the end of May (sent out to support the *Bismarck*) provided further access to Enigma settings, allowing teams at Bletchley Park (headquarters of British code-breaking efforts) to break into the German naval codes for the first time in the war. The first information from decrypted German transmissions allowed the Royal Navy to sweep up German supply and weather ships; the British destroyed six German tankers and three supply ships after determining their positions. Recognizing that such a clean sweep could hardly have been the result of luck alone, the Germans executed a major enquiry into the security of the message traffic but concluded that destruction of the tankers and supply ships resulted from the efforts of the British secret service.

The Germans had recognized that the British might capture Enigma settings and read transmissions for short periods of time, but they never believed that the British could do this on a sustained basis. They were wrong. Bletchley Park soon began reading U-boat message traffic on a regular basis. The opportunity came from Dönitz's close control of the U-boat war and the numerous transmissions to and from boats at sea, which provided the British with the cribs needed to break into the codes. The intelligence from these decrypts then allowed the British to maneuver convoys around U-boat patrol lines. Sinkings due to submarines dropped dramatically: in July 1941 down to 94,209 tons; in August to 80,310 tons; in September 202,554 tons; in October 156,554 tons; in November 62,196 tons; and in December 124,070 tons. The rise of losses in September reflected the fact that Luftwaffe long-range aircraft picked up the movement of Gibraltar convoys. This British success in the last half of 1941 is the only time in the war where intelligence was decisive by itself. In December 1941 the Germans introduced an additional rotor into the Enigma machine, and the British could not read U-boat message traffic for most of 1942.

The German High Point

The situation in the Atlantic took a drastic turn when Hitler declared war on the United States on December 11, 1941. Dönitz immediately sent a few long-range boats to the east coast of the United States. By mid-January five boats were off the coast from New York to Cape Hatteras, and the slaughter began. The Americans were totally unprepared. No convoy system existed. American destroyers plied up and down coastal waterways like clockwork, so that U-boat commanders always knew where they were. Some American cities along the coast refused to darken their lights. The five U-boats achieved stunning success; between the onset of Operation "*Paukenschlag*" on January 12 and the end of the month, the Germans sank forty ships, all sailing independently. Totals rose rapidly as the Germans reinforced and extended operations to the Caribbean and then to the north coast of South America. In February, U-boats sank 65 ships in American waters, in March 86, in April 69, in May 111, and June 121.

Despite the losses, the Americans stubbornly refused to establish convoys. The commander of defensive operations off the eastern seacoast believed "that a convoy without adequate protection is worse than none." Consequently he concentrated defensive forces in hunting down submarines by patrolling. Such efforts were uniformly unsuccessful; not until April did the Americans sink their first U-boat. The Americans also did not possess a system to integrate intelligence into operations. The British Operational Intelligence Center provided a guide for what was needed, but the U.S. Navy refused to heed British advice until late spring. Equally harmful was the lack of training and doctrine among the naval forces deployed against the U-boats. Initially in 1942 the Americans blamed their failures on a lack of resources, but as a veteran of the effort later admitted, the key factor was human error.

At the beginning of May, the U.S. Navy adopted convoys off the East Coast. That change led Dönitz to shift his emphasis to the Caribbean. Again the U-boats enjoyed a rich harvest of ships sailing independently. In May 1942 U-boats sank forty-one vessels of nearly 250,000 tons in the Gulf of Mexico; thirty-eight more of 200,000 tons went to the bottom in the Caribbean. The Germans had extended the range of U-boats into this area by use of submarine tankers, known as "milk cows." In May and June twenty U-boats operating in the West Indies and Caribbean sank nearly three quarters of a million tons of shipping, virtually all of it sailing independently. This catastrophe forced the Americans to begin convoys throughout the Caribbean; losses again dropped dramatically. The Germans now had to turn back to attacking convoys crossing the North Atlantic; the easy war was over.

The use of U-boats for purposes other than attacking sea lines of communication hampered the campaign in the Atlantic. In winter 1942, Hitler ordered a number of submarines to move into the Mediterranean to help Rommel. Similarly in spring and summer 1942, Hitler held back some U-boats to cover Norway. Then in November 1942, in response to Allied landings in North Africa, he ordered U-boats to attack the landing force. This redeployment cut down on the boats available in the Atlantic precisely at the moment when Allied convoys had lost many escorts to protect the North African landings.

But German difficulties in the North Atlantic were not entirely due to the diversion of submarines. Dönitz's method of controlling his boats created a situation advantageous to Allied intelligence, both in fixing enemy

Convoy Routes, 1942–1943

boats by direction finding and in breaking German naval codes. Further-more, Dönitz attempted to win the war in the Atlantic with a minuscule staff. For the first several years of the war that approach sufficed, but with no organic research unit, with a narrowly focused intelligence effort, and with its small number of officers immersed in day-to-day operations, the German submarine command fell behind the smoothly running organization that the Allies eventually put together. As one opponent remarked, Dönitz's system was "an eighteenth-century way of war in a twentieth-century age of technology."

During 1942, nevertheless, the Germans sank no less than 8 million tons of shipping and suffered few losses. Dönitz possessed approximately 150 U-boats in commission or being constructed in September 1941, and the operational fleet reached 212 boats by September 1942, with an additional 181 preparing for sea duty. By mid-1942 approximately thirty new boats joined the fleet each month. In November total sinkings reached 729,000 tons despite the diversion of many U-boats to North Africa. The climactic moment was now approaching in the Atlantic.

Allied Victory

Despite the large numbers of German submarines, several factors favored the defenders. In December 1942, Bletchley Park again broke into German naval codes, but that intelligence became available sporadically. On some days code breakers could break in quickly, on other days only after long delays. Nevertheless the British and Americans could build up a more complete picture of German operations in the Atlantic, and they now cooperated daily in exchanging intelligence about U-boat operations. The presence of so many U-boats in the Atlantic, however, made it difficult for the Allies to slip a convoy through without its being sighted.

But in 1943 other factors also affected the balance. The number of escorts increased dramatically; nearly all now possessed radar. An improvement to radar—the shifting of microwave frequencies to higher levels—rendered the German detection and jamming equipment useless. Sonar capabilities had considerably improved; depth charges were also better, and some escorts possessed "Hedgehog" rockets that allowed them to attack submarines without losing sonar contact. Allied antisubmarine doctrine and training had also noticeably improved, so that escort groups worked as effective and efficient teams. Finally, escort carriers provided air cover throughout the mid-Atlantic gap where land-based air power had not reached, while long-range aircraft equipped with radar proved a deadly danger to U-boats caught on the surface.

In January 1943 evasive routing of convoys, based on Ultra intelligence, combined with bad weather to lower shipping losses to 200,000 tons. In February losses rose to 360,000 tons, and in March they reached 627,000 tons. In March a series of convoy battles favored the Germans. In a period during which no Ultra intelligence was available to Allied naval commanders, forty German U-boats concentrated on convoys SC-122 and HX-229. In a four-day battle they sank twenty-one merchant ships for the loss of only one boat.

April saw more great battles, but this time the Germans were the losers. In the last week of April, two wolf packs totaling forty-one boats attacked convoy ONS-5. The attackers sank twelve merchant vessels, but the reinforced escort group sank seven U-boats, while severely damaging another five. In April the Germans lost the same number of boats as in March, fifteen. Then in May the battle went completely in favor of the defenders. A combination of escort and air attacks imposed an unacceptable level of losses on U-boats. Allied antisubmarine forces sank forty-one boats during the month. Dönitz concluded that his submarines could no longer meet the Allies on an equal footing; he withdrew them from the North Atlantic.

The battle of the Atlantic was by no means over. Unable to attack Allied convoys in mid-Atlantic, U-boats sought targets in distant waters. Here again, intelligence played a crucial role in leading Allied escort groups to German supply submarines on which long-distant voyages depended. But raids by U-boats off the coast of South Africa and into the Indian Ocean represented only pinpricks that did little overall harm to the Allies. Dönitz had to wait for technological changes to alter the balance. By mid-1945 the Germans were on the point of launching submarines that could move at fifteen knots underwater for short periods of time. Had these boats been available in 1944, the Germans might have negated Allied advantages and resumed a full-scale offensive against Allied commerce.

Allied success in the North Atlantic in May 1943 came at a point at which the American shipyards had begun turning out 10,000-ton *Liberty* ships in enormous numbers. The opening of the Mediterranean, which destruction of Axis forces in Tunisia had made possible, freed up millions more tons of shipping. Through the sea lanes of the world, America could now project its immense military and industrial power in both European and Pacific theaters. With their failure in the Atlantic, the Germans lost their only hope of blocking American troops and industrial products from the coasts of Europe. Significantly, the German navy had played a major role in persuading Hitler to declare war on the United States to prevent such movement. Just as in World War I, the German submarine campaign had failed to live up to the navy's expectations.

The Air War

The Opening Moves

The air war began later than prewar theorists had expected and took much time to work into high gear. Through May 1940, RAF Bomber Command found itself hamstrung by rules of engagement forbidding attacks even on warships tied up at dock. With the German onslaught in May 1940, these restrictions disappeared. For the next ten months, Bomber Command attacked precision targets in Germany, especially oil plants and transportation. But Bomber Command, because its past experiences in the war indicated clearly that daylight bombing attacks would suffer prohibitive casualties, decided to make its attacks at night for most of the rest of the war. The hope was "that the accuracy of night bombing [would] differ little from daylight bombing." Not until summer 1941 did the British discover how unrealistic such hopes were. Then an analysis of mission photographs indicated that only one in three bombers was hitting within five miles of the target; in other words, Bomber Command had a difficult time even in hitting cities.

Such inaccuracy pushed the British toward what they euphemistically described as "area bombing" to "dehouse" the German population. The British decided to undertake a bomber offensive because they wanted to escape the terrible casualties of the last war and because the collapse

Air Marshal Sir Arthur T. Harris fervently believed that only a strategic air offensive could win the war for the Allies in a reasonable amount of time and at an acceptable cost. He also believed, "One cannot win wars by defending oneself."

of France made strategic bombing the only avenue for striking Germany directly. The meager results obtained in 1941 led to pressure for utilization of bomber aircraft in other areas, such as the battle of the Atlantic. Moreover, by the end of 1941 loss rates for bombers had risen significantly as German night defenses improved.

In January 1942 disenchantment with bombing results led to appointment of Air Marshal Arthur T. Harris to head Bomber Command. Harris possessed an unshakable belief in strategic bombing. Fortified by a strong personality and intolerant of differing views, he was an ideal candidate to shake the command's lethargy. Harris understood the need for operational successes both to bolster the morale of his crews and to counter those who argued for diversion of bombers to other tasks. The development of the first significant navigational aid, Gee, allowed the British to bomb with greater accuracy for short distances onto the Continent. In March 1942, the first demonstration of Gee's effectiveness came when Bomber Command took out the Renault factory near Paris. One month later, Bomber Command destroyed Lübeck; postraid reconnaissance indicated that the attack had destroyed 40 to 50 percent of the city. At the end of April, British bombers blasted Rostock and a nearby Heinkel factory.

But Harris's greatest triumph of the year came in May. By scraping together training units and every bomber in his command, he put 1,000 aircraft over Cologne and swamped the night defenses. The British achieved an unheard-of concentration in bombing; with a low loss rate (3.8 percent), Bomber Command devastated the city but killed only 384 civilians, small casualties compared to what was to come. Photo reconnaissance indicated the attack destroyed 600 acres of Cologne. Bomber Command, nevertheless, did not achieve a similar success for the remainder of the year, and the cost remained high. From May to September the British lost 970 bombers; in May 1942 the Command's average number of aircraft had been only 417. The loss rate for the period was 233 percent.

Selected Aerial Targets in Germany

As the bomber offensive expanded, the Luftwaffe responded. In September 1939, Germany did not possess an air-defense system similar to that of Fighter Command. To defend the Reich, the Germans deployed a large number of searchlights and antiaircraft guns. The Luftwaffe also possessed single-engine fighters but committed few of them to home defense because it saw the mission of its fighters as winning air superiority over enemy airspace. In July 1940 the Luftwaffe established the 1st Night Fighter Division under General Joseph Kammhuber. Its mission was to protect Germany from RAF incursions. Kammhuber received a disparate group of aircraft, none of which carried radar. He introduced intruder missions into British airspace to attack RAF bombers taking off; this line of attack showed promise until Hitler ordered it discontinued in summer 1941. Thereafter the Germans never resumed intruder attacks in British airspace.

Throughout 1941, Kammhuber introduced an increasingly effective air-defense system that soon posed a formidable threat to British night operations. Using a belt of radar stations from Denmark to northern France, the system provided early warning as well as ground-control intercept to night fighters equipped with radar. It possessed one considerable weakness: each ground-control site controlled only one fighter and thus one intercept at a time. If the British concentrated their bombers in time and space, they could swamp defenses; but through the end of 1941, that occurred rarely.

In 1942 Bomber Command became a formidable weapon. Despite the heavy damage to Lübeck and Rostock, the OKW did not become alarmed. The devastating attack on Cologne was another matter. Believing these raids signaled a British attempt to start a second front, the Führer decided to reply to the attacks with retaliatory raids and "revenge" weapons such as the wasteful V-2 rocket. Regardless of the vulnerability of the Allied bombers, the Germans remained faithful to Douhet's theories about the futility of countering offensive air power and refused to devote significant resources to their night-fighter defenses.

The Bombing Campaign in Full Gear: Bomber Command

1943 saw an upswing in Allied air attacks on the Germans. Beginning in March 1943 Harris's force battered the Ruhr for three months. These raids marked the beginning of a series of Bomber Command successes. In May 1943 a highly select bomber group took out several dams in the Ruhr River valley, but German air defenses imposed a loss rate on attacking bombers that was close to unbearable. Then in July 1943 the British introduced "Window" (strips of aluminum that reflected to German radar the same signature as a bomber). By dropping out bales of these strips the British blinded the air-defense system. Combined with the arrival of new four-engine bombers, the Halifax and Lancaster, the British dealt out sledgehammer blows.

On the evening of July 27–28, Bomber Command delivered a devastating attack against Hamburg. Conditions were perfect. Hamburg was easy to find; the weather was warm and dry; Window blinded German defenses; and the city's firefighters were on the west side of the city putting out persistent, smoldering coal and coke fires. The marker flares went down perfectly in the center of the city, probably on the great lumberyard where Baltic timber arrived for distribution to Germany. Most of the following bombers dropped their loads of incendiaries and high explosives into the glowing cauldron. The fire then pumped superheated air straight up into the stratosphere, at the same time sucking in fresh air from outside the city. Winds approached 300–400 miles per hour, while temperatures reached close to 1,000 degrees. The raid burned a four-mile hole in the city's center; between 30,000–40,000 perished. After the war Speer claimed that if Bomber Command had repeated its Hamburg success four or five times in succeeding weeks, Germany would have collapsed. But Bomber Command could not repeat its success. In August it took out the bomb research and experimental station at Peenemünde on the Baltic coast. Since German night defenses were recovering from Window, the attacking force of

Destruction in Hamburg. Sir Arthur Harris believed such destruction pointed the "certain, the obvious, the quickest, and the easiest way to overwhelming victory."

597 lost forty bombers (6.7 percent). In October Harris's forces created another firestorm at Kassel.

At this point Harris determined to destroy Berlin. Though his offensive did not win the war, it came close to destroying his command. Berlin lay deep in Germany and Luftwaffe defenses could pick up and follow the great bomber stream throughout its course over the Reich. Rather than guide individual fighters to bombers, the Germans now guided night fighters into the bomber stream and then allowed the fighters to identify and attack individual aircraft. Also, a new German radar, SN2, allowed night fighters to tear away Window's veil. The weather in winter 1943–1944 was appallingly bad, so that virtually all bombing took place through clouds. Although Harris's attackers damaged Berlin extensively, their target was enormous, and the British did not attain the concentration achieved over Hamburg.

British losses rapidly rose. In December 1943 the British lost 170 bombers; in January 1944, 314; in February, 199; and in March, 283. Considering that the Command had a front-line bomber strength of 1,224 in January 1944, such losses were staggering. On the evening of March 30, 1944, Bomber Command struck Nuremberg; many of the attackers hit Schweinfurt instead; the Germans shot down 108. Such disastrous losses forced Harris to call off nighttime area bombing attacks on central Germany. While Bomber Command had dealt out devastating blows, it had not broken enemy morale, and by March 1944 its rate of attrition had reached unsupportable levels.

The Bombing Campaign in Full Gear: The American Effort

In summer 1942 the first bomber units of the U.S. Army Air Forces (USAAF) arrived in England to begin daylight operations on the Continent. The Americans brought with them a belief that during daylight hours they could fight their way through German defenses with great formations of heavily armed B-17s. These bombers would then attack the vital centers of Germany's industry and, by destroying certain crucial targets, cause the collapse of the enemy's economic system. While American air commanders recognized that the Luftwaffe was a formidable force, they believed that their numbers and disciplined flying could overwhelm the German air defenses without the support of long-range escort fighters. Initially, however, they had too few bombers to launch B-17s into German airspace; American raids thus initially struck at Nazi-occupied France within supporting range of friendly fighters. Nevertheless, this rather limited experience led Brigadier General Ira C. Eaker, Eighth Air Force commander, to write his superiors that "bombardment in force—a minimum of 300 bombers—can effectively attack any German target and return without excessive or uneconomical losses." Eaker's strength, however, did not reach that level until late spring 1943 because of the diversion of bombers to support "Torch" and operations in the Mediterranean.

The question of what to attack became a divisive issue. The German aircraft industry had to be a primary target because the Luftwaffe was a far more ferocious opponent than expected. Attacks on other industries offered the possibility of weakening the German economy, but most industries, such as oil, contained a larger number of targets than Eighth Air Force's force structure could attack. Consequently, through a selection process largely determined by the number of targets, the Americans settled on the ball-bearing industry as the weak link in the German economic structure.

At Casablanca in early winter 1943 British and American political and military leaders agreed that Allied air forces should wage a "combined bomber offensive" by day and night to put relentless pressure on the Reich's population and industry. Unfortunately the agreement in principle proved difficult to implement, at least as far as finding a common focus for the offensive. Harris stood firm in his belief in "area bombing" and in his contempt for attacks on specific targets, which he derisively described as "panacea targets." The Americans, on the other hand, persisted in their belief that by making precision attacks on industrial targets they could cause the collapse of the German economy. There was thus little room for a common approach until 1944.

American raids began reaching into Germany in early summer 1943. Heavy blows fell on the Ruhr in July; on August 17, Eaker dispatched a massive force to take out the Messerschmitt factory at Regensburg and the ball-bearing works at Schweinfurt. The latter complex produced half of Germany's ball bearings. But the attacks ran into a slew of German fighters. Of 146 bombers in the Regensburg force, the Germans shot down twenty-four

(16.4 percent). Because the bombers continued on to North Africa, thereby disconcerting the defenses, they avoided higher losses, but sixty of the bombers that reached Africa had to remain to be repaired or salvaged. The forces attacking Schweinfurt (230 bombers) lost thirty-six more aircraft (15.7 percent). Twenty-seven more bombers had to be written off after returning to England because of extensive damage.

From August through October 1943, Eaker threw great unescorted formations of B-17s into German territory without support from long-range escort fighters. Surprisingly the provision of such fighters remained low on his list of priorities. American aircraft continued to attack Luftwaffe production facilities and ball-bearing factories. Losses, however, were horrendous. In maintaining its aerial offensive, Eighth Air Force suffered a nearly 30 percent crew loss each month—a rate ensuring that few bomber crews ever completed the twenty-five missions required to return home. On October 14, "Black Thursday," Eighth again attacked Schweinfurt; the long flight across Germany took a terrible toll. Luftwaffe fighters and antiaircraft shot down sixty bombers, seventeen more were written off, while 121 were damaged but repairable. So heavy were the losses that Eighth had to call off deep-penetration raids. The Luftwaffe had won one of the last, but temporary, victories achieved by Germany in the war.

The Schweinfurt raids of 1943 against the ball-bearing industry represented a terrible threat to the German war economy. After the war, Speer admitted that continued attacks on the industry would have brought the economy to a halt. But Eighth Air Force could not endure such losses from continued attacks. Moreover, the Germans discovered that their industrial concerns possessed large backlogs of ball bearings, that the Swedes and Swiss were willing to sell them to the Reich, and that in some weapons they could substitute roller bearings (easier to manufacture) for ball bearings.

Yet for all its failings in 1943, the air offensive provided substantial benefits to the Allied cause. Attacks on the aircraft industry caused German production of new fighters to fall by an average of 200 fighters per month from its peak in July 1943. In November 1943 new fighter production was 300 under the total for July (576 versus 873). While attacking American forces suffered high losses, they inflicted heavy casualties on the enemy. Admittedly, they could not maintain that effort in the face of such losses, but the attacks seriously affected the Germans.

The British raids also had a serious, though indirect, impact. Well into 1944 the Germans emphasized production of bombers to strike back at the Allies. Moreover, by 1943 they embarked on an enormously costly program to build V-1 and V-2 rockets to pay the British back for area bombing. In the end the V-1 and V-2 program used up resources equivalent to the production of 24,000 fighter aircraft.

But the largest diversion of German military strength came in the area of antiaircraft defenses. In 1940 the air-defense system consisted of 791 heavy batteries, equipped with high velocity 88-mm, 105-mm, and 128-mm guns; by 1943 the number of batteries had risen to 2,132 with over 10,000 antiaircraft guns. That total represented a considerable investment in manpower and material that the Germans desperately needed elsewhere. This was especially so since, from a German point of view, Flak was not cost effective against high-flying aircraft. The 88-mm Flak weapon, for example, required 16,000 shells to hit an aircraft at high altitude. Every night these weapons fired large amounts of ammunition into the skies over the Reich to reassure the population that the Luftwaffe was defending the country against enemy bombers.

The Luftwaffe

From the beginning of the war, the Luftwaffe suffered from a poor support structure. Göring was incapable of providing long-term guidance; General Hans Jeschonnek, the chief of staff, focused entirely on operational concerns; and intelligence was a disaster. Most seriously, the production and maintenance structure was in complete shambles. One of Göring's closest confidants, General Ernst Udet, controlled this crucial sphere of Luftwaffe activity. Udet had been a great ace in World War I, a barnstormer in the 1920s and 1930s, and then a rising star in the resurrected Luftwaffe, but he possessed few managerial skills. Göring selected him nevertheless in 1938 to run the Luftwaffe's production and design establishment. Udet soon had more than forty different offices reporting directly to him. By summer 1941 production programs were way off target; technological development had stalled; and confusion reigned. In the summer of 1941, Göring finally reinstated Field Marshal Milch in the process; soon afterward, Udet committed suicide.

Milch possessed great managerial skills, and since the air war rested on industrial management, Milch's appointment was crucial to getting the Luftwaffe back on track. But the Germans had lost one full year and were already behind the British and Americans. In a hurried trip to the Eastern Front in September 1941, Milch discovered hundreds of broken aircraft littering forward airfields because of shortages in spare parts; the supply system had almost entirely broken down in the vastness of Russia. By December operationally ready rates for German bombers had fallen to 32 percent, for fighters to 52 percent, and for the whole Luftwaffe to 45 percent. These figures underline the difficulties that the Luftwaffe, conceived in terms of central European requirements, now confronted in fighting a conflict possessing continental distances.

For the Luftwaffe the war now became one of three fronts: the Eastern Front against an increasingly effective Red Air Force, equipped not only with its own production but with American and British aircraft as well; the Mediterranean against a growing tide of Anglo-American air power; and the great night and day attacks of the Combined Bomber Offensive. Against this massive threat, Milch struggled to increase aircraft production. Since Germany controlled the industrial capacity of central Europe, he achieved considerable increases in aircraft production. But British and American bombing did retard those efforts in 1943. More important, Germany's enemies had already geared up their economies for massive production increases.

In 1942 the Germans felt the first pressure from Allied production superiority. In Russia the quality of German aircrews made up for the Red Air Force's superiority in numbers. In the Mediterranean, however, the RAF exercised increasing influence over the conduct of operations. Air Marshal Sir Arthur Tedder, perhaps the greatest airman of the war, developed a force that could gain and maintain air superiority over the battlefield, while the desert air force's interdiction and close air-support strikes rendered crucial support to the army. Moreover, its antishipping attacks, supported by Ultra, undermined Rommel's logistical support.

At the end of 1942 the roof fell in on the Luftwaffe. Hitler and the senior military leaders made two serious mistakes. In response to Operation Torch, the invasion of North Africa by the British and Americans, the OKW moved large forces across to Tunisia. To support the commitment, the Luftwaffe had to use much of its Ju 52 transport fleet; that commitment shut down the training program for bomber pilots. The air battle to protect the tenuous logistic lines to Tunisia put the Luftwaffe at a severe disadvantage, especially since Ultra intelligence kept the Allies fully informed of Axis supply movements. Undersupplied and vulnerable on North African airfields, the Luftwaffe confronted increasingly effective Allied air attacks on its supplies and base structure. By March 1943 the Germans and Italians had to stop ship movements to Tunisia; movement of supplies by transport aircraft proved equally as costly. The air battle in the Mediterranean continued through the summer, when the Germans finally conceded defeat in the Mediterranean.

Events on the Eastern Front followed a similar pattern. Almost concurrently with Torch, the Soviets launched a counteroffensive against German Sixth Army at Stalingrad. Hitler, bolstered by Göring's promise that the Luftwaffe could keep Sixth Army supplied, refused any thought of abandoning Stalin's city. The transport fleet, already stretched by Tunisia, had to rush into the breach. Despite heroic efforts, the Russian winter made airlift operations impossible. Operationally ready rates plummeted, losses mounted. The Luftwaffe never came close to providing the 600 tons per day that Sixth Army required. Throughout the winter, fighting swirled around Stalingrad and forced the Luftwaffe to provide constant support for hard-pressed ground troops. In March 1943, the spring thaw brought a short pause to ground operations in the east. The air battles, however, continued, and the Luftwaffe took particularly heavy losses over the Caucasus.

Meanwhile, Army Group Center prepared for the climactic battle of the Eastern Front, the clash of armor at the Kursk salient. The Luftwaffe concentrated nearly 2,000 aircraft over Kursk. *Luftflotte* Six supported Army Group Center's drive with 750 aircraft, while *Luftflotte* Four supported Army Group South's attack with 1,100 aircraft. In 1943 a substantial proportion of Luftwaffe frontline strength still remained committed on the Eastern Front: 84.5 percent of all dive bombers, 27 percent of all fighters, and 33 percent of bombers. On the first day of Kursk, German pilots flew 3,000 sorties and fought a great air battle over the salient. But the Germans never established air superiority, and the Red Air Force interfered significantly with German air and ground operations. After the failure of the German offensive at Kursk, the Soviets launched counteroffensives against Army Group Center and Army Group South. The Luftwaffe desperately attempted to stave off defeat on the ground but suffered heavy losses that severely affected its capabilities. At the same time, its best fighter squadrons moved from the Eastern Front to meet the American bombing offensive.

In July and August of 1943 the Luftwaffe fought three great air battles. In the Mediterranean the Anglo-American attack on Sicily and air raids into Italy cost the Luftwaffe 711 combat aircraft in July and 321 in August (1,032 for the two months); in defending the skies over western Europe, it lost 526 in July and 625 for August (1,151 for the two months); and in the east the Luftwaffe lost 558 in July and 472 in August (1,030 for the two months). The loss of 3,213 combat aircraft in two months out of a force structure of approximately 5,000 combat aircraft was simply no longer supportable. Given the threat to Germany's cities and industries, the Luftwaffe had to come home to defend its base. After September 1943, German soldiers on the Italian and Eastern fronts would seldom see their air force. The skies over the battlefield belonged to the Allies.

*   *   *   *

The entry of the United States into World War II resulted from substantial miscalculations on the part of two Axis partners, Nazi Germany and Imperial Japan. In the end success in the war rested on the great industrial mobilization of the Allies' economies on which military might depended. For the Americans as well as the British the second piece of the puzzle was the ability to project military power over the world's oceans, and that required mastery over the substantial U-boat threat. Until their naval forces had mastered that threat, the economic and military potential of the Western Powers remained open to question.

For the Americans and the British, the defeat of France in May 1940 meant that their ground forces could not engage the enemy on the European Continent until 1943 or 1944. That in turn forced the Anglo-Saxon powers to rely on air power to strike at the sources of Nazi military power. From the retrospective view of fifty years, the Combined Bombing Offensive failed to achieve its stated operational objectives in 1942 and 1943. But it did at least strike the Germans hard, and it moved from being a considerable nuisance to posing a real threat to the stability of the Reich's war economy.

What was indeed remarkable was the unprecedented scale of the Allied effort in harnessing men, women, machines, and raw materials to the war effort. The successes of German and Japanese armies and navies in the first war years provided the incentive and popular support in Allied countries. The political skill and ruthlessness of the American, British, and Soviet leaders then provided the framework and means to translate large populations and economic power into military might.

SUGGESTED READINGS

Beesley, Patrick. *Very Special Intelligence: The Story of the Admiralty's Operational Intelligence Center* (London: Hamish Hamilton, 1977).

Buell, Thomas B. *Master of Sea Power: A Biography of Fleet Admiral Ernest J. King* (Boston: Little Brown, 1980).

Fuchida Mitsuo. *Midway, the Battle That Doomed Japan* (Annapolis: Naval Institute, 1955).

Hastings, Max. *Bomber Command* (New York: Dial Press, 1979).

Hayashi Saburo. *Kogun: The Japanese Army in the Pacific War* (Westport, Conn.: Greenwood Press, 1978).

James, D. Clayton. *The Years of MacArthur.* 2 vols. (Boston: Houghton Mifflin, 1970).

Millett, Allen, and Williamson Murray. *Military Effectiveness*, vol. III, *World War II* (London: Allen and Unwin, 1988).

Milward, Alan. *The German Economy at War* (London: Athlone Press, 1965).

Morison, Samuel Eliot. *The Two-Ocean War: A Short History of the United States Navy in the Second World War* (Boston: Little Brown, 1963).

Murray, Williamson. *Luftwaffe* (Baltimore: Nautical and Aviation Publishing Co., 1985).

Prange, Gordon W., with Donald M. Goldstein and Katherine V. Dillon. *At Dawn We Slept: The Untold Story of Pearl Harbor* (New York: McGraw-Hill, 1981).

_____. *Miracle at Midway* (New York: McGraw-Hill, 1982).

Ienaga Saburo. *The Pacific War: World War II and the Japanese, 1931–1945* (New York: Pantheon Books, 1978).

Spector, Ronald H. *Eagle Against the Sun: The War with Japan* (New York: The Free Press, 1985).

Townsend, Peter. *Duel of Eagles* (New York: Simon and Schuster, 1970).

U.S. Army Air Forces. *Ultra and the History of the United States Strategic Air Force in Europe vs. the German Air Force* (Frederick, Md.: University Publications of America, 1980).

Webster, Sir Charles, and Noble Frankland. *The Strategic Air Offensive Against Germany, 1939–1945* (London: Her Majesty's Stationery Office, 1962).

Winton, John. *Ultra at Sea: How Breaking the Nazi Code Affected Allied Naval Strategy During World War II* (New York: William Morrow and Co., 1988).

24

THE EASTERN AND MEDITERRANEAN FRONTS: WINNING BATTLES OF MEN AND MACHINES

To Stalingrad

Defeat in the East,
November 1942–
October 1943

The Mediterranean,
1942–1943

The East, 1944

By early 1942 the Nazi surge toward the frontiers of Europe had exhausted itself. The Wehrmacht, nevertheless, possessed the capability to launch major offensives and represented a determined opponent, capable of defending its position with tenacity even though at the far reaches of its logistic capabilities. But the productive and mobilized strength of the Allies exercised a growing and eventually overwhelming impact on operations. Moreover, Allied superiority in personnel and logistics allowed them to fight massive battles that played to their strengths, while minimizing those of their opponents. Along with these advantages went Allied superiority in intelligence and deception. Virtually every action that the German military undertook was now open to the prying eyes and ears of Allied intelligence. Moreover, the Allies could screen their intentions and plans almost entirely. Only Hitler's "intuition" at times caught glimpses of what was coming, but the Führer possessed neither the discipline nor consistency to act coherently on such visions.

In the Mediterranean, the British defeated Rommel at El Alamein and drove Axis forces from Egypt and Libya. As the British pushed the enemy back, the Allies used their advantages in sea and air power to land on the coast of North Africa. For the first time, the Americans entered the land battle against the Germans and after some initial difficulties played a major role in the Axis defeat in North Africa and then in the landings in Sicily and Italy. On the Eastern Front, the Soviets, through the skillful use of deception, magnified their growing superiority in weapons and their improving operational performance. In their offensives, they drove the Germans back hundreds of miles. In the end the Allies battered the Wehrmacht back to the Reich and ended whatever chance the Germans had of escaping their fate.

To Stalingrad

As spring 1942 approached, the Germans surmounted the desperate situation on the Eastern Front; they had prevented the terrible conditions of the winter campaign from degenerating into a collapse. Nevertheless, they confronted difficult challenges for the upcoming spring offensive. Halder, still chief of the general staff, and senior ground commanders argued that the army should remain on the defensive, rebuild the forces shattered by the winter, and await increases in production. Hitler, however, believed that Germany must destroy Soviet military potential before American industry came into play. By this point Hitler's word almost always carried the day.

In early April the OKH issued Directive 41 for a summer campaign. In the north, German forces were to link up with the Finns and finish the destruction of Leningrad. Army Group Center would stand on the defensive, while the major effort occurred in the south. There mobile units would clear the Soviets from west of the Don River and then strike into the Caucasus. Initially Hitler accorded Stalingrad little importance. The main objective was Soviet oil with the proviso that Stalingrad's capture might block movement of petroleum up the Volga River.

Several factors underlined how much Nazi capabilities had declined since 1941. Operation Barbarossa had called for a German offensive along the entire front, but by 1942 the Wehrmacht could launch a major offensive only in the south. Moreover, as German armies advanced into the Caucasus, their left flank would become increasingly exposed to Soviet counterblows from the north, and the Germans lacked sufficient troops to cover that flank. As a result, only by persuading their Romanian, Italian, and Hungarian allies to provide armies could Hitler launch the summer 1942 offensive. More ominously, the OKH had to strip other armies in the east of equipment and troops to prepare Army Group South for its role.

Before that offensive began, however, two major battles occurred. The Soviets picked up German preparations and at Stalin's direction launched a spoiling attack at Kharkov, Army Group South's main logistics base. The *Stavka* argued against the attack, for it believed that the Red Army should hold onto its reserves until German intentions became clear. On Stalin's orders, however, the offensive began on May 12; it soon broke through the German front. For a short period it appeared that the Russians

German Advance to Stalingrad,
May 7 – November 18, 1942

might reach Kharkov and its crucial supply dumps. But strong German forces contained the breakthrough and then launched a counterstrike at the salient's thin neck. Soviet commanders pleaded to retreat, but Stalin demanded that the attack continue. In effect, Soviet forces had advanced into a sack, and the German counterattack cut them off. Not only did the Germans capture 240,000 Soviet troops, but they also destroyed most of the Soviet armored reserves (1,200 tanks).

A second disaster for the Soviets followed on the heels of the first. In June 1942, Manstein, now commander of Eleventh Army, conducted a skillful attack on Sevastopol, the main Soviet naval base on the Crimean Peninsula. In ferocious fighting, German troops broke through the port's fortifications and crushed the Soviet garrison. As a reward for the successful siege, Hitler promoted Manstein to field marshal. The Führer, however, vetoed the new field marshal's suggestion that Eleventh Army form a reserve behind Army Group South's drive into the Caucasus. Instead most of the army's infantry and artillery (and Manstein) moved north to conduct siege operations against Leningrad. The few units remaining found themselves parceled out among the attacking armies of Army Group South.

On June 28 the summer offensive began. The Germans planned on launching a multiphased operation that would include sequential attacks from the left to right of Army Group South, followed by an advance into the Caucasus. On the left, in the first phase of the campaign, three panzer, three motorized, and nine infantry divisions struck due east toward Voronezh. By July 2 the Germans were on the city's outskirts, and by July 6 they had taken the city. Their success froze the *Stavka* because the German attack suggested an opening move against Moscow. However, the Germans turned south down the Don, while Hungarian divisions moved to cover the widening northern flank. On June 30, Sixth Army jumped off from the center of Army Group South and attempted to encircle Soviet units along the Don; but the *Stavka* finally persuaded Stalin to order a timely retreat and the German pincers closed on thin air.

As the Nazi advance accelerated, OKH divided Army Group South into Army Groups A and B, and on July 13 Hitler fired Field Marshal Bock for a second time. In effect, the Führer became commander of Army Group South and directed the offensive from his East Prussian headquarters. In the south Army Group A battered its way into Rostov, crossed the Don, and turned south. The gateway to the Caucasus was open. As Bock commented shortly before his relief, however, the battle had been "sliced in two." While Army Group B moved east toward Stalingrad and the Volga River, Army Group A moved south into the Caucasus. For the present, Hitler focused on the southern advance and shifted forces to Army Group A; this delayed the eastward move toward Stalingrad. Other delays came from both army groups having already encountered serious logistic difficulties, particularly the lack of fuel. The capture of Soviet oil fields in the Caucasus failed to alleviate these problems, since the Soviets did a thorough job of sabotaging wells and refining equipment.

In August, Hitler's erratic attention swung from the Caucasus to Stalingrad. On August 23, Sixth Army reached the Volga River north of the

Though the Germans occupied the center of Stalingrad, the Soviets refused to stop fighting. The Germans described the subsequent combat as a *Rattenkrieg*, a war among rats.

city; on the 24th it launched its first attacks on the suburbs and began fighting its way into the city. As fighting intensified, Hitler pulled forces out of the Caucasus and funneled them into the cauldron of Stalingrad's built-up area. The Soviet defenders prepared to hold out to the last. In the wreckage caused by constant air attacks and artillery bombardments, they established strong defenses and scattered numerous snipers. Street by street, building by building, German infantry dug the Soviets out of their defensive positions. Particularly savage fighting took place in Stalingrad's tractor works and in the city's great grain elevator. The close combat and hand-to-hand fighting, in some areas from floor to floor, maximized Soviet strengths of dogged stoicism and determination while minimizing German tactical flexibility and mobility.

Driven by Hitler's fanatical determination, the bitter battle had considerable strategic effects. The fighting ended whatever chance the Germans had to cut the Soviets off from oil supplies of the Caucasus. Moreover it reduced German reserves across the Eastern Front, while exhausting the Wehrmacht in a pointless battle of prestige. By early November Sixth Army had fought its way across the lunar landscape of Stalingrad. Although the Soviets held only a tenuous position on the banks of the Volga, they had pulled Sixth Army into a vulnerable position. Ill-equipped and poorly trained Romanian, Italian, and Hungarian formations protected its flanks; German forces in the Caucasus were exhausted; virtually no reserves were available; and winter was again closing in on a supply system stretched to the breaking point. Hitler, however, believed that the summer offensive had fought the Soviets to exhaustion. The generals were not so sure, but by this point in the war, they had learned to keep their opinions to themselves. German intelligence picked up some Soviet troop movements north of Stalingrad but reported that "only local attacks are expected."

Defeat in the East, November 1942–October 1943

Disaster at Stalingrad

In September 1942 the Soviets began preparations for a massive counteroffensive. Over the next two months, *Stavka* deployed nearly one million men, 900 tanks, and a vast array of artillery forces, including one-third of their rocket launchers, on Sixth Army's flanks. Their plan had limited aims—to break through the defenses north and south of Stalingrad and then to encircle German forces in the city. In the offensive the Soviets displayed significant improvements over the tactical and operational performance of earlier efforts.

On November 19, in the midst of a swirling snowstorm, units from five Soviet armies, including a tank army—a sign of growing Soviet operational skills—smashed into the Romanians north of Stalingrad. By early afternoon they had destroyed Romanian defenses and were in the open; their advance gained an average of fourteen miles on the first day. The XXXXVIII Panzer Corps attempted to plug the breach, but its obsolete collection of tanks had little chance against Soviet armor, equipped with T-34s. On the 20th two Soviet armies broke the Romanians south of Stalingrad. The Soviets split Fourth Panzer Army and drove some of its units into the pocket with Sixth Army. On November 23, Soviet spearheads advancing from north and south met late in the afternoon forty miles west of Stalingrad and isolated Sixth Army.

Decision making within the German high command now broke down, a sure indication of Hitler's destructive influence. On November 19 the Führer was in Berchtesgaden attempting to repair a deteriorating situation in the Mediterranean. As reports of trouble in the east arrived, he hurried north in his command train to OKH headquarters in East Prussia to deal with the Soviet emergency. During much of that trip, however, he was out of touch with the various command sections. Hitler provided no instructions to the commander of Sixth Army, General Friedrich Paulus, and by this point in the war no one remained in the high command willing to make independent decisions. On November 21, Hitler ordered Paulus to stand fast in Stalingrad "regardless of the danger of a temporary encirclement." When one of Paulus's corps commanders, General Walter von Seydlitz-Kurzbach, ordered his troops to retreat in preparation for a breakout, Hitler reacted angrily.

To deal with the deteriorating situation, Hitler created Army Group Don, consisting of four armies, and appointed Manstein to its command, but it took the field marshal nearly one week to assume control. During that period, Manstein advised Hitler that while a withdrawal from Stalingrad might be necessary, it would be best to wait until reinforcements arrived, since Sixth Army was tying down huge Soviet forces. The OKH, supported by many ground and air commanders on the scene, argued for an immediate breakout. Hitler, committed to holding on the Volga, temporized.

Göring, with the aid of some army commanders, provided the final ingredients for disaster. As early as November 21 Sixth Army had examined the possibility of an aerial bridge. The Luftwaffe's General Wolfram von Richthofen immediately warned Sixth Army that the Luftwaffe did not possess sufficient strength. Göring, however, assured Hitler that the Luftwaffe could supply Sixth Army, just as it had supported a corps and a half of German soldiers in the Demyansk pocket over the previous winter; the Luftwaffe chief of staff, despite a massive commitment of transport aircraft to Tunisia, offered no opposition to Göring's promise.

For the time being the Soviets strengthened their hold on Stalingrad. The Germans desperately attempted to patch together a relief force—not surprisingly, few of the reinforcements promised by Hitler arrived. The besieged required an airlift of 600 tons per day; under the best conditions the Luftwaffe could supply 350 tons. Airlift forces consisted of a hodgepodge of Ju 52s, Ju 86s, and He 111s. To cobble together even these aircraft the Luftwaffe stripped its bomber transition schools of their inexperienced crews; maintenance conditions were appalling, and operational rates fell to 10–20 percent during periods of bad weather. On only three days in December did transports reach a 300-ton level; on most days less than 100 tons arrived in Stalingrad.

In mid-December, Manstein launched his offensive to break through to Stalingrad; LVII Panzer Corps drove to within thirty-five miles of the city on December 19, but no farther. Manstein appears to have urged Hitler to order a breakout, but the Führer refused because neither Manstein nor Paulus would assure him that one would succeed. One observer of the Führer during this period concluded that he "seemed no longer capable of making a decision." On December 26, Paulus reported his army incapable of a breakout unless German troops outside the city first opened up a supply corridor.

In fact, it was too late. On December 16 the Soviets attacked the Italian Army along the Don northwest of Stalingrad. The Soviets ripped a one-hundred-mile gap in Army Group Don's flank, and Manstein had to shift forces to contain the breakthrough and abandon all ideas of relieving Sixth Army. The collapse along the upper Don placed an even greater burden on air supply, while Soviet capture of the airfields at Tatsinskaya and Morozovsk in early January forced the Luftwaffe to move its bases almost 200 miles from the pocket. This relocation ended any significant air bridge to Stalingrad.

Soviet Winter Offensive, 1942–1943

Throughout January, Soviet forces drove toward Rostov and the Donets Basin. The question now was whether the Red Army would reach Rostov and cut off Seventeenth and First Panzer Armies in the Caucasus. The defenders at Stalingrad would have to hold to the end, in hopes of tying up Soviet forces, while Army Group Don desperately attempted to stabilize a collapsing situation. After Paulus rejected the final surrender ultimatum, the Soviets began their last attack on January 10. By February 2, the Germans had surrendered. Out of 250,000 soldiers trapped in the Stalingrad pocket, approximately 90,000 became prisoners; barely 5,000 survived the war.

The Germans Recover

As Stalingrad capitulated, the Germans strove to stabilize the situation along the southern front. Hitler did allow Army Group A to withdraw from the Caucasus, but part of it became shut up on the Kuban peninsula opposite the Crimea. During the third week in January, a new series of Soviet attacks ripped into Army Group B and virtually destroyed the Hungarian Second Army. The Soviets had achieved operational freedom from Voronezh to Voroshilovgrad, a distance of over two hundred miles. By mid-January, they had captured Belgorod and almost reached Dnepropetrovsk. The Germans had to abandon Kharkov on February 15.

Despite Soviet gains, the Germans managed a recovery; they were falling back on their supply dumps, while the Soviets were outrunning their supply lines. A lack of focus also worked against the Soviets; their spearheads were neither mutually supporting nor strong enough to achieve independent success. Significant German reinforcements also arrived. Hitler permitted the transfer to Manstein's Army Group of about 100,000 soldiers from Army Group A in the Crimea and seven fresh divisions from western Europe. In addition, Luftwaffe forces, reorganized under Richthofen's driving leadership, provided enhanced air support. From February 20 to March 15, Luftwaffe squadrons provided 1,000 combat sorties per day versus an average of only 350 in January. By this point the Soviet advance had left the bases of the Red air force far behind, thereby making air support incapable of intervening in the battle.

Despite Hitler's anger at the loss of Kharkov, Manstein persuaded him that Army Group South (now reformed from Army Group Don and parts of Army Group B) could reestablish control of its northern flank only by temporarily relinquishing control of that city. Supported by Richthofen's aircraft, a German counteroffensive began on February 19. The sudden eruption of the German forces caused a collapse of the overextended Soviet forces. By mid-March, Army Group South had recaptured Kharkov and driven the Soviets back to the Donets River, a gain of almost one hundred miles. The spring thaw finally arrived, and both sides, exhausted after fighting that had lasted continuously from July 1942, collapsed.

The Battle of Kursk, July 1943

Even as SS troops battered their way into Kharkov, Hitler issued a directive for the coming summer. Since the Wehrmacht no longer possessed the offensive power to win a decisive victory in a short campaign, the Führer's directive suggested instead a series of limited offensives, first at Kursk then at Leningrad, to reduce Soviet reserves and to improve defensive positions. After discarding several options, Hitler settled in mid-April 1943 on a major offensive, "Citadel," against the Kursk salient north of Kharkov.

The original conception was that Citadel would begin as soon as spring conditions provided solid ground for maneuver. But there were risks; the sectors north and south of Kursk were vulnerable to a Soviet counter-strike. The overall situation led Manstein to suggest that the Wehrmacht remain on the defensive and counterattack any Soviet summer offensive. Such an approach, however, would have entailed considerable risks and perhaps even the surrender of territory, the last thing Hitler was willing to

The Battle of Kursk, July 4 – August 1, 1943

0   30   60 mi
0   20   40 km

XXXX
Second

Orel

XXXX
Ninth

XXXX

Kursk

XXXX
Second

Center
South

XXXX
Fourth

Belgorod

Donets R.

Kharkov

XXXX
Group Kempf

Front lines
Panzer army
German attacks

countenance. In the end the plan called for the major effort to occur on the southern shoulder of the Kursk salient. Army Group South would break through Soviet positions and then drive deep behind Kursk to link up with another drive launched on the northern shoulder by Army Group Center's Ninth Army. The hoped-for result would pinch off the Kursk salient and Soviet forces defending it.

Above all, Hitler hoped to achieve a major psychological victory over the Red Army. He argued, "The victory at Kursk must have the effect of a beacon seen around the world." In May he postponed Citadel until June or July despite opposition from some generals, including the OKH chief of staff, Colonel General Kurt Zeitzler. Hitler believed the postponement would allow a buildup of the armored forces with Tiger tanks and the new Panthers. Manstein and Günther von Kluge, commanders of the army groups involved in the operation, disagreed, believing that any delay would result in Soviet countermeasures. Nevertheless, Hitler postponed Citadel to early July. An uneasy calm settled on the Eastern Front as both sides prepared for the coming battle.

The Soviets had improved considerably in operational skill and in their use of intelligence. In April they picked up German intentions to launch a major strike at Kursk and in May began preparations on both shoulders of the salient. German intelligence never divined the massive scale of Soviet defensive and offensive measures to meet the attack. By this point in the war, Stalin was displaying greater trust in his generals. Zhukov and others advised him to remain on the defensive, and he accepted their advice.

The extent of Soviet preparations underlines the trap into which the Germans were walking. Soviet first-line defenses on both sides of the salient were two to three miles deep and contained three to four trench lines with numerous bunkers and strong points. Behind this line the Soviets constructed a second defensive zone at depths varying between six and eighteen miles. Twenty-five miles farther back they laid out three more lines on a similar scale. The fortification zone extended more than one hundred miles and included more than half a million mines. On the northern shoulder the Soviets achieved a density of forty-eight antitank guns per mile of front. Four armies, including a tank army, defended the northern shoulder of the Kursk salient; six armies held the southern side, while five armies of the Steppe Front stood immediately in reserve. Three more armies stood north of Kursk and two south; these forces could reinforce the salient should things turn bad. If the front held, the Soviets intended to use these reserves in major counterattacks. German intelligence gave no indication about the extent of enemy preparations.

On the German side, the growing strength of ground forces reflected the success that Speer had had in mobilizing the European economy. The Luftwaffe possessed nearly 2,500 combat aircraft, more than half of which would support Citadel. In the north, Field Marshal Walter Model's Ninth Army contained three panzer corps with twenty-one divisions, including one panzer grenadier and six panzer divisions, as well as 900 tanks; Manstein's Army Group South contained four panzer corps with twenty-two divisions,

Konstantin K. Rokossovskii wore a set of stainless steel false teeth as a result of his imprisonment and torture by the secret police before World War II for "anti-Soviet" activities. After regaining Stalin's favor he displayed a great flair for mobile warfare and played a key role in the battles of Moscow, Stalingrad, and Kursk, as well as Operation Bagration.

including six panzer and five panzer grenadier divisions, as well as 1,000 tanks. The entire battle would involve some 4,000 Soviet and 3,000 German tanks and assault guns.

On July 5, Citadel began. On the northern shoulder, Ninth Army attacked on a thirty-five-mile front and initially enjoyed limited success. Its attack broke through Soviet front-line defenses and had reached the second line by day's end. By July 6, Marshal Konstantin K. Rokossovskii, commander of Soviet forces in the north, had put in two tank corps and an infantry corps from his reserves, while *Stavka* moved additional units forward. By the next day Ninth Army's assault had stalled along a heavily fortified ridge thirteen miles beyond its start line and still well short of Rokossovskii's third defensive line; attempts to break through on July 10 and 11 failed entirely and Model could characterize the battle only as "a rolling battle of attrition"—exactly the kind of battle that played to Soviet strengths and minimized German mobility.

In the south, Manstein's offensive hardly got off to an auspicious start. As German troops moved into jump-off positions in the predawn hours of July 5, General Nikolai F. Vatutin, commander of Soviet forces in the south, unleashed a massive preemptive artillery bombardment. The surprise bombardment inflicted heavy casualties on German troops and demonstrated that the Soviets were fully informed about the coming attack. Nevertheless, the first hours went well. Fourth Panzer Army, consisting of XXXXVIII Panzer Corps and II SS Panzer Corps, attacked along a thirty-mile front. Within two hours they had penetrated front-line positions and had seemingly broken through. But by early afternoon the Germans began to recognize the weaknesses in their intelligence picture. They were, in fact, in the midst of a defensive position, the depths of which they scarcely could imagine. Moreover, in early afternoon a drenching thunderstorm flooded the battlefield and halted XXXXVIII Panzer Corps. Finally, while Fourth

Panzer Army made relatively good progress, Detachment Kempf (a temporary combination of two corps under General Werner Kempf) on its right flank had hardly advanced. In the air the Luftwaffe provided 3,000 sorties a day over the salient; however, even this level of effort was insufficient to eliminate Soviet aircraft that were defending their ground forces and attacking advancing Germans.

On July 6 and 7, Manstein made some progress in the south. The II SS Panzer Corps led the movement forward. Detachment Kempf continued to have difficulties, and Fourth Panzer Army had to detach a division to secure its flank. The ferocious fighting and extensive mine fields throughout the enemy's deep defensive positions imposed terrible losses on German tank forces. By July 9, the army's *Grossdeutschland* Division had already lost 220 out of 300 tanks.

Manstein's attacks from the south finally began to show results. By July 11, II SS Panzer Corps had advanced about twenty-five miles, and the Soviets were forced to use reserves from the Steppe Front. On the same day Kempf's III Panzer Corps had finally broken into the open. Despite desperate Soviet resistance, Kempf linked up with II SS Panzer Corps and trapped a substantial number of Soviet troops. On July 12 nearly 1,800 German and Russian armored vehicles clashed on a small battlefield near Prokhorovka in the largest tank battle of the war. When it was over, the Germans had lost over 300 tanks, and the Russians 400; but the Russians had held. Manstein still had two fresh divisions and believed that his forces could reach Kursk. He was undoubtedly wrong because the Soviets still held four armies in reserve.

Beginning on July 10, however, events elsewhere intervened: Anglo-American armies landed in Sicily, and Mussolini's regime teetered on the brink of collapse. Amidst concerns about Soviet forces north and south of Kursk, Hitler terminated Citadel to reinforce the Mediterranean. Only Manstein urged continuation of the Kursk battle, but his reasoning largely rested on a belief that no other alternatives existed. In retrospect, Kursk was a disastrous failure, for it had consumed most of the German army's replenished reserves and armored forces. It was the last important German offensive in Russia.

The Soviets Counterattack

After halting Citadel, the Soviets seized the initiative and launched a series of attacks across the breadth of the Eastern Front. They relied on methods quite different from those of the Germans; instead of boldly relying on deep penetrations and double envelopments, the Red Army utilized several thrusts that aimed to push back the enemy on a broad front. If the Germans halted one thrust, the Russians shifted to another. With a 2.5:1 advantage in the air, the Soviets used their air forces for close ground support and air defense, and with an even greater advantage in artillery, they used preparatory fires on the same scale as those used in World War I.

The first Soviet move came against the Orel salient lying directly north of Kursk. Three Soviet armies attacked the northern side of the salient on July 12, 1943. By using forces previously committed to the Kursk battle, Model prevented a Soviet breakthrough. In this rare case Hitler sanctioned retreat from the salient, for he desperately needed troops to shore up a collapsing Fascist Italy (Mussolini fell from power on July 25).

Manstein confronted more daunting problems in the south. Soviet attacks stung his forces at their northern and southern extremities. Hitler refused to make the hard decisions demanded by the desperate plight of German forces; Manstein warned that the Führer must either provide his army group with twenty divisions or abandon the Donets Basin. The best solution might have been a phased retreat of about 150 miles to the Dnieper and reinforcement of that line. Hitler dithered, however, and the northern flank of Army Group South dissolved. Soviet forces took Belgorod on August 5, drove west, and forced the Germans to evacuate Kharkov for the last time on August 21. A desperate counterattack by two divisions finally halted the Soviet advance and permitted Eighth Army and Fourth Panzer Army to reestablish contact and new defensive lines, but the Soviets had advanced nearly eighty miles.

Along the Mius and Donets rivers, Soviet offensives rocked First Panzer Army and a reconstituted Sixth Army. First Panzer Army held; on August 18, however, the Soviets broke through Sixth Army by concentrating massive artillery on a narrow front. Germans attempts to pinch off the breakthrough with attacks on its shoulders almost succeeded, but fierce Soviet attacks blocked the counterattack. Manstein urged Hitler to abandon the Donets Basin. The Führer remained obdurate; not until August 31 did he approve withdrawal of First Panzer and Sixth armies forty miles to a new defensive line. As the two armies pulled back, their desperate plight finally forced Hitler to abandon the Donets Basin and permit a withdrawal of about 140 miles. Sixth Army had to hold in front of the Dnieper because its retreat would isolate the Crimea; Hitler was desperately afraid that the Russians would use that peninsula to launch air attacks against Romanian oil fields.

Despite his permitting abandonment of the Donets Basin, Hitler refused to allow Fourth Panzer and Eighth armies on Army Group South's northern flank to fall back on the Dnieper, but that flank unraveled so fast that by late September, the Red Army and the Wehrmacht were in a desperate race for the Dnieper. Many retreating Germans escaped to the far side, but the Soviets made several hasty river crossings and established bridgeheads from which they could resume their advance.

The bridgeheads made the German position desperate. North of Kiev the Soviet advance severed connections between army groups South and Center; on the lower Dnieper, the Soviets crossed the river and seized a bridgehead north of Dnepropetrovsk thirty miles wide and ten miles deep. By this time they had already won a great victory against Army Group South. Their forces had advanced an average of 150 miles on a front of 650 miles and had regained the Ukraine's most valuable agricultural and industrial areas. Despite Hitler's demands for scorched earth, the hastiness and lack of planning characterizing Army Group South's retreat minimized the damage that the Germans could inflict.

Unrelenting Soviet pressure eventually cut off German forces in the Crimean peninsula. Against thirteen German and two Romanian divisions, the Soviets on October 9 launched forty-five infantry divisions, three tank corps, and two mechanized corps, supported by 400 batteries of artillery. As the Soviet drive gathered momentum and approached the Black Sea west of the Crimea, Kleist and the Romanian dictator, Marshal Antonescu, begged Hitler to abandon the peninsula and allow Seventeenth Army to retreat. Hitler, however, refused, and by November the Soviets had isolated Seventeenth Army in the Crimea. The entire position along the lower Dnieper had now unraveled. One hundred miles to the north, Soviet forces expanded the size of their bridgehead across the Dnieper. Another two hundred miles to the north, Soviet forces seized Kiev; nowhere on the southern front could the Germans stabilize the situation. Only the arrival of autumn rains eventually brought relief to the hard-pressed Wehrmacht.

The fighting over summer and fall 1943 represented the first stage in the collapse of the Nazi position in the east. The constant battles wore German infantry down and forced the panzer divisions to act as fire brigades.

The 2.5 million German soldiers on the Eastern Front had been insufficient to alter the growing imbalance. The OKW considered conscripting women but dropped the idea because of Hitler's violent opposition. As for the Soviets, they had had about 6 million soldiers and had learned their lessons well over the past two years. Their massive attacks and multiple thrusts effectively combined armor, infantry, and artillery and overwhelmed German defenders. On the intelligence side, they enjoyed an enormous superiority, and they skillfully used deception to blind their German enemy almost entirely.

The Soviets also used partisan operations to advantage. Hitler's racial policies and brutal treatment pushed many Russians into guerrilla warfare. By early 1943 approximately 250,000 Soviets operated as partisans behind German lines. Usually organized into brigades of 1,000 men and women, the partisans extended Soviet power into Nazi-occupied territory, conducted raids, demolished roads and railroads, cut telephone lines, and provided intelligence. Those near the front lines usually took orders from the staffs of the closest Soviet armies and launched operations in coordination with major offensives. Their superiors passed commands by radio and air; supplies came from low-flying aircraft. In the two years of most intense partisan warfare, German forces suffered approximately 300,000 casualties, including thirty general officers and more than one thousand officers. Although partisan operations did not change the course of the war in the east, they compelled the Germans to diffuse their already overextended forces.

While extraordinary battles in Russia continued with savage fury, Hitler drove his police and military—willing participants—to complete the racial cleansing of eastern Europe. This extermination of the Jews and the further enslavement of the Slavic masses continued until the final collapse of the Nazis. By 1942–1943 the great killing camps such as Auschwitz and Treblinka were spewing their ashen clouds of slaughtered Jews and other unfortunates over the landscape of eastern Europe; long trains of cattle and freight cars transported the victims—a diversion of scarce transport that even affected the Wehrmacht's logistics. Meanwhile, Ukrainians, Russians, Poles, and others in slightly higher racial categories—as defined by Hitler—were dragooned by the millions to serve as slave laborers in the great industrial undertakings of the SS and German industry. If not murdered, they were brutalized, starved, and mistreated. If Germany could not win the war, then at least the Reich could live up to the Führer's promise given before the war that he would free Europe of all its Jews however the war might turn out.

Although Hitler's racial policies and refusals to abandon territory contributed to the catastrophe, the problem lay deeper. The extent of German miscalculations in planning and executing Barbarossa were now apparent. Above all, the Germans were not fighting "subhuman" barbarians, but an enormously gifted people, whose military efforts early in the war had been seriously impaired by the mistakes and prejudices of Stalin. The Soviets had now emerged as a skillful and resourceful foe.

The Mediterranean, 1942–1943

While Soviet armies had begun the arduous task of retaking territory, the Western Powers finally were able to overcome German tactical and operational performance by improved battle effectiveness of their own, as well as increasing numerical superiority in manpower and equipment. Still unprepared for a direct assault on Fortress Europe, British and American commanders undertook to push the Axis from North Africa, open the Mediterranean to Allied shipping, and drive Italy out of the war. In this they were to be successful, but only after heavy fighting. The battles of North Africa would prove particularly important to correct the significant deficiencies that had appeared with the first commitment of American troops to battle.

El Alamein

The disastrous defeat on the Gazala Line and at Tobruk in June 1942 threatened to undermine the British position in the Middle East. At this point, the British theater commander, General Sir Claude Auchinleck assumed control of Eighth Army. As its beaten remnants streamed eastward, he determined to stand at El Alamein, sixty miles west of Alexandria. Unlike other defensive positions in the desert, El Alamein had the advantage that it could not be flanked; to the south lay the Qattara Depression, a great dry salt sea that could not support heavy vehicles.

Furious at the May and June defeats, Churchill sacked Auchinleck and appointed General Harold Alexander in his place as the theater commander. On August 13, Lieutenant General Bernard Law Montgomery assumed command of Eighth Army. Montgomery was an inspired choice. Admittedly he was a careful, prudent general who rarely took risks, but his approach reflected the caliber of his forces. In his memoirs, Montgomery explained that he built up the Eighth Army by concentrating "on three essentials: leadership, equipment, and training. All three were deficient."* Other problems identified by Montgomery included discipline, confidence, and morale. As he acted to restore Eighth Army, he made the ground and air forces work closely together and ended the practice of fighting in brigade-sized units. In the future divisions would fight as divisions. As additional supplies and new weapons poured into Egypt, Montgomery overcame deficiencies in equipment and established huge supply dumps. Over a period of three months, he fought the battles of Alam Halfa and El Alamein with a flawed instrument, but his success reflected a realistic appreciation of British weaknesses.

At the end of August, Rommel began the battle of Alam Halfa with an attack similar to the one he had used along the Gazala Line in May 1942.

---

*Bernard L. Montgomery, *Memoirs* (London: Collins, 1958), p. 103.

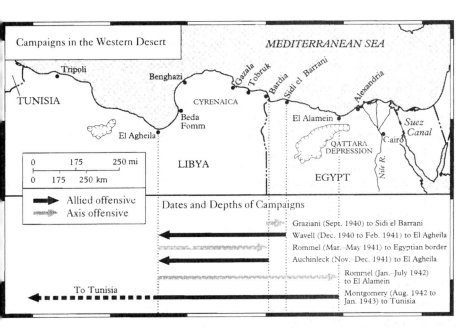

Campaigns in the Western Desert

MEDITERRANEAN SEA

TUNISIA

Tripoli

Benghazi

Gazala
Tobruk
Bardia
Sidi el Barrani
Alexandria

CYRENAICA

Beda
Fomm

El Agheila

El Alamein

Suez
Canal

QATTARA
DEPRESSION

Cairo

Nile R.

LIBYA

EGYPT

| 0 | 175 | 250 mi |
| 0 | 175 | 250 km |

→ Allied offensive
⇒ Axis offensive

Dates and Depths of Campaigns

Graziani (Sept. 1940) to Sidi el Barrani
Wavell (Dec. 1940 to Feb. 1941) to El Agheila
Rommel (Mar.–May 1941) to Egyptian border
Auchinleck (Nov.–Dec. 1941) to El Agheila
Rommel (Jan.–July 1942) to El Alamein
Montgomery (Aug. 1942 to Jan. 1943) to Tunisia

To Tunisia

That is, he launched a diversionary attack along the coast and on the British center and then sent his main attack against their southern flank. As the Germans drove into the British rear, RAF fighter bombers hammered their columns. Extensive minefields hampered the Afrika Korps' effort to cut off British forces, while British armor fought a solid defensive battle. On September 2, Rommel pulled back after suffering heavy losses and established defensive positions between the coast and the Qattara Depression.

Montgomery now began preparing Eighth Army for what would be his most famous battle, El Alamein. His initial concept involved an attack on each flank of the German position, but reservations about the readiness of his armor to fight a mobile battle resulted in a more straightforward plan. The main attack would occur against Rommel's northern flank, while diversionary attacks pinned German units in the south. Artillery would batter enemy defenses, engineers would clear lanes through enemy mine fields, infantry would then drive through those defenses, and finally the armor would break out. It was a simple plan that relied on firepower and numerical superiority.

The operation, however, failed to go according to plan. With Montgomery having some 230,000 troops and Rommel only 80,000, the set-piece attack began on October 23 with a powerful artillery bombardment, followed by infantry assaults. But gaps cleared by the engineers were too narrow, and the infantry failed to secure the far ends of the lanes. As a result, British armor became entrapped in mine fields. Fortunately for the British, Rommel was home on sick leave, and German commanders responded slowly. They launched a series of piecemeal attacks and suffered heavy casualties; by the end of the first day 15th Panzer Division had lost three-quarters of its

General Bernard L. Montgomery usually wore a black beret, a pullover sweater, and khaki pants. Though he seemed a cranky eccentric, he improved the performance of his units, generated greater confidence among his troops, and soon drove Rommel out of Egypt and Libya.

tanks. But the Germans continued fighting, while British armor remained stuck in mine fields.

To weaken German infantry and tanks, Montgomery began what he called a "dog fight." On November 2, after one week's hard fighting, he launched a powerful thrust against the German center. With the British possessing 600 tanks and the Germans only 30, Rommel, who had rushed back to Africa, started pulling his infantry back on November 3. But Hitler stopped him. Amidst the confusion, Montgomery launched another attack and broke through German defenses. Subsequent efforts to cut off the Afrika Korps, however, failed because British forces moved too slowly. Rommel began a rapid retreat across Egypt into Libya, eventually reaching Tunisia. Montgomery's pursuit was slow and methodical as he established airfields along his route of advance and opened ports for logistical support. But he had achieved what none of his predecessors had managed; he had defeated Rommel.

Operation "Torch"

Meanwhile on the western coast of North Africa major events were in motion. During the Arcadia Conference in December 1941, Churchill had proposed a landing on the shores of French North Africa. The Americans, however, displayed scant interest; from the first, they felt that a "Germany-first" strategy demanded immediate action in Europe. In May 1942, Roosevelt even promised Vyacheslav Molotov, the Soviet foreign minister, that the Western Powers would open a second front in 1942. Planning did begin for a descent on the French coast, should the Soviet Union appear on the brink of collapse, but such a venture represented only a desperate effort to distract the Germans.

The strategy preferred by the American military leaders, particularly General Marshall, the U.S. Army's chief of staff, was to build up military capabilities for a direct assault on western Europe sometime in 1943. However, the U.S. Navy, feeding on prewar preparations and popular attitudes,

In North Africa, General Dwight D. Eisenhower gained experience and developed the skills in high-level command and coalition warfare that were essential for his future success as Supreme Allied Commander.

pushed for a Pacific strategy; and the British doubted whether a landing in western Europe could be successful in 1943. For a while, Marshall moved toward the navy's urgings that the United States turn to the Pacific. Roosevelt, however, refused to countenance such a recasting of American strategy. Instead he demanded a major initiative in Europe in 1942—if not against German-occupied France, then in the Mediterranean—because he recognized the political necessity of a commitment of American troops in Europe to keep his nation focused on defeating Germany. American military leaders eventually agreed to Torch, landings to occupy Algeria and Morocco and co-opt the Vichy French.

The commander of Torch was an obscure American general, Dwight David Eisenhower. Ike had not seen combat in World War I, but he possessed gifts of diplomacy and tact as well as operational competence. His political skills were essential to getting Anglo-American forces to work together on the operational level. Initially, he had some weaknesses as a commander, but he displayed great capacity to learn. If not Rommel's equal on the battlefield, he far surpassed most German generals in his political and diplomatic skills and in his understanding the wider aspects of war.

Considerable wrangling took place between American and British leaders about the location of the landings; the final plan focused on Algeria and Morocco. Following landings at Casablanca, Oran, and Algiers, Allied forces would advance east by land and sea against Tunisia. The initial landings in North Africa on November 8 went well, especially considering the Allied troops' lack of combat experience. The French resisted the invasion tenaciously at first; Hitler's lack of trust in the Vichy regime, however, resulted in those forces possessing obsolete matériel and inadequate ammunition stocks. Coincidentally, Vichy's number-two man, Admiral François Darlan, was present in North Africa and eventually agreed to an armistice.

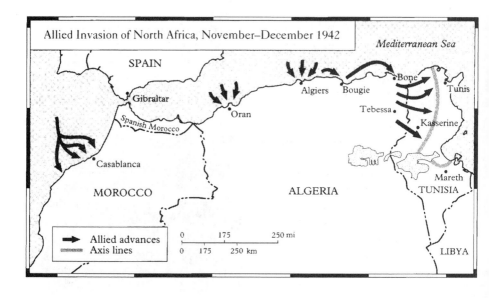

Allied Invasion of North Africa, November–December 1942

Hitler's response was, as usual, swift and ruthless. While Nazi troops occupied Vichy France, paratrooper and Luftwaffe units, flying from Sicily, won "the race of Tunisia" before the Allied forces could get there. By seizing Tunisia, the Germans kept the Mediterranean closed to Allied shipping for another six months and thereby exacerbated worldwide shipping shortages plaguing Allied logisticians. But the price was too high. The decision to fight in Tunisia resulted from Hitler's desire to support Mussolini's decrepit regime; it was perhaps the worst decision that Hitler made in 1942. It committed the remainder of Fascist Italy's military power and substantial numbers of German troops to defend a hopeless position, and it forced Axis naval and air power to fight at a severe disadvantage. The result was a defeat almost as great as Stalingrad, one entirely resulting from German miscalculations.

Though the opening moves in Tunisia had favored the Allies, German paratroopers and armor halted and then pushed the Americans and British back to Tunisia's western frontier. By January, Rommel had escaped from Libya and arrived in southern Tunisia where all the Axis forces in North Africa concentrated. However, Rommel commanded only a portion of Axis forces, while units in northern Tunisia fell under command of Colonel General Jürgen von Arnim. Immediately after his arrival in Tunisia, Rommel sensed an opportunity; Montgomery's hesitant pursuit gave the Germans a relatively free hand, while Anglo-American forces in Algeria were strung out along the Tunisian frontier. The Allied First Army included the American II Corps, commanded by Major General Lloyd R. Fredendall, who refused advice, deployed his troops badly, and located his headquarters deep underground and far behind the front lines. Rommel suggested an armored drive sweeping up from southern Tunisia to destroy Allied supply dumps in eastern Algeria and perhaps even to trap First Army against the coast. In addition, he hoped to give the Americans a severe mauling that would affect their confidence for the rest of the war. Fortunately for the

Allies, the Desert Fox received little support for the proposed attack, and much of the German armor remained under Arnim.

The battle began on February 14 when Rommel's 10th and 21st Panzer divisions punched through thinly held passes in central Tunisia. After pushing back Combat Command A of the U.S. 1st Armored Division and surrounding the 168th Regimental Combat Team, the Germans advanced west toward Kasserine. A counterattack by Combat Command C of the 1st Armored Division failed disastrously, and veteran German forces fought their way through Kasserine Pass. After Arnim had convinced Italian headquarters in Rome to deny Rommel's proposal for a deep encirclement, and after Arnim had refused to release one of his panzer divisions, Rommel advanced north in two columns. One column turned north ten miles east of Kasserine, while the other turned north at Kasserine. Both columns encountered spirited resistance from British units in prepared defensive positions and were halted; on February 22 German forces began withdrawing. Allied ground strength, Arnim's refusal to support Rommel, and German weaknesses had enabled Rommel to achieve only a tactical success.

Immediately after Kasserine, Rommel turned south against the British who had finally arrived from Egypt. Though he attempted to knock them off balance, intelligence from Ultra alerted his opponents, and Montgomery dealt the Afrika Korps a stunning defeat. German forces lost more than one-third of their tanks. Seriously ill, Rommel left Africa a few days later.

With Rommel's defeat, the Axis position in North Africa steadily deteriorated. Ultra allowed Anglo-American air power to interdict the Axis supply lines from Italy. By March the Germans had abandoned the sealift; thereafter, the Luftwaffe's hard-pressed air transports had to provide logistic support: ammunition, fuel, food, and personnel. Again Ultra provided ample intelligence, and Allied fighters destroyed protective screens of Axis fighters as well as the transports themselves. The end came in early May, as the Allies mopped up the remnants in Tunisia. The Germans had lost heavily in the air; the Wehrmacht's ground losses represented the OKH's Mediterranean reserves, while the destruction of Italian ground forces, the last to surrender, left Mussolini with little to defend the homeland. After Tunisia, the Duce's regime enjoyed neither respect nor authority among a disillusioned population.

The victory in North Africa was particularly important for American ground and air forces. Their opening exposure to combat had not been auspicious; some U.S. units in Kasserine Pass had collapsed under the pressure of what was a large-scale raid by German forces. But American commanders set about with determination to repair their deficiencies and learn from experience. As Rommel suggested shortly before his death, American ground forces had been inferior to those of the British when the Germans first encountered them, but the Americans had shown a great capacity to learn. The story of the U.S. Army was thus one of steady, consistent improvement in battlefield performance. Typical of this American improvement was that of air-ground cooperation in Tunisia. The system in place as the campaign began proved generally unworkable; but the Americans had the very effective model of the RAF-British army system to copy. Not only did they dispense with the old, but they improved the British system and subsequently used it with enormous effectiveness in Normandy.

Attack on Sicily and Italy

After the Axis surrender in Tunisia in May 1943, the Allies began preparing for the next phase in the European war. At the Casablanca Conference in January 1943, General Marshall had made a last appeal for a cross-channel invasion in 1943, but Churchill's eloquence convinced Roosevelt that the Allies should maintain their momentum in the Mediterranean and direct their efforts toward Italy. Though American military leaders still preferred an early cross-channel invasion, the advantages of defeating the Italians, opening the Mediterranean to Allied shipping, and enlarging the air offensive

Sicily and Italy, July–October 1943

against Germany were obvious. At the Trident Conference in May 1943, the Americans accepted the strategic goal of eliminating Italy from the war but demanded that the forces involved consist only of those already in the Mediterranean. At Trident the Americans and British also agreed that planning begin for a cross-channel invasion in May 1944. The British, nevertheless, pressed for operations in the eastern Aegean and possibly in the Balkans. Finally, at the Teheran Conference in November 1943, Roosevelt, Churchill, and Stalin agreed to a cross-channel invasion—Operation "Overlord"—in spring 1944 in conjunction with an Anglo-American attack on southern France and a major offensive by the Soviets on the Eastern Front. This was the final blueprint for Allied strategy in Europe.

On July 10, 1943, the British Eighth Army under Montgomery and the U.S. Seventh Army under Major General George S. Patton stormed ashore on Sicily in Operation "Husky"—the largest amphibious assault in the war. Seven divisions made amphibious landings (compared to five divisions later at Normandy). The landings occurred on the southeast corner of the island, the British on the right, the Americans on the left. Montgomery, as the senior ground forces commander, had devised a straightforward plan for conquering Sicily; Eighth Army would drive up from the southeast corner of Sicily toward Messina, while Patton's army provided a flank guard. There seemed no reason why Montgomery could not execute his plan; only a small force of German and Italian troops defended the island. But the Germans proved as tenacious and combat-effective as usual; hilly and broken terrain aided their defensive efforts.

When Montgomery's attack slowed, Patton, who had no intention of acting as flank guard, raced west, captured Palermo, and then pushed east along the northern coast of the island. He got to Messina before Montgomery, but not before German ground forces escaped. Flak batteries on both sides of the straits of Messina protected this escape, while Allied air and naval units failed to intervene with sufficient vigor. In this operation as in everything he did, Patton projected flamboyance as well as leadership. But his political sensitivity was, unfortunately, considerably less than his military genius. He came close to ending his career by slapping two enlisted soldiers suffering from shell shock.

Whatever its failures, Husky gained considerable strategic and political advantages. It forced Hitler to shut down Citadel and confirmed his fears about the political stability of Mussolini's regime. On July 25, King Victor Emmanuel III dismissed Mussolini from office. Immediately thereafter, military police arrested the fallen dictator and whisked him away to a variety of secret locations (Luftwaffe paratroops and SS commandoes liberated him in September 1943, but he would perish at the hands of Italian partisans in April 1945). The king called on Marshal Pietro Badoglio, who had presided over the disasters of 1940, to get Italy out of the war.

By summer 1943, losses of manpower and equipment in Tunisia had destroyed the Wehrmacht's strategic reserves throughout the Mediterranean. Thoroughly distrustful of the Italians, Hitler understood the meaning of the coup against Mussolini; the new government would make a deal as soon as possible with the Allies—a deal that could place the British and Americans on the Alps and provide them bases in Italy at minimum cost. He immediately ordered the buildup of sizable forces under Rommel to intervene, while German units infiltrated to strategic locations throughout the peninsula. Hitler had every reason to worry. Though Badoglio reaffirmed Italy's loyalty, he immediately opened negotiations to switch sides. But Italy's new leaders failed to act decisively, and negotiations dragged into August and early September. By then the possibilities that Italy offered had almost slipped away.

On September 3, Eighth Army landed on the toe of Italy. Six days later an Anglo-American force under General Mark Clark in Operation "Avalanche" landed in the Gulf of Salerno, south of Naples, while the British Broadcasting Corporation, to Badoglio's horror, announced Italy's acceptance of an armistice. Italian dithering and incompetence, however, had convinced the Americans that a drop by the 82nd Airborne Division on Rome's airfields would result in disaster. The king, Badoglio, and other Italian leaders promptly decamped, leaving the army with no orders, and made their way south to Allied lines. The Wehrmacht disarmed the leaderless Italian military with minimum difficulty.

Meanwhile, Field Marshal Kesselring responded vigorously to the landings at Salerno. Well-organized counterattacks threatened to drive Clark's forces into the sea, while Montgomery's Eighth Army advanced at a snail's pace up the Italian toe. Supporting Allied naval and air forces prevented the Germans from exploiting their advantage. With the linkup of Clark and Montgomery's forces, the Germans began a slow retreat northward and eventually abandoned Naples. The Allied advance, however, turned into a nightmare as the Germans dug in on one ridge line after another. By late 1943 the advance had stalled seventy miles north of Salerno and eighty miles short of Rome. The only significant gain was Foggia and its airfields (opposite Salerno, on the eastern side of the peninsula). For the next year and a half the Allies fought their way slowly north over the peninsula and destroyed much of Italy in the process.

The East, 1944

Fall and Winter Disasters for the Wehrmacht

In October 1943 arrival of bad weather had ushered in a temporary slackening of fighting in the east. Army Group South lay battered and bleeding. Neither troops nor commanders had illusions about what was coming. Manstein, still the army group's commander, argued that the Red Army disposed of enormous reserves behind its front; on November 20, he warned OKH that in addition to the forty-four divisions and numerous armored brigades established in 1943, the Red Army had thirty-three infantry divisions and eleven tank and mechanized corps in reserve on the southern front. Only the provision of "sufficient and powerful reserves," he noted, would allow Army Group South to hold the line. He had no chance of getting such reserves given the grave state of German forces in other theaters;

Manstein's demands underline how woefully ignorant the German generals were of the Reich's strategic situation.

On Christmas Eve 1943, the Soviets launched the winter's offensive, aimed at regaining the rest of the Ukraine. South of the Pripet Marshes and west of Kiev, First Guards and First Tank armies under General N. F. Vatutin pushed Fourth Panzer Army back. Hitler again refused to authorize any retreats or to approve Manstein's request to withdraw Army Group South's right flank. By early January the Soviets had opened up a 110–mile gap between army groups Center and South. Though Army Group South's left was dissolving, Hitler refused to abandon the lower Dnieper so forces could be assembled to meet the growing emergency. As the situation became fluid, the Germans closed a small encirclement around a portion of First Tank Army and destroyed a sizable number of tanks and assault guns, while inflicting heavy casualties. But the Red Army trapped two German corps, over 56,000 troops, near Cherkassy, in the center of Army Group South. The Germans got 30,000 men out, but most had to swim to safety and were completely broken by the experience.

At the end of March 1944, Hitler finally had had enough of Manstein's streak of independence and relieved the field marshal. But Manstein's relief did not presage any fundamental changes in how the Germans fought on the Eastern Front. By this point Manstein's opponents were fully his equal, with a broader understanding of the logistic, intelligence, and deception needs for any successful operation. One must also recognize that there was little political or strategic disagreement between Manstein and Hitler, as the former's wholehearted cooperation in the murderous actions of the SS in 1941 and 1942 underlined.

Things did not go better in Army Group A along the Black Sea. The Soviets struck Sixth Army on January 10 and 11. When Hitler allowed a

Throughout the war the Germans had fewer trucks than the Allies and often used horse-drawn wagons to carry equipment and supplies.

withdrawal, the order came so late that Sixth Army abandoned much of its heavy artillery, engineering equipment, and even armored fighting vehicles. In mid-February the Soviets reorganized for a major effort to recapture the rest of the Ukraine before the spring thaw. By this point, Soviet mechanized forces enjoyed greater mobility than their German opponents. Using sturdy American trucks for logistical support, Soviet tanks maneuvered in alternating conditions of thaw, freeze, snow, and rain. Since the Germans had designed most of their vehicles for western European conditions, their trucks often broke down. For example, 24th Panzer Division lost 1,958 of its vehicles during the winter, more than half of its authorized number. Some German panzer divisions were reduced to using horse-drawn peasant carts for supply.

Over the next month and a half Soviet commanders concentrated on destroying the two enemy army groups in the Ukraine. Between the Pripet Marshes and Black Sea, the Red Army deployed from north to south First, Second, Third, and Fourth Ukrainian fronts, each about double the size of a German army. West of Kiev, First Ukrainian Front drove deep into German positions, and by late March First and Second Ukrainian fronts had encircled First Panzer Army and smashed across the Dniester River. Only a desperate counterattack extricated the encircled Germans. Meanwhile Third Ukrainian Front, having taken Nikopol, drove on to take Odessa and reach the Romanian border. Soviet advances lapped to the passes over the Carpathian Mountains leading into Hungary, but the Germans and Hungarians, aided by the spring thaw, blocked that route.

Elsewhere in the east the Red Army scored its first major advances outside of Army Group South since winter 1941–1942. In the north, the Germans still besieged Leningrad, although the Soviets had opened a corridor to the city. In late December 1943, Army Group North's commander, Field Marshal Georg von Küchler, almost convinced Hitler to authorize a withdrawal of approximately 150 miles to a newly fortified position, known as "Panther." However, Eighteenth Army's commander, Colonel General Georg Lindemann, argued that his forces could hold their well-fortified but exposed positions. Always willing to take the optimistic point of view, Hitler supported Lindemann. But the latter and his intelligence officers had missed extensive Soviet preparations for an offensive. With a three-to-one superiority, the Soviets attacked both sides of the besieging forces at Leningrad on January 14. Second Shock Army struck out from the Oranienbaum enclave west of Leningrad, while Forty-Second Army attacked south of the city. At the same time, heavy Soviet attacks put German positions around Novgorod (one hundred miles to the south) in mortal danger. When Küchler pressed Hitler to authorize a short pullback, the Führer reluctantly agreed, but the Germans could not disengage cleanly. By January 19 the Russians had surrounded substantial numbers of Germans at Novgorod. Though concerned about the fall of another important Russian city, Hitler finally authorized a breakout.

Meanwhile the situation remained desperate in front of Leningrad. Küchler begged for permission to fall all the way back to the Panther line. By the end of the month Eighteenth Army had disintegrated into three separate groups, all facing encirclement. On January 30, Hitler finally permitted Küchler to pull back about fifty miles. At that point he fired Küchler and replaced him with Colonel General Walter Model, who had gained a reputation as a great defensive expert, but who also remained a favorite of the Führer because of his fanaticism. Model immediately wired his new headquarters, "Not a single step backward."

Despite Model's optimism and the arrival of reinforcements, strong Soviet pressure forced Army Group North back to the Panther position on March 1. The Germans held in this position, which extended north and south of Lake Peipus. An early spring thaw covered the frozen lake with water and halted the Soviet advance.

One last disaster befell German forces in the spring. Since fall 1943, Seventeenth Army had clung to the Crimea. Despite the pleas of his staff and Marshal Antonescu, Hitler insisted that the peninsula, which he described as an "aircraft carrier aimed at the Romanian oil fields," hold to the last. On April 7, 1944, the new commander of Army Group A, Colonel General Ferdinand Schörner, inspected the Crimea defenses and declared them in excellent shape, so excellent that they could hold "for a long time." Schörner was one of a new breed of generals promoted by Hitler for their enthusiasm and fanaticism. His prediction proved one of the shortest lived of the war.

On April 8 the Soviets attacked the German and Romanian defenders on the peninsula. Schörner at last recognized that Seventeenth Army would have to retreat to Sevastopol and the sooner the better. Hitler, of course, refused to authorize a withdrawal. Only under intense pressure did he finally sanction retreat but then demanded Sevastopol be held indefinitely. Schörner argued for a total withdrawal from the Crimea; but Hitler marshaled counterarguments from the air force and navy that they could supply Sevastopol. In early May the Soviets broke through the city's defenses. Only at this point did Hitler authorize a pullout, but the navy, while under heavy air attack, botched the operation. Although enough ships were available to transport the troops only 38,000 out of 64,700 escaped. The original strength of Seventeenth Army had been 75,546 Germans and 45,887 Romanians.

Operation "Bagration"

At Teheran in November 1943, Stalin, Churchill, and Roosevelt approved a common strategy for the coming year: the Western Powers would land forces in France and open a second front, while the Soviets launched a great offensive to coincide with it. Roosevelt assured Stalin that the invasion would occur in spring 1944.

As the Soviets prepared for their offensive, they focused on the area north of the Pripet Marshes, the only substantial portion of Soviet territory still under German occupation, since much of the significant fighting since 1942 had occurred in the south. Consequently, as Stavka established priorities for summer 1944, the front opposite Army Group Center received the highest priority. Following an offensive against the Finns to fix German attention, the Red Army would attack Army Group Center and advance to East Prussia, a distance of approximately 225 miles. After destroying Army Group Center, the Soviets would be well positioned for a move into the Balkans.

Code-named "Bagration," the upcoming operation against Army Group Center included two phases. In the first, Soviet forces would break through enemy defenses and envelop German forces at Vitebsk on the Dvina River and at Bobruisk on the Beresina River. They would then strike deeper and encircle German units east of Minsk. When Marshal Rokossovskii presented the plan to Stalin, he encountered strong doubts about the two-pronged envelopment of Bobruisk. Stalin approved the plans only after sending Rokossovskii out of the room twice to "think it over."

Preparations for Bagration began in the spring. Against Army Group Center's 700,000 soldiers, Stavka concentrated 1.2 million men on the front with another 1.3 million in reserve. It assembled 124 divisions, 4,000 tanks, 24,400 artillery pieces, and 5,300 aircraft. German intelligence picked up little information about the concentration; its estimates swallowed a superb Soviet deception plan that suggested another offensive against Army Group South. What few movements German intelligence picked up in the center, it dismissed as "merely a deception." This miscalculation of the situation resulted in a maldistribution of German forces. Army Group Center, defending a 488-mile front, possessed only thirty-eight divisions in the first line and five divisions in reserve; three Hungarian and five security divisions guarded its rear areas. By contrast, Army Group North Ukraine (previously Army Group South), defending a shorter front than Army Group Center, had thirty-five German and ten Hungarian divisions of which ten were panzer. Together the two southern German army groups contained eighteen panzer and panzer grenadier divisions.

But the greatest deficiency of Army Group Center lay in the slavish devotion of its commander, Field Marshal Ernst Busch, to Hitler's directives. Even in 1940, Busch had displayed a remarkable lack of imagination; by 1944 the war had entirely passed him by. Busch accepted Hitler's directive to establish "fortresses" around important centers and to hold them to the last man. He insisted on such a rigid defense that Ninth Army complained that it was "bound by orders to tactical measures which it cannot in good conscience accept and which in our own earlier victories were the causes of the enemy defeats."

By this point in the war, the qualitative as well as quantitative balance had swung against the Germans in the east. Soviet commanders down to the divisional level had mastered the conduct of the operational art; the *Stavka* could prepare, conduct, and exploit extraordinarily complex operations ranging hundreds of miles. Soviet deception entirely blinded German commanders as to Soviet operational intentions until the hammer blows fell. Once *Stavka* unleashed its forces, a skillful conduct of operations (sustained by an efficient and mobile support structure—largely due to American lend-lease trucks) enabled full exploitation of breakthroughs. Only at the tactical, small-unit level did German units enjoy some small advantage, but even here the Soviet quantitative edge gave German soldiers a sense of impending doom.

On June 22, 1944, the third anniversary of Barbarossa and two weeks after the landings in Normandy, Soviet armies attacked Army Group Center, which had its Third Panzer, Fourth, and Ninth armies deployed from Vitebsk to Bobruisk. After ripping through the Third Panzer Army's positions, Soviet spearheads closed around Vitebsk and trapped five German divisions. On the 24th, the next phase of Bagration began against Ninth Army; First Belorussian Front broke open its left flank. When Ninth Army requested permission to escape, the army group commander replied that "the army's mission was to hold every foot of ground." In fact, the speed of the Soviet offensive had already shattered Ninth Army and trapped its broken units in several small pockets around Bobruisk. At the last minute the OKH permitted a withdrawal, but again too late. The Soviets encircled two corps, 70,000 troops, and continued their drive toward Minsk. Positioned between Third Panzer and Ninth armies, Fourth Army tried to pull back, but the advancing units of Soviet armor were already closing the trap.

As the situation became increasingly confused, Hitler intervened and ordered Third Panzer, Fourth, and Ninth armies to hold east of Minsk, sixty miles behind their original positions. In fact, all three armies—or at least those units not yet captured, surrounded, or destroyed—were in desperate shape. By now OKH had finally concluded that the Soviets were launching an ambitious offensive, aimed at retaking Minsk. Hitler fired Busch, the army group commander, and replaced him with Model, but the latter confronted a catastrophic situation. On July 3, the Soviets captured Minsk amidst scenes of indescribable collapse and confusion that marked desperate German attempts to flee. In twelve days Army Group Center had lost twenty-five divisions; out of 165,000 soldiers Fourth Army alone had lost 130,000. The other armies in Army Group Center were in little better shape.

Still, OKH drew some comfort from its hope that the Soviet advance of 125 miles would cause the attackers to run out of supplies. Again the Germans were wrong. On July 8, Model reported that he could not hold a line 175 miles west of Bobruisk. A yawning chasm separated the remnants of Army Group Center from Army Group North. Model requested that Army Group North withdraw to the Riga-Dvinsk-Dvina River line, thereby shortening its front and freeing troops for use in the center. Hitler refused, this time because the Baltic coast was crucial to launching new U-boats and securing Swedish iron ore shipped through the Baltic. At the end of July the Soviet drive, having advanced some 200 miles, began to slow. The Soviets had finally outrun their supply system.

With German reserves drawn to the center, the Soviets attacked the flanks. In the south, Army Group North Ukraine lay exposed; by the end of July, Soviet forces had advanced sixty miles across a broad front. Likewise in the north, Soviet attacks unhinged Army Group North's flank and almost reached the Baltic.

Meanwhile, Soviet forces approached Warsaw. On July 30, elements of Second Tank Army reached within seven miles of the Polish capital; south of Warsaw Soviet units actually crossed the Vistula River. But at this point, short of fuel and with political concerns in mind, the Soviets stopped and refused to liberate the Polish capital. The Poles themselves had little desire for a Soviet liberation of Poland. Certainly, memories of Stalin's actions in September 1939, as well as the ferocious purges in eastern Poland in 1939 and 1940, left them none to eager to exchange one tyranny for another. Consequently, as the Red Army approached, the Poles rose in furious revolt in an attempt to liberate their capital before the Soviets arrived. Shortly before Soviet armor reached the outskirts of Warsaw, Stalin established his own Polish government, consisting of Communists obedient to him. The dictator certainly had no interest in helping anti-Communists establish themselves in Poland. Despite desperate Polish resistance, with Soviet forces totally quiescent, the Germans had little trouble crushing the rebellion.

An attempt on Hitler's life on July 20 added to the already difficult relations between the Führer and his officer corps. A small group of anti-Nazi officers placed a bomb in Hitler's daily conference. It exploded, killing a number of those present, but only slightly injuring Hitler. The SS quickly arrested the plotters and extinguished all hopes of a coup. General Guderian then became the army chief of staff and sought to rectify Germany's desperate situation by Nazi fanaticism and enthusiasm. Generals loyal to the regime, such as Guderian and Rundstedt, sat on courts of honor that stripped their comrades of rank and privilege before turning them over to Nazi "justice." Most conspirators suffered hideous deaths. Rommel was accused of cooperating with the conspiracy, but Hitler permitted him to commit suicide on October 14, 1944. Treachery and treason became Hitler's explanation for all Germany's defeats.

By early September, the Germans faced the Soviets with a patched together front. A message from the commander of Army Group North, Field Marshal Schörner, to a division commander suggests the kind of leadership that the German army had by 1944: "Major General Charles de Beaulieu is to be told that he is to restore his own and his division's honor by a courageous deed or I [the army commander] will chase him out in disgrace. Furthermore, he is to report by 2100 which commanders he has had shot or is having shot for cowardice."*

Collapse in the Balkans

In Romania the front had been quiet since April. Army Group South Ukraine had watched as a steady drain of its forces occurred. Its staff worried about the collapse of Marshal Antonescu's authority in Romania; defeats over the past two years and arrival of Soviet armies on the frontier had convinced most Romanians that they must abandon the disastrous German alliance. But commanders on the spot could convince neither Hitler nor OKH of the serious political situation since German experts in Bucharest reported all was well.

By early August the Germans had picked up indications that the quiet spell in the south would soon end. Given the catastrophes in the center and in Normandy, OKH could not reinforce Romania. On August 20, 1944, two Soviet fronts with ninety divisions, six tank and mechanized corps, and more than 900,000 troops attacked. By nightfall Soviet forces were in the open. The Romanians resisted at first but then refused to fight; Soviet spearheads were already encircling Sixth Army.

On the 23rd, worse news awaited the Germans. The young king, Michael, called Antonescu to the palace; as had happened with Mussolini, the king dismissed the marshal, arrested him, and dissolved the government. That night Michael announced that Romania would join the Allied nations and denounced the Treaty of Vienna, which had given Transylvania to Hungary. To free the German mission and overthrow the new government, Hitler authorized German air and ground forces to attack Bucharest.

---

*Earl F. Ziemke, *Stalingrad to Berlin: The German Defeat in the East* (Washington: Office of the Chief of Military History, 1968), p. 342.

However, fighting on the outskirts of Bucharest, as well as the bombing of the royal palace, only solidified support for the king.

As the Germans struggled to cope with political collapse, the military situation went from bad to worse. Romania's defection, followed by its declaration of war on August 25, placed every German unit in Romania at hazard. By the 27th, Army Group South Ukraine had collapsed. The Soviets cut Sixth Army into two separate pockets; in the debacle the Wehrmacht lost eighteen divisions and the headquarters of five corps. Moreover, the Romanians surrounded German forces in Bucharest, while at Ploesti they drove the 5th Flak Division from the oil refineries. Remnants of Army Group South Ukraine withdrew northwest and by September 15 had occupied positions along the spine of the Carpathian Mountains in a new line east of Budapest.

Bulgaria's defection followed on the heels of the Romanian collapse. The Bulgarians had never declared war on the USSR, and on September 2 they unilaterally ended their state of war with the Western Powers. But that was not enough for Stalin. On September 8 Third Ukrainian Front moved into Bulgaria, and the Bulgarians declared war on Germany. German forces in Greece and Macedonia were now in danger of isolation. Even Hitler recognized that there was no hope of holding the southern Balkans. A desperate retreat north began through the partisan-infested countryside of Yugoslavia. Yugoslav partisans harassed the retreating Germans but could not cut them off. The British, landing in Greece, pursued hesitantly, and Allied air power missed some substantial opportunities to interdict the escaping Germans. By mid-October most of the German forces had escaped from Greece and Macedonia.

But this temporary success did little to improve the situation. In early October the Hungarian leader, Admiral Miklos Horthy, signed an armistice with the Soviets. His government and the Hungarian army remained badly divided. Some Hungarians wanted to fight on, but many recognized Germany's hopeless position. Quick action by SS commanders overthrew Horthy's regime and installed a pro-Nazi puppet government. But Hungarian morale hit rock bottom as many senior generals, including the chief of staff, deserted. In some cases whole units went over to the Soviets.

Meanwhile the Red Army began a relentless push toward Budapest. The Germans, given their defeats elsewhere, lacked sufficient strength for a successful defense, while the Hungarians were on their last legs. In early November the Red Army fought its way into the suburbs of Budapest. By late December Soviet spearheads had closed around the city and surrounded four German and two Hungarian divisions. Hitler regarded Budapest as a symbol like Stalingrad, one that represented Germany's fanatical determination to see the war through to the end. While the Germans had made extensive preparations to withstand a siege, they did little to prepare for the needs of Budapest's one million civilians. Guderian, summing up the moral sensibilities of Hitler's military circle, commented that the requirements of the civilian population were immaterial.

☆   ☆   ☆   ☆

Events in the Mediterranean and on the Eastern Front represented a series of unmitigated disasters for the Germans from 1942 to 1944. By the winter of 1944 the Soviets had regained the Ukraine, and in the summer of 1944 they executed one of the most successful offensives of the war, Bagration, destroying all of Army Group Center and twenty-eight German divisions. In fall the Red Army liberated much of the Balkans and added that region to Stalin's empire. The Allies also made major gains in the Mediterranean, but they engaged considerably smaller German forces than the Soviets. By late 1943, British and American forces had driven Axis forces out of North Africa, captured Sicily, knocked Italy out of the war, and seized the air bases in southern Italy necessary to attack Romanian oil targets and Austria. Nevertheless, hard fighting remained before the entire Italian peninsula fell into Allied hands.

As the Allies pushed back Axis forces, the war attained new levels of scale and mechanization. At the battle of Kursk, the combatants employed about 7,000 tanks; in Operation Bagration, the Soviets committed 124 divisions and 4,000 tanks; in the landings on Sicily, the Allies launched an immense amphibious assault of seven divisions. On the Eastern Front, the Soviets overwhelmed the Germans with vast armies, supported by thousands of aircraft, while in North Africa, Sicily, and Italy, the Allies used enormous amounts of firepower to batter their way forward. As the toll of numerous battles reduced the Axis forces, the Germans slowly lost their qualitative edge, and the Allies became more proficient in planning and executing complicated and effective campaigns.

SUGGESTED READINGS

Bidwell, Shelford, and Dominick Graham. *Tug of War: The Battle for Italy, 1943–1945* (New York: St. Martin's Press, 1986).

Blumenson, Martin. *Kasserine Pass* (Boston: Houghton Mifflin, 1967).

_____. *Mark Clark* (New York: Congdon & Weed, 1984).

_____. *Masters of the Art of Command* (Boston: Houghton Mifflin, 1975).

Erickson, John. *The Road to Berlin* (Boulder, Col.: Westview Press, 1983).

_____. *The Road to Stalingrad* (New York: Harper & Row, 1975).

Hardesty, Von. *Red Phoenix: The Rise of Soviet Air Power, 1941–1945* (Washington: Smithsonian Institution Press, 1982).

Howard, Michael. *The Mediterranean Strategy in the Second World War* (New York: Praeger, 1968).

von Mellenthin, Friedrich W. *Panzer Battles: A Study of the Employment of Armor in the Second World War*, trans. H. Betzler (Norman: University of Oklahoma Press, 1956).

Sajer, Guy. *The Forgotten Soldier*, trans. Lily Emmet (New York: Harper & Row, 1971).

Wray, Timothy A. *Standing Fast: German Defensive Doctrine on the Russian Front During World War II* (Fort Leavenworth: Combat Studies Institute, 1986).

Zhukov, Georgii K. *Marshal Zhukov's Greatest Battles*, trans. Theodore Shabad (New York: Harper & Row, 1969).

Ziemke, Earl F., and Magna E. Bauer, *Moscow to Stalingrad: Decision in the East* (Washington: Office of the Chief of Military History, 1987).

Ziemke, Earl F. *Stalingrad to Berlin: The German Defeat in the East* (Washington: Office of the Chief of Military History, 1968).

25

VICTORY IN EUROPE: BRUTE FORCE IN THE AIR AND ON THE GROUND

The Air War, 1944

The Campaign in the
West, 1944

The Collapse of Germany

The battles on the periphery of Fortress Europe substantially wore down Germany's military forces. The Wehrmacht's battlefield excellence was no longer so sharply defined as in the earlier years of the war. Moreover, the overwhelming Allied quantitative superiority due to economic mobilization and vast resources provided a factor that no battlefield performance could match. In the west a sustained air battle began in February 1944 and continued for the next three months. When it was over, Allied air forces had broken the Luftwaffe and gained air superiority over the European continent. A successful amphibious landing on the beaches of Normandy immediately followed that success. From the east and west, Allied armies could now batter their way to and across the frontiers of the Reich.

Allied military operations, particularly those of Anglo-American forces, involved a close working of the services in a joint arena; air, sea, and land worked intimately to achieve larger purposes. Nowhere was this clearer than in Normandy and in the subsequent fighting and buildup. Naval and air forces got the ground forces ashore; naval support provided the great highway to the West's industrial might; and air power made the movement and supply of German troops a nightmare. In the end, infantry had to dig the Germans out of their positions in Normandy, hedgerow by hedgerow, but that infantry battle was possible due only to close interservice cooperation within the Allied forces.

The Air War, 1944

The Americans Defeat the Luftwaffe

Throughout fall 1943 and into early 1944, RAF's Bomber Command had waged a relentless campaign to destroy Berlin. But German night defenses recovered from the difficulties of summer 1943, and British losses mounted alarmingly. Nevertheless, as Bomber Command confronted defeat in its night offensive, the U.S. Eighth Air Force, supported by Fifteenth Air Force in Italy, returned to the attack. Not only had American bomber strength reached new levels, but now long-range escort fighters, in particular the P-51 Mustang, accompanied bomber formations all the way to targets deep in Germany. The P-51, the best piston-engine fighter of World War II, had outstanding aerial combat capabilities and the range with drop tanks even to reach Berlin.

In February 1944 the weather cleared sufficiently for Eighth Air Force to begin attacks on the German aircraft industry. The result was a massive battle of attrition that cost both sides heavily; the battle lasted until May when the German fighter force finally collapsed. Aiming to strangle production and deprive the Luftwaffe of its aircraft, the Americans initially attacked the factories manufacturing Luftwaffe fighters, but the raids failed to accomplish the objective. Despite savage pounding, the Germans raised

Due to flaws in doctrine and limitations in technology, Americans failed to develop an effective long-range day light escort fighter until early 1944. By May, however, fighters like the P-51 Mustang had won general air superiority over Europe.

fighter production by 55.9 percent during 1944, but only by shutting down production of other aircraft. The overall weight of airframes produced actually rose only 20 percent in 1944 and reflected a heavy emphasis on single-engine fighters. The new fighters also showed a marked decline in quality compared to earlier production runs.

Ironically, the offensive destroyed the Luftwaffe's air defenses, but in an entirely unforeseen fashion. The appearance of escort fighters deep in Germany represented a catastrophe for the Luftwaffe. The experience of one Bf 110 Group that scrambled twenty-one aircraft against B-17s in March was not atypical. In that incident the Germans shot down two B-17s but suffered heavily: four aircraft missing (three pilots bailed out), one crash-landing (pilot killed), another written off on landing, and three aircraft crashes on takeoff.

By early March, Eighth Air Force's new commander, Major General Doolittle, ordered his fighters to attack German airfields with low-level strikes. American fighter and bomber formations suffered heavy losses, but the Germans lost more heavily. Luftwaffe fighter-pilot losses reached an unsustainable level. In January the Germans lost 12.1 percent of their fighter pilots, killed, missing or wounded; in February, 17.9; in March, 21.7; in April, 20.1; and in May, 25 percent. From January to May the Luftwaffe averaged 2,283 pilots available in the fighter force; in that same period it lost 2,262 fighter pilots. In May 1944 the defenders cracked; the heavy losses that Allied bombers had been suffering dropped dramatically. From this point, while some daylight raids did suffer heavy losses, the Americans had won general air superiority over Europe.

Supporting the Invasion

In April, Allied air strategy changed direction. "Overlord," the invasion of the European continent, was finally ready. With achievement of air superiority over Europe, airmen had met the crucial precondition for a successful invasion. By the decision of the combined chiefs of staff, Overlord's supreme commander, General Dwight Eisenhower, commanded all air assets as of April 1, 1944. His chief deputy, RAF Marshal Sir Arthur Tedder, with advice from the scientist, Solly Zuckerman, had designed a plan to isolate Normandy by means of air interdiction. If successful, the air campaign would enable the Allies to win the logistic buildup once the battle began.

Eisenhower and Tedder ran into considerable opposition from Allied airmen. Lieutenant General Carl A. Spaatz, commander of U.S. Army Air Forces in England, argued for continuing the attack on the German aircraft industry. His planners, however, were already turning toward a new target, the German petroleum industry—which they believed represented the crucial weak link in the enemy's economy. Not surprisingly, Air Marshal Arthur Harris, commander of Bomber Command argued vociferously against air cooperation with Overlord. In particular, he worried disingenuously that attacks on French railroads would kill tens of thousands of innocent Frenchmen. Harris knew that Churchill desperately feared the postwar repercussions of such casualties.

Eisenhower and Tedder responded easily to the objections of American airmen: raids against German aircraft targets would continue, and in May attacks on oil targets would begin. Harris's claims were more difficult because of their political ramifications. However, Zuckerman discovered that Bomber Command based its estimates of French casualties on the pattern of night raids with many hundreds of bombers, when in fact French railway targets demanded attacks of no more than 100 to 200 bombers. Moreover, by this point British navigational devices were so accurate that Bomber Command could execute its attacks with great precision. The first tests showed that Bomber Command could hit targets even more accurately than Eighth Air Force. With his arguments disproved, Harris fell into line. Among the many night attacks, one on Vaires not only demolished the marshaling yard, but also caught trains from the 10th SS Panzer Division (*Frundsberg*) intermingled with a consignment of naval mines. When it was all over, the Germans collected identity disks from nearly 1,200 dead.

Out of the eighty most important transportation targets, Bomber Command attacked thirty-nine, Eighth Air Force, twenty-three, and tactical air forces, eighteen. Losses were heavy. Between April 1 and June 5, Allied air forces lost nearly 2,000 aircraft and 12,000 officers and enlisted men. But the attacks proved crucial. Beginning in early April, a precipitous drop in French railway traffic occurred. Attacks by fighter bombers on the Seine River bridges and trains further accelerated the decline. By late May, just prior to the attacks on the Seine bridges, rail traffic in France had dropped to 55 percent of January levels. By June 6, the destruction of the Seine bridges had reduced traffic levels to 30 percent, and by the end of July to 10 percent. By mid-June trains had virtually ceased to operate in western France. As the campaign progressed, Ultra intercepts and decrypts provided air commanders with crucial insights into the campaign's progress.

Air interdiction placed the Germans in an impossible situation. Since much of the Wehrmacht consisted of infantry divisions with horse-drawn equipment, the Germans depended on railroads to move reserves and supplies. Removal of that support made it difficult to redeploy forces once the invasion began. Destruction of the transportation network also forced German infantry to fight without adequate artillery support and even at times basic infantry supplies. Moreover, damage to roads and bridges made it difficult for motorized and mechanized units to reinforce the front. Thus air interdiction proved invaluable in winning the battle of France.

The Offensive Against the Petroleum Industry

Since 1939 the Germans had worried about petroleum. Romanian oil production was declining and difficult to get up the Danube River, and much of the Reich's oil came from synthetic plants that required great amounts of coal, the one natural resource Germany enjoyed in abundance. But the manufacture of synthetic fuels required refineries with miles of pipelines and production facilities, all vulnerable to air attack. In April 1944 a Luftwaffe staff officer warned that Germany's refineries and fuel plants lay within "the

The Boeing B-17 Flying Fortress was the workhorse of the American strategic bombing campaign in Europe. The normal maximum radius of action for the B-17 and B-24 was 850 miles; this range could be extended with auxiliary fuel tanks or reduced bomb loads.

zone threatened by air attack," and he found it inexplicable that the Allies had not yet attacked the oil industry—a target that would jeopardize Germany's entire war effort.

One month later his warnings came true. Eisenhower released Eighth Air Force from invasion preparations to attack oil targets. On May 12,935 B-17s and B-24s attacked the major synthetic oil plants. American losses were heavy, forty-six bombers and twelve fighters. The results were encouraging but not decisive, for the plant at Leuna, although damaged, lost only 18 percent of capacity. Ultra, however, reported a major redistribution of Luftwaffe Flak units to protect the synthetic refineries; this report alerted Allied airmen to the seriousness with which the Germans viewed the attacks. Nine days later another Ultra message indicated that Allied air attacks on oil facilities, including those in Romania, had forced the German high command to reduce fuel allocations.

After feverish efforts to repair the damage, production had almost returned to normal by the end of May. On May 28–29, Eighth and Fifteenth air forces launched another series of attacks. In the two-day air battle, both sides suffered heavy losses. The Americans lost eighty-four bombers, but the Germans lost thirty-nine single-engine fighter pilots killed or missing (twenty-one more wounded) and a further thirty-three crew members of twin-engine fighters either killed or wounded. These two attacks combined with raids against the Romanian oil fields at Ploesti to reduce German petroleum production by 50 percent. Since the Germans had virtually no oil reserves, they faced a catastrophic situation.

The attacks in May were a prelude to devastating, follow-on raids in succeeding months. New attacks in mid-June knocked out 90 percent of aviation fuel production; by the end of July successive Allied raids had lowered aviation gas production by 98 percent. When Ultra detected German efforts to restore production, follow-on attacks wrecked the repair work and what little capacity remained.

The impact of these oil attacks on Germany's strategic situation was enormous. The raids severely restricted the Luftwaffe's frontline force in its ability to defend the Reich against strategic bombers. By mid-summer, Speer's desperate efforts to restore fighter production had borne bitter fruit. New aircraft were available in increasing numbers, but insufficient fuel grounded most of them. Furthermore, without fuel the Luftwaffe could no longer train new pilots. Thus the Luftwaffe, battered into desperate condition by its mauling in the spring, could not maintain the uneven contest.

Fuel shortages were no less serious for the army. Combat operations suffered immediately; training became impossible. The Ardennes offensive, launched in December 1944, had enough fuel to get panzer spearheads only to the Meuse River; the attackers hoped to advance the rest of the way to Antwerp by capturing Allied fuel dumps. In February 1945 the German defenders of Silesia possessed over 1,100 tanks. Nevertheless, the Soviets conquered much of the province in less than one week, because the defenders had virtually no fuel. The German soldier rarely, if ever, saw the Luftwaffe overhead; throughout 1944 and 1945 he was pounded on every front by enemy aircraft, while supplies, attacked by both day and night, reached him with decreasing frequency.

The Campaign in the West, 1944

Italy

At the end of 1943 a major reshuffling of Allied commanders took place between the Mediterranean and Britain. Eisenhower became the Supreme Commander Allied Forces Europe. In every respect, he was an inspired choice. He was a first-rate strategist and operational commander, but above all he possessed political gifts that allowed him to lead and work with a quarrelsome group of senior Allied commanders. A number of other commanders moved from the Mediterranean. Tedder became Eisenhower's deputy; Montgomery became the land force commander. Among other Americans, Patton, still on probation, and Lieutenant General Omar N. Bradley journeyed to London, while Spaatz and Doolittle assumed control of American air forces in Britain. The Italian campaign, however, was not over; it continued as a secondary theater as Allied forces fought their way up the Italian peninsula.

Late 1943 and early 1944 found Anglo-American forces in Italy in a disconcerting position. The drive of the 15th Army Group under General Sir Harold Alexander had stalled well short of Rome. In four months the Allies had advanced only seventy miles beyond Salerno. The Gustav Line, a German defensive position set in the rugged Apennines, proved impervious

The Italian Campaign, October 1943 – June 1944

to attack. Frustrated, the Allies decided to make an amphibious landing south of Rome in coordination with another assault on the Gustav Line. They expected the amphibious assault to force the Germans to evacuate the Gustav Line and withdraw north of Rome. The target of the amphibious landing was the small town of Anzio, about sixty miles behind the Gustav Line. Chosen to command the landing was Major General John P. Lucas with his VI Corps. The attack was a combined operation with the British 1st and the American 3rd divisions making the initial landings. Assisting were commando and ranger units, a parachute regiment, and two tank battalions. Two more divisions were immediately available, U.S. 1st Armored and 45th Infantry divisions.

Unfortunately the landings in January 1944, known as Operation "Shingle," replayed the Suvla Bay fiasco of the 1915 British attack on Gallipoli. The first day went like clockwork; the landings at Anzio caught the Germans completely by surprise; the only Germans in the immediate vicinity were three drunken officers in a Volkswagen command vehicle who drove down the beach and into an LST. Within twenty-five miles of the beach were members of an engineer battalion who offered little or no resistance. By the end of the first day the Allies had landed 36,034 troops and over 3,000 vehicles. At the end of the second day VI Corps occupied a beachhead seven miles deep. The road to Rome lay open, and VI Corps was in a position to cut supply routes to the Gustav Line.

But before the invasion, Lucas expressed profound misgivings at its prospects. The Fifth Army commander, Lieutenant General Mark Clark, added to Lucas's caution by advising him not to stick his neck out. As a result, Lucas refused to exploit favorable circumstances and ordered his forces to remain inside the beachhead. The Allies did little more than consolidate their positions. But the Germans, never ones to waste time, reacted with dispatch, and by midnight on the day of landing, they had 20,000 troops closing in on Anzio. Within one week, they had concentrated elements from eight divisions and launched a series of counterattacks that nearly drove the Allies into the sea. Far from opening up the front, the Anzio landings soon represented a substantial liability.

Just prior to the Anzio landing, the Fifth Army attacked the lower half of the Gustav Line with a British, an American, and a French corps. As part of this operation, the U.S. 36th Infantry Division attacked across the Rapido River on January 20; its efforts failed miserably with almost 1,700 casualties. Neither this attack nor others broke German lines. Interdiction by Allied air forces also had little effect on the defenders; in some cases Allied air power even helped the Germans. At the abbey of Monte Casino, German paratroopers threw back every attack by Fifth Army; a major air raid on February 15 then destroyed the abbey completely. But in the scattered wreckage, German paratroopers waged an even more effective defense.

In May the balance of forces between the opposing sides finally reached the point where Allied air power, interdicting supplies from the north and pounding the front lines, combined with the overwhelming superiority of ground forces to break the deadlock. On May 11, the Allied offensive began. For three days attacks made little progress against stiff enemy resistance; but the ill-equipped Free French broke the stalemate by driving over the mountains where the Germans least expected an advance. Their success opened the Gustav Line to penetrations elsewhere. American forces at Anzio, now ably commanded by Major General Lucian K. Truscott, broke out of the beachhead, and German defenses collapsed. Truscott's VI Corps was positioned to trap many of the German defenders had it driven inland, but Clark ordered Truscott to turn north and capture Rome instead, which VI Corps did on June 5. Though Clark's capture of Rome grabbed the front pages of America's newspapers, much of the German Tenth Army escaped to fight another day.

Still, the Allies pushed the Germans northward until the front line stabilized on the Gothic Line north of Florence. In mid-August many of the U.S. and all of the Free French combat units moved off to participate in landings in southern France as part of Operation "Anvil" (later renamed "Dragoon"). The Italian theater again settled into stalemate. Some historians have claimed that Anvil prevented the Allies from driving through the Po River valley and on into the Alps and Austria. Such claims seem improbable. Not until the following April did the Allies finally break the deadlock and surge into Austria, but by that point the Wehrmacht was collapsing on every front.

What did the Italian theater contribute to victory? Through summer 1943 it proved an excellent training ground for Anglo-American forces.

The rough terrain of Italy restricted the mobility of the highly motorized American troops. In terrain where trucks could not move, mules provided valuable assistance in transporting weapons and supplies.

Moreover, the casualties the Allies inflicted on German ground and air forces in Tunisia and Sicily were a significant return on investment. After that point, however, Italy cost more than it gained. The skill and tenacity of German troops combined with difficult terrain and weather to make this a dismal theater indeed.

Northern France

In a speech to the French people in October 1940, Winston Churchill said: "Good night, then: sleep to gather strength for the morning. For the morning will come. Brightly will it shine on the brave and the true, kindly upon all who suffer for the cause, glorious upon the tombs of heroes. Thus will shine the dawn." Dawn came June 6, 1944, but only after immense preparations and a massive mobilization of manpower and resources in both Britain and the United States. The complexity of a cross-Channel invasion did not become fully apparent until after the Dieppe raid of August 1942. In that attack British commandoes and Canadian troops attempted to seize the French port of Dieppe. Anticipating less than 1,500 German defenders, they encountered three times that many, plus ample reserves, most of whom were third-line infantry. The Dieppe defeat suggested that an invading army could not gain a French port in the invasion's first days; an extremely powerful landing force would have to make the invasion over open beaches. In the end, the planners for Normandy had almost two years to absorb Dieppe's lessons, as well as those of other amphibious landings the Allies executed in the European and Pacific theaters. Consequently, the Normandy landing was perhaps the most thoroughly planned battle in the history of warfare.

A cross-Channel invasion presented enormous logistic difficulties. Not only men but also supplies would have to be down-loaded into landing craft and then moved to beaches in small boats for another unloading. Moreover, the northern French beaches fronted directly on the English Channel, which was famous for its rough and unpredictable seas. Consequently, the Allies required landing craft in far greater numbers than planners had initially envisaged. A worldwide shortage of such craft and demands from the Pacific created major hurdles. Only in 1944 did the Allies possess sufficient landing craft to make an invasion possible. Beyond landing craft, the planners decided to supply the beachhead through artificial harbors. In the first days of Overlord, Allied naval forces thus had the task of funneling hundreds of thousands of men and tons of equipment into France and of constructing two "Mulberry" artificial harbors, including breakwaters, piers, and landing facilities to speed the buildup.

The size of the invasion demanded general air superiority. During the Dieppe landing, the Luftwaffe had caused serious losses among landing

The Coast of France, June 1944

craft and naval vessels supporting the raid. But the victory of American air power over the Luftwaffe in spring 1944 removed that threat; the Luftwaffe would hardly get an aircraft over the crowded beaches of Normandy on June 6.

By summer 1943 planning was well underway; in November 1943 the planners received approval for the initial design for Overlord. They had rejected the easily accessible area around Pas de Calais, because that area was also obvious to the Germans, had received much of the effort to fortify the coast, and could be attacked from three different directions by German reserves. Instead the planners selected Normandy: it was farther removed from enemy reserves, the ocean could protect the invading force's western flank, and Allied air power could more easily isolate the battlefield from enemy reinforcements and resupply.

Logistic planning rested on a belief that once ashore the advance into France would be slow. Anticipating a methodical, rather than mobile campaign, the logisticians failed to prepare for swift movements that could consume vast quantities of gasoline. Exacerbating this miscalculation was the fact that through the end of July the battles in Normandy consumed more ammunition and less fuel than predicted. At the beginning of August, Allied logisticians increased ammunition allocations and decreased those of fuel—at precisely the moment when the campaign turned mobile.

By January the Allied high command was in place. Eisenhower commanded Supreme Headquarters Allied Expeditionary Forces, while Montgomery commanded 21st Army Group with responsibility for the landing. Under Montgomery was the British First Army (Lieutenant General Sir Miles C. Dempsey) and the U.S. First Army (Lieutenant General Bradley). Upon arrival in Britain, Eisenhower and Montgomery examined and rejected plans to land three divisions over the beaches and to drop one airborne division inland. They believed that such forces were inadequate to the task and that the initial landings would have to consist of five divisions, supported by three airborne divisions dropped inland.

The Allies would come ashore on five separate beaches; from east to west they were Sword, Juno, Gold, Omaha, and Utah. The British and Canadians would land on the three eastern beaches, the Americans on the two western beaches. On the eastern side, the British 6th Airborne would seize the Orne River bridges. On the other end of the front, the American 82nd and 101st Airborne would shield the westernmost beaches—the most exposed landing site. Above all, the Allies would have to get maximum men and equipment ashore before the Germans launched a strong counterstroke.

In the German high command, disunity and disharmony marked Nazi preparations. Field Marshal Rundstedt was in overall command in the west, but he lacked control over air and naval units and had only limited control of SS and parachute units. His chief subordinate was Rommel, who as commander of Army Group B, held responsibility for the immediate defense of western Europe. Above both hovered Hitler's disruptive influence; the Führer was determined to keep the levers for defending France firmly within his grasp. Consequently, neither Rundstedt nor Rommel had authority to move the mobile formations that made up the reserves. Moreover, they differed on how best to defend France. Rundstedt believed that German forces should conduct a mobile defense to inflict maximum casualties on the Allies; Rommel argued that superior Allied resources, air power, and manpower demanded that the Wehrmacht stop the invasion on the beaches. Should the Anglo-American force gain a foothold, he believed the war would be lost.

Rommel threw himself into the task of defending France with his usual energy. Under his inspiring leadership, German engineers laid millions of mines; beach defenses and obstacles sprouted; and "Rommel asparagus" (telephone poles with wire strung between them) spread across French fields to destroy Allied gliders. The construction of beach obstacles below the high-tide line forced the Allies to land at low tide; consequently, the landing had to take place between June 4 and 8, when low tide and dawn coincided.

The weather almost did not cooperate. After excellent weather in May, storms blew in from the Atlantic, and only on June 5 did conditions clear up sufficiently for Eisenhower to launch the invasion. However, the period of bad weather helped the Allies achieve tactical surprise. Rommel was in Germany visiting his wife, while the commander of Seventh Army and most of his corps and division commanders were away from their headquarters to participate in a war game.

Normandy

As dusk settled over airfields in England on June 5, paratroopers from three airborne divisions clambered aboard their aircraft. The first pathfinders were down in France before midnight. The British Sixth Airborne Division quickly seized the key bridges on the landing's eastern flank. The two American divisions were more dispersed on landing. In some areas heavy Flak greeted American transport aircraft; as a result troops from the 82nd and 101st divisions dropped all over western Normandy. But their spread confused the Germans, and the Americans achieved their purpose of preventing reinforcements from moving on Utah beach.

In the grey dawn of June 6, Allied troops came ashore on five different landing beaches. The assault went well on the British beaches and on Utah. Nevertheless, despite their gains, the British and Canadians failed to take full advantage of the situation. One Canadian battalion almost reached Caen but was ordered to pull back by the brigade commander because such a move was not in the plans. That night, the 12th SS Panzer Division (*Hitler Jugend*) moved into place, and the British and Canadians did not capture Caen for a month and a half. British official history attributed the failure to capture Caen on the first day to the unexpectedly high tide, congestion on the shore, strength of opposition, and a lack of urgency.

Only on Omaha did the Germans hold the attackers on the beach for a substantial period of time. Instead of encountering light defenses, the U.S. 1st Infantry Division, reinforced by elements of the 29th Infantry Division, ran head on into the 352nd Division, which had recently moved into the area. Because of strong currents and poor navigation, the Americans landed

American paratroopers prepare to jump from C-47 Dakota transport planes. Airborne forces in the enemy's rear areas in Sicily, Salerno, and Normandy confused and harassed the enemy and gave the Allies a greater chance of success.

on different parts of the beach than planned and then came under withering fire from well-placed Germans. Most of the special tanks that could supposedly "swim" sank in heavy swells, as did much of the artillery carried in amphibious trucks. For a time Bradley considered diverting follow-on forces from Omaha to other beaches. But small groups of soldiers began advancing under fire and somehow drove the Germans from the heights. By the end of the day infantry from the two divisions had pushed two miles inland, and bulldozers were clearing paths to the heights. By the morning of D+1, the Allies had over 177,000 troops ashore in four secure beachheads, and the buildup was already well underway.

The Allied success received considerable help from the Germans. As early as 0400 hours, German commanders on the scene requested release of the armor to launch a counterblow. But Hitler was asleep, and the OKW's chief of operations, General Alfred Jodl, refused to release the reserves or to wake the Führer. Not until late in the afternoon did the German high command allow 21st Panzer Division to attack, while other armored divisions were too far away from Normandy or released too late to participate in the first day's fighting.

Two distinct battles soon developed in Normandy, the British and Canadians fighting in the east, and the Americans in the west. Both efforts

While balloons provided protection against low-flying aircraft, an armada of ships poured thousands of men and tons of equipment and supplies onto the Normandy beaches.

involved a massive application of firepower, air power, and superior resources against the Germans. In the west, before driving south, the Americans were supposed to turn right, advance across and then up the Cotentin Peninsula to capture Cherbourg, but the port did not fall until June 27. To make matters worse, the Germans sabotaged the port facilities thoroughly, and Allied ships could not use its piers until August 7. In July the Allies had hoped to land some 725,000 tons of supplies but managed to land only 446,852. After capturing Cherbourg, the Americans concentrated on driving south and breaking through German defenses in western Normandy. Here they ran up against the worst of the *bocage* country and its thick hedgerows; virtually every field and village offered heavy cover for the defenders. Nevertheless, slowly, but inexorably, the Americans drove the Germans back.

On the eastern side, the British and Canadians fought in terrain more open and favorable than the hedgerow country. Dempsey, the British ground force commander, had his chances to make more substantial gains near Caen. On June 12, XXX Corps sensed a weakness in German positions. Seventh Armored Division got its lead brigade through German lines in undamaged condition. But upon reaching Villers-Bocage, the lead column consisting of tanks, soft-skinned vehicles, and supply trucks in peacetime formation came under fire on its flank from five Tiger tanks from the

501st SS Heavy Tank Battalion. In a one-sided action, the Tigers caught the British completely by surprise and destroyed almost the entire column. By the time the battle was over, the German tankers had destroyed twenty-five tanks and twenty-eight other armored vehicles and thrown 7th Armored back to its start line.

By July 1 the Allies held only a small portion of the area anticipated by Overlord planning. Caen remained in German hands. Seeking to capture that city, the British launched major offensives on July 8 and 18. Finally capturing Caen but failing to break through the enemy's positions, they drew German armor piecemeal into a battle of attrition that wore away the enemy's armored reserve.

Eisenhower identified three factors that made fighting in Normandy extremely difficult: "First, as always, the fighting quality of the German soldier; second, the nature of the country; third, the weather." The tired, weary, outnumbered, and outgunned German infantry displayed superior tactical skills and initiative compared to their opponents, and the terrain of the bocage country served only to exacerbate the imbalance. Operating in small units, they relied on an active defense and made limited counterattacks with local reserves and small groups of tanks. Soft ground limited the mobility of the highly mechanized Allied forces, and hedgerows divided the battlefield into numerous rectangular compartments that the Germans skillfully tied together. As for the weather, the amount of wind and rain in July exceeded that of any time in the past half-century and hampered air support and mobility. In the month of July, the U.S. First Army suffered about 40,000 casualties, 90 percent of whom were infantrymen. One American infantry regiment that entered combat shortly after D-day had only four officers remaining from its original complement in the third week of July.

As the Germans reinforced Normandy, extensive damage to the transportation system and road network made movement difficult. Allied fighter bombers dominated the daylight hours, while night movement was difficult. The French resistance added to German discomfiture by sniping and creating numerous obstacles. Units of 2nd SS Panzer Division (*Das Reich*) took nearly two weeks to arrive in Normandy from Limoges, a journey that should have taken two days. Along the way they committed a number of atrocities, the worst of which occurred at Oradour-sur-Glane and involved the murder of about 650 French civilians. The men were machine-gunned in open fields, and the women and children were burned to death in the village church.

As Allied forces poured into Normandy, German difficulties mounted. Ultra picked up the location of Panzer Group West's Headquarters, and an immediate strike by Allied tactical air destroyed the only headquarters in the west capable of coordinating movement of large panzer formations. The supply situation was catastrophic; only desperate measures kept the front lines from collapsing. Rommel was at his wits' end; on July 17 a fighter bomber attack badly wounded the field marshal and sent him home where Hitler would order him to commit suicide for participation in the July 20 assassination attempt. Hitler also relieved Rundstedt. In his case, in reply to Jodl's rhetorical question, "What shall we do?," the blunt old field marshal had replied: "End the war. What else can you do?" Rundstedt's replacement was Field Marshal Hans Günther von Kluge, one of Hitler's favorites. After taking over, Kluge told Rommel, "Even you will have to get used to obeying orders." After Rommel's wounding, Kluge also assumed command of Army Group B. The field marshal's experience since 1940 had been exclusively on the Eastern Front, so he had little idea of the immense superiority of Allied air power and its capabilities. He soon learned.

The Breakout

On July 25 the U.S. First Army launched Operation "Cobra," which sought to break through the German defenses at St. Lô. Major General J. Lawton Collins's VII Corps made the main attack with three infantry divisions leading and two armored and one motorized infantry divisions following. A massive bombing of German defenses was to precede the attack. On July 24, however, a major bombing went awry due to bad weather; American bombs killed twenty-five soldiers and wounded another 131. On the next day, under ideal conditions, 1,800 bombers from Eighth Air Force repeated the errors of the preceding day and dropped many bombs within American lines. This time, they killed 111 soldiers, including Lieutenant General

The Normandy Campaign,
June 30 – August 13, 1944

Allied attacks
Allied front lines
Carpet bombing by Allies

0   10   20 mi
0   10   40 km

Cherbourg
Normandy
Le Havre
June 30
Bayeux
Caen
June 30
St. Lô
July 25
July 25
Coutances
Aug. 13
Vire R.
Orne R.
Falaise
Gulf of
St. Malo
Vire
Argentan
Avranches
St. Malo
Mortain
Aug. 13
July 31

Lesley J. McNair, and wounded 490 others. The attack by the 30th Infantry Division went in anyway against the *Panzer Lehr* division. The Germans, though bloodied and battered, did not break at first. But on July 26 German resistance crumbled. VIII Corps, which was to the west of VII Corps, broke through the defenses on its front, and 4th Armored Division entered Coutances on the 28th and Avranches on the 30th. The swift advance of about thirty-five miles almost doubled the amount of terrain under Allied control.

As Cobra ended, key changes in command occurred. Under a barrage of protests from Montgomery, Eisenhower activated 12th Army Group under Bradley; with Bradley's promotion, Lieutenant General Courtney H. Hodges assumed command of First Army. Bradley in turn activated Patton's Third Army and released Patton from his role as a decoy. To trick the Germans into believing that a second invasion was coming at a location other than Normandy, the Allies had placed the flamboyant American in command of a nonexistent army group and allowed the Germans to collect information about its preparations for assaulting Pas de Calais.

On August 1, American forces poured through the bottleneck at Avranches. To secure the ports in Brittany, the first corps in Patton's Third Army turned west toward St. Malo, Brest, and Lorient. Concerned with logistical support, Overlord planners had aimed for Cherbourg to be turned over to the British as a supply base and for Brittany's ports to serve as a supply base for the Americans. To some, such as Major General John S. Wood, commander of the 4th Armored Division, the move toward the west was in the wrong direction, but the Allies remained concerned about gaining large port facilities. Recognizing the strategic importance of the ports, the Germans ordered them defended to the last man. After rushing through Avranches, 6th Armored Division raced almost 200 miles to reach Brest on August 6. Because Brest was well protected by several hills and streams, as well as numerous defensive positions, VIII Corps brought up three infantry divisions and amassed considerable ammunition reserves before it began a sustained attack on August 25, the day Paris fell. Brest finally fell on September 19, costing almost 10,000 American casualties. In retrospect, the costly siege of Brest seems wasteful and a blind adherence to plans that events had overtaken, especially since the Allies were unable to restore Brest to operating condition before the war ended.

As the area under Allied control expanded dramatically, Bradley decided on August 3, with Montgomery and Eisenhower's concurrence, to stop the movement west into Brittany and to turn American forces to the east. While the Canadian First, British Second, and U.S. First armies continued to battle the Germans in Normandy, three of the corps in Patton's Third Army raced south and then east, one corps driving south to seize Rennes (forty miles from Avranches) on August 3 and another corps driving southeast to seize LeMans (ninety miles from Avranches) on August 8.

Hitler recognized the threat posed by the breakthrough at Avranches. He ordered Kluge to pull the panzer divisions out of the battle against the British and concentrate on cutting off American forces rolling through Avranches. The target for their counterattack was the Norman village of

Mortain (twenty miles east of Avranches). Fortunately for the Allies, Ultra picked up enemy intentions, and Bradley placed strong forces on Mortain's dominating terrain to meet the attack. Moreover, American air power made German daylight movements a nightmare. The offensive failed to reach even its first objectives.

The counterattack at Mortain, however, placed German armor in danger of encirclement. With the Americans at LeMans and with the Canadians south of Caen, Fifth Panzer Army, Seventh Army, and Panzer Group Eberbach were in the middle of a rapidly closing pocket. Hitler reluctantly agreed to withdraw, but the escape exit from the pocket was narrow indeed. Neither Bradley nor Montgomery forced the closure of the pocket, or the "Falaise gap," as it became known. On orders from Bradley, Patton's forces halted at Argentan on August 13 to await the British and Canadians, driving from the north. The Canadian First Army drove south of Caen toward Falaise. On August 14, 800 heavy bombers attacked targets in front of the Canadians, but as at St. Lô, some bombs hit friendly troops, killing or wounding nearly 400. The next day the Canadians continued south but faced strong enemy resistance. At the end of the day on the 15th, they still remained two to three miles from Falaise. Meanwhile, Allied air strikes and artillery hit the mass of Germans fleeing the pocket.

Although the Germans lost more than 60,000 soldiers (killed or captured) and abandoned vast quantities of equipment in the Falaise pocket, large numbers of their best troops escaped. The loss of quantities of weapons did not create insurmountable problems, because German industry was producing vast amounts through Speer's effort. The Allies had let a golden opportunity slip through their fingers by the failure to close the Falaise-Argentan gap.

Advancing Toward the Rhine

The German collapse in France, nevertheless, was complete. Allied armies surged out across France in a wild drive toward the German frontier. On August 15, American and French troops landed in southern France in Operation Dragoon (previously known as Anvil), and German defenses collapsed as the Allies drove up the Rhône River valley. Paris fell on August 25; the Seine represented no obstacle. Unfortunately, the euphoria gripping Allied commanders and troops approaching the Reich turned into overconfidence and a belief that the war was won. The Allies correctly sensed the desperate state of the Wehrmacht, but their overconfidence carried with it seeds of failure.

As Allied forces approached the Seine, Eisenhower reconsidered his campaign strategy. The original plan had called for a halt on the Seine and buildup of supplies for three weeks before a resumption of the advance. Eisenhower knew that once a pursuit had begun, his forces should advance relentlessly, so he decided to press eastward as far as logistics would allow. But he had to decide whether to move on a broad front beyond the Seine River or whether to give priority to a single thrust into Germany.

The Allied Race Across France, August 26 – September 15, 1944

The ensuing debate about "Broad Front" versus "Single Thrust" strategy revealed much jealousy and friction between Americans and British. Prior to crossing the Seine, the Allies had envisaged their advancing along two axes into Germany. The northern route went through Amiens, Mons, and Liège to the Ruhr industrial region; the southern one went through Reims, Metz, and the Saar to Frankfurt. On August 23, Montgomery proposed that the bulk of Allied divisions and supplies concentrate under his command for a single thrust along the northern route. On August 29, Eisenhower decided to adhere to the original plan but add weight to the north by having Hodges's First Army move along the northern, rather than southern axis. Montgomery would take Antwerp and drive toward the Ruhr, while Bradley's forces spread across the Ardennes—Hodges's First Army moving north, and Patton's Third Army toward Metz. The decision angered Bradley and Patton, for it weakened 12th Army Group and gave Third Army a low priority for gasoline supplies. On September 1, Eisenhower assumed control of the ground campaign, but not before calling a press conference in London and warmly praising Montgomery. Both 21st and 12th Army groups now reported directly to Supreme Headquarters, Allied Expeditionary Force (SHAEF). Eisenhower insisted that this was not a demotion for Montgomery, who was promoted to field marshal to assuage his ego.

Montgomery drove into Belgium, all the while complaining about shortages of supplies and fuel. He still was pressing for a single thrust—under his command. Arguing that insufficient logistical support existed for more then one major drive, he proposed that Bradley's forces should halt and that all logistic support go to 21st Army Group for the last, decisive blow against a tottering Wehrmacht. Although Montgomery received nearly 80 percent of the logistical support he requested, he missed a golden opportunity to shorten the war. On September 3 British forces captured Brussels; on September 4, 11th Armored Division seized Antwerp so quickly that the Germans could not destroy the port facilities. Everything fell into British hands in undamaged condition; only the opening of the Scheldt estuary stood between the Allies and the relief of their growing supply difficulties. But Montgomery, focusing his attention entirely on the Rhine, missed the logistic implications of Antwerp's capture. Furthermore, by capturing Antwerp, the British were in position to put the German Fifteenth Army in the bag. That sizable force had guarded Pas de Calais and was now fleeing up the coast. An advance of less than ten miles beyond Antwerp would have sealed off the Walcheren and South Beveland peninsula and bottled up Fifteenth Army. But Montgomery halted at Antwerp. Consequently Fifteenth Army, ferrying across the Scheldt at night, escaped to Walcheren Island and then back into Holland.

Montgomery's pause reflected his desire to tidy up the battlefield and bring his forces under tighter control. He proposed to Eisenhower an armored thrust, supported by British and American airborne forces, across Holland and the Rhine into the Reich. Eisenhower agreed to the operation which became known as "Market Garden." From its inception it proved to be badly thought out and, moreover, plagued by bad luck. Similar in conception to the German attack on Holland in May 1940, Montgomery's plan aimed for three airborne divisions to capture the bridges leading up to and over the Rhine. Then, his XXX Corps would drive through the Dutch countryside to the north German plain. The last, crucial bridge lay across the Rhine at Arnhem. Significantly, Montgomery's proposal meant that the Allies would not be able to clear the Scheldt estuary and therefore use Antwerp to relieve growing supply difficulties.

The British needed almost two weeks to get attacking forces ready. While preparations proceeded, the Germans replenished and reorganized their beaten units back into effective fighting formations. The pause also

Operation Market Garden, September 17 – October 4, 1944

Arnhem

Rotterdam   *Lower Rhine R.*

Waal R.

Nijmegen

North
Sea

Rhine R.

Maas R.

NETHERLANDS

Breda

Willems Canal

Wilhelmina Canal

Walcheren
Island

Schedt Estuary

Eindhoven

Maas R.

West Wall

Antwerp   Sept. 17   Neerpelt

GERMANY

BELGIUM

Albert Canal

— Allied lines, Sept. 17
⊕ Airborne operation

0   15   30 mi

0   15   30 km

Brussels

allowed a number of panzer divisions, including 9th and 10th SS Panzer, to withdraw for rest and refit; those two divisions went to southern Holland, while units from Fifteenth Army worked back into fighting trim in the same area. As early as September 5, Bletchley Park indicated that 9th and 10th SS Panzer were in the Arnhem area. Further Ultra decrypts, as well as intelligence from the Dutch underground, reinforced the first warning, but such intelligence made no impression on the British generals.

Montgomery and his airborne commander, Lieutenant General F. A. M. Browning, selected the inexperienced British 1st Airborne Division to capture the most difficult bridge at Arnhem. The more experienced American divisions, the 82nd and 101st, received the easier tasks of securing the bridges at Nijmegen and Eindhoven. Allied airmen then persuaded the inexperienced commanders of 1st Airborne to accept a drop zone six miles from their target because the flight path to the excellent drop zone immediately south of the bridge would expose aircraft to heavy antiaircraft fire.

Market Garden began on September 17 after extensive air attacks prepared the way. It went badly from the first; poor weather interfered with air reinforcements and supply. Despite stringent prohibitions, an American officer carried a complete set of the plans on board one of the attacking gliders; it crashed, killing him and the other occupants. Within hours, those plans were in the hands of General Kurt Student, commander of German paratroopers, who was in the area. The British 1st Airborne got only one battalion to the Arnhem bridge before the Germans sealed off the drop zone. In the south, XXX Corps advanced extremely slowly in its drive north to support the paratroopers; units from the German Fifteenth Army put up a tenacious resistance. Mud and water constrained XXX Corps' movement and forced armored vehicles to advance along a single road, an ideal killing zone for German antitank guns. Market Garden failed short of the Rhine. Though it opened a salient deep into German lines, XXX Corps never reached Arnhem, and the Allies failed to establish a bridgehead across the lower Rhine. Montgomery had prepared everything thoroughly but had wasted the most important commodity in war, time.

On September 22, Eisenhower directed Bradley to support Montgomery's operation with a drive toward Cologne. Bradley in turn ordered First Army to fight its way through the West Wall at Aachen. From October 13 to 21, some of the most bitter house-to-house fighting in the war occurred in that demolished city. As the Allied offensive slowed, it became apparent that the Germans had pulled off what Goebbels termed "the miracle of the west." The German West Wall and fighting around Arnhem, Aachen, and Metz brought the Allied offensive to a halt.

Logistic realities caught up with British and American forces who had outrun their supply system. Allied air power had wrecked the French railroad and road network in preparation for the invasion and breakout and had exacerbated the difficulty of moving Allied supplies. To shorten supply lines and ease the logistic situation, Montgomery had to open the Scheldt, but the Germans had had plenty of time to prepare defenses. Thus the failure to open the Scheldt in early September resulted in bitter and costly fighting. Not until mid-November did the Canadians finish the job. The first supply ship docked in Antwerp on November 28—nearly three months after the British had captured the port.

Weather added to Allied discomfort. British and Americans battered at weary German troops but could not break the deadlock. Swollen rivers and streams made movement difficult. The Germans hung on tenaciously in the hope that the Führer would deliver the promised miracle weapons. The widespread knowledge of the army's and Nazi Germany's criminal behavior throughout the war undoubtedly encouraged many Germans to resist to the bitter end. Moreover, the West Wall, constructed in 1938–1939 along the Reich's western frontier, provided the Wehrmacht with well-positioned defenses, although the Germans had moved most of its guns to the Atlantic Wall in 1943 and 1944.

In an attempt to move forward toward the Ruhr, Eisenhower assigned Bradley responsibility for the main effort. In mid-November the Ninth and First armies on Bradley's left launched an attack on a narrow front near Aachen in another attempt to break through the West Wall. Preceded by the heaviest close-air support bombing attack of the war, American troops encountered strong opposition, particularly in the Huertgen Forest. By early December they had advanced no more than twelve miles. Meanwhile, Patton fought his way beyond Metz. The French First Army, part of Lieutenant General Jacob M. Devers' 6th Army Group, failed to overcome strong German resistance around Colmar and created what became known as the Colmar Pocket west of the Rhine. Despite significant gains, the euphoria that had gripped Allied troops as they raced across France and Belgium had evaporated.

The Collapse of Germany

The Air Contribution

By December 1944 the Allied forces had battered the German army back to the Reich. Now the many pressures brought to bear on Germany worked in combination to broaden the effect of individual efforts. In early September 1944 control of Allied strategic bombing forces returned to the airmen. With the loss of its long-range warning network on the French coast and a sharp decline in oil production, the Luftwaffe could hardly wage an effective air defense. Moreover, Allied tactical air could also strike targets in Germany. The result was a three-pronged offensive by Allied air forces that contributed considerably to Nazi Germany's collapse.

Tedder argued strongly for a focused effort to destroy the German transportation system. His argument emphasized the Allied success in attacking French transportation. He received some support from airmen, but the strategic bombing barons had their own agenda. Harris obdurately clung to "area" bombing, but as most major railway stations lay in the center of German cities, he agreed to use them as aiming points. Spaatz still pushed for the oil campaign; nevertheless, when conditions did not permit precision bombing, he agreed to attack transportation targets. Much of the tactical air efforts also went into support for the transportation plan. The impact of such attacks on the Reich's rail and road system represented the single most effective use of air power in the war.

By early September 1944, air attacks against German transportation targets were well underway, and by October they were having considerable impact. For the week ending August 19, 1944, the German railroads had loaded and dispatched 899,091 cars; by the end of October that figure had fallen to 703,580 cars; by the end of December the total had fallen to 547,309 despite the demands of the Battle of the Bulge, the German winter counteroffensive. In that month, marshaling capacity of rail yards had declined to 40 percent of normal; in February 1945 it had fallen to 20 percent. The Battle of the Bulge indicated that attacks on transportation could not yet prevent the Germans from executing military operations. On the other hand, according to the Strategic Bombing Survey, these attacks "had reduced the available capacity for economic traffic in Germany to a point at which [the war economy] could not hope to sustain, over any period of time, a high level of military production." And, of course, the diversion of declining transport resources to supporting the Battle of the Bulge exacerbated the difficulties that German industry was already experiencing.

The steady decline of the transportation network gradually strangled the war economy by disorganizing and reducing the flow of raw materials and finished goods necessary for the production of weapons and munitions. Under such conditions neither planning nor production took place in an orderly fashion. The precipitous decline of coal transportation, essential to continued functioning of the economy, underlines the extent of the problem. In January 1944 the Essen division of the German railway system had loaded an average of 21,400 coal cars per day; by September that total had dropped to 12,000, of which only 3,400 were long-haul cars. By February 1945, Allied air attacks had cut the Ruhr off from the rest of Germany, while German railroads often had to confiscate what little coal they loaded just to keep locomotives running. The Ruhr was swimming in coal that it could no longer transport even to the industries in the region, much less to the rest of Germany.

The evidence suggests a general collapse of the war economy by mid-winter 1945. Since it was not a sudden and cataclysmic collapse, it remained difficult to discern even to those conducting the campaign. In July and August 1944 both the Eastern and Western fronts had suffered enormous defeats with great loss of equipment. Nevertheless, because German armaments production in summer 1944 remained at a relatively high level, the Wehrmacht reequipped the survivors and the new men (mostly boys) called upon to defend the frontier. There the Germans offered tough resistance and even launched the Ardennes offensive. However, beginning in January 1945 in the east, followed within a month and a half in the west, German armies again lost major battles, but this time neither on the Rhine nor on the Oder rivers were they able to reknit for a last stand. The collapse came because air attacks on the transportation network had successfully shut down the war economy, and the Wehrmacht no longer had the weapons, munitions, or petroleum necessary to fight. Even blind fanaticism could not maintain a struggle under such conditions.

Battle of the Bulge

The idea of counterattacking in the west had come to Hitler in early September 1944, even as his armies streamed back toward the German frontier. He believed that the Wehrmacht could still achieve a decisive battlefield victory that would drive the Western Powers from the war. Ever the gambler, he selected the Ardennes as the location of the main attack. The target would be Antwerp to destroy a vital logistic link for the Allies and to entrap much of the British army. But to get to Antwerp the Germans had to capture Allied fuel dumps, and the Wehrmacht possessed only enough petroleum to get to the Meuse.

On the Allied side, senior commanders remained optimistic despite German resistance on the frontier. Few could conceive that the enemy would be able to assemble the necessary resources for a major offensive. In early December, Eisenhower met with Montgomery and Bradley and outlined plans for an attack in early January 1945. The Allies would retain the broad-front strategy, but the main effort would be in the north. As Anglo-American armies prepared to launch another offensive, there were indications that the Germans were also preparing an attack. Even though the Wehrmacht faced desperate shortages of supplies, Ultra intercepts indicated major buildups of ammunition and fuel dumps opposite the Ardennes, the one place where the Allies were not attacking. But preoccupied with their own offensive and confident the Germans could not attack, Allied commanders missed the warnings. In late fall the vulnerability of the Ardennes increased with the insertion of inexperienced divisions into that quiet sector. Only the 82nd and 101st Airborne divisions were in reserve; the Allied high command had committed everything else to the front.

On December 16 the Germans struck between Monschau and Echternach along a fifty-mile front in the Ardennes. The weather cooperated by providing a heavy, thick blanket of clouds to obscure the battlefield and prevent the intervention of U.S. air power. Sixth SS Panzer Army attacked in the north but met stiff resistance on its right from the U.S. 99th and 2nd divisions, part of V Corps. Fifth Panzer Army to the south, however, broke through the U.S. 106th and 28th divisions. The Germans advanced rapidly, for the U.S. divisions were spread thinly across wide fronts and were inexperienced or weakened from previous fighting.

On the northern shoulder, the 99th and 2nd divisions held the critical Monschau and Eisenborn Ridge area and thereby denied use of its critical roads to the Germans. Because of the difficult terrain in the Ardennes, the main German advance was along secondary roads, but American troops offered strong resistance at several key road junctions, most notably St. Vith and Bastogne. At St. Vith, American soldiers blocked the vital road junction for six days. At Bastogne, a small armored detachment held the Germans long enough for the 101st Airborne Division to arrive. Though surrounded, the defenders at Bastogne refused to surrender. On the southern shoulder of the penetration, U.S. forces retreated, but as in the north, they eventually held. Thus strong defenses on the shoulders and at several critical road junctions limited the width of the German penetration and disrupted the enemy's advance.

The Allied high command responded more swiftly than the Germans had expected. Since the Germans had cut off Bradley's communications with the northern flank of the Bulge, Eisenhower turned the battle there over to Montgomery, while Bradley coordinated the battle in the south. Montgomery eventually brought in his XXX Corps to help strengthen the defenses.

In the south, Patton had his finest hour. His initial reaction when told of the attack in the Ardennes was to commit all his units in heavy fighting so that he would not lose any to the fighting farther north. When he recognized, however, that a full-scale enemy offensive had begun, he shifted units of Third Army on his own authority to counterattack the breakthrough from the south. He advised Eisenhower: "Hell, let's have the guts to let the sons of bitches go to Paris. Then we'll really cut 'em off and chew 'em up." When the weather failed to cooperate, he had his chaplain compose a particularly bloodthirsty prayer. On December 23, the weather cleared, and Allied tactical and strategic air forces pounded the Germans throughout the Ardennes. Patton decorated his chaplain.

By Christmas Eve elements of Fifth Panzer Army had reached within three miles of Dinant and the Meuse River, an advance of about sixty-five miles, but that was as far as they got. Along the way Waffen SS troops under Lieutenant Colonel Jochen Peiper massacred American prisoners near Malmédy; the SS troops also murdered Belgian civilians as they advanced.

News of the atrocities and the presence of Germans in American uniforms and vehicles created considerable turmoil; sentries energetically questioned unknown Americans passing through their position about who played first base for the Cubs or how many home runs Babe Ruth had hit in 1927.

As Allied units attacked the northern and southern flanks of the Bulge, Allied aircraft raked the exposed German units. On December 26, Patton's 4th Armored Division made contact with the defenders of Bastogne. By mid-January Allied counterattacks had pushed the Germans back, and the bulge had disappeared. Hitler's desperate gamble had gained the Reich nothing. Instead he had wasted the Wehrmacht's mobile reserves and lost 100,000 men, and the Allies were on the western frontier of Germany with their forces poised for the final campaign and with their logistic base steadily improving.

Collapse in the East

The German offensive in the Ardennes led the Western Powers to request the Soviets to launch their long-expected winter offensive. The Red Army had preparations well in hand. On January 12, 1945, it struck along the Vistula; the number of forces was totally in the Soviets' favor, for the Germans had bled off most of their reserves for the Ardennes offensive. What little remained went to Hungary to fight around Budapest. The Soviets launched two concurrent offensives. The first, on the central portion of the front, saw the First Belorussian and First Ukrainian fronts break out between Warsaw and the Carpathian Mountains. They intended to drive through central Poland into Germany to the Oder River. The second, north of Warsaw, resulted in the Second and Third Belorussian fronts striking East Prussia and Pomerania. Up to now the Red Army's watchword in its conduct of operations had been "liberation"; now it was "vengeance." Soviet troops entered German territory fully encouraged to pay the Germans back for their momentous crimes in the Soviet Union.

The offensive on the central portion of the front opened with the First Ukrainian Front's attack, which hit seven weak German divisions with nearly five armies, two tank armies, and over 1,000 tanks. Within a day it had opened a forty-mile hole through which its troops and tanks poured into Silesia and raced toward the Oder River. On January 14, the First Belorussian Front launched its attack; within a day it had broken through German lines north of Warsaw. Guderian warned Hitler that Soviet attacks had shattered Army Group Center and that weakened German forces could not halt the Red Army unless reinforced. Hitler released some forces from the west but promptly shipped them off to Budapest.

By January 17, the Soviets had taken Warsaw and were approaching Cracow. Hitler sent Field Marshal Schörner to restore the situation and blamed the OKH for Warsaw's fall. After having three OKH staff officers arrested, he ordered that henceforth no command be given that could not be countermanded from above. Schörner brought unwarranted optimism and a fanatical belief in Naziism to a hopeless situation. By January 19, Army

Central Europe, 1945

Group A, defending Upper Silesia and central Poland, had lost contact with Army Group Center. Soviet forces had ripped Army Group A's front to shreds; only logistical limitations could halt their advance. In Hitler's headquarters, the Führer appointed Heinrich Himmler to restore the front on the Oder. As commander of Army Group Vistula, Himmler's mission was to maintain an open corridor to East Prussia and prevent breakthroughs to Danzig and Posen. But his experience as the head of the SS did not translate into battlefield competence.

Before Himmler arrived to take command, the dam broke. Soviet forces attacked German units protecting East Prussia. Though Hitler had diverted divisions from East Prussia to central Poland, he refused permission for any withdrawals; German defenses again unraveled. On January 24 the Soviets reached the coast west of Danzig and the mouth of the Vistula; this advance isolated East Prussia from the rest of Germany. On the 25th the Soviets drove past Posen.

By early February 1945 the Soviets had pushed 200 miles west of Warsaw. Their leading units rested on the Oder within forty miles of Berlin; they had surrounded large German garrisons in Posen and Breslau. Though on the brink of final collapse, the Germans pulled themselves together for a final stand in front of Berlin. Not surprisingly the Soviets themselves were experiencing logistical difficulties, given the distances they had covered. In February and March, the Red Army cleaned up East Prussia, except for Königsberg and a small coastal strip. As the main body of the Russians closed on the Oder-Neisse line (the eventual Polish-German boundary), they did not resume their offensive toward Berlin. Perhaps close to the wolf's lair, they did not want any failures to dampen their triumph at war's end. Since Western ground forces still remained on the west bank of the Rhine, there seemed little need for haste.

Despite what subsequently happened to the Germans, many found it hard to sympathize with them, since they had committed such horrible crimes in the east. Nevertheless, a terrible revenge fell on eastern Germany, as Soviet troops began systematically looting and raping the territories they conquered. Soviet soldiers, often in a drunken stupor, murdered tens of thousands of civilians. Estimates of civilian casualties are as high as 3,000,000. Whatever the total, it represented the hideousness of the ideological war unleashed by the Nazis on June 22, 1941.

Collapse in the West

Meanwhile, German defenses in the west unraveled at a fast rate during January and February 1945. In the south Devers's 6th Army Group reduced the Colmar Pocket in the first week of February, while in the north and center, Allied units began closing in on the Rhine. By early March British and American units had battered their way into the Rhineland. By March 11, 21st Army Group held the Rhine between Düsseldorf and Nijmegen. Eisenhower planned on encircling the Ruhr by having Montgomery make the major crossing of the Rhine north of the Ruhr, and having Bradley make secondary crossings to the south with First and Third armies. Montgomery ordered a pause to prepare the massive assault across the Rhine, but the Americans moved more quickly.

In early March Third Army cracked German defenses in the Eifel (northeast of Luxembourg) and in three days reached the Rhine. Hodges's First Army did even better: on March 7, 9th Armored Division reached the Rhine at the moment that the Germans were blowing up the Ludendorff railroad bridge at Remagen. German engineers had placed their charges too evenly on the bridge supports. After pressing the plunger, the appalled defenders watched with amazement as the bridge, with much smoke and noise, rose several feet in the air and then settled back on its pilings. U.S. infantrymen rushed the bridge and then seized the cliffs overlooking the river. They now commanded the approaches and reinforcements surged across.

Hodges, with Bradley's support, rushed a large number of units across without fully informing SHAEF, for fear that the Allied high command might not recognize the opportunity. Eisenhower's operations officer lived up to expectations. He told Bradley: "Sure, you've got a bridge, Brad, but what good is it going to do you. You are not going anyplace down there at Remagen. It just doesn't fit into the plan."* But Eisenhower proved more flexible, allowing Hodges and Bradley to push strong forces over the Rhine.

An enraged Hitler ordered an immediate search for traitors. With no reserves, the Nazi army could do little to contain a growing American

*Omar N. Bradley, *A Soldier's Story* (New York: Holt, 1951), p. 500.

bridgehead. The Luftwaffe launched a number of sorties against the bridge and even fired off V-2s, while the navy floated mines and frogmen downriver in desperate efforts to cut the cord across the Rhine. Eventually the bridge collapsed, but by then the Americans had pontoon bridges and four divisions across the Rhine.

To the south Patton moved down the Rhine valley and in cooperation with Seventh Army cleaned up the left bank. To Goebbels' outrage German civilians greeted the Americans everywhere with white bed sheets displayed from windows; there was no fanatical resistance in the Rhineland. Not to be outdone by Hodges's accomplishment at Remagen, Patton threw a bridge across the Rhine at Oppenheim on March 22 and rushed everybody he could across the river. That day, in reference to Montgomery's coming assault across the Rhine on March 24, Patton's briefing officer reported: "Without benefit of aerial bombing, ground smoke, artillery preparation, and airborne assistance, Third Army at 2200 hours, Thursday, March 22, crossed the Rhine River." The rapid advance of the U.S. First, Third, and Seventh armies through the Rhineland had killed, wounded, or captured 225,000 Germans at a cost of 5,000 casualties.

After two weeks of intense preparations, Montgomery was finally ready to launch his blow. Against five ill-equipped, weakly manned divisions holding a thirty-mile front, the British used an artillery bombardment of 3,300 guns, Allied strategic and tactical air forces, and two airborne divisions. The weight of the offensive initially slowed its forward movement, but the British soon broke out into the open. The combined effect of Mont-

Allied forces made rapid progress in Germany. Many towns decked themselves in white flags whereas others offered only token resistance.

gomery's advance and the Americans' advance south of the Ruhr placed the Germans in a hopeless position. The exploitation occurred at an even faster pace than in the Normandy breakout. On April 1, the U.S. 2nd Armored Division from the north met First Army's 3rd Armored Division at Lippstadt, seventy-five miles east of the Rhine, thereby encircling the Ruhr. Within the wreckage of Germany's industrial heart lay Field Marshal Model's Army Group B. Nothing remained in western Germany except a few pockets of fanatical Nazis to hinder Anglo-American forces.

The Allied advance followed political realities as well as operational concerns. Since the political agreements at Yalta had already placed the area around Berlin within the Soviet sphere, it made little sense for Allied soldiers to die capturing territory that would end up under Soviet control. Consequently, Allied troops halted along the Elbe River. In the south the Red Army had already reached Vienna's outskirts; it made equal sense not to reach for what was within Soviet grasp. Only by seizing Prague could the Western Allies perhaps have made a difference in the postwar settlement, but Eisenhower halted Patton's Third Army before it reached the Czech capital.

One last act remained. As Anglo-American forces rampaged through western and central Germany, the Red Army launched its forces on Berlin. The Germans had no prospect for delaying the coming blow. Their Ninth Army, defending the capital, consisted of fourteen understrength divisions; Third Panzer Army on its left flank had eleven divisions. In total, the Germans possessed 754 tanks, 344 artillery pieces, and 900–1,000 antiaircraft guns. Their opponents, First and Second Belorussian fronts, disposed of 110 infantry divisions, eleven tank and mechanized corps, and eleven artillery divisions (4,106 tanks and self-propelled guns, and 23,576 artillery pieces).

The main Soviet offensive across the Oder came on April 16. Despite initial difficulties and fanatical resistance, the Soviets by April 20 had won the battle of Berlin. On the 21st, Soviet artillery shells began falling on the German capital. In the bizarre atmosphere of his bunker, Hitler maneuvered nonexistent units on his battle maps, but there was no hope of relief. On April 25, Soviet and American units met on the Elbe and cut Germany in half. On the afternoon of April 30, Adolf Hitler, having just married his mistress Eva Braun, committed suicide; he was soon followed by Goebbels and his family. The nightmare in Europe was finally over.

*   *   *   *

The collapse of Germany reflected a war waged by one major industrial power against three of the world's other major industrial powers, including one that by itself could outproduce most of the world. Allied air had brought Germany's transportation network to a halt by winter 1945, which in turn caused the collapse of war production, while the destruction of petroleum facilities grounded much of the Luftwaffe and robbed the German army of its mobility. On the Eastern and Western fronts, Allied superiority wrecked the German Army. Hitler's strategic and operational direction of the war made a bad situation worse, but his fanatical will drove the German nation to fight to the end. Nevertheless, the Wehrmacht's competence at tactical and operational levels mitigated some of Hitler's decisions and prevented Allied thrusts from breaking into Germany until 1945.

The battles in Europe in the last year of the war reflected the narrowing of the gap between German battlefield performance and the performance of the opposing armies. The steadily improving tactical and operational capabilities of Allied forces was, of course, substantially aided by their overwhelming superiority in numbers and firepower. The invasion of Normandy, the expansion of the beachheads, and the breakout and surge across western Europe demonstrated the Allies' improved ability to join infantry, tanks, and artillery into effective combined arms teams and to use air power to extend the performance of their ground forces. Particularly noteworthy was the capacity of Allied forces to work together in a joint environment in which the services complemented the capabilities of each other. Combined with the advantages of superior intelligence and deception on a massive scale, these capabilities had placed the Germans in a hopeless situation.

SUGGESTED READINGS

Ambrose, Stephen E. *The Supreme Commander: The War Years of General Dwight D. Eisenhower* (Garden City, N.Y.: Doubleday, 1970).

Bennett, Ralph. *Ultra in the West: The Normandy Campaign, 1944–45* (New York: Scribner, 1979).

Blumenson, Martin. *Breakout and Pursuit* (Washington: Office of the Chief of Military History, 1961).Bradley, Omar N. *A Soldier's Story* (New York: Holt, 1951).

Eisenhower, Dwight D. *Crusade in Europe* (Garden City, N.Y.: Doubleday, 1948).

Harrison, Gordon A. *Cross-Channel Attack* (Washington: Office of the Chief of Military History, 1951).

Hastings, Max. *Overlord: D-Day and the Battle for Normandy* (New York: Simon and Schuster, 1984).

Hechler, Ken. *The Bridge at Remagen* (New York: Ballantine, 1957).

MacDonald, Charles B. *The Mighty Endeavor: American Armed Forces in the European Theater in World War II* (New York: Oxford University Press, 1969).

———. *Time for Trumpets: The Untold Story of the Battle of the Bulge* (New York: Morrow, 1984).

Montgomery, Bernard L. *The Memoirs of Field-Marshal the Viscount Montgomery of Alamein* (New York: World, 1958).

Patton, George S. *War as I Knew It* (Boston: Houghton Mifflin, 1947).

Pogue, Forrest C. *The Supreme Command* (Washington: Office of the Chief of Military History, 1954).

Ryan, Cornelius. *A Bridge Too Far* (New York: Simon and Schuster, 1974).

Weigley, Russell F. *Eisenhower's Lieutenants: The Campaign in France and Germany, 1944–1945* (Bloomington: Indiana University Press, 1981).

Wilmot, Chester. *The Struggle for Europe* (New York: Harper, 1952).

Ziemke, Earl F. *Stalingrad to Berlin: The German Defeat in the East* (Washington: Office of the Chief of Military History, 1968).

26

VICTORY IN THE PACIFIC: NAVAL AND AMPHIBIOUS WAR ON THE OPERATIONAL LEVEL

The South Pacific, August 1942–December 1943

The Submarine Campaign

Advance Across the Central Pacific, November 1943–February 1944

Continuing the Two Drives Across the Pacific, 1944–1945

The Invasion of the Philippines

The Final Campaigns

World War II

The Americans committed large forces to the Pacific even though U.S. grand strategy was one of "Germany first." No matter how appealing such an approach might be in strategic terms, the strategy of "Germany first" flew in the face of the fundamental political reality that it was Japan against whom the American public directed its anger. The strategy also encountered the military reality that a major invasion of the European continent could not have occurred before spring 1944. Thus throughout the war, Japan received a higher priority in terms of the commitment of U.S. military forces than the grand strategy seemingly dictated. Many of the debates about strategy focused less on strategic objectives and courses of action than on the allocation of scarce resources. In the end it worked out, but there were times when American strategy and operations in the Pacific possessed a distinctly ad hoc nature.

The war in the Pacific differed greatly from most other wars in the twentieth century. After the battle of Midway in early June 1942 halted the tide of Japanese victory, U.S. commanders in the Pacific possessed only the slimmest of resources; the move against Guadalcanal with one marine division underlined this fact. Though the Americans initially could do little more than defend the sea lines of communication to Australia, the mobilization of manpower and industrial production eventually allowed them to take the offensive. Partially due to interservice rivalries, U.S. forces made two great drives—one from the south Pacific, one across the central Pacific—to destroy Japanese military power. As the Americans confronted their Pacific enemies, the number of naval battles and ships sunk exceeded the combined totals of all other twentieth-century conflicts. Nonetheless, the Americans combined air, land, and sea forces in an unprecedented manner for giant leaps across the ocean. In the end the war in the Pacific concluded the same way it had begun, by air attack, but the explosion of two atomic bombs over Japan heralded the unleashing of new levels of destructive power.

The South Pacific, August 1942–December 1943

The Allied moves against Guadalcanal in August 1942 and into New Guinea in October–November occurred because of the strategic requirement to protect sea lines of communication to Australia. Although American leaders gave Europe first priority, they could not permit the Japanese to consolidate their position in the Pacific. Moreover, public opinion in the United States, still outraged by Pearl Harbor, demanded revenge. The South Pacific saw a series of inconclusive air and naval battles that collectively turned the tide against Japan. There were no decisive victories, but American naval, air, and ground forces emerged from these battles in greater strength, whereas the opposite occurred with the Japanese. Above all, the growing American superiority reflected the awesome industrial capabilities of the United States.

Guadalcanal

In August 1942, U.S. Marines found themselves haphazardly deposited on Guadalcanal. The naval disaster at Savo Island forced the transport fleet to leave, and marines ashore received only half the equipment they required. Fortunately for the Americans, the Japanese had almost completed the airfield on the island; within two weeks the U.S. Navy Seabees had completed it, and fast destroyers brought in fuel, bombs, and ground crewmen. Soon marine aircraft arrived, and from that point on American air reigned over the Solomon Islands. Japanese arrogance and miscalculations also aided the Americans considerably. The Imperial high command, misled by Savo Island, believed the American attack against Guadalcanal was nothing more than a raid; the Japanese army estimated that a reinforced regiment would suffice to regain the airfield on Guadalcanal. Consequently the Japanese launched an ill-prepared countermove on August 21; the marines almost wiped out the attackers in a night of savage fighting. That defeat finally woke up the Japanese high command to the seriousness of the threat; both sides rushed to build up forces on Guadalcanal—the Japanese at night, the Americans by day. Meanwhile a series of naval and air battles swirled around Guadalcanal. On August 24, in the battle of the eastern Solomons, the Americans sank the small carrier, *Ryujo*; the U.S. carrier *Enterprise* in turn received three bomb hits that put it out of action.

By the end of August, the Japanese had built their forces up to 6,000 men. In a series of ferocious attacks on September 13, they came close to breaking through to Henderson Field, but the marines held. The attackers lost 50 percent of their men; the marines lost nearly 20 percent. In early October the U.S. Navy slipped the 164th Regiment of the Americal Division into Guadalcanal. The Japanese by now had over one division ashore and prepared a three-pronged attack on the defensive perimeter despite insufficient artillery. The attacks on October 23–26 came in disjointed fashion. The main attack hit the south side of the perimeter which one marine battalion, reinforced by a battalion from the 164th, held. Throughout two nights of fierce fighting, the well-entrenched Americans beat off the attack. Nearly 3,500 Japanese died in the unsuccessful attempts. The line on Guadalcanal had held.

When American marines landed on Guadalcanal on August 7, 1942, 75-mm pack howitzers came ashore with the assault battalions to provide fire support. Heavier 105-mm howitzers landed later in the day.

From September through November, naval battles continued in furious but indecisive fashion. The Japanese sank carrier *Wasp* and badly damaged carrier *Saratoga* and new battleship *North Carolina*. Off Cape Esperance, northwest of Guadalcanal, American cruisers and destroyers bested their Japanese opponent for the first time at night on October 11–12; their success was largely a result of radar and of Japanese confusion rather than of improvement in U.S. tactical skill. As the Japanese attacks against Henderson Field failed in late October, another inconclusive naval clash occurred north of Guadalcanal. In the battle of the Santa Cruz Islands, 350 miles east of Guadalcanal, the Japanese sank carrier *Hornet* and again damaged *Enterprise*; in turn, American aircraft damaged two Japanese cruisers. Though the U.S. Navy had suffered heavier losses, both sides pulled back.

Recognizing the need for new leadership, Nimitz fired the naval commander of the South Pacific who had originally objected to the campaign in the Solomons and who had become exhausted and indecisive from the strain. His replacement was Vice Admiral William F. "Bull" Halsey, an aggressive combat sailor. As he told the marine commander on Guadalcanal, Major General Alexander A. Vandegrift: "Go on back. I'll promise you everything I've got."

By now the Japanese were not only slipping reinforcements down the Solomons by night but were also bombarding Henderson Field with heavy cruisers and battleships. In November they attempted to land large numbers of reinforcements on Guadalcanal. They began their effort on the night of November 12–13 with an attack against American ships off Guadalcanal and an attempt to land troops on the island by transports. The Americans suffered heavily but forced the enemy to turn back. They badly damaged battleship *Hiei*, and U.S. aircraft sank it the next day. The Japanese returned on November 14, but the Americans sank seven of eleven troop transports. A clash of battleships, one of the few in the entire war, also took place: on the American side battleships *South Dakota* and *Washington*; on the Japanese side, *Kirishima*. Although the Japanese had to scuttle the badly damaged *Kirishima*, they beached four transports on Guadalcanal. Thereafter they risked no more capital ships in the Solomons campaign. The Japanese attempted to send reinforcements by troop transports on December 3, 7, and 11, but heavy losses forced them to abandon the effort to reinforce Guadalcanal.

By early January 1943 the situation completely favored the Americans. The 2nd Marine Division had replaced the 1st, while the 25th Division and the remainder of the Americal Division had arrived. Under the command of Lieutenant General Alexander M. Patch, the Americans drove west to push the Japanese off the island. The Japanese conceded defeat, however, and pulled off 11,000 weary, beaten troops in the first week of February 1943. Of 60,000 American marines and soldiers who fought on Guadalcanal, 1,600 died and 4,200 were wounded; of 36,000 Japanese, 15,000 were killed or missing, 9,000 died of disease, and 1,000 were captured. The air and naval contest had also ended in an American victory; there the results were even more decisive. Air battles over the Solomons cost the Japanese 1,000 naval aircraft and a further 1,500 in defending New

Guinea and Rabaul. The fighting cost the Japanese navy nearly half its fighter pilots and an even greater percentage of dive bomber and torpedo crews; those losses, combined with Midway, undermined the Japanese navy's capacity to fight a naval air battle on anything approaching equal terms with its American opponents.

Papua

The American victory in the battle of the Coral Sea in May 1942 momentarily halted the drive on Port Moresby in New Guinea, and victory at Midway in June swung the initiative tentatively to the Americans. The Japanese, however, did not abandon their hopes of seizing Port Moresby and thereby threatening Allied lines to Australia. On July 21 they landed 11,000 troops on New Guinea and marched south over the mountains toward Port Moresby. After the Japanese got within twenty miles of their goal in mid-September, Australian forces drove the enemy back to the northeast coast where the Japanese established a defensive perimeter. They intended to renew their offensive once they had beaten the Americans on Guadalcanal.

Since MacArthur believed the best way to defend Australia was to control New Guinea, he reacted strongly. In October and early November, the Australian 7th Division and the American 32nd Division moved across from Australia to Port Moresby and on to the northeast coast of Papua (the easternmost extension of New Guinea). When the 32nd Division attacked Buna on November 19, it discovered the Japanese solidly dug in, surrounded by a huge swamp. Without heavy artillery, flamethrowers, or tanks, American attacks gained little. Unwilling to tolerate delays, MacArthur sent Lieutenant General Robert L. Eichelberger to remedy the situation.

While the Australians attacked Japanese forces west of Buna, Eichelberger replaced the 32nd Division's commander and swiftly improved the supply situation and combat power of his forces. In addition to providing better food and ensuring that his soldiers rested, Eichelberger obtained tanks to support the infantry and developed more effective methods for capturing enemy bunkers. Thirty-two days after his arrival, Buna fell. One month later Australians and Americans captured Sanananda, three miles northwest of Buna and the strongest Japanese position in Papua. The Allies had learned important lessons about reducing Japanese defensive positions, but the cost was heavy—8,500 casualties, over 3,500 dead. Nonetheless, the Allies had held at Guadalcanal and driven the Japanese from Port Moresby; they now held the initiative.

Operation "Cartwheel"

These successes raised the question of what to do next. At the Casablanca Conference in January 1943, the Americans lost most of the strategic arguments, but the Combined Chiefs of Staff agreed to retain the initiative in the Pacific. Admittedly, this decision reflected political realities; it also reflected the fact that the great fleet the U.S. Navy was assembling could

Isolation of Rabaul, June 1943 – March 1944

serve no other purpose. The Combined Chiefs of Staff, however, did not envisage a full-scale offensive against Japan until after Germany's defeat.

Soon after Casablanca, the issue of unity of command in the Pacific arose. The army favored MacArthur, the navy Nimitz. Washington had not yet reached a decision when representatives of the Pacific commanders gathered in the U.S. capital. There, MacArthur's chief of staff asked for much larger forces for a drive on Rabaul: no less than five additional divisions and 1,800 aircraft. Appalled at the magnitude of MacArthur's request, the Joint Chiefs of Staff concluded that there were not enough planes, ships, or divisions available in the Pacific to capture Rabaul in 1943. In March they postponed plans to seize Rabaul and accepted MacArthur's new proposal for a two-pronged drive converging on the Japanese base. With MacArthur in overall command of Operation "Cartwheel," Halsey would advance up the Solomons as far as Bougainville, while forces under MacArthur would move along the coast of New Guinea before attacking the western end of the island of New Britain. Whether or not to attack Rabaul on the eastern end of New Britain would depend on the availability of additional forces.

Operation Cartwheel established a model that Pacific commanders would use for the rest of the war. The Americans would advance by great bounds due to their air superiority, hit the Japanese at weak spots, seize existing airfields and ports, and then use their newly acquired bases to support the next leap forward.

Air Power

Air power played a key role in Cartwheel, as well as subsequent Pacific operations. Much of the Allied effort aimed to cut Japanese lines of communication—the air, sea, and land routes over which troops and equipment moved—and to prevent Japanese reinforcement or escape. In August 1942, MacArthur had received a new air commander, Major General George C. Kenney. Kenney may have been the premier airman of World War II; he was certainly the best in the Pacific. Unlike many other airmen, he was no ideologue; he understood the need to adapt military forces to actual conditions and to use air power to accomplish overall theater objectives. Kenney took over a weak organization: combat crews were discouraged and dispirited, maintenance was in shambles, and supply channels were inefficient and incompetent. He gave his air units a thorough housecleaning and relieved no fewer than five generals and an even larger number of colonels. But Kenney made his greatest contribution in air tactics and operations. High-level bombing of ships had thus far killed mostly fish, and Kenney determined to change his forces' tactical approach. Among other improvements, he retrained medium bomber crews and modified their aircraft to attack at low level. B-25s now carried eight .50-caliber machine guns in their noses and six 100-pound bombs that could be skipped into targets.

Meanwhile the Japanese replied to the increasing American threat in the South Pacific by moving forces from as far away as China to the theater. They placed their Eighth Army at Rabaul, Seventeenth Army in the Solomons, and Eighteenth Army in New Guinea and New Britain. In April 1943, they moved the 51st Division from Rabaul to New Guinea; eight transports and eight destroyers provided sea lift. Nearly one hundred fighters were to provide continuous cover for the convoy as it rounded New Britain. "Magic" (the breaking of Japanese codes) picked up Japanese plans. Forewarned of enemy intentions, Kenney studied past experience with Japanese convoys. These assessments along with further Magic intelligence allowed U.S. aircraft to strike with devastating effectiveness. Japanese fighters looked for high-altitude bombers; instead, B-25s attacked at low level from head on. Machine-gun fire and fragmentation bombs rained death on crowded transport decks, while 100-pound bombs skipped into the enemy ships. In one day's air attacks, Kenney's aircraft sank all the transports and four destroyers; the Japanese lost about 3,000 soldiers and most of the 51st Division's staff. Besides demonstrating Kenney's skills, the battle of the Bismarck Sea represented a decisive success for land-based air against naval power.

The Japanese concentrated much of their land-based air at Rabaul and Wewak (an island off the north-central coast of New Guinea). To halt erosion of the Japanese situation, Admiral Yamamoto Isoroku launched a series of massive air raids—the "I" operation—against New Guinea and Guadalcanal in April 1943. The raids achieved little. Moreover, by utilizing Magic the Allies learned of a visit by Yamamoto to the theater and shot down his aircraft. Despite Japanese opposition, Kenney built air bases in

New Guinea, gained air superiority above MacArthur's ground forces, and attacked the Japanese bases. American raids not only destroyed one hundred enemy aircraft on the ground at Wewak on August 17 but also wrecked the enemy's base and supply organization. Consequently the Japanese no longer could shuttle air units back and forth within the theater.

A deteriorating operational situation led the Japanese to undertake desperate remedial measures. The navy committed its new carrier pilots to defend Rabaul's airfield; code name for the counterattack was "RO." A series of savage air battles occurred over Rabaul and New Britain in October and November. Again there was no clear winner; both sides suffered heavy losses, while claiming even heavier ones for their opponents. But in the end, the Americans could replace crews and aircraft without difficulty; the Japanese, their naval air units decimated by the fighting, lost the full combat value of their carriers for the remainder of the war.

The Amphibious Campaign

By early summer 1943, MacArthur and Halsey had begun Operation Cartwheel. The arrival of additional landing craft made movement and commitment of amphibious forces far easier. Specially designed craft such as the Landing Ship Tank (LST), Amphibious Tractor (Amtrac), and Landing Craft Infantry (LCI) moved men and equipment from ship to shore. Halsey's forces had more new craft than MacArthur's forces did in the southwest Pacific, but MacArthur had an Engineer Amphibious Brigade, which carried troops and equipment to shore and organized the beachhead. Such support left the landing troops free to fight the battle.

Halsey's first amphibious strike went against the Munda airfield on New Georgia, which threatened Guadalcanal. Landing on a small, nearby island in late June, about 32,000 soldiers and 1,700 marines moved to New Georgia but took several weeks to dislodge the Japanese from the dense jungle. The next target was Kolombangara with 12,000 Japanese troops in strong defenses. Instead of attacking the enemy force directly, Halsey skipped Kolombangara and landed on the next island, Vella Lavella, where there were no Japanese. Though enemy land-based air posed some risk, the move caught the Japanese off guard. They had no choice but to evacuate the isolated troops on Kolombangara.

MacArthur's forces achieved similar success in New Guinea. Late in January a small contingent of Australian forces repulsed an attack on Wau (about 150 miles northwest of Buna). Allied reinforcements arrived by air, while Kenney's destruction of enemy transports carrying the 51st Division halted Japanese reinforcements. In late June, Allied forces landed on the New Guinea coast east of Wau. On September 5, the 503rd Parachute Regiment dropped on the airfield at Nadzab (fifty miles north of Wau); Kenney's transports then flew in the Australian 7th Division. Combined with another amphibious assault, this vertical envelopment forced the Japanese to abandon strongly held positions at Salamaua and Lae on the coast. A few weeks later the Allies grabbed the Huon Peninsula north of Salamaua and Lae.

The peninsula lay just west of New Britain, which had Rabaul on its eastern tip. Taking advantage of the favorable situation, Kenney's aircraft dropped 685 tons of bombs on Rabaul in October.

Halsey now moved against Bougainville; on November 1, 1943, 3rd Marine Division landed at Empress Augusta Bay. In eight hours both troops and equipment were ashore, a considerable improvement over Guadalcanal. Offshore, the navy, with radar's assistance, fought the Japanese on even terms at night. Staying outside the range of "Long Lance" torpedoes, American ships blasted Japanese light cruisers and destroyers that had come from Rabaul to attack the transports. The Japanese responded by sending a larger naval force to reinforce Rabaul and attack the Allied naval forces near Bougainville. On November 5, violating previous practice, Halsey sent almost one hundred carrier aircraft against Japanese ships anchored at Rabaul. The raid damaged six cruisers and two destroyers and ended the enemy threat to Empress Augusta Bay. Meanwhile the 37th Infantry Division with a New Zealand brigade arrived to assist the 3rd Marine Division in clearing Bougainville, a task not completed until the war's end. As the Allies expanded control over the island, they built an airfield that placed them in an even better position to attack Rabaul.

In mid-December, the 112th Cavalry Regiment landed on the south coast of New Britain. Two weeks later the 1st Marine Division landed at Cape Gloucester on New Britain's western tip. These landings effectively neutralized Rabaul. MacArthur saw no need to undertake a costly assault on the fortified port; the Americans could leave the Japanese to wither on the vine and move to more distant and significant targets. After mid-February 1944 no Japanese warships remained in Rabaul, and no aircraft rose from Rabaul to challenge Allied bombers.

The island-hopping campaign was underway. The Americans, where possible, now avoided Japanese strong points and struck deep into the Japanese island empire. The carriers or land-based aircraft provided air superiority to suppress enemy ground-based air in the area and to fend off enemy naval forces. The amphibious forces, army or marine, would then capture the base, and Allied logistical forces would move up to support the next jump. Without aircraft and cut off from support, the isolated Japanese posed no threat to the Allied advance.

The Submarine Campaign

While two great American drives pushed up the Solomons and New Guinea and across the central Pacific, the U.S. Navy waged one of the most effective campaigns of World War II—one that brought the Japanese to the brink of collapse. That campaign was the submarine offensive against enemy commerce. Before the war, the Japanese had recognized that commercial shipping would play a crucial role in bringing raw materials from the "Greater East Asia Co-Prosperity Sphere" to keep the war economy functioning.

Therefore, in their prewar buildup they expended considerable resources on modernizing their merchant fleet.

Ironically, the Japanese made virtually no preparations to defend commercial shipping. In fall 1941 only two junior staff officers in the naval high command were responsible for protecting the entire Japanese merchant fleet from enemy submarines. The title for their area of responsibility was "rear area" defense; within their sphere lay not only antisubmarine warfare but also antimining and antiaircraft operations. One officer with the derogatory title of "staff officer for training" was responsible for all commercial shipping along the Honshu coast and from Tokyo to Iwo Jima. Despite the obvious success of German submarines against British shipping in the Atlantic, the Japanese failed to provide escorts for merchant shipping at the onset of war. Not until six months after Pearl Harbor did they establish an escort fleet at Formosa, but it consisted of only eight destroyers.

At the beginning of the war the U.S. Navy could not take advantage of such weaknesses. It possessed excellent submarines with enough range and load capacity to operate in the wide expanses of the Pacific, but most submarine commanders were overage and lacked a killer instinct. It took the war's first year to create a cadre of younger, more aggressive skippers. But the problem was not just one of leadership; American torpedoes simply failed to work. The magnetic device designed to make them explode underneath enemy ships rarely functioned because the navy had tested torpedoes inadequately before the war. The navy's Bureau of Ordnance refused to believe reports coming from the Pacific about defects and blamed misses on the submarine commanders. When the evidence finally became too overwhelming to deny, another equally serious defect cropped up: the contact firing pin, designed to explode the torpedo by direct hit, was too delicate; direct hits jammed the firing mechanisms without an explosion. Not until July 1943 was the second problem recognized at Pearl Harbor, and not until September 1943 did U.S. submarines finally have effective torpedoes.

The failure of U.S. boats in their attacks on merchant shipping lulled the Japanese into a false sense of security; they waited until March 1943 to establish a second escort fleet. Even then their escorts numbered only sixteen destroyers, five coast-defense frigates, and five torpedo boats. In no fashion could they handle the storm that now broke. In September 1943 the Japanese lost a record 172,082 tons of merchant shipping; by November that total had climbed to 265,068 tons. Magic and other signals intelligence revealed the routing of Japanese merchant vessels; consequently U.S. submarines easily intercepted enemy shipping. In 1944, American submarines formed wolf packs in response to increasing use of convoys by the Japanese. The slaughter continued; in 1944 the submarine offensive sank more tonnage than the Japanese had lost in the entire 1941–1943 period. By the end of 1944, American submarines had sunk half the Japanese merchant fleet and two-thirds of their tanker fleet. Movement of oil from the Dutch East Indies stopped; shipments of raw material to the Home Islands slowed to a trickle.

Overall, American submarines sank 1,113 merchant vessels over 500 tons, a total of 5,320,000 gross tons. In addition they sank 201 naval vessels, including battleship *Kongo* and supercarrier *Shinano*. The total naval tonnage sunk reached 577,000 tons. All of this cost the U.S. Navy only fifty-two submarines. Considering that American losses included 22 percent of the sailors in the submarine force (the highest casualty rate of any branch), one should not minimize the cost, but the succes of the submarine campaign more than repaid the investment in resources and manpower.

Advance Across the Central Pacific, November 1943–February 1944

In May 1943 at the Trident Conference in Washington, the Combined Chiefs of Staff set long-range objectives for the defeat of Japan: while the Allies would continue to pursue a strategy of Germany first, they would maintain relentless pressure on Japan. The first aim would be to cut the Japanese Empire off from the raw materials of Southeast Asia; the second to launch a strategic bombing campaign against Japan; and the third to invade Japan and break its military power. To achieve these goals the Allies planned to build upon British efforts in Burma, American successes in the South Pacific, and Chinese military power in East Asia for a final offensive against the Home Islands of Japan.

But Admiral King had his own conception. Beginning in January 1943 he pressed for a drive across the Central Pacific by naval forces. This drive would move toward Japan over the coral atolls scattered across the

Admiral Ernest J. King believed, as a distinguished naval historian has explained, that "what was good for the Navy was good for the United States, and indeed the world." Never a seeker of publicity, he was an enormously talented officer who had a firm grasp of naval strategy and tactics.

Pacific. During the same period, MacArthur proposed an advance across the South Pacific via New Guinea and the Philippines. While King emphasized the advantages of leaping vast distances across the Pacific, MacArthur emphasized Allied obligations to the Filipinos, the advantages of maintaining pressure against an already retreating enemy, and the possibility of a renewed Japanese threat to Australia. Even Nimitz had qualms about two Pacific drives. In the end the American chiefs of staff performed a delicate balancing act; King would get his way, but the drive across the central Pacific would move first against the Gilbert Islands and then advance toward the Philippines, as would MacArthur. The move against the Gilberts and then the Philippines would leave considerable sea lift for MacArthur's forces.

Sea Power

While Halsey's and MacArthur's successes in Cartwheel were wearing away Japanese ground and air power, the naval balance swung drastically in favor of the Americans. The first Essex-class fleet carriers arrived at Pearl Harbor; at 27,000 tons, with a top speed of thirty-two knots and one hundred aircraft, they represented a major increase in naval air power. American industry was producing them at the rate of nearly one a month. At the same time the Independence-class light carriers of 11,000 tons with a similar speed and a capacity of fifty aircraft were also arriving. By autumn 1943, Fifth Fleet under Admiral Raymond A. Spruance had grown to six fleet carriers, five light carriers, five new and seven old battleships, nine heavy and five light cruisers, and fifty-six destroyers—all of which required an enormous support system of tankers, supply ships, and tenders. The carriers, moreover, possessed the F6F Hellcat fighter, which finally gave navy pilots a fighter superior to the Zero. All of this reflected design and production decisions made in the late 1930s and early 1940s. The new carriers provided the navy the capability to advance across the central Pacific toward Japan.

    One of the great triumphs of the Pacific war was the fact that the U.S. fleet remained at sea on a constant basis with only individual ships returning for refit and with Halsey's and Spruance's headquarters rotating command. While Halsey's headquarters, Third Fleet, was commanding at sea, Spruance's headquarters, Fifth Fleet, would be in Pearl Harbor planning the next operations; and when Spruance and his headquarters went to sea, Halsey and his headquarters returned to Pearl.

    No matter who commanded, a vast armada of supply ships sustained the fleet across the immense distances of the central Pacific. The unsung story of the drive across the central Pacific was the logistic support for that fleet, a fleet that quite literally never returned to its bases. It represented a triumph that no other nation could match. In a manner not anticipated in the 1920s and 1930s, the fleet could exist by itself in enemy waters for indefinite periods of time; it required anchorage only for resupply and refit, but more often than not the former took place while ships were underway in the open ocean. Island bases provided only the logistic structure from which the fleet drew its sustenance.

In October 1943 Nimitz created two mobile service squadrons. By the end of the year three squadrons contained thirteen large fleet oilers, innumerable stores and ammunition ships, and a whole host of smaller repair barges and tugs. These squadrons enabled the American attack fleet to cut its ties with the shore. Individual ships, of course, returned to port for overhaul and refitting, but the fleet remained at sea. The attack on the Mariana Islands in June–July 1944 suggests the immensity of the logistical operations. Some 535 combat and auxiliary ships carried 127,571 troops to island targets 1,000 miles from Eniwetok and 3,500 miles from Pearl Harbor; they then executed a massive set of landings *and* fought a series of great naval and air battles to protect the landings. By 1945 logistic capabilities of the U.S. fleet had reached an undreamed of extent. On July 21–22, for example, Task Force 38, after completing a series of air strikes on Tokyo, replenished at sea less than 450 miles from the Japanese capital. In less than two days supply ships transferred 6,369 tons of ammunition, 379,157 barrels of oil, 1,635 tons of stores and provisions, and 99 replacement aircraft. The Japanese had no chance against such capabilities.

Tarawa

The first target of King's Central Pacific drive was the coral atoll of Tarawa. The assault on Tarawa on November 21, 1943, was a costly but necessary learning experience for American amphibious forces. The preinvasion bombardment was too short, lasting only two-and-one-half hours. It stunned the enemy but failed to impair fighting capacity. Unfortunately for the attacking marines, the planners had underestimated enemy defenses. Equipped with 200 artillery pieces, including some 8-inch guns removed from the British defenses at Singapore, 5,000 Japanese troops defended Tarawa. As the landing craft moved toward shore, communications problems caused the bombardment to lift too early. Advancing in Amtracs, the first of three waves of marines reached the shore safely, but low tide prevented following landing craft from crossing the barrier reef. Some marines had to leave their landing craft 700 yards short of the beach; Japanese defenders slaughtered them as they waded ashore and pinned others into a narrow beachhead less than 300 yards deep. At the end of the first day the marines had 5,000 men on Tarawa, but 1,500 were dead or wounded. In the end, however, superior American firepower destroyed the defenders. When it was over only seventeen Japanese soldiers had survived, while the marines had lost 1,000 dead and 2,000 wounded.

As the marines suffered heavy casualties on Tarawa, the army's 165th Regimental Combat Team and 105th Infantry Regiment landed on Makin in the Gilberts. There the Japanese possessed fewer troops and virtually no heavy weapons. Nevertheless, the soldiers took four days to reduce the garrison. While their deliberate, careful approach kept the casualty rate low, naval support had to remain overly long on station. As a result, a Japanese submarine got in among the invasion fleet and sank escort carrier *Liscome Bay*, killing nearly 650 sailors. With control of Tarawa and Makin, the Americans had control of the Gilberts; the Marshalls were the next target.

Kwajalein and Eniwetok

Almost immediately after Tarawa, American naval leaders debated where to strike next in the advance across the central Pacific. Previous plans had called for a two-step operation aimed at two atolls at the eastern edge of the Marshalls, followed by seizure of Kwajalein in the chain's center. But Nimitz believed the Japanese had strengthened the eastern Marshalls and preferred Kwajalein as the next target. Spruance and Admiral Richmond Kelly Turner, commander of amphibious forces, argued that an attack on Kwajalein would expose U.S. forces to enemy air attacks from bypassed positions in the eastern Marshalls. When Nimitz insisted on moving directly on Kwajalein, Spruance received permission to seize an unoccupied atoll in the eastern Marshalls to provide a protected anchorage.

Accompanied by Task Force 58 with twelve carriers and 650 aircraft, the amphibians attacked the Marshalls at the end of January 1944. Although the defenders possessed formidable defenses, more than three-quarters of the 8,000 Japanese defenders were supply and administrative rather than combat troops. Moreover, the Americans had thoroughly studied Tarawa and other recent landings and succeeded in overcoming many problems that had occurred in earlier operations. Some improvements included a more

A battleship fires salvos onto a beach as Amtracs loaded with infantry move forward for the amphibious assault.

thorough reconnaissance of beaches and reefs, more extensive naval support fire, and enhanced communications between those landing and those supporting. Following three days of bombardment, the 4th Marine Division and the army's 7th Division captured Kwajalein at a fraction of Tarawa's cost in lives.

Success at Kwajalein led to a move within a month against Eniwetok, an atoll west of the Marshalls, while at the same time fast carriers neutralized Truk, 750 miles farther to the west. In a series of heavy blows, they destroyed 200 enemy aircraft, damaged the island's airfields, and then sank fifteen naval vessels and twenty-four cargo vessels and tankers. This ended Japanese use of Truk as an operating base and effectively isolated Eniwetok. On February 19, 1944, marines and soldiers hit the beaches at Eniwetok. Though a strong Japanese garrison occupied the island, the enemy had not prepared extensive defenses; and incessant air attacks hindered what efforts they did make before the invasion. Nevertheless, fighting was heavy but not nearly as heavy as might have occurred had the Japanese had time to strengthen their positions. Consequently the decision to attack Eniwetok in February 1944 rather than May saved a large number of American lives. By seizing Eniwetok the Americans had moved nearly one thousand miles from Tarawa. The Mariana Islands were next; once there, the Americans could begin aerial bombardment of Japan.

Continuing the Two Drives Across the Pacific, 1944–1945

By early 1944, relations between the army and navy were so delicate that the Joint Chiefs gave no clear priority to either drive across the Pacific. Their strongest guidance was that "due weight should be given to the fact that operations in the Central Pacific promise more rapid advance." At the Quadrant Conference at Quebec in August 1943, the British expressed concern about the twin drives and suggested that the Americans halt MacArthur. When King and Marshall defended the U.S. approach by arguing that the drives were mutually supporting, the British responded that they were also mutually competing.

MacArthur's Advance in the Southwest Pacific

While the Central Pacific thrust picked up speed, MacArthur's drive also accelerated. By avoiding enemy strong points and moving forward in leaps, he sought to advance the fighter-escorted bomber line until it could cover an invasion of the Philippines. In February 1944, Kenney reported that there was no sign of major Japanese units in the Admiralty Islands, 400 miles west of Rabaul. Anxious to complete his isolation of Rabaul and to accelerate the advance, MacArthur accompanied 1,000 assault troops from the 1st Cavalry Division to the Admiralties and landed on February 29. The attackers hit Los Negros Island, held by a Japanese garrison nearly four times U.S. strength. Fortunately for MacArthur, the enemy had deployed to protect the other side of the island. By the time the Japanese had reorganized, American destroyers had brought in 1,500 additional cavalrymen and 400 Seabees. Japanese counterattacks failed. By mid-March another brigade had landed, and the islands were securely in American hands.

MacArthur's risky but successful stroke encouraged another move. It also focused Washington's attention on the Southwest Pacific; thus MacArthur found support to strike at Hollandia, far up the coast of New Guinea. The new target, 580 miles from American bases, was barely within range of Kenney's fighters, but the capture of Hollandia would isolate 40,000 enemy troops and provide American control of three Japanese-built airstrips. Nimitz offered support from fleet carriers, but Kenney argued that his fighters could achieve air superiority by themselves. They did.

In mid-April the landing force departed from the Admiralty Islands. The main attack targeted Hollandia and a smaller force targeted Aitape (125 miles to the east of Hollandia) on the coast of New Guinea. The Japanese had 11,000 men in the Hollandia area, but few were combat troops. Achieving surprise, two infantry divisions under Eichelberger landed on April 22. By the 26th the Americans held all three airfields. The landing by a regiment at Aitape also achieved surprise. The Allies poured in additional troops, however, when they learned that the Japanese Eighteenth Army was moving west toward Aitape. After about a month's intense fighting and a loss of nearly 9,000 soldiers, the Eighteenth Army withdrew.

In late May, MacArthur's forces seized Wakde (150 miles west of Hollandia) off the coast of New Guinea, and a small beachhead on New Guinea to protect the island. On May 27 the Americans struck Biak (325 miles west of Hollandia). Both Wakde and Biak had airfields, but from Biak American aircraft could reach the Philippines.

At this point the Japanese were expecting to fight a major naval battle in the Central Pacific, but they recognized the threat posed by American land-based bombers on their southern flank. Consequently the Imperial navy assembled powerful amphibious and naval forces and moved against Biak in late May, but false reports about sizable Allied naval forces near the island convinced them to withdraw. After assembling an even larger force, including battleships *Musashi* and *Yamato*, the Japanese again prepared to move. Just before they could move, however, the Japanese received word of Spruance's strike against the Marianas in the Central Pacific. They immediately called off the attack on Biak, set in motion "A-GO," code name for a decisive fleet operation, and prepared for a battle in the Central Pacific. These events point out the risks as well as the benefits of having two Pacific drives. Had the attack on Biak begun earlier or had Spruance moved later, the Japanese might well have dealt MacArthur a serious blow—one that could have set the Pacific advance back by a number of months. Such an event would have also given Japanese morale an enormous boost.

Saipan

In the Central Pacific, the next objective was Saipan in the Marianas, one thousand miles west of Eniwetok. Even Nimitz doubted the wisdom of the move, for all the protecting air power would come off carriers. Aware of the impending landing in Normandy, King made clear that the fleet must reach for the Marianas and gain a significant victory. Only 1,200 miles from Japan, Saipan was the closest major island in the Marianas to the Home Islands; the new American superbomber, the B-29, could strike Japan from airfields located there. Along with Saipan, the Americans planned to seize Guam and Tinian as well. Protection for landing forces consisted of Spruance's Fifth Fleet. The attack force for Saipan included the marines' 2nd and 4th divisions and the army's 27th Infantry Division. After taking Saipan that force would assault Tinian. To the south 3rd Marine Division and 77th Infantry Division attacked Guam. On Saipan itself, the Japanese had 32,000 troops, but they had not completed their defenses. Again the Americans had moved faster than their enemy expected.

Overall commander at Saipan was the marine amphibious expert, Lieutenant General Holland M. Smith, referred to behind his back as "Howling Mad" Smith. The plan called for landing two marine divisions in the southwest corner of the island. New lightly armored amphibian tractors were to drive deep into the beachhead. A two-day bombardment by battleships, cruisers, and destroyers, as well as air strikes, preceded the landing.

The bombardment, however, had not concentrated sufficiently on the immediate beachhead and had been too brief; heavy enemy fire and rough terrain prevented the amphibians from driving inland. By nightfall, June 15, 1944, the Americans had 20,000 troops ashore, but the beachhead was 1,000 yards deep, half the distance anticipated by planners. Within two days, Smith brought in the 27th Division to reinforce the marines. That division had moved too slowly at Makin Island and Eniwetok, and on Saipan with a marine division on each flank, its performance was again marginal. At this point, Holland Smith did what MacArthur and Eisenhower regularly did in their theaters: he relieved the division commander. The result, however, was a cause célèbre, one that caused unnecessary bad blood between army and marine corps.

Outside the 27th Division and one or two other anomalies, army and marine divisions performed similarly in the Pacific. The divisions in the Pacific had an advantage over those in the European theaters, for once committed to the battle, army divisions in Europe remained in sustained, unremitting combat, in which replacements had to be integrated directly on the battle front. In the Pacific, fighting for the most part involved sharp bitter engagements over Japanese-held islands where casualties were usually high. But substantial periods of noncombat usually followed, during which units could adapt to new conditions, retrain their combat personnel on the basis of lessons learned in the last campaign, and integrate replacements in a coherent and effective fashion. The result was a steady and impressive improvement in the combat effectiveness of army and marine units in the Pacific.

By early July, the Americans had pushed the Japanese to the northern tip of Saipan. From there the enemy launched the largest banzai attack of the war. When the battle was over, the Americans had suffered 14,000 casualties, while most of the 32,000 Japanese were dead. To add to the tragedy, many Japanese civilians committed suicide or were killed by their own troops to avoid falling into American hands.

On July 24, 4th Marine Division attacked Tinian. The marines hit the narrow beaches opposite Saipan (within artillery range) where the Japanese did not expect a landing. Within eight days Tinian and its valuable airfields were in American hands. Meanwhile, 3rd Marine Division and the army's 77th Infantry Division took Guam. Here soldiers and marines got along without difficulty; the 77th, although never before in combat, was an exceptionally well-trained outfit, and its performance was every bit as good as its more-experienced marine counterpart. By early August the Americans had secured the island. Within several months, B-29s would begin the great aerial bombardment of Japan.

Battle of the Philippine Sea

As noted earlier, the American advance on the Marianas and the landing on Saipan caused the Japanese to halt their move against Biak and send the First Mobile Fleet of nine carriers, five battleships, thirteen cruisers, twenty-eight destroyers, and over 400 aircraft to fight a decisive battle in the Central

Pacific. In the subsequent battle of the Philippine Sea from June 19–21, the Americans enjoyed numerous advantages: their pilots were more experienced; their aircraft were superior; and they outnumbered the Japanese in almost every category. While the Japanese counted 222 fighters and almost 200 bombers, the Americans possessed 500 fighters and over 400 bombers. Enemy aircraft were superior only in range, but that superiority came from a lack of self-sealing fuel tanks and armored protection. Nevertheless, Japanese carriers could launch aircraft against American carriers while remaining outside the reach of U.S. aircraft from those carriers.

The battle of the Philippine Sea occurred after Spruance held his fleet between the Japanese and the American forces attacking Saipan and refused to sail west in search of the enemy. On the afternoon of June 18 the Japanese spotted the Americans. On the next morning they launched heavy air attacks but had to fight their way through a dense screen of F6F Hellcats, and then through heavy antiaircraft fire from American fast battleships before reaching the carriers. Relying on radar, American naval pilots intercepted and destroyed four successive waves of attacking aircraft; less than one hundred enemy aircraft survived out of 373. The Americans lost only twenty-nine aircraft; the pilots nicknamed their victory the "Great Marianas Turkey Shoot." Late that afternoon, American reconnaissance aircraft located the enemy carriers. Although the Japanese were almost out of range, the commander of Task Force 58, Vice Admiral Mark A. Mitscher, launched his aircraft and sank one carrier and damaged three others; U.S. submarines had already sunk two enemy carriers. Much of the Japanese fleet escaped, but it had lost the bulk of its trained aviators. As a result, enemy carriers had entirely lost their combat effectiveness.

The performance of American carriers in the battle of the Philippine Sea deserves note. No fewer than five subdivisions of Task Force 58 operated in close coordination, four containing fast carriers and fast battleships. Each carrier group contained between three and four carriers, fifteen fleet and light carriers altogether, while the fast battleship group possessed no fewer than six battleships. This conglomeration of capital ships, all completed and manned since Pearl Harbor, worked in close cooperation to provide the combat air patrols to shield the fleet, to cover the carriers with antiaircraft gunnery, and eventually to attack the Imperial fleet as it approached. In every respect the American performance reflected not only an awesome projection of military power across Pacific distances but an organizational triumph of impressive magnitude.

The Invasion of the Philippines

During summer 1944, the Americans squabbled over their next major target. King advocated a continuation of "island hopping" by seizing a foothold on Mindanao in the southern Philippines and then making a long leap to Formosa and the China coast; not surprisingly, MacArthur disagreed and argued that the United States could not leave the Filipino people under Japanese control. By and large, naval commanders in the Pacific supported MacArthur.

In September a raid by aircraft from Halsey's carriers suggested (wrongly) that the Japanese lacked strong forces in the Philippines. Halsey recommended cancellation of a number of secondary operations and a direct attack on the Philippines. Nimitz approved, moved the invasion to an earlier date, and canceled secondary attacks—except one. In September, following a three-day bombardment, the 1st Marine Division landed on Peleliu in the Palau Islands; this time, however, the Japanese had withdrawn from the beaches and established strong defenses inland. The marines that made the amphibious assault suffered more than 40 percent casualties, the highest casualty rate of any assault in the war. A joint force of soldiers and marines finally secured the island at the end of November but lost over 1,000 dead and 5,000 wounded. Unfortunately the island proved of little use in the invasion of the Philippines. Peleliu was probably Nimitz's worst mistake.

Leyte

Meanwhile, American planning and preparations proceeded for a landing on Leyte in the central Philippines as a stepping stone to Luzon, the main island in the northern Philippines, which included both Manila and the Bataan Peninsula. The invasion of the Philippines married the two Pacific drives. MacArthur's staff would control ground fighting, while his air commander, General Kenney, would be responsible for land-based air. Rear Admiral Thomas C. Kinkaid's Seventh Fleet, which had older battleships, would provide direct support. Finally, Halsey's Third Fleet with its fast carriers and new battleships would provide long-distance cover.

In early October 1944, Halsey's ships moved between the Philippines and Formosa, and a huge air battle took place. When it ended, American naval air had destroyed much of the enemy's land-based and naval air in the area. Inexperienced Japanese crews gave wildly optimistic but false reports of the damage inflicted on American ships. Meanwhile the Imperial navy returned its carriers to Japan for repairs and pilot training; the "Marianas Turkey Shoot" and Halsey's raids in October had stripped Japanese carriers of their air crews. The remainder of the fleet moved to Lingga Roads, near Singapore. Although the Japanese would have preferred to concentrate their fleet in home waters, the loss of tankers to American submarines forced the surface fleet to remain close to Borneo's oil.

The Imperial navy, nevertheless, prepared for a decisive battle. As usual, the Japanese drew an excessively complex plan, code-named "Sho-1," which was the Philippine variation of its overall defense plan called "Sho." Four separate task forces would move against the Americans: the carriers would sortie from the Home Islands and draw the American carriers away from the landings; the Japanese surface fleet, including super battleships, would move through San Bernadino Strait (south of Luzon) and attack the landing forces; a smaller task force would move through Surigao Strait (south of Leyte); and finally, another small force of destroyers and cruisers from the Home Islands would also move through Surigao Strait. For once the complex plan came dangerously close to success.

On October 20, MacArthur attacked Leyte. Under the command of Lieutenant General Walter Krueger, Sixth Army struck the northeast coast of Leyte. After the 6th Ranger Battalion cleared several off-shore islands, X Corps (1st Cavalry and 24th Infantry divisions) landed near Palo, while XXIV Corps (96th Infantry and 7th Infantry divisions) landed ten miles to the south. In the face of moderate Japanese opposition American infantry fought their way inland.

The Japanese responded immediately. On October 23 two U.S. submarines reported the main Japanese fleet north of Borneo; the Americans

The Philippines, October 1944 – July 1945

0   100   200 mi
0   100   200 km

Lingayen Gulf
Jan. 9
Luzon

PHILIPPINES

PACIFIC OCEAN

San Antonio
Jan. 29
Manila

Jan. 31

Mindoro

San Bernadino Strait

Samar

South China Sea

Dec. 15

Leyte
Oct. 20

Surigao Strait

Sulu Sea

Mindanao

➤ U.S. attacks

Celebes Sea

then attacked and sank two heavy cruisers and badly damaged another. Admiral Kurita Takeo, commander of the main San Bernadino task force, was using one of the heavy cruisers, the *Atago*, as his flagship. He transferred his flag to battleship *Yamato*, but the sinking clearly unnerved him at the start of the battle.

On the morning of October 24, the battle of Leyte Gulf moved into high gear. Japanese aircraft, based in the Philippines, found Halsey's fleet and launched a series of attacks. Hellcats destroyed most of the attackers, but one enemy aircraft got through to hit carrier *Princeton*, which eventually had to be scuttled. Meanwhile, Halsey's aircraft found Kurita's battle fleet west of San Bernadino Strait and sank super battleship *Musashi*. Although most of Kurita's force escaped serious damage, the admiral lost his nerve and turned back. American pilots reported his move but considerably exaggerated the damage they had inflicted on his other ships.

Now began a series of miscalculations that nearly resulted in disaster. Halsey had finally picked up the Japanese carriers to the north. Satisfied that he had taken care of Kurita, he moved to the north and took with him all the carriers and fast battleships. He left nothing behind to guard San Bernadino Strait and failed to inform other naval commanders. Meanwhile, the Japanese naval high command communicated its displeasure to Kurita about his retreat, and Kurita reversed course to the east toward the unguarded San Bernadino Strait.

The first contact between surface fleets came on the night of October 24–25 in Surigao Strait. Two Japanese task forces entered the strait separately, but battleships from the Seventh Fleet crossed the enemy "T" and sank all of the enemy except one destroyer. Shortly after dawn on the 25th, escort carriers supporting landings off Leyte suddenly spotted Kurita's force of heavy cruisers and battleships. Kurita had passed unopposed through San Bernadino Strait and turned south toward the invasion fleet where only a few destroyers and escort carriers stood in his way. Weak American forces desperately harried the Japanese and even sank three heavy cruisers, but if the Japanese steamed on, there was no chance of stopping them. Under continuous attack from American aircraft and weary after the pounding of the previous days, however, Kurita turned back. That ended the naval battle, although it did considerable harm to Halsey's reputation.

But attacks on the American fleet protecting the Leyte invasion had not ended. On that same day, the Japanese delivered the first *kamikaze* (divine wind) attacks. Though the suicidal pilots managed to damage some American ships and sink escort carrier *St. Lô*, their attacks marked the end of the battle of Leyte Gulf.

As the invasion of Leyte proceeded, the Japanese made other responses. Reinforcements arrived through early December and more than tripled the forces defending the island to about 55,000 troops and elements of five divisions. To achieve this level of reinforcement the Japanese stripped their forces from other islands, including Luzon and Okinawa. American air power, unfortunately, failed to interfere with the reinforcement because of the battering that the kamikaze attacks were giving the escort carriers. Moreover, it took a considerable period to construct air bases for the army's

On October 25, 1944, a bomb dropped by a plane from the USS *Essex* hit the *Ise*, a Japanese battleship to which flight decks had been added.

Fifth Air Force on Leyte. Following the arrival of the Japanese reinforcements, the operation became much more difficult for the Americans.

Krueger's objective was the port of Ormoc on the western coast of Leyte through which the Japanese had shipped reinforcements onto the island. Fearing the possibility of an enemy landing in his rear, Krueger moved slowly until the arrival of additional American forces. With the arrival of the 7th Infantry, 11th Airborne, and 32nd Infantry divisions, the Americans pressed forward. Nevertheless, the Japanese had used the time to strengthen their defenses along the mountains that extended north to south through the center part of the island. On December 7, the 77th Division landed just south of Ormoc and three days later captured the city. At about the same time the Japanese made a combined ground and airborne attack against the airfield at Burauen in the center of the island. After the seizure of Ormoc, however, Japanese resistance collapsed, and on Christmas Day the Americans seized the last port on the island. The Leyte campaign had cost the Japanese dearly; in addition to losing most of five divisions, their naval and air losses had doomed their other forces in the Philippines.

Luzon

Early January 1945 saw MacArthur finally in a position to redeem his pledge to return to the heart of the Philippines: Luzon. This campaign was the largest of the Pacific war with two armies (ten divisions and five regimental combat teams) fighting their way across a battle-scarred landscape. Nonetheless the campaign would still see Japanese forces in the field when the emperor finally surrendered in August 1945. For his amphibious landing, MacArthur selected the beaches of Lingayen Gulf on the western coast of Luzon; that location offered him access to the best road and railroad network in the islands as well as to Manila and its port facilities.

Had the Japanese attempted to defend Manila and Bataan as MacArthur had in December 1941, they would have suffered an even quicker defeat. But they did not. The Japanese commander in the Philippines, General Yamashita Tomoyuki, who had gained a brilliant victory over the British in Malaya and Singapore early in the war, yielded the main cities, particularly Manila, as well as the coastal lowlands, in favor of a prolonged resistance in the mountainous region of northern Luzon.

In early January 1945 the American invasion fleet sailed against Luzon. From the first, kamikazes subjected it to savage attacks; the U.S. Navy had no fewer than twenty-five ships sunk or damaged by these suicide attacks. Despite the kamikazes, Krueger's Sixth Army made an amphibious assault on January 9 against the beaches of Lingayen Gulf with four infantry divisions and a regimental combat team. Within several days the Americans had 175,000 men ashore. Facing only light opposition, Krueger's forces advanced south more than forty miles within two weeks.

Despite dense jungle and difficult terrain, American infantry relied on tanks for support. Tanks often destroyed enemy pillboxes and strong points or covered enemy positions with fire as American infantry advanced.

On January 29 the Americans made the first of two landings intended to keep the Japanese off balance. As part of Eichelberger's Eighth Army, XI Corps landed near San Antonio, sixty-five miles northwest of Manila. Two days later a regiment of 11th Airborne Division made an amphibious landing forty miles southwest of Manila. On February 3 another regiment of 11th Airborne made a parachute landing twenty miles inland. On that same day the first units from the landing at Lingayen Gulf reached Manila. Despite Yamashita's order to abandon the capital city without a fight, Japanese marines, not under his command, fought to retain the city. The resulting month-long battle wrecked Manila almost as completely as Warsaw. As many as 100,000 Filipino civilians died in the carnage.

Meanwhile, American forces rapidly liberated Bataan and Corregidor, names that still resonated from the dark days of the war. MacArthur also set in motion reconquest of the remaining Philippine Islands; in a month and a half, Eighth Army under Eichelberger made almost forty amphibious landings and swiftly liberated the remaining islands. The subsequent campaign in the mountains of northern Luzon, however, proved to be almost as difficult as the fighting in Manila. Yamashita dug his forces in and fought a skillful delaying action against the Americans. Despite severely pounding their Japanese opponents, MacArthur's forces never succeeded in breaking Yamashita's hold on the northern mountains. The end of the war would find the Japanese still tenaciously holding on, but by that time the fighting had passed well beyond the Philippines to the very gates of Japan.

The Final Campaigns

Iwo Jima

In fall 1944, B-29s began operations against Japan from the Marianas; by January 1945 the bombers were suffering heavy losses without achieving significant results. One reason was that Japanese radar on Iwo Jima (midway between the Marianas and Japan) provided the Home Islands with advance warning of impending attacks. Intending to halt this early warning, the Joint Chiefs ordered Nimitz to seize Iwo Jima. Planners also recognized that airfields on the island could provide emergency landing strips for damaged B-29s returning from Japan.

The Japanese recognized the danger; from June 1944 they had prepared to meet an American landing. The garrison commander, Lieutenant General Kuribayashi Tadamichi, utilizing already existing caves, turned Iwo Jima into a fortress with deep redoubts. As on Peleliu, the Japanese launched no suicide charges and did not attempt to hold the Americans on the beaches; instead, Kuribayashi chose to allow the attackers to come ashore and then to impose the highest possible casualties on them. The geography of the island helped the defenders. The Japanese placed their main defenses in a volcanic peak, Mt. Suribachi, which overlooked the entire island and provided an excellent view of the landing beaches.

Iwo Jima, February 19 – March 11, 1945

Major General Harry Schmidt's V Amphibious Corps received the mission to take Iwo Jima. With the 3rd, 4th, and 5th Marine divisions, the corps was the largest force the marines had ever assembled. Though Schmidt requested a ten-day bombardment, Spruance agreed to only three days with a possible fourth. Instead of supporting the marines, Spruance used his carriers for an attack on Japanese aircraft factories; one suspects that the navy wanted to show what naval air could accomplish in comparison with the failures that B-29s had thus far encountered. On February 19, 4th and 5th Marine divisions stormed ashore after a four-day bombardment. They initially encountered light enemy fire, but soon a virtual storm swept up and down the beaches. Among the nearly 30,000 marines who had reached shore by evening, casualties were heavy, especially from artillery dug into the caves of Mt. Suribachi. The conquest of the flatter terrain was relatively easy, but the attack on Japanese troops dug in on the sides of the volcano was a nightmare. After four days of heavy fighting some marines worked their way to Suribachi's summit and planted the American flag. However, not until the end of March did the marines end Japanese resistance on Iwo Jima. The casualty bill was horrendous: 6,821 marines dead; nearly 20,000 wounded. Few Japanese from a garrison of 21,000 survived. Admiral Nimitz best described the sacrifice of the marines: "Among the Americans who served on Iwo Island, uncommon valor was a common virtue."

Okinawa

Barely had the fighting on Iwo Jima subsided when the next major amphibious assault began. This time the target was Okinawa, an obvious jumping-off position for the invasion of Japan. Defending the island was Lieutenant General Ushijima Mitsuru's Thirty-Second Army with over 70,000 troops. Ushijima recognized that he did not possess sufficient troops to defend the whole island; therefore he determined to fight for the southern portion to inflict maximum casualties on invading Americans. He also hoped that kamikazes would damage supporting naval forces sufficiently to reduce air and gunfire support. The attacking American Tenth Army, under Lieutenant General Simon Bolivar Buckner, Jr., attacked with a corps of two marine divisions and another of two army divisions. Two additional army divisions remained in reserve. Offshore no fewer than forty fleet and light carriers, eighteen battleships, and nearly 200 destroyers bolstered the landing force.

Okinawa, April–June 1945

On April 1 the armada reached Okinawa and began landing soldiers and marines on the west coast of the narrow, long island. About 50,000 Americans landed the first day; by the second they had reached the east coast. While III Amphibious Corps turned north, XXIV Corps turned south. On April 6 the invasion fleet came under intense attack from kamikazes flying from Japan. On that day alone, 700 enemy aircraft—over half of them suicide aircraft—attacked the American fleet. Nine other kamikaze attacks, altogether numbering over 1,000 aircraft, hit the fleet standing off Okinawa in succeeding weeks. These ferocious attacks sank thirty ships, damaged 368 vessels, killed 5,000 American sailors, and injured a further 5,000.

On Okinawa, the marines cleared the northern half of the island in two weeks. But when XXIV Corps closed on Japanese defenses in the south, the killing began. The 96th Infantry Division ran into the main Japanese defenses first; soon three infantry divisions battered at the enemy's elaborate defenses. Some staff officers urged Buckner to use his reserve to make an amphibious assault and take Japanese defenses in the rear. Buckner believed such a landing would be difficult and costly and continued attacking straight ahead. As the Americans pressed forward, the Japanese launched two counterattacks, one of which cost them nearly 6,000 dead.

The Americans fought their way through the Machinato Line and then encountered the even stronger Shuri Line, which consisted of a web of mutually supporting strong points with artillery and mortars firing from caves. It was probably the strongest defensive position encountered by the Americans in the Pacific. But they continued pressing forward. By the end of June 1945, the U.S. Tenth Army had destroyed the Japanese Tenth Army of 70,000 troops. At least 80,000 Japanese civilians died in the fighting. The U.S. Army and Marines lost nearly 7,000 dead, with total American casualties (including the navy) 65,631 killed or wounded. Okinawa provided a frightening forecast of the coming invasion of the Home Islands.

Strategic Bombing

Strategic bombing attacks on Japan had begun in June 1944 with B-29s flying from bases in China, yet the problems in supplying that force from India over the Himalaya mountains presented insurmountable difficulties. Moreover, the Japanese army in China launched an offensive and took out the air bases, as Chinese nationalist forces proved incapable of serious resistance. But as Chinese bases fell, air bases in the Marianas (Saipan and Tinian) became available to the B-29s.

The bombing from the Marianas initially reflected the precision bombing doctrine with which U.S. Army Air Forces had entered the conflict. However, both weather and the nature of Japanese industry made such a campaign a dubious proposition. Much of the enemy's production occurred in small decentralized factories, the location of which was almost impossible to identify. In February 1945 a new commander, Major General Curtis E. LeMay, decided to launch incendiary raids on Japanese cities instead of precision attacks. Two high-altitude raids against Kobe and Tokyo proved encouraging.

Then LeMay changed the pattern of American bombing. The B-29s, now stripped of armor and defensive armament, attacked with incendiaries at night and at low altitude. In effect these attacks were indistinguishable from those of RAF's Bomber Command against Germany's cities. On March 8 the B-29s again struck Tokyo. Though attacking individually, LeMay's aircraft concentrated their bombs in the center of the capital; within minutes they had started a great firestorm. Japanese defenses were as incapable of stopping the attacking planes as the firefighting units were incapable of stopping the fires. By morning 83,000 Japanese had died, while a further 41,000 were injured; the attack burned out the center of Tokyo.

American bombers then proceeded to destroy Japanese cities, one after another. By July they had gutted the major industrial cities. Hundreds of thousands were dead, millions homeless. To add insult to injury, B-29s dropped mines and closed down Japanese shipping in the inland sea.

By summer 1945, Japan was prostrate. Industry was entirely isolated from the raw materials of Southeast Asia; cities were burning deserts; the Imperial navy no longer existed; and the tide of enemy conquest had reached Okinawa. Only the army remained intact, but much of it remained in China. If the Americans chose not to invade but rather to blockade the Home Islands, millions of Japanese would face starvation in the near future.

With this catastrophic military situation, one would expect the Japanese to seek an end to the war. They did not. They prepared, instead, to make a last-ditch stand. Some Japanese officers argued that such resistance would force Americans to concede more favorable terms. But most looked on further resistance as a matter of honor. A few Japanese, particularly in the foreign ministry, hoped to escape a final cataclysm; the Japanese did put out feelers to the Soviets, but Stalin had no interest in helping, since he had his own desiderata in the Far East. Moreover, even those interested in getting out of the war were generally unrealistic in the terms that they proposed.

Meanwhile, the Japanese military had arranged a deadly reception for the Americans. As a staff officer indicated after the war:

> We expected an allied invasion of southern Kyushu and a later invasion of the Tokyo plain. The entire army and naval air forces had volunteered for an all out Kamikaze defense, and each had from four to five thousand planes. Five thousand pilots were available with 3,000 in training. We planned to send over waves from 3–400 at a rate of one wave per hour. On the basis of Leyte and Okinawa we expected about one out of four planes to hit a ship.

The naval staff estimated that these attacks would damage somewhere between 30 and 50 percent of the attacking fleet. In addition there were nearly half a million regular troops in Kyushu, plus innumerable local militiamen. Finally the Japanese had packed hundreds of suicide speed boats with high explosives.

As the Japanese expected, the Americans planned to come ashore on southern Kyushu. In Operation "Olympic," Sixth Army with eleven army and marine divisions (650,000 troops) would execute the landing. The first wave would consist of three separate landings of three divisions each. To ensure availability of adequate forces, a steady flow of veterans from Europe began moving across the Pacific. Some senior officers in Washington estimated the conquest of Japan would double American casualties in the war, thus far approximately 700,000; even the much lower figures favored by some historians interested in minimizing the contribution of the atomic bomb would have represented a terrible price. What the Japanese casualties, civilian as well as military, would have been is unimaginable.

At this point the atomic bomb made its appearance. As the result of a warning from Albert Einstein to President Roosevelt, the Americans had started a major atomic weapons development program in the early 1940s. Code-named the "Manhattan Project," the program received vast resources from the U.S. government throughout the war. Nevertheless, U.S. scientists, aided by scientists from other nations, did not solve the intractable scientific and engineering problems until summer 1945. A successful testing at Alamogordo in New Mexico in July 1945 proved that atomic weapons had a good chance of working.

The new American president, Harry S Truman, then confronted the question of whether to use this terrible new weapon against the Japanese. Truman had learned about the A-bomb project only after succeeding to the presidency upon Roosevelt's death. In World War I he had served as an artilleryman on the Western Front and consequently had a real appreciation of the sharp end of combat. Some scientists argued against using the bomb; others argued that the Japanese should receive a warning or a demonstration of the new weapon.

In the end, Truman, influenced by the potential carnage of an invasion, decided to drop the bomb. On August 6, 1945, three B-29s flew over Hiroshima; the small size of the formation occasioned no fear among the Japanese. Over 90,000 people died in a flash brighter than the sun; three days later the Red Army rolled across the Manchurian frontier from Siberia and rampaged through Japanese defenses on the mainland of Asia. That same day another B-29 dropped the second atomic weapon on Nagasaki; another 35,000 Japanese died.

Amazingly, even after Hiroshima, the Imperial government still did not seek peace. The Japanese military had questioned whether the Americans really had such a weapon; then when incontrovertible evidence came in about Hiroshima, they claimed that the enemy could possess only one such weapon. The second bomb convincingly undermined that argument, but the Japanese cabinet remained deadlocked on whether to surrender. The deadlock, however, allowed Emperor Hirohito to take matters into his own hands. He ordered his advisors to surrender on American terms if he could retain a ceremonial position. Hirohito's decision was immensely courageous; for several weeks it was unclear whether the military, particularly the junior officers, would obey his command. In the end most did, and on

The second atomic bomb was dropped on Nagasaki on August 9, 1945. The fire-bombing of Tokyo in March 1945 killed and injured more Japanese and destroyed more square miles of urban area than either of the atomic bombs on Hiroshima and Nagasaki.

September 2, 1945, representatives of the Imperial government signed the surrender on the decks of the battleship *Missouri*. The six-year conflict was finally over.

World War II

On the decks of the *Missouri* in September 1945, World War II came to an end. By any criterion it was the most destructive conflict in human history, and the damage it had caused extended from one end of the globe to the other. Only North and South America had escaped the full impact of the fighting. Almost immediately after the war, the Cold War—overshadowed by the threat of atomic war—began. Consequently, World War II did not provide an enduring peace, yet it did see the destruction of one of the world's most pernicious and dangerous tyrannies, Adolf Hitler's Third Reich, as well as the destruction of Benito Mussolini's Fascist government and the Japanese Imperial government. Those accomplishments alone justified the war.

In the larger framework of military history, World War II was the most fluid of all major wars. Aircraft and tanks, as well as concepts for using them, restored mobility to land warfare. Gliders, parachutes, and airborne units greatly increased the reach of armies. More capable aircraft lifted larger bomb loads and flew greater distances, thereby exposing unconquered nations to sustained attack. Aircraft carriers and carrier-based planes permanently enlarged the dimensions of war at sea. Equipment and techniques for replenishing ships at sea allowed fleets to remain nearly permanently at sea and gave fleets almost unlimited range. Landing craft became large and seaworthy enough to sustain highly ambitious amphibious operations across open beaches. Improvements in sonar, submarines, and antisubmarine weapons and doctrine intensified the struggle for sea lanes. Radar helped airmen and sailors see beyond the horizon to find and destroy enemy forces. Improved communications permitted commanders to be better informed and to move units and equipment to critical areas. Altogether these developments ensured that air, land, and sea campaigns remained mobile.

Other developments gave the war a different character from previous conflicts. The Allies' ability to intercept and decode radio transmissions—Ultra and Magic—gave intelligence a timely and important effect on operations and provided the Allies significant advantages. In both the Atlantic and the Pacific, successful campaigns required an unprecedented interdependence of air, land, and sea forces—never before had large armies been transported over such great distances and landed on hostile shores with support from aircraft and warships. Waging war on a global scale also required unparalleled harnessing of men, women, machines, and raw materials. Ultimately it was the superiority of the Allies' production that gave them a decisive advantage.

World War II, nevertheless, represented an evolutionary change in the nature of warfare. Many key developments in the war that seemed revolutionary were in fact a continuation and an amplification of developments that had occurred in World War I. For example, the seemingly "revolutionary" operational employment of tanks by the Germans in 1940 in fact represented the fruition of tactical and operational concepts developed by the Germans in the latter part of World War I. Even strategic bombing, which carried the war directly to the enemy's homeland, had appeared in the last war, as had the relentless campaigns that American and German submarines executed against the commerce of their opponents. Developments did result, however, in substantially improved methods and equipment. One has only to compare the awkward armored attacks of 1918 with those of 1940, or the amateurish landings at Gallipoli in 1915 with those of 1945 to recognize the improved performance.

What was truly different about World War II was the unparalleled destruction it wrought, particularly on civilians and their possessions. Much of the devastation originated in Nazi Germany's fight for an ideology that aimed at destroying the liberal heritage of the nineteenth century and replacing it with a monstrous polity based on race. The Holocaust and the German crimes against the people of eastern and southeastern Europe were a direct result of the Nazi crusade. When the Soviets brought their own communist ideology to bear on the Eastern Front, the scene was set for an unrestrained and merciless war. The Allies added to the slaughter with strategic bombing, their air forces unleashing the whirlwind that the Axis had sowed at Rotterdam, London, Belgrade, and hundreds of other places. Raids by hundreds of bombers against German and Japanese cities killed and injured hundreds of thousands of civilians.

Adding to the devastation, the explosion of atomic bombs at Hiroshima and Nagasaki represented a true technological and philosophical revolution in war. These two explosions suggested that a war between powers possessing the bomb might lead to the annihilation not only of the opponents, but of humankind itself. By its development, the atomic bomb increased humanity's destructive power so greatly that it constricted warfare and ushered in an age where war between the Great Powers became unlikely.

The war also significantly affected political boundaries after 1945; the course of military events in the last months of the war in Europe and Asia largely established the borders between the new superpowers, the United States and Soviet Union. Soviet strategy and operations in the last years of the war had deliberately aimed at assuring firm control over much of Europe. The Yalta Conference in February 1945 occurred at a moment when Soviet forces were almost on the Oder River, a short hop from Berlin, while Anglo-American troops were barely breaking through the frontier defenses of western Germany. The resulting division seemed favorable to the West at the time, and the subsequent surge of Western forces almost to Berlin should not obscure the grim military realities of February 1945. In the Pacific the outcome reflected the consequences of military events. Since the destruction of Japanese military forces had resulted almost exclusively from American operations, the occupation of Japan became a U.S. concern and brought sweeping political and social change. On the continent of Asia, however, the hasty intervention of the Soviet Union ensured that Manchuria and northern Korea would fall into the hands of political movements favorable to the Soviets. The scene was set for future confrontations between the new superpowers.

The war also had an unexpected and crucial effect on the colonial powers and their dominions. The fall of France in 1940 loosened its control over its possessions in Africa and Southeast Asia, and the stunning successes of Japanese arms in 1941 and early 1942 against British and other colonial regimes further undermined their credibility in Asia and the Pacific. As a result, the dismantling of the great Western colonial empires began during the war and accelerated thereafter. In some cases that process was accomplished in a peaceful fashion (India and other British possessions being the foremost examples), but in other cases (Indochina and Algeria in particular), the process of decolonization proved extraordinarily costly and painful. In the long term, the war brought an abrupt end to Western political domination of Asia.

The settlement of World War II, nevertheless, proved to be surprisingly durable despite the Soviet-American confrontation in the Cold War. Conflicts would occur on the periphery and on occasion threaten cataclysmic war. But such a war never occurred. In that sense, World War II represented an enormous political and strategic success for the victors.

SUGGESTED READINGS

Appleman, Roy E., et al. *Okinawa: The Last Battle* (Washington: Office of the Chief of Military History, 1948).

Barbey, Daniel E. *MacArthur's Amphibious Navy: Seventh Amphibious Force Operations, 1943–1945* (Annapolis: Naval Institute Press, 1969).

Blair, Clay. *Silent Victory: The U.S. Submarine War Against Japan* (Philadelphia: Lippincott, 1975).

Buell, Thomas B. *The Quiet Warrior: A Biography of Admiral Raymond A. Spruance* (Boston: Little, Brown, 1974).

Cook, Charles. *The Battle of Cape Esperance: Strategic Encounter at Guadalcanal* (New York: Crowell, 1968).

Crane, Conrad C. *Bombs, Cities, and Civilians: American Airpower Strategy in World War II* (Lawrence, Kans.: University Press of Kansas, 1993).

Dower, John W. *War Without Mercy: Race and Power in the Pacific War* (New York: Pantheon Books, 1986).

Eichelberger, Robert L. *Our Jungle Road to Tokyo* (New York: Viking Press, 1950).

Frank, Richard B. *Guadalcanal* (New York: Random House, 1990).

Isely, Jeter A., and Philip A. Crowl. *The U.S. Marines and Amphibious Warfare* (Princeton, N.J.: Princeton University Press, 1951).

James, D. Clayton. *The Years of MacArthur*, 2 vols. (Boston: Houghton Mifflin, 1970).

Krueger, Walter. *Down Under to Nippon: The Story of the Sixth Army in World War II* (Washington: Combat Forces Press, 1953).

Lewin, Ronald. *The American Magic: Codes, Ciphers, and the Defeat of Japan* (New York: Farrar Straus Giroux, 1982).

Morison, Samuel Eliot. *The Two-Ocean War: A Short History of the United States Navy in the Second World War* (Boston: Little, Brown, 1963).

Potter, Elmer B. *Bull Halsey: A Biography* (Annapolis: Naval Institute Press, 1985).

————. *Nimitz* (Annapolis: Naval Institute Press, 1976).

Inoguchi Rikihei, and Nakajima Tadachi with Roger Pineau. *The Divine Wind: Japan's Kamikaze Force in World War II* (Annapolis: Naval Institute Press, 1958).

Roscoe, Theodore. *United States Submarine Operations in World War II* (Annapolis: Naval Institute Press, 1949).

Slim, William S. *Defeat into Victory* (London: Cassell, 1956).

Smith, Robert R. *The Approach to the Philippines* (Washington: Office of the Chief of Military History, 1953).

————. *Triumph in the Philippines* (Washington: Office of the Chief of Military History, 1963).

Spector, Ronald H. *Eagle Against the Sun: The War with Japan* (New York: The Free Press, 1985).

Thorne, Christopher G. *The Issue of War: States, Societies, and the Coming of the Far Eastern Conflict of 1941–1945* (New York: Oxford University Press, 1985).

VI

★ ★ ★ ★

Warfare in the Nuclear Era

27

THE COLD WAR AND THE NUCLEAR ERA: ADJUSTING WARFARE TO WEAPONS OF MASS DESTRUCTION

The Birth of the Atomic Arms Race

Placing Increased Reliance on the Bomb

Achieving Strategic Parity and Controlling Nuclear Weapons

The Cold War was a clash of interests and ideas that dominated international relations from 1945 until 1990. As antagonisms between the United States and the Soviet Union hardened in the late 1940s, a series of crises sharpened ideological differences and heightened tensions. With the Soviet Union leading communist states and the United States leading Western democratic states, the first crises occurred in Europe, but the establishment of the People's Republic of China in 1949, followed by the North Korean invasion of South Korea, intensified and expanded the Cold War. While the Soviet Union and other communist powers attempted to consolidate and expand their influence, the United States and its allies sought to "contain" communism. For more than four decades, the confrontation between the two camps yielded numerous conflicts, such as the ones in Korea and Vietnam, as well as those in the Middle East and Southwest Asia. Some of these conflicts were "campaigns" in the broader and more dangerous Cold War, and they occurred despite the threat of a small crisis escalating rapidly into a world war.

Through the decades of rivalry, the existence of atomic or nuclear weapons shaped the nature of the Cold War and influenced virtually every issue in international security. For a brief period the United States held a monopoly on the atomic bomb, but the Soviets exploded their first atomic device in August 1949. That explosion signaled the beginning of a remarkable arms race that would extend over the next four decades. From the mid-1950s to the early 1960s political and military leaders considered the effect of the new weapons and resigned themselves to the use of those weapons in an emergency. After the Cuban Missile Crisis in October 1962, the Soviet Union embarked on a massive program to modernize its nuclear arsenal. As the Soviets approached strategic parity with the Americans, both sides began accepting arms control limitations over their nuclear arsenals. Only the eventual disintegration of the Soviet Union ended the Cold War and reduced the danger of a nuclear holocaust.

Since the use of nuclear weapons created the possibility of an Armageddon, the superpowers sought to deter their use but nonetheless grappled with each other by every means short of direct combat or nuclear exchange. Each provided military and economic assistance to its allies, and each sought to gain influence in the newly emerging nations of Africa and Asia. Although direct armed conflict between the superpowers never took place, Moscow and Washington provided direct and indirect support to opposing sides in numerous conflicts around the world. Using the number of war-related deaths as the criterion for defining a major conflict, the Stockholm International Peace Institute identified more than 160 major conflicts between 1945 and 1990. Though many were regional or were civil wars with no apparent link to the Cold War, others created the possibility of escalation, superpower involvement, and the spilling over of war into Europe, where the vast forces of the North Atlantic Treaty Organization and the Warsaw Pact faced each other across the boundary of a divided Germany. Almost no one doubted that a conflict between these huge forces would escalate into a nuclear holocaust.

In the end, the introduction of atomic and nuclear weapons revolutionized the nature of strategy and imposed limitations on war to avoid the employment of these weapons. The value of nuclear weapons lay in their not being used and in their power to deter an opponent from using them or even using conventional weapons. Their introduction made the era of the Cold War unlike any other in the history of warfare.

The Birth of the Atomic Arms Race

Before the United States entered World War II, scientists had worked out the theoretical foundations of an atomic bomb. Fearful that Germany would develop and use an atomic bomb first, the physicist Leo Szilard convinced Albert Einstein to send a letter to President Franklin D. Roosevelt that explained the nature of atomic energy and how it could be fashioned into a weapon of unprecedented power. This letter led to the creation in 1942 of a highly secret program named the Manhattan Project, which became the largest, most expensive, and most secret program of World War II. Placed under the overall direction of the U.S. Army and led by Major General Leslie R. Groves, the army engineer who had just finished designing and building the Pentagon, and Dr. J. Robert Oppenheimer, a brilliant theoretical physicist, the project commanded the highest priorities for scarce wartime resources and involved many leading physicists, mathematicians, and chemists from the scientific community. Oppenheimer and his colleagues tested an atomic device for the first time in the desert of southern New Mexico on July 16, 1945.

After Germany surrendered in May 1945, some American scientists questioned whether the new weapon should be used against Japan; they believed Japan would fall inevitably to conventional forces. Political and military leaders believed, however, that using the bomb on Japan would shorten the war, save the lives of American soldiers, and perhaps influence the postwar expansionist behavior of the Soviets. The subsequent dropping

Major General Leslie R. Groves and Dr. J. Robert Oppenheimer in September 1945. The two hardly could have been less alike in appearance, personality, and politics.

of an atomic bomb on Hiroshima, Japan, on August 6, 1945, and another one on Nagasaki three days later brought the existence of the atomic bomb into the open and engendered much concern about its use. Though more people had died in some conventional bombing raids—Dresden, for example—the shock of Hiroshima and Nagasaki and the possibility of such weapons being employed in the future horrified the world.

The Americans Adapt to the Atomic Bomb

Following World War II, President Harry S Truman laid the groundwork for American atomic policy. From the beginning he regarded the atomic bomb as fundamentally different from other military arms. For a time he hoped that diplomatic initiatives at the United Nations (the Baruch Plan) would convince the Soviets to accept international control of atomic weapons, but deepening hostilities doomed the proposal. Concerned about the effects of atomic warfare, he reserved for himself the authority to order use of the bomb. Under the provisions of the Atomic Energy Act of 1946, Congress vested a completely civilian commission with control over the American atomic energy program. Scientific and technical knowledge about the atomic program, as well as production decisions, became hidden behind an unprecedented wall of secrecy. As a consequence, American war planners often worked in the early years of the atomic era without specific reference to the size, character, and capabilities of the American atomic arsenal. Recently declassified documents suggest that not even President Truman received a formal accounting until 1947 of how many weapons the United States actually possessed at any time.

As the Cold War intensified, the United States confronted the question of its role in the nuclear age. Americans watched uncomfortably as the Soviets refused to withdraw from Iran and then took over Czechoslovakia; they became even more concerned when Greek Communists attempted to overthrow Greece's government. Concluding that the United States had to take action against what seemed to be Soviet expansionist policies, Truman appeared before a joint session of Congress on March 12, 1947, and said, "I believe that it must be the policy of the United States to support free peoples who are resisting attempted subjugation by armed minorities or by outside pressures." In an attempt to revive Europe, the United States subsequently announced the Marshall Plan in June 1947. The core of the new policy of "containment" appeared in a famous article in *Foreign Affairs* in July 1947. The anonymous author, who was later identified as George F. Kennan, stated, "[T]he main element of any United States policy toward the Soviet Union must be that of a long-term, patient but firm and vigilant containment of Russian expansive tendencies." Kennan proposed opposing force with force and preventing the Soviets from expanding.

The atomic bomb provided partial answers to the question of how the United States could "contain" the USSR. In August 1947, strategic planners in the Joint Chiefs of Staff completed a war plan—code-named "Broiler"—which attempted to integrate atomic weapons into the American war machine. Recognizing that the bomb conferred a "tremendous strategic advantage" upon the United States and its allies, the planners of Broiler called for an "air-atomic campaign" very early in a war against Soviet targets that were chosen less for their military than their psychological importance. The campaign focused upon key governmental and other targets whose destruction would shock and unhinge the Soviet government. Though the target list in Broiler called for dropping thirty-four bombs on twenty-four cities, the United States had no fully assembled bombs and no capability to produce any quickly, and its more traditional means of military power had declined precipitously.

One of the first crises in which atomic weapons played a role—though an ambiguous one—occurred in the spring of 1948 when Truman responded to the Berlin Blockade. The Soviets had cut off all rail and road traffic to the western sections of Berlin, and he ordered an airlift of food and fuel supplies for the beleaguered people of the city. Part of his response included the deployment of sixty B-29s to airbases in Great Britain. Even though no atomic bombs actually left the United States, an administration spokesman pointedly announced that the aircraft were "nuclear capable." On May 12, 1949, the Soviets ended the blockade by once again permitting movement by land from West Germany into West Berlin and restoring gas and electric service. Flying more than 1.4 million metric tons of food, coal, and other supplies into Berlin apparently did more to end the blockade than deploying nuclear aircraft to Britain.

Toward the close of 1948 the United States had about one hundred atomic bombs in its stockpile, and its war plans emphasized a sudden atomic attack against the Soviet Union. Under the demanding leadership of General Curtis LeMay, the Strategic Air Command had developed the capability of delivering 80 percent of the American atomic stockpile in a single strike on the Soviet Union. One war plan—code-named "Fleetwood"—called for the delivery of 133 atomic bombs on seventy Soviet cities. Despite the emphasis on an "air-atomic campaign," the United States did not reject the possibility of a limited conventional campaign. It believed a future war would begin with a surprise attack by an enemy, to which the United States would respond with a massive atomic attack. As the aggressor reeled under an atomic attack, the United States would mobilize and employ its conventional forces. This view of future war permitted the United States the luxury of giving priority to strategic forces, while providing only minimum support to conventional forces. After all, planners argued, the employment of the bomb would provide the time necessary to prepare U.S. conventional forces.

An even greater emphasis on the atomic bomb, however, appeared in late 1949 in a new war plan code-named "Offtackle." Despite serious interservice differences, the 1950 budget reduced conventional capabilities even further. From the perspective of air-power advocates, atomic weapons seemed to need no assistance from armies except perhaps to occupy the smoking ruins of devastated cities. Air-power advocates also envisaged only limited roles for navies, including atomic bombs dropped from carrier aircraft. In what was later called the "Admirals' Revolt," the navy attempted to roll back the air-atomic emphasis, characterizing the new B-36 bombers as a "billion-dollar blunder." Nonetheless, American strategic forces flourished while conventional forces withered.

The Soviet Bomb, the Thermonuclear Bomb, and NSC-68

After failing to establish international control over atomic energy, the United States expected to maintain a monopoly over the bomb for some time and ruled out sharing scientific information with the USSR. General Groves confidently predicted it would take the Soviets ten to twenty years to produce a bomb. As early as 1939, however, Soviet scientists had started their own project to develop a bomb. By 1941, they had a cyclotron ready for experiments. The German invasion of the USSR stalled the Soviet atomic project until 1943, when the physicist Igor V. Kurchatov began directing a rejuvenated program. On August 29, 1949, in Central Asia, the Soviet Union exploded its first atomic device. The shock of America's losing its monopoly over atomic weapons was magnified by the fall of Nationalist China to the Chinese Communists in late 1949.

In response to these events, Truman formally authorized in January 1950 the building of the thermonuclear, or hydrogen, bomb—even though the Soviet Union would not have atomic weapons in large numbers or the capability to deliver them against the United States for several years. He also directed the formation of an ad hoc group of officials from the state and defense departments to conduct a review of American national security policies. This group would ultimately produce a memorandum designated NSC-68, which was to become one of the most important policy documents of the Cold War.

Presided over by Paul Nitze of the State Department's Policy Planning Staff, the ad hoc group's final report emphasized the expansionist nature of the Soviet Union and the danger such a power posed when armed with atomic weapons. Assuming the Soviets would eventually achieve atomic parity with the United States, the group considered prospects for defending Western Europe bleak. If the United States could not count on atomic weapons as its ultimate card, then conventional forces had to be ready to bear added burdens. The only recourse, Nitze's group believed, was to improve atomic and conventional forces simultaneously. The report also emphasized the adequacy "for the moment" of the American atomic retaliatory capability, but in the event of a "surprise blow," the United States had to be capable of surviving this attack and mounting an immediate counterattack. The authors of NSC-68 argued for the rejuvenation of the defense establishment so its ready combat power could deter the Soviets from a direct confrontation. With the Soviets' continuing to improve their atomic capabilities, the report signaled the eventual emergence of deterrence as a prime feature of American policy. The Americans would soon conclude that the value of their atomic weapons lay less in their actual use than in the threat of their use and that fear of retaliation would constrain an enemy from using them or creating a crisis in which they might be used.

Even though President Truman and the National Security Council formally approved NSC-68 in April 1950, chances were remote that this ambitious and expensive program would ever come to fruition. The United States still had vast superiority in atomic weapons over the Soviet Union, at least for a time, and possession of the bomb still worked as a powerful incentive for those who sought to limit government spending. To these critics, the time required for the Soviets to gain the capability to inflict significant damage on the United States seemed too long to warrant the kind of expensive defense buildup recommended by NSC-68. Truman himself was not entirely convinced of the need for rearmament.

And there the matter would have rested but for the attack, barely two months later, upon South Korea by the North Korean army on June 24, 1950. The limitations of the bomb were about to be made manifest.

The Korean War and the Truman Rearmament

Following the North Korean attack, many American political and military leaders feared that Moscow had directed the invasion as a diversionary move in preparation for a Soviet advance against Western Europe. Aware of the limitations of American power, the Joint Chiefs recommended the prompt abandonment of South Korea if the Soviets moved against Europe. Additional questions about Soviet motivations appeared in November 1950 when the Chinese Communists intervened in the war.

As a hedge against the much-feared invasion of Western Europe, Truman deployed atomic weapons to forward positions in Great Britain and the Mediterranean; however, he sent none to the western Pacific. The Joint Chiefs of Staff decided that the Korean peninsula was unsuitable for the use of atomic weapons. They believed Korea had no worthy targets, no industrial complexes or centers of military power that would warrant the use of any atomic weapon then in the arsenal. Additionally, they believed the rugged Korean terrain would limit the full effect of any atomic weapon, even against such targets as large troop concentrations. General Omar Bradley considered the idea of using these weapons in this conflict as "preposterous."

At a news conference in November 1950, President Truman nevertheless hinted broadly that atomic weapons might in fact be used in Korea. The North Koreans gave no sign they had heard, or taken seriously, the president's veiled threat, but Truman's comment alarmed the public in both the United States and Europe. British Prime Minister Clement R. Attlee immediately flew to Washington for talks with Truman, who reassured him that he would not really use the bomb. Like General Bradley and most of his other military advisors, the president feared that the real war lay elsewhere in the uncertain future and that America's atomic advantage would only be wasted on the Chinese. The Korean War thus remained limited, but it served as a catalyst for the implementation of the provisions of NSC-68, including a massive rejuvenation of the American armed forces.

The Truman administration realized that atomic weapons did not provide answers to every national security question. In fact, the brief atomic monopoly had given the United States a false sense of security and power and failed to avert military confrontation. Nor had possession of atomic weapons changed operational or tactical methods, as proven by the fighting on the Korean peninsula, which differed little from that of earlier wars.

Placing Increased Reliance on the Bomb

When Truman left office in 1953, he left nearly 1,000 atomic weapons to his successor, Dwight D. Eisenhower. Though Truman never overcame his awe of the atomic or nuclear bomb, his successor would demonstrate no such discomfort (at least in public). Nuclear weapons were about to become the centerpiece of the new administration's foreign and military policies. In the process, nuclear power would take on a much more pervasive character than what would have been believed possible in the early days of the Cold War.

During the presidential campaign of 1952, Eisenhower had campaigned on promises to end the war in Korea and to reduce the federal budget significantly. When he took office, military costs accounted for 70 percent of federal spending. Eisenhower did not think American foreign and defense policy took advantage of nuclear weapons and disagreed with the Truman administration's attempts to balance nuclear and conventional arms; reducing conventional forces would pay the bill for Eisenhower's campaign promises. By placing greater reliance on nuclear arms, Eisenhower believed the risk of reducing American conventional combat power could be minimized.

Throughout 1953, the Eisenhower administration worked to establish a "New Look" in national security policy. Hints about a new strategy suggested a stronger reliance on strategic nuclear power and less reliance on traditional ground and naval forces. In October 1953, the chiefs of the military services received a National Security document called NSC 162/2, which provided clear guidance from the Eisenhower administration. NSC 162/2 stated: "In the event of hostilities, the United States will consider nuclear weapons to be as available for use as other munitions." In an address before the United Nations, Eisenhower, reflecting his recent approval of NSC 162/2, observed that "atomic weapons have virtually achieved conventional status within our armed forces." Additional information came from Secretary of State John Foster Dulles in January 1954 when he called for "massive retaliation" in response to Soviet aggression.

"Massive Retaliation" became a shorthand description of the new strategy. It did not mean, however, that the United States would automatically respond to Soviet aggression with a massive nuclear strike; instead, it meant the Americans might reply in kind or raise the stakes by employing nuclear weapons. In other words, an American response was certain, but its nature was not. Critics of the strategy, however, perceived it as an "all-or-nothing" strategy, particularly when public comments by Dulles hinted that an aggressor had to remain uncertain about how close to the "brink" the United States would go.

Limited Nuclear War

When the Eisenhower administration adopted NSC 162/2 in 1953, the concept of "limited nuclear war" emerged as an alternative short of general nuclear war. The first concepts for limited nuclear warfare had appeared in the years immediately after World War II. One of the key figures in the development of the atomic bomb, J. Robert Oppenheimer, for example, stated in the late 1940s that existing bombs were "too big" for the "best military use." As technical advances permitted the development of smaller and more rugged nuclear devices, interest in the United States in tactical nuclear weapons accelerated. Faced with the Soviets' having significant advantages in conventional forces, analysts argued that an army equipped with tactical nuclear weapons could defend successfully against an enemy many times its

The firing of the first atomic artillery shell from a 280-mm artillery gun. Such tests demonstrated the availability of nuclear weapons and the possibility of their being employed throughout a battle area.

own size and that such weapons could enable Western military forces to halt communist aggression. Robert E. Osgood, in his influential book *Limited War*, explicitly linked tactical nuclear weapons and limited war. He wrote, "Tactical nuclear weapons, especially the low-yield battlefield weapons, can play a decisive role in supporting containment by giving the United States an adequate capacity for limited war at a tolerable cost."

Technological advances quickly provided tactical nuclear weapons. In May 1953, a U.S. Army 280-mm gun became the first artillery piece to fire a nuclear round successfully. Shortly thereafter, the army deployed half a dozen of the huge guns to Europe, even though they had a range of only seventeen miles and weighed eighty-three tons. It also equipped some of its units with Honest John rockets, which had a range of about twenty-two miles. Recognizing the need for smaller and more mobile nuclear delivery means, the army eventually introduced nuclear rounds for artillery pieces as small as 155-mm and introduced a nuclear-capable, short-range rocket, the Davy Crockett, into maneuver battalions. The Davy Crockett had a yield of .02 kilotons and a range of 650–4,400 yards.

As the army added tactical nuclear weapons to its inventory, it also reconfigured its infantry divisions by creating "Pentomic Divisions," which contained five "battle groups" (actually reinforced battalions). The new design eliminated the brigade echelon and added tactical mobility and other assets in an attempt to construct an organization that could disperse and concentrate rapidly. Theorists believed the division could survive and fight on the nuclear battlefield by spreading its forces in a "checker board," rather than linear fashion. Relying on new equipment, much of which never became available, the Pentomic Division proved to be difficult to command and not at all mobile, and its existence turned out to be mercifully brief.

Increases in the number of tactical nuclear weapons, nonetheless, created great concerns about escalation, particularly as Soviet capabilities increased. American critics argued that any tactical nuclear exchange would invariably lead to an all-out nuclear exchange. And Europeans feared the possibility of numerous tactical nuclear explosions on their crowded continent. More important, the Soviet Union paid little attention to tactical nuclear considerations, believing any use of nuclear weapons would initiate general nuclear war. In a key speech before the Supreme Soviet of the USSR in January 1960, the Soviet minister of defense ruled out "limited nuclear warfare" and "tactical use of nuclear weapons." Despite the obvious danger of escalation, tactical nuclear weapons remained an important part of the American arsenal.

Technological Advances

Eisenhower's two terms as president included not only a revolution in strategy but also a revolution in the technology of nuclear weapons and in the means of delivering them. Since the beginning of the nuclear era, air force bombers in Strategic Air Command had played the most important role in plans for delivering nuclear weapons. When Eisenhower took office, the United States had a mixed fleet of one thousand strategic and not-so-strategic bombers, and he lost no time in approving development of a truly strategic manned bomber, the all-jet B-52 Stratofortress, due to reach operational status by 1955. About 500 of these intercontinental bombers supplemented the more limited B-47 Stratojets, and by 1959 the United States had approximately 1,850 bombers.

As the United States improved its bombers, it also developed smaller, more powerful nuclear devices whose effect would be measured in megatons, rather than kilotons. In 1951, on the small Pacific island of Eniwetok, the United States detonated two small fusion devices, and the following year it detonated at Eniwetok a thermonuclear device with a force equal to 10 million tons of TNT, which was vastly larger than the bomb dropped on Hiroshima (equivalent to 14,000 tons of TNT) and the one dropped on Nagasaki (equivalent to 20,000 tons of TNT). The Soviet Union tested its own nuclear device in 1953. The United States tested an air-deliverable nuclear bomb in March 1954 but did not drop one from an airplane until May 1956. By the late 1950s, a B-52 bomber could deliver four nuclear bombs.

As technological improvements made nuclear weapons much smaller and also much more powerful, the missile began to challenge the manned bomber as the best means of delivery. By the mid-1950s, the air force was at work on two different Intercontinental Ballistic Missiles (ICBMs), the Titan and the Atlas, meant to deliver a one-megaton warhead at ranges of 5,500 and 6,250 miles, respectively. The first Atlas ICBMs became operational in the United States in 1959. The army entered the age of nuclear missiles in earnest with its own intermediate-range missiles. The Corporal became operational in 1953 with a 75-mile range, the Redstone in 1956 with a 225-mile range, and the Jupiter in 1957 with a range of 1,500 miles. Such missiles could reach far beyond the traditional area of concern of even the most senior ground commanders, leading to an intense debate between the army and air force about areas of responsibility.

The navy took a different atomic tack, investing initially in atomic propulsion for its fleet, especially its submarines. As early as 1951, however, it deployed nuclear-capable aircraft on its carriers, and three years later all carriers bore nuclear weapons and the aircraft to deliver them. Though the navy did not commission the world's first nuclear-powered aircraft carrier, the USS *Enterprise*, until November 1961, it commissioned the world's first nuclear-powered submarine, the USS *Nautilus*, in September 1954. At the end of the decade, the navy's Submarine-Launched Ballistic Missile (SLBM) program became feasible for submarines after smaller warheads and solid propellants became available. Initial plans called for the first missile-carrying submarine to be available in 1963, but increased concerns about the Soviet Union resulted in the first Polaris submarine, the USS *George Washington*, successfully launching its first missile while submerged in July 1960. Later versions of the missile increased its firing range from 1,375, to 1,700, to 2,850 miles. The age of the submarine-launched ballistic missile clearly had arrived.

The emergence of a Soviet nuclear threat made the gathering of intelligence particularly important. The United States created the National

Admiral H. V. Rickover directed construction of the USS *Nautilus*, the first nuclear-powered submarine. Its capability for sustained underwater operations was constrained only by the human limitations of its crew.

Security Agency in 1952; its mission was to conduct electronic eavesdropping on Russian communications systems. The new agency established radar stations in friendly countries along the Soviet perimeter and skirted Soviet borders with reconnaissance aircraft. As traditional sources of information—spies and refugees—began to dry up, the intelligence services resorted more and more to advanced technology to retrieve information. In 1956, the U-2, as the plane was called, became operational; it was capable of cruising above 70,000 feet, well beyond the ranges of Soviet air defenses. During the next four years, U-2s made dozens of spy flights over the Soviet Union before one was shot down by a new air-defense missile. By one informed estimate, the U-2 gleaned more than 90 percent of the West's strategic intelligence on the Soviet missile program before the flights ended. In time, satellites became the prime source of intelligence for both sides.

Meanwhile, like the Americans, the Soviets initially emphasized the long-range bomber. Their first important bomber was the Tu-16 Badger, which was similar to the American B-47 in performance. Entering into service in 1954–1955, it had the range to reach some cities in the United States on one-way flights from northern Siberia. In 1955, the Soviets introduced the Tu-20 Bear, which had a greater range and payload than the Badger, but not the American B-52. Although the Soviets had only a few hundred Bears and Badgers in service at the end of the 1950s, an intense debate erupted in the United States about the existence of a "bomber gap." A bomber gap did exist, but it was in favor of the Americans, not the Russians.

Motivated by inflated fears of Soviet bombers, the United States expended considerable effort and resources to defend itself against bombers with its Distant Early Warning line, numerous aerial interceptor squadrons, and land-to-air missiles that were nuclear armed.

As the United States prepared to defend itself against bombers, the Soviets made significant progress in the development of missiles. In August 1957 a Soviet SS-6 Sapwood ICBM traveled several thousand miles from its launch pad to its target in Siberia. Two months later, on October 4, 1957, an SS-6 rocket threw a 184-pound satellite called *Sputnik* into Earth orbit. One month later, the Soviets launched another satellite, weighing 1,121 pounds and carrying a live dog, into space. Though the Americans managed to launch a satellite, *Explorer I,* weighing thirty-one pounds, on January 31, 1958, they did not test the Atlas ICBM over its entire range for another year. Almost immediately, the "missile gap" replaced the bomber gap as Americans concluded that Soviet successes in space signaled their superiority in missile technology and numbers. Eisenhower, however, refused to panic. The U-2s, whose operations were known only to a few of the highest officials, had provided him with enough intelligence to know that the Soviets remained considerably behind the United States in strategic nuclear forces.

While Americans debated the implications of *Sputnik,* the Soviets began making slow progress in submarine-launched ballistic missiles. Between 1954 and 1957, the Soviets fitted several submarines with SS-N-4 Sark missiles, which had to be fired from the surface, rather than from underwater. The missile carried a nuclear warhead and had a range initially of 350 and later of 750 miles. Between 1958 and 1962, the Soviets equipped about thirty Golf and Hotel submarines with the SS-N-4 Sark. Not until 1968 did the Soviet navy complete a more modern submarine (the Yankee-class submarine) which carried sixteen missiles capable of being launched underwater and having a range of about 1,500 miles. The requirement for surface launching—in addition to the significant antisubmarine capability of the U.S. Navy—made the earlier Soviet submarines only a limited strategic threat to the United States. Nonetheless the Soviets had acquired the capability by the mid-1950s to inflict considerable damage on the United States, and that capability continued to expand.

Throughout much of the 1950s and 1960s, as demonstrated by the delusions associated with the "bomber gap" and the "missile gap," a significant difference existed between actual Soviet capabilities and American perceptions of those capabilities. The continued growth of Soviet missiles, however, dispelled all American hopes of fending off a Soviet nuclear strike. When the Soviets relied solely on bombers, the Americans could have destroyed many of the bombers before they dropped their bombs, but they had little or no defense against missiles. Though the United States maintained an overwhelming superiority, nuclear planners in the late 1950s recognized that the United States could not escape substantial damage in the event of a nuclear exchange.

Even though the Soviets remained far behind the Americans, a revolution in military affairs—according to Soviet writings—occurred in the Soviet armed forces between 1953 and 1960. Writers often compared the extent of the change to that which accompanied the introduction of gunpowder. In January 1960, Nikita S. Khrushchev underlined the extent of the change in an address to the Supreme Soviet of the USSR. He emphasized the decisiveness of nuclear weapons and threatened that if attacked, the Soviets would "wipe the country or countries attacking us off the face of the earth." A subsequent speech by the minister of defense highlighted the formation of new Strategic Rocket Forces and described them as "unquestionably the main service of the armed forces." In essence, the Soviets shifted from a primary focus on continental land warfare to a focus on global nuclear warfare. Military leaders believed that the revolution in military affairs compelled complete revisions in strategy, tactics, and force structure. As part of these revisions, the Soviets modified their thinking about the conduct of ground operations in the nuclear age and emphasized dispersion, mobility, high operating tempos, and multiple attacks on broad axes.

Thus, like the Americans, the Soviets acknowledged the profound effects of nuclear weapons on warfare. Changes in policy—influenced by the reduced size and increased power of nuclear weapons, the improved capabilities of manned bombers, the enhancement of missile range and accuracy, and the introduction of submarine-launched ballistic missiles—had achieved a military revolution, even if the only atomic bombs employed in combat were the two dropped on Japan at the end of World War II. For the moment the United States retained a position of superiority in nuclear affairs, but improvements in Soviet nuclear capabilities through the 1960s would eventually compel the United States to reevaluate its strategy of Massive Retaliation and to choose a different strategic path.

The Rise of the Defense Intellectuals

From the beginning, but particularly in the 1950s, much of the most important thinking in the United States about nuclear warfare was done by civilian intellectuals who traditionally had made a contribution to military thought but had never dominated the development of doctrine and equipment. Arguing that nuclear warfare was unique and answered to its own particular logic, civilian specialists provided much of the intellectual framework for nuclear thinking. They struggled to fit nuclear weapons within the framework of foreign policy and military affairs.

In a book entitled, *The Absolute Weapon*, Bernard Brodie laid down the fundamental outlines of nuclear deterrence—that the costs of retaliation in kind were too high for nations to contemplate using atomic warfare as a traditional means of defending their foreign policy interests. Brodie and his associates concluded that the real value of the atomic bomb lay not in its actual employment in war, but in the *threat* of its employment. In a now-famous passage, Brodie crafted the fundamental concept guiding what came to be called deterrence theory: "Thus far the chief purpose of our military establishment has been to win wars. From now on its chief purpose must be to avert them. It can have almost no other useful purpose." Additional thoughts came from other individuals, including J. Robert Oppenheimer, the physicist who had led the Los Alamos team during the Manhattan Project. In an essay published in *Foreign Affairs*, he depicted the Russians and Americans as "two scorpions in a bottle, each capable of killing the other, but only at the risk of his own life."

From these and other studies, the defense intellectuals conceived a wholly new vocabulary for the nuclear age and deployed it against the unconvinced defense establishment with breathtaking skill. "Counterforce" became the shorthand term for attacks against military targets. "Countervalue" was the touchstone for intentionally punitive attacks against "soft" targets such as cities and other psychologically valuable sites. "Stability" came to mean not a comfortable superiority such as the United States had enjoyed during the early years of the atomic era, but a kind of equilibrium reached when both sides were equally confident of destroying the other. Many outsiders found it difficult to accept the cold, logical language of nuclear theorists, some finding it as arcane as medieval scholasticism.

Particularly in the 1950s, Brodie and his colleagues—Albert Wohlstetter, Herman Kahn, and others—produced some of the most intellectually sophisticated work of the nuclear age. With their academic backgrounds, general contempt for traditional military thought, and quasi-official standing, the civilian strategists had a remarkable influence over nuclear thinking—and by extension, thinking about defense in general—from the Korean through the Vietnam wars.

Early Efforts to Rattle the Nuclear Saber

As for the effect of nuclear weapons on foreign policy, Eisenhower took advantage of the diplomatic power of the bomb early in his term. Attempting to unstick deadlocked negotiations with the Chinese, Eisenhower issued a discrete, ambiguous warning through the government of India that he might use atomic weapons against Chinese cities to force the Korean War to a conclusion. To back up his warning, he deployed atomic weapons to Okinawa, which was well within bomber range of both Korea and China. Though the effect of Eisenhower's atomic threat remains unclear, the Chinese did relent; several months later, the Korean armistice was announced.

The first full-fledged test of Eisenhower's new policy occurred early in 1954, a few months after the conclusion of the Korean armistice. In Indochina, the French army was gradually losing ground to a Vietnamese communist insurgency. The situation reached a crisis point in April 1954, when the French garrison at Dien Bien Phu seemed more than likely to succumb to its communist besiegers. Despite concerns about the effect of a French defeat on NATO's cohesion, Eisenhower refused to send American troops to bolster the French army in Indochina. He also refused to permit the employment of tactical nuclear weapons, even though Dien Bien Phu eventually fell.

A more direct contest with the Chinese Communists occurred over two small islands, Quemoy and Matsu, a few miles offshore from the Chinese mainland. Nationalist Chinese troops under Jiang Jieshi (Chiang

Kai-shek) had occupied the islands when they had lost the civil war in 1949. By September 1954, the Chinese Communists had concentrated troops on the mainland opposite these islands and had begun bombarding the Nationalist garrisons with artillery. Although Eisenhower never intended to use atomic weapons to solve the Quemoy-Matsu crisis, he equivocated in public. At a press conference in March, 1955, Eisenhower was asked to respond to a broad hint made earlier by Secretary of State Dulles that America would use some "small atomic weapons" if necessary. Eisenhower replied that smaller weapons could be used in such a case, "just as you would use a bullet or anything else."

The public furor that erupted over Quemoy and Matsu, along with all the talk about atomic weapons by administration officials and members of Congress, may well have been enough to dissuade the Chinese from invading the islands and attempting to take Formosa. All along, however, Eisenhower seemed to have no intention of committing American power, chiefly because he understood that the Chinese had no means of crossing the Formosa Strait against the opposition of the U.S. Seventh Fleet. The Chinese gave up their bombardment of the islands by April 1955 and agreed to diplomatic talks a while later.

The emergence of the Soviet Union as a strategic nuclear power altered the strategic equation. During the Suez Crisis of 1956, Israeli forces pummeled Egyptian forces in the Sinai while Anglo-French expeditionary forces seized the northern end of the Suez Canal and moved south quickly. With Egypt facing decisive defeat, the United States pressured the Israelis, British, and French to withdraw. Khrushchev went a step farther, however, and hinted of Soviet nuclear weapons landing in Paris and London and of Soviet "volunteers" pouring into Egypt. As with other crises, the effect of the nuclear threat was uncertain, but it was clear that more than one power could now rattle the nuclear saber.

Achieving Strategic Parity and Controlling Nuclear Weapons

Throughout the 1950s the strategy of Massive Retaliation came under severe criticism. As Soviet advances reduced American advantages in strategic arms, it no longer seemed credible to attempt to deter limited aggression by possibly escalating to a massive nuclear response. Thus, the likelihood of nuclear weapons, according to the critics, being employed against Soviet aggression decreased, as did the chances of effectively resisting communist aggression. Among those objecting most strenuously to American emphasis on strategic nuclear forces was a succession of U.S. Army general officers, including two chiefs of staff, General Matthew B. Ridgway and General Maxwell D. Taylor. To them, limited conflicts—particularly those in which conventional forces played a key role—seemed the way of the future, and they argued that the United States had to build strategically mobile conventional forces capable of meeting threats to national interests wherever they might appear.

During his campaign for the presidency, John F. Kennedy committed himself to reversing Eisenhower's Massive Retaliation strategy and substituting in its place a new strategy of "Flexible Response." Shortly after entering office in January 1961, he stated, "Any potential aggressor contemplating an attack on any part of the free world with any kind of weapons, conventional or nuclear, must know that our response will be suitable, selective, swift, and effective." In essence the president resolved to create multiple options so an American response could be tailored to a Soviet challenge. The new strategy required a larger number and variety of conventional forces, eventually leading the army, for example, to abolish its Pentomic divisions and to focus on conventional warfare.

When commissioned in 1961, the USS *Enterprise* was the largest ship ever built. It displaced 85,600 tons, measured over 1,100 feet, and carried a crew of 4,600, including 2,400 air personnel. Its vast range and great speed enabled the United States to project force over the entire globe.

The adoption of Flexible Response did not reduce the importance of nuclear weapons. Robert S. McNamara, the new secretary of defense, began developing the nuclear dimension of Flexible Response and emphasized the requirement, if deterrence failed, for greater flexibility and discrimination in the selection of nuclear targets. In June 1962, he said that "principal military objectives in the event of nuclear war . . . should be the destruction of the enemy's military forces, not of his civilian population." By refraining from an attack against enemy cities and by holding a large, strategic nuclear force in reserve, McNamara sought with a counterforce strategy to provide an adversary "the strongest possible incentive" to avoid striking American cities and to agree quickly to ending a war.

The new counterforce strategy proved to be expensive, for it required "powerful and well-protected" American nuclear forces. Additionally, the targeting of Soviet forces required more accurate and reliable delivery systems than targeting larger and more easily hit cities. The Kennedy administration took office at a time when the last of the first-generation ICBMs became operational (Atlas E in 1960, Titan I in 1962, and the Atlas F in 1962). Despite the costs involved, McNamara accelerated the entry of more accurate second-generation missiles (Minuteman I and Titan II) into the American arsenal and began eliminating first-generation missiles. He also reduced the number of manned bombers, primarily by phasing out the older B-47s. Recognizing the advantages of submarine-launched ballistic missiles, McNamara accelerated the development of Polaris submarines. The SLBMs represented the "third leg" (along with land-based ICBMs and manned bombers) of what became known as the TRIAD. To avoid substantial damage from a retaliatory or second strike, an adversary would have to destroy each leg of the TRIAD in a first strike. With the Americans' possessing three separate strategic systems for delivering nuclear weapons, however, the possibility of multiple strikes against the same target—or "overkill"—appeared, so in 1962 McNamara approved the Single Integrated Operational Plan (SIOP), which had been developed during the Eisenhower administration. By incorporating controlled options into the SIOP, the United States could hold in reserve a large strategic nuclear force and could manipulate nuclear warfighting instead of simply pulling a single trigger. By the mid-1960s, the United States had about 1,000 ICBMs, 650 SLBMs, and 650 manned bombers.

The Cuban Missile Crisis

The closest brush with nuclear Armageddon came not in the Eisenhower administration but in the Kennedy administration when the new president found few options to his liking in the Cuban Missile Crisis. The crisis grew out of Khrushchev's decision in early 1962 to place nuclear missiles in Cuba. Russian advisors, aircraft, and air-defense weapons accompanied the missiles, and in August 1962, an American U-2 spotted suspicious construction sites. As the reconnaissance flights continued, intelligence analysts identified more and more sites.

Despite Soviet assurances that no offensive missiles had been deployed in Cuba, a U-2 flight returned on October 14, 1962, bearing photographs that definitively revealed launch sites being prepared in western Cuba for medium-range (1,000 miles) ballistic missiles as well as long-range (2,200 miles) missiles. If the Soviets finished the sites and placed nuclear weapons at them, they would have the capability of covering with nuclear weapons much of the continental United States. Believing he could not permit the weapons to remain in Cuba, President Kennedy ordered a naval "quarantine" on October 22, 1962, to prevent Cuba from receiving any more Soviet equipment. He also insisted that any nuclear weapon launched from Cuba would be considered to have been launched from the Soviet Union and placed U.S. nuclear forces on the highest level of alert ever ordered, DEFCON-2 (Defense Condition 2), including the maintenance of fifty-seven nuclear bombers on a twenty-four hour flying readiness schedule. Another quarter of a million American troops also were placed in higher states of readiness. Meanwhile, Soviet commanders in Cuba received permission to use nuclear weapons in the event of an American invasion.

As the crisis intensified, Khrushchev offered to withdraw the missiles from Cuba in exchange for the Americans' removing Jupiter missiles from Turkey, lifting the naval blockade, and promising not to invade Cuba. Kennedy eventually accepted the offer but did not make his own concession public. After some tense moments at the naval picket lines, when Soviet and American ships faced off, the crisis passed. By October 27, all parties had backed off gingerly from the nuclear brink.

Both superpowers emerged from the Cuban Missile Crisis with a revitalized fear of nuclear consequences. Though Secretary of State Dean Rusk believed the Americans and Soviets came away from the crisis "more cautious and more thoughtful," the Soviets concluded that the American advantage in nuclear weapons had forced them to yield, and they subsequently embarked on an ambitious program to modernize their nuclear arsenal. Shortly after the crisis, a senior Soviet official told his American counterpart, "You Americans will never be able to do this to us again." A new period in the nuclear era had begun.

Mutual Assured Destruction

Though the American modernization program in the 1960s was impressive, that of the Soviets was even more so. A succession of new ICBMs entered the Soviets' Strategic Rocket Forces in the late 1960s. The SS-11 became operational in 1966, the SS-9 in 1967, and the SS-13 in 1969. The SS-11 became the most extensively employed Soviet ICBM. At the same time, the Soviets began to place their strategic weapons in hardened underground silos. Moreover, the Soviet Union accelerated in the mid-1960s the construction of submarines capable of launching strategic missiles. By 1970 the Soviet Union had surpassed the United States in number of operational ICBMs, 1,299 to 1,054.

As the Russians acquired a greater capability to retaliate directly against American cities, the Americans began to question a purely counterforce strategy and to look for other options. In February 1965 Secretary McNamara announced that the United States would rely on "Assured Destruction" to deter a Soviet attack. In essence, this meant the Americans would respond to an enemy nuclear attack by inflicting unacceptable damage on the Soviets, that is, an attack upon civilian as well as military targets. McNamara believed the possibility of massive destruction of Soviet cities would deter the enemy from launching a first-strike attack.

After the Soviets acquired an assured second-strike capability, the Americans modified their strategy again. In September 1967, McNamara added the word "mutual" to "assured destruction," thereby creating the unfortunate acronym, MAD, which suggested to many the insanity of holding the populations of both countries hostage. Nevertheless, Mutual Assured Destruction signaled an acceptance by the United States of its own vulnerability and the emergence of what McNamara called a "stable balance of terror." According to some analysts, the Soviet Union achieved "strategic parity" or a "rough equilibrium" in the early 1970s.

The Proliferation of Nuclear Weapons

For nearly two decades, the history of the nuclear era played out chiefly in the United States and the Soviet Union, but other powers began acquiring atomic or nuclear capability. Several months before the Soviets tested their atomic bomb in 1949, the British announced they would build their own atomic weapons. In October 1952, they tested their first atomic bomb on a small island northwest of Australia.

France's explosion of a bomb in the Sahara Desert in February 1960 signaled major changes in the nuclear arena. In his memoirs, Charles de Gaulle stated that one of his objectives had been for France "to acquire a nuclear capacity such that nobody could attack us without risking frightful wounds." It quickly became clear that the "nobody" included the United States. In November 1968, the French army's chief of the general staff published an article in which he announced that French nuclear forces, the *force de frappe*, would be capable of covering all points of the compass. In essence, he declared the independence of French nuclear forces. Other powers also acquired nuclear capabilities. In 1957, the Soviet Union agreed to provide defense assistance to Communist China, including assistance in nuclear matters. The Soviets cooperated fully with Chinese specialists who exploded their first nuclear device in October 1964.

With the number of nuclear powers increasing, many political and military leaders became increasingly concerned about the dangerous proliferation of nuclear technology. In August 1967, the United States and the Soviet Union jointly submitted to the U.N. Disarmament Commission a treaty to halt the spread of nuclear weapons. When ratified, the Nuclear Nonproliferation Treaty bound the signatory states with nuclear weapons not to supply them to other nations and those without nuclear weapons not to manufacture them. Though the pact was hailed as an epochal event, states throughout the world continued to seek nuclear technology. Communist

China denounced the treaty as a "plot," and in May 1974, India exploded its first nuclear device. Despite the sincerest of efforts, the "nuclear genie" had escaped from the bottle.

Arms Control Comes of Age

For almost two decades after World War II, little or no progress occurred in arms control. During the years when the United States had obvious superiority over the Soviet Union, Moscow often called for general and complete disarmament, but neither Moscow nor Washington accepted any real limitations or controls. In 1946, Bernard M. Baruch presented to the United Nations an American proposal for international control over the development and use of atomic energy, but the proposal foundered when the Soviets objected to on-site inspections. In 1955, President Eisenhower, hoping to lessen the danger of surprise attack, suggested having "Open Skies" over the USSR and the United States by permitting each to conduct flights over the other. The Soviets, however, denounced the plan as an espionage plot. Following the Cuban Missile Crisis, the two sides swiftly approved the Limited Test Ban Treaty of 1963. With over one hundred signatories, the treaty prohibited the testing of nuclear devices in space, the atmosphere, and underwater but allowed underground testing. Additional progress occurred as the two superpowers approached strategic parity, most notably the 1967

As the range of Polaris missiles grew from 1,375 to 2,850 miles, nuclear submarines carrying the missiles became more difficult to locate since they could hide in vastly larger areas of the ocean.

Nonproliferation Treaty. Several years of subsequent talks, however, failed to produce a breakthrough on limiting nuclear arms. In these and other efforts at arms control, distrust between the superpowers and the technical difficulties of verifying numbers and controlling technological advances created insurmountable obstacles.

Throughout the arms control discussions, verification of the number of an opponent's warheads remained impractical but became even more problematic when the United States began deploying missiles with multiple warheads. In 1964 it introduced the Polaris A-3 missile, which carried a multiple reentry vehicle (MRV) payload. When fired, the MRV would separate into individual reentry vehicles, or "bomblets," and strike an area in "shotgun" fashion. In 1968 the United States tested a multiple independently targeted reentry vehicle (MIRV) with the Minuteman III, which was an intercontinental ballistic missile with a range of about 9,300 miles. More accurate than the bomblets in the MRV warheads, the bomblets in the MIRV warheads could be directed with surprising precision against individual targets. The warhead of the Minuteman III carried three reentry vehicles, or bomblets, each with an estimated yield of about 200 kilotons. In 1970 the United States fitted its submarines with the Poseidon C-3 missile, which had a MIRV capability. The Soviet Union soon matched the technological developments in American strategic weapons. Testing of the SS-9 with a MRV warhead began in late 1968, and the fielding of Soviet missiles with MIRVs began in 1974.

The implications for nuclear strategy and arms control were enormous. Analysts contended that a preemptive nuclear strike by ICBMs with multiple warheads could inflict significant damage to fixed missile silos. Some concluded that immobile, undefended, land-based ICBMs were obsolete. Also, the existence of multiple warheads on a single missile made the number of warheads almost impossible to verify. Using satellites, both sides could detect and count missile launchers, but they could not count warheads. Technological advances had changed the rules for the nuclear game.

Despite the problems posed by MIRVs and verification, both sides slowly came to recognize in the late 1960s the "advantages" of a strategic balance and dreaded the costs of another round of nuclear improvements. For the most part, subsequent discussions between the superpowers took little notice of the increasing spread of nuclear weapons to other countries. Nonetheless, the bilateral superpower negotiations for the Strategic Arms Limitation Treaty (SALT), which began in Helsinki in late 1969, were not concluded until nearly three years later. SALT I, as it came to be known, called only for a freeze on building more ICBMs by both sides and restricted the United States and the Soviet Union to two Antiballistic Missile (ABM) sites each. The treaty did not include a limit on numbers of warheads. Despite its modest achievements, SALT I was an important first step in arms control.

The next round of SALT discussions also proceeded slowly. Meanwhile the Soviets tested a new, more powerful family of ICBMs: SS-17, SS-18, and SS-19. All of them had MIRVs. In June 1979, Jimmy Carter and Leonid Brezhnev finally signed the SALT II agreements, which capped strategic delivery systems for each side at no more than 2,250, and established a specific ceiling of 1,320 missiles with MIRVs.

Despite the apparent progress, controversy plagued the arms control process. One sensitive issue was that of U.S. plans to field the enhanced radiation bomb, which was also known as the "neutron bomb." This new device produced much greater radiation than a traditional weapon and thus had a greater effect on personnel in armored vehicles, which were relatively resistant to blast effects. This made it a useful weapon against the huge Soviet armored forces. Critics argued, however, that the new device made nuclear war more likely by blurring the distinction between nuclear and conventional war. The introduction of the cruise missile also added complexity to the nuclear equation. The missile used forward-looking radar to guide itself along the nap of the Earth to its target. Though many analysts doubted its capacity to kill hard targets such as ICBMs deep within their silos, its existence blurred the distinction between strategic and theater-level nuclear delivery systems. A protocol attached to the SALT II agreement established temporary bans on the deployment of mobile ICBM launchers and on longer-range cruise missiles. After an intense debate in the U.S. Senate about whether SALT II should be ratified, the treaty fell victim to renewed American doubts about Soviet intentions following their invasion of Afghanistan in December 1979.

Continued Innovation in Nuclear Technology

In the 1960s and 1970s, key American officials concluded that assured destruction was not enough and that the United States needed a wider range of options. In 1973, James Schlesinger, secretary of defense under President Richard M. Nixon, stated, "[W]e ourselves find it difficult to believe that we would actually implement the threat of assured destruction in response to a limited attack on military targets that caused relatively few civilian casualties." He then called for "a series of measured responses to aggression which bear some relation to the provocation." In July 1980, President Carter signed Presidential Directive 59, which incorporated many of Schlesinger's ideas; the document called for a "countervailing" nuclear strategy in which the United States would arrange its future arsenal so that it could fight a nuclear war at "any level of intensity," from limited nuclear exchange, to a theater-level war, to all-out nuclear war. Improvements in command and control, delivery systems, and accuracy had enabled the Americans to develop the capability to use their nuclear weapons in limited nuclear options against Soviet nuclear forces, conventional forces, or other military targets, and perhaps to control escalation all the way from the most limited use through an all-out nuclear exchange. In essence, the new policy signaled a move away from countervalue toward counterforce in U.S. strategy; it relied on delivery means for nuclear weapons becoming more precise and controls becoming more flexible. Nevertheless its announcement brought on a storm of criticism from those who believed the new policy increased the likelihood of nuclear weapons being employed in the future.

When Ronald Reagan became president in 1981, he was convinced that the Soviet nuclear forces were superior to those of the U.S., and he soon took steps to strengthen the U.S. nuclear arsenal. While refusing to revive SALT II, Reagan accelerated the employment of Trident nuclear submarines and Trident II missiles (an undersea long-range missile system that was begun in the early 1970s) and stood solidly behind the decision to deploy Pershing II and Tomahawk cruise missiles in the defense of Europe. He also poured money into the MX missile. Although Carter had initiated most of the new programs, it was Reagan who pushed them. From the Soviet perspective, the new president seemed to be waging economic warfare.

Among the most dramatic steps taken by President Reagan was the Strategic Defense Initiative, which initially envisaged a strategic missile defense in space using directed energy or lasers. After the use of laser weapons proved infeasible, a concept for kinetic energy interceptors replaced the notion of using lasers. Whatever its methods, the announcement of SDI created an international uproar and popular dissent. Critics saw the SDI program as a dangerous change, for the prospect of the United States' having a shield against a nuclear attack seemed to increase the chances of the Soviets' attacking before the shield was completed or to encourage the Americans to launch a first strike after the shield was erected. Either scenario could result in a nuclear holocaust. As the Soviet Union began to desintegrate and the threat of a Soviet attack receded, questions about the utility and expense of SDI increased. When Iraq's effort to develop nuclear weapons became apparent in the Persian Gulf War, however, proponents of SDI pointed out that nuclear weapons were no longer the monopoly of the superpowers and that up to fifteen states could possess nuclear weapons in the near future. They believed SDI could provide valuable protection against an attack from one of these powers.

As the 1980s ended, Mikhail S. Gorbachev, the Soviet head of state, eagerly sought additional curbs on nuclear weapons. In December 1987, Gorbachev and Reagan agreed to destroy all U.S. and Soviet intermediate-range nuclear missiles (300–3,000 miles). In July 1991, Gorbachev and President George Bush signed the long-awaited Strategic Arms Reduction Treaty (START). In essence, START cut Soviet strategic nuclear warheads from 11,012 to 6,163 and American warheads from 12,646 to 8,556. Following the dissolution of the Soviet Union, President Bush and President Boris N. Yeltsin of Russia signed START II in January 1993. The treaty limited Russia to 3,000 warheads and the United States to 3,500. The treaty also banned all long-range land-based missiles with multiple warheads. Bush concluded, "Today, the Cold War is over."

The proliferation of nuclear arms around the world, however, ensured that concerns about nuclear weapons did not disappear with the ending of the Cold War. In an indication of the increasing complexity of the nuclear environment, three of the successor states to the Soviet Union—Ukraine, Kazakhstan, and Belarus—expressed reservations about the START agreements. As the United States confronted the new strategic environment, it refocused the SDI program from providing protection against a Soviet attack to providing protection from "limited ballistic missile strikes, whatever their source." The new strategy of Global Protection against Limited Strikes (GPALS) signaled how dramatically the international situation had changed.

∗ ∗ ∗ ∗

Through the second half of the twentieth century, nuclear weapons affected many decisions and actions relating to international security and had dramatic effects on strategy and force structure. After World War II, the United States had only a few atomic weapons, but it had a monopoly over them. In subsequent years as the Cold War heated up, and as the United States adopted a policy of containing the USSR and communism, atomic weapons played an increasingly larger role in American military thinking. When the

Observers watch the explosion of an atomic shell. In mid-1955, the U.S. Army positioned a task force three kilometers from an exploding 30-kiloton atomic device and had them advance to within 900 meters of ground zero. Such exercises supposedly demonstrated the ability of ground forces to operate on a nuclear battlefield.

Soviet Union exploded an atomic and then a nuclear device, the United States lost its monopoly over the enormously destructive weapons, and deterrence became particularly important. For the rest of the Cold War, containment and deterrence remained significant American goals.

Following the Korean War, Eisenhower emphasized a strategy of Massive Retaliation, and nuclear weapons assumed a position of primacy in American military thinking. As the Soviets improved their nuclear capabilities, the Americans moved toward a strategy of Flexible Response, which relied on more balanced conventional and nuclear forces. After the Cuban Missile Crisis, the Soviet Union accelerated the development of its nuclear capabilities, and the United States adopted Assured Destruction and then Mutual Assured Destruction as its new strategy. Recognizing it could no longer maintain overwhelming superiority, the United States prepared to respond to a Soviet attack by destroying much of Soviet society.

The United States maintained its nuclear superiority until the early 1970s when the Soviet Union gained strategic parity. With nuclear forces in rough equilibrium and new technological advances threatening to upset the delicate balance or require vast new resources, political leaders became more agreeable to nuclear arms limitations. Meanwhile, the long-term evolution of American nuclear policy formally entered a new phase with the adoption of a countervailing strategy in July 1980. Instead of relying on Mutual Assured Destruction, the Americans had developed the capability to use nuclear weapons in limited nuclear options and sought to avoid an all-out nuclear exchange. Finally, the dissolution of the Soviet Union and the proliferation of nuclear weapons created a new strategic environment; the United States began shifting from an emphasis on retaliation against nuclear attack to defense against nuclear attack.

Though numerous wars occurred between 1945 and 1990, the only two bombs used in combat were those dropped on Hiroshima and Nagasaki, and thus concepts for nuclear war remained largely theoretical. The United States and the Soviet Union expended vast resources to develop strategies and forces for nuclear war, but they also devoted considerable effort and resources to avoiding such a war and to preventing a small war from escalating into a larger war. The initiation of an era of limited war thus emerged as one of the most important effects of the introduction of nuclear weapons.

SUGGESTED READINGS

Armacost, Michael H. *The Politics of Weapon Innovation: The Thor-Jupiter Controversy* (New York: Columbia University Press, 1969).

Bacevich, A. J. *The Pentomic Era: The U.S. Army between Korea and Vietnam* (Washington, D.C.: National Defense University Press, 1986).

Brodie, Bernard, ed. *The Absolute Weapon: Atomic Power and World Order* (New York: Harcourt, Brace and Company, 1946).

Brodie, Bernard. *Strategy in the Missile Age* (Princeton, N.J.: Princeton University Press, 1959).

Bundy, McGeorge. *Danger and Survival: Choices About the Bomb in the First Fifty Years* (New York: Random House, 1988).

Freedman, Lawrence. *The Evolution of Nuclear Strategy* (New York: St. Martin's Press, 1981).

Gaddis, John L. *Strategies of Containment* (New York: Oxford University Press, 1982).

Herken, Gregg. *The Winning Weapon: The Atomic Bomb in the Cold War, 1945–1950* (New York: Vintage Books, 1982).

Holland, Lauren H., and Robert A. Hoover. *The MX Decision: A New Direction in Weapons Procurement Policy* (Boulder, Col.: Westview Press, 1985).

Kaplan, Fred M. *The Wizards of Armageddon* (New York: Simon and Schuster, 1983).

Kissinger, Henry. *Nuclear Weapons and Foreign Policy* (New York: Harper, 1957).

Mandelbaum, Michael. *The Nuclear Question: The United States and Nuclear Weapons, 1946–1976* (Cambridge: Cambridge University Press, 1979).

Midgley, John J., Jr. *Deadly Illusions: Army Policy for the Nuclear Battlefield* (Boulder, Col.: Westview Press, 1986).

Neufeld, Jacob. *Ballistic Missiles in the United States Air Force, 1945–1960* (Washington, D.C.: Government Printing Office, 1989).

Newhouse, John. *War and Peace in the Nuclear Age* (New York: Alfred A. Knopf, 1989).

Osgood, Robert E. *Limited War: The Challenge to American Strategy* (Chicago: University of Chicago Press, 1957).

Porro, Jeffrey, ed. *The Nuclear Age Reader* (New York: Alfred A. Knopf, 1989).

Prados, John. *The Soviet Estimate: U.S. Intelligence Analysis and Russian Military Strength* (New York: Dial Press, 1982).

Rhodes, Richard. *The Making of the Atomic Bomb* (New York: Simon and Schuster, 1986).

Rose, John P. *The Evolution of U.S. Army Nuclear Doctrine, 1945-1980* (Boulder, Col.: Westview Press, 1980).

Rosenberg, David A. "The Origins of Overkill: Nuclear Weapons and American Strategy, 1945–1960," *International Security*, vol. 7, no. 4 (Spring 1983), pp. 3–71.

_____. "American Atomic Strategy and the Atomic Bomb Decision," *Journal of American History*, vol. 66, no. 1 (June 1979), pp. 62–87.

Sherwin, Martin J. *A World Destroyed: Hiroshima and the Origins of the Arms Race* (New York: Vintage Books, 1987).

Stares, Paul B. *The Militarization of Space: U.S. Policy, 1945–1984* (Ithaca, N.Y.: Cornell University Press, 1985).

Talbott, Strobe. *Deadly Gambits: The Reagan Administration and the Stalemate in Nuclear Arms Control* (New York: Alfred A. Knopf, 1984).

————. *Endgame: The Inside Story of SALT II* (New York: Harper & Row, 1979).

Werrell, Kenneth P. *The Evolution of the Cruise Missile* (Maxwell Air Force Base, Ala.: Air University Press, 1985).

Wohlstetter, Albert. "The Delicate Balance of Terror," *Foreign Affairs*, vol. 37, no. 2 (January 1959), pp. 211–34.

28

KOREA: LIMITING WAR TO AVOID ARMAGEDDON

Rushing to War: The High
Cost of Unpreparedness

Changing War Aims and
a Changing War

Ending the War:
Politics as War

The Korean War was the first major conflict of the Cold War; it began on June 25, 1950, when North Korean ground forces invaded South Korea. Armed forces from the United States and other members of the United Nations came to the aid of the South Koreans, and a three-year war resulted. After fighting a war of maneuver up and down the Korean peninsula for about a year, the combatants settled into deeply entrenched positions, reminiscent of World War I. As negotiations for ending the war began and the war became a stalemate, bitter battles erupted over minor outposts for small negotiating advantages. The issue of exchanging prisoners of war became a major obstacle to final agreement, prolonging the war until an armistice stopped the fighting on July 27, 1953.

While the Korean War witnessed few innovations in warfare, it demonstrated methods for gaining national objectives in the newly born atomic era. For the United States, the war was a "limited" war. To avoid provoking retaliation from the Soviet Union, American political leaders limited the geographic areas in which military commanders could operate, the strength of their forces, and the weapons to be used against the enemy. Communist forces suffered huge losses in the fighting and sought to achieve, through prolonged armistice negotiations, what they could not gain on the battlefield. They sought an advantageous political outcome by manipulating public opinion in the United States and among its allies, as well as throughout the nonaligned nations of the world. Thus the Korean War was less about tactical evolution than about political goals, the strategy to achieve those goals, and the operations designed to make the strategy succeed.

Rushing to War: The High Cost of Unpreparedness

After World War II, antagonism between the Soviet Union and the United States grew as the two former allies became increasingly distrustful and suspicious of the other's motives. The first notable confrontation occurred in 1946 when the Soviets briefly refused to withdraw from Iran. More acute problems occurred in Turkey and Greece. The Soviets pressured the Turks for control of the straits of the Bosporus and Dardanelles and the return of territory lost at the end of World War I. When Greek Communists attempted to overthrow Greece's government, the Americans became particularly concerned, and President Truman pledged support to "free peoples who are resisting attempted subjugation by armed minorities or by outside pressures." This pledge came to be known as the Truman Doctrine. In an attempt to revive Europe, the United States established the Marshall Plan in 1947 and provided the economic base on which democratic reforms could be made. But international tensions increased with the Berlin Blockade in the spring of 1948, the explosion of a Soviet atomic device in August 1949, and the communist takeover of China in December 1949. During this series of crises, the United States adopted the policy, defined by George F. Kennan, of "a long-term, patient but firm and vigilant containment of Russian expansive tendencies."

In January 1950 President Truman directed officials from the departments of state and defense to conduct a broad assessment of American military needs. The resulting document, known as NSC-68, was the first comprehensive statement of national security policy since the end of World War II. To meet the threat posed by rapidly expanding Soviet capabilities, NSC-68 advocated an immediate buildup of U.S. and allied military strength in hopes that the United States might induce a change in Soviet policy while avoiding all-out war. The document called for the United States to have the capacity to wage either general or limited war and clearly emphasized that atomic weapons by themselves were insufficient for American national security needs. War broke out in Korea, however, before military readiness could be improved significantly.

Rapid demobilization after World War II had greatly affected American armed forces, but of all the services, the U.S. Army was in the worst shape to fight a war. In total, there were ten army divisions and eleven separate brigades on active duty in the spring of 1950. Of those forces, four infantry divisions were in Japan and immediately available to General of the Army Douglas MacArthur, Commander-in-Chief, Far East, and thereby the theater commander. But these forces were far from being combat ready. Except for the 25th Infantry Division, all were below their authorized peacetime strength of 12,500 men. Within the regiments, the number of battalions had been reduced from three to two and the tank company eliminated. The divisions' artillery was scaled down, and there were shortages of antitank mines, high explosive antitank ammunition, and spare parts for weapons. The divisions also had serious training problems. Although individual soldiers were reasonably well trained, units were not. When Lieutenant General Walton H. Walker took command of Eighth Army in the summer of 1949, training for combat finally took priority over occupation duties, but the demands of occupying and administering Japan continued to take their toll on combat readiness.

Failing to recognize the likelihood of war in Korea also had an effect on readiness. When World War II ended, the Soviets and the Americans entered Korea to administer the surrender of Japanese forces. At that time the 38th Parallel had no significance other than dividing Korea in such a way as to give the United States ports at Inchon and Pusan to facilitate the repatriation of Japanese troops. As the possibility of Korean unification became more remote, the South Koreans held elections in May 1948, and after the U.N. General Assembly recognized the newly elected government of Syngman Rhee in South Korea, the Soviets created and recognized the Democratic People's Republic of Korea. The 38th Parallel divided the two Korean states.

Throughout this period, the United States remained primarily concerned with unfolding events in Europe and demonstrated little interest in becoming deeply involved in Korea. By 1950, Kim Il Sung had risen to the top of the communist forces in North Korea and had assembled a relatively small but highly capable army of 135,000 men. With Moscow's approval, he began preparations for unifying Korea by force. Neither the Soviets nor the North Koreans expected the United States to oppose the Communists with military forces. Meanwhile the South Koreans—with American advice and assistance—organized a small ground force of about 65,000 troops equipped well enough to prevent border raids and to preserve internal security, but not to fight a hard war. Ready or not, the American and South Korean armed forces were about to be involved in a life and death struggle.

The War Begins

North Korea had completed preparations for an offensive against South Korea by June 23, 1950. The main attack, which was conducted by the 3rd and 4th North Korean divisions, aimed at Seoul on the west coast and began at about 0430 hours on June 25. Farther to the east in the mountains, the 2nd and 7th North Korean divisions drove toward Yoju and Wonju, and on the east coast, the 5th Division (reinforced) headed for Samch'ok. Second echelon regiments followed closely, prepared to attack through the lead units to objectives deep in the South Koreans' rear. Advancing on a broad front, the North Koreans achieved success everywhere. The South Korean forces, which were also known as Republic of Korea (ROK) forces and which were defending along the 38th Parallel, fell back in the face of superior enemy strength, hardly delaying the North Koreans.

As North Korean troops advanced south toward Seoul, President Truman concluded that the United States—as part of a United Nations'

President Truman reports to the nation on the actions taken by the United States. He had earlier stated, "The attack upon Korea makes it plain beyond all doubt that Communism has passed beyond the use of subversion to conquer independent nations and will now use armed invasion and war."

effort—had to oppose communist aggression in the Far East. In a complete reversal of policy, he decided American forces would intervene to save South Korea. Opposition to U.N. involvement came from the communist states, but because the Soviets had walked out of the U.N. Security Council the preceding January, their resistance was uncoordinated and ineffective. On Sunday, June 25, the U.N. Security Council adopted an American-sponsored resolution branding the North Korean attack as a breach of the peace and calling on the North Korean government to cease hostilities and withdraw behind the 38th Parallel. On the following Tuesday, the Security Council approved a follow-on resolution calling on members of the United Nations to help South Korea "repel the armed attack and . . . restore international peace and security in the area." The U.N. Security Council designated the president of the United States as its executive agent for the war in Korea. Truman, in turn, appointed General MacArthur as the Commander-in-Chief, United Nations Command (CINCUNC).

MacArthur's mission was to stop the North Koreans and eject them from South Korea. Somehow he had to slow down the North Koreans sufficiently to give him time to mount a counterattack against their flanks or rear. His first act was to delay what appeared to be the enemy's main attack on the Seoul-Suwon-Ch'onan-Taejon axis leading to the port of Pusan in the south. On the last day of June, MacArthur ordered Major General William F. Dean, commanding general of the 24th Infantry Division, to send an infantry-artillery task force to Korea as the vanguard for the division. The task force—known as Task Force Smith, after Lieutenant Colonel Charles B. Smith, commander of the 1st Battalion, 21st Infantry—consisted of about half the battalion. It reached Taejon on July 2 and moved toward a defensive position about five kilometers north of Osan. Though greatly diminished in strength, the Americans were confident that they could halt the North Koreans. One general officer told Smith, "All we need is some men up there who won't run when they see tanks." By first light on July 5, Colonel Smith's units were in place, and Battery B, 52nd Field Artillery, was prepared to provide fire support.

Beginning around 0700 on July 5, the task force received an attack from North Korean tanks, all of which tried to drive through the American position. About twenty of Smith's infantrymen were killed or wounded in the fight. Damaged but not defeated, with enemy tanks somewhere in its rear, Task Force Smith received another attack several hours later. Attacking frontally, the leading North Korean infantry units took heavy casualties; they then managed to envelop Smith's position and seize high ground on both flanks. Around 1430 hours, Smith decided that his small command had done all it could and ordered his troops to withdraw. As the infantrymen attempted to pull back, enemy pressure increased and prevented some of the Americans from making a fighting withdrawal. A few of them abandoned their crew-served weapons and their rifles. They also left some of their dead and wounded behind. Fortunately for the Americans, the North Koreans chose not to pursue aggressively. The next morning, remnants of Task Force Smith reached Ch'onan. After other survivors made their way back, the final count of missing was 148 soldiers and five officers. Any notion that the North Koreans would pull back at the sight of Americans had disappeared.

Establishing the Pusan Perimeter

Though MacArthur's knowledge of the enemy was incomplete in the first few days of the war, he formulated a broad operational plan containing three clearly identifiable phases. The first was to delay the enemy on his main approach and thereby to buy time needed to rush reinforcements to Korea. The second phase was to defend a toehold on the Korean peninsula to allow the buildup of forces through the port of Pusan. The final phase was an amphibious turning movement by a corps raised in Japan that would strike at the waist of Korea and trap the North Koreans between the new beachhead and Pusan.

For the three-phased operation, MacArthur had advantages in his air and naval forces. Aircraft from the Far East Air Force (FEAF) and the navy soon controlled the sky and provided close air support to Koreans and those few Americans then on the ground. By July 3, Australian air units joined the growing U.N. air force. U.S. carriers launched aircraft to strike targets in North Korea on July 4 and 5. Naval surface forces quickly assembled in Korean waters and secured the sea routes between Japan and Korea. Naval

The Korean War: June 28 – September 15, 1950

CHINA

Manchuria

Yalu R.

Ch'ongch'on R.

Hamhung
Hungnam

Sea of Japan

P'yongyang

Wonsan

Imjin R.

June 25, 1950

June 25, 1950

38th Parallel

Panmunjom

Seoul
Hoengsong
Inchon
Wonju
Samch'ok
Han R.
Suwon
Osan
Yoju
P'yongt'aek
Chech'on

X X X
X
U.S.

Sept. 15, 1950

Ch'onan
Choch'iwon

Kum R.
Taejon

X X
25
U.N.

Aug. 1, 1950

X X
24
U.S.

X X X X
Eighth
U.S.

Yellow Sea

Naktong R.

Pusan
KOJE-DO

TSUSHIMA

0	50	100 mi
0	50	100 km

U.N. forces
North Korean attacks

patrols halted the movement of supplies from China and the USSR into North Korea and prevented the infiltration of troops and supplies by sea to the North Koreans south of the 38th Parallel.

U.N. air and naval superiority enabled ground forces to fight numerically superior enemy formations successfully throughout the war. Time and again, even when U.N. forces were in retreat and facing serious setbacks, tactical aircraft and naval gunfire saved the ground forces from being overwhelmed. Beyond the battlefield, supporting aircraft and ships carried war matériel to the combat zone in record-breaking time. The arrival of reinforcements and equipment around the first of August, when Eighth Army and the ROK army were backed into their defensive perimeter around Pusan, saved the whole war effort. Such was the power of air and naval superiority.

In addition to the United States, other members of the United Nations sent forces to aid South Korea. In the end fifty-three nations responded favorably even though actual contributions were slow in coming. Among those sending contingents were Great Britain, Australia, New Zealand, Canada, the Philippines, Sweden, the Netherlands, Belgium, France, Turkey, Thailand, Belgium, Greece, India, and South Africa. Some eventually sent combat forces that played significant roles fighting alongside American regiments.

While the U.N. allies marshaled forces, General Walker and his soldiers in Eighth Army shouldered the crucial task of holding on in Korea long enough to mount the amphibious counteroffensive. The North Koreans proved to be strong, numbering perhaps 80,000 troops and up to 150 tanks. Walker had four U.S. divisions at his disposal—the 7th, 24th, 25th, and the 1st Cavalry Division—but they were spread across the length of Japan and had to be transported to Korea. First he pushed the rest of the 24th Infantry Division into Korea to join Task Force Smith in blocking the enemy's main axis of advance. The division fought the North Koreans in a series of delaying actions at P'yongt'aek and Ch'onan on July 8, at Choch'iwon on the 11th, and on the Kum River between the 13th and 15th. The North Koreans pressed ahead, attacking much as they had against Task Force Smith: advancing along main roads in valleys; striking the American front with tanks, infantry, and artillery; enveloping the flanks with infantry who swarmed across the rugged hills; destroying command posts, supporting artillery, and mortars in the rear; and blocking escape with powerful roadblocks to unnerve the defenders.

When the 25th Division arrived, Walker sent it north to join the 24th in delaying the enemy. To move the 1st Cavalry Division into the country and on line with the 24th and 25th, Walker needed a delay of two days at Taejon. Dean and the 24th Division provided the two days even though they were hopelessly outnumbered. With the 1st Cavalry Division now positioned to its rear, the battered 24th gave up Taejon on July 20 and fell back to the Naktong River. Among its casualties was General Dean, who became engaged in the fight, was cut off, and escaped, only to be captured after weeks of evading the North Koreans. As the enemy continued attacking, Walker slowly gave up ground until his forces were pushed into the

"Pusan Perimeter," as it came to be known. U.S. troops occupied the western part of the defensive perimeter, while the South Koreans covered the northern part.

As reinforcements poured into Pusan and combat strength began to favor Walker, MacArthur assembled forces in Japan for his amphibious operation, now planned for mid-September. Despite the deep concern of the Joint Chiefs of Staff (JCS) for the fate of Eighth Army in the Pusan Perimeter, MacArthur was convinced that his complete superiority of air power and growing strength in tanks, artillery, and infantry would enable Eighth Army and the South Koreans to hold Pusan. His confidence was soon to be tested.

Beginning on August 5 the North Koreans launched violent, piecemeal attacks against the perimeter. Walker parried their thrusts by skillfully shifting his meager reserves between threatened points. Better organized and more savage attacks began on August 31. By this time Walker enjoyed greater combat power, particularly in tanks and artillery. By September 12, the North Korean offensive had spent itself on all fronts against Walker's skillful defense. Best of all, virtually all the enemy's units were concentrated against Pusan. The time for a counteroffensive had arrived.

The Inchon Landing

Though Inchon had the worst physical characteristics that could be imagined in an amphibious objective, MacArthur was convinced that the advantages of seizing it were worth the risk. He believed that the North Koreans, concentrated around the Pusan Perimeter in the south, would be vulnerable to an amphibious turning movement aimed so far to the north. Their vulnerability would be increased because Inchon was so close to the capital city of Seoul. Not only would the capture of Seoul be an important psychological victory, but even more important, Seoul was the intersection of most of the major roads and railroads in South Korea. To capture this intersection would force the North Koreans to surrender or escape to the mountains, abandoning all their heavy equipment.

Detractors of the plan, however, made strong arguments against Inchon as an objective. It had treacherous hydrographic conditions including nine to eleven meter tides, strong tidal currents caused by channel islands, and mud flats that stranded ships at low tide. To gain the most advantage from otherwise difficult tidal conditions, the attack had to begin on September 15. After that the weather turned cold, and rough waters made a landing more hazardous. At best, conditions required a daylight approach past the island of Wolmi-do, which if defended would be a dangerous obstacle. Even worse, a second wave could not follow the first until the next high tide, twelve hours later. Concerns about the defenders at Pusan and the risks inherent in the Inchon landing bothered the Joint Chiefs of Staff and General Walker, as well as some of MacArthur's naval and marine commanders who had to carry it out. Only MacArthur maintained a public air of confidence, so bold that it bordered on arrogance.

Beginning early in September, according to plan, naval air forces struck targets up and down the west coast of Korea; the U.S. Air Force provided general air support farther inland. As the days passed, naval air attacks converged on the Inchon area. Surface gunfire support ships took station off the harbor and began to add their weight. On September 15, Major General Edward M. Almond's X Corps made the amphibious assault at Inchon. The 1st Marine Division made the ship-to-shore landing under the cover of heavy naval gunfire and close air support. Early in the morning, marines took Wolmi-do, and on the next high tide they landed in Inchon north of the Wolmi-do causeway and then fought through the southern edge of the city. The 7th Division landed in Inchon after marines had cleared the city and then moved south of the marines to secure the south bank of the Han River and the high ground between Seoul and Suwon. Though the North Koreans were surprised, they fought fiercely to hold Seoul. Almond's X Corps nevertheless prevailed, and the city fell on September 28.

Despite the landing at Inchon, the heaviest concentration of North Koreans remained around the Pusan Perimeter, and Eighth Army had difficulty breaking out. Finally, a week after X Corps landed at Inchon, the North Koreans began to waver. On September 23, they started a general withdrawal, and Eighth Army units advanced. Within hours, the North Korean withdrawal turned into a rout as enemy soldiers sought refuge across the 38th Parallel or in the mountains of South Korea.

MacArthur's success was largely due to the confidence he had in the strategy and methods employed in the Pacific during World War II. His turning movement at Inchon completely reversed the strategic situation, giving U.N. forces the initiative for the first time. By October 1 he had expelled the aggressors from South Korea. Had nothing happened to change his mission, MacArthur could have counted this battle as a decisive victory. A change in MacArthur's mission, however, soon obliged him to continue the war with new constraints and new methods.

Changing War Aims and a Changing War

Even though the allies had achieved their strategic objectives, the war was not over. In retrospect, the turning point in the Korean War occurred when the allies decided to cross the 38th Parallel, to invade North Korea, and to pursue new strategic objectives. Conventional military wisdom demanded the destruction of the North Korean army to prevent a renewal of its aggression. On September 11—four days before the Inchon landing—President Truman approved MacArthur's pursuing the enemy into North Korea, but he adopted prudent restraints to avoid provoking the Chinese and Soviets. No U.N. troops would enter Manchuria or the USSR, only South Koreans would operate along the international border, and if the Soviets or Chinese intervened before the crossing of the 38th Parallel, the operation would be cancelled. The president also changed the national objective from saving

U.N. Drive over the 38th Parallel and
Advance Toward the Yalu River,
October–November 1950

CHINA

Manchuria

Yalu R.

Ch'ongch'on R.

Survivors of
North Korean
Army

Hamhung

Hungnam

Sea of
Japan

P'yongyang

Wonsan

XXX
X
U.S.

Imjin R.

XXXX
Eighth
U.S.

XXX
I
ROK

Panmunjom

38th Parallel

Seoul

Hoengsong

Inchon

Han R.

Wonju

Samch'ok

Suwon

Osan

Yoju

Chech'on

P'yongt'aek

Naktong R.

Ch'onan

Yellow
Sea

Kum R.

Choch'iwon

Taejon

Pusan

KOJE-DO

TSUSHIMA

| 0 | 50 | 100 mi |
| 0 | 50 | 100 km |

U.N. attacks
North Korean front line

South Korea to unifying the peninsula. After the United Nations passed a resolution calling for unification of the peninsula on October 7, MacArthur sent his forces into North Korea.

MacArthur's operations in North Korea never achieved the success of his earlier operations. He sent the exhausted Eighth Army in the main attack against the North Korean capital of P'yongyang and mounted a new amphibious assault by X Corps against the east coast port of Wonsan. Although Eighth Army advanced rapidly against light resistance, the amphibious assault by X Corps was six days late because mine sweepers ran into an elaborate mine field. Almost two weeks before the marines could land, Wonsan fell to a South Korean corps that had advanced north along the coast. After the capture of P'yongyang and Wonsan, allied troops streamed north virtually unopposed. In a conference with President Truman at Wake Island on October 15, MacArthur was optimistic about an early victory. Beginning on the 25th, however, a reinvigorated enemy struck Eighth Army and X Corps in a brief but furious counterattack. By November 2, intelligence officers had accumulated undeniable evidence from across the front that Chinese Communist Forces (CCF) from the People's Republic of China had intervened.

Before U.N. forces crossed the 38th Parallel, Chinese leaders had tried to ward off a direct confrontation with the Americans by warning them in September not to cross the 38th Parallel. American leaders interpreted these statements as bluff rather than policy. But they were wrong. Alarmed at the collapse of the North Koreans and concerned about the possible presence of American forces on China's borders, Mao Zedong—the supreme political and military leader of China—received promises of air support from Stalin and decided to intervene. Between October 14 and November 1, some 180,000 Chinese crossed the Yalu River and secretly massed in front of the U.N. Command.

Not knowing the full extent of the Chinese commitment, MacArthur believed their late October attack was a limited gesture rather than a serious intervention. After a three-week delay, while Eighth Army finally replenished its depleted supplies, the U.N. Commander resumed the advance. On November 24 the troops of Eighth Army, supported by an all-out effort by air forces, launched a rapid attack toward the Yalu River. Within twenty-four hours after Eighth Army jumped off, the Chinese struck; they aimed their main attack at the ROK II Corps on the army's right flank. Two days later the CCF hit X Corps as well. Stunned, American and South Korean units recoiled and began a long retreat that did not end until early January 1951.

Effective close air support enabled MacArthur's ground forces to escape. For days at a time, air forces were the only U.N. opposition to the advancing enemy. Timely and accurate attacks by relays of fighter bombers stopped the enemy in front of U.N. defenders. The Chinese, in their haste to close with Eighth Army in the west, abandoned their habitual concealment and marched night and day along primary and secondary roads. Casualties among men and vehicles from air attacks mounted so high that Chinese commanders had to confine road movement to nighttime, thus slowing the advance significantly. As the troops of Eighth Army put some distance

Chinese and North Korean Offensive and U.N. Withdrawal Below 38th Parallel, November 1950 – January 1951

between themselves and the Chinese, the air forces attacked and destroyed Chinese supplies and equipment. Then in mid-December FEAF launched a coordinated interdiction campaign against railway yards and bridges, highway bridges, tunnels, and supply dumps. Eighth Army owed its survival and subsequent resurgence in January 1951 to overwhelming air support during its retreat.

Defeat in North Korea forced the United Nations to reexamine its war aims in light of Chinese involvement. MacArthur quickly charged that he was facing "an entirely new war" and that the strategy for war against North Korea did not apply in a war against China. MacArthur wanted more forces and a broader charter to retaliate against the Chinese. But even in the darkest days before the Inchon landing, American leaders believed that restraint was necessary to avoid widening the war. Within the broader scope of the Cold War, Europe remained the main concern of American policy, not Asia; attacks on China could bring on Soviet involvement and even expand the war to Europe. MacArthur's proposals to increase his forces and to retaliate against the Chinese were therefore completely at odds with those of his president and other U.N. leaders.

During the first week of December, when reports from the front were grim, President Truman met Prime Minister Clement R. Attlee of the United Kingdom in Washington. Attlee had flown to the United States after Truman had hinted publicly that atomic weapons might be used in Korea. Speaking for some other U.N. members, he questioned American direction

Chinese soldiers proved tough, skillful, and numerous. To neutralize U.N. advantages in fire power, they advanced by stealth and infiltration and often attacked at night while making wild bugle calls and barbaric screams. They steadily increased their artillery, firing a record of more than 93,000 rounds on one day in October 1952.

of the war. His principal interest was to induce the Chinese to stop fighting and withdraw. Truman entered the talks committed to sticking it out in Korea and even continuing the war against China if forced off the peninsula. Initially the two allies could not have been farther apart. After four days of intense discussions, however, the two reached a compromise solution: they would continue to fight side by side in Korea, find a line and hold it, and wait for an opportunity to negotiate an end to the fighting from a position of military strength. Moreover, they reaffirmed their commitment to "Europe first" in the face of Soviet hostility toward NATO. In essence the decision to unify Korea was abrogated and a new war aim adopted.

Significantly, the most immediate military effect of the talks was to prevent MacArthur from exacting revenge for his humiliating defeat. The Joint Chiefs limited his reinforcements to replacements, shifted the priority of military resources to strengthening NATO forces, and wrote a new directive for MacArthur that required him to defend in Korea as far to the north as possible. MacArthur was outraged. He disagreed with giving priority to Europe at the expense of the shooting war in Korea. He smoldered at the thought of going on the strategic defensive and fought determinedly against the new directive. Nevertheless, on January 12, 1951, the JCS sent him the final version of the order to conduct a strategic defensive. In essence, U.N. forces had a new war aim designed to bring about a negotiated settlement.

Ridgway's War

Just two days before Christmas in 1950, the command of Eighth Army passed to Lieutenant General Matthew B. Ridgway after General Walker died when a Korean truck hit his jeep. Ridgway arrived at his new headquarters determined to halt the retreat and to attack north as soon as possible. Somehow he had to reunite X Corps with Eighth Army, stop the retreat, and turn the army around. He also had to revive the fighting spirit of his troops.

General Douglas MacArthur and General Matthew B. Ridgway. Ridgway carefully tailored operations to correct the problems of Eighth Army. His self-assurance and his success soon restored the confidence of Eighth Army.

One of the immediate problems he faced was the separation of X Corps in Hungnam on the east coast from Eighth Army on the western flank. As Eighth Army fell back, the gap between the two forces increased, and on December 13, X Corps was evacuated by sea from Hungnam. As Eighth Army continued falling back, Ridgway's American I and IX Corps held the western sector, while a ROK Corps held the eastern end of the line. Two other ROK corps stretched themselves over the extended mountainous center. Unfortunately for the U.N. forces, Chinese and North Korean units could easily penetrate the center in a southwesterly direction and force Eighth Army to move farther south to avoid being trapped in the Seoul area by having its right flank enveloped or turned. The difficulties of this tactical situation had plagued Walker, and now, even as FEAF conducted a furious five-day air assault to halt the enemy's advance, a Chinese and North Korean penetration forced Ridgway to give up Seoul and fall below a line between Osan and Samch'ok (on the east coast).

After Ridgway pulled back, his front-line units reported only light contact with the enemy, leading him to conclude that Chinese units were unable to maintain pressure. Sensing the opportunity to turn on the Chinese, Ridgway halted on a line from P'yongt'aek in the west to Samch'ok on the east coast. When American divisions, withdrawn from Hungnam with X Corps, moved up to thicken the line in the lightly held center, Ridgway ordered his forces to patrol north and find the enemy. His offensive campaign began with an attack by the tank-supported 27th Regimental Combat Team on January 15. He next sent IX Corps units toward Inchon on the 22nd. An attack by I and IX Corps units then aimed north of Suwon and Yoju toward the Han River on the 25th. By February 10, I Corps had reached the Han River and captured Inchon and Kimp'o Airfield near Seoul.

Ridgway now looked to X Corps in the central sector to drive north against Wonju and Hoengsong. Although X Corps enjoyed early success, two CCF armies and a North Korean corps attacked south through gaps in the ROK sector to the east. They broke through three ROK divisions and forced X Corps to withdraw to Wonju. As the enemy attempted once again to drive southwest, bitter fighting raged around Wonju and Chip'yongni, the southern and northern shoulders of the penetration. Ridgway filled the gap between the two towns, defenders held the shoulders by heroic sacrifice, and the U.N. command defeated the enemy attack.

In what amounted to a renewal of his previous attack, Ridgway sent IX and X Corps north in Operation "Killer" on February 21. After Chinese and North Korean pressure subsided along the new front stretching from Chip'yongni southeastward through Wonju to Chech'on, extensive patrolling by U.N. forces disclosed that the enemy was pulling back from the salient created by their attack. Patrols reported bits of information that painted a fairly convincing picture of an army badly in need of reorganization and resupply. Though intelligence officers could not account for all the enemy forces in Korea, they nonetheless identified five Chinese armies and three North Korean corps in front of the allies. Ridgway judged the potential gains of a quick offensive to be worth the risks of an incomplete intelligence picture. He believed a rapid resumption of the U.N. offensive would take

U.N. Counteroffensive, January 24 – April 21, 1951

advantage of the weakened condition of the Chinese and North Korean soldiers and inflict a large number of casualties.

Ridgway's plan included an objective line known as Arizona, that ran
from Yangp'yong on the Han River, to north of Chip'yongni and Wonju, and
then to Kangnung on the east coast. Line Arizona was about twenty kilometers north of the U.N. front lines. The main effort would move along two
axes of advance, the westernmost by U.S. IX Corps, aiming from Wonju
north to Hoengsong. In the eastern sector, U.S. X Corps was to attack north
to a road junction just south of Line Arizona and then attack west across the
corps front to block further enemy withdrawal. The west flank of the attack
was to be protected by U.S. I Corps and the east flank by the ROK III
Corps. In all, eight American and ROK divisions and a British brigade
would comprise the attacking force, and the rest of the army would support.
The operation was code-named Killer to emphasize its main purpose.

Ridgway wanted Eighth Army units to learn from the mistakes of
previous operations. He warned corps commanders to maintain tight contact between adjacent frontline units and to avoid the gaps that had doomed

South Koreans poured forth by the thousands to repel the invaders, but they initially
performed poorly because of inexperienced leaders and inadequate training. Not until
entire ROK divisions were withdrawn from the lines and sent through training programs
did they become—to use Ridgway's words—"first rate fighting forces."

the previous attack. He wanted units to advance along the high ground and
envelope enemy positions rather than assault them frontally. As was his custom in Korea, Ridgway saw the ground advance as a series of short, methodical steps, controlled by phase lines and characterized by heavy air and
artillery fire on enemy positions before the infantry advanced.

Operation Killer began precisely as planned before dawn on February
21, except for one unforeseeable event. Up to that day, snow had covered
the ground, roads were frozen hard, and rivers and streams were covered
with thick ice. On the 21st, the temperature soared to 50 degrees Fahrenheit
and remained above freezing during daylight for the rest of the month. The
falling snow became rain, the ground thawed, roads turned into deep mud,
melting snow filled streambeds, and breaking ice rushed downstream destroying bridges and making fords impassable. Each night the surface froze
again, only to melt at sunup. Thus Operation Killer, conceived as a rapid
strike to cut off enemy forces, became a plodding advance at a speed dictated
by nature.

U.N. forces advanced toward Line Arizona against scattered delaying
forces left behind by the enemy. By the end of February, Ridgway had made
significant gains but could not catch the enemy. As the two corps labored
forward, rain, mud, and high water became the real enemies. The 1st
Marine Division of IX Corps finally reached the hills overlooking Hoengsong,

and the 7th Infantry Division of X Corps turned west to begin sweeping across the corps front. By March 6 all the objectives had been achieved. Though the infantry of Eighth Army never closed decisively with the enemy, forward units found heavy casualties littering the hills and buried in shallow graves; most were attributable to intense artillery fire and close air support.

On March 7, Ridgway launched another carefully controlled attack. When U.S. forces crossed the Han River east of Seoul, the CCF abandoned the capital; allied forces continued moving north. In early April the U.N. advance slowed as units prepared strong defensive positions in anticipation of an enemy counteroffensive. Surprisingly, the shock came not from the enemy as expected but from Washington when Truman dismissed MacArthur.

The Relief of MacArthur

One way to view MacArthur's relief is to consider it as the last step necessary to adapt the war effort to the new war aims. MacArthur bristled under the new directive requiring him to defend South Korea rather than rebuild an offensive capability to unify the peninsula. With his outrage so close to the surface, it was only a matter of time before he gave the president good reason to dismiss him.

MacArthur had been a difficult subordinate. He had clashed with Truman over U.S. policy toward Formosa early in the war and complained about the restrictions placed on his forces and his freedom to wage the war. Occasionally he had been uncommunicative with the JCS. Then after the retreat of Eighth Army, he publicly suggested that the policies of the Truman administration had been responsible for the defeat. Truman was angered by this charge, and on December 6, 1950, he published an executive order—aimed at MacArthur—requiring all government officials to clear their public statements on foreign and military policy with the administration. Mac-Arthur then objected to the JCS directive of January 12, 1951, written to implement the Truman-Attlee agreements. By requiring MacArthur to go on the defensive, that directive squelched any hope of unifying the peninsula and defeating the Chinese and North Koreans. In February and again in March, MacArthur called for a new strategy, presumably one that would permit him to attack the Chinese in their sanctuary north of the Yalu River.

As Ridgway neared the 38th Parallel again, a position of military strength seemed near at hand. President Truman took advantage of Ridgway's success to invite the Communists to negotiate a cease-fire. After reading the text of Truman's proposed message, MacArthur broadcast a bellicose ultimatum to the enemy commander undermining the president's plan. Truman was furious; MacArthur had preempted presidential prerogative, confused friends and enemies alike about who was directing the war, and directly challenged the president's authority as commander-in-chief. As Truman pondered how to handle the problem, Congressman Joseph W. Martin, Minority (Republican) Leader of the House of Representatives, released the contents of a letter from MacArthur in which the general repeated his criticism of the administration. The next day Truman began the process that was to end with MacArthur's relief from command on April 11.

Ending the War: Politics as War

After MacArthur's relief, Ridgway took his place as Commander-in-Chief, Far East and CINCUNC. Lieutenant General James A. Van Fleet, an experienced and successful World War II combat leader, took command of the Eighth Army. On April 22, as Van Fleet's army edged north, the CCF opened the expected general offensive, aiming their main attack toward Seoul in the west. The Chinese, numbering almost a half-million men, drove the U.N. defenders south. Followed closely by this formidable force, Van Fleet had to withdraw once again below the 38th Parallel, finally halting a bare eight kilometers north of Seoul.

On May 10 the Chinese jumped off again, this time concentrating seven armies in their main effort in the east-central and eastern sector of the U.N. line. They drove X Corps and two ROK corps south of the 38th Parallel

Chinese-North Korean Spring Offensive, April 21 – May 19, 1951

but paid a heavy price for thinning their front in the west. Taking advantage of the Chinese concentration in the east, Van Fleet attacked suddenly in the west, north of Seoul. The rest of the Eighth Army attacked to the front. The effect was dramatic; surprised CCF units pulled back, suffering their heaviest casualties of the war, and by the end of May found themselves retreating into North Korea. By mid-June 1951, U.N. forces had regained a line, for the most part north of the 38th Parallel. There they remained. The yearlong mobile phase of the Korean War had ended, and a strange war in which most battles were fought over the control of outposts between front lines had begun. The outpost war would continue for the next two years.

Negotiations and Stalemate

Regardless of U.N. success on the battlefield, ending the war turned out to be a maddeningly long process. U.S. planners knew that because of the Truman-Attlee agreement, the war would probably not end in a conventional victory. Obtaining a cease-fire had become an implicit war aim of the United Nations. Moreover, Chinese and North Korean commanders needed a respite from the heavy casualties sustained in Van Fleet's recent offensive. Consequently both sides agreed in late June 1951 to begin negotiations. The subsequent negotiations were initially hampered by haggling over matters of protocol and the selection of a truly neutral site. On July 26, 1951, the two sides finally agreed on an agenda containing four major points: fixing a demarcation line and demilitarized zone, supervising the truce, handling prisoners of war, and making recommendations to the governments involved in the war. With an agenda in hand, negotiators at Panmunjom began the lengthy process of debating each item. Meanwhile, the fighting continued.

After receiving reinforcements in early summer, Van Fleet conducted limited attacks to strengthen his defensive line and keep pressure on the Communists. All across the front, divisions sent combat teams forward to capture key terrain features. By the end of October, Van Fleet had a new and more commanding line that provided tactical advantage to Eighth Army. He wanted to continue his attacks, but Ridgway directed him to stop and carry on an "active defense." At stake was the success of negotiations aimed at establishing a demarcation line.

On November 17 the U.N. delegation presented the Communists with a proposal to designate the current line of contact as the demarcation line, provided that all remaining agenda items were resolved within thirty days. The allies believed this proposal would make possible an early resolution of differences and a quick end to the war. But it also provided the Communists a windfall opportunity, for they could negotiate the agenda items while strengthening their defensive positions. At the end of the thirty days, the U.N. would have no agreement and would face a defensive zone too formidable to crack with the forces at hand. The communist negotiators accepted the proposal on November 27; on December 27 the United Nations faced an enemy defensive line so deeply dug in that both sides had to accept a stalemate. From that moment on, the battlefield regressed to a static kind of war, reminiscent of World War I.

As ground action waned, the United Nations turned to powerful air and naval arms for military pressure to support its negotiating team. In August 1951, air, naval, and marine commanders concentrated all available aircraft on the interdiction of Communist-controlled bridges, highways, railroad lines and yards, and supply points. Most of the air assets took part in Operation "Strangle," a road and rail-cutting scheme designed to slow down the southward movement of enemy troops and matériel. Operation "Saturate," which followed Strangle, placed even greater emphasis on the railway-interdiction effort. During the day, fighter-bombers raked the railroad lines; at night, B-26s scoured the countryside for trucks. Approximately ninety-six fighter sorties a day continued to provide close air support to the ground war. Despite the heavy bombing, enemy work details devised ingenious ways to repair the railroad overnight. The North Korean Railroad Bureau employed three brigades full time on railroad repair and, at the height of the air campaign, used as many as 500,000 soldiers and civilians to keep the lines open. The sustained bombing campaign also forced the communist air forces out of their Manchurian sanctuary in an attempt to stop interdiction of roads and rail lines. Beginning in September 1951, communist MiG-15s became more aggressive and more numerous—as many as ninety at a time entered North Korean airspace—bringing an end to the allies' uncontested control of the air. When communist fighters chose to challenge U.N. aircraft, however, they suffered heavy losses.

Beginning in May 1952, the United Nations used air power more forcefully to place greater pressure on the Communists. Despite numerous attacks on supply centers, transportation networks, and personnel, neither the North Koreans nor the Chinese acceded to the U.N. armistice terms; on the contrary, both became more intransigent and refused to yield to such pressure. As a result, aerial bombing added to the Communists' difficulties but it did not succeed in driving them from the war.

Achieving a Cease-Fire

After the winter of 1951–1952, the war in Korea became a seemingly endless succession of violent fire fights, most of them at night, to gain or maintain control of hills that were a little higher and ridges that were a bit straighter. Sharp fighting occurred over places with such names as Pork Chop Hill, Sniper's Ridge, Old Baldy, T-Bone, White Horse, and a hundred other hilltops between the two armies. In some cases, both sides piled on reinforcements until "terrain grabs" turned into prolonged and bloody fights. All of them, no matter how large the forces engaged, were deadly encounters designed to provide leverage for one side or the other in the protracted political war going on at Panmunjom. In an era when technology provided great mobility, tactical warfare in Korea went through a regression that can be explained only in terms of its close relationships to the negotiations. Constant pressure was its purpose, not victory on the battlefield. Pressure in such a stalemated war proved difficult for a democracy to maintain.

U.N. Offensive over the 38th Parallel May 19, 1951; and Stalemate, June 24, 1951 – July 27, 1953

Outpost Eerie, a battle fought in March 1952, is a good example of a small-unit action typical of the fighting during the stalemate. Eerie was located on the southernmost hilltop on a T-bone shaped complex of ridges and hills. The Chinese held the top of the "T," about 1.5 kilometers to the north of Eerie. The Americans on Outpost Eerie came from Company K, 179th Infantry Regiment, 45th Infantry Division. They normally occupied the hill with two rifle squads, a light machine gun, a 60-mm mortar, and a platoon command group. Supporting fires came from .50-caliber machine guns on the main line of resistance, mortars from the K Company weapons platoon, and artillery from a direct-support battalion. To strengthen their position, the Americans on Eerie dug trenches, built bunkers, and encircled their position with three barbed-wire fences.

Lieutenant Omer Manley's 3rd Platoon of Company K occupied the outpost on March 21. At about 2300 hours, Manley received reports of the Chinese setting up a machine gun on a hill about 600 meters from Eerie. An

American patrol also encountered a platoon-sized enemy formation moving south. After two trip flares went off, the Chinese poured machine-gun fire onto the American position and began trying to break through the wire in two places. Lieutenant Manley called for artillery support and illuminating rounds, while his soldiers fired at the oncoming Chinese. By 0100 hours, the Americans had run out of illuminating rounds, and the Chinese had breached the wire. The Chinese seized the north end of the outpost and advanced across the top of the bunkers. The Americans were pushed to the southern end of the position and soon ran out of ammunition. Manley disappeared after throwing his empty carbine at a Chinese soldier.

At 0120 hours, communications with Eerie ended, and the commander of Company K called for artillery concentrations directly on the outpost. As soon as the artillery firing began, the Chinese withdrew. Company K then advanced to clear the outpost and search for survivors. Of the twenty-six men in Eerie, eight were dead, four wounded, and two missing. Manley could not be found. After discovering thirty-one enemy bodies inside and around the position, Company K repaired the defenses of the outpost and prepared to defend it against the next attack.

As fights such as the one at Outpost Eerie continued nightly, negotiators in Panmunjom plodded through the remaining agenda items. Results came slowly. One extremely contentious issue pertained to the supervision of the armistice agreement. Ridgway wanted an armistice commission with free access to all of Korea and an agreement to ban reinforcement of men and matériel. The Communists countered with a proposal that denied free access and contained no provision for reinforcements or replacements of any kind. Finally a compromise emerged that permitted rotation of 35,000 troops and supplies each month through specified ports of entry. Both sides accepted Swedish, Swiss, Polish, and Czech membership on an armistice commission. The last agenda item on political recommendations was settled quickly; both sides called for a conference to convene three months after a cease-fire. All political issues not settled during the negotiations would be discussed at that conference.

What to do about prisoners of war became the final obstacle to an agreement to end the war. Fearing mistreatment by the Communists, the U.N. Command wanted prisoners to decide for themselves whether or not they would return home. The Communists insisted on forced repatriation as was called for in the Geneva Convention. To restore movement to the talks, the U.N. delegation proposed that prisoners be polled by the International Red Cross about where they wanted to go. The Chinese and North Koreans agreed. When the Red Cross made interim results of the screening known early in April 1952, the data surprised everyone. Of 132,000 Chinese and North Korean prisoners screened, only 54,000 North Koreans and 5,100 Chinese wanted to go home. The communist delegation was incredulous and accused the United Nations of influencing the poll. From that moment on, negotiations bogged down on the prisoner-of-war issue.

At about this same time, May 1952, General Ridgway left Tokyo to become Supreme Allied Commander, Europe. General Mark Clark, who

A U.S. rifle squad attacks. As the stalemate continued, fighting often degenerated into clashes between patrols. Eighth Army sometimes conducted raids by concentrating artillery and air strikes and then sending in small ground forces against the enemy.

had made his reputation during World War II in Italy, replaced Ridgway as CINCUNC. Ridgway's last problem, and Clark's first, was to settle an uprising by hard-core prisoners on Koje-do, an island off the coast of South Korea. In an attempt to derail screening of all prisoners, leaders inside the prisons deliberately provoked their guards. Their crowning success was capturing the camp commander in an unguarded moment and forcing him to terminate forcible screening and to negotiate for humane treatment of prisoners. The Communists trumpeted acceptance of these terms as an admission of inhumane treatment and tampering with the Red Cross poll. Clark was furious and relieved the camp commander. After being reinforced with combat troops, the new camp commander stormed the compounds with tank-infantry teams and isolated the hard-core communist leaders in separate compounds.

The Koje-do incident hurt the negotiating position of the U.N. delegation. Friends, enemies, and neutrals decried the violent suppression of the prisoners, and communist negotiators became intractable on the prisoner-of-war issue. Over the summer of 1952, the language of negotiation became more abusive and inflammatory. Clark had had enough. In exasperation, he ordered the U.N. delegation to walk out of Panmunjom on October 8. With no one to refute their assertions, the Communists gained a major political victory and hammered away at U.N. treatment of prisoners and alleged U.N. violations of the neutral zones surrounding the negotiating site.

Early in 1953 the newly elected president, Dwight D. Eisenhower, increased pressure on the Communists. He believed that the Truman strategy was the only practical one but also believed that something had to be done to give the Communists an incentive to reach agreement. He permitted the air force to bomb dams in North Korea and to flood the countryside. He instructed the JCS to prepare plans for more intensive and mobile battles should negotiations break down. He deployed atomic delivery aircraft to the Far East and ordered them to train for low-level attacks with atomic bombs. And he let it be known that the United States was prepared to renew the war at a higher level unless progress was made at Panmunjom. As the Americans signaled their intentions to expand the war, the death of Joseph Stalin on March 5, 1953, brought on a deadly power struggle in the Kremlin that probably focused Soviet leaders' attention on internal problems rather than a prolonged war. With economic problems adding to political and military concerns, communist leaders in the Soviet Union, China, and North Korea had sufficient reasons to question the continuation of the war.

On March 28, 1953, China and North Korea agreed to an exchange of sick and wounded prisoners and suggested that this might lead to settlement of the entire prisoner-of-war issue and a cease-fire. On April 20, 684 Americans returned to U.N. control and 5,194 North Koreans, 1,030

An army nurse providing care to a soldier. With its helicopters, radio dispatch system, and treatment facilities, the Mobile Army Surgical Hospital (MASH) provided better medical care than what had been available in previous wars.

Chinese, and 447 civilians went over to the communist authorities. On April 26, negotiating sessions resumed at Panmunjom. In the following months, negotiators agreed that repatriation was to be offered to all prisoners and that those who chose not to return home were to be turned over to a neutral commission that would hold them for interview by their respective countrymen before releasing them.

While the United Nations worked diligently toward an armistice, Syngman Rhee, the South Korean president, became obstructive; he had long demanded the withdrawal of the Chinese from the Korean peninsula and the disarming of the North Korean army. On the night of June 18, Rhee ordered his guards on the prisons to release the friendly North Koreans. During the hours of darkness, 25,000 prisoners disappeared, absorbed into South Korean society. Though Eisenhower was outraged, he convinced Rhee not to undermine the armistice.

As the final details of the agreement were negotiated, the Communists sought one last military advantage. Their goal was to mount an offensive that would end at the same time that the truce agreement was signed, thus giving the illusion of a peaceful settlement following a communist victory. They sought to straighten the line in front of the ROK II Corps. Terrain objectives were limited to outpost hills in adjacent American sectors. The attacks began against the ROK II Corps on June 10, and by June 16 the U.N. line had been pushed 4,000 meters south. Eighth Army reinforced the ROK II Corps sector for a counterattack, but it was too late. Although some ground was recovered, fighting slackened as commanders of the contending armies prepared to sign the truce.

On July 27, 1953, Mark Clark signed the armistice documents to end the fighting in the Korean War.

*   *   *   *

For a war intended to be limited, the Korean War exacted a staggering human toll. Although CCF and North Korean casualties are unknown, estimates of total losses range between 1.5 and 2 million, plus perhaps 1 million civilians. The U.N. Command suffered a total of 88,000 killed, of whom 23,300 were American. Total casualties for the U.N. (killed, wounded, missing) were 459,360; of these 300,000 were South Korean. For decades after the war, the two armies continued watching each other over the demilitarized zone and waiting for the day when fighting might begin again.

Until the outbreak of the Korean War, the Cold War had been waged mainly with economic, political, and psychological weapons. War in Korea, however, redefined the conflict between the United States and the Soviet Union as a much more dangerous contest in the nuclear age. Virtually all international incidents thereafter became crises that had the potential for global consequences. No inhabited region of the world was exempt. The antagonists and their allies in NATO and the Warsaw Pact armed themselves and enlisted other states to take sides.

Not surprisingly, after five years of minimal spending for defense, the Korean War also changed the military policy of the United States. Out went austerity as big defense budgets permanently rearmed American as well as allied forces. The war increased the number of U.S. military forces stationed overseas, particularly in Europe. It fostered a peacetime selective service system, the largest standing military force in the nation's history, and the growth of an unprecedented military-scientific-industrial alliance that greatly influenced the world economy thereafter. And it created effective military readiness aimed at going to war with little or no warning.

Perhaps most important in the history of warfare, Korea became a model for limited war and demonstrated alternative ways of gaining national objectives without resorting to atomic war. For the United States, it had been a war limited in scope and violence and fought for alliance objectives. For the communist forces, it had been a war that relied on prolonged armistice negotiations to gain what could not be gained on the battlefield. Thus the significance of the Korean War is less about changes in the technical methods of waging war than about the difficulties and complexities of attaining political goals through the use of military force.

SUGGESTED READINGS

Appleman, Roy E. *South to the Naktong, North to the Yalu, June-November 1950* (Washington, D. C.: Government Printing Office, 1961).

Clark, Mark W. *From the Danube to the Yalu* (New York: Harper, 1954).

Collins, J. Lawton. *War in Peacetime: The History and Lessons of Korea* (Boston: Houghton Mifflin, 1969).

Foot, Rosemary. *A Substitute for Victory: The Politics of Peacemaking at the Korean Armistice Talks* (Ithaca, N.Y.: Cornell University Press, 1990).

Futrell, Robert F. *The United States Air Force in Korea, 1950-1953* (Washington, D.C.: Government Printing Office, 1983).

Goodrich, Leland M. *Korea: A Study of U.S. Policy in the United Nations* (New York: Council on Foreign Relations, 1956).

Goulden, Joseph C. *Korea: The Untold Story of the War* (New York: Times Books, 1982).

Hermes, Walter G. *Truce Tent and Fighting Front* (Washington, D.C.: Government Printing Office, 1966).

Kaufman, Burton I. *The Korean War: Challenges in Crisis, Credibility, and Command* (New York: Knopf, 1986).

Marshall, S. L. A. *The River and the Gauntlet* (New York: Morrow, 1953).

Mossman, Billy C. *Ebb and Flow, November 1950–July 1951* (Washington, D.C.: Government Printing Office, 1990).

Rees, David. *Korea: The Limited War* (New York: St. Martin's Press, 1964).

Ridgway, Matthew B. *The Korean War* (Garden City, N.Y.: Doubleday, 1967).

Schnabel, James F. *Policy and Direction, The First Year* (Washington, D.C.: Government Printing Office, 1972).

29

THE VIETNAM WAR, 1961–1975: REVOLUTIONARY AND CONVENTIONAL WARFARE IN AN ERA OF LIMITED WAR

The war in Vietnam represented a clash between two very different types of warfare. Fought on the Indochinese peninsula during the years 1961–1975, a direct offshoot of the Cold War, it matched the "revolutionary war" techniques of North Vietnam and the National Liberation Front of South Vietnam (NLF) insurgents against the limited war doctrines and modern, high-technology conventional forces of the United States and its South Vietnamese ally. Militarily, the two sides fought to a prolonged and bloody stalemate. As a consequence, the political dimensions of the war ultimately proved decisive. As long as the North Vietnamese and NLF did not lose, they won, and they successfully employed a protracted war strategy to take advantage of American impatience. Unwilling to expand the war to win in the traditional sense, the United States could do no better than a stalemate, and the war's increasing unpopularity at home eventually forced a U.S. military withdrawal. The United States' military power had never been able to compensate for the political weakness of its client government, and when the United States withdrew, the Saigon regime collapsed in the face of a full-scale North Vietnamese invasion. Whether the war validated North Vietnam's revolutionary war doctrines remains very much in doubt in light of the end of the Cold War. It did prove the difficulty of fighting a limited war in the Cold War setting, and it provoked a major reconsideration of U.S. military doctrine, the outcome of which also remains quite uncertain.

Vietnam and "People's War"

During their thirty-year war against France and the United States the Vietnamese applied a concept variously labeled "People's War" or "Revolutionary War." The Vietnamese approach to warfare was multifaceted, combining military, political, and diplomatic measures in a tightly integrated manner. Even in the military realm, it involved guerrilla warfare as well as more conventional methods. The Vietnamese relied especially on a mobilized citizenry and the application of a protracted war strategy, and in both their wars with France and the United States, they counted on wearing down less patient enemies fighting unpopular wars far from their shores.

A Martial Tradition

The Vietnamese drew on a rich military tradition that was an essential part of their heritage. For roughly one thousand years, the land of Nam Viet (later Vietnam) was the southernmost province of China. During much of that time, the Vietnamese had fiercely resisted the domination of their larger northern neighbor. Perhaps the most famous of Vietnamese heroes, the Trung sisters, mounted elephants to lead the first major rebellion against a much superior Chinese force and, when defeated, drowned themselves in a lake in Hanoi. Another woman, Trieu Au, led yet another unsuccessful revolt in 248 A.D. In the tenth century the Vietnamese won their independence by luring an attacking Chinese fleet into a river bed in which they had planted iron-tipped spikes, impaling the ships of the invaders.

In the thirteenth century, the Vietnamese repulsed the legendary Mongol warrior Kublai Khan three times. Using the inhospitable climate and terrain to advantage, their leader, Tran Hung Dao, pioneered methods of guerrilla warfare later used against the French and Americans, avoiding head-on engagements and employing hit-and-run tactics to exhaust a stronger enemy. In his *Essential Summary of Military Arts*, Dao observed that "The enemy must fight his battles far from his home base for a long time. . . . We must further weaken him by drawing him into protracted campaigns. Once his initial dash is broken, it will be easier to destroy him." In the climactic battle against the Mongols in the Red River Valley in 1287, the Vietnamese defeated three hundred thousand enemy troops. Finally, in 1426, another legendary figure, Le Loi, defeated the Chinese and secured independence for Vietnam.

The years of resistance to China and the victories over the Mongols comprise an essential part of Vietnamese folklore. "Through the millennia of their history the Vietnamese people have struggled incessantly against foreign invaders . . . in great battles that took place one century after another," a contemporary history observes. In their own mythology, the Vietnamese repeatedly win against stronger enemies through cleverness, ingenuity, and virtue, and because of their ability to mobilize all the people, to make every citizen a soldier. "We fight and win . . . because we are . . . moral, loyal, patient, strong, indomitable, filled with compassion," Communist party chief Le Duan told soldiers during the American war. "We have been fighting for our independence for four thousand years," Premier Pham Van Dong warned the Americans through two French emissaries in 1967. "We have defeated the Mongols three times. The United States Army, strong as it is, is not as terrifying as Genghis [sic] Khan."

Although it is less celebrated by the Vietnamese, expansion to the south forms as important a part of their military heritage as resistance to northern invaders. After defeating the Mongols, they moved southward to conquer the kingdom of Champa and after nearly two centuries of fighting destroyed its capital of Indrapura and killed 40,000 people. National unity was always a fragile matter, however, and civil war continued until the French imposed peace on Vietnam through colonization.

Ironically in view of their long history of conflict, the Vietnamese approach to warfare also drew heavily on Chinese models, especially the ideas developed by Mao Zedong during the Chinese civil war. Maoist doctrine emphasized the formation of a broad united front comprised of all elements of the population with the goal of national liberation, recognized the equal importance of political and military struggle, and relied on protracted war to exhaust stronger enemies.

Mao's classic *On Protracted War* set forth three stages of revolutionary warfare. In the first, essentially defensive stage, the revolutionary force was to withdraw, hide from the enemy, and mount sporadic hit-and-run attacks, the main goal being survival. During this phase, the focus was on revolutionary activity among the people to establish a secure base for future operations. Terrain was to be exchanged for time. Second came a stage of equilibrium, when caution began to give way to boldness and the defensive to the offensive. The guerrillas in this stage would extend their hold across the countryside and force the enemy to retreat into shrinking urban enclaves. Battles were larger, more frequent, and more conventional. The third and final stage of Maoist protracted warfare was the counteroffensive, when politics gave way to military operations and guerrilla warfare to full-scale conventional war.

The First Indochina War, 1946–1954

The three-decade struggle for Indochina began September 2, 1945, when the charismatic nationalist leader Ho Chi Minh declared the independence of Vietnam. The Vietnamese revolution was in many ways the personal

During World War II, Nguyen Ai Quoc changed his name to Ho Chi Minh ("he who enlightens") to conceal his communist background from his Chinese sponsors in the war against the Japanese. Beginning in spring 1945, Americans from the Office of Strategic Services served at Ho's headquarters in an effort to hasten the defeat of the Japanese.

creation of Ho Chi Minh. Born in the province of Nghe An, the cradle of Vietnamese revolutionaries, Ho settled in France and after World War I joined the French Communist Party. During the 1920s and 1930s, he served as a party functionary and revolutionary organizer in the Soviet Union, China, and Thailand. He returned to Vietnam in 1940 to found the Vietminh (League for the Independence of Vietnam) and organize yet another Vietnamese revolution against outside control. For a brief period after World War II, Ho attempted to negotiate a settlement with the colonial power, France, but the two sides could not agree on the most basic issues. In November 1946 mounting tensions sparked a war that in its various phases would last for nearly thirty years.

In their revolutionary war against France, the Vietnamese adapted Maoist doctrine to their own needs and conditions. Space was at a premium in Vietnam, and instead of trading terrain for time, as Mao had proposed, the Communist-led Vietminh rebels emphasized in the first stage organization and clandestine activity. From small cells of three to five people, they constructed "liberated areas." Avoiding pitched battles, they cultivated support among the people and where feasible ambushed exposed enemy forces. The Vietnamese also placed greater emphasis than Mao on external forces, increasingly relying on moral and material support from the Soviet Union and after 1949 from Mao's China. Perhaps even more important, public opinion in France was deemed crucial in influencing French policy, and the Vietnamese calculated that the longer the war lasted the more support would be generated for their cause. Given these factors, party theoretician Truong Chinh reasoned, absolute military superiority might not be necessary to launch the third and climactic phase of revolutionary war. To the Vietminh also, the third stage, although predominantly military, remained a civil war in which political struggle continued to be vital.

The Vietminh applied these ideas with some modification in the conflict against France. After the outbreak of war in late 1946, they melted into the countryside, concentrating on avoiding pitched battles, mobilizing the population into a united anti-French front, and harassing French forces. In January 1948, the Vietminh leadership announced the second stage of equilibrium warfare where they sought to regain the initiative, wear down enemy forces, and expand the territory under their control. The emphasis was still on guerrilla warfare, but larger units were created to mount mobile operations over large areas. The communist victory in China in 1949 significantly altered the character of the war in Vietnam, making available to the Vietminh material aid and protected sanctuaries. Thus buoyed, they prematurely shifted to the third phase in 1951, launching an offensive that proved disastrous. After three more years, in which they combined vigorous political activity in the countryside, guerrilla warfare, and conventional operations, the Vietminh mounted the climactic battle. General Vo Nguyen Giap pulled off a logistical miracle by moving vast numbers of men and quantities of supplies through mountainous terrain into a position to attack. Surrounding isolated French forces at the remote outpost of Dien Bien Phu in the northwestern corner of Vietnam, they gradually closed the ring and, while the world watched, decisively defeated a major European power.

The war won by the Vietminh at Dien Bien Phu was lost at the conference table in Geneva. Largely at the insistence of its allies, the Soviet Union and China, the Vietminh was compelled to accept a temporary partition of its country with national elections to be held in 1956. It took control of the area above the seventeenth parallel. In the south, however, a government headed by Ngo Dinh Diem and backed by the United States used the two-year interval to establish a separate South Vietnam, undermining the spirit if not the precise letter of the Geneva Accords. The Diem government ignored the call for elections in 1956. It also launched a ruthless and highly effective campaign to root out former Vietminh operatives who remained in the south.

Origins of the Second Indochina War

On the verge of extinction by 1957, the southern Vietminh launched a rebellion that would eventually grow into the Second Indochina War. Seeking merely to salvage what remained of the revolution of 1945, they mounted an armed struggle against the government, reactivating the intelligence and propaganda networks that had fallen into disuse after Geneva and initiating a vigorous campaign of political agitation in the villages. Largely as a result of Diem's oppressive policies, they found a receptive audience in the countryside—the peasants were like a "mound of straw ready to be ignited." The Vietminh attracted thousands of adherents and established a presence in numerous villages. The level of violence increased dramatically. In 1958, an estimated 700 government officials were assassinated; in 1960, 2,500. In

December 1960 the insurgents formed the National Liberation Front (NLF), a broad-based organization led by Communists but designed to rally all those disaffected with Diem by promising sweeping reforms and genuine independence.

North Vietnam gradually committed itself to the southern insurgency. In March 1957, Hanoi approved plans to modernize its own armed forces. Two years later, it formally authorized the resumption of armed struggle in the south and took measures to back it. The North Vietnamese established a special force to construct a supply route into the south—what would become the famed Ho Chi Minh Trail. They gradually increased the flow of men and matériel into the south and in September 1960 formally approved the shift to armed struggle.

From 1960 to 1965, the insurgency grew dramatically. Following the overthrow and assassination of Diem in a coup backed by the United States, South Vietnam degenerated into chaos, government succeeding government as through a revolving door. In December 1963, Hanoi instructed the NLF to step up its political agitation and military operations against the embattled South Vietnamese government. More important, it expanded infiltration into the south and even began to commit units of its own regular army. Over the next two years, the NLF extended its political control over the countryside, and its military units mounted increasingly bold attacks against South Vietnamese forces. The People's Army of North Vietnam (PAVN) was prepared for battle in the south. United States officials concluded by early 1965 that if they did not take drastic measures, South Vietnam would soon fall to the insurgents.

The NLF, PAVN, and Revolutionary War

To gain the upper hand in South Vietnam, NLF forces skillfully combined political and military "struggle." Their aims were to undermine the enemy's military and political positions and rally the people to their cause. In the political realm, NLF cadres created special organizations to give status to groups such as farmers, women, and youth. They used agitation and propaganda—"agitprop"—to arouse the people to the government's oppressiveness and lack of responsibility. They played to local grievances and used songs, skits, and speeches to explain their own program in terms the people could understand. Creating a mass organization where none had existed, they established a tightly knit political-military movement operating with often deadly efficiency from the village level to the central committee. By 1963, NLF strength in the rural areas of South Vietnam had grown to an estimated 300,000 people.

The NLF also assembled a highly disciplined and potent military organization. NLF main forces comprised some forty-seven battalions organized into five regiments and numbering by 1965 an estimated 80,000 of the "toughest, most experienced guerrilla fighters to be found anywhere in the world." Lightly equipped, usually clothed in the traditional black pajamas rather than uniforms, they relied on speed, surprise, and deception. Targets were chosen for maximum psychological significance, the NLF attacking villages and killing people who were deemed the greatest threats to their cause. They used violence selectively and judiciously to attain specified political ends—in general, to coerce or win over the population and undermine the legitimacy of the Saigon government. NLF units ambushed the forces of the South Vietnamese army (ARVN), attacked government-controlled hamlets, and sabotaged government communication links such as bridges, roads, and telephone or telegraph installations. They sought to provoke government officials to take oppressive measures that could be exploited politically. They assassinated and kidnapped village leaders who might cause problems for them, singling out those good officials whose removal could weaken the government and bad ones whose elimination could gain support for their cause.

The Main Forces were backed up by a popular army that operated at the village and hamlet level, a poorly equipped part-time guerrilla force of some 85,000 that worked the fields by day and ambushed and sabotaged by night.

By 1965, NLF forces were supported and in some areas supplanted by North Vietnamese regulars. Trained, organized, and equipped along Chinese lines, the People's Army of Vietnam numbered as many as 500,000 men and was supplemented by a ready reserve also of close to a half-million. Its divisions each possessed an authorized strength of 10,000 men, lightly armed and equipped for maximum mobility. Infantrymen generally carried Chinese-made pistols, 7.62-mm rifles, and three to five "potato-masher" grenades. Infantry divisions consisted of three infantry regiments when in the south, backed by weapons companies armed with 60-mm and 82-mm mortars, 57-mm and 75-mm recoilless rifles, and heavy machine guns. Training emphasized camouflage, the use of explosives, and small-unit tactics; field exercises were often conducted at night and under the most adverse conditions. The North Vietnamese made a virtue of the necessity of their light armament by constantly emphasizing that men, not weapons, constituted the decisive element in war. "People's war, not modern weapons and techniques, decides victory because war is the most acute form of struggle between man and man," party theorist Truong Chinh proclaimed in 1965.

The PAVN attempted to compensate for its weakness in firepower with rigorous discipline, tactical superiority, and careful preparation. As much as 50 percent of the training time of the PAVN soldier was spent in political education, and political commissars accompanied every unit above the company level. In battle, the North Vietnamese attempted to use the terrain to their best advantage, digging in even during rest periods and developing camouflage into a fine art. They tried to avoid battle except under favorable conditions and attacked the enemy at weak points rather than strong ones. They did not attempt to hold ground but rather sought to attack and withdraw before the enemy could react, hoping to inflict maximum casualties with rifles and automatic weapons in the opening moments of the fight. They were masters of the ambush. Actions of all sorts were planned and rehearsed with painstaking care. North Vietnamese units might take as much as a month to prepare the battlefield, massing ammunition and supplies, digging intricate systems of underground trenches, and stocking food and ammunition at attack points, ambush sites, and along withdrawal routes.

Mobility and small-unit maneuver were the hallmarks of North Vietnamese tactics. To minimize the impact of enemy firepower, PAVN forces attempted to close with the enemy as quickly as possible and to maintain close contact, even to the point of "hugging" and hand-to-hand combat. They preferred to overwhelm enemy forces by massing strength at a single point, and they excelled at encircling maneuvers with fifty to seventy-five men. Survival on the battlefield often depended on the ability to disengage, and North Vietnamese tactical doctrine held that the withdrawal was as important as the advance. At times, PAVN forces counterattacked to permit disengagement. If escape routes were blocked, they might attack a weak spot and slip away through the hole. Delaying forces were usually assigned the task of ambushing and harassing pursuers. Despite the lightness of its arma-

A detachment from the People's Army of Vietnam marches down a road as North Vietnamese civilians watch.

ments and a tendency to be repetitive and mechanistic in its tactical moves, the North Vietnamese army was a formidable fighting force. The French-born combat historian Bernard Fall did not exaggerate when he described it in September 1965 as "one of the best infantry combat forces in the world, capable of incredible feats of endurance and raw courage even against vastly superior firepower and under the worst physical conditions."

The United States: Counterinsurgency and Limited War

By the mid-1960s, Vietnam had become a focal point of United States' foreign policy. Perceiving the Soviet Union as a mortal threat, the Truman administration, in the aftermath of World War II, had committed itself to the containment of communist expansion. From the outbreak of revolution in Vietnam, U.S. policy makers had viewed Ho Chi Minh's Vietminh as an instrument of Moscow's larger global designs. Thus in early 1950, the United States began to provide military and economic aid to the French to assist in the suppression of the Vietminh insurgency. By 1954, Washington was paying nearly 80 percent of the cost of the war. When the French were defeated, the United States filled the vacuum, assisting the Diem government to solidify its position and providing lavish aid to sustain in South

Vietnam an independent, non-communist government that could stand as a bulwark against further communist expansion in Southeast Asia.

In the 1960s, Vietnam became a test case for new U.S. counterinsurgency doctrines. The Eisenhower administration had responded to the outbreak of war in Vietnam by providing the Diem government additional aid and U.S. military advisers. The Kennedy administration went further. Kennedy and his advisers were persuaded that so-called "brush-fire" wars such as the one taking place in Vietnam represented the new Soviet strategy for world domination. By fighting at a low level in peripheral areas, the communist adversary could avoid a nuclear confrontation and chip away at free-world strength. Kennedy and his advisers therefore scrapped Eisenhower's New Look defense policy, which had emphasized nuclear weapons and Massive Retaliation, and adopted a strategy of "Flexible Response" that permitted different types of military moves at different levels. They launched in 1961 a massive buildup of conventional forces to balance America's nuclear arsenal and implement Flexible Response.

The Kennedy administration also placed great emphasis on counterinsurgency. The president himself took a keen interest in the subject, and the works of Mao Zedong became required reading for top U.S. officials. Kennedy gave his blessings to the U.S. Army's elite Green Berets and required all the military services to develop counterinsurgency doctrine.

The administration first applied its new ideas and methods in Vietnam. As a senator, Kennedy had once referred to Vietnam as the "cornerstone of the free world in Southeast Asia." He and his advisers increasingly viewed it as a test case of America's determination to uphold its commitments and its capacity to meet the challenges of guerrilla warfare in the emerging nations. Between 1961 and 1963, the president thus launched a full-scale counterinsurgency program in Vietnam, approving a massive increase in U.S. military and economic aid and enlarging the number of U.S. advisers to more than 16,000.

The Kennedy program attacked the NLF insurgency on several fronts. Militarily, the United States provided the South Vietnamese army the latest hardware including armored personnel carriers, helicopters, and aircraft. Buoyed by American aid and advisers, the South Vietnamese armed forces took the offensive against the guerrillas. U.S. advisers performed ever-widening tasks. Special Forces units conducted civic action programs among the primitive peoples of the Central Highlands. Helicopter pilots dropped detachments of South Vietnamese troops into battle zones deep in the swamps and picked up the dead and wounded. Americans went with Vietnamese trainees on bombing and strafing missions and, when the Vietnamese ran short of pilots, flew the planes themselves. Army officers and enlisted men conducted expanded training programs for the South Vietnamese army, and advisers down to the battalion level accompanied its units on combat missions.

U.S. military and civilian advisers also assisted the South Vietnamese government in implementing the so-called Strategic Hamlet program. Developed by the British counterinsurgency expert Sir Robert Thompson on the basis of experiences in Malaya, the program was designed to isolate the

NLF from the people of South Vietnam. Peasants from scattered villages were brought together into hamlets surrounded by moats and bamboo stake fences and defended by military forces. The hamlets were intended to protect the people against the guerrillas and also to serve as an instrument for a social and economic revolution to draw the people to the government. Village elections, land reform, and the establishment of schools and medical services were to persuade the people that life under the South Vietnamese government offered more than the NLF. The objective, U.S. counterinsurgency expert Roger Hilsman observed, was to reduce the guerrillas to "hungry, marauding bands of outlaws devoting all their energies to remaining alive," forcing them out into the open where they would have to fight the South Vietnamese army on its terms.

The Kennedy counterinsurgency program failed. The Strategic Hamlet program was flawed both in conception and execution. It had worked well in Malaya, where Malay villages were fortified against Chinese insurgents, but in Vietnam the hamlets were to be erected against Vietnamese, many of whom had lived among the villagers for years, and they were easily infiltrated. In some regions, the hamlets could not be established without massive uprooting of the peasantry, and the displacement of people from ancestral lands added to the discontent that already pervaded the countryside. In many cases, the government moved too far too fast in implementing the program, establishing hamlets in areas where no real security existed. The vulnerable settlements were thus quickly overrun or infiltrated by the insurgents. Many of the hamlets lacked adequate defenses. Some were spread over such a large area that it would have required a full division to defend them. In the hands of Diem and his sinister brother-in-law, Ngo Dinh Nhu, moreover, the program alienated the people rather than attracted them to the government.

Militarily, the Kennedy program also failed. Despite relentless pressure from the White House, the armed services refused to embrace counterinsurgency and insisted on fighting the war the way they knew how. Even with modern aircraft, it proved impossible to locate the guerrillas amidst the dense forests and swampy paddy lands. The very nature of U.S.–South Vietnamese operations, an air strike followed by the landing of troops, gave the insurgents warning and permitted them to slip away. ARVN forces would often bomb and strafe large areas and land sizable detachments of troops with little result, and when they withdrew the guerrillas simply reoccupied the region. The insurgents learned how to bring down slow, clumsy helicopters with small arms. Sometimes they would lie in hiding until the helicopters had departed and then ambush the landing force. As operations became more costly, ARVN commanders, apparently under orders from Diem, relied more and more on air power and refused to risk their troops in battle.

The Battle of Ap Bac, 1963

The shift in the fortunes of war was dramatically revealed in January 1963. An American adviser, the legendary Colonel John Paul Vann, pressed his

South Vietnamese division commander to attack three guerrilla companies near the village of Ap Bac. The South Vietnamese commander delayed for a day, giving the NLF time to learn of the operation and prepare deadly defenses. Outnumbering the enemy ten to one—the classic ratio for success against guerrillas—the South Vietnamese planned a three-pronged assault. At the first signs of resistance, however, the attacking forces balked. One prong simply refused to attack. Other units failed to block enemy escape routes. The battle ended ingloriously with the South Vietnamese firing on each other while the enemy slipped away. The vastly superior ARVN forces suffered sixty-one dead and one hundred wounded, while the NLF left only three bodies behind. Continuing to think in conventional warfare terms, the U.S. command in Saigon claimed victory because the enemy had abandoned its territory. Those in the field and the American reporters who covered the action knew better.

By 1965, the United States faced a major turning point in Vietnam. Following the overthrow and assassination of Diem and the instability that followed, the NLF insurgency had gained momentum. Supported by a steadily growing flow of men and supplies from North Vietnam, the insurgents took advantage of the near anarchy in the south. By early 1965, the NLF had secured uncontested control of the vital Mekong Delta region south of Saigon and appeared capable of splitting the country in half. The corruption-ridden South Vietnamese army, even with sharply increased U.S. aid, could not slow, much less stop, the enemy onslaught.

The administration of Lyndon Baines Johnson saw little choice but to escalate the U.S. commitment. Responding to the urgent warnings of his advisers that South Vietnam was on the verge of collapse, the president in February 1965 mounted regular, sustained bombing raids against North Vietnam. The bombing had only a marginal impact on the war, however, and by late spring General William Westmoreland, head of the U.S. military assistance program in Vietnam, requested a massive increase in American military forces and the commitment of U.S. combat units to reverse a rapidly deteriorating situation. After several weeks of intensive deliberations, the president in late July made what amounted to a decision for full-scale war in Vietnam, committing himself to provide U.S. combat support as needed.

Limited War in Theory and Practice

Responding to the challenge in Vietnam, Johnson and his advisers were deeply influenced by the limited war theory so much in vogue in the United States during the 1950s and 1960s. When the Soviet Union developed effective delivery systems for nuclear weapons, it was obvious to many military theorists that the Eisenhower administration's emphasis on Massive Retaliation could not work. With nothing but nuclear weapons as a deterrent, the United States in responding to communist challenges in peripheral areas would face the unthinkable choice of starting a nuclear war or doing nothing.

To escape that dilemma and find the means to contain communist expansion without risking a nuclear holocaust, civilian and military theorists advocated the alternative of limited war. Such a strategy would harness the nation's military power more closely to the attainment of its political objectives. Through Flexible Response, a variety of military instruments would be readied to respond to different types of threats at different levels. The amount of force to be employed in any situation would be limited to that necessary to achieve the political aim. The objective was not to destroy an opponent but to persuade him to break off the conflict short of achieving his goals and without resorting to nuclear war.

The limited-war theorists provided a set of broad guidelines for the conduct of that sort of conflict. Statesmen must "scrupulously limit" the political objectives and clearly communicate them to the enemy. They must make every effort to keep open diplomatic channels to terminate the war through negotiations on the basis of limited objectives. They must keep the war precisely limited in terms of geography and must restrict the force used to that amount necessary to attain the political objectives. Limited war must be directed by the civilian leadership. The special needs of the military should not affect its conduct, and indeed the military must be a controllable instrument of national policy.

Limited-war theory also set forth methods for using military power to persuade an adversary to act in the desired way. Military action was less important for the damage it did, according to this reasoning, than for the message it sent. War became a sort of bargaining process through which force was employed to persuade an enemy that persisting in what he was doing would be too expensive to continue. "The object," political scientist Thomas Schelling observed, "is to exact good behavior or to oblige discontinuance of mischief, not to destroy the subject altogether." The implicit assumption was that the use of force could be orchestrated in such a way as to communicate precise and specific signals and that an opponent would back down in the face of such threats or pressure.

Limited-war theory had numerous flaws. It was primarily an academic, rather than a military concept, and it drastically misunderstood the dynamics of war. Its authors seemed to say that since limited war was mainly about bargaining and diplomacy, it required no knowledge of military matters and indeed military considerations should not affect its conduct. Despite the popular frustrations caused by fighting a limited war in Korea, the theorists seemed grandly indifferent to the domestic political problems it posed. Political scientist Robert Osgood conceded that this type of conflict ran counter to the American way of war and that Americans might not easily accept the "galling but indispensable restraints" required by it. But he neatly dodged the problem with platitudes, calling for candor and courage on the part of leaders and surmising that if Americans were treated as adults they would respond accordingly. Limited-war theorists also devoted more effort to explaining why this type of war should be fought rather than how it was to be fought. In terms of bargaining theory, moreover, they assumed a greater capacity than was warranted on the part of a gigantic bureaucracy like the United States government to send clear, precise signals, and they reduced the behavior of potential enemies to that of laboratory rats. These problems, however, are more obvious in retrospect than they were at the time.

The Johnson administration's strategy in Vietnam was deeply influenced by limited-war theory. Fearful that the actions they were taking to prevent a third world war might themselves provoke a dangerous confrontation with the Soviet Union and China, the president and his top civilian advisers put precise geographical limits on the war. They kept their military commanders on a tight rein, rejecting proposals to invade enemy sanctuaries in Laos, Cambodia, and North Vietnam, mine Haiphong Harbor, and bomb near the Chinese border. Vividly recalling the Korean War and the bitter controversy between President Harry S Truman and General Douglas MacArthur, Johnson and his civilian advisers fretted about military recklessness and a MacArthur-like challenge to civilian authority. "General, I have a lot riding on you," the president told Westmoreland in February 1966. "I hope you don't pull a MacArthur on me."

The administration fought the war according to the political dictates of limited-war theory. The theory of gradual escalation presumed that a steady increase in the level of military pressure would coerce an adversary into compliance. Thus the United States slowly increased the bombing and steadily expanded the number of U.S. troops and the intensity of ground operations. At no point did the president accede to the full requests of his military commanders. Yet once underway, the process of escalation achieved a momentum of its own, the failure of one level of force providing justification for the next level. By 1967, the United States had concentrated in Vietnam close to 500,000 men, roughly one-half its tactical airpower, and 30 percent of its naval strength. It was spending more than 2 billion dollars per month on the war.

A Modern, High-Tech Military Machine

The forces the United States sent to Vietnam were the best that money and modern technology could provide. During the Kennedy years, Secretary of Defense Robert S. McNamara had presided over a dramatic expansion and reorganization of the U.S. military to meet the perceived threats of a direct Soviet attack on Western Europe, limited conventional wars like Korea, and "brush-fire" wars in the Third World.

Although Vietnam was primarily a land war, air and sea power played an important role. Refitted World War II battleships pounded North Vietnamese bases from offshore. Conventional and nuclear-powered aircraft carriers were deployed in the Gulf of Tonkin, and their aircraft conducted Operation "Rolling Thunder" against North Vietnam from March 1965 until October 1968. Air force F-105 Thunderchiefs (known as "Thuds" by their pilots) carrying 7,500 pounds of bombs were also workhorses in the air war against North Vietnam. Air force and navy aircraft bombed enemy supply lines and staging areas in North and South Vietnam and flew close air-support missions for American and South Vietnamese forces in the field. The most formidable weapon—and most feared by the enemy—was the giant B-52 bomber that flew at 30,000 feet, carried a payload of 58,000 pounds, and left enormous craters in its path of destruction.

In what Westmoreland described as "the most sophisticated war in history," the United States attempted to exploit its technological superiority to cope with the peculiar problems posed by a guerrilla war. To locate an ever-elusive enemy, the military used small portable radar units and "people sniffers," which picked up the odor of human urine. IBM 1430 computers were programmed to predict likely times and places of enemy attacks. Herbicides were used on a wide scale and with devastating ecological and human consequences to deprive the NLF of natural cover. C-47 transports were converted into awesome gunships called "Puff the Magic Dragon" that could fire 18,000 rounds per minute.

The army that fought in Vietnam was one of the best clothed, best equipped, and best prepared the nation had ever sent to war. McNamara had increased the strength of the army to nearly one million men, raised the number of combat-ready divisions from eleven to sixteen, vastly expanded airlift capacity, and stockpiled huge quantities of equipment. The army was reorganized to create a flexible, adaptable organization capable of meeting its varied missions.

Innovations in equipment drastically increased its mobility and firepower. The advent of armored personnel carriers and troop-carrying helicopters significantly altered the nature of infantry operations. Helmets, pistols, and mortars were similar to those used in Korea, and machine guns and artillery were improved versions of weapons long in use, but two new

U.S. soldiers dismounting from a helicopter in a search and destroy operation. Airborne insertions often occurred when intelligence reported the presence of enemy soldiers. If the landing unit made contact with enemy forces, additional units "piled on" in an attempt to surround and destroy the enemy.

weapons vastly increased the firepower of the individual infantryman. The M-79 grenade launcher permitted the use of grenades at ranges up to 350 meters with far greater accuracy and were particularly useful in ambushes and against machine-gun nests. Claymore mines, which weighed only 3.5 pounds, were easy to place, had a destructive area of up to fifty meters, and were valuable in ambushes.

A major innovation of the 1960s was the creation of an air-cavalry division by the U.S. Army. Helicopters had been used effectively in restricted roles in Korea, and as their technology improved their potential began to seem almost limitless. They were widely employed during the advisory years in Vietnam and seemed increasingly to provide the solution to the difficult problem of locating and engaging elusive guerrillas in difficult terrain. After a period of tests, McNamara activated the 1st Cavalry Division (Airmobile) in June 1965. The new division made large-scale airmobile operations possible. Although lightly armed, it compensated with its fast-strike capability; its helicopters could land as many as 10,000 troops in battle zones within hours. Its greatest assets were its ability to cover all types of terrain, maneuver over large areas, react quickly to enemy attacks and reinforce embattled units, and conduct raids behind enemy lines. Thus by July 1965, two nations with very different military traditions and two powerful and quite different military forces were set to engage each other in Vietnam.

Escalation and Stalemate, 1965–1968

By the time the United States escalated the war in 1965, North Vietnam and the NLF appeared on the verge of victory. Sensing in the growing chaos in South Vietnam a splendid opportunity to attain long-sought goals, Hanoi had sharply escalated the war. North Vietnamese leaders still thought in terms of Maoist doctrine, a protracted struggle with victory to be attained through a series of stages. Always flexible in their thinking, however, their new strategy called for a gradual shift from low-level action to the use of large-scale military forces to annihilate enemy main forces. The final stage would be a military offensive in the rural areas and a popular uprising in the cities that would leave the United States no choice but to pull out of South Vietnam. In 1964 and 1965, the North Vietnamese implemented their strategy with great success. PAVN and NLF main forces gradually extended their control over the strategic Central Highlands of South Vietnam while NLF guerrillas scored equally impressive gains in the Mekong Delta south of Saigon. By early 1965, the insurgents controlled half the population and more than half the territory of South Vietnam. The only secure areas were the major cities, and they were increasingly threatened by civil disturbances.

In escalating the war, the Johnson administration sought to head off what seemed a certain enemy victory and to preserve an independent, non-communist South Vietnam. The administration's strategy was based on the assumption that if the United States slowly increased the level of military pain, it would reach a point at which the North Vietnamese would decide that the costs were greater than the potential gain. The Rolling Thunder bombing program initiated in March 1965 and gradually expanded thereafter was designed to reduce the infiltration of men and supplies into South Vietnam and to pressure North Vietnam into stopping its support of the insurgency. With the increased ground forces provided him in July 1965, General Westmoreland sought first to stem the momentum of communist advances in the countryside and to provide security in the urban areas. This accomplished, he planned to launch a number of major search-and-destroy operations to cripple enemy main-force units and break the NLF hold on the countryside. Once the enemy's regular forces had been destroyed, he reasoned, the South Vietnamese government would be able to stabilize its position and "pacify" the countryside, and the enemy would have no choice but to negotiate on terms acceptable to the United States. The marines were given responsibility for operations in the northern provinces (I Corps), while the army was assigned the task in the Central Highlands, along the central coast, and in the region around Saigon. In the meantime, the ARVN, with the support of U.S. civilian and military advisers, was to launch a "pacification" program to break the NLF hold on the countryside and build support for South Vietnam's government.

Battle of the Ia Drang, 1965

The first major clash of opposing armies came in the Ia Drang valley in the Central Highlands in late 1965. As part of its winter-spring campaign of 1965–1966, Hanoi ordered a PAVN army corps to execute a series of operations around Pleiku in the Central Highlands with the object of striking a knockout blow. The first stage of the operation was an attack on a U.S. Special Forces camp near Plei Me near the Cambodian border. Using a classic lure-and-ambush tactic, the North Vietnamese followed with the real object of their plan, a major attack against the South Vietnamese relief column sent to save the base. Using ground forces, artillery, and especially tactical air support and relying—as they would throughout the war—on the superiority of their firepower, the United States and South Vietnam launched a furious counterattack on the forces besieging Plei Me and repulsed the North Vietnamese ambush of the relief column. Their plan frustrated, the PAVN forces slipped away to their base areas in Cambodia. According to U.S. estimates, in this first encounter, the North Vietnamese lost as many as 850 killed and 1,700 wounded.

Seeking to follow up this initial success, Westmoreland dispatched the 1st Cavalry Division on search-and-destroy operations against retreating enemy forces. From October 28 to November 14, U.S. forces conducted a series of air and ground searches in the Ia Drang valley punctuated by sporadic and violent clashes. The largest action occurred on November 14 when four American companies fell upon a North Vietnamese regiment at

Ia Drang, November 1965

To Pleiku (40 km)

Albany

Artillery Base

Plei Me

Ia Drang R.

Ia Tae R.

X-Ray

Chu Pong Massif

Victor

North Vietnamese advances
U.S. landing zones

0   2.5   5 mi
0   2.5   5 km

CAMBODIA   SOUTH VIETNAM

landing zone X-Ray. As at Plei Me, U.S. firepower eventually saved the day,
artillery from nearby landing zones pouring more than 8,000 rounds against
enemy positions, and air force fighter-bombers and even giant B-52s from
Guam flying close air support. Pounded relentlessly for nearly two days, the
battered North Vietnamese eventually withdrew to their sanctuaries. The
following day, an American battalion stumbled into a disastrous ambush a
nearby landing zone Albany, suffering huge casualties. In all, the North Viet
namese lost an estimated 3,000 killed in the Ia Drang fighting, the United
States 300.

It remains difficult even today to assess this first (and one of the few)
major battles of the Vietnam War. Thinking in entirely conventional terms,
the U.S. military claimed victory because of the heavy losses it inflicted and
because the enemy had been forced to withdraw from the battlefield. Some
commentators also hailed as unusual if not indeed unique among America's
first battles the outstanding performance of U.S. troops in this, their "blood-
ing." North Vietnam indeed suffered staggering losses. In the aftermath of
the Ia Drang, Giap reverted to guerrilla warfare and made major tactical
adjustments to better cope with U.S. firepower. Still, U.S. officials were also
stunned by the severity of their losses and abandoned any hope that success
could be achieved at light cost. Americans failed to recognize, moreover,
that in this kind of warfare if the enemy did not lose, it won. Finding in the
Ia Drang confirmation of his belief that a search-and-destroy strategy would
break the enemy's will to fight, Westmoreland made no major adjustments in
his approach to the war. The Ia Drang battle thus set the tone for much of
what lay ahead: more and larger search-and-destroy missions, numerous
"victories"—and ultimately frustration.

Throughout 1966 and 1967, the United States continued to escalate
the war. Rolling Thunder bombing sorties increased from 25,000 in 1965 to

U.S. Air Force F-5 Freedom Fighter engaged in close air support. Ground troops particularly valued missions against enemy bunkers and fortified positions. Air attacks proved less successful, however, in interdicting supplies from North Vietnam.

108,000 in 1967, and the tonnage of bombs dropped increased from 63,000 to 226,000. The number of ground troops grew from 184,300 at the end of 1965 to 485,600 at the end of 1967. Furnished with thousands of new ground troops and a massive arsenal of modern weaponry, Westmoreland took the war to the enemy. Throughout 1966 and 1967, intensive fighting raged across much of South Vietnam. Along the demilitarized zone, marines and North Vietnamese regulars were dug in like the armies of World War I, pounding each other relentlessly with artillery. In the jungle areas, small American units probed for a hidden enemy in a manner comparable to the Pacific island campaigns of World War II.

Increasingly, however, Westmoreland concentrated on large-scale search-and-destroy missions against enemy base areas. Operation Cedar Falls, a major campaign of early 1967, sent some 30,000 U.S. troops against the Iron Triangle, an NLF stronghold just north of Saigon. After B-52s saturated the area with bombs, U.S. troops surrounded it, and helicopters dropped large numbers of specially trained combat forces into the villages. Following removal of the population, giant Rome plows with huge spikes on the front leveled the area, destroying what remained of the vegetation and leaving the guerrillas no place to hide. The region was then burned and bombed again to destroy the miles of underground tunnels that formed the enemy military complex.

The most that could be achieved was a stalemate. North Vietnam was stunned by American intervention in 1965 and alarmed by the effectiveness of U.S. firepower in the Ia Drang. Hanoi thus abandoned any hope of an early victory and settled in for a protracted struggle against a greatly strengthened enemy. Learning from their war against France, the North Vietnamese leadership increasingly counted on the weakness of the South Vietnamese regime and antiwar opposition in the United States. The key to exploiting these advantages, they reasoned, was to keep maximum military pressure on the enemy without needlessly exposing their own forces to destruction. PAVN and NLF units thus retreated to their sanctuaries, seeking to avoid U.S. search-and-destroy operations. At the same time, they constantly harassed exposed U.S. and ARVN troops and launched attacks of up to regimental size at times and places of their own choosing. Hanoi's strategists concentrated against the South Vietnamese government and army to exploit their weaknesses and ultimately force their collapse. To keep the American casualty lists as high as possible and thereby keep the war on the front pages in the United States, they also attacked U.S. forces. They used tactics of "clinging to the G.I.s' belts" to minimize the effectiveness of U.S. artillery and air support. High priority was still given to political agitation, especially in the cities of South Vietnam that were swollen with increasing numbers of restless and disaffected refugees.

North Vietnam effectively countered the U.S. air war. By 1967, the tonnage of bombs dropped on North Vietnam exceeded that dropped on Germany, Italy, and Japan during World War II. America's heavy reliance on air power seriously underestimated the commitment of the North Vietnamese and overestimated the capabilities of strategic bombing. The gradual escalation of the bombing permitted the North Vietnamese to protect vital resources, and losses were more than made up by expanded aid from China and the Soviet Union. The North Vietnamese showed a remarkable capacity for coping with the bombing, repairing bridges and railroads within hours after destruction. The daily pounding from the air seemed to stiffen their will, and they showed no sign of bending under the pressure. The rate of infiltration into the south increased after the bombing was started and continued to increase as it expanded. By late 1967, North Vietnamese forces were four times greater than in 1965.

The North Vietnamese also blunted U.S. operations on the ground. Westmoreland's strategy of attrition assumed that the United States could inflict intolerable losses while keeping its own losses within acceptable bounds, an assumption that flew in the face of past experience with land wars on the Asian continent and the realities in Vietnam. An estimated 200,000 North Vietnamese came of draft age each year, and Hanoi was able to match each American escalation. Moreover, the conditions under which the war was fought permitted North Vietnam to control its losses. The North Vietnamese and NLF were generally able to avoid contact when it suited them. They fought at times and places of their own choosing and on ground favorable to them. If losses reached unacceptable proportions, they melted into the jungles or retreated into sanctuaries in North Vietnam, Laos, or Cambodia. North Vietnamese and NLF forces were hurt, sometimes badly, but their main forces could not be destroyed. They retained the strategic initiative and could strike sharply when and where they chose. Westmoreland did not have sufficient forces to wage war against enemy regulars and control the countryside. The NLF political structure thus remained intact, and even in areas such as the Iron Triangle, when American forces moved on to fight elsewhere, the NLF quietly slipped back in. It all added up to a "state of irresolution," journalist Robert Shaplen observed in 1967.

With the military situation a stalemate, the political aspect assumed greater importance, and the fundamental problem, the Saigon government, remained unresolved. A coalition of generals headed by Nguyen Cao Ky and Nguyen Van Thieu finally emerged from the long series of coups and countercoups from 1963 to 1965, but it represented none of the multiplicity of political factions in the south. Neither the government nor the United States was capable of broadening South Vietnam's narrow political base. The huge influx of Americans after 1965 and expansion of the war created problems that even the most responsible and effective government would have found difficult to handle. The massive bombing and artillery fire drove thousands of sullen refugees into already overcrowded cities. The South Vietnamese economy was geared around providing services to the Americans and quickly reached the point where it could not absorb the ever-expanding volume of money and goods. In the cities, corruption, profiteering, and vice ran rampant.

As the war dragged on inconclusively, moreover, popular support in the United States began to erode, and by the end of 1967 the American

In April 1967, General William C. Westmoreland briefed President Johnson and his top advisors on the need to send additional troops to Vietnam. By approving an increase of 50,000 instead of 200,000, the president refused to expand the war dramatically, but he also refused to accept Robert S. McNamara's advice about making basic changes in policy toward Vietnam.

people had become polarized over Vietnam as no other issue since their own Civil War a century earlier. Those labeled "hawks" protested the restraints imposed on the military and demanded that Johnson do what was necessary to win or get out of Vietnam. At the other extreme, growing numbers of so-called "doves" protested that the war was immoral or unnecessary or both and demanded that the United States get out of Vietnam. At this point in the war, the great majority of Americans rejected both extremes, but as the war dragged on and the debate became more divisive, disillusionment increased markedly. Public support for the war dropped sharply in 1967, and Johnson's approval rating fell even further, dipping to a low 28 percent in October.

The Tet Offensive, 1968

In the spring and summer of 1967, the North Vietnamese decided to attempt to break an increasingly costly deadlock. To lure American troops away from the major population centers and maintain high U.S. casualties, a series of large-scale diversionary attacks was to be launched in remote areas. These would be followed by coordinated NLF assaults against the major cities and towns of South Vietnam designed to weaken the government and ignite a "general uprising" among the people. At the same time efforts would be made to open negotiations with the United States. Hanoi probably hoped through these coordinated actions to get the bombing stopped, weaken the Saigon regime, exacerbate differences between the United States and its South Vietnamese ally, and intensify pressures for a change in U.S. policy. Its ultimate objective was to secure an acceptable settlement, the minimum ingredients of which would be a coalition government and U.S. withdrawal.

The first phase of the North Vietnamese plan worked to perfection. In October and November, PAVN forces attacked the Marine base at Con Thien across the Laotian border and the towns of Loc Ninh and Song Be near Saigon and Dak To in the Central Highlands. Shortly after, two PAVN divisions laid siege to the Marine garrison at Khe Sanh near the Laotian border. Westmoreland quickly dispatched reinforcements to these embattled areas, in each case driving back the enemy and inflicting heavy losses, but in the process dispersing his forces and leaving the cities vulnerable. By the end of the year, moreover, the attention of Westmoreland, President Johnson, and indeed much of the nation was riveted on Khe Sanh, which many Americans assumed was General Giap's play for a repetition of his smashing victory at Dien Bien Phu.

During the Tet holiday of early 1968, the North Vietnamese and NLF launched the second and major phase of their offensive. On January 30, 1968, the NLF carried out a series of attacks extending across the length of the country. In all, they struck thirty-six of forty-four provincial capitals, five of the six major cities, sixty-four district capitals, and fifty hamlets. In Saigon, they mounted a daring raid on the U.S. embassy, briefly penetrating

Tet Offensive, 1968

the compound, and assaulted Tan Son Nhut airport, the presidential palace, and the headquarters of South Vietnam's general staff. In Hue, 7,500 NLF and PAVN troops stormed and eventually took control of the ancient Citadel, the interior town that had been the seat of the emperors of the ancient kingdom of Vietnam.

Although taken by surprise, the United States and South Vietnam recovered quickly. The initial attacks were poorly coordinated, and premature assaults in some areas enabled Westmoreland to get reinforcements to vulnerable spots. In addition, the attackers were slow to capitalize on their early successes, giving the U.S. and South Vietnam time to mount strong defenses. In Saigon, U.S. and ARVN forces held off the initial attack and within several days had cleared the city, inflicting huge casualties, taking large numbers of prisoners, and forcing the remnants to melt into the countryside. Elsewhere, the result was much the same. ARVN fought better under pressure than anyone could have anticipated, and the United States and South Vietnam used their superior mobility and firepower to devastating advantage. The NLF launched a second round of attacks on February 18, but these were confined largely to rocket and mortar barrages against military installations and had little effect.

The Battle for Hue

Hue was the major exception. The battle to liberate that city pitted two PAVN regiments and two NLF battalions against eight U.S. and thirteen ARVN battalions, lasted from January 31 to March 2, and was one of the most savage and destructive battles of the entire war. For those ARVN forces and U.S. Marines who participated, the struggle for Hue involved some of the most brutal and deadly fighting since World War II.

Recognizing the value of holding even temporarily the cultural and religious center of the nation, North Vietnamese and NLF forces had infiltrated Hue before Tet, carefully stockpiling weapons and ammunition. They attained near-complete surprise, and as advance units took key points, reinforcements poured into the city. Undermanned because of holiday furloughs, ARVN responded ineffectually. Within hours of the opening of the battle, North Vietnamese and NLF units controlled all of the Citadel and much of the city south of the Perfume River, even threatening the headquarters of the U.S. military command.

Initial U.S. and South Vietnamese efforts to retake the city failed. ARVN units dispatched to liberate Hue were battered by carefully planned enemy ambushes. United States and ARVN forces staged a major attack on February 1, but met fierce resistance from well-emplaced enemy forces. They made painfully slow progress, only to be hurled back on February 6 by a PAVN/NLF counterattack.

Eventually, massive force and heavy fighting were needed to retake the city. At first reluctant to destroy Hue's architectural treasures, the United States and South Vietnam in time bowed to expediency. Ships from the U.S. Seventh Fleet, aircraft, and artillery pounded enemy positions, and tanks and flamethrowers cleared the way for attacking forces. Both sides used tear gas, and Hue was the only battle of the war where gas masks were regularly worn. Backed by massive firepower, South Vietnamese and U.S. forces launched a full-scale attack on February 9 against dug-in enemy forces and well-concealed snipers. The enemy responded the following day, counterattacking and decimating an entire ARVN battalion. Slowly, U.S. and South Vietnamese forces clawed their way, house by house, into the city, reaching the moat of the Citadel by February 21. After a night of bitter, hand-to-hand combat, advance ARVN units raised the South Vietnamese flag over the Citadel. That same day, another South Vietnamese unit retook the Imperial Palace. After more than a week of mopping up operations, Hue was finally liberated on March 2.

It remains difficult twenty-five years after the event to assess the impact of the battles of Tet. The North Vietnamese and NLF did not force the collapse of South Vietnam. They were unable to establish any firm positions in the urban areas, and the South Vietnamese people did not rise up to welcome them as "liberators." NLF and PAVN battle deaths have been estimated as high as 40,000, and although this figure may be inflated, the losses were huge. The NLF bore the brunt of the fighting throughout South Vietnam. Its main force units were decimated and would never completely recover, and its political infrastructure suffered crippling losses.

If in these terms Tet represented a defeat for North Vietnam and the NLF, it was still a costly and in some ways hollow victory for the United States and South Vietnam. ARVN forces had to be withdrawn from the countryside to defend the cities, and the pacification program incurred another major setback. The destruction visited upon the cities heaped formidable new problems on a government that had shown only limited capacity to deal with the routine. American and South Vietnamese losses did not approach those of the enemy, but they were still high: in the first two weeks of the Tet campaigns, the United States lost 1,100 killed in action and South Vietnam 2,300. An estimated 12,500 civilians were killed, and Tet created as many as one million new refugees. In Hue during the period of PAVN/NLF "liberation," 2,800 civilians were massacred and buried in mass graves. As with so much of the war, there was a great deal of destruction and suffering, but no clear-cut winner or loser.

Perhaps the major impact of Tet was in the United States. Westmoreland insisted that the attacks had been repulsed and that there was no need to fear a major setback, and administration officials publicly echoed his statements. Johnson and his advisers were shocked by the suddenness and magnitude of the offensive, however, and intelligence estimates were much more pessimistic than Westmoreland. Among the general public, Tet caused a mood of gloom. For those who had long opposed the conflict and some who had supported it, Tet seemed to provide compelling evidence of its folly. "The war in Vietnam is unwinnable," the columnist Joseph Kraft concluded, "and the longer it goes on the more the Americans . . . will be subjected to losses and humiliation." Approval of Johnson's handling of the war, which had risen significantly in late 1967, again plummeted sharply in 1968, hitting an all-time low of 26 percent during Tet. Senator Eugene McCarthy's strong showing against the president in the New Hampshire primary suggested the political damage done by the war. Johnson was further threatened by Senator Robert Kennedy's announcement that he too would run on an antiwar platform.

Tet eventually forced Johnson to approve important changes of policy. After nearly two months of soul-searching and intensive internal debate, the president rejected his military advisers' proposals for a major escalation of the war. In a dramatic speech on March 31, 1968, he went still further, cutting back the bombing to the area just north of the demilitarized zone, making clear his willingness to negotiate, and, to underscore his seriousness, withdrawing from the presidential race.

Johnson's speech is usually cited as a major turning point in the war, and in some ways it was. It brought an end to the policy of gradual escalation, yet it did not represent a change of goals. Apparent U.S. success in the battles of Tet reinforced the conviction of the president and some of his advisers that they could yet secure an independent, non-communist South Vietnam. By rejecting major troop reinforcements, reducing the bombing, shifting some of the fighting to the South Vietnamese, and withdrawing from the presidential race, Johnson hoped to salvage his policy at least to the end of his term. The president's March 31 speech did not represent a change of objective as much as a shift of tactics to sustain a policy that had come under bitter attack.

For the North Vietnamese and NLF as well, Tet produced disillusionment, even despair. The failure of the offensive to attain its major goals and the heavy losses suffered appear to have provoked heated internal debate. The Vietnamese recognized, as one document put it, that "Victory will come to us, not suddenly, but in a complicated and tortuous way." The North Vietnamese and NLF were no more prepared than Johnson to abandon their goals, however, and they recognized that unless they were able to maintain a high level of pressure on the United States and South Vietnam, victory would not come at all. Thus while the North Vietnamese accepted American proposals for negotiations, they determined to maintain maximum military pressure. Keeping their main force units out of battle, they sought to sustain small-scale attacks throughout South Vietnam, most of them conducted by paramilitary units.

As a consequence, while in many ways Tet represented a major turning point, it merely elevated the war to a new level of stalemate. During the last eight months of 1968, North Vietnamese and U.S. negotiators met in Paris. Neither was willing to make concessions that would jeopardize achievement of their goals, however, and the negotiations made little progress. When Johnson stopped the bombing of North Vietnam entirely on October 31, the South Vietnamese balked. Fearing that the United States might sell out South Vietnam, the government of Nguyen Van Thieu raised objections that blocked the opening of substantive negotiations until the end of Johnson's term of office.

In the meantime, military activity in South Vietnam grew to unprecedented levels. The air war in South Vietnam reached a new peak of intensity B-52s and fighter-bombers relentlessly attacked infiltration routes, lines of communication, and suspected enemy base camps in South Vietnam and Laos. The number of B-52 attacks tripled in 1968, and the bombs dropped on South Vietnam exceeded one million tons. In the spring and summer, the United States and South Vietnam conducted the largest search-and-destroy missions of the war. The year 1968 was thus the "bloodiest year" of the war, in the words of historian Ronald Spector, and both sides suffered heavy losses. Each could thus claim victory in the campaigns of Tet, but the position of each was also significantly weakened, and neither emerged with sufficient leverage to force a settlement. Tet merely hardened the deadlock, and it would take four more years of "fighting while negotiating" before it was finally broken.

Fighting While Negotiating, 1968–1975

In the aftermath of Tet, the United States and North Vietnam adjusted their strategies to the changed circumstances. After an unsuccessful attempt to win the war through intimidation, the new administration of Richard M. Nixon resorted to a "Vietnamization" strategy designed to hold the line in South Vietnam while easing antiwar pressures at home. In the meantime, Hanoi settled into a classic "fighting while negotiating" strategy, closely coordinating its military, political, and diplomatic moves to maximize pressures on the United States and exacerbate differences between Washington and Saigon.

Certain that they could succeed where their predecessors had failed, Nixon and his national security adviser, Henry A. Kissinger, at first attempted to end the war through threats and diplomacy. The Saigon government appeared stronger than ever in 1969 and with U.S. backing might hang on indefinitely. Nixon and Kissinger also hoped to use the prospect of trade and arms control agreements to secure the Soviet Union's assistance in forcing Hanoi to make major concessions. Comparing his situation to that of Dwight D. Eisenhower with the Korean War in 1953, Nixon concluded that the threat of "massive retaliation" might sway the North Vietnamese, as he believed it had the North Koreans a decade earlier, and he counted on his image as a hard-line anticommunist to make it credible.

In the summer and fall of 1969, Nixon and Kissinger put their plan into action. Through intermediaries, they conveyed to the North Vietnamese their desire for peace and proposed the mutual withdrawal of troops from South Vietnam and restoration of the demilitarized zone. To signal that he meant business, Nixon ordered intensive, secret bombing attacks against North Vietnamese sanctuaries in neutral Cambodia. Publicly, he unveiled what he described as a comprehensive peace plan, revealing proposals he had made privately and then announcing the withdrawal of 25,000 U.S. troops. Through French and Soviet intermediaries, he warned Hanoi that if a settlement were not attained soon he would be compelled to employ "measures of great consequence and force."

Nixon's secret diplomacy and military threats failed to wrench concessions from Hanoi. From the North Vietnamese standpoint, the president's proposals were no better than those of Johnson, and to accept them would be to abandon goals they had been pursuing for nearly a quarter century. Throughout 1968 and into 1969, North Vietnam had tried to sustain maximum military pressure on the United States and South Vietnam, but the results were disappointing. Still hurting from the horrendous losses suffered at Tet but stubbornly clinging to its goals, the leadership reevaluated its strategy. Militarily, it reverted to the defensive and to guerrilla warfare. At the same time, it sought to rebuild the political apparatus in the south so badly damaged by Tet and to drag out the negotiations in a way that would put pressure on the United States to make concessions. Still confident that public opinion would eventually force an American withdrawal from Vietnam, Hanoi ignored Nixon's threats and prepared to wait him out.

"Vietnamization"

His end-the-war strategy frustrated, Nixon fell back on the Vietnamization concept introduced by Johnson on a small scale after Tet. To quiet popular opposition to the war, he initiated a phased withdrawal of U.S. troops and a gradual transfer of primary military responsibility to the South Vietnamese. While U.S. combat forces sought to keep the enemy off balance by relentlessly attacking their supply lines and base areas, American advisers worked frantically to build up and modernize the South Vietnamese armed forces. The force level was increased to more than one million, and the United States turned over to South Vietnam vast quantities of the newest weapons. Nixon hoped that by mobilizing American opinion behind his policies and building up South Vietnam's military strength, he could persuade the North Vietnamese that it would be better to negotiate with him now than with South Vietnam later, and he could extract the concessions necessary to secure an honorable U.S. withdrawal.

In part as a means of supporting Vietnamization, in part to pressure the North Vietnamese, Nixon authorized in April 1970 an invasion of previously neutral Cambodia. The venture backfired. From a purely military standpoint, it achieved modest results, buying some time for Vietnamization. At home, however, the unexpected expansion of a war the president had promised to end enraged his critics, causing massive antiwar demonstrations across the country. The killing of six students during demonstrations at Kent State and Jackson State added to the furor. The Cambodian venture brought the most serious congressional challenge to presidential authority since the beginning of the war. And it merely hardened the diplomatic deadlock. North Vietnamese and NLF delegates boycotted the Paris peace talks until American troops had been withdrawn from Cambodia.

The result was more stalemate. A disastrous ARVN invasion of Laos in 1971 ended in a humiliating retreat back into South Vietnam and made clear that Vietnamization was a long-term undertaking if it could be accomplished at all. Despite continued troop withdrawals, opposition to the war in the United States rose to an all-time high in the summer of 1971. As the purpose of the war became more murky and protest mounted at home, rampant demoralization set in among U.S. troops in Vietnam. Enlisted men refused to obey orders, and "fragging" of officers reached unprecedented proportions. Problems with drugs and racial conflict among G.I.s further highlighted the breakdown of morale. Under these circumstances, Hanoi remained content to bide its time, more and more certain that domestic pressures would eventually force a U.S. withdrawal.

The Easter Offensive

In 1972, each side took measures to break the long-standing stalemate. Since 1969, North Vietnam had carefully built up its resources and manpower for a final military offensive to topple the South Vietnamese regime and force the United States from Vietnam. While attempting to keep Vietnam on the back burner, Nixon and Kissinger sought to negotiate major changes in U.S. relations with the Soviet Union and China, ensuring the president's reelection, isolating North Vietnam from its major allies and suppliers, and leaving it no choice but to come to terms. Neither side would achieve what it hoped with its dramatic moves of 1972, and each would pay a high price trying. But they did bring the war into a final, devastating phase that would ultimately lead to a compromise settlement.

In March 1972, North Vietnam launched a massive, conventional invasion of the south. Hanoi correctly assumed that domestic pressures would prevent Nixon from putting U.S. forces back into Vietnam. The invasion, like that of 1968, was also probably timed to coincide with the presidential campaign in hopes that, as before, a major escalation would produce irresistible pressures for peace in the United States. The North Vietnamese aimed the offensive at the ARVN main force units, hoping to further discredit the Vietnamization policy and leave the countryside open for the NLF.

B-52 Stratofortress bombers played a key role in operations Linebacker and Linebacker II in 1972. A modified B-52D carried as many as 108 500-pound bombs; this bombload almost equaled that of a squadron of B-17s in World War II.

In its first stages, the offensive enjoyed great success. ARVN held off a major assault at An Loc, just sixty miles north of Saigon, but PAVN units forced abandonment of South Vietnamese strongholds at Quang Tri near the demilitarized zone and Kontum in the Central Highlands.

Although stunned by the swiftness and magnitude of the invasion, Nixon responded vigorously. Unwilling to send U.S. troops back to Vietnam, he nevertheless lashed out furiously. He quickly approved B-52 strikes across the demilitarized zone and followed with the most drastic escalation of the war since 1968, the mining of Haiphong harbor, a naval blockade of North Vietnam, and massive, sustained bombing attacks under the code name "Linebacker." The conventional military tactics employed by North Vietnam in the offensive required vast quantities of fuel and ammunition, and the bombing and blockade made resupply extremely difficult. Backed with devastating U.S. air power and fighting the conventional war for which they had been trained, the South Vietnamese stabilized lines in front of Saigon and Hue and even mounted a counteroffensive.

The military campaigns of 1972 raised the stalemate to a new level of violence. Both sides suffered heavily, the North Vietnamese losing an estimated 100,000 men and South Vietnam 25,000, but neither emerged appreciably stronger than before. North Vietnam had demonstrated ARVN's continued vulnerability and the NLF had scored some gains in the countryside, but the South Vietnamese government remained intact and Nixon had not given in. Despite heavy casualties and massive damage from U.S. bombing, the North Vietnamese retained sizable forces in the south, and intelligence reports indicated they could fight on for at least two more years.

Peace and More War, 1973–1975

Thus by the fall of 1972, each side found compelling reasons to compromise. Nixon recognized that an indefinite continuation of the air war might cause serious problems at home. He was eager to uphold earlier promises to end the war, and he wanted a settlement before the election if it could be achieved without embarrassment. North Vietnam had suffered terribly from the latest round of U.S. bombing and also wanted peace if it could be attained without abandonment of long-term goals. Battered, exhausted, and increasingly isolated from its allies, Hanoi apparently concluded that it might get better terms from Nixon before rather than after the election.

Each side thus moved cautiously toward a compromise. The United States had already made a major concession, agreeing to allow North Vietnamese troops to remain in the south after a cease-fire. It also retreated from its absolute commitment to the Thieu regime by agreeing to a tripartite electoral commission that would arrange a political settlement after the cease-fire. In the meantime, the North Vietnamese dropped their insistence on the ouster of Thieu, accepting the principle of a cease-fire that would leave him temporarily in control but would give the NLF status as a political entity in the south. After more than six months of tortuous, on-and-off negotiations, complicated by strenuous objections and obstructionism on the part of the Thieu regime and yet another round of massive bombing of North Vietnam—"Linebacker II," the so-called Christmas bombing—an agreement was signed in January 1973 providing for U.S. military extrication from Vietnam.

The Paris peace agreements did not bring an end to war. The Nixon administration still hoped to keep the Thieu government in power. The United States used various subterfuges to provide continued military assistance to the Saigon government, and civilian advisers assumed the role formerly played by military officials. Both the Thieu government and the North Vietnamese and NLF jockeyed for position in South Vietnam militarily and politically and refused to cooperate in furthering the peace process. Finally, in early 1975, North Vietnam launched another massive military offensive. Without U.S. support, South Vietnam could not withstand the onslaught. Nixon had been forced to resign the previous year because of the Watergate scandals, themselves in part a product of his efforts to control domestic opposition to the war in Vietnam. His successor, Gerald Ford, presiding over a nation traumatized by war-weariness and economic recession, could do nothing. To a large extent America's creation, and never able to stand without massive American support, South Vietnam fell on April 30, 1975, ending a war that in its various phases had lasted for nearly thirty years.

*   *   *   *

The legacy of Vietnam for warfare was as ambiguous as the war itself. At the tactical level, the utility of the helicopter was validated, and it seemed likely to assume an even greater role in the warfare of the future. The effectiveness of the so-called "smart" bombs first used by the United States in 1972, precisely guided to their targets by computers receiving signals from television cameras and laser beams, foreshadowed a new era in air warfare.

Such new technology failed to produce military success, however, and in the realm of strategy the significance of Vietnam was less certain. Flushed with victory, the Vietnamese hailed the triumph of people over technology, proclaimed the superiority of their revolutionary war doctrines, and heralded a new era in the unrelenting struggle against capitalism. The Vietnamese did wage war with skill and determination, to be sure, and they showed adaptability and even at times genius in conceiving and applying what turned out to be a successful strategy. As Martin van Creveld has observed, moreover, in all the low-intensity wars of the post–World War II era, the less-advanced nation has won, demonstrating the limits of sophisticated weaponry and conventional military forces.

In retrospect, however, the Vietnamese victory appears to owe as much to the unique circumstances of that war and the balance of forces prevailing in Vietnam as to ideology or abstract principles of warfare. Revolutionary war doctrine prevailed nowhere else, and the collapse of the Soviet Union and its eastern European empire less than fifteen years after the fall of Saigon left the Socialist Republic of Vietnam, along with China, North Korea, and Cuba, communist anachronisms in a world dominated by alien political and economic systems. The devastating display of high-technology military weaponry put on by the United States in the Persian Gulf War of 1991 at least called into question simplistic Vietnamese notions that people would always prevail over weapons.

Failure normally provokes more in the way of soul-searching than success, and in the aftermath of their first defeat in war, Americans engaged in an extended and at times agonizing reappraisal of their involvement in Vietnam. Some critics insisted that instead of attempting to wage a conventional war in the guerrilla-war setting of Vietnam, the United States should have recognized the sort of war it was in and employed counterinsurgency methods better designed for it. Others insisted that the United States had failed because timid civilian leaders, by imposing crippling restrictions, had prevented the military from using American power effectively to attain victory. The one thing on which most Americans could agree was that Vietnam had discredited the limited-war doctrines so much in vogue in the 1950s and 1960s. Politicians and military thinkers, liberals and conservatives, all generally concurred in the aftermath of America's failure in Vietnam that limited war was unworkable, even immoral. In going to war in the Persian Gulf in 1991, President George Bush made clear that he would not permit "another Vietnam" and gave his military commanders freedom to use American power swiftly and decisively.

The long-range implications of such conclusions nevertheless remained quite unclear. American success in the Persian Gulf War owed more to the circumstances peculiar to that war than to successful application of lessons from Vietnam. More important, the end of the Cold War eliminated the geopolitical setting in which limited-war doctrines had been conceived and the Vietnam War had been waged. The "lessons" of Vietnam thus remained as murky as the nature of warfare in the post–Cold War world.

SUGGESTED READINGS

Bergerud, Eric. *The Dynamics of Defeat: The Vietnam War in Hau Nghia Province* (Boulder, Col.: Westview Press, 1991).

Clodfelter, Mark. *The Limits of Air Power: The American Bombing of North Vietnam* (New York: Free Press, 1989).

Davidson, Phillip B. *Vietnam at War: The History, 1946–1975* (Novato, Calif.: Presidio Press, 1988).

DeBenedetti, Charles, and Charles Chatfield, assisting author. *An American Ordeal: The Antiwar Movement of the Vietnam Era* (Syracuse, N.Y.: Syracuse University Press, 1990).

Duiker, William. *The Communist Road to Power in Vietnam* (Boulder, Col.: Westview Press, 1981).

Giap, Vo Nguyen. *People's War; People's Army* (New York: Praeger, 1962).

Herring, George C. *America's Longest War: The United States and Vietnam, 1950–1975* (New York: McGraw-Hill, 1986).

Krepinevich, Andrew. *The Army and Vietnam* (Baltimore: Johns Hopkins University Press, 1986).

Pike, Douglas. *PAVN: People's Army of Vietnam* (Novato, Calif.: Presidio Press, 1986).

————. *Viet Cong* (Cambridge, Mass.: MIT Press, 1966).

Race, Jeffrey. *War Comes to Long An: Revolutionary Conflict in a Vietnamese Province* (Berkeley: University of California Press, 1972).

Sheehan, Neil. *A Bright Shining Lie: John Paul Vann and America in Vietnam* (New York: Random House, 1988).

Spector, Ronald H. *After Tet: The Bloodiest Year in Vietnam* (New York: Free Press, 1993).

Westmoreland, William C. *A Soldier Reports* (Garden City, N.Y.: Doubleday, 1976).

Young, Marilyn B. *The Vietnam Wars, 1945–1990* (New York: HarperCollins, 1990).

30

WAR IN THE MIDDLE EAST: VIOLENCE ACROSS THE SPECTRUM OF CONFLICT

The Arab-Israeli Wars

The Iran-Iraq War

The War in Afghanistan

The Cold War in Retrospect

During the Cold War from 1945 to 1990, wars tended to occur more frequently and to last longer than earlier in the century. By the late 1980s, some thirty-two major and seventy-five minor conflicts were being fought each year at widely varying scales of violence and for reasons often having little or nothing to do with the Cold War. Of the numerous conflicts during the post–World War II period, several of the most significant occurred in the Middle East and Southwest Asia, areas which had long been the scene of religious and ethnic wars. As colonial powers lost their control over this region after 1945, deep-rooted hostilities emerged among the diverse religious and ethnic groups, as well as the newly independent states. With the establishment of the state of Israel in 1948 and a refusal by neighboring Arab states to accept its existence, the region's instability increased. As tensions rose, international interest in the volatile area remained high because of its rich oil reserves and because three of the world's major religions (Islam, Judaism, and Christianity) had their roots in the area. Adding to the region's international importance were its position on the southern flank of the Soviet Union, the presence of Soviet and American client states, and the prominence of the Suez Canal as a vital link between the Red and Mediterranean seas. The strategic importance of the area increased the chances of superpower involvement, but that involvement usually remained indirect given the desire of the superpowers to avoid a direct confrontation and to prevent regional wars from getting out of hand.

935

The Middle East and Southwest Asia

    The presence of advanced weapons and methods added to the sig-
nificance of conflicts in the Middle East and Southwest Asia. In the
post–World War II period, important advances in military technologies produced remarkably accurate and extremely lethal weapons, most notably, a
new generation of precision-guided munitions. By the late 1980s, sophisticated electronics and computers promised even greater range, accuracy, and
lethality in a wide range of lightweight and rugged weapons. Most of the
economies in the Middle East and Southwest Asia had little or no capability to manufacture high-technology weapons and equipment, but foreign
arms suppliers, especially the two superpowers, provided the latest arms
to the belligerents, often as soon as those arms were fielded. When the superpowers refused to provide the most advanced weapons and equipment,
regional powers were able to purchase them elsewhere with vast oil profits.
With the employment of precision-guided munitions, medium-range missiles, and chemicals and with the use of constantly changing and improving
methods, conflicts in the Middle East and Southwest Asia proved to be
crucibles in which the most advanced ideas and technologies were tested
and demonstrated.
    Despite the numerous wars, continued violence, and active interest
of the superpowers in these two regions, conflicts did not spill over into other
areas and did not escalate to the point of direct superpower confrontation.
Nuclear weapons remained unused, even though the threat of nuclear escalation by the superpowers remained constant. Nonetheless, the combatants
often committed their entire populations and resources to the war effort and,
in the case of Iraq in the Iran-Iraq War and Russia in the Afghanistan War,
used chemical agents against their enemies. Thus, the various conflicts may
have been "limited" in the eyes of the superpowers, but to the combatants
there was little that was limited about them.

The Arab-Israeli Wars

Of the various conflicts in the Middle East, the Arab-Israeli wars came closest to causing a confrontation of the superpowers. Although the long-term roots of the Arab-Israeli conflict after World War II had little to do with the interests of the superpowers, and although neither superpower desired a confrontation, both provided much equipment and aid to their friends in the region. Many of the tensions stemmed from Jewish efforts to establish an independent state in Palestine and from the Arab rejection of such a state. For nearly two thousand years some Jewish people had yearned to return to the land of their origin and at the end of the nineteenth century began migrating to Palestine. European anti-Semitism in the 1930s and the Nazi Holocaust of World War II increased Jewish migration. The rise of Islam in the seventh century, however, had transformed the Middle East into a predominantly Islamic region, and Jerusalem had become one of Islam's holy cities. Though the Arabs tolerated the return of a small number of Jews to Palestine, they objected to large numbers of Jewish immigrants and rejected the idea of an independent Jewish state in what had become an Arab-Islamic region.

Following World War I and the dismantling of the Ottoman Empire, a League of Nations' mandate gave Great Britain control of Palestine. After World War II, the British reluctantly concluded that they could no longer contain the escalating violence between the Arabs and Jews and turned the problem over to the United Nations, which voted in November 1947 to partition Palestine. This partition intensified the war of guerrillas and terrorists, and savage attacks by both sides increased. When British forces withdrew, the Jews proclaimed on May 14, 1948, the establishment of the state of Israel. Minutes after the establishment of the new state, President Truman announced its recognition by the United States.

The next day Egyptian aircraft struck Tel Aviv, and soon thereafter forces from Egypt, Transjordan, Syria, Lebanon, Iraq, and Saudi Arabia attacked the new state. Most analysts expected the more numerous and better equipped Arabs to defeat the Jews easily. The Arabs, however, delivered a series of poorly coordinated attacks with only part of their forces, and the Israelis committed as many soldiers to battle as the attacking Arabs and fought with great courage and skill. The battles turned out to be a series of disorganized clashes between small units. After four weeks of fighting, both sides accepted a cease-fire sponsored by the United Nations.

Following 1948, tensions between Israelis and Arabs remained high but increased after 1954 when Gamal Abdel Nasser gained control of the Egyptian government. When Nasser's attempts to acquire weapons from the West failed, he turned to the Soviet Union for assistance in modernizing Egyptian forces. A September 1955 agreement between Egypt and Czechoslovakia enabled the Soviets to supply, indirectly, arms to Egypt for the next twenty years. Meanwhile, France objected to Egypt's providing arms to insurgents in Algeria and supplied arms to Israel. Seeking to end the British presence in Egypt and the Suez Canal zone, Nasser unexpectedly national-ized the Suez Canal on July 27, 1956. The British and French decided to intervene militarily, and the Israelis joined them in an attack against Egypt.

After calling up reserves on October 28, the Israelis began their attack against Egypt with a daring airborne landing deep inside the Sinai east of the Mitla Pass. Concurrent with the landing, a small Israeli force of infantry and tanks crossed into the Sinai on the southern part of the Israeli frontier, drove across the desert, and linked up with the paratroopers on October 30. In the center of the Sinai front, the Israelis moved around the strong Egyptian defenses at Abu Ageila and attacked them from the rear; they then drove west toward Bir Gifgafa. In the south, they sent a small col-umn toward Sharm el-Sheikh, the strategic point at the mouth of the Gulf of

1956 Sinai Campaign

Mediterranean Sea

Gaza

Anglo-French landings, Nov. 5

Port Said

Suez Canal

Qantara

Abu Agelia

ISRAEL

Ismailia

Bir Gifgafa

Anglo-French air attacks Oct. 31 – Nov. 4

Bir Gidy Pass

Mitla Pass

Suez City

SINAI

EGYPT

Gulf of Suez

Gulf of Aqaba

Main roads
Secondary roads
Israeli attacks
Airborne drop

0   25   50 mi
0   25   50 km

Sharm el-Sheikh

Aqaba. On October 31, French and British bombers began their attacks against Egyptian airfields and destroyed most of the Egyptian air force. Fearing that Egyptian forces in the Sinai would be cut off by the French and British seizure of the Suez Canal, Nasser ordered a withdrawal. Israeli forces eventually halted about fifteen kilometers east of the Suez Canal. As the Israelis expanded their control over the Sinai, the British and the French landed one-and-a-half divisions of infantry on November 6 near the northern mouth of the Suez Canal. After these forces started advancing down the canal, the French and British accepted a United Nations cease-fire.

Despite the decisiveness of the British, French, and Israeli victory, the United States—followed by the Soviet Union—demanded that they relinquish captured Egyptian territory. This was the first and only time the Americans sided with the Soviets against their closest allies. President Eisenhower believed that Western aggression would pressure Third World nations into the Communists' arms and opposed the reassertion by force of colonial control over less-developed nations. He warned the Russians, however, that if they placed troops in the Middle East, the United States would oppose them with force. Reflecting the explosiveness of the situation, a Soviet diplomat stated in a letter to Eisenhower, "If this war is not curbed, it . . . can develop into a third world war." The British, French, and Israelis had no choice but to accede to the American and Soviet demands. In the end, the Israelis withdrew from the territory they had seized, and the British and French lost much of their influence in the region.

Whatever the outcome of the war, the Israelis had developed an effective military force between 1948 and 1956. They organized a small, high-quality standing army always ready for action, and they used universal military conscription of men and women to form reserve units that could be ready for combat in seventy-two hours. With rigorous training and frequent active-duty tours by the reservists, the Israelis prepared their armed forces for extremely demanding operations. The 1956 campaign, however, had not been without difficulties. The Israelis had not forged a clear doctrine on the operations of armor and infantry in mobile warfare and had encountered problems with their loose system of command and control. The Israeli performance had been impressive, but it would be even more so in the future.

1967: The Six-Day War

A fragile peace existed in the Middle East until 1967. A United Nations force patrolled Israel's border on the Sinai and along the Gaza Strip, but along Israel's border with Syria and Jordan, ambushes, firings on civilians, and reprisal raids occurred frequently. The series of events that led to the 1967 war began in early May when Moscow informed Nasser that the Israelis were massing troops for a strike against Syria. Nasser responded to the report—which turned out to be false—by mobilizing his reserves and moving units into the Sinai. He also pressured the United Nations into withdrawing its troops from the Sinai and soon occupied Sharm el-Sheikh, the strategic point at the mouth of the Gulf of Aqaba. As soon as Egyptian units had control of Sharm El-Sheikh, Nasser cut off Israeli shipping through the Gulf of Aqaba, sparking the 1967 war.

The Arabs recognized that the defeat of Israel would require unity. Shortly before the outbreak of hostilities, they established a semblance of unity of command by having the Jordanian king accept an Egyptian general as commander of Arab forces on the Jordanian front. Iraq also permitted its troops to come under Egyptian command; contingents from Kuwait and Algeria joined the Arab forces encircling Israel. Prior to the war, the Arabs—according to an Israeli analyst—had some 250,000 troops, 2,000 tanks, and 700 aircraft available for use against Israel. Despite the nominal authority of the Egyptian general, no true unity of command ruled the diverse forces.

Facing an extremely unfavorable situation but with the advantages of central position, centralized command, and effective intelligence, the Israelis quietly mobilized their reserves to defend against the impending Arab attack and then launched a preemptive air strike. The attack began early on June 5, hit eleven Egyptian airfields, and caught the Arabs completely by surprise. In a matter of hours, the Israelis destroyed most of the Egyptian air force and then turned their attention to the other Arab air forces. By the evening of the second day the Israelis had destroyed more than 400 Arab aircraft, while losing only twenty-six. This remarkable performance provided the Israelis complete air superiority for the remainder of the campaign and was the key to their victory.

Relying on their central position, the Israelis intended to shift forces from one front to another and to defeat Egypt, Jordan, and Syria in turn. The Egyptians were first. In the northern part of the Sinai, an Israeli armored division attacked along the coast and then turned to secure Bir Gifgafa. In the central part of the Sinai, another armored division fought a desperate battle against Egyptian defenses around Abu Ageila and finally managed to capture the main enemy positions. After securing Abu Ageila, armored units raced southwest to secure the Bir Gidy and Mitla passes. By capturing Bir Gifgafa and the Mitla and Bir Gidy passes about fifty kilometers from the Suez Canal, the Israelis trapped most of the Egyptian forces. As the Egyptians attempted to flee, their columns became easy targets for the Israeli Air Force; Nasser later acknowledged that the Egyptian army lost about 80 percent of its equipment in the Sinai. On the fourth day of the war, June 8, some Israeli forces reached the Suez Canal and exchanged artillery and antitank fire with Egyptians across the canal.

On the central front, which included Jerusalem and the West Bank along the Jordan River, Jordan entered the battle around noon on June 5, the day the Israelis' preemptive strike destroyed most of the Arab air forces. Hesitant to cross the border with a sizable assault, the Jordanian army fired artillery and small arms into Israel and crossed the border with a small force south of Jerusalem. The Israelis responded by capturing Jerusalem and then isolating the high ground that runs north of Jerusalem, parallel to the Jordan River valley. After launching attacks on the north and south ends of the high ground, the Israelis gained control of all the bridges over the Jordan River. This cut off the Jordanians on the west bank of the river and ensured their complete defeat.

Having defeated Egypt and Jordan, the Israelis concentrated against the Syrians who had done little to aid their allies in the first days of the war. On the morning of June 9, the Israelis attacked, beginning their efforts with heavy air strikes. Despite strong Syrian fortifications, the Israelis seized the forward slope of the northern Golan Heights by the end of the first day's fighting. The next morning, they fought through the Syrian defenders. To the south of the Sea of Galilee, an Israeli armored division broke through the Syrians, and Israeli paratroopers, using helicopters, assaulted rear positions. As Syrian resistance crumbled, a United Nations cease-fire went into effect at 1830 hours on June 10.

Israeli tanks entered Jerusalem on June 7, 1967. The seizure of the Wailing Wall in the Old City of Jerusalem marked the emotional climax of the war for the Israelis.

Israel's decisive victory changed its strategic situation dramatically. For the first time, it controlled the Golan Heights, the West Bank, and the Sinai; it now had depth for its defense. It also had a very competent air force and army that functioned smoothly together in highly mobile operations. Additionally, the army had developed a strong armored force, improved its command and control system, and polished its methods for attacking fortified positions. Despite some progress, the Arabs still had not coordinated their efforts effectively and had not mastered armored operations. Their piecemeal and tentative attacks had given the Israelis time to mobilize and the opportunity to defeat each opponent in succession. Arab commanders had also displayed less confidence and initiative than their Israeli counterparts.

The 1967 war complicated the Arab-Israeli conflict and brought increased superpower involvement in the region. New controversy focused on the return of the Sinai and the Golan Heights and the status of the West Bank and the Gaza. The Arabs refused to accept the loss of additional territory to the Israelis and began a so-called "War of Attrition" that lasted for three years. This included numerous cross-border raids, artillery barrages, and air strikes. Washington supported Israel's demand for a negotiated peace settlement in exchange for the occupied territories and increased its shipment of arms to Israel. The Soviets also became more involved and agreed to rearm Egypt and Syria; no longer funneling their weapons through Czechoslovakia, they shipped them directly to the Arab states. The discontent of the Arabs uprooted by the establishment and expansion of Israel complicated the situation further. Known as Palestinians, they had formed the Palestine Liberation Organization. Most lived in neighboring Arab states and increasingly used terrorist tactics against the Israelis. Both the Arabs and Israelis soon became weary of the stalemate and casualties, and in August 1970, another cease-fire went into effect.

1973: The Yom Kippur War

After Nasser died in 1970, Anwar Sadat became the president of Egypt. More moderate than his predecessor, he nevertheless felt compelled in October 1973 to go to war against Israel, but he did not seek a decisive defeat of the Israelis. Instead, he sought to break down the aura of Israeli invulnerability. Recognizing that a limited military victory would provide significant political gains, Sadat coordinated his actions effectively with Syria and Jordan so that the Israelis would have to fight a debilitating war of attrition on two fronts.

Sadat also provided his forces with sophisticated weapons and energetically improved their readiness. When the Soviets refused to provide their most advanced weapons, he ordered Soviet advisors out of Egypt. Despite the shock of this expulsion, the Kremlin continued providing weapons, and oil money from other Arab states enabled the Egyptians to purchase arms from different sources. As Sadat worked to improve Egyptian forces, one of his most important steps was to draw officers and soldiers from the better-educated segments of Egyptian society. He recognized the importance of intelligent, well-trained soldiers capable of handling sophisticated weapons. He prepared his army to fight a set-piece battle in which superior numbers of personnel and weapons would wear down the Israelis and brunt the effectiveness of their mobile units.

In the Sinai, Israeli strategy played into the hands of Sadat, primarily because the Israelis had emerged overly confident from their 1967 victory. To defend the Sinai, the Israelis constructed the Bar-Lev line on the east bank of the Suez Canal. They first built huge ridges of sand with a few reaching as high as twenty-five meters. They then prepared small fortified positions every ten to twelve kilometers behind the ridges of sand. The small forces in these positions had the mission of delaying the Egyptians until the Israelis mobilized and deployed sufficient ground forces. Reflecting the prevailing overconfidence, one general officer remarked that the line would be "the Egyptian army's graveyard."

Though Israeli intelligence had performed well in 1967, it did not do so in 1973, and the Egyptian attack surprised the Israelis. As early as October 1, the Israelis had observed increased activity on the western edge of the canal, and on October 2 the commander of the Southern Command ordered a higher state of alert. The Israelis also brought their forces along the Golan Heights to a higher state of readiness. Intelligence officers, however, doubted that the Arab armies would attack during Ramadan, Islam's month of fasting which occurred in October. On the morning of the Arab attack,

1973 Sinai Campaign

MEDITERRANEAN SEA

Port Said

Suez Canal

Second

Ismailia

Bir Gifgafa

Great Bitter Lake

Bir Gidy Pass

Third

To Cairo (40 mi)

Mitla Pass

Suez City

Gulf of Suez

Egyptian line
Egyptian attacks
Israeli attacks
Later Israeli attacks

Prime Minister Golda Meir approved a partial mobilization but ruled out a preemptive strike. In the approaching conflict, the Israelis would not have several of the key advantages they had had in 1967.

The Egyptians attacked along the entire front of the canal at 1405 hours on Saturday, October 6, the Jewish Sabbath as well as the Day of Atonement (Yom Kippur). Syria simultaneously struck in the Golan Heights. Preceded by air strikes throughout the Sinai and a huge artillery barrage, five infantry divisions, using about 1,000 rubber assault boats, crossed the Suez Canal. Engineers used high-pressure water hoses to wash away the ridges of sand and open crossing sites through which vehicles could pass; they also began constructing twenty bridges across the canal. After six hours of fighting, the Egyptians had established several bridgeheads with a depth of three to four kilometers. By October 9 the bridgeheads had a depth of about ten to twelve kilometers. Only after consolidating their position across the canal did the Egyptians expect to advance toward Bir Gifgafa and the Mitla and Bir Gidy passes. They intended to remain under the protection of their air defense and repel the expected Israeli armor and air attacks when they came.

The effectiveness of the Arab antiaircraft and antitank defenses shocked the Israelis. During the first week of fighting, the Israelis lost eighty aircraft, about one-quarter of all their front-line planes. With direct Russian participation and assistance, the Egyptians used a variety of surface-to-air missiles to establish an air barrier thirty kilometers wide and 140 kilometers long, along the canal. The Egyptians also beat back three Israeli armored brigades that launched several loosely coordinated attacks without infantry and artillery support. Following the victory of 1967, the Israelis had downplayed the need for infantry and artillery to support armor, and in the first days of the 1973 war, Sagger antitank missiles caused heavy damage to the Israeli tanks. Though awkward to fire, the Sagger had a range of about 3,000 meters and could be manually guided to a target with a hand-controlled stick. For the first time, the individual infantryman had a long-range, highly lethal antitank weapon, and the Israeli tanks found themselves in unfavorable circumstances without infantry and artillery support in a combined-arms team.

On Sunday, October 14, the Egyptians charged out of their bridgeheads in six major thrusts. In the subsequent battle, about 2,000 tanks on both sides fought the largest tank battle since Kursk in 1943. Though the Egyptians penetrated about fifteen to eighteen kilometers, they lost about 200 tanks. Instead of making one or two strong armored thrusts, they diluted the effect of their offensive by splitting their forces into six weaker efforts. Perhaps more important, the Egyptians moved outside the umbrella of their highly effective air defenses and suffered heavily from Israeli air strikes. They also encountered Israelis armed with newly arrived TOW (tube-launched, optically tracked, wire-guided) antitank missiles from the United States.

As soon as the opportunity appeared, the Israelis went on the offensive. At 1700 hours on October 15, the Israelis began a daring and bold operation to cross the Suez Canal north of the Great Bitter Lake. Brigadier

General Ariel Sharon's division cleared a corridor through the Egyptian forces on the east bank of the canal. Despite fierce fighting, the division crossed the canal and caused pandemonium among several Egyptian divisions that were surprised by its sudden appearance. As Sharon's division began expanding the bridgehead to the west of the canal, elements from two additional Israeli divisions crossed the canal. These forces destroyed air-defense sites on the west bank of the canal and thereby enabled the Israeli Air Force to operate more effectively. In addition to threatening the logistical support of the entire Egyptian army, the three divisions turned south and cut off the Egyptian Third Army, which was on the eastern bank of the canal.

Though huge forces participated in the Sinai action, some of the most critical fighting occurred on the Golan Heights, where the Israelis had very little space to trade for time. The Israelis initially had only two infantry battalions in the Golan Heights, reinforced by two tank battalions from the 188th (Barak) Brigade. In late September, the 7th Armored Brigade arrived, bringing the total number of tanks to about 175. On October 6 three Syrian mechanized divisions, reinforced by two armored divisions, attacked these small forces, which had to hold until reinforcements rushed to their assistance. With about 1,500 tanks, the Syrians greatly outnumbered the Israelis. During the desperate fighting, which lasted for three days and two nights without respite, the Israelis threw newly mobilized squads, platoons, and companies into the battle as soon as they arrived on the front. Israeli and Syrian units became intermingled, and artillery from both sides pounded the battlefield continuously. Despite the odds, the Israelis halted the Syrians, and by October 10 had driven them behind the 1967 truce line. The Syrians lost almost 900 tanks and hundreds of weapons and vehicles.

On October 11 the Israelis attacked Syria. Despite heavy losses, units from the 188th and 7th brigades led the attack. On the morning of October 13, the Israelis destroyed most of an Iraqi armored brigade that was attempting to reinforce the Syrians. That night, the Israelis punched through enemy defenses along the main Damascus road. Although a combination of Syrian, Jordanian, and Iraqi forces made several counterattacks, they failed to crack the Israeli positions. On October 22 the Israelis captured Mount Hermon on the northern end of the Golan Heights, but it was clear that any further advance into Syria would stretch Israeli logistical support beyond its limits and provoke an even stronger reaction from the Arabs.

As the Israeli victory became apparent, the United States and the Soviet Union called for an end to the fighting; even though Israel and Egypt agreed to a cease-fire, the fighting continued. Fearful of a complete destruction of Arab forces, the Soviet Union threatened to act "unilaterally" and to send in troops to enforce a cease-fire. This provoked a worldwide alert for U.S. armed forces; the crisis passed when Moscow agreed to an international peacekeeping force without American or Soviet participation. On October 24, the day prior to the alert of American forces, the Israelis reluctantly accepted a cease-fire. Despite overwhelmingly unfavorable odds, they had won a remarkable victory. As in the earlier Arab-Israeli wars, the key was their aggressive, highly mobile, hard-hitting style of fighting that placed a special premium on individual initiative.

Though the Israelis had won the war, Sadat had achieved his strategic objective of destroying the aura of Israeli invulnerability. As many as 12,000 soldiers from both sides lost their lives in the 1973 war, and Egypt and Syria lost about 2,000 tanks and 500 aircraft. Despite these losses, many Arabs believed they had won an important psychological victory. Their near-success demonstrated how some of them—particularly the Egyptians—had improved their loosely coordinated, oftentimes tentative style of fighting that had characterized earlier wars. Although the Israelis had gained territory on the Golan Heights and had halted only one hundred kilometers from Cairo, they had suffered a relatively large number of casualties (almost 3,000 killed), paid a high economic cost, and seen their regional and international position weakened at the expense of the Arabs. Their margin of victory would have been narrower if the United States had not rushed weapons and supplies to them.

Subsequent events also confirmed the reliance of the United States, Western Europe, and Japan on Middle Eastern oil and the utility of oil as a weapon to influence their behavior. To punish Israel's supporters, Arab members of the Organization of Petroleum Exporting Countries shut off the flow of oil in 1973 to the United States and the Netherlands (which had permitted the shipment of American military supplies to Israel across its territory). Though brief, the oil embargo demonstrated that whatever the outcome of future battles, the Arab countries had a powerful means to influence Western political priorities.

Following the 1973 war, the Camp David Accords of September 1978 provided for the establishment of normal relations between Egypt and Israel and resulted in the signing of a peace treaty between the two states in March 1979. The peace treaty caused great anguish among the other Arab states and did not solve the intractable problem of the Palestinians. The Palestine Liberation Organization (PLO) exercised considerable influence among the large numbers of Palestinian refugees in Lebanon. More a revolutionary military force than a classic military force, the PLO relied on subversion, kidnappings, and terrorism. With the presence of the PLO exacerbating relations in an already splintered society, a civil war erupted in Lebanon in early 1975. Responding to terrorist attacks, the Israelis launched air strikes and commando raids into Lebanon and in March 1978 and June 1982 invaded southern Lebanon. Thus even though Egypt and Israel established normal relations after the 1973 war, violence between the Arabs and Israelis did not end, and strife continued on Israel's northern border.

Between 1948 and 1973, the waging of war had changed dramatically in the Middle East. While the belligerents in 1948 engaged in numerous small, disorganized battles, the battles and campaigns of the 1956, 1967, and 1973 wars became larger, more complicated, and more sophisticated. For the extremely mobile campaigns of these wars, the Israelis were the first to recognize the need for high-quality leaders, capable of using their initiative and acting independently, but the Arab forces, particularly the Egyptians, slowly improved their forces. Nonetheless, the Arabs never displayed the flexibility and daring of the Israelis; they also never had unity of command. In each of the successive wars the combatants used increasingly complex and sophisticated weaponry. The 1967 campaign, in particular, demonstrated the remarkable ability of the Israelis to integrate air and ground operations and to wage mobile warfare reminiscent of the German *Blitzkrieg* of World War II. In 1973 about 2,000 tanks on both sides became engaged in the largest tank battle since Kursk in 1943. As is evident from Israeli successes in 1967 and 1973, they mastered armored operations before their opponents and employed their air and ground units in a more tightly coordinated and effective fashion; they also rapidly adapted to the requirement for combined-arms teams. The Egyptians, however, achieved great surprise with their use of precision-guided munitions and highly effective air-defense weapons in the 1973 war. Given the Middle East's strategic importance and the sophistication of the weapons employed, military leaders throughout the world carefully studied the Arab-Israeli wars for insights into how warfare was evolving and, particularly after the 1973 war, used that conflict as a benchmark to measure the readiness of their own forces.

The Iran-Iraq War

Another significant war in the Middle East and Southwest Asia during the Cold War was the Iran-Iraq War of 1980–1988. Though superpower involvement was limited, Iran and Iraq devoted their entire efforts to what was for them a total war without nuclear weapons. The fighting included a curious mixture of high-technology weapons and gruesomely bloody infantry assaults that seemed more appropriate for 1914 than for 1980. For the first time since World War I, chemicals were widely used, and for the first time since World War II, heavy aerial attacks hit population and economic centers. The Iraqis, having assembled a huge arsenal of modern weaponry, maintained an edge in the quality of their weapons, but the willingness of the Iranians to die for their nation and their religion enabled them to overcome significant disadvantages. The professionalism of the operations and the quality of generalship on both sides, however, were inferior to those of the Israelis in the Arab-Israeli wars.

The Iran-Iraq War stemmed from many centuries of religious (Sunni vs. Shi'ite) and ethnic (Persian vs. Arab) conflict, but President Saddam Hussein of Iraq attacked Iran for more immediate reasons. Concerned about Iran's efforts to undermine his regime, he hoped to curtail the spread of Islamic fundamentalism to which Iraq's Shi'ite population seemed particularly vulnerable. Seeking to increase his influence over the Persian Gulf area, he also wanted to seize key geographic areas that would enhance the political and economic power of Iraq.

Optimistic because of accounts of political, economic, and military turmoil in Iran, Saddam evidently expected a short, limited war. His confidence stemmed from the vast sums he had spent improving his armed forces and equipping them with more than 1,700 Soviet T-54, T-55, and T-62 tanks, 1,800 armored personnel carriers, and 340 combat aircraft. Saddam also knew that Iran had been weakened by the upheaval of its 1979 Islamic revolution and by the chaos engendered by Ayatollah Ruhollah Khomeini's efforts to subordinate Iranian political and military power to Islamic fundamentalists. As part of U.S. containment policy, the Americans had built up Iranian forces in the post–World War II period, but following the Islamic overthrow of the Shah of Iran, Khomeini had severely reduced the size of the Iranian armed forces, while dramatically increasing the number of militia and simultaneously replacing scores of officers with religious leaders who had little or no military experience. Despite Saddam's expectations of a quick and easy victory, the war would drag on for years and ultimately would cause somewhere between 600,000 and 970,000 deaths.

After a surprise air attack against ten Iranian air fields on September 22, 1980, the Iraqis launched ground attacks into Iran along four separate axes. Because many of Iran's most advanced planes were in protective hangars, the preemptive aerial attack failed to yield any real advantages. The ground attack also produced little, and about one week after the invasion began, Saddam called for a cease-fire. The Iraqis attempted several subsequent attacks, but by March 1981 they had exhausted themselves. The attacks had gained little more than a narrow strip of Iranian territory along the 1,100-kilometer border. Instead of giving the Iraqis an important strategic advantage or a swift victory, the attacks provided the revolutionary regime in Teheran with a rallying cry for the mobilization of its people. A huge outpouring of patriotism and fury brought forth thousands of volunteers willing to die for their nation and the Islamic faith. Having failed to win a swift victory, the Iraqis struggled to avoid defeat and survive against Iran's far greater population and resources. Optimistic hopes for a short, limited war were replaced by the dreadful specter of a long war involving all of Iraq's population and resources.

As governments throughout the world watched the unfolding events, many feared the spread of Ayatollah Khomeini's influence in the Middle East more than Saddam's record of aggression and human rights abuses. Consequently, most members of the international community refused to sell Iran arms and equipment even though Saddam had initiated the war. The lack of international support caused the Iranians significant logistical problems for the remainder of the war. In particular, the inability to obtain repair parts quickly decreased the combat effectiveness of their air force.

From September 1981 through May 1982, Iran seized the initiative with a series of poorly coordinated and executed attacks. The inferior quality of its operations came from its inadequately trained commanders and staffs and its shortage of equipment. In some cases, the Iranians used human wave attacks. These attacks sometimes began with hundreds of children and old men, motivated by religious fervor, racing forward and using their bodies to detonate concealed mines. Then waves of poorly trained militia threw themselves on the barbed wire and attempted to cut the wire while under the fire of the Iraqis. Finally, better equipped and trained soldiers attacked over the mangled bodies of the initial waves of children, old men, and militia.

Iranian leaders hoped the religious zeal and nationalism of their people would enable them to expel the invaders, but such emotions did not overcome serious organizational and operational weaknesses. As Iranian commanders and staffs gained experience and became more effective, they used other methods such as the launching of night infantry assaults, supported by tanks and attack helicopters. Despite huge losses, the Iranians pushed the Iraqis back. At the end of June 1982 Saddam Hussein ordered the evacuation of most of the territory seized from Iran. This withdrawal, however, did not end hostilities, and Iran soon shifted from attempting to drive the invaders from its territory to defeating Iraq and deposing Saddam.

In July, the Iranians launched a huge offensive to capture Basra, Iraq's second largest city. After this attack failed, they began an offensive in October 1982 on the central front, seeking to drive toward Baghdad. Other attacks along the long front followed, but strong Iraqi defenses held the Iranians to relatively insignificant gains. By December 1982, the Iraqis were using limited amounts of mustard gas to repel night attacks and disrupt human wave assaults. They may also have used nerve gas. One Iraqi general officer compared the use of chemicals against the Iranians to the use of "pesticides" against "insects." Despite huge losses and no significant gains, the Iranians continued to press forward.

The war entered a new phase in 1984 when Saddam began using his superior air power to halt the shipment of Iranian oil through the Persian Gulf. In February, Iraq launched attacks on the Kharg oil terminal in the Gulf, and in subsequent weeks attacked several tankers with Exocet air-to-surface cruise missiles. Since the Iraqis shipped their oil by pipeline, mainly through Turkey, the Iranians could not attack Iraqi tankers, but they could attack the shipping of Iraq's allies, Kuwait and Saudi Arabia. Subsequent attacks against tankers were condemned by the United Nations' Security Council and began what came to be known as the "Tanker War." Throughout the remainder of 1984, attacks on commercial shipping and population centers continued. While Iran held the initiative on the ground, Iraq controlled the skies, and oil from Iraq and its allies continued to flow to the outside world.

From March to June 1985, the "War of the Cities" occurred. As early as 1980–1981, Iraq had used Frog 7A missiles against Iranian cities and in 1982 began using Scud missiles (a NATO code name for the Soviet-designed SS-1 missile). In 1985, however, Iraq intensified its attacks, including more than forty air strikes against Teheran. After Iran acquired its own Scud missiles from Libya, it too began firing missiles at Iraq's cities, mainly Baghdad. Both sides improved their tactics in 1984 and 1985, but no dramatic changes occurred. In early 1986 improvements in the quality of Iranian commanders and staffs enabled them to launch two major offensives simultaneously for the first time in the war. They made one attack north of Basra and the other in the Fao peninsula, to the west of the Shatt-al-Arab waterway. Despite strong Iraqi counterattacks, the Iranians clung to the Fao peninsula and severed Iraq's direct access to the Persian Gulf. The impression that things were going badly for Baghdad was heightened when an Iraqi offensive in May against Mehran in the central sector was driven back in July with heavy losses. Saddam had little choice but to intensify air attacks.

The key development in 1987 was the increasingly active role played by the United States. Washington reluctantly concluded that an Iranian victory was contrary to its interests and threatened the stability of the Middle East. After Kuwait transferred ownership of half its tankers to a U.S. shipping company, American warships began providing them security in the Persian Gulf. In May an Iraqi aircraft launched two Exocet cruise missiles—

The Exocet missile proved deadly against ships in the Falklands and in the Persian Gulf conflicts. The missile had a range of thirty-five to forty miles, and a pilot could launch a missile toward a target ship without making visual contact. After being launched, the missile traveled to its target only six to ten feet above the water at a speed of more than 600 miles an hour.

supposedly accidentally—against the USS *Stark*, killing thirty-seven crewmen and badly damaging the ship. When a tanker escorted by three U.S. warships hit a mine on July 22, a direct U.S.-Iran naval confrontation occurred. American forces made several attacks, including one against an Iranian gunboat laying mines and another against two offshore platforms being used as bases for Iranian gunboats. By the end of 1987, the United States had over thirty warships (but no aircraft carriers) in the Gulf, and Iran confronted the possibility of even greater American involvement.

In 1988 the strategic situation began to favor Iraq. The early part of that year brought a lull in the fighting, primarily because the Iranians could not mount their usual offensive. Increasing domestic discontent with the war hampered the mustering of sufficient forces. As the Iranians began to weaken, Iraq escalated its aerial attacks on Iranian cities. An important offensive occurred in the Fao peninsula on the night of April 16 when the Iraqis pushed the Iranians across the Shatt-al-Arab waterway. Iran's concerns were heightened by U.S. Navy attacks on April 18 that sank two of Iran's four frigates and one of its armed speedboats. These attacks forced Iran to confront the awful possibility of having to fight Iraq and a superpower at the same time.

Beginning in May, Saddam launched offensives in the north and central sectors, and then in the south. Perhaps more ominously for the Iranians, the Iraqis attacked at dawn in June against the southern part of the Haur-al-Hawizeh marshes. In addition to dropping airborne troops inside Iran, the Iraqis mounted an amphibious attack with Hovercraft. In about a day, they won one of their most important victories, but they soon withdrew from the captured territory. Saddam evidently sought to signal the Iranians his willingness to end the war.

Amidst the background of an increasingly bleak situation for the Iranians, the USS *Vincennes* mistakenly identified an Iranian airplane with 290 people aboard as a war plane and shot it down. The downing of the civilian aircraft sapped the morale of Iranian leaders, for it signaled the possibility of increased superpower involvement in the war. At the same time Iran experienced even more formidable problems in obtaining military supplies from other countries and adequately equipping its armed forces. Mismanagement and corruption magnified the effect of the international community's refusal to provide arms, spare parts, and supplies.

In late July, the Iraqis attacked in the northern, central, and southern sectors. In one case they penetrated more than sixty kilometers into Iran and came within twenty-five kilometers of a provincial capital, making it clear that they had the initiative on the ground and in the air. The Iranians managed to regain their lost territory by July 25, primarily through the use of human wave attacks. Unlike the initial outpouring of volunteers in 1980, however, the Iranians came forward less willingly. As Iran's situation became more desperate, cracks began to appear in Khomeini's tight control.

Having no real alternative, Iran finally accepted a truce. At 0300 hours on August 20, 1988, the long war ended. For years the war had provided Iranian leaders the opportunity to consolidate and expand the Islamic revolution, but the possibility of losing on the battlefield threatened the revolution's existence. In the end, neither country gained from the long and bitter war, and both plundered their economies and wasted thousands of lives. Some analysts, aware of the long enmity between the two countries and of the inconclusive ending of the war, wondered when it would resume.

The war itself witnessed few innovations, but the Iraqis used the latest chemicals, missiles, and high-technology weapons. They relied on their superior air power to attack Iranian cities and halt the shipment of Iranian oil through the Persian Gulf. They also integrated rudimentary airborne and amphibious operations into their campaigns, particularly in the latter part of the war. Nevertheless, neither Iraq nor Iran demonstrated a high level of operational proficiency during the war, though both did slowly improve their performance. When the United States became involved, the Americans' advanced naval weapons and methods dominated the Persian Gulf, but the damaging of the USS *Stark* by Iraqi Exocet missiles and the downing of the Iranian civilian airplane by a missile from the USS *Vincennes* demonstrated the complexities and dangers of employing such weapons in combat. In the broadest sense, however, the nature of the war and its place within the history of warfare is suggested more by the Iranians' human-wave attacks than by high-technology weapons or sophisticated operations.

The War in Afghanistan

A different type of war occurred in Afghanistan where Afghan guerrillas fought the Soviets from 1979–1988. For many reasons, the war bears a closer resemblance to the Vietnam War than to other conflicts in the Middle East and Southwest Asia. Strategically located between Russia, Persia (Iran), and India, Afghanistan had long been the scene of international conflict and intrigue, even though it was a backward, divided country with numerous quarrelsome tribes. A new conflict began in April 1978 with the overthrow of the government of Mahammed Daoud (who had overthrown the monarchy in 1973) and the seizure of power by the People's Democratic Party of Afghanistan. Armed resistance against the new Marxist government broke out quickly, and the situation deteriorated steadily, particularly when the ruling government split into factions openly contending for power. In December 1979, the Soviets, concerned about the key region on their southern border, supported a coup. While Soviet units already in Kabul seized control of key sites, two swiftly moving columns crossed the border, traveled along traditional invasion routes, reinforced the Soviet units already in Afghanistan, and seized important provincial cities. These actions neutralized the Afghan armed forces, established Soviet control over major urban centers, and enabled the Soviets to install Babrak Karmal as president of the Democratic Republic of Afghanistan (DRA). Some Afghan units resisted, but the Soviets disarmed them quickly.

Though hoping for a quick collapse of resistance similar to Czechoslovakia in 1968, the Soviets provoked a struggle that lasted until 1988 and pitted regular troops and advanced technology against divided bands of guerrillas operating out of difficult mountainous terrain. Initially the Soviets were not overly concerned about Afghan resistance. The 15 million people living in Afghanistan seemed miniscule in comparison to the 265 million people in the Soviet Union and their vast industrial and military power. Soviet military leaders believed the various Afghan tribes had little unity and had only obsolete rifles and equipment left over from World War II. They did not anticipate the fierce resistance to Karmal's government from numerous factions of Afghan guerrillas, or Mujahideen. They also overlooked the Afghans' traditional hatred for foreign interference and the disastrous experience of the British in 1842 and 1879–1880.

During the first four years of the war, the Soviets and their Afghan allies held the major urban centers and launched attacks against the Mujahideen in remote and often mountainous areas. Opposition increased during this period as more than half of the 80,000 soldiers in the Afghan army deserted or joined the Mujahideen; many of the deserters brought their weapons with them. Relying on classic guerrilla tactics, the Mujahideen made numerous small-scale attacks and conducted ambushes of Soviet and DRA convoys along the major roads. Along with their indomitable fighting spirit, which was partially sustained by a wide wave of Islamic fundamentalism, the

Mujahideen possessed one other very important advantage—their ability to use sanctuaries in Pakistan and Iran as bases for support and training. Bands of guerrillas crossed the border with impunity and struck without warning throughout Afghanistan.

The initial Soviet and DRA tactics relied on standard techniques of mechanized warfare—a preliminary bombardment from artillery, helicopters, and airplanes, followed by a ground assault with tanks and armored personnel carriers. Especially in the first years of the war, Soviet and DRA forces often conducted division-sized offensives against Mujahideen sanctuaries. They also used large cordon and search operations in which they encircled an area and then combed it thoroughly for the elusive guerillas. Particularly in the central and eastern portions of Afghanistan, however, the guerrillas found many hiding places among the rocks, crevices, and valleys of the rugged countryside. With their detailed knowledge of the area, they could operate easily in the mountainous areas and were not confined to the roads, but the Soviets usually had to move by helicopter or use road-bound vehicles.

Within months after arriving in Afghanistan, the Soviets slowly began modifying the structure of their units and changing their tactics. When they first intervened in Afghanistan, they employed an airborne division and four motorized rifle divisions, but they soon discovered that mechanized units and conventional attacks did not yield substantial success. They turned to decentralized, mobile operations with battalions and regiments reinforced by artillery, engineers, and helicopters. They also quickly increased their helicopters and trained their infantry for heliborne operations. Though still relying on mechanized infantry, they used air-transported infantry to strike swiftly at unsuspecting Afghan guerrillas. As time passed, their airmobile tactics resembled those employed by the Americans in Vietnam.

As the Soviets and DRA modified their organizations and tactics, the Mujahideen began receiving weapons from the west, including mines, recoilless rifles, and small antiaircraft guns. Though some unity of command would have ensured better coordination and perhaps greater effectiveness, most of the guerrilla factions operated independently. They moved back and forth across the border from Pakistan and Iran and launched operations with virtually no strategic or tactical purpose other than the killing of Soviet soldiers and their supporters. Rocket attacks against Kabul and other important cities became a standard practice. To starve and terrorize the guerrillas into submission, the Soviets used "scorched earth" tactics and destroyed villages and crops. They also used chemicals, particularly in the first three years of the war, but the Mujahideen stubbornly continued to resist and despite heavy losses controlled significant parts of Afghanistan.

By 1984 the Soviets had to choose between a massive increase in forces or a different strategy. Reluctant to accept higher casualties and to increase the size of their forces beyond 125–140,000, they adopted a different strategy. They shifted from destroying individual guerrillas to destroying the infrastructure needed by the guerrillas for survival and to disrupting their supply lines and bases in border provinces. To accomplish this, they attacked the supply lines along which men and equipment flowed from Pakistan; they also unleashed attacks against areas in the border provinces that previously had been sanctuaries for the guerrillas. Air and artillery strikes against hostile population centers became routine. Soviet troops attacked villages suspected of having sheltered guerrillas and destroyed their livestock and crops. For a time the Soviet and DRA forces seemed to have gained the upper hand. As attacks against villages increased in frequency and destruction, more and more Afghans fled Afghanistan. Analysts estimated that about 30–50 percent of the populace had departed by 1986. Nonetheless, the Soviets and DRA still had little control outside the urban centers.

In 1986, it became more and more apparent that battlefield victories and ruthless destruction of civilians and their property could not destroy the insurgents' will to fight. New air-defense weapons also began to have a significant effect. As early as February 1982, the Mujahideen had used the SAM-7 surface-to-air missile against Soviet aircraft, but in February 1986 the United States decided to send high-technology weapons to Afghanistan. By mid-1987 the Soviets were losing about one aircraft per day to shoulder-fired air-defense missiles, particularly the American-made Stinger. They quickly learned that aircraft had to take evasive measures and could not operate effectively near guerrilla units armed with the highly effective air-defense weapons.

The disruption of aerial operations reduced the Soviets' freedom to maneuver and forced them to launch ground attacks with less air support and fewer heliborne assaults. In 1987 and 1988, most operations reverted to reliance on mechanized infantry formations, supported by artillery. In

The first 340 Stinger missiles fired by Afghan rebels brought down 269 Soviet aircraft. These losses forced the Soviets to change their aviation tactics completely.

reality, the Soviets no longer had the mobility of the lightly equipped Afghan guerrillas. In November 1988, they began using Scud missiles—despite their inaccuracy—to provide fire support for units and to increase terror among the Afghan people. As the mobility of the Soviets decreased, they reluctantly withdrew from many remote areas and sought to secure urban areas, thereby permitting the Mujahideen slowly to gain the upper hand. The Mujahideen began using trucks rather than pack animals and main roads rather than trails. They also began using heavier weapons.

Karmal's presidency ended in November 1986. His replacement, Mohammed Najibullah, head of the secret police, adopted a more Islamic public image in November 1987 in an attempt to sway the Mujahideen. Though under Soviet control, he made another attempt at "national reconciliation" by dropping the word "democratic," which supposedly suggested Marxist leanings, and adopting the name, Republic of Afghanistan.

Continuing to search for alternatives, the Soviets and their Afghan allies launched air raids against Mujahideen bases in Pakistan. They stepped up attacks on villages controlled by guerillas and air-dropped thousands of mines along suspected supply routes. Despite these last-ditch efforts, the strategic initiative had shifted to the Mujahideen. The Soviet and Afghan forces still lacked popular support, and they had little control outside the major urban centers. In early 1988, the Mujahideen estimated that they controlled 80 percent of the countryside. Battlefield victories by the Soviets and heavy casualties among the Afghan people had neither ended the flow of troops and supplies across the border nor increased popular support for the new government. The deteriorating Soviet situation worsened as soldiers' morale dropped, discipline dwindled, and drug use became more prevalent.

Like the Americans after the Tet Offensive in Vietnam, the Soviets refused to increase the number of forces involved in the war. Facing overwhelming economic problems at home, they finally decided to withdraw. After signing an accord in Geneva in April 1988, they staged a farewell parade in Kabul in May and began to transfer equipment to the Kabul government and withdraw Soviet troops. The last Soviet soldiers departed Afghanistan on February 15, 1989. With the Cold War ending and the Soviet empire disintegrating, the government in Kabul remained faithful to the Soviets, and the war continued even though the Afghans were now fighting a civil war among themselves.

In April 1992, fourteen years after the Soviet-backed coup plunged Afghanistan into war, Najibullah gave up power, tried to flee, and ended up seeking refuge in a United Nations' building. As thousands of Mujahideen poured into Kabul, rival factions fought for control over the Afghan capital. An uneasy truce finally emerged, but factional strife—ethnic, tribal, and religious—continued. The outlook for Afghanistan remained bleak.

In the Afghanistan War, the Russians experienced numerous difficulties as they initially attempted to fight the Mujahideen with forces designed for combat in central Europe. Even after changing their methods and relying more on airmobile operations, the Russians failed to defeat the highly mobile Mujahideen and found themselves at a disadvantage when shoulder-fired air-defense weapons destroyed many of their aircraft and restricted the role of air support. Though facing defeat, the Russians refused to expand the war significantly in order to end the flow of weapons and supplies to the Mujahideen. In the end, the Russians limited their forces and objectives and by exercising self-restraint chose defeat rather than escalation.

The Cold War in Retrospect

The most unique aspect of the Cold War was the role played by nuclear weapons. From the dropping of the first atomic bomb in August 1945 to the formal dissolving of the Warsaw Pact in July 1991, atomic and then nuclear weapons exercised a dramatic influence over national security policy, military strategy, and the organizations and equipment of military forces. The influence of nuclear weapons over national security policy expanded as technological advances extended the range, improved the accuracy, and increased the payloads of nuclear delivery systems, vastly multiplying the destructive power of nuclear devices. Many changes in the nuclear era came from one of the superpowers reacting to actions or advances by the other. After the Soviet Union exploded an atomic and then a nuclear device, the Americans lost their monopoly over nuclear weapons, and deterrence became crucially important, particularly as Soviet nuclear forces approached parity with those of the Americans. Foremost among other factors influencing questions relating to nuclear weapons were concerns about the morality of destroying millions of people, military and civilian. To many critics, the acronym for Mutual Assured Destruction, MAD, aptly described the reasoning, or lack thereof, that underpinned theories relating to nuclear warfare. Nonetheless, changes in ideas and technologies pertaining to nuclear weapons greatly influenced the policies, strategies, and forces of both sides during the Cold War.

One of the most important consequences of the introduction of nuclear arms was the opening of an era of limited war. Throughout the Cold War, both the Americans and the Soviets feared the consequences of nuclear escalation and sometimes found themselves having to yield or compromise rather than raise the stakes in a crisis. Though both sides sought advantages in regional conflicts, neither wanted a crisis to draw the superpowers into a direct confrontation. Aware of the dangers of escalation and nuclear warfare, political and military leaders acknowledged the existence of various levels of conflict, ranging from low-intensity, to mid-intensity, to high-intensity, to general nuclear war. To avoid general nuclear war or high-intensity conflict (which presumably could escalate quickly), the superpowers limited their objectives or the size and nature of their military forces involved in a conflict. Nevertheless, both devoted considerable resources and efforts to the development of new weapons and methods, and both sold or shared these with friendly or client states. As a result, modern arms spread around the world at an unprecedented rate, and regular and irregular forces used them with terrifying effect in some 160 major conflicts and numerous minor ones between 1945 and 1990.

Though the superpowers avoided a direct confrontation, numerous revolutionary wars occurred in the post–World War II decades as European colonial empires dissolved and new successor states appeared. After Mao and the Communists successfully seized power in China in 1949, Mao's ideas wielded great influence. Along with other leaders such as Ho Chi Minh, he recognized the difficulty of achieving a quick victory against better-armed opponents, so he placed equal emphasis on political and military efforts and relied on a protracted struggle to exhaust his enemies and permit the seizure of power. In the ensuing decades of violence, dealing with guerrillas became not only the most common but also one of the most complex aspects of the Cold War. Amidst increased concern about low-intensity conflict in protracted wars, military forces developed special expertise and capabilities to deal with guerrillas. The Americans learned hard lessons about guerrilla warfare in Vietnam, while the Soviets learned similar lessons against the Mujahideen in Afghanistan.

Terrorism also became common. Though radicals had long used sustained, clandestine violence—murders, kidnappings, bombings, skyjackings—to achieve their political purposes, incidents of terrorism surged to historically high levels in the late 1960s and 1970s and became even more frequent in the 1980s. As acts of terrorism spilled outside the boundaries of ongoing conflicts, governments responded to the increased levels of violence by exchanging information about terrorist groups and accumulating intelligence about their membership and activities. Normal police procedures prevented some incidents. Israel, the United States, Great Britain, and Germany went a step farther and formed highly trained and specially equipped counterterrorist units to combat some of the gravest threats. In July 1976 an Israeli Army unit flew to Entebbe, Uganda, and freed a plane full of Jewish hostages. In October 1977, a West German counterterrorist group successfully stormed a Lufthansa aircraft held by terrorists at Mogadishu in Somalia. And in May 1980 members of the British Special Air Service killed six terrorists who had seized twenty-six hostages in the Iranian Embassy in London. While efforts to eradicate terrorism did not yield complete success, the number of incidents seemed to ebb by 1990.

Along with the willingness to use violence against innocent civilians came an erosion of previous restraints on the use of chemicals. The Iraqis used chemicals against the Iranians and compared this use to the use of "pesticides" against "insects." The Soviets also used chemicals in Afghanistan, particularly in the first three years of the war. Additionally, the Egyptians used chemicals in Yemen, the Vietnamese in Kampuchea and Laos, the Libyans in Chad and Northern Uganda, the Cubans in Angola, and the Iraqis against the Kurds. The United States often used riot control gasses and hebicides in Indochina during the Vietnam War. In every case, the use of chemicals occurred in situations in which an opponent lacked adequate means of protection or retaliation. The apparent willingness to employ chemical weapons reflected in part some states' viewing chemical weapons as a "poor man's" nuclear weapon, but it also reflected a widespread willingness to use nearly any means available to achieve victory.

Most major conflicts during the Cold War proved to be protracted rather than brief. The United States hoped to end the Korean War quickly after the landing at Inchon and the breakout from the Pusan perimeter, but the entrance of the Chinese into the war and the complications of political questions and prisoner-of-war issues prevented an early termination of the war. In Vietnam, the Americans had even less success in ending the war early on favorable terms. At the beginning of the Iran-Iraq War, the Iraqi attack against Iran failed despite Iraq's possession of advanced weapons and despite the disorganized state of Iran's forces, and the war dragged on for years. Also, the Russians, despite their numerous advantages and initial success, failed in Afghanistan after years of fighting against a populace determined to pay any price to avoid defeat. Numerous other conflicts, many of which were civil wars stemming from the collapse of colonial empires, tended to last for years. Notable exceptions to long wars occurred with the Israeli victories in 1956, 1967, and 1973, but even these could be considered incidents in a much longer conflict extending over several decades.

In an age of astonishing progress in science and technology, the introduction of advanced weapons and equipment had a particularly significant effect on operations throughout the Cold War. In the Korean War, the combatants used weapons very similar to those of World War II, but in Vietnam the United States fielded a very different force that relied primarily on the helicopter for battlefield mobility. The United States also introduced some rudimentary precision-guided munitions in that war, but the potential of such weapons became most evident in the 1973 Arab-Israeli War. In the Afghanistan War, the Mujahideen used sophisticated and highly mobile air-defense weapons, which relied on advanced electronics, to transform the nature of the fighting. In the last two decades of the Cold War, electronic advances enhanced the ability of commanders to control their forces. With much-improved radios, commanders could maintain better contact with their subordinate units and often had a better grasp of the flow of events. Information about the enemy also increased as the introduction of remarkably capable cameras and high-flying, supersonic aircraft and then satellites permitted the gathering of critical intelligence by the most advanced armed forces. Similarly, advances in computers and information processing permitted improvements in logistical systems. By 1990, the capability of weapons and equipment, as well as intelligence and logistical systems, far exceeded those of 1945.

Despite some significant anomalies, as combat became more lethal, operations became more mobile and linked to air power. Reaching beyond the experience of World War II, battles truly became three-dimensional with the tightening of links between air and ground operations and the introduction of airmobile operations. The Israelis, particularly in the 1967 and 1973 wars, demonstrated their proficiency in conducting lightning-fast campaigns, relying on tightly integrated air and ground forces. Their successes in 1967 and 1973 stemmed more from their superior organizations, strategy, and doctrine than from their superior technology. Advantages in air power and in air mobility, however, did not enable the Americans to overcome the strategic advantages of the North Vietnamese or the tactical mobility of their lightly equipped infantry. Under similar circumstances the Russians failed to overcome the Mujahideen. Iraqi advantages in air power over the Iranians also did not inject mobility into the Iran-Iraq war.

In the final analysis, the conduct of war varied so greatly from conflict to conflict in the Cold War that no single example can serve adequately as a representation of all operations in the era. The key changes in warfare, nevertheless, were both conceptual and technological. Emphasis on limited war reflected the desire of the superpowers to avoid a direct confrontation and escalation to general nuclear war. And the notion of a spectrum of conflict—including low-, mid-, and high-intensity—reflected the various levels of conflict possible prior to all-out nuclear warfare. Within this spectrum, low-intensity conflict—including insurgency, counterinsurgency, and terrorism—received special attention as revolutionary groups often used violence to gain power or achieve their political aims. In an era of remarkable scientific and technological advances, new weapons and equipment frequently appeared, and numerous states fielded modern armed forces equipped with sophisticated arms. The Cold War was thus an era of innovation and change in which military leaders constantly confronted new ideas and weapons, as well as new challenges.

SUGGESTED READINGS

Amstutz, J. Bruce. *Afghanistan: The First Five Years of Soviet Occupation* (Washington, D.C.: National Defense University Press, 1986).

Badri, Hassan el, et al. *The Ramadan War, 1973* (Boulder, Col.: Westview Press, 1977).

Bradsher, Henry S. *Afghanistan and the Soviet Union* (Durham, N.C.: Duke University Press, 1985).

Carver, Michael. *War Since 1945* (London: Ashfield Press, 1990).

Chubin, Shahram, and Charles Tripp. *Iran and Iraq at War* (Boulder, Col.: Westview Press, 1988).

Collins, Joseph H. *The Soviet Invasion of Afghanistan: A Study of the Use of Force in Soviet Foreign Policy* (Lexington, Mass.: Lexington Books, 1986).

Department of National Defence, Canada, Operational Research and Analysis Establishment, ORAE Report No. R 95, G. D. Kaye, D. A. Grant, E. J. Emond. *Major Armed Conflict: A Compendium of Interstate and Intrastate Conflict, 1720 to 1985* (Ottawa, Canada: Orbita Consultants LTD, 1985).

Gawrych, George W. *Key to the Sinai: The Battles for Abu Ageila in the 1956 and 1967 Arab-Israeli Wars* (Fort Leavenworth, Kans.: Combat Studies Institute, 1990).

Hauner, Milan. *The Soviet War in Afghanistan: Patterns of Russian Imperialism* (Philadelphia: Foreign Policy Research Institute, 1991).

Herzog, Chaim. *The Arab-Israeli Wars: War and Peace in the Middle East* (New York: Random House, 1982).

_____. *The War of Atonement: October, 1973* (Boston: Little, Brown and Company, 1975).

Hiro, Dilip. *The Longest War: The Iran-Iraq Military Conflict* (New York: Routledge, 1991).

Kahalani, Avigdor. *The Heights of Courage: A Tank Leader's War on the Golan* (Westport, Conn.: Greenwood Press, 1984).

Klass, Rosanne, ed. *Afghanistan: The Great Game Revisited* (New York: Freedom House, 1987).

Laqueur, Walter. *The Age of Terrorism* (Boston: Little, Brown and Company, 1987).

Luttwak, Edward, and Dan Horowitz. *The Israeli Army* (Cambridge, Mass.: Abt Books, 1983).

O'Ballance, Edgar. *No Victor, No Vanquished: The Yom Kippur War* (San Rafael, Calif.: Presidio Press, 1978).

Small, Melvin, and J. David Singer. *Resort to Arms: International and Civil Wars, 1816–1980* (Beverly Hills, Calif.: Sage Publications, 1982).

Thompson, Robert. *War in Peace: Conventional and Guerrilla Warfare Since 1945* (New York: Harmony Books, 1985).

Zabih, Sepehr. *The Iranian Military in Revolution and War* (London: Routledge, 1988).

31

THE AGE OF INTERVENTIONS: PROJECTING POWER AND MAINTAINING PEACE

Interventions in the Cold War

Beyond the Cold War: The Persian Gulf

The United Nations: From Peacekeeping to Peace Enforcement

By the final decade of the Cold War, the major economic and military powers of the West had developed the capability to project force quickly over great distances. Improvements in air and sea transport had enhanced strategic mobility and enabled a few countries to move and support units across thousands of kilometers. In an age of science and technology, these same powers had built arsenals of high-technology weapons with remarkable accuracy and long range. Additionally, advances in electronics and communications permitted more effective command and control of units located at great distances from their homelands. In essence, rapid transport, advanced weapons, and modern communications provided a few countries the capability to project force almost anywhere on the globe. The states possessing this capability—primarily the United States, the Soviet Union, Great Britain, and France—often transported forces during the Cold War to distant regions to protect their own interests, limit the outbreak or spread of violence, or combat aggression. They consequently became embroiled in small conflicts in areas such as the Falklands, Grenada, and Panama.

When the Cold War ended in 1989–1990, the likelihood of interventions did not diminish. Although the confrontation between the two superpowers and their allies disappeared, a more complicated world, split by national, religious, ethnic, and regional differences, appeared. As the constraints of the Cold War dissolved, long-suppressed animosities and aspirations resurfaced, and violence broke out in several regions. Particularly in the Balkans and in the southern part of the former Soviet Union, civil strife, massacres, and pitched battles produced considerable turmoil. Fearing that the violence and turmoil would spread, almost like a cancer, to previously stable regions, some political and military leaders proposed interventions by national and multinational forces to end the violence and restore peace. To most observers' surprise, however, the first major conflict of the post–Cold War era began on August 2, 1990, when Iraq invaded and seized Kuwait. The international community responded to this aggression by transporting massive forces to Southwest Asia and then—in an astounding display of advanced weaponry—destroying much of the Iraqi armed forces with first an aerial attack and then a joint air and ground attack. The swift campaign revealed that not even a relatively wealthy and advanced country like Iraq could match the forces of the major military powers.

The ending of the Cold War also brought changes in the role of the United Nations and its use of intervening forces. No longer constrained by the likelihood of a veto in the U.N. Security Council or by the dangers of a superpower confrontation, U.N. leaders called for "peace-enforcement" operations in which multinational forces would intervene in conflicts, using appropriate levels of force, and restore peace. The reluctance of the United Nations to go beyond providing humanitarian aid in Bosnia-Herzegovina and the difficulties encountered with peace enforcement in Somalia demonstrated the complexities and problems of using international forces in interventions. These conflicts also reminded political and military leaders of the difficulties of employing force in regions riven by strong nationalistic, ethnic, or religious differences.

Interventions in the Cold War

During the Cold War, the major military powers often used their armed forces to support their foreign policy or to achieve specific political objectives. Many of these actions came from the effort to "contain" communism or to prevent a small crisis from erupting into a worldwide conflagration. Actions by the United States, for example, ranged from making a visit to a foreign port with a single warship, to reacting to the seizure of the USS *Pueblo* by the North Koreans in January 1968, to rushing supplies and equipment to Israel in October 1973 during the Arab-Israeli War. About forty crises reached the point where the United States had to confront the possibility of combat.

The U.S. Navy and Marines participated in most of the operations in which Americans were involved. The United States maintained fleets in most major oceans, and the Fleet Marine Force (which was established in

1933) provided battalions of marines that remained afloat with each fleet. In a crisis, marines could move quickly to an area as part of a fleet and could draw upon the fleet's firepower, aviation, and logistical support as they moved ashore. Such forces often proved ideal for dealing with small crises, and other countries such as Great Britain followed the American lead in increasing their fleet's capability to send units ashore.

Following World War II, airborne units and long-distance military air transport provided new means for interventions in distant regions. Much of the increased emphasis on airborne insertions came from the improved range and carrying capacity of military air transport. Particularly in the United States, each new aircraft (such as the Fairchild C-119 Flying Boxcar, the Lockheed C-130 Hercules, the Lockheed C-141B Starlifter, and the Lockheed C-5 Galaxy) provided greater range and carrying capacity than its predecessor. The transition from the C-119, widely used in the Korean War, to the C-5, widely used in the Persian Gulf War, included the change from a cruising speed of 325 kilometers per hour (200 miles per hour) and a range of 1,500 kilometers (900 miles) with a 20,000-pound cargo, to a cruising speed of 830 kilometers per hour (518 miles per hour) and a range of 5,600 kilometers (3,500 miles) with a 170,000-pound cargo. As the capability for air transport of large forces over long distances increased in the mid-to-late 1950s, military leaders recognized that improved transportation enabled light ground units to respond swiftly to an emergency, participate in a small war, or provide initial reinforcements in a much larger war.

An early example of the use of both air- and sea-transported forces occurred in April 1965. In the first American intervention in the Caribbean since U.S. Marines departed from Haiti in 1934, Washington dispatched troops to the Dominican Republic in April 1965. After a revolution broke out in the island nation, President Lyndon B. Johnson, fearing a communist takeover, decided to use military force to restore order. On April 28, 3rd Battalion, 6th Marines flew in helicopters from nearby American ships and landed in Santo Domingo. They assisted in the evacuation of Americans and reinforced the security guard at the U.S. Embassy. After being alerted on the night of April 26, elements of the U.S. Army's 82nd Airborne Division flew on C-130 aircraft from the United States to Puerto Rico and then landed at an airfield near Santo Domingo at 0216 hours on April 30. Members of 7th Special Forces Group and 5th Logistics Command followed. By May 4, more than 17,000 Americans were in Santo Domingo, and by May 17 more than 24,000.

The United States was not the only state to develop the capability for projecting power over great distances. In November 1956, after Gamal Abdel Nasser unexpectedly nationalized the Suez Canal, British and French forces seized the Canal. The operation included French and British airborne battalions jumping onto key targets while British marine battalions came ashore in amphibious landings and heliborne air assaults. Another multinational intervention occurred in November 1964, when U.S. Air Force C-130 aircraft flew 12,000 kilometers from Belgium to the Republic of the Congo and air-dropped a battalion from the Belgian Paracommando Regiment in an attempt to rescue 1,600 European and American hostages. Of those states intervening far outside their own frontiers, France demonstrated a special willingness to intervene in Africa, for it engaged in more than a dozen interventions from 1962 to 1994 in Dakar, Gabon, Chad, Zaire, the Central African Republic, Togo, and Rawanda.

The Falklands

Not all crises had direct ties to the Cold War. When Great Britain responded in 1982 to Argentina's seizure of the Falkland Islands, the roots of the conflict stretched back for more than a century. Known as Las Malvinas in Argentina, the Falklands are an archipelago of some 200 small and two large islands—East Falkland and West Falkland—located about 600 kilometers off the eastern shore of Argentina and 12,000 kilometers from the British Isles. The British claimed sovereignty over the islands, for they had occupied them for more than 150 years and most of the approximately 2,000 inhabitants were of British origin. Argentina denied London's claims and insisted that when Argentina became an independent republic in 1816, it had assumed title to those territories formerly ruled by Spain from Buenos Aires, including the Falklands. As early as 1965, the U.N. General Assembly recognized the dispute between the two states, and for almost two decades the two states discussed the islands' future. In December 1981, however, Argentina began preparing to seize the islands.

On April 2, 1982, the Argentines landed about 1,000 men at Port Stanley on the island of East Falkland and quickly overcame the small Royal Marine detachment. The next day the Argentines seized South Georgia, an island 1,300 kilometers east-southeast of the Falklands and a direct dependency of Britain. They then transported troops and supplies by air and sea until they had about 13,000 troops on the Falkland Islands. British leaders faced the uncomfortable choice of accepting the Argentine action or going to war nearly 12,000 kilometers from Britain with no force organized or prepared for such a contingency, no shore-based air, and little or no knowledge of their enemy.

The importance of sea power for the projection of power over great distances became particularly evident in subsequent British actions. Refusing to accept the Argentine action, the British quickly put together a "retrieval force," the lead elements of which departed Portsmouth on April 5. The task force eventually included a landing force of some 8,000 soldiers and marines and a naval force of more than one hundred ships, including two small aircraft carriers, eight destroyers, fifteen frigates, and six submarines. Fortunately for the British, they had not completed the previously arranged sale of the HMS *Hermes*, a small aircraft carrier, to the Australians. Much of the subsequent campaign would turn on control of the air provided for the British by Vertical/Short Take-off and Landing (VSTOL) aircraft from the HMS *Hermes* and the HMS *Invincible*.

British strategy first sought to isolate the Argentine forces on the Falklands. In early April, London announced that a "maritime" exclusion

The Falklands, April–June 1982

GREAT BRITAIN

Portsmouth

ATLANTIC OCEAN

6,000 km

ASCENSION ISLAND

ATLANTIC OCEAN

ARGENTINA

6,000 km

| 0 | 500 | 1000 mi |
| 0 | 500 | 1000 km |

600 km

1,300 km

FALKLAND ISLANDS

SOUTH GEORGIA

SOUTH SANDWICH ISANDS

zone with a 200–nautical mile (370 kilometer) radius would go into effect around the islands on April 12; on April 30 they expanded this into a "total" exclusion zone. Any Argentine aircraft or ship entering this zone would be treated as hostile and could be attacked. On May 1 the British began air and sea bombardment of Port Stanley and Goose Green. The following day, a British nuclear-powered submarine sank the Argentine cruiser, *General Belgrano*, well outside the exclusion zone; 323 members of the Belgrano's crew perished. For the next three weeks the British continued softening up the Argentine defenders on the Falklands.

Meanwhile, the British used Ascension Island, a small air and naval base in the Atlantic midway between Britain and the Falklands, as a staging base for the operation. After hastily assembling the requisite ships and personnel, the main task force, under Rear Admiral John Woodward, sailed from Ascension Island on April 18, even though additional personnel and ships continued to depart Britain for Ascension Island and the Falklands. As the main forces assembled in the South Atlantic, British special operating forces seized South Georgia on April 26, and on May 15 they struck a small Argentine airfield on Pebble Island, just off the north end of West Falkland, and destroyed eleven propeller-driven aircraft.

The Argentines did not remain passive. On May 1, when the British began their attacks on the Falklands, the Argentines launched fifty-six aerial sorties against the enemy's warships. Much to their dismay, they discovered that their best fighters, Mirages and Skyhawks, were no match for British Sea Harriers, which were armed with more advanced AIM-9G Sidewinder heat-seeking missiles. Part of the Argentines' problem came from their keeping their most advanced aircraft at airbases on the continent as many as one thousand kilometers from the Falklands, thus limiting these aircraft to only a few minutes in which they could loiter over a target or engage in a dogfight. In essence, the Argentines could not gain air superiority and could do little more than damage British naval forces and disrupt an amphibious landing. On May 4, from a range of about thirty-five kilometers, however, two Super Etendard aircraft fired two Exocet missiles at British ships; one missed the HMS *Hermes*, but the other struck the HMS *Sheffield*, a destroyer. The

Argentine air force personnel load antipersonnel rockets onto a propeller-driven aircraft. Despite the lethality of such weapons, attacks against British ships came closest to turning the war in Argentina's favor.

British had to abandon the burning *Sheffield*, which had twenty of its crew members killed. Despite the short loiter time, the Argentines continued launching strikes against British warships. On May 25, the Argentines sank the HMS *Coventry* and the *Atlantic Conveyor*, the first with 1,000-pound bombs and the second with an Exocet missile. Throughout the campaign, courageous Argentine pilots would sink six British ships and damage eighteen others. Had they possessed more than five of the French-manufactured Exocet missiles, they might have inflicted even greater damage.

By mid-May, the British had advanced into the South Atlantic, isolated Argentine forces on the Falklands, recaptured South Georgia, and launched commando raids and aerial reconnaissance in preparation for an amphibious landing. At dawn on May 21, after a diversionary operation farther south, British forces began landing at Port San Carlos and San Carlos on the northwest corner of East Falkland. The landing of the 3rd Commando Brigade (a marine unit commanded by Brigadier Julian Thompson) and two parachute battalions went smoothly and met almost no opposition, but Argentine pilots braved heavy antiaircraft fire to strike British ships. The British intended to consolidate their beachhead, unload supplies, and advance only a short distance until the 5th Infantry Brigade arrived. Although under heavy aerial attack, the British unloaded 12,000 tons of cargo in the first five days.

Concerned about British losses and desiring to show greater progress, London ordered the capture of Darwin and Goose Green, twenty kilometers south of the beachhead. Advancing on the night of May 27, the

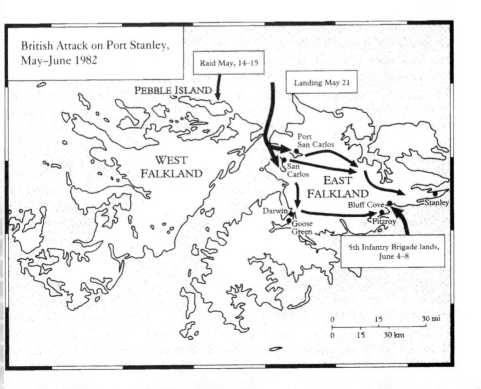

British Attack on Port Stanley, May–June 1982

2nd Battalion of the Parachute Regiment attacked early on May 28 and encountered strong opposition. Though their battalion commander was killed, the British continued pressing the Argentine defenders until they offered to surrender. Much to the paratroopers' surprise, more than 1,200 Argentines, some of whom were from the air force, surrendered their weapons and marched into captivity. With little support, a single British battalion had defeated a force triple its own strength.

The battle, however, produced considerable strain between the British military and the news media. Shortly before the attack on Goose Green, the BBC World News Service announced the location and mission of the 2nd Battalion. Other difficulties stemmed from few of the reporters having a sophisticated understanding of military affairs, and fewer still being prepared for the rigors of marching across the Falklands. Some reporters in the South Atlantic became particularly angry when they realized that their reports were being heavily censored and that some of the information removed by censors in the South Atlantic was being released by the Ministry of Defence in London.

After Goose Green, the British turned their attention to the capture of Port Stanley on the opposite side of East Falkland. Located at the tip of a twenty-five kilometer peninsula, Port Stanley had three chains of mountains between it and the approaching enemy. The Argentine commander, Brigadier General Mario B. Menéndez, had about 9,000 troops and placed them in well-organized and strong defensive positions in these mountains. Though apprehensive about an amphibious landing near Port Stanley, he evidently thought these mountainous positions were impregnable, and he expected his defenses and the approaching winter to force the British to seek a diplomatic end to the war. His lack of confidence in his soldiers, mostly conscripts, and the absence of air and sea support convinced him to wage a passive campaign and to keep his forces in static defenses. The morale of the defenders was very low. Few had proper cold-weather clothing, and many suffered from inadequate rations. Most apparently felt abandoned.

For the assault on Port Stanley, the British had intended to transport their troops by helicopter, but the sinking of the *Atlantic Conveyor*, a container ship, had resulted in the loss of critical helicopter support. Consequently many soldiers and marines had to trudge across some eighty kilometers of cold, wet, difficult terrain. The British advanced on two routes, one along the northern coast of East Falkland and the other along the southern coast. On June 1 they used helicopters to land troops on two mountains in the most westward chain, and other forces arrived by foot a few days later. On June 5 a battalion from the 5th Infantry Brigade landed on the coast to the south of the 3rd Commando Brigade, and two later days, another battalion landed but suffered heavily from an Argentine air strike.

The British land-force commander, Major General Jeremy Moore, eventually had two brigades in place for the final assault on Port Stanley. After doing everything possible to convince the Argentines to surrender, he decided to make a night attack on a broad front. On the night of June 11–12, the 3rd Commando Brigade, reinforced by the 3rd Parachute Battalion, attacked with three battalions abreast and seized, after some difficult

fighting, the second chain of mountains. Two nights later the 5th Brigade passed through the marines and attacked the third chain. The British battalion in the north encountered strong opposition, but the two battalions in the south met little resistance. The Argentine defenders struck the northern battalion in two minor counterattacks, but heavy fire broke them. The failure of these counterattacks left the British in command of high ground from which they could dominate all the open ground to the west of Stanley. Within minutes, Argentine defenses collapsed. As the defenders fled in panic toward Port Stanley, white flags appeared throughout the Argentine positions. At 2100 hours on June 14, Menéndez signed an "instrument of surrender" given him by Moore.

In a stormy, mountainous, freezing environment, the British had won a difficult campaign. They had defeated a numerically superior force and had overcome the significant logistical problem of transporting and supporting large forces 12,000 kilometers from their home base. The war demonstrated the strengths of a well-trained, prepared force. British soldiers and marines, all of whom were volunteers, performed much better than the Argentines, most of whom were conscripts. Only the Argentine pilots performed on a par with the British. The war also demonstrated the importance of joint operations. Unlike the Argentines, who encountered problems in getting their services to cooperate, the British military achieved excellent cooperation among air, land, and sea elements as they waged a relatively short-warning, intense operation against an unexpected adversary. Another significant feature of the war was the demonstrated effect of the high-technology weapons entering the world's arsenals in the 1980s. The lethality and effectiveness of the Exocet over great distances cost the British dearly, just as the technical advantages of the more advanced Sidewinder missile cost the Argentines dearly. In the final analysis, however, the British won because of their ability to project power over great distances and their mastery of basic military skills.

Operation "Urgent Fury" in Grenada

Another significant intervention during the Cold War occurred in October 1983 when the United States relied on air and sea transport to intervene on extremely short notice in Grenada, a small island in the Caribbean. With marine units relying on naval transport, and army units relying on air transport, the brief conflict turned out to be unexpectedly difficult because of limited planning time, the great distances involved, the variety of forces participating, and the lack of adequate intelligence. Around noon on Saturday, October 22, President Reagan ordered the intervention in Grenada. Because of the breakdown of order on the island, he was initially concerned with the safety of Americans, but he soon expanded the operation's objectives to include restoring democratic government in Grenada and eliminating current and future Cuban intervention on the island. The Cubans were building a major air base in Grenada, and he feared the spread of Cuban and communist influence in the Caribbean.

A military policeman guards prisoners in Grenada. Planning for Urgent Fury included preparation not only for transport and combat but also for logistical support, medical care, civil affairs, and a host of other requirements.

The Joint Chiefs of Staff issued the formal order around 1700 hours on Saturday for Operation "Urgent Fury." Anticipating a mission to ensure the safety of Americans, the Commander-in-Chief of the Atlantic Command (CINCLANT) had already organized a joint force (designated Joint Task Force 120, under the command of Vice Admiral Joseph Metcalf, III) and sent it toward Grenada. Subsequent intelligence estimates of enemy forces in Grenada, however, identified about 700 Cubans (of whom 25 percent were military), 1,200–1,500 members of the People's Revolutionary Army (PRA), and 2,000–5,000 members of the People's Revolutionary Militia (PRM). Though the figures turned out to be inflated, the opposition appeared to consist of about ten combat battalions, plus supporting units. Responding to broader goals and facing what they thought was a large enemy force, planners increased the size of the American force by adding army units, flown in by the air force, to the operation. What had initially been envisaged as a relatively small and simple navy-marine rescue of American students became a much larger and more complicated operation.

Located about 200 kilometers off the coast of Venezuela, the island of Grenada is shaped like an oval, about thirty kilometers long and twelve kilometers wide, with a broad peninsula jutting out from the southwest corner. Much of the island consists of mountainous jungle, surrounded by a narrow coastal plain on which most of the island's towns are located. The Point Salines airfield with a 3,000-meter runway is on the peninsula in the southwest corner, and the capital city of St. George's is about seven kilometers north on the west coast of the island. Farther to the north and near the

The Caribbean

east coast is Pearls Airport. The airfields at Point Salines and Pearls and the city of St. George's became the focal points of American efforts. As planning proceeded, marine units received responsibility for the northern part of the island and army units for the southern part. Except for two small areas north and south of St. George's, the beaches were rocky, blocked by reefs, and unsuitable for amphibious landings.

The first force to move toward Grenada was an amphibious task force that—as a precaution—had been ordered around midnight on October 20 by CINCLANT to sail toward Grenada. The task force included the navy's Amphibious Squadron Four, consisting of five ships, and the 22nd Marine Amphibious Unit, consisting of an infantry battalion and a medium helicopter squadron. When the intervention began, however, Special Operations Forces led the Americans into Grenada. Among those participating were Delta Force, Seal Team 6, and C Company, 1st Battalion, 75th Rangers. The first attempt to use Special Operations Forces miscarried on Sunday night, October 23–24, when a joint Seal–air force combat-control team failed to land on Grenada and set up a sophisticated navigational aid for incoming aircraft. Early on Tuesday, October 25, other forces failed to seize the radio transmitting station north of St. George's and to release political prisoners from Richmond Hill Prison. A Seal team managed to seize the transmitting tower, but a counterattack by PRA soldiers forced them to withdraw. Nonetheless, the Seals destroyed the tower and prevented the PRA from transmitting any warning to the militia. In the one notable success of Special Operations Forces, a Seal team landed in helicopters at the Government House just outside St. George's and secured the safety of the British Governor General, Sir Paul Scoon. Despite strong counterattacks from PRA soldiers using Soviet armored personnel carriers, the Seals retained control over the Government House until rescued by marines the following morning.

Marine and army landings followed the actions of the Special Operations forces. Around 0730 hours on Tuesday, after receiving only a few small bursts of automatic weapons fire, heliborne marines secured Pearls Airport in the northeast corner of Grenada. Shortly thereafter, helicopters landed a company on a soccer field in the center of the town of Grenville about two kilometers to the south of Pearls Airport. The marines encountered no opposition and quickly secured the town and its port without taking any casualties. Farther to the south, U.S. Army units encountered much stronger opposition against well-prepared defenders. The first soldiers to arrive were from 1st Battalion, 75th Rangers; they had the mission of securing the Point Salines airfield before the arrival of 82nd Airborne Division. Not knowing whether they would land on the airfield or make an airborne drop, they flew about 3,000 kilometers from Savannah, Georgia, on C-130 aircraft. After the lead aircraft encountered strong antiaircraft fire, the ranger battalion commander ordered his soldiers to jump from 500 feet, thereby limiting their exposure to enemy fire. When the rangers landed around the airfield at 0530 hours on Tuesday, they received heavy automatic weapons and mortar fire from defenders on the high ground to the north of the airfield, but they quickly secured the airfield's periphery and cleared the runway of construction equipment, wire barriers, and metal stakes. Around 0900 hours, the rangers rescued 138 medical students at the True Blue campus just off the eastern end of the airfield.

While the rangers fought to expand the area under their control around the Point Salines airfield, the first elements of 82nd Airborne Division departed Fort Bragg, North Carolina, shortly after 1000 hours and landed at Point Salines around 1400 hours. Like the rangers, they had traveled more than 3,000 kilometers. When the first battalion from the 82nd landed, accompanied by the division commander, Major General Edward Trobaugh, sniper and automatic weapons fire continued sporadically from the high ground around the airfield. Despite the importance of pushing on to St. George's, Trobaugh focused on protecting the airfield and awaiting the arrival of another battalion before moving into the steep, heavily forested terrain along the route to Grenada's capital. Troop strength at Point Salines increased slowly because the unfinished runway had insufficient ramp space for parking landed aircraft, and a huge backlog of incoming forces and equipment quickly developed. The second battalion did not arrive until around 0300 hours on Wednesday.

On Tuesday afternoon, Admiral Metcalf decided to bypass the Cuban and PRA defenders around Point Salines and land marines at St.

George's. Around 1830 hours, without encountering any opposition, thirteen amphibian tracks landed about two kilometers north of St. George's. Using utility landing craft, a platoon of M-60 tanks and jeeps with heavy machine guns and antitank weapons followed. The next morning, around 0730 hours, one of the marine companies and the tank platoon reached the house where PRA soldiers besieged the Seals and Sir Paul Scoon. The appearance of the tanks and amphibian vehicles dispersed the PRA forces. On that day and the next, against little more than sniper fire, the marines secured the harbor works and the hilltops around St. George's.

At 0630 hours on Wednesday, two battalions of infantry from the 82nd Division attacked northeast out of the Point Salines airfield into the Calliste barracks, killing sixteen and capturing eighty-six Cubans. They then climbed a steep hill north of Calliste and captured a large ammunition depot about one and a half kilometers to the northeast. Six huge warehouses contained weapons, ammunition, uniforms, spare parts, and vehicles. As the paratroopers advanced, the rangers used marine CH-46s and CH-53s to travel to Grande Anse (about two kilometers to the north of the Point Salines airfield) and rescue additional students there. Despite the objections of one marine commander, who initially refused to transport army troops on marine helicopters, the rangers landed at about 1615 hours and quickly evacuated 224 students.

On Thursday, October 27, the 82nd, with six battalions on the ground plus its divisional artillery, pushed north toward St. George's. The operation went smoothly except for a navy A-7 aircraft accidentally strafing the headquarters of the 2nd Brigade and wounding sixteen soldiers, one of whom later died. At 1630 hours, the rangers launched an air assault into Calivigny Barracks, about five kilometers east of the Salines airfield. Though the rangers encountered no enemy, two helicopters collided, killing and injuring about two dozen men. The securing of the barracks around 2100 hours marked the end of significant military activity in Grenada.

Despite overwhelming superiority, the Americans had encountered many difficulties. Some problems stemmed from the operation's being cobbled together hastily without the participants having the time or opportunity for coordination. Other difficulties, particularly for the army and air force, revolved around the long distance—about 3,000 kilometers—between the units' home stations and Grenada. The complexities of launching an operation over such a long distance were accentuated by confusion over questions of command and control and by the lack of direct radio communications between the 82d Airborne, the marines, and Admiral Metcalf. As with many combat operations, intelligence could have been more accurate and timely. Urgent Fury became a controversial operation with criticisms surfacing for most aspects of the operation but focusing on the inability of the services to work together smoothly.

The October 1983 intervention in Grenada also marked a low point in relations between the U.S. armed forces and the news media. Heeding Department of Defense requests, President Reagan placed a total ban on press coverage during the first two days of the invasion and maintained tight restrictions on reporting in the following week. The Department of Defense provided several reasons for maintaining tight control over news reporting, including the necessity for secrecy and the inability to provide security for reporters. Some critics charged, however, that the American military leaders were suspicious of reporters and wanted to avoid negative media coverage. In the final analysis, strained relations between the military and the news media heightened criticism of the operation.

Operation "Just Cause" in Panama

Over the next few years the United States made some improvements in its conduct of joint operations and rapid interventions, and the effect of these changes was obvious in December 1989 when U.S. forces seized control of Panama. For several years tension had increased between Washington and Panama, and on Friday, December 15, the Panamanian National Assembly gave sweeping powers to General Manuel A. Noriega and declared Panama in a "state of war" against the United States as long as American "aggression" continued. On Sunday, December 17, President George Bush ordered U.S. military forces to intervene in Panama. In an address from the White House on the day of the operation, he explained that the objectives of "Just Cause" were "to safeguard the lives of Americans, to defend democracy in Panama, to combat drug trafficking, and to protect the integrity of the Panama Canal Treaty."

Unlike Urgent Fury in Grenada, Just Cause was smoothly and almost flawlessly executed. Those planning the operation relied on existing command relationships; they also had the crucial advantage of having sufficient time for planning and preparation and having 13,000 troops and a U.S.-controlled airbase immediately available. These advantages enabled most of the participating units to be well rehearsed for their combat mission and thoroughly familiar with the terrain. Even those units that parachuted onto key targets after being flown from the United States in transport planes had detailed information about their objectives. By striking twenty-seven targets almost simultaneously in the night, the Americans quickly gained control of Panama. Within seven hours after the assault began, the Panamanian Defense Forces no longer existed as a cohesive military organization and offered no organized resistance against U.S. forces.

Thus in the final decade of the Cold War, improvements in the ability to project force from fleets and increases in the cruising range and payloads of military air transport enhanced the capabilities of a few countries to intervene quickly in distant regions. Because of the need for rapid action over long distances, accomplishing critical planning and establishing effective command arrangements remained difficult. Problems with intelligence, logistics, communications, and coordination also appeared frequently. Interventions, nevertheless, continued to rely on offensive action and sought to overwhelm more poorly equipped and trained opponents swiftly.

Beyond the Cold War:
The Persian Gulf

As the Cold War ended, political and military leaders recognized the dangers of aggression from rogue states seeking territory, influence, or advantages. Common sense underlined the need to react swiftly with relatively large forces to counter such aggression. Hardly anyone, however, expected a major conflict immediately after the end of the Cold War. In many ways, the Persian Gulf War was as much a surprise as the Korean War, but unlike that experience, the United States, whose forces carried most of the weight of the war, proved to be far better prepared. Unfortunately for the Iraqis, the United States had developed the capability to reinforce Europe by transporting forces over great distances rapidly, and the campaign in Southwest Asia proved to be ideal for forces and doctrine designed to fight the Soviets in central Europe.

The war began when the military forces of President Saddam Hussein of Iraq invaded the tiny desert sheikdom of Kuwait on August 2, 1990. In a bold operation, Iraqi forces seized control of Kuwait's capital city and its rich oil fields and drove the emir of Kuwait into exile. With only 20,000 troops, thirty-six combat aircraft, and 275 tanks, Kuwait was no match for the Iraqis. Iraq's aggression and quick success convinced the international community that it threatened the traditional balance of power in the Middle East and Southwest Asia. Led by Egypt, Arab governments in the region sought an "Arab solution" to ease Iraq out of Kuwait, but Iraq announced on August 8 the annexation of Kuwait, dashing any hopes for peaceful resolution of the crisis. At a meeting of the Arab League shortly after the invasion, twelve of the twenty-one members expressed support for a United Nations embargo against Iraq and endorsed Saudi Arabia's invitation to the United States to send troops to deter Iraqi aggression. They also agreed to send Arab forces to defend Saudi Arabia. Many Arabs recognized that Saddam's ambitious desire to establish Iraq as the dominant power in the Middle East threatened their own way of life.

The seizure of Kuwait also captured the attention of much of the world. With the Soviet Union in disarray, with the Warsaw Pact crumbling, and with the two Germanys about to be reunited, the world seemed to be entering a period of peace. In what many hoped would be a new world order, aggression by one state against another could not be tolerated. For many, Saddam seemed to be nothing more than a "terrorist with an army." Moreover, Saddam's belligerence jeopardized much of the world's oil supplies. By seizing Kuwait and declaring it the nineteenth province of Iraq, Saddam doubled Iraq's oil reserves and gained control over 20 percent of the world's proven reserves. Even worse, his position in the Gulf, if unchallenged, could eventually allow him to dominate Saudi Arabia and increase his control to 40 percent of the world's oil reserves. The oil-dependent nations of the world could tolerate neither Iraq's aggression nor the threat of its controlling the world's oil supplies.

King Fahd of Saudi Arabia and General H. Norman Schwarzkopf. Keeping the diverse coalition together proved to be one of the most complex challenges of the war.

Much of the world united against Saddam. In a very important change closely associated with the ending of the Cold War and the willingness of Russia to oppose the Iraqi action, the United Nations Security Council adopted a resolution condemning the Iraqi invasion of Kuwait and soon imposed mandatory sanctions and an embargo against Iraq. After the United Nations adopted a resolution authorizing the use of force, thirty-six countries—not including Kuwait—dispatched forces to the Gulf.

Particularly during the period when the coalition was rushing ground forces to Saudi Arabia, the Iraqi ground forces, which had recently emerged from an eight-year war against Iran, seemed large and capable. Iraq's army dwarfed not only the other armies in the area—except for Iran's—but also many of those in Europe. As the fourth largest army in the world, it was bigger than those of Britain and France combined. It also possessed huge quantities of modern equipment and seemed to have a formidable tank force. U.S. intelligence agencies estimated that the Iraqis had some 4,550 main battle tanks and 2,880 armored personnel carriers in and around Kuwait. Though the great majority of the Iraqi tanks were older Soviet T-54 and T-62 models, about 500 of the main battle tanks were Soviet T-72 tanks, which weighed about 45 tons and were considered among the best tanks in the world. As for artillery, the Iraqis had 3,257 pieces in or near Kuwait; some analysts credited the Iraqis with a 7-to-1 advantage in artillery. The Iraqi air force had about 950 combat aircraft, and with more than 4,000 air defense guns and 300 long-range, Soviet-made SA-2 and SA-4 ground-to-air missiles, Iraqi air defenses seemed formidable.

Moreover, Saddam possessed a substantial store of chemical weapons and during the Iran-Iraq War had demonstrated his willingness to use them. The only thing lacking in Saddam's arsenal was nuclear weapons, but evidence strongly suggested that he was making a concerted effort to develop such weapons. On August 21, Pentagon officials acknowledged that the Iraqis had moved medium-range ballistic missiles into Kuwait. The missiles were Scud missiles which could carry conventional high-explosive warheads or chemical warheads with mustard or nerve gas. The possibility of Scud missiles spewing chemical or biological agents against coalition soldiers or against unprotected civilians caused considerable concern.

American Forces in the Gulf

The coalition facing Iraq established a centralized command system for Arab and Western air forces, but no single commander controlled all the coalition's ground forces. The coalition had two parallel commands for ground forces, one Arab and the other Western. A Saudi Arabian general officer maintained relatively loose command over the various Arab ground units. The Commander-in-Chief of U.S. Central Command, General H. Norman Schwarzkopf, commanded all American forces in the region of the Persian Gulf and Southwest Asia; the French and British governments also gave him control of their ground forces. As for air forces, U.S. Lieutenant General Charles A. Horner acted as the coalition's air commander and worked directly under Schwarzkopf.

Of those nations sending forces, the largest number by far came from the United States. With lead elements arriving on August 8, the 82nd Airborne Division was the first large American ground unit to arrive, followed by U.S. Marines. Virtually all of the first 35,000 American troops in Saudi Arabia were flown there by about sixty commercial aircraft chartered by the U.S. military, but the bulk of their equipment came by sea and arrived weeks later. When it became apparent that the U.N. embargo would not force the Iraqis to withdraw, the Americans increased their offensive capability. In November, President George Bush announced that the United States would substantially increase the size of its ground forces in Saudi Arabia by mobilizing additional reserve forces and by moving U.S. Army units from Europe. Shortly thereafter, armored units from the U.S. Army began to arrive.

The move of VII Corps from Germany was particularly challenging. After the public announcement on November 8 of VII Corps' deployment to Southwest Asia, the Americans moved 122,000 soldiers and 40,000 major pieces of equipment to the air- and seaports of embarkation, using 465 trains, 312 barges, and 119 convoys. From these ports, the corps used 578 aircraft and 140 ships to travel to Saudi Arabia. After arriving at ports in Saudi Arabia, some VII Corps units traveled as far as 500 kilometers in convoys along Saudi highways. Though the entire move took about twelve weeks, most tactical units arrived in sufficient time to conduct training in the desert in chemical protection, weapons firing, land navigation, breaching procedures, and tactical operations.

The Americans brought with them the technological weapons that they had created during the 1970s and 1980s. The air force's F-117A Stealth bomber was invisible to Iraqi defenses throughout the war. Precision-guided munitions from the F-117A and other aircraft allowed them to attack targets with unheard-of accuracy. Air-launched and sea-launched cruise missiles could strike targets from extreme distances and with accuracy similar to precision-guided munitions. Electronic warfare aircraft could jam and distort enemy radars, while air-launched missiles sought and destroyed active radars. The army also possessed weapons that allowed its troops to seek out and kill its opponents at great distances. Infrared and other devices allowed U.S. ground forces to "see" at night, while their opponents remained blinded by the darkness. Additionally, the Americans' training, doctrine, and operational conceptions provided them significant advantages. The competence, initiative, and flexibility of U.S. air and ground forces rendered irrelevant all considerations of Iraqi numbers, quality equipment, and battle experience.

From the beginning, it was clear that women would play a larger role in this war than any in history. Of the more than half-million American personnel in the Persian Gulf region at the height of the war, 35,000 were women. They operated air-defense systems, made intelligence assessments, drove trucks, sorted mail, operated water purification units, repaired equipment, acted as military police, and performed a host of other functions. Women helicopter pilots flew in combat zones, but not on direct combat missions; they moved supplies and soldiers around the battlefield and evacuated wounded soldiers. When the fighting began, five women were killed in hostile action; two others were captured by the Iraqis, one when her truck became lost and the other when her helicopter crashed.

Planning the Coalition's Defense and Attack

The outbreak of the war caught American military and diplomatic planners by surprise. Much of the prewar planning had viewed the Persian Gulf region as secondary to the European theater. Intelligence assessments in the region had focused mainly on the possibility of a Soviet advance, not on an Iraqi attack through Kuwait into Saudi Arabia. For most of August, as the

U.S. military deployed forces over enormous distances, the possibility of Iraq's moving south caused grave concern, but the situation was not as serious as it appeared at the time. While the Iraqis threatened Saudi Arabia, they possessed neither the training nor the logistical capabilities that such an operation would have required. By the end of August the Iraqis had settled into defensive positions in Kuwait to wait out the gathering coalition. Because of the solid performance of Iraqi defenses during the eight-year Iran-Iraq War, coalition commanders expected these positions to be strong.

The rapid buildup of U.S. combat aircraft initially focused General Schwarzkopf's attention on the use of air power. Six days after Iraq invaded Kuwait, he asked the air staff in Washington to prepare plans for aerial attacks against the Iraqis. Within a few days, a planning cell in the Pentagon produced a plan called "Instant Thunder" which envisaged a massive strategic air campaign against Iraq. Air planners believed that such a campaign would prevent a costly ground war and in six to nine days could achieve American national objectives, including "the immediate, complete, and unconditional withdrawal of all Iraqi forces from Kuwait." Schwarzkopf accepted the plan on August 10, apparently viewing it as a retaliatory plan. After briefing General Colin Powell, Chairman of the Joint Chiefs of Staff, planners added another phase to Instant Thunder, entitled "An Operational Air Campaign Against Iraqi Forces in Kuwait," which focused on destroying the Iraqi army. The air planners believed that Schwarzkopf intended to use only air power to force the Iraqis from Kuwait.

As events unfolded, however, Schwarzkopf conceived of the campaign against Iraq in four phases. In phase I, air attacks would strike Iraq. In phase II, coalition aircraft would gain air superiority over Kuwait. In phase III, air attacks would reduce Iraqi ground forces and destroy their ability to use chemicals. And in phase IV, ground forces with support from air forces would eject Iraqi forces from Kuwait. Schwarzkopf also made the crucial decision that Horner would run the air war and that the other air forces (marine and navy, but not army), as well as the other coalition air forces, would come under Horner's command. That decision allowed air planners to develop an integrated approach to air attacks against Iraq. To blend Instant Thunder into overall aerial planning, Horner established a special planning group in Saudi Arabia. The name Instant Thunder was dropped, and the air attack against Iraq—in essence a strategic campaign—became "Offensive Campaign Phase I." Before the first air attacks began, however, the idea of the air war being divided into distinct phases had almost disappeared, and target lists for phases I, II, and III had merged. Planners expected the focus of the aerial attacks to shift gradually from the strategic to the tactical arena and from Iraq to Kuwait.

Initial plans for the ground forces emphasized the defense, but early in September, Schwarzkopf's staff began planning for an offensive. On October 6, planners presented several alternatives to Schwarzkopf who selected an option calling for a two-week air attack followed by a ground attack that would penetrate Iraqi forces and advance into southern Kuwait. With the coalition's ground forces clearly outnumbered, planners ruled out a bold envelopment of the Iraqi forces. Concerned about the possibility of heavy casualties in such an attack, Schwarzkopf directed his staff on October 15 to begin planning for an attack with larger ground forces. His staff immediately began developing plans for an attack through the great Iraqi desert and around the flank of the Iraqis in Kuwait. In late October, Schwarzkopf approved the concept for an envelopment of Iraqi forces, and in mid-November, with President Bush having announced the commitment of VII Corps, he set mid-January as the time for the offensive.

The Coalition's Aerial Attack

Almost from the beginning of the crisis, the coalition had a distinct advantage in air power, concentrating 2,614 aircraft in the Persian Gulf area, 1,990 of which were American. Shortly before 0300 hours (local time) on January 17, 1991, the coalition's air plan unfolded when army AH-64 Apache helicopters attacked several frontier early-warning radar sites. The destruction of those sites created a corridor through which F-15Es were able to strike at Scud missile bases in western Iraq. A few minutes later, F-117A Stealth aircraft, undetected by Iraqi radar, arrived over Baghdad and other targets and began dropping precision-guided munitions. Minutes later, a wave of "Tomahawk" cruise missiles from naval vessels in the Gulf slammed into targets throughout Baghdad and elsewhere. At the same time, air-launched cruise missiles from B-52G bombers, which had flown from air bases as distant as Louisiana, hit their targets. The strikes caught the Iraqis completely by surprise, because they possessed no means of detecting the inward-bound missiles or Stealth aircraft.

The coalition made the destruction of the Iraqis' air defenses a high priority. From carriers in the Red Sea, the U.S. Navy sent F/A-18 Hornets and EA-6B Prowlers to strike Baghdad from the west; at the same time U.S. Air Force F-4G Wild Weasels approached the capital from the south. Decoys and drones gave the impression of even larger attacking groups, and chaff created additional confusion. As the Iraqi radar sites tracked the incoming aircraft, antiradar missiles homed in on their radar signals. Following this attack, many Iraqi air-defense units turned off their radar and fired their weapons aimlessly into the sky. Within hours, the Iraqi air-defense system ceased to operate as a coherent, functioning military system. Few Iraqi aircraft rose to meet the tide of aircraft sweeping over Saddam's lands; the few that did soon disappeared in explosions of air-to-air missiles.

When dawn came, amazed coalition air commanders discovered that they had lost only one aircraft during the night—far less than their prewar expectations of twenty-five to fifty aircraft. Most important, coalition air forces had achieved air supremacy over Iraq. Since coalition aircraft at heights above 10,000 feet could operate beyond the effective range of enemy antiaircraft guns, subsequent attacks suffered only minimal casualties. The coalition now had the luxury of continuing air attacks almost indefinitely.

The first night, coalition aircraft and missiles also hit a large number of special sites, particularly the nuclear, chemical, and biological special weapons programs on which the Iraqi regime was hard at work. Other strikes destroyed command-and-control centers, communications networks, and enemy airfields. Planners targeted Iraq's electrical network particularly heavily; they believed its destruction would lead to the collapse of communications, make it more difficult for the Iraqi military to function, and perhaps even lead to a collapse of national morale. By dawn on the morning of January 17, Iraq was well on its way to defeat.

Continuing the Air Attacks

From the allied perspective, the first few days of the air attack went like clockwork. Not only were losses well below expectations, but electrical power systems were down throughout much of Iraq. On day three weather began to interfere with air operations. Throughout the rest of the war, weather conditions created numerous difficulties for those planning and conducting air operations. Whatever the difficulties, the volume and accuracy of air attacks wore down the Iraqi military. At the end of the first week of air attacks, F-111Fs and the F-117As went after hardened shelters on Iraqi airbases. These attacks destroyed a substantial number of shelters on enemy airfields, as well as the aircraft parked inside. In a desperate move, Saddam

A Patriot missile leaps from its launcher. Initially designed to engage aircraft, the Patriot became the first successful antimissile system after modifications were made to the missile and its computers. Before the war its antimissile capability had undergone only limited testing.

ordered many of his remaining aircraft to fly to Iran. This action eliminated the Iraqi air force as a military factor in the war.

Despite the intensity of the coalition's air strikes, the Iraqis managed, beginning on January 18, to launch ninety-three Scud missiles, most of which were aimed at population centers in Saudi Arabia and Israel. Though lacking accuracy, the Scuds posed a strategic threat, for Saddam expected Scud attacks on Israel to bring Israeli forces into the war and thereby shatter the coalition. The U.S. Army's Patriot air-defense system intercepted 70 percent of the Scud missiles fired at Saudi Arabia and 40 percent of those fired at Israel. These were the first missiles ever intercepted in combat by an antimissile system, and the civilians and soldiers who had been the targets of Scud missiles loudly applauded the success of the Patriot. Nonetheless, the performance of the Patriot missiles was not flawless. Since the Patriot had been designed to explode near an incoming missile, not necessarily to destroy the warhead, some of the Scuds intercepted by the Patriots still caused damage on the ground. Due to a problem with computer software, a Patriot battery north of Dhahran failed to detect an incoming Scud missile on February 25, and the missile hit a barracks, killing twenty-eight American soldiers and wounding ninety-seven others.

On January 29, the Iraqis launched a raid with the 5th Mechanized Division, plus elements of two other divisions. They recognized that air attacks would continue for the foreseeable future. Moreover, air attacks had entirely shut down the Iraqi capacity to acquire intelligence. Consequently, they hoped the raid could gain valuable intelligence and perhaps force the coalition to begin the ground attack. Although the Iraqis got some troops into the Saudi frontier town of Khafji, most of the raiding force did not achieve even a brief success. One of the armored brigades got stuck in a minefield where coalition aircraft massacred vehicles and troops alike. Aircraft also hit units that were supposed to support the attack on Khafji and prevented them from reaching the front lines. By the end of the Khafji battle, the Iraqis had suffered several thousand casualties and lost several hundred armored vehicles. Khafji made clear that the Iraqis could not concentrate their armored and mechanized forces under a sky—night or day—dominated by coalition aircraft.

Air attacks thoroughly disrupted Iraq's command-and-control systems, political as well as military. Over the night of February 12–13, F117As executed a series of particularly heavy raids against Iraqi headquarters and bunker targets in the Baghdad area. One of those targets was the al-Firdos bunker; intelligence indicated that the Iraqis had just activated the bunker. Unfortunately, no one in either intelligence or in the planning cycle knew that the bunker also served as a shelter for families of the governmental elite (Saddam's regime constructed no bunkers for the general population of Baghdad). The result was a tragic loss of civilian lives that television immediately broadcast to the world. In response, political authorities in the United States forbade further attacks on Baghdad without Washington's approval; attacks on Iraq's political infrastructure virtually halted. Late in the war, F-117As did strike a few targets in Baghdad, but none that carried the risk of further civilian casualties.

As the time for the ground attack approached, coalition aircraft struck operational-level targets such as Iraq's military supply lines to Kuwait and the Republican Guard divisions in northern Kuwait. Among their targets, they destroyed thirty-one railway and highway bridges and thirty-two pontoon bridges. They also destroyed important fuel- and lubricant-distribution centers. At the end of the first week in February, the focus of the air campaign moved to preparing the battlefield for the ground attack.

Early in February, F-111F pilots discovered that their infrared sensors could accurately spot armored and other vehicles in the desert because of the heat differential between sand and metal. On February 5, F-111Fs attempted an experiment using their laser-guided bombs against enemy vehicles dispersed in the desert; these attacks were so successful that Horner, at Schwarzkopf's urgings, transferred the F-111Fs entirely into attacks in Kuwait. Dropping precision-guided bombs each night, the F-111Fs destroyed or damaged hundreds of Iraqi vehicles.

Aerial attacks significantly weakened the will to fight of Iraqi ground forces. Waves of B-52s pounded Iraqi positions, particularly the formidable Republican Guard units and the best Iraqi armored divisions. Meanwhile, psychological warfare efforts worked to weaken their morale further. Special radio programs broadcast antigovernment propaganda into Iraq, and aircraft dropped 30 million leaflets onto Iraqi positions. The constant bombardment severely demoralized the Iraqis, and a few deserters made their way across minefields into coalition hands in Kuwait. Larger numbers of deserters managed to flee into Turkey.

The Iraqis had entered Kuwait with a relatively well-equipped force manned by many combat-experienced soldiers and officers. At the end of the aerial operation, which lasted thirty-eight days and included more than 90,000 sorties, the coalition claimed to have destroyed 39 percent of the Iraqi tanks, 32 percent of the armored personnel carriers, and 48 percent of the artillery in Kuwait and southern Iraq. They also claimed to have destroyed more than one-third of the Iraqi aircraft, including thirty-five shot down in aerial combat. In addition to destroying much of the equipment and weakening the morale of the Iraqi army and air force, air strikes had destroyed key bridges across the Euphrates River, partially isolating the battlefield in preparation for the ground war. The final phase of the air attack, which gave priority to the support of ground operations, did not begin until after the launching of the ground attack.

The Hundred-Hour Ground Battle

Shortly before the ground assault, the Americans had about 527,000 troops in the Persian Gulf region, including those aboard ships. Among the U.S troops were seven U.S. Army divisions, three brigades from other divisions, two U.S. Marine divisions, and elements from a third marine division. Other large ground forces came from Great Britain, France, Egypt, and Syria, as well as Saudi Arabia and Kuwait. The coalition initially credited the Iraqis with having about 545,000 troops in southern Iraq and Kuwait, but by the time the ground assault began, the Iraqis may have had no more than 350,000 troops, including twelve armored divisions and thirty infantry divisions stationed in Kuwait and southern Iraq. Schwarzkopf later estimated that because of desertions and casualties, some Iraqi frontline divisions had less than 50 percent strength, and those in the second line had somewhere between 50–75 percent of their authorized strength.

To defend Kuwait, the Iraqis organized their defenses into three zones, similar to what they had done in the Iran-Iraq War. The first zone consisted of fortified defenses along the Saudi border and included two lines of infantry in bunkers and trenches behind huge sand berms, ditches filled with flammable oil, row after row of concertina wire, and minefields. The Iraqis expected these defenses to entangle the attacking coalition forces and expose them to massive artillery barrages, including chemicals. If the coalition's forces managed to penetrate this zone, they would then encounter the second defensive zone, which consisted of three Iraqi armored divisions poised to blunt any penetration. To the rear of these divisions, Republican Guard divisions occupied positions in a huge crescent pattern in southern Iraq. The Republican Guards functioned as a theater reserve, prepared to strike the coalition's forces with a massive counterattack if they managed to push through the forward two zones. Expecting an amphibious assault, the Iraqis also placed infantry divisions in strong defensive positions along the shores of the Persian Gulf. For reasons only Saddam understands, the western flank of the Iraqi forces had almost no defenses, providing the coalition an opening for a decisive blow.

To keep the Iraqis focused on the east, Schwarzkopf concocted an elaborate deception plan that convinced the Iraqis that the coalition's main attack would hit their main defenses in eastern Kuwait and that an amphibious assault near Kuwait City would also occur. Coalition forces remained in positions along the Kuwaiti border and conducted artillery raids and probes to create the impression that their attack would strike into the teeth of the Iraqi defenses in eastern Kuwait. At the same time, U.S. naval forces practiced for an amphibious landing along the Kuwaiti shoreline. These efforts convinced the Iraqis that major ground and amphibious assaults would advance directly into Iraq's strongest defenses and led them to hold six divisions in place along the coast of Kuwait.

Some observers described Schwarzkopf's campaign strategy as a "one-two punch" consisting of a "right jab" followed by a knockout blow from a "left hook." In the simplest terms, he concentrated his strength against the Iraqis' weakest point. With the Iraqis focused toward the east, Schwarzkopf intended to move west, sweep around front-line fortifications in Kuwait, and drive deep into Iraq in a gigantic envelopment. In preparation for the "left hook," Schwarzkopf began shifting forces far to the west of the Kuwaiti border with Iraq on January 17, three weeks prior to the launching of the ground attack. About 270,000 troops, complete with sixty days of ammunition and supplies, shifted west. The fact that the coalition had air supremacy made Schwarzkopf confident that the Iraqis would not detect this move, or if they did detect it, that they would not be able to shift most of their forces without exposing them to devastating air attacks.

Coalition Ground Attack,
February 24–28, 1991

The Attack Begins

The ground attack was scheduled to begin on G-day, which was initially set for February 21, but a Russian peace initiative pushed G-day back. The coalition's ground attack officially began at 0400 hours on February 24. As part of the "right jab," Joint Forces Command East, consisting of five Saudi, Kuwaiti, Omani, and United Arab Emirate brigades, advanced between the coast and the main road leading to Kuwait City. To their left were the 1st and 2nd U.S. Marine divisions, reinforced by a U.S. Army armored brigade. The Joint Forces Command North, consisting of a combined Egyptian-Syrian force, advanced to the left of the marines but began moving later than the other forces to avoid having the Syrians' Soviet tanks accidentally engaged by the coalition's other forces.

As marines and other coalition forces advanced into eastern Kuwait, they passed through paths cleared through minefields and initially met only sporadic and uneven resistance. Nevertheless, two Iraqi mechanized brigades launched a counterattack and managed to come within 300 meters of the command post of 1st Marine Division. In the advance into Kuwait, the marines captured thousands of prisoners, as did other coalition forces. The numbers were so large that they slowed the advance of the attacking units.

As for the "left hook," VII Corps had the mission of advancing about one hundred kilometers into Iraq and then turning east into the rear and flank of the Iraqis. XVIII Airborne Corps was on VII Corps' left and had the mission of protecting the flank of the coalition's forces as they moved into Iraq. XVIII Airborne Corps was supposed to begin its move on G-day and VII Corps on G+1.

From an initial position about 300 kilometers west of the Kuwaiti border, XVIII Airborne Corps raced north toward the Euphrates River when the ground attack began on G-day, February 24. The corps consisted of 101st Airborne Division (Air Assault), 24th Infantry Division (Mechanized), a brigade of the 82nd Airborne Division, 3rd Armored Cavalry Regiment, and the French 6th Light Armored Division. In the largest air assault operation since Operation "Junction City" in the Vietnam War, 101st Airborne Division flew about 275 kilometers through driving rain to cut off the main highway between Baghdad and Kuwait. As the 101st moved forward rapidly, the French 6th Light Armored Division and a brigade from 82nd Airborne Division established a screen farther west to cover the flank and rear of the corps. Once the screen was established, 24th Infantry Division, with 3rd Armored Cavalry Regiment on its right, raced across the desert to link up with the 101st and block a crossing site over the Euphrates River just west of an-Nasiriyah. As soon as the Americans reached the Euphrates, Iraqi units could no longer move along the highway south of the Euphrates. Because of the water barrier formed by the Euphrates, the Hawr al-Hammar Lake, and extensive swamps, the Iraqis could escape only by crossing over hastily erected pontoon bridges across the Euphrates or withdrawing to the northeast toward Basra.

VII Corps had responsibility for delivering the knockout blow to the Republican Guard. Though the plan called for VII Corps to begin moving on G+1, the rapid advance of XVIII Corps and light opposition encountered by the "right jab" led Schwarzkopf to order VII Corps to begin moving on G-day. VII Corps included 1st Armored, 3rd Armored, 1st Infantry (Mechanized), and the British 1st Armored divisions, as well as 2nd Armored Cavalry Regiment. The Corps was reinforced by a brigade from 3rd Infantry Division (Mechanized), four field artillery brigades, and an aviation brigade. It numbered more than 145,000 soldiers and had more than 48,000 vehicles and aircraft. The magnitude of the logistical effort can be seen in the corps' expecting to consume more than 5.6 million gallons of fuel, 3.3 million gallons of water, and 6,075 tons of ammunition each day. When VII Corps moved into Iraq, hundreds of trucks followed closely behind; they carried tons of fuel, ammunition, and water to keep the huge force moving.

Ground Combat

VII Corps' attack passed through Iraqi defenses along the border easily. As 1st Cavalry Division created a diversion to the right of VII Corps by advancing up the Wadi al-Batin corridor, 2nd Armored Cavalry Regiment breached the border defenses and protected the rest of VII Corps' units as they moved into Iraq. 1st Armored Division, after crossing the border, moved to the left of 2nd Cavalry, and the two units led VII Corps' advance.

As 1st Armored Division raced forward, its initial objective was the town of al-Busayyah, about 110 kilometers inside Iraq. The town was an Iraqi logistics center on a main supply route and served as the headquarters for an Iraqi division. 1st Armored moved in a "compressed division wedge" formation twenty kilometers wide and fifty kilometers deep. With its cavalry squadron screening to the front, the division had its 1st Brigade as an advanced guard, its 2nd Brigade on its left, its 3rd Brigade on its right, its artillery between the two flank brigades, and its support elements (totaling nearly 1,000 vehicles) following closely.

On February 25, the VII Corps commander, Lieutenant General Frederick M. Franks, Jr., began turning his units to the east and inserting 3rd Armored Division between 1st Armored Division and 2nd Cavalry Regiment. By the time 1st Armored Division began turning, it had already moved about 150 kilometers in forty-one hours. Using the analogy of a hand closing into a fist, General Franks sought to concentrate his divisions and to destroy the Republican Guard. He soon had four divisions on line, including the 1st Armored, 3rd Armored, 1st Infantry, and British 1st Armored, and pressed the attack against the Republic Guard units and the north-south Basra–Kuwait City highway.

Before General Franks concentrated his divisions into a fist, 2nd Armored Cavalry Regiment took part in some of the heaviest combat of the war. When the Iraqi 12th Armored and Republican Guards Tawakalna divisions, as well as other units, attempted to pull out of Kuwait, they ran directly into 2nd Armored Cavalry. Much of the fighting occurred in a blinding sandstorm on February 26 with sporadic concentrations of Iraqi artillery falling on the Americans' position. Though visibility in the sandstorm was sometimes less than 200 meters, the M1A1 tanks' thermal sights could see almost one kilometer, and the Americans extracted a terrible toll from the waves of tanks that came charging toward them. Despite desperate

Iraqi tank crews had little chance of success since they were out-gunned by American tanks and not prepared to fight large armored formations. Not one American M1A1 tank was lost to Iraqi tank fire.

charges and the sacrifice of many lives, the Iraqis never managed to break out of the deadly trap that had closed behind them.

Though pounded by coalition air forces for weeks, the Republican Guard managed to shift some units from a southeast to a southwest orientation and awaited the arrival of VII Corps. The Republican Guards sometimes occupied strong defensive positions, but the superiority of the M1A1 tank proved decisive. The M1A1 could fire at and hit armored vehicles three kilometers away, well beyond the effective range of the Iraqi T-72s. Aerial attacks increased the effect of the ground attack. While American ground forces engaged tanks and armored personnel carriers, coalition air forces destroyed numerous enemy vehicles as they attempted to maneuver or escape. By the end of the campaign, only 700 of Iraq's tanks survived.

As the final thrust of the "left hook" continued forward, elements from 24th Infantry Division and 3rd Armored Cavalry Regiment attempted to close up on VII Corps' left flank. As the coalition's forces moved forward on February 27, the fourth day of the attack, they met alternating pockets of Iraqi soldiers ready to fight or to surrender. Around 1800 hours on the 27th the cavalry squadron of 1st Infantry Division reached the Basra–Kuwait City highway; the bulk of the division was about ten kilometers to its rear. Throughout the night of February 27–28, elements in the corps wiped out pockets of resistance left in their rear until the "cessation of offensive operations," proposed by Washington and accepted by Schwarzkopf, occurred at 0800 hours on the 28th.

Assessing the Victory

Although elements of the "left hook" had moved a great distance (the 24th Division traveled about 370 kilometers) in an attempt to close the "trap" completely, a sizable number of Iraqi units escaped on the nights of February 26 and 27 by fleeing to the northeast toward Basra. This opened Schwarzkopf and Franks to criticism for having failed to close that escape route and for having failed to destroy even more of Iraq's forces. The magnitude of the coalition's victory after forty-two days, however, can be seen in the estimates of damage done to the Iraqis. About one month after the cease-fire, U.S. intelligence agencies estimated that 85 percent of the Iraqi tanks, 50 percent of the armored personnel carriers, and 90 percent of the artillery in southern Iraq or Kuwait were damaged or destroyed. More than 10,000 Iraqi prisoners were taken in the first twenty-four hours of the ground battle, and more than 70,000 by its end. Although no final figure could be obtained, the Defense Intelligence Agency (DIA) estimated several months after the end of the war that the Iraqis suffered 100,000 soldiers killed and 300,000 wounded, and that 150,000 Iraqis had deserted. Acknowledging the difficulty of making estimates of enemy casualties, the DIA stated that its estimate had an "error factor" of 50 percent or higher. In sharp contrast to the Iraqi losses, the coalition suffered few. A total of eighty-nine Americans died in the war, including thirty-eight in the four-day ground battle, and 324 were wounded, including seventy-eight in the ground battle.

Though exact Iraqi losses may never be known, the coalition had destroyed most of Saddam's armed forces and thereby significantly reduced his abili ty to threaten Kuwait. An advance on Baghdad, as some critics suggested, might have resulted in the overthrow of Saddam, but the coalition's goal had been to repel the Iraqi invaders from Kuwait, not to destroy Saddam's government.

Throughout the war, relations between the military and the news media were strained. Before the ground attack began, news reporters had only limited access to military personnel and were usually accompanied by escorts. In an attempt to fool the Iraqis into thinking that the coalition's main attack would hit the coast and would include an amphibious assault against Kuwait, however, Schwarzkopf permitted news reporters to broadcast live pictures of U.S. Marines conducting practice landings. Only after the ground battle began did news reporters gain greater access to other units participating in the operation. Another controversial aspect of war came from the broadcasting of reports from Baghdad. News reporters from the West provided live pictures of the aerial attack on Iraq and on bomb damage. Critics accused them of being used by the Iraqis to influence public opinion in the West; this led one news reporter to respond, "We're using them, they're using us." In the final analysis, the ability to transmit live television coverage from throughout the battle area intensified the desire of the military to control the access of reporters, while simultaneously increasing the desire of the news media for greater access.

In retrospect, Schwarzkopf's campaign strategy and the superiority of his forces were the keys to his victory. Weakened by thirty-eight days of air attack and surprised by the swiftness and the depth of the American move, the Iraqis simply could not respond adequately to the coalition's "left hook." The relentless aerial attack had severely weakened the Iraqi forces, and the ground attack defeated them completely. Though some of the Iraqi forces escaped, Saddam had foolishly placed his forces in a vulnerable position, had played to the strength of the coalition, particularly the Americans, and had offered a challenge the international community could not ignore.

The United Nations: From Peacekeeping to Peace Enforcement

During the Cold War, the United Nations often conducted peace-keeping operations where some semblance of peace existed and where the former combatants asked for U.N. assistance. Following the sending of officers into the Balkans and Indonesia in 1947, the U.N. began its first official peace-keeping operation in May 1948 with the establishment of the United Nations Truce Supervision Organization. U.N. forces subsequently participated in more than twenty-five peace-keeping missions in such diverse areas as Lebanon, the Congo, Yemen, Cyprus, the Dominican Republic, India-Pakistan, Angola, El Salvador, and Cambodia. Over half a million people served in U.N. peace-keeping forces after 1948, of which more than 800 from forty-three countries lost their lives. Always invited by both sides and always attempting to show impartiality, the U.N. forces sought to maintain peace by establishing a cease-fire between belligerents, serving as buffers between opposing forces, overseeing the implementation of peace plans, and providing humanitarian relief. Other missions included disarming guerrillas, preserving law and order, and monitoring elections.

After the Cold War ended in 1989–1990, the number of U.N. peace-keeping operations increased from an average of three or four in a year (several lasting for decades) to thirteen in December 1992. As the number of operations increased, and as violence and turmoil expanded in the aftermath of the Cold War, the United Nations asserted its right to intervene—without invitation—in the internal affairs of sovereign states. The U.N. Secretary General, Boutros Boutros-Ghali, emphasized the principle of "universal sovereignty" and the "legitimate involvement" of the United Nations "in issues affecting the world as a whole." Using the term "peace enforcement" to describe a military intervention by the United Nations, he called for multinational operations to end hostilities and enable diplomats to negotiate a final peace. He defined such diplomatic efforts as "peacemaking."

One of the first post–Cold War international interventions occurred at the end of the Persian Gulf War, when the Kurds in northern Iraq revolted against the authority of Saddam Hussein. The United Nations authorized humanitarian relief to the Kurds and forbade the Iraqis to interfere with relief efforts. The United States and other member nations soon conducted relief operations in Operation "Provide Comfort." A year later in Operation "Southern Watch," American and other nations' aircraft prevented the Iraqis from using air power against Shi'ites in southern Iraq. In essence, the U.N. enforced the peace over the objections of Saddam's government and went beyond providing observers for a cease-fire.

Somalia

Another crisis involving intervention by the U.N. occurred in Somalia. Despite the optimism of the international community, the complexities and difficulties of intervening with multinational forces quickly became apparent. The roots of the crisis came from prolonged drought, overpopulation, and decades of war—clan, ethnic, and religious—which turned Somalia into a scene of terrible human suffering. Although most Somalis speak the same language and are Sunni Muslims, the area has a long history of conflict between clan and tribal groups. Violence increased through the 1980s when the powers of the central government waned. As banditry and fighting between clans disrupted commerce and agriculture, many Somalis fled from their rural homes to cities or towns where they found some safety but little or no food. The situation worsened in 1991 when the central government

Somalia, December 1992

YEMEN

ERITREA

Gulf of Aden

DJIBOUTI

• Hargeysa

ETHIOPIA

SOMALIA

Shabeele R.

Jubba R.

INDIAN OCEAN

• Mogadishu

KENYA

0   125   250 mi
0   125   250 km

collapsed. By October 1992, hundreds of Somalis were dying daily from starvation. To alleviate the suffering, international relief agencies attempted to transport food to the starving Somalis, but bandits and clan members looted most of the supplies. A small U.N. force provided some security but had little effect. The United States dispatched large amounts of food to Somalia and saved numerous lives, but the violence and banditry continued.

As the situation in Somalia became more desperate and famine worsened, the United Nations decided to intervene. Though it had long refused to intervene in a sovereign country without an invitation, the U.N. Security Council decided that the magnitude of the "human tragedy" in Somalia had become a "threat to international peace and security" and thereby a legitimate object of U.N. action. Following the approval of a U.N. Security Council Resolution, President George Bush announced to the American people on December 4, 1992, that as part of the United Nations' effort he had ordered a "substantial force" to Somalia. The U.S. forces had the mission of creating "a secure environment in the hardest-hit parts of Somalia" and then passing the security mission to a U.N. peace-keeping force and withdrawing. Other states agreeing to send forces were France, Pakistan, Morocco, Malaysia, Italy, Belgium, Canada, Australia, and Egypt, but the largest number came from the United States.

As part of Operation "Restore Hope," the first Americans, U.S. Marines, landed at Mogadishu before dawn on December 9. The plan called for about 16,000 marines and 10,000 soldiers to land in Somalia. Americans established some control over Mogadishu and in subsequent days fanned out across the southern half of Somalia. By the end of December, the U.S. had 12,500 troops in Somalia, and seventeen other countries had 6,000. Planners envisaged a U.N. force of about 28,000 peacekeepers (3,000–5,000 Americans) eventually taking over the operation. In the middle of January 1993, the first Americans departed as military personnel from other countries began replacing them. By May most of the American personnel came from the U.S. Army's 10th Mountain Division.

Throughout this period, U.S. leaders resisted expanding their mission from providing humanitarian aid to disarming feuding clans. U.N. officials believed that if the Somalis were not disarmed, clashes between the clans would occur and starvation would return when international forces departed. Despite reservations about expanding their mission, American forces began seizing weapons, particularly in Mogadishu, after several incidents, but their focus remained on providing humanitarian aid.

In early May, the United Nations took control of the multinational effort, and Lieutenant General Cevik Bir of Turkey became its commander. Almost simultaneously, efforts to disarm the Somalis escalated, and low-level urban guerrilla warfare began. U.N. casualties also rose rapidly. In June, fighting erupted in and around Mogadishu between U.N. peace-keeping forces and Somalis loyal to General Mohammed Farah Aidid, one of the region's most powerful warlords. As U.N. forces operated in the Mogadishu area, they received sniper fire and became engaged in firefights. While returning on June 5 from an inspection, a Pakistani unit was caught in a three-sided ambush. By the end of the day, twenty-three Pakistani soldiers had died, and sixty-three other U.N. soldiers had been wounded.

The following day, the U.N. Security Council condemned the attacks and called for the "arrest and detention" of those responsible. In subsequent weeks, U.N. troops attempted to capture Aidid and had several skirmishes with his forces. Differences emerged among the coalition with the Italians' being particularly critical of the abandonment of neutrality and the shift away from humanitarian efforts. In mid-July, U.N. officials relieved the commander of the Italian contingent in the multinational force after he refused to engage his 2,500 troops in action against Aidid.

In late August, soldiers from the U.S. Army's Delta Force and 75th Ranger Regiment arrived and launched raids in search of Aidid and his top aides. On October 3, however, they suffered heavy losses in Mogadishu when a "snatch operation" went badly wrong. The raid went well at first, for the Americans captured several of Aidid's aides. But as they withdrew, the Somalis, using a rocket-propelled grenade, shot down a helicopter from 160th Special Operations Regiment. When the Americans moved to secure the helicopter, the Somalis shot down another helicopter. Then several hundred fighters loyal to Aidid rushed to the area and began pouring fire into the surrounded Americans. A rapid reaction force consisting of a company from the 10th Mountain Division attempted to rescue the surrounded rangers, but Somalis ambushed the truck-borne troops as they moved through the city's narrow streets. A relief column of American infantry, four Pakistani tanks, and Malaysian armored personnel carriers finally reached the Americans, but by the time the fighting stopped, eighteen American and one Malaysian peacekeeper had died and more than one hundred were wounded. During the battle, the Somalis may have captured and executed several Americans; they kept one pilot as a prisoner but finally released him. Estimates of the number of Somalis killed in the fighting on October 3 ranged from 200 to 300, including women and children.

Shortly after the battle, President Bill Clinton spelled out a more limited mission for American forces. This included keeping key roads and lines of communication open for relief workers and food supplies, maintaining pressure on those who had originally cut off the flow of relief supplies, and helping the Somali people "solve their own problems." In essence, the Americans had halted their efforts to capture Aidid and disarm the factions. Clinton also announced that American forces would withdraw prior to March 31, 1994. Other states eventually joined the exodus from Somalia. Despite the magnitude of the continuing human tragedy, members of the United Nations no longer perceived Somalia as a "threat to international peace and security."

Bosnia-Herzegovina

The United Nations also experienced difficulties in Yugoslavia where it found itself torn between—on the one hand—providing humanitarian relief and local security or—on the other hand—intervening and using force to halt a wave of slaughter, rape, and destruction. The crisis began in February 1991 when the northern republics of Slovenia and Croatia adopted measures that pushed them toward independence from Yugoslavia. After Slovenia and Croatia formally declared their independence in June, Yugoslavian federal troops intervened to halt the breakup of their state, but on December 19, Germany recognized the two breakaway republics. Two weeks later, after the United Nations promised to deploy peace-keeping forces in Croatia, the Yugoslav government accepted the breakup and agreed to a peace plan and a cease-fire.

The disintegration of Yugoslavia accelerated in early 1992 when citizens of the republic of Bosnia-Herzegovina held a referendum and overwhelmingly supported independence. With a population of about 4.4 million, 44 percent of the Bosnians were Muslim Slavs, 31 percent Serbs, and 17 percent Croats. Most of the Serbs belonged to the Eastern Orthodox Church, and most of the Croats to the Roman Catholic Church. Large-scale violence began in early April when Serbian militia and guerrillas seized control of much of Bosnia. In May, the president of Serbia (previously Yugoslavia) transferred substantial arms and ammunition and about 50,000 Yugoslav troops to the control of Bosnian Serbs. Widespread atrocities occurred as the Serbs tightened their control over most of Bosnia, occupied about 70 percent of the countryside, and forced about one million Muslims and Croats to become refugees. The fighting quickly degenerated into a three-sided civil war.

In May the United Nations imposed economic sanctions on Yugoslavia and established an embargo against the shipment of weapons to

Bosnia, August 1994

Legend:
- Bosnian Serbs
- Bosnian Muslims
- Bosnian Croats

Bosnia, but it stopped short of using force. While the Serbs received weapons from the Yugoslavian army and the Croats from Croatia, the Muslims had few weapons, and the U.N. embargo hampered their acquiring additional weapons. As the carnage continued, the United Nations issued an ultimatum in late June for the Serbs to stop shelling Sarajevo. When the bombardment slowed, the United Nations began airlifting food and medicine to Sarajevo. Meanwhile, Serbs continued terrorizing other Bosnian towns. The United Nations responded by banning military flights over Bosnia but initially did little to enforce the ban.

As the crisis intensified, evidence mounted of Serbian atrocities against civilians. Bosnian refugees reported that Serbian forces had massacred Muslims and Croats and established concentration camps in which they tortured and killed thousands. At the end of December the Bosnian government estimated that 150,000 Bosnians had been killed and 1.6 million made homeless. In early January 1993, a team of European Community investigators reported that approximately 20,000 Muslim women had been raped by Serbian soldiers. Many of the victims claimed that the Serbs had used rape as a "weapon of war." The investigators concluded that thousands of rapes had served the "strategic purpose" of "ethnic cleansing" by "demoralizing and terrorizing communities" and driving the Bosnians from their homes.

Despite evidence of slaughter, mass rapes, and "ethnic cleansing," the United Nations refused to use force or risk losing its neutrality. Believing the Bosnian problem could best be handled through negotiations, Boutros-Ghali insisted that U.N. military intervention could only make the situation worse and could draw the international organization into a long and costly war. Nonetheless, he placed U.N. forces in Bosnia but restricted their role; he made them responsible primarily for escorting relief supplies into Sarajevo and other besieged areas. Once on the ground, U.N. military commanders argued against the aerial bombing of Serbian positions around Sarajevo because of their fears of retaliation against U.N. ground forces. In late February 1993, with U.N. approval, U.S. Air Force planes began parachuting food and medical supplies to Muslim towns besieged by the Serbs. In March, French and German planes also began dropping relief supplies and in April, NATO aircraft began enforcing a "no-fly zone" over Bosnia's airspace. Beginning in June, talks in Geneva between the warring Serbian, Croatian, and Muslim factions of Bosnia-Herzegovina focused on dividing Bosnia into three ethnic states. With the talks yielding little, the U.N. Security Council declared Sarajevo and five other Muslim strongholds in Bosnia "safe areas" and agreed to send U.N. troops to guard them. Nevertheless, Serbian and Croatian forces prevented U.N. ground forces from entering Muslim enclaves, and the wanton killing continued.

As the horror of the international community increased, the U.N. began using limited force against the Serbs. After a mortar round killed 68 civilians in a public market in Sarajevo in February 1994, the United Nations, threatening air strikes, ordered the Serbs to withdraw heavy weapons from around Sarajevo or hand them over to U.N. forces; the Serbs reluctantly complied. In late February, NATO observers identified six Serbian planes blatantly violating the U.N. ban on flights over Bosnian airspace, and two American planes shot four of them down. Technically, it was the first combat operation by NATO forces. In April, with U.N. authorization, NATO planes bombed Serbian forces around Gorazde, a safe area, after they refused U.N. demands to stop shelling and withdraw. After some delays and negotiations, the Serbs finally agreed to withdraw their heavy weapons beyond twenty kilometers from Gorazde; nearly 400 U.N. troops deployed to monitor the Serbian withdrawal. In August and September, NATO planes hit Serbian heavy weapons when they entered a zone around Sarajevo from which heavy weapons had been excluded.

The conflict took an unexpected turn in November after Muslim forces attacked out of the safe area around Bihac and drove the Serbs back. The Serbs counterattacked and soon placed great pressure—including aerial attacks—on Bihac. In late November, NATO planes launched limited strikes against a Serbian-controlled airbase in Croatia, hitting the airfield and avoiding planes and fuel dumps; they also struck Serb missile sites on the outskirts of Bihac. The Serbs, however, continued attacking Bihac and detained more than 450 U.N. personnel as hostages. Air strikes against the Serbs quickly ended. The American secretary of defense, William J. Perry, stated publicly that Serbian gains could not be reversed, and some Western political leaders called for new peace proposals acceptable to the Serbs. In

Many of the combatants in the Balkans had little or no military training and had no reservations about destroying civilian lives and property and committing atrocities.

May 1995 the Serbs began bombarding Bosnian safe areas and forcibly taking back the heavy weapons they had previously yielded to U.N. custody. When the United Nations responded with NATO air strikes, the Serbs again seized U.N. troops as hostages and human shields. As the crisis worsened, the Serbs shot down a U.S. Air Force F-16 fighter.

Fifteen NATO and European defense ministers met to discuss the crisis and decided to increase the combat strength of U.N. forces in Bosnia by sending two rapid reaction brigades to Bosnia. While the British 24th Airmobile Brigade could respond rapidly to an attack on U.N. troops in a remote area, Task Force Alpha (a brigade consisting of French, British, and Dutch troops and light armored vehicles) could provide rapid reinforcement and armored protection. Some critics believed that by adding the two brigades U.N. forces risked crossing the "Mogadishu line" and forfeiting their neutrality. European leaders, however, insisted that the U.N. troops would remain peacekeepers and not become combatants.

Despite the United Nations' reluctance to use force, its role gradually had expanded from humanitarian relief to peace enforcement. It simultaneously had tried to use carefully calibrated air attacks to compel the Serbs to comply with its ultimatums and small ground forces to provide humanitarian aid and local security, particularly around the so-called safe areas. The unwillingness of U.N. members to be drawn into a wider war and the vulnerability of peace-keeping forces on the ground, however, restricted the peace enforcement efforts of the United Nations. The limited power of international forces became even more apparent in July when the Serbs captured the safe area at Srebrenica and expelled thousands of terrified Muslim refugess.

In both Bosnia and Somalia, military officials criticized the ad hoc nature and inefficiency of U.N. military operations. In their eyes, the conflicting interests and objectives of participating states made it difficult to identify clear missions for multinational military forces and precise conditions for their withdrawal. Moreover, the diversity of forces involved in U.N. operations made detailed coordination difficult; and a weak and diffuse chain of command, unreliable intelligence, incompatible communications equipment, and the absence of a common logistical system added further complexities. Not until operations were fully under way in Somalia and Bosnia, for example, did the U.N. establish a twenty-four-hour operations center in its headquarters. To some, deficiencies in the U.N. system ruled out swift, decisive interventions unless one or two states dominated the entire operation. Some analysts called for the establishment of a standing U.N. "rapid deployment force" or "peace-enforcement unit" which could deter or repel aggression by being transported to distant regions on short notice. Member states, however, remained opposed to a standing U.N. army. Despite the apparent limitations of multinational forces, U.N. Secretary General Boutros-Ghali remained convinced of their utility and did not abandon his call for international peace-enforcement operations with personnel from as many as "forty states."

*   *   *   *

Throughout the post–World War II period, major military powers often sent expeditions to distant regions to conduct combat operations. Relying on air and sea transport, most expeditions deployed rapidly on short notice to unfamiliar locations such as the Dominican Republic, the Falkland Islands, or Grenada. The expeditions usually sought to overwhelm a poorly armed or less capable opponent quickly. Despite the relative brevity of the campaigns, the expeditions faced complex challenges; intervening forces frequently had to transport troops and equipment hastily over long distances and rely on combinations of air, sea, and land forces to gain victory swiftly. Since the operations typically took place in unexpected and unfamiliar locations, the intervening forces often encountered significant difficulties in obtaining adequate intelligence, securing sufficient logistical support, establishing effective communications, and accomplishing proper coordination. Advances in strategic transport and communications, nevertheless, provided a few states a true "global reach." As the Cold War faded from the scene, interventions by national or multinational forces in regional conflicts appeared likely in a world plagued by national, religious, ethnic, and regional antagonisms.

Iraq's aggression against Kuwait, however, provoked the first major conflict of the post–Cold War era, the Persian Gulf War. Those opposing the Iraqis brought with them forces and methods designed for high-intensity conflict in central Europe, and in the subsequent fighting, they provided an impressive display of advanced methods and weapons. After witnessing the swift defeat of Iraq and the remarkable performance of the coalition's forces in the Persian Gulf War, some analysts suggested that weapons based on the electronic microchip would replace the low-cost, mass-production weapons of the industrial age that had dominated warfare through much of the nineteenth and twentieth centuries. Highly lethal and accurate weapons would supposedly enable leaders to wage intense battles of short duration, rather than grinding battles of attrition. Increases in tactical, operational, and strategic mobility also suggested new possibilities for using maneuver against an opponent. Other advances in intelligence-gathering systems and in communications systems suggested new means of commanding and controlling military units, and the wide use of computers facilitated the processing of massive amounts of information. Those believing a new age of warfare had begun saw the need for new strategies, new tactics, and new relationships between military organizations and societies.

Despite such expectations, the initial challenges of the new post–Cold War era found little use for new strategies and tactics and only limited use for high-technology weapons. Amidst the spread of violence and turmoil, armed forces found themselves acting as peacekeepers and having to deal not with disciplined, well-equipped opponents but with paramilitary forces, militias, and gangster-like elements. In this environment, the United Nations expanded its role from peacekeeping to peace enforcement. In Bosnia the United Nations initially provided relief supplies to people besieged by forces attempting to starve them into submission, but the U.N. secretary general gradually permitted U.N. forces to use limited force. In Somalia, the United Nations intervened without a formal invitation, and the role of the intervening forces also expanded from providing humanitarian aid to peace enforcement. The reluctance of the United Nations to act more forcefully in Bosnia and Somalia and the difficulties encountered in both areas, however, demonstrated the complexities of interventions—whether launched by a single state or by a multinational force.

SUGGESTED READINGS

Adkin, Mark. *Urgent Fury: The Battle for Grenada* (Lexington, Mass.: D.C. Heath, 1989).

Atkinson, Rick. *Crusade: The Untold Story of the Persian Gulf War* (Boston: Houghton Mifflin, 1993).

Blechman, Barry M., and Stephen S. Kaplain. *Force Without War: U.S. Armed Forces as a Political Instrument* (Washington, D.C.: The Brookings Institute, 1978).

Bolger, Daniel P. *Americans at War: 1975–1986, An Era of Violent Peace* (Novato, Calif.: Presidio Press, 1988).

Callwell, C. E. *Small Wars: Their Principles and Practice* (London: Her Majesty's Stationery Office, 1899).

Dunn, Peter M., and Bruce W. Watson, eds. *American Intervention in Grenada: The Implications of Operation "Urgent Fury"* (Boulder, Col.: Westview Press, 1985).

Friedman, Norman. *Desert Victory: The War for Kuwait* (Annapolis: Naval Institute Press, 1991).

Hallion, Richard P. *Storm over Iraq: Air Power and the Gulf War* (Washington, D.C.: Smithsonian Institution Press, 1992).

Hastings, Max, and Simon Jenkins. *The Battle for the Falklands* (New York: W. W. Norton and Company, 1983).

Koburger, Charles W., Jr. *Sea Power in the Falklands* (New York: Praeger, 1983).

Middlebrook, Martin. *The Fight for the "Malvinas": The Argentine Forces in the Falklands War* (New York: Viking, 1989).

Musicant, Ivan. *The Banana Wars: A History of United States Military Intervention in Latin America from the Spanish–American War to the Invasion of Panama* (New York: Macmillan, 1990).

Odom, Thomas P. *Dragon Operations: Hostage Rescues in the Congo, 1964–1965* (Fort Leavenworth, Kans.: Combat Studies Institute, 1988).

Scales, Robert H., Jr. *Certain Victory: United States Army in the Gulf War* (Washington, D.C.: Government Printing Office, 1993).

Shaughnessy, Hugh. *Grenada: An Eyewitness Account of the U.S. Invasion and the Caribbean History that Provoked It* (New York: Dodd, Mead and Company, 1984).

Spector, Ronald H. *U.S. Marines in Grenada, 1983* (Washington, D.C.: Government Printing Office, 1987).

Spiller, Roger J. *"Not War But Like War": The American Intervention in Lebanon* (Fort Leavenworth, Kans.: Combat Studies Institute, 1981).

Summers, Harry G., Jr. *On Strategy II: A Critical Appraisal of the Gulf War* (New York: Dell Publishing, 1992).

United Nations. *The Blue Helmets: A Review of United Nations Peace-keeping* (New York: United Nations Department of Public Information, 1990).

Watson, Bruce W., and Peter G. Tsouras, eds. *Operation Just Cause: The U.S. Intervention in Panama* (Boulder, Col.: Westview Press, 1991).

Yates, Lawrence A. *Power Pack: U.S. Intervention in the Dominican Republic, 1964–1966* (Fort Leavenworth, Kans.: Combat Studies Institute, 1988).

32

TERROR AND THE REDEFINING OF WAR

Global War on Terror

War in Iraq

Asymmetrical Warfare

As the twenty-first century opened, the world seemed to be entering a new era in which old theories of international relations and national security no longer applied. Most people hoped for a new era of peace, marred only by brief interventions by major powers into various corners of the globe. At the same time, political and military leaders foresaw a transformation of war stemming from the new international environment and from great scientific advances, especially those in electronics and information management. When President George W. Bush spoke at the United States Naval Academy on May 21, 2001, he said he was committed to having the world's finest navy and marine corps and stated: "To do so, we must build forces that draw upon the revolutionary advances in the technology of war that will allow us to keep the peace by redefining war on our terms. I'm committed to building a future force that is defined less by size and more by mobility and swiftness, one that is easier to deploy and sustain, one that relies more heavily on stealth, precision weaponry and information technologies."

As he spoke, terrorists were planning an attack against the United States and attempting to redefine war on their own terms. The attack on September 11, 2001, against the World Trade Center in New York City and other targets demonstrated that revolutionary

advances in the technology of war by themselves could neither redefine war nor keep the peace and that no one in the world was safe
or secure from acts of violence by terrorists. The subsequent global
war on terrorism also demonstrated that although the United States
could, as President Bush said at the United States Military Academy
on June 1, 2002, "strike at a moment's notice in any dark corner of
the world," it would face severe challenges clearing those "dark corners" of terrorists.

An era very different from the Cold War and immediate post–
Cold War emerged. The globalization of the world's economies, the
easy and quick movement of people across international borders,
and the availability of information instantly from almost anywhere
created conditions that brought into question the existence of many
states and revived old identities of tribal and ethnic groups. Amid
this enormous change, religious fervor stoked new passions. Previously considered a historical relic, violence for religious or ethnic
reasons dominated conflict at the beginning of the century. Chaos
within failed states added further complexities, particularly after
more powerful explosives became available and illicit arsenals of nuclear, chemical, and biological weapons became possible.

The world thus entered a new era of international relations
and national security, but not one that political and military leaders
in the West welcomed.

GLOBAL WAR ON TERROR

Terrorism

Studies on terror have acknowledged more than a hundred definitions of the word. Those who have offered definitions have often
crafted them to exclude their own acts or to include those of their
opponents. In 2001, the United States Department of Defense offered its own definition when it defined terrorism as a "calculated
use of unlawful violence to inculcate fear; intended to coerce or intimidate governments or societies in pursuit of goals that are generally political, religious, or ideological."

For millennia, numerous individuals, groups, or states have used terror or sponsored terrorist groups to inculcate fear, intimidate others, and achieve widely varying goals. Terrorists have come from most religions, from the political right and left, from rich and poor regions, and from states with authoritarian and democratic governments. Those using terror have sought occasionally to supplement conventional campaigns, but they often have been too weak to prevail in a clash of arms on a battlefield and considered terror the least costly and most effective alternative for them. Neither irrational nor lunatic, many terrorists have been young idealists willing to sacrifice themselves and others in pursuit of their goals.

The modern use of the word *terror* began during the French Revolution when the Committee of Public Safety executed thousands of citizens. In what was called the "Reign of Terror," many died under the blade of the guillotine, but others died in macabre circumstances such as in the mass drowning of prisoners in Nantes in 1794. The revolutionaries used the killings, as well as the threat of additional ones, in an effort to transform the entire society. They also used violence to reduce the number of counterrevolutionaries, intimidate reluctant citizens, and consolidate their power.

Before the invention of gunpowder, terrorists used weapons such as knives, swords, or arrows to wound or kill opponents and intimidate others. The introduction of gunpowder made bullets and bombs the preferred weapons of terrorists, and the invention of dynamite in 1866 gave them a small, powerful explosive. Evidence of the new explosive's power appeared in 1881 when Tsar Alexander II died from a bomb thrown by a member of a Russian terrorist group known as "People's Will." In the final decades of the nineteenth century, anarchists seeking to trigger mass uprisings and overthrow governments used powerful bombs to kill innocent people as well as leaders. In the post–World War II period, the invention of plastic explosives provided terrorists new means of destruction. Although suicide of terrorists was not new, the suicide bomber was. Terrorists learned how to wrap themselves in powerful explosives and metal shards and infiltrate and destroy unsuspecting crowds. Preventing suicide bombers from killing themselves and others proved extraordinarily difficult.

Analysts sometimes classify terrorist groups as state and non-state sponsored. An example of a state-sponsored group is the Baader-Meinhof Gang. In the late 1960s, the gang, which eventually became known as the Red Army Faction, waged a violent campaign against West German capitalists and United States military personnel in Europe.

With some assistance from East Germany, members of the Baader-Meinhof gang spent most of their time robbing banks, bombing buildings, and murdering business executives. Although the gang's goals remain unclear, some analysts believed members wanted to goad the West German government into draconian measures that would spark a civil war. An example of a non–state-sponsored group is the Japanese cult, Aum Shinrikyo, or Supreme Truth. In March 1995, members of the cult released sarin, a nerve gas, on a Tokyo subway and killed twelve people. In a five-year effort, members of the religious cult had developed an arsenal of chemical weapons and biological warfare agents. Radicals had transformed the cult from a yoga and meditation group into a far more sinister religious movement that combined elements of Buddhism and Christianity. Although the methods and agendas of terrorists have varied widely around the globe, almost all have exhibited no reluctance to kill innocent bystanders in pursuit of their goals.

Incidents of terrorism became common in the final decades of the twentieth century. Amid rising international discontent, reactions against Western colonization and imperialism created fertile fields for the planting of radical ideas. The increase in terrorist violence was not necessarily a by-product of poverty or of religious persecution, for some terrorists came from prosperous families and peaceful communities with little or no history of religious or ethnic intolerance. Yet, rising birth rates and declining infant mortality produced a large population of young people who suffered under intense competition for education and jobs and who responded to calls from radical groups. Although many terrorists rejected Western ideas and values, globalization created conditions making their violent acts possible. The ease of international travel and communications facilitated their recruitment, financial, and logistic efforts, and modern scientific advances provided them more powerful weapons. At the same time, radio, movies, and television spread images of violent acts and information about them almost instantly into all corners of the globe. The desire for publicity motivated some terrorists to commit heinous acts against innocent people who often knew little about them or their cause.

An especially dangerous brand of terrorism grew out of the Afghanistan war from 1979 to 1989. Hundreds of young Muslims traveled to Asia to become *mujahideen*, freedom fighters, and wage a *jihad*, holy war, against the Soviets and their Afghan allies. As a growing number of foreign fighters joined the fight, some of them wanted to expand their operations from establishing an Islamic state in Afghanistan to Islamic struggles elsewhere. Among those seeking to expand the struggle was Osama bin Laden, a wealthy Saudi whose primary role during the Afghan war was raising funds for recruiting and training *mujahideen*. Returning to Saudi Arabia after the Soviets withdrew from Afghanistan, he objected vehemently when the Saudi government invited the United States and its allies to enter Saudi Arabia in 1990 and drive Saddam Hussein from Kuwait. He accused the Saudi king of profaning sacred soil by inviting infidels to enter the "land of the two mosques, Mecca and Medina." Forced to leave Saudi Arabia, bin Laden traveled to Sudan and began calling publicly for attacks on the United States. He argued the United States had attacked Islam and blamed Americans for all conflicts involving Muslims, including Palestine, Chechnya, Kashmir, and the Philippines.

In late 1996, after garnering additional resources, bin Laden returned to Afghanistan with more than two hundred of his supporters and their families. During the next several years, he and other members of his organization, now known as al-Qaeda, or the base, trained and indoctrinated as many as twenty thousand individuals in special camps. Sheltered by the fledgling Taliban group, which ruled Afghanistan, al-Qaeda evolved into a nebulous, transnational organization not controlled or limited geographically by any single state. In February 1998, the "World Islamic Front," headed by bin Laden and Ayman al-Zawahiri, issued a *fatwa*, a legal pronouncement in Islam made by a leader capable of making judgments on Islamic law. The *fatwa* claimed the United States had declared war against God and Islam and called for Muslims everywhere to murder Americans. To end the war, bin Laden and his followers insisted the United States leave the Middle East, convert to Islam, and abandon its immorality and godlessness. The bombing of United States embassies in Kenya and Tanzania in August 1998, which killed approximately three hundred people, was al-Qaeda's first major terrorist attack. Two years later, al-Qaeda militants struck the USS *Cole* in Yemen with a suicide attack and killed seventeen American sailors.

A new era in the long history of terrorism had begun.

The Attack on the World Trade Center and the American Response in Afghanistan

On the morning of September 11, 2001, two airliners struck the Twin Towers of the World Trade Center in New York City; minutes later, another plane smashed into the Pentagon. Although terrorists wanted to fly a fourth plane into the White House or Capitol, passengers on the plane heroically fought to regain control of it and caused it to crash in a deserted field in Pennsylvania. About three thousand victims died in the crashes.

On the eve of the attack, the United States only partially understood the threat and capabilities of terrorists such as bin Laden. Although the 1995 National Intelligence Estimate had warned of a new type of terrorism and the White House's National Security Council had a Counterterrorism Strategy Group, no central strategy for a war on or defense against terrorism existed, and no effective method for combining domestic and foreign intelligence had been established. Most officials continued to think of terrorists as agents of states, not members of a loose, widely scattered, transnational organization. Very few in Washington viewed al-Qaeda as a significant threat.

As for the military, preparation for sustained operations against terrorists remained extremely limited. Created in April 1987, Special Operations Command could plan and execute strikes against terrorist networks, but the highly publicized failure of a raid in Mogadishu, Somalia, in October 1993 to kill or capture a warlord and his top lieutenants made policy makers reluctant to risk such operations. In the wake of terrorist attacks in the 1990s, the United States emphasized deterring such attacks with limited air power and, after the bombing of the United States embassies in Kenya and Tanzania in August 1998, used Tomahawk missiles from submarines to attack al-Qaeda's known training camps in Afghanistan and a suspected nerve gas manufacturing plant in Sudan. By the summer of 2000, the military had identified thirteen options for missile or special operations strikes and by December, after the bombing of the USS *Cole*, had a modest plan for a "phased campaign" of air strikes against targets in Afghanistan, including the Taliban. The level of effort devoted to other issues, such as confronting Serbia in the Balkans, however, was many times greater than that devoted to al-Qaeda.

As the United States considered its options, an array of countries and international organizations promised support. The United Nations Security Council quickly adopted resolutions not only affirming the right of states to defend themselves against terrorism but also labeling terrorism a threat to international peace and security and obliging member states to freeze the assets of terrorists and deny them safe haven. NATO declared that the attack on the United States represented an attack on every member of the organization. National leaders around the world recognized they could not stand by idly as grave threats coalesced around them. According to the United States Department of Defense, sixty-eight states joined the global war on terrorism as part of a military coalition, and twenty states deployed sixteen thousand troops to the United States Central Command's (CENTCOM) region of responsibility (Middle East, East Africa, and Central Asia).

Within hours after the attack on the World Trade Center, President Bush decided to use all elements of American national power to destroy al-Qaeda and other related terrorist networks. Through diplomatic channels, the State Department issued an ultimatum to the Taliban to surrender bin Laden and his lieutenants. Not expecting the Taliban to cooperate, the president directed Secretary of Defense Donald Rumsfeld to develop plans for operations against them. The CIA and CENTCOM quickly crafted plans for CIA teams and special operations units to work with Afghan warlords in a fight against al-Qaeda. When the Taliban defied the president's ultimatum by refusing to turn over bin Laden unless the United States provided concrete evidence of his involvement in the terrorist attack, Bush ordered General Tommy Franks, commander of CENTCOM, to launch military operations in Afghanistan and destroy al-Qaeda and the Taliban regime. He refused to distinguish between terrorists and those who sheltered them.

The ensuing campaign was a remarkable demonstration of logistics, air power, and special operations. Projecting power halfway around the globe proved daunting. Using diplomatic channels, the United States gained the cooperation of key states round Afghanistan—including Pakistan, Kyrgyzstan, Uzbekistan, and Tajikistan—to establish logistic bases and ports. Other regional states providing bases were Oman, Kuwait, and Qatar. After gaining permission to fly over numerous countries, the United States Air Force built an "air bridge" of C-5 and C-17 transports to bases in the Middle East. It then used C-17, C-130, and C-141 aircraft to transport troops and supplies to remote bases in Central Asia. Only Herculean efforts from Air Force logisticians supplied sufficient fuel and kept the complex aircraft flying.

Using long-range bombers, carrier-based aircraft, and Tomahawk missiles from American and British submarines, the attack against the Taliban and al-Qaeda began on October 7, 2001, twenty-five days after the attack on the World Trade Center. Some of the first strikes came from B-2 stealth bombers flying from Missouri; others came from naval aircraft flying one thousand kilometers from aircraft carriers to their targets. American and British warships also fired Tomahawk land-attack missiles. As the campaign progressed, more air support came from American and coalition planes flying from land-based air stations in the Gulf region. Many of the sorties came from the British-owned Indian Ocean atoll of Diego Garcia, a one-way distance of four thousand kilometers. With initial priority given to hitting the Taliban's command and control, early warning radar, and air defense systems, the air war changed rapidly from strikes against preplanned targets to a combination of preplanned and immediate targets. Especially noteworthy was the use of long-range bombers in a close air support role against targets identified only minutes before by United States personnel on the ground with anti-Taliban forces. Although cumbersome procedures for approving targets delayed some strikes and a few casualties from friendly fire occurred, pilots were consistently able to destroy enemy targets with precision. The airmen performed extraordinarily well in a challenging and complex environment.

A top-secret air war used satellites and unmanned aerial vehicles to identify time-sensitive targets and enable aircraft to strike them. At one point, a Predator unmanned aerial vehicle succeeded in locating the Taliban leader, Mullah Muhammad Omar. Through a video link with the Predator, General Franks watched Mullah Omar's small convoy and decided to strike the convoy using F-14 or F-18 aircraft instead of Hellfire missiles from the unmanned aerial vehicle. As he attempted to avoid damaging a mosque and sought President Bush's approval of the strike, Mullah Omar escaped. Franks did not get a second chance.

Within Afghanistan, the Northern Alliance offered prospects of cooperation. Comprised primarily of ethnic minorities such as the Tajiks and Uzbeks, the Northern Alliance was an extremely loose alliance of tribal warlords who opposed the Taliban, which consisted primarily of Pashtuns in southern Afghanistan. Members of the alliance held small areas in the northeastern and northwestern parts of the country. The United States decided to seek the help of the Northern Alliance in overthrowing the Taliban and attacking al-Qaeda but realized it had to tread carefully to avoid alienating the various tribes and warlords that made up the alliance. Rumsfeld and Franks did not want to repeat the Soviet Union's disastrous experience in Afghanistan and believed tens of thousands of troops would look more like an army of occupation to the Afghans than an army of liberation. Instead of a large, heavy force, they wanted a light, lethal force that could work with the Northern Alliance and deliver precision strikes.

On October 19, special operations forces began landing in Afghanistan. The bulk of these forces came from the 5th Special Forces Group, 160th Special Operations Regiment, and Special Tactics personnel from United States Air Force, but soldiers from other countries in the coalition participated. Teams landed at four main areas in Afghanistan. In the northeast, they landed near Mazar-e-Sharif and Taloqan; in the east, Kabul; and in the south, near Kandahar. Once on the ground, they quickly established contact with forces from the Northern Alliance and began calling in close air support. The air strikes had a devastating effect on the Taliban's fighters who soon began to withdraw before the troops of the Northern Alliance. In addition to long-range bombers and fighter-bombers, ground controllers called on AC-130 Spectre and Spooky aircraft to saturate enemy positions with thousands of Gatling gun and cannon rounds a minute. Often riding horses, the special operations personnel accompanied the attacking Afghans and, using air power, destroyed many enemy command posts, troop concentrations, armored vehicles, and anti-aircraft artillery. On November 10, the Afghans drove into Mazar-e-Sharif amid cheering local citizens who lined the streets. The following day, Taloqan fell easily, as did Kabul, the capital of Afghanistan. The last Taliban stronghold in northern Afghanistan, Kondoz, which was located to the west of Taloqan, did not fall until November 23 after extremely heavy aerial bombardment.

Farther to the south, Kandahar became the next objective. Planners expected its capture to be more difficult because Pashtuns, who made up 44 percent of the country's population, dominated the region and strongly supported the Taliban movement. After preparatory fires from AC-130 Spectre gunships, United States Army Rangers seized a remote airfield south of Kandahar. C-130, C-17, and H-53 aircraft then landed about a thousand marines and special operations soldiers who quickly covered the exits from Kandahar. On November 14, a special forces team linked up with Hamid Karzai and his small band of followers near Kandahar. A Pashtun who was pro-Western and anti-Taliban, Karzai proved vital to the coalition's success because he could attract fighters to his side from the Pashtuns. Against occasionally strong opposition, Karzai's force slowly increased in numbers and began advancing toward Kandahar. Facing relentless air strikes, the Taliban fighters abandoned the city on December 7, and Karzai, accompanied by coalition troops, entered.

To the east of Kabul, al-Qaeda and Taliban forces retreated into extremely rugged terrain and offered stiff resistance in early December. Since the time of the anti-Soviet *mujahideen*, terrorists had controlled the mountainous area, known as Tora Bora, and dug extensive fortifications and caves in which they stockpiled weapons and equipment. Not wanting to risk alienating the Afghans by sending additional American ground forces, General Franks decided to let anti-Taliban forces surround and assault the enemy's positions. As Afghan troops moved forward from boulder to boulder, special forces teams coordinated the delivery of hundreds of air strikes onto the mountainous terrain. In the end, anti-Taliban forces captured a few al-Qaeda fighters and killed many more, but some of the enemy—perhaps including bin Laden—slipped through the porous ring of anti-Taliban forces and fled into the mountains of Pakistan.

With the collapse of resistance around Tora Bora, the Taliban lost control of Afghanistan. In less than sixty days, coalition and anti-Taliban forces had removed the regime and severely disrupted al-Qaeda's operations. A number of prominent Afghans met in Bonn, Germany, to devise a plan for governing the country, and Karzai became head of a transitional government in Kabul. He quickly called for international assistance for the Afghan people who had suffered from decades of warfare and economic neglect. The United Nations responded by creating the International Security Assistance Force, which established security around Kabul and its surrounding territories. Neither the United States nor other Western countries, however, were willing to commit a large number of troops to stabilize and secure the entire country. In the absence of robust stability operations, coalition forces controlled only a small portion of Afghanistan.

In late February 2002, Taliban and al-Qaeda fighters entered the Shahi Kowt Valley south of Kabul and the city of Gardiz. As the

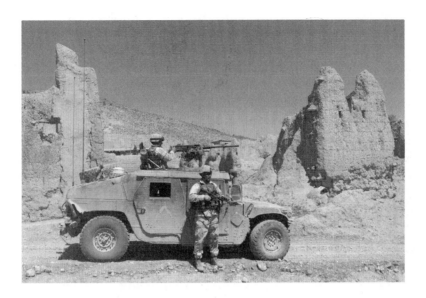

number of enemy increased, Major General Franklin L. "Buster" Hagenbeck, commander of the 10th Mountain Division, received the mission of destroying them in Operation Anaconda, which began on March 2. Under an operational concept calling for "nonlinear simultaneous operations in noncontiguous areas of operations," Hagenbeck attempted to isolate and encircle enemy forces in the valley and destroy them with converging attacks. Using a mixture of Afghan, American, and coalition (from Australia, Britain, Canada, Denmark, France, Germany, and New Zealand) forces, Hagenbeck succeeded in encircling the al-Qaeda forces in the rugged terrain but failed to destroy them completely.

In this first major battle in Afghanistan involving significant numbers of conventional troops, difficulties abounded in intelligence, command and control, and air control. Intelligence underestimated the numerical strength and ferocious resistance of the enemy, although the United States focused its most sophisticated electronic and satellite assets on the relatively small piece of terrain. Because of the faulty intelligence, Hagenbeck received barely enough forces to accomplish his mission. As for command and control, Hagenbeck did not control all the forces in the area, particularly special operations units who conducted high-risk missions in enemy territory and who were accustomed to working alone. Adding to the complexity, Hagenbeck's immediate land-forces superior was in Kuwait, the center for coordination of his air support in Saudi Arabia, and the CENTCOM commander, General Franks, in Tampa, Florida.

Franks used video teleconferences to delve into operational details, and numerous requests for information, much of which was demanded by the secretary of defense, burdened Hagenbeck's staff. Moreover, the theater air control system proved inadequate for very demanding and complex airspace control requirements. Numerous aircraft had to strike targets in a relatively small area, and a complex approval process slowed their arrival.

Once the operation began, little went as planned. The movement of Afghan forces was disappointing, as vehicular problems and mud delayed their deployment and friendly fire from an AC-130 aircraft halted their advance. More than a week later, a new Afghan commander and seven hundred soldiers arrived from Kabul, and the Afghans renewed their advance. Other coalition forces moved quickly into position, but in the initial fighting, fierce firefights on Takur Ghar, a mountain to the southeast of the valley, diverted air resources after a Navy SEAL fell from a helicopter and enemy fire shot down a CH-47 helicopter. With Afghan forces arriving late and air strikes diverted or sometimes arriving slowly, ground forces found themselves fighting under unfavorable circumstances. Because CENTCOM had denied Hagenbeck's request for artillery when his task force first deployed to Central Asia, the infantry had to assault prepared enemy positions with only mortars and air strikes. Although casualties were light, ground commanders later complained loudly about their not having artillery for more responsive, immediate fires.

All in all, Operation Anaconda took several days more than expected, required more support (logistics, air, and operational reserves) than anticipated, and proved more difficult than expected. Hagenbeck nonetheless delivered a destructive blow and drove al-Qaeda and Taliban forces out of the Shahi Kowt Valley.

Although Operation Anaconda marked the end of large operations in Afghanistan, low-level attacks by al-Qaeda and Taliban fighters continued and security outside Kabul remained poor. The United States and other powers were reluctant to commit substantial ground forces in stability operations in Afghanistan. Except for finger-pointing in the Pentagon between the Army and Air Force, however, no one in Washington doubted the efficacy and power of American armed forces. Rumsfeld and Franks, in particular, thought the war had demonstrated the transformation of the American military and its readiness for a new way of war.

A Broader Response to Terrorism

In the first days after the attack on September 11, President Bush recognized the war on terrorism required more than ridding Afghanistan of the Taliban regime. Among the issues receiving attention were improvements in security, many of which occurred relatively quickly and easily. The United States Coast Guard and Army National Guard proved invaluable for reinforcing security efforts of local authorities in air and sea ports and other sensitive points. Close cooperation with Canada also enabled the United States to enhance aerial and maritime defense against terrorists. While continuing to watch for threats emerging from other continents, the North American Aerospace Defense Command broadened its surveillance to threats appearing from within North America. Other improvements, such as checking the contents of thousands of containers arriving by air and sea in the United States, did not come easily. The Department of Homeland Security, which evolved from an "office" in the White House in September 2001 to a cabinet-level department in November 2002 with some two hundred thousand employees, had an extraordinarily complex mission. As the new department gained better cooperation among federal, state, and local governments and raised safeguards for domestic and international shipping and border control, security increased in the United States. Sharp controversy, however, surrounded questions of funding priorities.

With the broadening of the campaign against terror, traditional boundaries between the battlefield and the home front became blurred. Because terrorists in clandestine cells could be almost anywhere, the gathering of intelligence, the conduct of antiterrorist operations, and the holding of prisoners raised questions, not always new, between military authorities and domestic law enforcement officials. Some believed legal protections inherent in criminal law did not apply to terrorists who could use legal procedures to shield the planning and conduct of violent acts. Others believed Western judicial systems were obliged to guard fundamental human rights and civil liberties and provide protection to all those under the authority and control of civilian and military authorities, including possible terrorists. Fierce debates occurred in the United States and elsewhere over the gathering of intelligence (especially the electronic monitoring of private conversations by Americans) and the treatment of prisoners. Many of the sharpest debates concerned prisoners captured by the United States and its allies and held in a United States naval base at Guantanamo Bay in Cuba. Critics argued the prison eroded the world's faith in the American judicial system.

The war against terror quickly became a global effort that went beyond capturing and killing terrorists. Members of United States Special Operations Command, Pacific (SOCPAC), for example, deployed in the Philippines in January 2002 to assist Philippine forces in operations against terrorists. They focused their efforts on the island of Basilan in the southern Philippines, a stronghold of the terrorist group, Abu Sayyaf. In addition to advising Philippine forces, the Americans built roads, improved airfield and port facilities, and dug water wells. They also provided extensive medical assistance to local civilians. Elsewhere around the globe, other nations cooperated in unraveling terrorist networks. Geography encouraged the Indonesians and Australians, for example, to work together closely. After a terrorist bombing killed 202 civilians, including 88 Australians, on the island of Bali in October 2002, Indonesian and Australian police worked together to hunt down and capture those who had planned and executed the attack. Their combined counterterrorist effort also interrupted the financing of terrorist enterprises and improved the skills of the region's law enforcement officers.

Heightened fears of terrorism and weapons of mass destruction contributed to the United States' developing a new national security strategy. With the routing of the Taliban in Afghanistan fresh in mind, President Bush told a Joint Session of Congress in his State of the Union Address on January 29, 2002, that an "axis of evil" and its terrorist allies threatened the peace of the world. After identifying Iraq, Iran, and North Korea, the president said, "I will not wait on events, while dangers gather. I will not stand by, as peril draws closer and closer. The United States of America will not permit the world's most dangerous regimes to threaten us with the world's most destructive weapons." Traditional policies of containment and deterrence seemed useless against states who callously repressed their own people and slaughtered thousands of innocent human beings and against terrorists who had no nation or citizens to defend. Five months later, when speaking at the graduation ceremony at West Point, Bush used the words "preemptive action" and promised the United States would "confront the worst threats before they emerge." The new grand strategy emphasized, first, not allowing "rogue states" to threaten the use of weapons of mass destruction or provide them secretly to terrorists and, second, curtailing terrorist influence by spreading liberty and democracy. Implicit within the new strategy was the refusal of the United States to allow international organizations to constrain its actions in the face of an impending catastrophe.

THE WAR IN IRAQ

The new American strategy received its first test in Iraq. From the earliest moments of the September 11 attacks, President Bush and most members of Congress believed Iraq posed a threat to the United States. In October 2002, more than two-thirds of the Senate and House of Representatives voted to authorize the president to "use the armed forces of the United States as he determines to be necessary and appropriate in order to defend the national security of the United States against the continuing threat posed by Iraq." After the Gulf War of 1991, UN inspectors had worked in Iraq to ensure the dismantling of Iraq's weapons of mass destruction but received little cooperation from the Iraqis. They departed in 1998 only hours before American and British warplanes struck some one hundred targets across Iraq to "degrade Saddam's development of weapons of mass destruction." Facing a possible invasion by the United States, Iraq allowed UN inspectors to begin work anew in November 2002 and cooperated more extensively with them. Although inspectors had discovered evidence before 1998 of Saddam's attempts to develop chemical, biological, and nuclear weapons, they found no new evidence this time of secret programs and asked for more time to conduct additional inspections. Intelligence (which was later discredited) about Iraq's relations with al-Qaeda and its efforts to reconstitute its nuclear program, however, reinforced American sentiment for war.

In his State of the Union Address in January 2003, President Bush stated, "The dictator of Iraq is not disarming. To the contrary; he is deceiving." He added, "Trusting in the sanity and restraint of Saddam Hussein is not a strategy, and it is not an option." On February 5, Secretary of State Colin Powell went before the UN Security Council to lay out intelligence on Iraq's weapons programs, insist Iraq had failed to disarm, and win international backing for an invasion. He failed, however, to convince France, Russia, and China that military action against Iraq was necessary and justified. The United

States did not get a Security Council resolution providing international support for an invasion.

Six weeks later, however, a coalition headed by the United States attacked Iraq.

Operation Iraqi Freedom

Commanded by General Tommy Franks, CENTCOM spent almost sixteen months planning the Iraq invasion, Operation Iraqi Freedom. Although considerable pressure for an extremely small invasion force came from Secretary Rumsfeld, Franks believed a revolution in military affairs had occurred and American forces could defeat Iraq using new technology and methods and far fewer ground troops. He believed that United States forces were more lethal than in 1991 because of advances in precision weapons and improvements in command and control and that the Iraqi Army was smaller and less capable. He also believed that the threat of violence kept Saddam Hussein in power and that the Iraqi people would welcome the overthrow of his regime.

Not wanting to take months to deploy forces to the Middle East, Franks aimed for a flexible plan and for deployment on short notice. Beginning with a plan that called for at least four hundred thousand troops, staff officers at CENTCOM worked through several variations of war plans with different numbers of ground forces and with different sequences of ground and air assaults. They also considered different levels of coalition support and various lead times between the orders to deploy and invade. As they revised the basic design of the invasion, they spent relatively little time addressing questions pertaining to occupying and stabilizing Iraq after the seizure of Baghdad. Those ultimately responsible for planning, Rumsfeld and Franks, as well as many others in Washington, believed a campaign in Iraq would be as easy as the recent one in Afghanistan and demonstrated only modest interest in addressing the messy and difficult challenge of pacifying postwar Iraq.

Franks expected several simultaneous thrusts to enable him to dominate the Iraqis quickly. His final concept for Operation Iraqi Freedom envisaged "five fronts": simultaneous attacks coming from Kuwait and Turkey; special operations forces deploying in the western desert of Iraqi and destroying scud missiles aimed at coalition forces or Israel; special operations forces landing in northern Iraq and preventing Iraqi divisions north of Baghdad from moving south;

information and psychological operations eroding Iraqi forces' will to fight; and aerial strikes hitting the city of Baghdad and its defenses. Focusing on speed, Franks wanted to strike deep into Iraq before the Iraqis could react or employ weapons of mass destruction against forces assembling in the region. He later said the total strength of the invading force, including allies, numbered 292,000, and of these, 170,000 were United States soldiers and marines. At the beginning of the campaign, however, the numbers were smaller because Franks planned on building up part of the invasion force before the formal commencement of hostilities and, after the invasion began, passing combat units through ports and staging bases one after the other. Having large sea and aerial ports in Kuwait, as well as extensive logistics and command and control facilities, enabled him to commence ground operations while a significant portion of his forces continued to flow into the theater.

To command the operation, Franks divided his forces into three component commands: naval, air, and ground. Vice Admiral Timothy J. Keating commanded the Coalition Forces Maritime Component Command. In addition to keeping the sea lines of communication open, Keating conducted interdiction operations in the surrounding seas and guarded against environmental challenges such as the Iraqis' dumping oil into the Arabian Gulf. Working closely with ground and air forces, he also provided operational fires from ships, aircraft, and submarines.

Lieutenant General T. Michael Moseley commanded the Coalition Forces Air Component Command. Franks expected Moseley to use air power to compensate for a relatively small ground force. Unlike the first Gulf War, when air attacks had preceded the ground assault by thirty-eight days, Franks saw no need to begin the invasion with a lengthy aerial campaign and follow it with a ground campaign. For more than ten years, coalition aircraft had enforced two separate no-fly zones over Iraq, and only a narrow band of airspace over central Iraq remained untouched. Using the no-fly zones, Moseley weakened enemy air defenses before the invasion by cutting communication links and knocking out radar and air defense sites. Between March 1 and 20, coalition aircraft flew some four thousand strikes and support sorties in the no-fly zones.

Lieutenant General David D. McKiernan commanded the Coalition Forces Land Component Command and had responsibility for the attack from Kuwait. To prevent Saddam from employing weapons of mass destruction, he wanted to move ground forces as rapidly as possible across Iraq. The United States Army's V Corps would make the main attack through the desert west of the Euphrates River while the Marine Corps' I Marine Expeditionary Force (MEF) marched farther east between the Tigris and Euphrates rivers and while British forces, working under I MEF, isolated Basra and protected southern oil fields.

Operations in western and northern Iraq remained under Franks' control. After the Turkish government refused to let the United States 4th Infantry Division march through its territory, he took special steps to keep the northern "front" viable. He arranged for the 173rd Airborne Brigade to parachute into Iraq north of Kirkuk and join special operations forces and Kurdish rebels. Crucial support from the Italian and Turkish governments permitted the brigade to fly from Italy, through Turkey, to northern Iraq.

General Franks wanted to begin the air assault fifteen hours before the ground assault, but he had to change his plan when images from a Predator unmanned aerial vehicle suggested the Iraqis were setting afire oil wells in the south. Because of its complexity, the massive air campaign could not begin early, so he ordered General McKiernan to begin the ground campaign on the night of March 20, a day earlier than the air campaign. Special forces entered Iraq late on the night of March 19, 2003, and the "first shot" of the war occurred the following morning. Two F-117 stealth jets attempted but failed to decapitate the Iraqi regime when they dropped two thousand–pound bombs at 0530 on a bunker near Baghdad where Saddam and his two sons were reported to be sleeping. That evening, ground forces moved into Iraq.

On the evening of March 21, the air campaign, sometimes known as "shock and awe," began in earnest. The air component commander, General Moseley, sought to prevent the employment of weapons of mass destruction, disrupt Saddam's ability to control his forces, and erode the Iraqis' will to fight. The first strikes came from Tomahawk missiles launched from American and British ships in the Arabian Gulf and from cruise missiles launched by B-52 bombers flying from bases in Great Britain and the Indian Ocean. After some three hundred cruise missiles struck in and around Baghdad, F-117 and B-2 stealth bombers dropped precision munitions. Coalition aircraft also struck targets in other Iraqi cities, such as Mosul and Tikrit. While attempting to avoid unnecessary civilian casualties, they struck targets such as Saddam's palaces, the Ministry of Defense, military command posts, and industries supporting the war effort. They avoided hitting power plants, electric grids, and water distribution systems because attacking such targets would greatly complicate postwar humanitarian efforts. As ground forces moved deeper into Iraq, coalition aircraft devoted more resources to close-support missions.

In the initial moves into Iraq, coalition forces encountered little resistance, but the Iraqis had some surprises of their own. Although special operations forces kept the Iraqis from firing tactical ballistic missiles at Israel or Jordan, the Iraqis succeeded in firing five missiles at coalition forces on the first day of the campaign. Of the seventeen fired in the entire campaign, all were destroyed by Patriot air defense missiles or landed harmlessly in the desert or the Gulf. Each firing nonetheless caused coalition forces to suit up in their protective gear and take precautionary measures.

Before the invasion, Iraqi expatriates had convinced many in Washington that the Iraqis would welcome the invaders as liberators, but the reception proved far different. Iraqi commanders planned on a defense in depth in the Tigris-Euphrates valley, and they offered the strongest resistance on the outskirts of major cities and at bridges over the Euphrates River. Although most Iraqi units melted away after offering only token opposition, irregular units fighting unconventionally surprised coalition forces by their fierce resistance. Reinforced by non-Iraqi volunteers, "Saddam's Martyrs" proved fanatically determined and willing to die. Ironically, Saddam had sent the paramilitary forces south less to counter an invasion than to keep the Shiite population in check.

With Baghdad some five hundred kilometers from the Kuwaiti border and some units still arriving, the V Corps commander, Lieutenant General William Wallace, sent the 3rd Infantry Division west of the Euphrates toward Karbala, which was in the gap between Bar al-Milh Lake and the Euphrates River. After traveling more than 125 kilometers and fighting through the night of March 21–22, the mechanized division seized the Highway 1 bridge over the Euphrates (northwest of An Nasiriyah). The division passed control of the bridge to Task Force Tarawa of I MEF and continued moving northwest along the Euphrates River toward As Samawah (one hundred kilometers northwest of An Nasiriyah) and An Najaf (ninety kilometers northwest of As Samawah). The soldiers encountered strong resistance in As Samawah and An Najaf, and the marines had to fight their way through An Nasiriyah before entering the valley between the Tigris and Euphrates rivers. As fighting continued in the cities along the Euphrates, General Wallace sent the 11th Attack Helicopter Regiment north on the night of March 23–24 in a deep strike against the Medina Division in the Karbala Gap. The mission accomplished little, and of thirty-two aircraft in the mission, one was downed and thirty-one were damaged.

On March 25, a huge sandstorm struck southern Iraq and continued for three days. The surprisingly strong enemy resistance and the sandstorm stalled the coalition's advance. With the enemy still resisting in cities along the Euphrates, McKiernan was concerned about securing his lines of communication and feared enemy attacks would disrupt his establishing a logistic base near An Najaf for the final drive on Baghdad. On March 27, in a decision angering Franks, who wanted to accelerate the pace, McKiernan ordered V Corps and I MEF to halt their advance and clear the pockets of resistance threatening their supply lines. In the V Corps sector the 101st and 82nd divisions protected the corps' rear while in the I MEF sector Task Force Tarawa did the same for the marines.

As coalition forces closed in on Baghdad, the air campaign shifted its primary focus to close support for ground forces. Thinking coalition aircraft could not fly in the sandstorm, Saddam and his generals miscalculated and sent units forward to engage the coalition's forces. In a devastating attack against Republican Guard divisions, high-flying aircraft destroyed hundreds of Iraqi vehicles between the Karbala Gap and Al Kut. This enormous destruction left Saddam with fewer forces to defend his capital and opened the way for the coalition's ground forces.

In the final drive to Baghdad, General Wallace feinted a move northeast across the Euphrates and then sent his main attack north through the narrow two-kilometer gap between Karbala and Bahr al-Milh Lake. Soldiers of the 3rd Infantry Division fought their way through the narrow gap on the night of April 1–2 and rushed forward to seize a crossing over the Euphrates River and then the intersection of Highways 1 and 8 south of Baghdad. Continuing the attack, the soldiers seized the Baghdad International Airport on the western side of the city early on the morning of April 4 and began encircling the city. As I MEF approached from the southeast, the 3rd Infantry Division held positions on the south and west of Baghdad and began securing an objective to its northwest.

With relatively few ground forces available, General McKiernan did not relish the prospect of a house-by-house fight in a city of almost six million people. He decided to encircle Baghdad and launch raids into it. On April 5, the 3rd Infantry Division launched a "thunder run" through the city. With guns blazing, a tank battalion, minus its wheeled vehicles, made a bold march through the city, starting on the southern outskirts and ending at the airport to the west. On April 7, the division sent an entire brigade into the city on another thunder run, but this time, American forces remained. Although fighting was far from over, the pulling down of Saddam's statue in the heart of Baghdad by United States marines on April 9, 21 days after coalition forces crossed the Kuwaiti border, seemed to mark the end of the campaign.

During the next three weeks, coalition forces fanned out across Iraq and entered areas that had seen no fighting. Although their presence signaled the end of Saddam's regime, the failure to halt looting in Baghdad and other cities demonstrated the limits of the coalition's control over Iraq. With United States forces doing little more than protecting a few government buildings, thousands of Iraqis plundered hospitals, schools, power plants, and businesses.

A week after the pulling down of Saddam's statue in Baghdad, General Franks met with his subordinate commanders in a palace at Abu Ghraib. He expected the vast majority of United States forces to be withdrawn within three or four months and for only one United States Army division to be in Iraq by September. He anticipated the establishment of a functioning Iraqi government within one or two months. A week later, Secretary Rumsfeld canceled the deployment of the 1st Cavalry Division to Iraq. Planners had intended for the division to be part of an "insurance force," but he saw no reason to send additional troops to Iraq.

On May 1, President Bush landed on the USS *Abraham Lincoln* and announced the end of major combat operations. As he spoke, a banner behind him proclaimed, "Mission Accomplished." Although he warned of "difficult work ahead," most of those watching television that day did not realize that the most challenging and costliest part of the mission remained in the future.

From Combat to Stability Operations

By definition, an insurgency aims to overthrow an existing government through subversion and armed conflict. Thus, according to the definition, an insurgency against coalition forces could not have existed until after the Americans arrived in Baghdad and a new government was formed. Those trying to kill coalition troops in April and May, however, could not have discerned a difference between their actions before or after the coalition seized Baghdad. Secretary Rumsfeld initially dismissed the existence of an insurgency and insisted the attacks came from foreign fighters and "pockets of dead-enders." Paul Wolfowitz, the deputy secretary of defense, explained, "It's not an insurgency, in the sense of an uprising. It is a continuation of the war by people who never quit." Many of the irregular Iraqi and foreign forces who attacked at An Nasiriyah, As Samawah, and An Najaf continued attacking coalition troops in late April and May, and the widespread civil disorder and looting that followed the capture of Baghdad created a perfect environment for the seeds of an insurgency to flourish.

Several missteps contributed to the growth of the insurgency, the most significant of which was the absence of a robust stabilization effort in Iraq after the seizure of Baghdad. In essence, postwar preparation was based on the assumption that the Iraqis would welcome the arrival of foreign troops and cooperate in the building of democratic institutions. Beginning in October 2001, the State Department's "Future of Iraq Project" attempted to bring together Iraqi expatriates and international experts to consider how to create a new Iraq, but virtually none of the project's work was used after Saddam fell. At CENTCOM, General Franks created Joint Task Force IV to oversee Phase IV of the campaign, the period after the end of combat operations, but two months before the invasion, Rumsfeld brought postwar preparations under his own control by creating the Office of Reconstruction and Humanitarian Assistance (ORHA) and appointing General (Retired) Jay Garner as its head. During the planning phase, President Bush showed no interest in nation building, and Rumsfeld was primarily interested in getting troops to Baghdad and then removing them as quickly as possible from Iraq. With his superiors demonstrating little interest in Phase IV, Franks was far more interested in the planning and conduct of the operation than in post-invasion requirements for stabilizing and pacifying Iraq. After reaching Baghdad, he anticipated a rapid departure of United States troops.

The crucial transition from combat to stability operations was accompanied by important changes in American commanders and command structure. Instead of keeping General McKiernan and his large, experienced staff in Iraq to face the ongoing violence, General Franks created Combined Joint Task Force 7 (CJTF-7) and named Lieutenant General Ricardo Sanchez its head. A recently promoted lieutenant general who had not participated in the first phase of the war, Sanchez faced enormous challenges, initially with a relatively small staff. Compounding the turbulence, General Franks announced his retirement in May and retired in July. Franks' deputy, General John Abizaid, became the new CENTCOM commander. The new CENTCOM and CJTF-7 commanders faced the very difficult task of convincing political and military leaders in Washington that the war was not over and that stabilizing and pacifying Iraq required significant levels of troops and equipment.

Other changes disrupted political efforts in Iraq. In early May, cursory preparations made by ORHA were interrupted when L. Paul Bremer replaced Garner and received the title United States Presidential Envoy and Administrator in Iraq. Shortly thereafter, Ambassador Bremer was appointed head of the Coalition Provisional Authority, which subsumed ORHA and assumed responsibility for governing Iraq. His chain of command went through Secretary Rumsfeld to President Bush. On May 16, Bremer banned many former Ba'ath Party members from public office, and a week later, he formally dissolved the Iraqi Army, which already had evaporated, he insisted, on its own. The decisions pleased Iraqi Shiites and Kurds who feared leaving the Ba'athists in positions of power and who objected to reassembling the Sunni-dominated army. However, banning higher-level members of the Ba'ath Party threw out of office thousands of people who knew how to make the government work and provide basic services, and dissolving the armed forces disrupted efforts to use the army in stabilizing and reconstructing Iraq. During the next few years, getting the government to function and fielding a new Iraqi Army proved to be extremely difficult. The bans also left skilled soldiers and intelligence specialists available for recruitment by insurgents. Numerous Iraqis from general officers to schoolteachers no longer had a job or any real reason to support the occupying forces. Virtually all the structure of government disappeared, and the chaos that began when coalition forces seized Baghdad continued.

With coalition troops limited in numbers and Iraqi security forces almost nonexistent, many Iraqis faced the rising tide of violence alone—especially during the first weeks after the seizure of Baghdad. Numerous kidnappings, abductions, rapes, and robberies occurred. Revenge killings struck down not only former regime officials but also shop owners, business leaders, academics, teachers, and journalists. Many Iraqis eventually found a degree of safety in protection provided by warlords or militias split along tribal, ethnic, and sectarian lines, but they viewed foreign troops as occupiers rather than liberators and were angered by the disruption of their lives. With weapons and explosives easily available, some of those who had resisted coalition forces during the invasion never stopped their attacks. Additionally, some unemployed Iraqis carried out attacks for pay, whereas others sought to avenge destruction of their property or injury of their family members. Foreign fighters began flowing into Iraq in summer 2003 and garnered the spotlight frequently with their horrific acts, but they constituted only a small minority, although a very destructive one, among those causing havoc. As time passed, coalition forces faced a witch's brew of competing political groups, religious sects, former regime elements, foreign fighters, al-Qaeda terrorists, tribal communities, warlords, criminals, and vigilantes.

Several important missteps thus squandered any possibility of peace settling easily over Iraq. Hope proved not to be a strategy, and the war proved to be more complicated than seizing Baghdad.

Combating Guerrillas

Within three months of the invasion, an average of five insurgent attacks a day occurred. Attacks occurred primarily in Sunni Arab areas and in Baghdad and usually consisted of roadside bombings, sniper fire, ambushes, and mortar rounds. The initial attacks lacked sophistication, but insurgents gradually gained experience and greater success. The attackers' success demonstrated the weakness and vulnerability of coalition forces and encouraged additional attacks.

Amid the escalating violence, coalition forces initially focused on "former regime elements" and continued to search for Saddam Hussein and weapons of mass destruction. After a tip revealed the location of two of Saddam's sons in July 2003, coalition forces surrounded them in Mosul and, in the course of a gun battle, killed them. In December, American forces found Saddam hidden in a hole beneath a two-room house on a farm near Tikrit. For a brief moment, Washington optimistically hoped Saddam's capture would lower the level of violence, but as attacks increased, coalition forces realized they faced deadly opponents who were far more than Iraqi "dead-enders" who wanted to restore Saddam to power. Along with hopes of finding weapons of mass destruction and of receiving assistance from a Muslim peacekeeping force, unrealistic expectations in Washington about reducing the number of troops quickly disappeared.

Facing a growing insurgency in late 2003 and early 2004, American political leaders believed the geopolitical importance of Iraq compelled the United States to restore order. If Iraqi society descended into chaos, a humanitarian catastrophe could result, sending millions of refugees to neighboring countries. Instability could spread to other states, and a broad sectarian conflict could engulf the entire Middle East. Concerned about its own internal stability, Turkey could send forces into northern Iraq to prevent Iraqi Kurds from establishing an independent state, and Iran could send forces into southern Iraq to protect Shiites and gain control of important oil fields. Within their own borders, Sunni-controlled states feared a Shiite insurrection, perhaps supported by an Iranian government that was developing nuclear weapons. More like cancer than dominoes, chaos in Iraq, American officials feared, would have severe consequences for Iraq and the Middle East and significantly affect the United States' role in the world.

After considering options, American leaders decided to keep a modest number of troops in Iraq and expand Iraqi security forces so they could control the country and deal with the escalating insurgency. General Abizaid did not favor flooding Iraq with American troops. He knew the United States did not have enough ground forces to keep more than 130,000 Americans in Iraq for an extended period, and he believed Iraqis would react negatively to the presence of a large foreign force. He insisted that the solution to Iraq's security problem lay not with United States armed forces but with the Iraqis. Keeping a large number of troops in Iraq, however, placed a heavy burden on United States ground forces. Although multiple deployments around the world reduced the number of soldiers available for service in Iraq and taxed the endurance of service members and their families, Secretary Rumsfeld adamantly refused to increase the size of the active Army and Marine Corps.

As coalition forces attempted to stabilize Iraq, they had little choice but to wage an antiguerrilla campaign, not a counterinsurgency campaign. Especially in the Sunni triangle, there were barely enough troops to conduct raids against "former regime elements" and definitely not enough to saturate large areas, clear them, and then occupy them for an extended period. The relatively small number of troops could protect only a small portion of the population. Valuable assistance could have come from the "New Iraqi Army," which was formally established in August 2003, but the new force expanded slowly in numbers and even more slowly in capability.

Arguing that coalition forces were facing "a classical guerrilla-type campaign," General Abizaid emphasized carefully aimed operations based on good intelligence and surprise. To confront the escalation of attacks, General Sanchez shifted forces from one particularly violent area to another and required division commanders to provide some protection to Iraqi civilians in their area of responsibility. In a series of raids, American commanders attempted to destroy insurgents, seize weapons caches, and enhance local security. Ranging across much of Iraq but focusing primarily on Sunni areas, the operations often consisted of establishing a security cordon around an area, searching a village or community, seizing war-making materiel, and arresting people suspected of being insurgents.

Air power added considerably to the coalition's operations by enhancing intelligence, movement, logistics, and fires. Intelligence from aerial platforms provided valuable information about civilian and enemy activities and helped commanders move ground forces to where they were needed. Transporting troops and supplies by fixed- or rotary-wing aircraft accelerated the pace and mobility of operations and reduced opportunities for insurgents to strike vulnerable convoys. When ground forces came under enemy fire, they received air support quickly. From an average response time of twenty to twenty-five minutes early in the campaign, response time for air support was reduced to six or seven minutes. Precision air attacks destroyed insurgent positions or buildings and inflicted considerably less damage to nearby structures than in past wars. Aircraft made other important contributions by helping protect vulnerable infrastructure and by flying numerous missions over electric systems and oil pipelines. Rapid aerial evacuation saved the lives of many soldiers by reducing the time between their being wounded and their receiving high-quality medical care.

Amid the antiguerrilla campaign, coalition forces tried to pacify Iraq using methods the Americans had practiced in the Balkans. Strongly believing in "boots on the ground," commanders attempted to increase security by running patrols through villages and neighborhoods. They also tried to rebuild local governments and emphasize "hearts and minds." That is, they tried to win public support by improving basic services (water, electricity, and garbage collection), reopening schools and hospitals, establishing an Iraqi police force, restoring the country's oil production, and encouraging the growth of commerce. A veritable "war of the pipelines" existed between saboteurs and repair teams along the main pipelines carrying crude oil. Using money taken from Saddam's hoards, commanders undertook small construction projects; larger construction and infrastructure projects required formal approval and allocation of funds. Commanders also placed greater emphasis on gathering intelligence and limiting civilian casualties and destruction. They learned to weigh the advantages of target destruction against the disadvantage of creating additional insurgents. Although some progress occurred, especially in Kurdish and Shiite regions, having too few troops and resources limited the coalition's efforts. Insurgents frequently destroyed improvements or coerced or killed those who cooperated with coalition forces. Many gains made in hearts and minds shriveled away in the insecure environment.

Despite the coalition's positive goals, some operations deepened hostility to the presence of foreign troops. Some commanders failed to emphasize sufficiently the importance of treating Iraqis with dignity and respect. As soldiers kicked down doors and gates and handled people roughly, they increased the resentment of the Iraqis and directly and indirectly contributed to the growth of the insurgency. Similarly, arresting and imprisoning thousands of able-bodied men who were suspected of being insurgents did little to reduce the number of insurgents. For many of the insurgents, imprisonment provided important networking and training opportunities.

Rotating units between the United States and Iraq and shifting units from quiet to violent regions also worked against the coalition's goals. Moving units interrupted the development of close relations with local authorities and oftentimes allowed insurgents to resume their violent ways. Some cities, such as Mosul, which had seemed peaceful after the 101st Airborne Division occupied it and restored basic service in spring 2003, fell victim to new attacks. In Mosul's case, a brigade equipped with the eight-wheeled Stryker Light Armored Vehicle replaced the 101st, and its smaller number of infantry could not maintain the same level of security. Assassination of the Iraqi governor of the province also removed a strong advocate of cooperation with the Americans. In essence, coalition forces could not provide local security uniformly and consistently across Iraq.

As Iraqi discontent mounted, reports of abuse and humiliation of Iraqi prisoners at Abu Ghraib, as well as graphic photographs of these abuses, flashed around the world in April 2004. The detention of thousands of suspected insurgents had overwhelmed the prison, which was thirty kilometers west of Baghdad, and the guards at the prison had willingly cooperated with interrogators to "loosen up the prisoners." In testimony before the Senate Armed Service Committee, Major General Antonio Taguba, who conducted a formal investigation on the abuse of prisoners at the prison, stated: "A few soldiers and civilians conspired to abuse and conduct egregious acts of violence against detainees and other civilians outside the bounds of international law and the Geneva Convention. Their incomprehensible acts, caught in their own personal record of photographs and video clips, have seriously maligned and impugned the courageous acts of thousands of United States and coalition forces." Questions quickly rose about Secretary Rumsfeld's and General Sanchez's roles in approving harsh interrogation techniques, but they were cleared eventually of any wrongdoing. The damage to the coalition's effort, however, was significant. Images from Abu Ghraib horrified many devout Muslims, weakened the credibility of the United States, and confirmed what many Iraqis had suspected.

Politics, Religion, and Major Battles

In the political arena, the situation varied greatly across Iraq. One can better understand Iraqi politics by artificially dividing Iraq into Sunni, Shiite, and Kurdish regions, although such a division risks oversimplifying an extraordinarily complex society. Much of the armed resistance to coalition forces initially came from the "Sunni triangle," which stretched from Baghdad in the east, to Ar Ramadi in the west, to Tikrit in the north. Sunni Arabs saw themselves as targets of the American-led invasion and refused to accept their loss of power and status. In the north, the Kurds, 75 percent of whom were Sunnis, welcomed the overthrow of Saddam and generally worked smoothly with coalition forces. In the south, the Shiites also welcomed the overthrow of Saddam, but their long persecution under the Ba'athists led them to demand their rights as a majority. They wanted to mold the state in their own image and avoid any chance of their being persecuted again. In those areas with mixed populations, extreme violence became normal. For example, in the area that stretched fifty kilometers south of Baghdad along the Euphrates River, known as the "triangle of death," Sunni extremists murdered and tortured Shiites and bloody clashes occurred between Sunnis and Shiites.

As the insurgency gathered momentum in 2003 and 2004, the United States moved slowly toward the establishment of an Iraqi government that could garner sufficient support to derail it. Ambassador Bremer inherited a chaotic situation from General Garner when he arrived in Baghdad in May 2003, and in his year in Iraq, he made only modest progress in establishing a functioning Iraqi government supported by most of the people in the country. Although the Bush administration had talked idealistically before the invasion about bringing democracy to Iraq, Bremer found blazing a path to democracy through the thicket of ethnic and religious groups extremely difficult. The question of political authority was crucial, for in a classical counterinsurgency campaign, success depends as much or more on political achievements as on military operations.

A few weeks after arriving, Bremer formed the Governing Council and ruled out the possibility of quick national elections. Iraq, he said, was too turbulent for full elections. Additionally, Sunni and Kurdish leader did not want elections to occur until safeguards for their regions were in place. Composed largely of exiles who returned to Iraq after Saddam's fall, the twenty-five–member Governing Council provided advice to the Coalition Provisional Authority and had little real authority. It had even less credibility among the Iraqi people. The council nonetheless criticized coalition forces in one of its first meetings for using "cruelty and violence" while searching citizen's homes.

With little leadership coming from the Governing Council, the influence of Islamic clerics became particularly significant. Although many had suffered under Ba'athist rule, most Sunni clerics almost immediately denounced the United States and the occupation of Iraq. Within weeks after Saddam's fall, some called for active opposition to the occupying forces and declared a *jihad*; Sunni mosques soon served as recruitment centers for the insurgency. Becoming more deeply religious and fighting for Islam appealed to many Sunnis who joined the insurgency. Radical Islamic ideas flourished amid the effort to drive "infidels" from Iraq.

In contrast, Shiite clerics urged moderation although almost all of them criticized the presence of foreign troops. While formally rejecting the occupation, Ayatollah Mohammed Baqir al-Hakim, head of the Supreme Council for the Islamic Revolution in Iraq, preached restraint until he died in a car bombing. His brother, Ayatollah Abdul Aziz al-Hakim, succeeded him as the head of the Supreme Council and served as a member of the Iraqi Governing Council. He argued not for an Islamic state but for a state that did not contradict Islam. Grand Ayatollah Ali al-Sistani, the senior Shiite cleric in Iraq and the most influential person in postinvasion Iraq, also preached restraint. He never issued a *fatwa* or *jihad* against the occupying forces. An Iranian who lived in An Najaf, al-Sistani did not seek an Iranian-style theocracy; he believed religious authorities should give advice and guidance to those in power, not exercise power directly themselves. He nonetheless insisted on holding general elections and having Iraqis write their own constitution.

A young Shiite cleric, Moqtada al-Sadr, sought a more active role. His father had been murdered, apparently by agents of Saddam Hussein, and he used his father's reputation and his own fiery sermons to gain support among impoverished Iraqis and those interested in establishing a strict Islamic state. In late 2003 and early 2004, al-Sadr built up his militia, known as the Jaysh al-Mahdi, or the Mahdi Army, and established control over a section of Baghdad known as Sadr City. Named after a religious leader who was killed by Saddam Hussein but not the young cleric's father, Sadr City was a slum in which a third of Baghdad's population lived. After several deadly bombings, militias loyal to al-Sadr established security around Shiite neighborhoods in Baghdad. Acting as death squads, some of his militiamen attacked Sunnis and drove many of them from Baghdad. This violence was an early step in what soon became a civil war.

As the Mahdi Army grew, al-Sadr became more aggressive. In October 2003, he announced the appointment of an "alternative government" and his supporters ambushed a column of United States forces in Sadr City. A few days later, his supporters attempted to seize an important Shiite shrine in Karbala. Despite al-Sadr's violent record, the Coalition Provisional Authority failed to act decisively against him.

In March 2004, the strength of the Mahdi Army had increased enough for al-Sadr to unleash a larger attack against coalition forces. For several weeks, firefights broke out between members of the Mahdi Army and Spanish-Salvadoran soldiers at An Najaf, Italians at An Nasiriyah, Ukrainians in Al Kut, British in Amara, Bulgarians and Polish in Karbala, and Americans in Sadr City. The Iraqi police and military disintegrated when confronted by the ragtag Mahdi Army. Demonstrating that the Shiites were far from being a monolithic body, however, other Shiite militias stood aside as the clashes occurred. Reinforced by the 1st Armored Division, multinational forces regained control of most areas except An Najaf, where a standoff occurred around the Imam Ali shrine, one of the holiest sites for Shiite Muslims. During the crisis, coalition forces confiscated arms and ammunition, much of which was found in mosques. After losing hundreds of followers and facing the prospect of a combined Iraqi-American assault, al-Sadr agreed in June to stop fighting, withdraw from An Najaf, and join the political process. Although he had failed to spark a widespread revolt among the Shiites, his Mahdi Army kept many of its weapons and retained significant influence, if not control, in An Najaf.

During the same period, a significant crisis also occurred in Fallujah, a city of some three hundred thousand, most of whom were Sunnis, west of Baghdad. In the early days of the occupation, local residents did not welcome United States forces, but leading citizens rejected the call of hard-line Ba'athists who wanted to continue to fight coalition forces. Then, on April 28, 2003, troops from the 82nd Airborne Division killed about a dozen civilians in an unfortunate incident during an anti-American rally in the city. Although American and Iraqi accounts differ and exact casualties remain uncertain, there is no doubt the incident derailed any chance of the city's being easily pacified. Between April 2003 and March 2004, four different United States Army units tried to quell violence in the city but failed. None stayed in the city long enough to establish a strong, personal relationship with local leaders.

When United States marines arrived in the area in March 2004, they planned on accelerating reconstruction projects and building rapport with the city's citizens. They wanted to drive a wedge between the insurgents and ordinary Iraqis by emphasizing cooperation, not coercion. Within weeks after arriving, they faced a crisis engendered by an Iraqi mob killing four American security contractors and mutilating their bodies. With Secretary Rumsfeld, Ambassador Bremer, and General Abizaid demanding action, General Sanchez ordered the marines to subdue the city and capture the killers. A fierce battle quickly ensued. American authorities hoped elements of the new Iraqi Army would help, but one battalion transported to Fallujah refused to fight and others refused to board transportation. Within days, marines had secured nearly a third of the city, but images of destroyed homes and streets and interviews with wounded civilians incensed common citizens throughout Iraq and sparked an international outcry against American excesses. Although the marines were pleased with the progress of their attack and believed they had minimized damage to the city, Sunnis on the Governing Council demanded a halt in the offensive. They believed, as did the UN special envoy to Iraq, Lakhdar Brahimi, that the United States was attempting to punish the city. On April 9, 2004, Ambassador Bremer announced a unilateral "suspension of offensive operations," a decision that brought strong complaints from marine commanders.

The halt marked what Bremer later called "the most critical crisis of the occupation." With al-Sadr's Mahdi Army battling coalition forces across southern Iraq, as mentioned above, and with Iraqi security forces having failed not only against the Mahdi Army but also in Fallujah, Sunni members of the Governing Council threatened to resign if the offensive continued in Fallujah. Facing a collapse of the entire political process, Bremer and Sanchez feared Sunnis and Shiites would combine and rise together in a full-scale revolt against coalition forces.

As American and Iraqi authorities sought a way out of the difficult situation in Fallujah, Lieutenant General James T. Conway, commander of I MEF, began secret negotiations with former Iraqi Army generals who proposed assembling a brigade of former Iraqi soldiers to control the city and combat the insurgents. Conway wanted to avoid reducing the city to rubble in a block-by-block fight and welcomed the idea of establishing a force within the city that would be trusted by the people. He soon agreed to the formation of what became known as the "Fallujah Brigade" and to withdraw marines from the city. He provided the brigade weapons, trucks, and radios and directed its leaders to report directly to him. He expected the brigade to secure the city and patrol its streets alongside Iraqi policemen and soldiers. Conway informed generals Abizaid and Sanchez of the Fallujah Brigade shortly before its formation, but Ambassador Bremer was not informed until after its formation, and he was furious. Yet, his response was less harsh than that of Iraqi political leaders who believed Conway had turned over the city to terrorists and Ba'athists.

Despite initial reports of progress, the Fallujah Brigade never operated as planned. Most members of the brigade were former Saddam loyalists who had taken part in previous operations against United States forces. Wearing old Iraqi Army uniforms, its members attempted to calm the city, but within weeks they were intimidated by or had joined the insurgents. The city became a haven for insurgents, such as Abu Musab al-Zarqawi who believed the marines' withdrawal signaled a victory for them. Within the city, extremist Islamic elements issued harsh religious edicts governing daily life and edged out moderate groups, as well as tribal leaders.

Amid the An Najaf and Fallujah crises, the coalition's leaders decided to shift power more quickly to the Iraqis. A new Iraqi government, they hoped, would attract the support of Iraqi people and parties and reduce support for violent groups. In a shadowy process in which the British and the UN special envoy to Iraq, as well as others, played a role, Ambassador Bremer formed the Iraqi Interim Government. Unlike the Governing Council, the Interim Government had real authority to govern and consisted of individuals from a somewhat broader section of Iraq. Iyad Allawi, a secular Shiite and former Ba'athist who had lived most of his life outside the country, became

Iraq's interim prime minister. In a formal ceremony on June 28, 2004, Bremer passed control of Iraq to the Interim Government and the new prime minister and quickly departed for the United States. The United States ambassador to Iraq, John Negroponte, assumed responsibility for many of the tasks previously handled by Bremer.

The ceremony marked the formal return of sovereignty to Iraq. The Interim Government planned national elections in January 2005 to select delegates for writing and approving a constitution and expected subsequent national elections to choose members of a freely elected government. With only the beginnings of a new Iraqi Army and no real government bureaucracy, the Interim Government had little or no power to enforce its decisions. Because it was appointed and not elected, it also lacked the authority of a national consensus. Yet, Allawi faced two unresolved crises, one in An Najaf and the other in Fallujah. In effect, Allawi inherited a worse situation from Bremer than Bremer had inherited from Garner.

Shortly after the formation of the Interim Government, Moqtada al-Sadr declared it illegitimate and demanded coalition forces withdraw immediately from Iraq. In early August, firefights again broke out between the Mahdi Army and coalition forces. Soon thereafter battles occurred in Sadr City, Al Diwaniya, and An Nasiriyah. In several towns, followers of al-Sadr attacked the offices of Prime Minister Allwawi's party. In An Najaf, where most of the fighting occurred, al-Sadr's forces again used the city's holiest site to protect themselves. Although destruction of the holy shrine was possible, the Interim Government sent Iraqi forces to join the battle and eliminate the upstart rival. Critics denounced this action and insisted the government was trying to establish a strongly centralized, authoritarian government. Ignoring the criticism, coalition and Iraqi forces continued their attack, killing or capturing hundreds of Mahdi Army militiamen. On August 26, they halted their attack in An Najaf, and Grand Ayatollah al-Sistani negotiated an agreement with al-Sadr. To the dismay of the Interim Government, he let al-Sadr remain at large and his followers keep their weapons. By accepting al-Sistani's intervention in the crisis, however, the government had acknowledged his authority and highlighted the power of Shiite clerics.

In September, the Interim Government began negotiations with civic leaders in Fallujah to get insurgents to abandon the city. With the talks yielding nothing, Prime Minister Allawi demanded that Zarqawi, the al-Qaeda leader, be turned over, and when nothing happened, he ordered the attack on Fallujah. Although the Interim

Government survived, several Sunni groups withdrew from the government in protest and threatened to boycott Iraqi national elections in January 2005.

In November, immediately after the United States national elections of 2004, the offensive began. The Americans attacked with six marine, three army, one British, and three Iraqi battalions. As the date of the attack loomed, fewer than thirty thousand residents remained, and electricity and water were cut off to induce the last ones to leave. Supported by aerial precision bombing, the ground assault began after dark on November 8. In some of the heaviest fighting of the war, the attacking force cleared the city house by house and block by block. The insurgents could not stand up to the attackers' massive firepower. On November 13, the Iraqi government declared the city secure, but clearing every part of the city took another six weeks. In the process, more than half of Fallujah's thirty-nine thousand buildings were seriously damaged and ten thousand destroyed or rendered uninhabitable. Although the offensive did not cripple the insurgency, it did demonstrate the combat power of the coalition and the refusal of the Iraqi Interim Government to accept the uprisings in An Najaf and Fallujah.

Counterinsurgency

During the presidential campaign of 2004, Senator John Kerry accused President Bush of having no strategy in Iraq, and the administration responded by carefully crafting a policy for supporting Iraq. The policy emphasized developing sound governance in Iraq, strengthening the Iraqi economy, neutralizing insurgents, and increasing international support. It also emphasizing having the Interim Government take the lead in political decisions. In essence, the policy established the framework for a new emphasis on counterinsurgency.

In June 2004, General George Casey replaced Lieutenant General Sanchez who departed about the same time as Ambassador Bremer. A seasoned veteran of the Pentagon who had served as vice chief of staff of the United States Army and director of the Joint Staff, Casey began a strategic review not long after arriving in Baghdad. Casey's strategy, which was published in August 2004, initially focused on containing the insurgency by clearing important cities, hunting down insurgent and terrorist leaders, and expanding Iraqi security forces. With strong blows against al-Sadr's militia in An Najaf in August and the insurgent enclave in Fallujah in November, he demonstrated his refusal, as well as that of Prime Minister Allawi, to tolerate safe havens for insurgents. Later versions of his strategy explicitly placed more emphasis on counterinsurgency and on having the Iraqis take responsibility for their own security. Coalition forces, Casey said, remained in Iraq at the "behest" of the Iraqi government, and their mission was to train Iraqi security forces and supplement them in ongoing operations, especially against al-Qaeda. Prime Minister's Allawi's government had to assume responsibility for protecting cities cleared by coalition and Iraqi forces.

As part of the renewed interest in counterinsurgency, the United States Army published a draft field manual in October 2004 entitled "Counterinsurgency Operations." Impetus for the new field manual came from the Iraqi insurgency and the realization that American forces could face other insurgencies in the global war on terrorism. Two years later, a new field manual appeared, this time with cooperation from the United States Marine Corps. It was the first field manual on counterinsurgency published by the Army in twenty years and by the Marine Corps in twenty-five years. Although long overdue, its publication reflected the effort by the American armed forces to think through the challenges inherent in a counterinsurgency environment. The new manuals noted that "political power" is the "central issue" in an insurgency, and both editions emphasized the importance of "host nation security forces." The final edition noted, "In the end, the host nation has to win on its own." The manual also noted, "The protection, welfare, and support of the people are vital to success." To emphasize the complexity of counterinsurgency operations, the final edition stated that the conduct of counterinsurgency operations is "counterintuitive to the traditional United States view of war." Among the several "paradoxes" noted was, "Sometimes, the more force is used, the less effective it is."

To strengthen Iraq's ability to withstand insurgent attacks on its own, Casey strongly supported Lieutenant General David Petraeus who had arrived in June 2004 to take command of the "Multinational Security Transition Command." Petraeus's mission was to assist the Iraqis in organizing and training their armed forces. After dissolving the Iraqi Army in May 2003, Ambassador Bremer had announced the creation of the "New Iraqi Army" three months later, but building an effective force proved to be an extraordinarily complex, frustrating endeavor. The insurgency prospered more than the new force. Many Iraqis joined only for the pay and refused to use arms against their own ethnic or religious group. Although rigorous training could ensure recruits acquired necessary combat skills, it could not overcome a lack of motivation or will to fight. It also could not prevent sectarian militias from infiltrating and dominating Iraq's security forces; animosity among Sunnis, Shiites, and Kurds did not disappear when soldiers put on uniforms. Additionally, corruption proved difficult to eliminate. Although leaders of the new Iraqi Army demanded better pay for their soldiers and more modern weapons and equipment, much of the funding seemed to disappear in their own pockets. Some soldiers demonstrated greater interest in robbing civilians than protecting them.

In late 2005, General Casey said Iraqi armed forces were not ready to take responsibility for the fight against insurgents. Yet, he refused to request additional American troops. Keenly aware of one of the "paradoxes" of counterinsurgency operations, he—like General Abizaid—thought a large, intrusive American force would delay Iraq's taking responsibility for its own security and could even fuel the insurgency. For most of 2004 and 2005, the number of American ground troops in Iraq hovered between 130,000 and 140,000, although the numbers increased to more than 150,000 in the months surrounding the elections of January and December 2005.

Generals Abizaid and Casey hoped national elections in 2005 would strengthen counterinsurgency efforts and bring the Iraqi people together. Although the elections succeeded in making the government legitimate in the eyes of some Iraqis, they failed to defuse the violence or produce compromise and reconciliation. In the elections of January 2005 for a "Transitional National Government," almost 8.5 million Iraqis voted, or about 60 percent of those eligible, although most Sunni Arabs boycotted the elections. Of 275 seats in the National Assembly, the United Iraqi Alliance (consisting of the main Shiite parties except Prime Minister Allawi's) won 148 seats, the Kurdish Alliance 75, and Allawi's list 40. Grand Ayatollah al-Sistani supported the United Iraqi Alliance. In late April Ibrahim al-Jaafari, a Shiite whose public comments were filled with religious terms and symbols, became prime minister of the Transitional National Government. After drafting a constitution, the new government had it ratified by the National Assembly and approved in October in a national referendum. With 63 percent of registered voters turning out, including Sunni Arabs, the constitution was approved by a wide margin, 79 percent for and 21 percent against. When national elections occurred again in December, the Sunnis participated and, except for bombings by al-Qaeda, the insurgents stood aside. This time, the United

Iraqi Alliance and its allies won 130 seats, the Kurdish Alliance 53, and Allawi's list only 25. Two Sunni parties won 55 seats. Although failing to win support from the Sunnis and Kurds, al-Jaafari would remain prime minister through May 2006.

As elections took place in 2005, severe fault lines in Iraqi society became more apparent. Instead of strengthening multicultural, quasi-secular elements seeking to unite Iraq, the elections favored sectarian elements wanting to expand their power at the expense of others. Fundamental differences of opinion existed on the strength of the central government, autonomy of different regions, power of local governments, and role of religion. Sharp differences also existed on control of Iraq's oil reserves, most of which were in Kurdish and Shiite-dominated regions. American officials repeatedly urged the Iraqis to make reforms that would encourage insurgents to lay down their arms and join the political process, but Iraqi leaders refused to compromise. No significant reforms—except for a modest relaxation of the ban on Ba'athists—occurred.

Amid escalating violence and sharp debates among the bickering factions, militias assumed increasing importance. As sectarian hatred shredded communities, a destructive cycle of violence pitted Sunni against Shiite as well as Sunni against Sunni and Shiite against Shiite. Violence between competing militias increased in number and scale and began to overshadow the insurgency. Americans demanded the militias be disbanded, but Iraqi leaders refused. The Kurds insisted their militia was the foundation of their tranquility and prosperity, and the two largest Shiite militias (the Badr Organization and al-Sadr's Mahdi Army) were controlled by parties supporting the ruling Shiite government. Much to the dismay of the coalition's leaders, the demarcation between militias and security forces became increasingly blurred.

Meanwhile, coalition forces had attempted throughout 2005 to clear cities crucial to the outcome of elections and place greater emphasis on counterinsurgency. Adopting a tactic known as "clear, hold, and build," the 3rd Armored Cavalry Regiment gained considerable success in the important insurgent stronghold of Tal Afar. Its operation in that city became a widely cited example of counterinsurgency doctrine in action. Located in Nineveh Province in northern Iraq, not far from Mosul, the city had a population of two hundred thousand, 70 percent of whom were Sunni Turkmen and 25 percent Shiite Turkmen. Along with the Arabs and Kurds, the Turkmen were one of the three largest ethnic groups in Iraq. Most insurgents in Iraq were Sunni Arabs, but Sunni Turkmen played an important role in the insurgency. In the summer of 2005, the city of Tal Afar provided insurgents a safe haven in which they could organize, train, and equip insurgents for deployment throughout northern Iraq. Cooperation between former regime elements and Islamic extremists kept the population tightly under control.

In May 2005, the 3rd Armored Cavalry Regiment, under the command of Colonel H. R. McMaster, arrived in Tal Afar. The most important dimension of McMaster's method was his focus on providing security for the population, not killing or capturing insurgents. With two cavalry squadrons, an infantry battalion, a reconnaissance squadron, and an aviation squadron, McMaster began clearing the area by cutting the links of insurgents in the city to outside or foreign sources of support. His task was simplified by his having a high ratio of troops to residents and by Tal Afar's being surrounded by a desert. After using a combination of air and ground assets to isolate the city, he beefed up controls along the nearby border and destroyed a network of safe houses between Syria and Tal Afar. Next, he encircled the city with an eight-foot berm that could be crossed only at designated points. With most of the insurgents having fled, a combination of Iraqi and American forces cleared the city by moving civilians safely aside, conducting house-to-house searches, and using precision fires against any resistance. McMaster did his best to avoid alienating residents by destroying their homes or hurting innocent family members.

The "hold" and "build" phases focused on protecting the residents of the city and took advantage of their revulsion against the extremely brutal insurgents. In the holding phase, McMaster placed about thirty combat outposts in the city. Iraqi and American forces occupied the combat outposts and provided local security. He also worked to enhance the legitimacy, credibility, and effectiveness of the police. The Interim Government provided new leaders from outside the city, and new recruits transformed the police from a sectarian to a more representative force. From an all-Shiite force of 150, the police grew to a more diverse 1,765 Iraqis. Assisted by Americans, the mayor, police leaders, and Iraqi Army commanders worked together to protect all residents.

In the building phase, Colonel McMaster focused on bettering the lives of Tal Afar's residents by providing municipal services and strengthening the economy. From only 60 percent of the people having electricity and 40 percent water, services improved until almost all of the residents had electricity and water. Schools reopened and reconstruction of damaged buildings began. As security increased and the quality of life in the city improved, residents provided important intelligence, and insurgent attacks went from a high of 170 in a month to 35–40 a month. Encouraging signs of reconciliation between Sunnis and Shiites appeared, and many families who had fled the city returned. In March 2006, the regiment returned to the United States and a brigade from the 1st Armored Division replaced it. Residents of the city fretted about the prospect of security unraveling and violence returning.

At Tal Afar and elsewhere, air power added an important dimension to counterinsurgency efforts. In many operations, aircraft reported the movement of people (combatants and civilians), thereby aiding ground commanders in positioning their forces or securing positions. Pilots also identified enemy soldiers concealed on the ground and provided overhead protection for patrols and convoys. Transporting personnel, equipment, and supplies with helicopters and aircraft reduced opportunities for insurgents to attack convoys along predictable routes. In several cases low-flying aircraft helped disperse angry crowds without dropping bombs. Limiting collateral damage with precision munitions proved key to clearing areas held by insurgents. Beyond a doubt, ground forces would have been far less effective without the strong air support they received.

Throughout Iraq, a stronger emphasis on counterinsurgency prevailed from late 2004 through 2006. A newly established school north of Baghdad indoctrinated incoming unit commanders in insurgency, and the rules of engagement were tightened to preclude the unnecessary use of force. As the number of troops in the new Iraqi Army increased, American units focused more and more on providing them support, and combined Iraqi-American patrols became common. Yet, there were not enough troops to "clear, hold, and build" in every Iraqi city, and violence between competing militias threatened to undo the progress made in stabilizing Iraq. Suicide bombers wearing vests filled with explosives or driving trucks and cars packed with bombs destroyed markets and streets. Explosions ripped apart recruiting stations for police and security forces. "Improvised explosive devices" punched holes through Iraqi and American vehicles, and "explosively formed penetrators" proved deadly even against M-1 Abrams tanks. Amid the broad counterinsurgency effort, units continued to launch raids against insurgent networks, strongholds, and bomb factories. Although some progress occurred in cities such as Tal Afar, Iraq was still far from stable, much of its population remained exposed to danger, and relatively few steps toward political compromise and national reconciliation took place.

Insurgency Within a Civil War

At the beginning of 2006, American officials expected Iraqi security forces to take greater responsibility for the war against the insurgents and provide more security for the Iraqi people. In February 2006, however, a terrorist bomb destroyed the golden dome of one of the Shiites most revered shrines, the Golden Mosque in Samarra, one hundred kilometers north of Baghdad. The mosque's destruction unleashed an outpouring of rage across Iraq, and thousands of Shiites, many of whom blamed the Americans, poured into the streets demanding revenge. Within a few days, retaliatory attacks of bombs, gunfire, or arson struck twenty Sunni mosques across the country. Although some considered the bombing of the Golden Mosque the beginning of a civil war, the bombing marked only the escalation of an existing civil war. Significant clashes between Shiites and Sunnis already had occurred, and a low-level, multifaceted civil war had long complicated the coalition's efforts to neutralize the witch's brew of insurgents.

Coalition forces could not keep the Iraqis from killing one another. By early 2006, sectarian violence had torn apart the cities, especially Baghdad. As hatred hardened boundaries between Shiite and Sunni neighborhoods, violence or threats of violence forced many Iraqis to flee their homes, sometimes emptying entire neighborhoods of one of the sects.

During Saddam's reign, some tensions had existed between Shiites and Sunnis, especially after Saddam had given Sunnis preferential treatment and suppressed Shiites violently. Bloody clashes between Sunnis and Shiites, however, were rare. Families had intermarried and mixed communities had emerged throughout Iraq. After Saddam's fall, sectarian hatred escalated as extremists kidnapped, tortured, and killed Iraqis from other sects. Such violence provoked retaliatory attacks from militias and local vigilante groups, and some extremists struck both sides in an effort to create chaos and generate more reprisals. Seeking to make people hate the government, insurgents disrupted government services by attacking anyone, Sunni or Shiite, considered a collaborator or anyone who worked with the government. Although their main targets were members of the Shiite-dominated Iraqi Army and the police, Sunni insurgents also killed fellow Sunnis from government offices who repaired water and electrical lines in Sunni neighborhoods or who collected garbage. In the wake of the deadly violence, hundreds of thousands of Iraqis fled, mostly to Jordan, Syria, and Lebanon. The refugees included large numbers of business leaders, engineers, physicians, and other professionals who were vital for Iraq's recovery and whose departure made its prospects bleak.

The failure to curtail violence in Iraq and improve public services resulted in the Kurds and Sunnis, as well as the Americans, harshly criticizing the Iraqi prime minister, Ibrahim al-Jaafari, who refused to step down. In May 2006, al-Jaafari finally relinquished his position, and Nuri al-Maliki replaced him. A Shiite, al-Maliki announced a national reconciliation program and an anticorruption plan and also promised to rein in militias.

In an attempt to restore stability and improve the quality of life in Baghdad, Prime Minister al-Maliki launched Operation Together Forward in June 2006. More than fifty thousand personnel were supposed to participate in the operation, including 8,500 Iraqi Army soldiers, 13,000 national police, and 21,000 local police, as well as more than 7,000 coalition troops. In an indication of the difficulty of the operation and the unreliable nature of Iraqi security forces, several Iraqi battalions deserted rather than go to Baghdad, and several brigades slated to take part in the operation never arrived. The operation went little beyond establishing checkpoints manned by Iraqi policemen and soldiers.

In August, al-Maliki launched Operation Together Forward II. An additional six thousand Iraqis and thirty-five hundred Americans joined the operation. Using the "clear, hold, and build" tactic, the operation aimed at clearing Iraqi neighborhoods of militias and insurgents, holding them primarily with Iraqi forces, and winning the allegiance of the Iraqi people with security, reconstruction, and services. Although American forces succeeded in clearing some areas of insurgents, poor performance of Iraqi security forces allowed the insurgents to return, and results failed to meet expectations. In October, the official spokesman for multinational forces in Iraq publicly expressed disappointment with the operation's success. The acknowledgment of failure contrasted sharply with previous public announcements that had painted a positive portrait of improvements in security in Baghdad. Holding sectors with unreliable Iraqi soldiers and with police infiltrated by militias proved impossible. More ominously, between August and November 2006, attacks against Americans in Iraq reached the highest level thus far recorded.

In early 2007, four years after invading Iraq, coalition forces began a new effort to secure Baghdad in Operation Enforcing the Law. The "surge," as it became known, temporarily raised the United States troop levels by 28,000, resulting in a total of 169,000 Americans in Iraq. To add the additional American troops, President Bush approved sending five more brigade combat teams to Iraq (raising the total from fifteen to twenty), and extending the tours of some units already in Iraq. Although some of the newly arriving American troops went to Al Anbar Province, most went to Baghdad or its immediate vicinity. Generals Abizaid and Casey, who had consistently opposed adding more American ground forces, moved on, Abizaid to retirement and Casey to Washington as the United States Army Chief of Staff.

With the additional troops, General Petraeus, who replaced General Casey in February 2007, intended to launch a counteroffensive and, by bringing down the level of violence in Baghdad, gain enough time for the Iraqis to implement reforms and pursue reconciliation among warring factions. Instead of relying almost solely on Iraqis to secure Baghdad, Petraeus ordered American units to play a larger role in clearing the capital city of insurgents and preventing them from returning. The surge of troops, although temporary, would "bridge" the time it took to improve Iraqi security forces sufficiently for them to maintain security after United States troop levels returned to presurge levels.

Petraeus's operational concept resembled not only the method used by Colonel McMaster in Tal Afar but also the *tâche d'huile*, or oil-spot method, used by French generals Joseph Gallieni and Hubert Lyautey at the end of the nineteenth century in North Africa and Indochina. To hold cleared areas, Petraeus created "joint security stations" (known as "combat outposts" when only Americans occupied them) in key sectors of the city. Manned by a combined force of Iraqi police, Iraqi Army, and American soldiers, the joint security stations became focal points for maintaining order and improving the local economy and government services. Petraeus expected the joint security stations to make Iraqis safer, especially those in troubled neighborhoods, but he recognized scattering the security stations through Baghdad put United States troops at greater risk.

As part of the new effort, President Bush and the new ambassador to Iraq, Ryan Crocker, put more pressure on the al-Maliki government to achieve important "political benchmarks" such as sharing oil revenue, holding local elections, and advancing national reconciliation. They also demanded better performance from Iraqi security forces. Responding to the pressure, Prime Minister al-Maliki appointed an Iraqi lieutenant general to command all Iraqi forces in the operation—including army and local and national police. The Iraqi commander assigned an Iraqi Army or police brigade to each of the nine security districts in Baghdad. Of the nine brigades, six were already present in the capital. Although fewer Iraqi police and army units arrived than promised, and some performed poorly, Iraqi security forces performed better overall than they had the previous summer in operations Together Forward I and II. Al-Maliki ordered militias to disarm or face attack when the operation began, but he made it clear that he wanted to fight insurgents, not militias.

As in Tal Afar, the operation started outside Baghdad in an effort to reduce movement of insurgents into the city itself. Northeast of Baghdad, Diyala Province and its capital, Baqubah, received special emphasis as insurgents fled from Baghdad and Al Anbar Province to Diyala and evidence mounted of Iran's funneling weapons and people across its border into that area. Although isolating Baghdad was impossible, operations in the belt around the city removed sanctuaries from which insurgents could launch attacks into the city. Using the "clear, hold, and build" tactic, the operation next aimed to clear Iraqi neighborhoods of militias and insurgents. Instead of surging, coalition and Iraqi forces trickled into Baghdad and slowly expanded their area of influence. In some districts, Americans built walls around Sunni enclaves to prevent Sunni insurgents from bringing in supplies and keep marauding Shiite militias from attacking. The operation also included strikes against rogue members of the Mahdi Army who refused to lay down their arms or who committed criminal acts such as murder, kidnapping, or torture.

The newly arriving forces established more than forty joint security stations in Baghdad, as well as additional combat outposts manned only by Americans. Living in isolated joint security stations across Baghdad made American soldiers more vulnerable, and an increase in raids on Shiite militias brought retaliatory attacks against the stations. Concrete barriers, sand berms, and barbed wire converted the stations into fortresses. On several occasions, Americans caught Iraqi policemen setting explosive devices to kill American soldiers and damage their vehicles. Some United States commanders within the stations displayed their doubts about their Iraqi counterparts' loyalties by posting sentries around the Americans' section, and at least one group of soldiers referred to their station as "the Alamo." The tedious, dangerous routine and poor living conditions also took a toll on the morale of those inside the fortified positions. Even worse, the presence of Iraqi forces did not reassure some residents. The arrival of security forces that had been infiltrated by Shiite militia, for example, provoked a strong reaction and deadly attacks in Sunni neighborhoods. Some Shiite-dominated security forces viewed all Sunnis as insurgents.

The surge nonetheless dealt a blow to the insurgency by increasing security of the civilian population in Baghdad, and the additional combat capability of United States forces, as well as the better performance of Iraqi security forces, made a difference. As the effort to secure Baghdad proceeded, United States commanders saw "some positive signs" and claimed "some success." They cited, for example, an increase in merchants and shoppers in markets and children in parks and on soccer fields. They also cited a decrease in car bombings. Yet, they acknowledged an increase in suicide bombings. Insurgents used spectacular attacks against public markets and bridges to demonstrate weaknesses in the security plan and keep Baghdad residents fearful for their safety. Whether the surge would make a big difference or dampen violence on a long-term basis was not at all clear.

The most notable progress, much of which occurred before the additional United States troops had an effect, came in Al Anbar Province. A desert region that included 30 percent of Iraq's land mass, the province stretched from west of Baghdad to Jordan and Syria and comprised much of what was known as the "Sunni triangle." A mix of Islamic militants, former Ba'athists, and recalcitrant tribesmen thrived among the overwhelmingly Sunni population. Although relatively few Sunni-Shiite clashes occurred, al-Qaeda terrorists and Sunni extremists savagely attacked anyone cooperating with coalition forces or the Iraqi government. After the fall of Baghdad, the 3rd Armored Cavalry Regiment initially covered the vast area and had its main base at Ar Ramadi, the capital of Al Anbar, one hundred kilometers west of Baghdad. In 2004, United States marines had moved into the area, and by 2007, twenty-five thousand of the thirty-five thousand United States troops in the region were marines. In the fall of 2006, a pessimistic intelligence report from the chief of Marine Corps intelligence in Iraq said prospects for securing Al Anbar Province were dim and the United States could do little to improve the situation there.

At about the same time, Colonel Sean MacFarland, commander of the 1st Brigade, 1st Armored Division, arrived in Ar Ramadi. He was told, "Fix Ramadi, but don't destroy it. Don't do a Fallujah." Lacking sufficient troops for a large offensive, MacFarland began securing Ar Ramadi one small area at a time. He used combat outposts to push into areas of the city dominated by the insurgents and al-Qaeda. Gaining the confidence and support of residents proved difficult, as did finding volunteers to join the police and security forces. To gain more volunteers, MacFarland agreed to let them serve only in their tribal areas or communities.

Not long after the 1st Brigade's arrival, tribal leaders approached MacFarland and offered to form an alliance against al-Qaeda and hard-line Sunni extremists. The offer came from sheiks reacting strongly against the violence used by extremists to coerce people into supporting their agenda. In one tribe alone, insurgents had killed more than two hundred people and kidnapped many others. Additionally, some of the tribal leaders did not support al-Qaeda's goal of establishing a fundamentalist Islamic state in Al Anbar Province. In essence, the tribal sheiks had realized they faced an enemy worse than the Americans.

MacFarland's superiors in I MEF reacted warily because they knew tribal leaders had supported the insurgency in the past and had long been involved in smuggling and other criminal activity. They also did not want another Fallujah, especially another Fallujah Brigade, and they feared a tribal alliance could pose a threat to the authority of the Iraqi government. Despite the reservations, MacFarland convinced his bosses to support the sheiks wanting to form a tribal alliance against al-Qaeda.

When the tribal alliance came together, its leaders sought financial and military support from the Iraqi and American governments. In return, the sheiks, whose power lay more outside the cities than within them, volunteered hundreds of tribesmen for duty as police officers and agreed to allow construction of joint American-Iraqi military and police security stations throughout their tribal territories. A visit from Prime Minister al-Maliki and General Petraeus brought promises of additional economic and military support and encouraged the sheiks to continue their cooperation.

With the help of the sheiks, the situation facing the Americans became simpler and the number of enemy smaller. Colonel MacFarland already had built small combat outposts in Ar Ramadi's most dangerous neighborhoods, and additional recruits from tribal leaders gave him enough troops to construct and operate joint security stations in other areas cleared by Iraqi and American forces. Important assistance came from newly recruited police who had a working knowledge of the local population and terrain and a commitment to establishing security. At the same time, United States and Iraqi forces launched major operations outside of Ar Ramadi. They sought to stop al-Qaeda militants from intimidating the local population through murder and kidnapping.

Early in 2007, there were some signs of progress in Ar Ramadi. Almost all of the thirty-one tribes (actually subtribes) pledged to fight the insurgents. Acts of violence dropped from as many as eighty-four each week in the summer of 2006 to six each week. Before 2007, the government center in downtown Ar Ramadi, which was little more than a bullet-ridden bunker of shattered concrete, had been under continuous siege by insurgents. As the violence ebbed, the Iraqis renovated the government compound and nearby buildings to create offices for the province's governor, council, and administration. Schools and shops reopened. American and Iraqi leaders hoped other tribes would cooperate with them and allow them to expand the police and construct garrisons in other areas.

Violence, however, did not end in Al Anbar Province. Extremists used assassinations, suicide bombers, and trucks filled with chlorine gas canisters to kill hundreds of Sunnis. American leaders hoped the brutal attacks would cost the insurgents additional public support. They also hoped the sheiks would not change sides again.

In Diyala Province, which is located northeast of Baghdad adjacent to Iran, American commanders had additional forces, thanks to the surge, to take advantage of a rift in mid-2007 between Iraqi insurgents and al-Qaeda. Local leaders had previously complained of the insurgents establishing a "Taliban Republic" in the province, especially after militants fled there from Al Anbar Province and Baghdad. The situation began to change in Diyala when al-Qaeda attempted to take control of the insurgency by assassinating several insurgent leaders and bombing tribes that refused to submit to their will. As in Ar Ramadi, the brutality of al-Qaeda, especially the wanton killing of innocent civilians, caused some of the insurgents to seek assistance in ending the reign of terror. Most of them were Sunnis who remained critical of the Iraqi government, but they provided intelligence about al-Qaeda, participated in combined patrols, and identified the location of improvised explosive devices. Although progress came slowly and some assistance proved useless, American commanders welcomed the prospect of insurgent groups turning against al-Qaeda and eventually reconciling with the Iraqi government. They hoped Diyala Province would evolve in the same manner as Al Anbar Province. Some Iraqi leaders, however, feared the Americans were establishing new Sunni militias that eventually would oppose the Shiite-dominated central government and escalate the civil strife.

★ ★ ★ ★ ★

Serious flaws in prewar planning contributed to the coalition's difficulties in Iraq. The Iraqis did not welcome the invading force, coalition forces were not able to withdraw quickly after seizing Baghdad, and Iraqi society did not remain stable after the overthrow of Saddam. After the successful seizure of Baghdad in April 2003, several missteps added to the coalition's difficulties in Iraq. Failing to stabilize or pacify Iraq after the seizure of Baghdad opened the door to greater violence from al-Qaeda and die-hard Saddamists. Then, dismantling the Iraqi armed forces and banning members of the Ba'athist Party from positions of responsibility made many Iraqis more willing to support the insurgents. As violence escalated General Abizaid attempted to quell the bourgeoning insurgency with carefully aimed operations and "hearts and minds" programs. His efforts, however, were limited by his never having enough troops for a vigorous counterinsurgency campaign and by the rotating of American commanders and units in and out of Iraq. Although he sought assistance from the Iraqis, creating and building effective Iraqi security forces proved extremely slow and complex. Beginning in late 2004, a stronger emphasis on counterinsurgency, especially to "clear, hold, and build," resulted in some gains, but there were not enough ground troops to yield significant success. With Iraqi security forces remaining unreliable, most gains proved short-lived unless coalition forces, mostly Americans, maintained a long-term presence in cleared areas.

In an attempt to gain broader Iraqi support the Coalition Provisional Authority created the Governing Council and then the Interim Government, but the return of sovereignty to the Iraqis in June 2004 and the conduct of national elections in 2005 failed to reduce the violence and resulted in a strongly sectarian Shiite coalition assuming power. Over time, the Iraqi people became more sharply divided, and militias of various ethnic and sectarian persuasions assumed greater importance. By early 2006, a low-level, multifaceted civil war existed. Thousands of Iraqis had fled after the fall of Baghdad in April 2003, but the number of refugees, perhaps totaling more than 2 million, increased dramatically as violence became more extreme.

By mid-2007, the outcome of the Iraq conflict was far from certain. Partially as a result of the surge, coalition forces made limited gains in Baghdad and key areas such as Al Anbar Province, and genuine rifts seemed to exist between al-Qaeda and some elements within the insurgency. Yet, the Americans could not stop the Iraqis from killing one another, and translating operational success into political momentum proved difficult. The reliability and capability of Iraqi security forces, especially the police, remained uneven, and progress toward "political benchmarks" established by the United States Congress and considered key to Iraqi national cohesion and economic recovery remained elusive. Amid dwindling public support in the United States for the war, Congressional leaders demanded more progress from the Iraqis and threatened to withdraw funding. A complete withdrawal of American forces from Iraq seemed possible, but the prospect of full-scale civil war within Iraq and chaos spilling over into neighboring countries left American and coalition leaders searching for alternatives.

ASYMMETRICAL WARFARE

At the beginning of the twenty-first century, analysts used the term *asymmetrical* to describe a conflict in which opponents of unequal power or capability use different methods to take advantage of their strengths and their enemy's weaknesses. In the broadest sense, asymmetrical warfare is as old as warfare itself because opposing armies are rarely equal in capability and always have devised innovative ways of inflicting losses on an opponent. Weaker forces, for example, have often used terrorist attacks and guerrilla operations to offset the advantages of a larger, more powerful opponent. Yet, theorists foresaw a new dimension in asymmetrical warfare coming from radically new technologies and a remarkable willingness of militants to kill themselves and others. Using scenarios of chemical, biological, or nuclear attack more reminiscent of science fiction than historical conflicts, theorists foresaw transnational terrorists and gangster cartels, for example, launching biological attacks or exploding primitive, dirty nuclear weapons to blackmail corporations or governments. No scenario seemed completely implausible to theorists.

The War in Lebanon

A historical example of an asymmetrical conflict that did not enter the realm of science fiction occurred in Lebanon where a weaker opponent gained an especially notable success against a stronger opponent. The war in Lebanon had long roots. After the creation of Israel and the Arab-Israeli conflict of 1948, thousands of Palestinian refugees fled to various locations in the Middle East. Taking up arms, Palestinians launched raids in subsequent years from Lebanon, Jordan, and Gaza and committed or sponsored international acts of terrorism, such as the hijacking of aircraft, to strike not only Israelis but also Jews around the world. The Palestinian Liberation Organization (PLO), which was led by Yasser Arafat and served as an umbrella organization for various Palestinian political and military groups, gained control over Palestinian refugee camps in Lebanon and directed many raids into Israel. As the number of attacks from Lebanon rose, Israel became more aggressive and, for example, launched a deadly raid into Beirut after the 1972 massacre of Israeli athletes in the Munich Olympics.

Within Lebanon, the power of the central government deteriorated as Christians and Muslims clashed over Christian control of the government and formed militias for protection. Lebanon descended into a civil war in 1975 that lasted until 1990. At the invitation of Lebanon's president, Syria occupied northern Lebanon in 1976 and with a mandate from the Arab League attempted to quell the violence. Fighting continued, however. Much of northern and east-central Lebanon was controlled by Syria, southern Lebanon by Christian militias, and west-central Lebanon by Palestinian militias who were mostly Sunnis. Beirut, a city once known as the "Paris of the Middle East," became a land of rubble, snipers, and fear.

To curtail Palestinian terrorists and guerrillas, Israeli forces launched Operation Litani in 1978 and seized much of the area south of the Litani River. Facing intense pressure from the United States and the United Nations, Israeli forces withdrew without having driven the PLO from its base and were replaced by the UN Interim Force in Lebanon (UNIFIL). The UN force was supposed to watch over the departure of Israeli forces and allow Lebanon's own army to move to the south. Much of the area previously occupied by the Israelis, however, came under the control of a militia known as the South Lebanon Army, which was composed primarily of Christians and received financial and logistic support from Israel.

In 1982, the Israelis again advanced into Lebanon, this time to force the PLO's political and military leaders out of Lebanon. After Israeli forces besieged Beirut, Arafat agreed to leave, and with the assistance of some two thousand UN peacekeepers, including eight hundred Americans, he and other PLO leaders departed for Tunis. Arafat cleverly gained a moral victory by claiming he was leaving to "rescue" the city from Israeli shelling.

An asymmetrical war began as Palestinian leaders withdrew, but Lebanese Shiites, not Palestinian Sunnis, dominated this conflict.

Although some Shiites had welcomed the Israelis when they first arrived in Lebanon, resentment against the occupying forces, as well as the example of Shiite success in Iran, slowly but surely transformed them into implacable foes. One of the Shiite groups that began attacking the Israelis was Hezbollah, or Party of God, which gradually gained influence over many Lebanese Shiites. Hezbollah was inspired by the revolutionary ideas of Iran's Grand Ayatollah Ruhollah Khomeini and supported by Iranian arms and money. It saw terrorist and guerrilla attacks as first steps in a long conflict that would culminate in an Islamic army destroying Israel and establishing an Islamic republic free of Western influence and imperialism.

Although American and French forces in Lebanon were part of a multinational peacekeeping effort, Hezbollah militants viewed them as pawns of the Israelis. On April 18, 1983, a suicide bomber exploded a truck filled with explosives in the compound of the American Embassy in Beirut, killing sixty-three people, including seventeen Americans. Six months later, two suicide bombers driving trucks filled with explosives destroyed buildings housing multinational forces. The Americans lost 241, who were killed, and the French, 58. After withdrawing from Beirut, the United States concluded Hezbollah was behind the bombings.

Israeli forces faced a foe who initially fought amateurishly but who gradually became more proficient with deadly sniper fire, ambushes, remotely controlled roadside bombs, booby traps, and raids. Between 1982 and 1985, the Israelis withdrew incrementally to a small security zone in Lebanon (ranging in depth in from five to twenty kilometers) paralleling the northern border of Israel. The security zone proved quite effective at halting infiltration in Israel, but it was not deep enough to prevent mortar and rocket attacks from Lebanon. With Hezbollah's increasingly sophisticated and effective attacks, the security zone also proved unsafe for Israelis and members of the South Lebanon Army who assisted them. Attempting to halt Hezbollah's attacks, the Israelis advanced deeper into Lebanon in 1993 and again in 1996, the first operation lasting one week and the second two weeks. Tired of having twenty to thirty soldiers killed each year, Israel finally withdrew from Lebanon in May 2000. By pulling back to its own border, Israel complied with UN Security Council resolution 425, dating from 1978, and calling for its complete withdrawal from Lebanese territory. In the eyes of many, Hezbollah, waging asymmetrical warfare, had won an important victory over a powerful foe.

During the next five years, the number of cross-border incidents decreased, but tensions mounted as attacks and counterattacks by Hezbollah and Israel continued. In May 2006, a major exchange of fire occurred after rockets fired from Lebanon landed in Israel. Although previous incidents similar to this had usually resulted in a limited exchange of fires, Israel responded more powerfully with air strikes, artillery, mortars, and tanks, and Hezbollah upped the ante with its own rockets, mortars, and small arms. After a short period, UNIFIL, the "interim" UN force that still occupied positions along the Lebanon-Israel border, arranged a ceasefire.

A serious crisis began on July 12, 2006, when Hezbollah fighters fired rockets into Israel from southern Lebanon and simultaneously conducted a raid across the border. Mimicking an attack in late June from the Gaza Strip in which two Israeli soldiers were killed and one captured, Hezbollah fighters attacked an Israeli patrol and killed three and captured two soldiers. The Israelis responded immediately with air and artillery fires and sent a platoon into the area from which Hezbollah fighters had launched their attack. By the end of the engagement, the Israelis had suffered a total of eight killed, and they had not rescued the two captured soldiers.

A sharp escalation occurred almost immediately. Fed up with Hezbollah's operating freely without interference from the Lebanese Army, the prime minister of Israel, Ehud Olmert, said, "Lebanon is responsible and it will bear responsibility." With extensive plans in hand for striking Hezbollah throughout Lebanon, the Israeli chief of staff, Lieutenant General Dan Halutz, an air force officer, stated, "If the soldiers are not returned, we will turn Lebanon's clock back 20 years." Having launched operations into Lebanon on several occasions over the years, the Israelis intended to use air power to damage Hezbollah and inflict enough pain on Lebanese civilians to turn them against Hezbollah. The Israeli government nonetheless announced publicly it was not fighting Lebanon but was attacking terrorists who held Lebanon "hostage" and who occupied "enclaves of murder."

Israeli's plan rested heavily on using air power across Lebanon and firing artillery from northern Israel into Lebanon. Using precision munitions, devastating air strikes soon hit Beirut's main electricity plant, fuel storage sites, international airport, and transportation and communication networks. Air strikes also destroyed Hezbollah targets. Because Hezbollah did not have industrial facilities or robust command and control centers, the Israelis concentrated their attacks on leaders, occupied positions, and weapons, many of which were hidden in Lebanese civilian neighborhoods. Air strikes also hit Dahi-yeh, a suburb of Beirut where many militants lived. Instead of under-mining support for Hezbollah, however, the attacks had the opposite effect. After viewing numerous video and photographic images of the bombing, sometimes manipulated for anti-Israeli effect, critics asked sharp questions about whether the situation merited such a drastic response. Anti-Israeli sentiment increased within Lebanon, as well as throughout the Middle East.

During the thirty-four–day campaign, Hezbollah fighters fired some four thousand rockets, most of which were 122-mm Katyusha rockets with a range of thirty kilometers. Hezbollah also fired about 450 to 500 rockets with ranges longer than the Katyusha but varying from 45 to 115 kilometers. Almost a quarter of all the rockets landed in Israeli cities or villages. Although inaccurate, salvoes of rockets went deeper into Israel than in the past, caused more damage, forced thousands to move or seek shelter, and disrupted economic activ-ity. Hezbollah fighters also used a handful of unmanned aerial ve-hicles, cruise missiles, and antiship guided missiles. Along the border Hezbollah fighters occupied strongly fortified positions, arranged in depth and reinforced with large mines and deadly antitank guided missiles. They hoped rocket attacks would bait the Israelis into a costly attack on their strong positions.

Although preempting or suppressing the rockets dominated the Israelis' efforts, they failed to stop the attacks, the intensity of which grew steadily throughout the campaign. Although they reduced to about a minute the time between sighting a rocket launcher and destroy-ing it, they failed to halt the launching of rockets. Civilian casualties among the Lebanese mounted as the Israelis attempted to destroy Hezbollah rocket launchers near holy sites, civilian neighborhoods, and schools.

Aiming to do more than disrupt rocket attacks, the Israelis launched limited ground attacks and destroyed some of Hezbollah's fortified positions near the Israeli border. They also conducted raids against Hezbollah positions, including a strike against a hospital in Beirut, where they seized several Hezbollah "officials." On August 3, the Israeli defense minister announced Israeli forces would move deeper into southern Lebanon and seize the area south of the Litani River (an advance of about thirty kilometers). The offensive aimed at overrunning the area from which almost three-quarters of Hezbol-lah's rockets were fired. In subsequent days, the Israelis sent more than ten thousand troops into the area south of the Litani River, but they failed to halt the firing of rockets, and their casualties mounted.

On the last day of the campaign, Hezbollah fired more than 250 rockets into Israel.

Although a UN-brokered ceasefire began on August 14, the Israelis continued small raids into Lebanon and did not lift their naval and aviation blockades until early September. When Lebanese troops entered the area south of the Litani, Israeli forces began pulling back and completed their withdrawal on October 1.

The total number of civilian and military deaths on all sides numbered about two thousand, but the war's effect seemed much larger. To Israel's dismay, the campaign exposed the limits of its military power, and Hezbollah's success almost guaranteed similar campaigns in the future. Skillfully manipulating public opinion, Hezbollah's leaders had neutralized the advantages of a conventionally superior force, and Hezbollah's fighters had aroused enthusiasm around the world for their cause by continuing to resist and fire rockets in the face of substantial Israeli military might. Sensing a defeat, Israelis were disappointed by the failure of their vaunted military to obtain a quick victory, and they were disheartened by the unexpected surge in international support for Hezbollah. The Israeli chief of the general staff, General Halutz, resigned in mid-January 2007, and several formal reports condemned the government's handling of the war.

★ ★ ★ ★ ★

The waging of war in the beginning of the twenty-first century proved as complicated and difficult as in previous centuries. In relatively easy campaigns, the United States and its allies succeeded in removing regimes in Afghanistan and Iraq, but subsequent efforts to defeat terrorism, end sectarian violence, and spread democratic ideals proved far more difficult and costly. The highly competent Israeli military also failed to gain a clear victory over an asymmetrical foe in Lebanon. Although strengthened security measures made terrorist attacks more difficult around the world, the wars in the Middle East, especially the one in Iraq, created a breeding ground for terrorists and a more dangerous situation internationally. And Hezbollah's example provided a model of success for those wanting to stymie or defeat a major power.

Under the pressure of practical demands, as opposed to theoretical frameworks, the United States slowly adapted its strategy, doctrine, and weapons to the new strategic environment, but it found no magic potion for neutralizing the destructive currents bubbling up from terrorists around the world. The fighting in Iraq also consumed important resources and diverted the attention of American military forces from Afghanistan and al-Qaeda. By early 2007, al-Qaeda and the Taliban appeared to be regaining strength. Al-Qaeda not only rebuilt some of its notorious training camps, this time in Pakistan's loosely governed tribal regions near the Afghan border, but also created or established relations with affiliated groups in multiple regions. A new generation of terrorists filled leadership positions vacated by casualties, and a stream of suicide bombers who believed the global war on terror was a war on Islam caused havoc in unexpected places.

Fundamental misconceptions about the nature of war contributed to the problems confronting the United States and its allies. As the United States attempted to redefine war on its own terms, it expected its adversaries to operate in ways that would leave them vulnerable to American strengths. In essence, American decision makers forgot that war is waged against an opponent who acts and reacts on his own and that war is the most complex, demanding, and unpredictable of all human endeavors. In the end, it was the terrorists who redefined the waging of war and who compelled the United States and its allies to fight on their terms.

SUGGESTED READINGS

Gilbert Achar and Michael Warschawski, *The 33-Day War: Israel's War on Hezbollah in Lebanon and Its Consequences* (Boulder, Colo.: Paradigm, 2007).

Ali A. Allawi, *The Occupation of Iraq: Winning the War, Losing the Peace* (New Haven, Conn.: Yale University Press, 2007).

Paul Aussaresses, *The Battle of the Casbah: Terrorism and Counter-Terrorism in Algeria, 1955-1957* (New York: Enigma Books, 2002).

L. Paul Bremer III, *My Year in Iraq: The Struggle to Build a Future of Hope* (New York: Simon & Schuster, 2006).

James S. Corum and Wray R. Johnson, *Airpower in Small Wars: Fighting Insurgents and Terrorists* (Lawrence, Kans.: University Press of Kansas, 2003).

Michael Delong, *Inside CentCom: The Unvarnished Truth About the Wars in Afghanistan and Iraq* (Washington, D.C.: Regnery, 2004).

Gregory Fontenot et al., *On Point: The United States Army in Operation Iraqi Freedom* (Annapolis, Md.: Naval Institute Press, 2005).

Tommy Franks, *American Soldier* (New York: Regan Books, 2004).

David Galula, *Counterinsurgency Warfare: Theory and Practice* (Westport, Conn.: Praeger, 2006).

Michael R. Gordon and Bernard E. Trainor, *Cobra II: The Inside Story of the Invasion and Occupation of Iraq* (New York: Pantheon Books, 2006).

Ahmed S. Hashim, *Insurgency and Counter-Insurgency in Iraq* (Ithaca, N.Y.: Cornell University Press, 2006).

Matt M. Matthews, *Operation Al Fajr, The Battle for Fallujah: A Study in Army and Marine Corps Joint Operations* (Fort Leavenworth, Kans.: Combat Studies Institute, 2006).

Williamson Murray and Robert H. Scales, Jr., *The Iraq War: A Military History* (Cambridge, Mass.: Belknap Press, 2003).

Sean Naylor, *Not a Good Day to Die: The Untold Story of Operation Anaconda* (New York: Berkley Caliber, 2006).

Richard Norton, *Hezbollah: A Short History* (Princeton, N.J.: Princeton University Press, 2007).

Nicholas E. Reynolds, *Basrah, Baghdad, and Beyond: The U.S. Marine Corps in the Second Iraq War* (Annapolis, Md.: Naval Institute Press, 2005).

Louise Richardson, *What Terrorists Want: Understanding the Enemy, Containing the Threat* (New York: Random House, 2006).

Thomas E. Ricks, *Fiasco: The American Military Adventure in Iraq* (New York: Penguin Press, 2006).

U.S. Army Center of Military History, *Operation Enduring Freedom, October 2001–March 2002* (Washington, D.C.: United States Government Printing Office, 2004).

Bing West, *No True Glory: A Frontline Account of the Battle for Fallujah* (New York: Bantam, 2006).

Lawrence A. Yates, *The US Military's Experience in Stability Operations* (Fort Leavenworth, Kans.: Combat Studies Institute Press, 2006).

CONCLUSION

In the past four centuries warfare in the West has changed gradually but fundamentally—the result of changes both in the way humans have lived and in the way that they have chosen to fight. From the early seventeenth to the mid-twentieth century, warfare tended to increase in scale, speed, complexity, and power. That tendency was sometimes interrupted, especially after the Thirty Years' War when states reacted against the enormous destruction of that war and after World War II when fears of nuclear war forced the superpowers to limit warfare. Underlying the increases in the scale, speed, complexity, and power of military operations since the seventeenth century were the continued development of the nation state and popular participation in government (essential to the mobilization of people and resources); the steady and then phenomenal growth of population in Europe and North America (the foundation for mass armies of the nineteenth and twentieth centuries); revolutionary changes in agriculture, industry, transportation, and communications (changes that since the late eighteenth century have made it possible to feed, equip, move, and control ever larger forces); and the invention of weapons that were unusually well suited to war (muskets and cast-bronze cannon, rifles and rapid-fire artillery, smokeless powder and machine guns, tanks and airplanes, nuclear warheads and missiles). But such underlying developments in politics, society, industry, and technology would not automatically have altered warfare. Someone still had to develop ways of exploiting emerging resources for war, to develop ways of organizing, equipping, and employing people to wage war more effectively. Consider once again how some of the most important changes came about.

For more than a century before Gustavus Adolphus became King of Sweden, Europe had been undergoing a military revolution—a prolonged adjustment to improvements in firearms that had led in part to a stagnation of land warfare. The development of more powerful handguns and artillery by the early sixteenth century made battles increasingly lethal and medieval stone fortresses obsolete. While commanders learned to avoid large scale engagements, the most prosperous states of western Europe invested in new angled-bastion fortresses and ever larger armies to garrison and attack those fortresses. Wars became long, indecisive, and expensive struggles with few battles and many sieges and skirmishes. Late in the sixteenth century the Dutch used superior discipline, smaller units, and the countermarch to make firearms more effective tactically. But the Dutch employed their improved tactics only on the defensive and remained mired in sieges and skirmishes well into the seventeenth century.

It remained for Gustavus Adolphus, campaigning in central Europe where there were few modern fortresses to impede the movement of armies, to develop the operational possibilities of the military revolution. He, more than any other figure in that revolution, was able to exploit improvements in weapons, tactics, and military administration to increase the scale and decisiveness of warfare. Borrowing freely from the Dutch and other Europeans and drawing on his own considerable experience with war, he mobilized the resources of his small state and created an inspired, disciplined army of Swedish volunteers and conscripts to serve as the nucleus for a much larger army of German mercenaries. He equipped these forces with improved handguns, pikes, and light artillery and trained them to fight with their arms combined—with infantry, artillery, and cavalry thoroughly integrated. He also trained them to exploit firepower and shock, offensively as well as defensively. And, once he intervened in the Thirty Years' War and was able to draw resources from Germany, he not only used firepower, discipline, and tactical flexibility to win great battles but also undertook campaigns on an unprecedented scale.

After the Thirty Years' War, Europeans rejected the mercenary armies, sweeping campaigns, and costly battles that had plagued Germany for more than a generation. To provide security at home and abroad, states invested in larger standing armies (permanent professional forces as large as 390,000 men supported by regular taxes and a central bureaucracy) and in more elaborate fortifications; these investments led gradually toward a new and more limited way of war. Because standing armies were expensive and could not be replaced easily and because improvements in weapons increased firepower and therefore casualties, commanders became reluctant to risk their armies in battle. Moreover, the proliferation of fortresses and the dependence of armies on a magazine system of supply restricted the movement of all forces. Even the most aggressive commanders were hard pressed to precipitate a battle or exploit a victory. For more than a century after the Thirty Years' War, Europeans waged war mainly by maneuver, skirmish, and siege. Such measures produced few decisions. Wars became long and expensive, tests as much of a state's financial resources as of the skill of its commanders. Even the most powerful and aggressive head of state, even a man like Frederick the Great of Prussia who relied more on battle than any of his contemporaries, was constrained by the conventions of limited war.

While European states employed standing armies in limited wars, their colonies in North America developed a less formal and far less limited form of warfare—a form that would touch European armies occasionally in the War for American Independence and that would nearly engulf them in the wars of the French Revolution. For most of the seventeenth and half of the eighteenth century, the English colonies of North America relied on poorly trained volunteers and militia to provide for their security. These popular forces knew little about European warfare; they succeeded mainly by attacking the whole of the enemy's population—by destroying the crops, stores, and dwellings of American Indians and other European colonists in brutal wars of conquest. In the War for American Independence the English colonists continued to fight for high stakes—the allegiance of the people and the preservation (or destruction) of the United States. Patriots did create a regular army that was eventually able to stand against the British, but the Continental army never employed the harsh discipline or complicated drill of European professionals and had to rely on the militia to do much of the fighting. By the final campaigns of the War for American Independence both sides had learned to blend regulars and militia, to organize their forces so they could live off the countryside and gain mobility, and to risk battle to destroy the enemy's forces.

On a small scale both sides in the American Revolution had anticipated the changes in warfare that would come to Europe a decade later with the French Revolution. When French Revolutionary governments were threatened by the principal states of Europe, they embarked on wars of survival and conquest. The Revolution employed people, weapons, and ideas that had served the Old Regime, but the Revolution's leaders relied mainly on the citizens and resources of France and on a new way of war to protect and expand their Revolution. They employed conscription, republican ideology, and simplified drill and tactics to create armies of unprecedented size and power; they called upon every citizen to support those armies; and they ordered their commanders to engage and destroy enemy forces. French military leaders did not squander their armies in ponderous conventional campaigns of maneuver and siege. Rather, by living off the countryside, their armies acquired the mobility needed to precipitate battle—to create the circumstances where superior numbers, morale, and firepower could win decisive victories. Thus, French forces, relying on skirmishers, mobile field artillery, and loosely organized columns and lines of infantry, overwhelmed the standing armies of Europe and, temporarily, extended French frontiers to the Rhine, Alps, and Pyrenees.

The French Revolution opened many careers to men of talent. No one benefited more than Napoleon Bonaparte, who rose from a captain of artillery to head of state in just over six years and who subsequently drew on the military legacy of the Revolution to make startling changes in the scale, speed, and decisiveness of warfare. His Italian campaign of 1796–1797, one of the most extraordinary campaigns in European military history, gave new meaning to the concept of maneuver and went well beyond the operational conventions of limited war. In a brief period and with limited resources, he fought eighteen major battles and forty-seven engagements, destroyed the First Coalition, and insured France's territorial integrity under a revolutionary government. In subsequent years, Napoleon used the armies of the Revolution as a nucleus for large, patriotic conscript forces that were subdivided into corps to live off the countryside and gain the mobility to win decisive battles. In the campaigns of 1805, 1806, and 1807 he employed his corps in armies that were twice the size of the largest forces from the age of limited war, that could march twice as far and twice as fast, and that could make a battle truly decisive.

Napoleon's system of operations, however, had limits. When he tried to campaign in the sparsely populated and barren peripheries of Europe where roads were poor and his armies could not move rapidly or obtain sufficient food and fodder, and when his forces roused spontaneous and fanatical popular resistance, he found himself mired in wars of attrition that eventually eroded the quality of his troops and the will of his countrymen. And when his enemies learned to exploit sea power and manage large forces, they were able to offset the advantages of his operational system. Even so, he had taught Europe how to make war on a scale and with a speed and decisiveness that would have been unthinkable before the French Revolution.

Within a half century of Napoleon's defeat, citizens of the new United States significantly increased the comprehensiveness and destructiveness of warfare. Those citizens had managed, after winning their independence, to hold their own against the British in the War of 1812, drive American Indians west of the Mississippi River, and develop a professional officer corps that would prove itself in directing the conquest of much Mexican territory in 1846–1847. But Americans were not prepared for their Civil War for a war which would be fought by large armies of inspired volunteers equipped with powerful rifled weapons. In the decades before the Civil War the Americans had learned to benefit from railroads, steamships, and telegraph lines. They had tried to adjust some of their methods to rifled muskets and artillery. When the Civil War began, however, both sides were shocked by the lethality of their weapons and the advantages that those weapons gave to an army on the defensive. Nonetheless, since both sides felt passionately about the causes of the war and admired the aggressiveness of Napoleonic warfare, both willingly endured heavy casualties and extensive mobilization of their male citizens and economic resources. Northern commanders tried for at least a year to win the war without alienating Southerners—to win by blockading Southern ports and capturing Richmond. After this strategy clearly failed, the North gradually began to wage a hard, destructive war against the South. They sought not just to destroy Confederate forces in campaigns of attrition but also to exhaust the South by freeing their slaves, obliterating their farms and factories, and breaking the will of their people. Such a strategy was costly—especially when Northern armies attacked entrenched Confederate forces—and it produced campaigns that seemed frustratingly indecisive. But after four years the North won the war, preserved the United States, and carried offensive warfare beyond anything that the Europeans had been willing or able to do.

European wars of the mid-nineteenth century were much more limited in aim, duration, and intensity than the American Civil War. Yet during those limited wars, European armies made changes in the equipment, mobilization, and employment of their forces that significantly altered warfare. In the Crimean War, Britain and France employed rifled muskets as well as steamships, railroads, and telegraph lines to defeat Russia; after the war they adopted new manufacturing techniques to equip their forces with ever better weapons. But it was Prussia that showed best how to combine the benefits of the Industrial Revolution with a growing population to wage war more effectively. The Prussians used a comprehensive system of conscription and training to create a large reservoir of soldiers; they equipped those soldiers with breech-loading rifles and artillery; they developed a series of schools and examinations for their officers; and they created a general staff to make detailed plans and to lead their forces in war. The Prussians did not always have the best weapons, and they sometimes took heavy casualties in attacking troops with breech-loading rifles; but so superior was their mobilization, so effective their use of railroads in sustaining an offensive, and so well trained and led were their huge conscript armies that they defeated Austria in 1866 and France in 1870–1871 with remarkable ease.

Toward the end of the nineteenth century, the development of more effective and lethal weapons continued to modify warfare. The introduction of smokeless powder, machine guns, and rapid-fire artillery forced armies to rethink—if not revise—their tactical and operational methods. During the same period, advances in weapons and ship design altered naval operations. For a brief period Western powers possessed an overwhelming advantage over other regions, and they used this advantage to spread their empires over much of the world. The victory of Japan in the Russo-Japanese War, however, signaled the emergence of significant military power outside the West and should have forced a thorough revision of military and naval operations.

But most armies failed to understand how destructive and how much less decisive warfare had become. Many military leaders expected that by inculcating their soldiers with an offensive spirit, by adopting a comprehensive system for conscription and training, by improving officer education and establishing a more effective general staff for planning, they could wage war quickly, successfully, and economically, provided they were able to mobilize before their enemies. They did not foresee that improvements in rifles, machine guns, and artillery—improvements in range, accuracy, and rates of fire—would increase the strength of the defense, offset superior planning and organization, and crush poorly organized attacks relying on élan. Most military leaders ignored the difficulties that armies on the offensive experienced during small wars at the turn of the century; most continued to believe that well-motivated troops could attack successfully against the latest machine guns and artillery.

World War I was, then, very disillusioning for all who had planned carefully for a short, decisive war. After the first month, that war degenerated into a costly stalemate in western Europe, into the most costly war that mankind had yet known. States succeeded in organizing their citizens and economies for near total war on an unprecedented scale. But no amount of ingenuity or suffering could find a strategic, tactical, or technological way to break the deadlock of trench warfare. Weakened by the effects of the Allied blockade but emboldened by the withdrawal of Russia from the war, Germany drove the Allies back in the spring of 1918 with massive offensives, but tactical gains did not yield strategic success. The entry of the United States into the war, when the other belligerents were exhausted, helped the Allies halt the German attacks and launch the final victorious offensives of the war.

Despite the stalemate of the trenches, World War I proved to be a period of remarkable innovation. New methods for organizing, equipping, supplying, and moving huge armies were devised. New weapons were introduced, including the tank, flamethrower, and light machine gun. For the first time, the airplane made war three-dimensional, and many of the most fundamental ideas about air power, including strategic bombing, made their appearance. Though rudimentary, the aircraft carrier became a reality, and the submarine proved deadly against surface shipping. Other improvements included better coordination between artillery and infantry and the introduction of the elastic defense and infiltration tactics. In ideas and weapons the armies, navies, and air forces of 1918 bore little resemblance to those of 1914.

In important respects—strategic and operational—World War II was a continuation of World War I. Once again states mobilized people and resources comprehensively for war. Most of the belligerents relied on procedures developed in 1914–1918 to employ their citizens and to develop and protect their war industries and raw materials. Similarly, in 1939 as in 1914, war was waged with air, land, and sea forces. After 1939 it became increasingly difficult for a state to succeed on air, land, or sea without considerable strength in all three; and the Allies' victory depended in no small measure on their ability to manage such joint operations as the invasions of France and the Philippines. Additionally, a number of operational methods that came to fruition between 1939–1945 had first appeared in World War I: strategic bombing, submarine warfare, and offensive tactics that would become the foundation for *Blitzkrieg*.

But warfare also changed substantially between the two world wars. Larger, more powerful, and, above all, more mobile forces made operations in World War II increasingly fluid and destructive. After 1939 military leaders used improved ideas and weapons to restore mobility to war and to prevent any prolonged return of the stagnant warfare of World War I. Better tanks and the methods of using them, as well as the development of mechanized infantry, mobile artillery, airborne forces, close air support, and amphibious operations, helped armies penetrate or bypass all defenses except those of extraordinary depth and kept land warfare fluid on nearly all fronts. Fast-carrier task forces, supplied and repaired while underway, were able to do much the same for war at sea; they operated with greater freedom from bases than any warships since the age of sail and—with the help of aircraft, radar, and long-range submarines—found and attacked enemy forces hundreds of miles beyond the horizon. Such fleets were also able to protect transports and landing ships as they established invasion forces on beaches thousands of miles from ports of embarkation. The opposing forces were usually too evenly matched and tactical defenses too strong, however, for either side to exploit mobility dramatically or to make more than gradual gains in a fluid global war.

More than any other war in history, World War II was a total war. The French Revolutionary and Napoleonic Wars, the American Civil War, and World War I had witnessed in turn the gradual harnessing of more and more resources and ever greater portions of the participants' populations in the war effort, but World War II surpassed all of them in the move toward total war. As the capabilities of industry increased between the eighteenth and twentieth centuries, vast quantities of weapons and equipment became available for the armed forces, and as the powers of central governments expanded during the same period, more and more people—directly and indirectly—became involved in their nation's war. The number of people and the amount of resources committed to the war effort made World War II the most destructive of all wars. Nonetheless, some states resisted complete mobilization. The United States continued to rely on voluntary actions by its populace, and though desperately outnumbered, Germany took only modest steps to involve women in the war-time effort.

The development of nuclear weapons at the end of World War II served not only to accelerate the end of that war but also to shape warfare for nearly a half century. During the Cold War, Americans and Soviets avoided any direct confrontation and sought to limit conflicts that could escalate into nuclear wars. They, nevertheless, engaged in a nuclear arms race, took part in several wars (Korea, Vietnam, and Afghanistan), and supported friends and client states in other conflicts. In this strategic environment, protracted wars of mid- to low intensity became particularly prevalent. With assistance or opposition from the superpowers, leaders such as Mao Zedong and Ho Chi Minh waged protracted struggles in which they combined political and military efforts and often relied on guerrilla forces. Other types of conflicts also occurred. Some wars, especially in the Middle East, involved large forces and advanced weapons and equipment, and restraints against the use of chemicals as weapons of mass destruction slowly eroded. From the superpowers' perspective, however, the wars remained limited—confined to particular places, conducted with forces of finite size and composition, and fought with restricted objectives in mind.

The ending of the Cold War removed some of the restraints on warfare exercised by the United States and Soviet Union because of their fears of a nuclear war with each other. In parts of eastern Europe, the Balkans, and Africa, national, religious, and ethnic differences resurfaced and exploded into brutal regional conflicts. As violence and turmoil threatened to spread, national and international leaders considered military interventions, relying on gains in strategic mobility developed during the Cold War. The first major conflict occurred, however, when an international coalition responded to Iraqi aggression against Kuwait. In the campaign that drove the Iraqis from Kuwait, the Americans in particular relied on remarkably sophisticated weapons that had been developed during the Cold War for use in central Europe. Despite the spread of highly advanced weapons, other regional conflicts in the new era initially involved quite limited warfare—warfare that required modest operational skills and that was waged by paramilitary forces and militias with unsophisticated conventional weapons in confined spaces. The United Nations sought to contain or end some of these conflicts with negotiations, peace-keeping operations, or the limited use of force in peace-enforcing measures. Nevertheless, its initial performance raised some doubts about whether the international community had the unity, resolve, and resources to keep local conflicts from escalating beyond the usual bounds of limited warfare, from drawing in states with nuclear weapons and medium-range missiles, and from turning local conflicts into much larger and more destructive wars.

Thus, the waging of war has changed dramatically over the past four centuries. Changes have occurred for a variety of reasons, and no war has been a carbon copy of a previous war. In most cases the waging of war has evolved unevenly as new ideas, methods, or weapons spread from state to state or region to region in an uneven fashion. Methods or equipment that worked in one conflict or region often could not be used successfully in other conflicts or regions. When confronted with the need to change, most armed forces remained conservative until the need for modification became obvious, but those states remaining abreast of the latest innovations in warfare often found themselves with an advantage over their opponents. In the future as changes continue to occur in the way humans live—in their politics, society, industry, and technology—military leaders will need great skill and imagination in choosing how to fight, in developing more effective ways to organize, equip, and employ their forces for war. The waging of war may well remain the most demanding and dangerous of all human endeavors.

PHOTOGRAPH CREDITS

Chapter 16: p. 499, National Archives; p. 511, National Archives; p. 512, Theodore Roosevelt Collection, Harvard College Library; p. 514, Wide World; p. 518, The Bettmann Archive; p. 520, National Archives. **Chapter 17:** p. 524, The Bettmann Archive; p. 532, Hulton Deutsch Collection Limited; p. 536, The Bettmann Archive; p. 546, Library of Congress; p. 549, The Bettmann Archive. **Chapter 18:** p. 556, Hulton Deutsch Collection Limited; p. 561, Australian War Museum; p. 570, National Archives; p. 574, Imperial War Museum; p. 579, The Bettmann Archive; p. 580, Hulton Deutsch Collection Limited; p. 582, Tank Museum Collection. **Chapter 19:** p. 588, National Archives; p. 594, National Archives; p. 598, National Archives; p. 602, Library of Congress. **Chapter 20:** p. 613, National Archives; p. 618, National Archives; p. 621, National Archives; p. 628, The Bettmann Archive; p. 632, Bayerisches, Hauptstaatsarchiv, Munich. **Chapter 21:** p. 639, UPI/Bettmann; p. 645, Wide World; p. 652, UPI/Bettmann; p. 660, Bundesarchiv, Koblenz; p. 664, Imperial War Museum. **Chapter 22:** p. 670, Imperial War Museum; p. 673, Hulton Deutsch Collection Limited; p. 679, Imperial War Museum; p. 680, UPI/Bettmann; p. 686, UPI/Bettmann; p. 691, National Archives; p. 696, UPI/Bettmann. **Chapter 23:** p. 704, National Archives; p. 713, Coast Guard; p. 718, UPI/Bettmann; p. 730, Hulton Deutsch Collection Limited; p. 733, Hulton Deutsch Collection Limited. **Chapter 24:** p. 744, National Archives; p. 751, Wide World; p. 758, National Archives; p. 759, Library of Congress; p. 765, UPI/Bettmann. **Chapter 25:** p. 776, The Bettmann Archive; p. 779, Library of Congress; p. 783, National Archives; p. 787, National Archives; p. 788, National Archives; p. 804, UPI/Bettmann. **Chapter 26:** p. 811, National Archives; p. 819, Library of Congress; p. 823, National Archives; p. 831, National Archives; p. 832, National Archives; p. 839, National Archives. **Chapter 27:** p. 847, Los Alamos National Laboratories; p. 853, National Archives; p. 856, National Archives; p. 861, The Bettmann Archive; p. 865, National Archives; p. 869, National Archives. **Chapter 28:** p. 876, National Archives; p. 885, Wide World; p. 886, National Archives; p. 889, National Archives; p. 896, Wide World; p. 897, UPI/Bettmann. **Chapter 29:** p. 904, Wide World; p. 909, UPI/Bettmann; p. 915, UPI/Bettmann; p. 919, UPI/Bettmann; p. 921, Frank Wolfe/LBJ Library Collection; p. 930, UPI/Bettmann. **Chapter 30:** p. 942, UPI/Bettmann; p. 952, Wide World; p. 957, Gamma Liaison. **Chapter 31:** p. 970, UPI/Bettmann; p. 973, UPI/Bettmann; p. 975, © 1995 Abbas/Magnum Photos, Inc.; p. 981, Wide World; p. 986, Courtesy of Raytheon; p. 992, Wide World; p. 1001, Reuters/Bettmann.

Index